THE PAPERS OF MARTIN LUTHER KING, JR.

Sponsored by

The Martin Luther King, Jr.,
Center for Nonviolent Social Change, Inc.,

in association with

Stanford University and Emory University

Ralph David Abernathy, Martin Luther
King, Jr., and Bayard Rustin leave the Mont-
gomery courthouse on 24 February 1956.
Photo and permission courtesy of Associated
Press/Wide World Photos.

THE PAPERS OF MARTIN LUTHER KING, JR.

VOLUME III:

Birth of a New Age

December 1955–December 1956

Senior Editor

Clayborne Carson

Volume Editors

Stewart Burns
Susan Carson
Peter Holloran
Dana L. H. Powell

UNIVERSITY OF CALIFORNIA PRESS

Berkeley   Los Angeles   London

University of California Press
Berkeley and Los Angeles, California

University of California Press, Ltd.
London, England

Library of Congress Cataloging-in-Publication Data

King, Martin Luther, Jr., 1929–1968.
    The papers of Martin Luther King, Jr.
    Includes bibliographical references and index.
    v. 3. Birth of a new age, December 1955–December 1956.
    Contents: v. 1. Called to serve, January 1929–June 1951—
    v. 2. Rediscovering precious values, July 1951–November 1955.
    1. Afro-Americans—Civil rights.   2. Civil rights move-
ments—United States—History—20th century.   3. King, Martin
Luther, Jr., 1929–1968—Archives.   4. United States—Race relations.   I. Carson, Clayborne, 1944–   .   II. Burns, Stewart.
III. Carson, Susan.   IV. Title.
        p.   cm.
    ISBN 0–520–07951–5 (cloth : alk. paper)
    E185.97.K5A2   1996   323′092   91–42336

Printed in the United States of America
9 8 7 6 5 4 3 2 1

The paper used in this publication meets the minimum requirements of American National Standards for Information Sciences—
Permanence of Paper for Printed Library Materials, ANSI Z39.48–
1984. ♾

*If we are to speed up the coming
of the new age we must have
the moral courage to stand up
and protest against injustice
wherever we find it.*

MARTIN LUTHER KING, JR.
3 December 1956

The editors of the Martin Luther King, Jr., Papers Project wish to acknowledge the financial and material support of the following major contributors, without whose support this volume would not have been possible:

Major Contributors

National Endowment for the Humanities
National Historical Publications and Records Commission
James Irvine Foundation
Lilly Endowment
Stanford University
Emory University
John T. Rockefeller Foundation
Peter Kovler
Judith L. Lansing
Nordson Corporation Foundation
H. W. Wilson Foundation
David and Lucile Packard Foundation

Patrons

Ruth M. Batson Educational Foundation
Diane F. and James A. Geocaris, Jr.
William P. Madar
San Jose Mercury News
Elizabeth Traugott

ADVISORY BOARD

Coretta Scott King (chair)
Christine King Farris
Lerone Bennett, Jr.
Ira Berlin
John W. Blassingame
Samuel Dubois Cook
John Hope Franklin
David J. Garrow
Robert L. Green
Vincent Harding
Louis R. Harlan
Robert A. Hill
Darlene Clark Hine
Bernard Lafayette, Jr.
John D. Maguire
Otis Moss, Jr.
Joseph Roberts, Jr.
Harry H. Wachtel
Preston N. Williams
Harris Wofford
Andrew J. Young

The publishers gratefully acknowledge the many individuals and foundations that have contributed to the publication of the Papers of Martin Luther King, Jr., and the General Endowment Fund of the Associates of the University of California Press for its contribution toward the publication of this volume.

Our special thanks to Maya Angelou, Mary Jane Hewitt, Sukey Garcetti, Maxine Griggs, Franklin Murphy, Joan Palevsky, and Marilyn Solomon for their leadership during the campaign.

Challenge Grant
Times Mirror Foundation

Leadership Grants
The Ahmanson Foundation
AT&T Foundation

Partners
ARCO Foundation
William H. Cosby, Jr., and Camille O. Cosby
The George Gund Foudnation
The Walter & Elise Haas Fund
LEF Foundation
Sally Lilienthal
J. Michael Mahoney
The Andrew W. Mellon Foundation
National Historical Publications and Records Commission
Peter Norton Family Foundation
Joan Palevsky
The Ralph M. Parsons Foundation

CONTENTS

List of Illustrations   xxiii
Acknowledgments   xxv
Introduction   1
Chronology   35
Editorial Principles and
     Practices   55
List of Abbreviations   61
The Papers   65
Calendar of Documents   499
Index   547

Illustrations follow p. 64

2 Dec 1955   Leaflet, "Don't Ride the Bus" (facsimile)   67

5 Dec 1955   Minutes of Montgomery Improvement Association Founding Meeting, by U. J. Fields   68

5 Dec 1955   MIA Mass Meeting at Holt Street Baptist Church   71

8 Dec 1955   To the National City Lines, Inc.   80

10 Dec 1955   "Statement of Negro Citizens on Bus Situation"   81

12 Dec 1955   From H. Edward Whitaker   83

15 Dec 1955   Program for MIA Mass Meeting at First Baptist Church   84

15 Dec 1955   To M. C. Ballenger   87

21 Dec 1955   To Ralph W. Riley   87

21 Dec 1955   From Walter C. Carrington   88

25 Dec 1955   "To the Montgomery Public"   89

27 Dec 1955   To Archibald James Carey, Jr.   93

3 Jan 1956   From Aubrey Willis Williams   95

4 Jan 1956   FBI Special Agent in Charge, Mobile, to J. Edgar Hoover (facsimile)   96

9 Jan 1956   To the Commissioners of the City of Montgomery   97

11 Jan 1956   From Earl B. Dickerson   98

18 Jan 1956   From H. Edward Whitaker   99

22 Jan 1956   MIA Press Release: The Bus Protest Is Still On   100

23 Jan 1956   Notes on MIA Executive Board Meeting, by Donald T. Ferron   101

26 Jan 1956   From Martin Luther King, Sr.   105

26 Jan 1956   Complaint, *City of Montgomery v. Martin L. King* (facsimile)   106

27 Jan 1956   "To the Citizens of Montgomery"   107

28 Jan 1956   To Roy Wilkins   108

30 Jan 1956   Notes on MIA Executive Board Meeting, by Donald T. Ferron   109

30 Jan 1956   To H. Edward Whitaker   113

30 Jan 1956   Notes on MIA Mass Meeting at First Baptist Church, by Willie Mae Lee   113

31 Jan 1956   "Blast Rocks Residence of Bus Boycott Leader," by Joe Azbell   114

31 Jan 1956   From Pinkie S. Franklin   115

31 Jan 1956   From J. Pius Barbour   116

1 Feb 1956   From Major J. Jones   116

1 Feb 1956	From Walter R. McCall	117
2 Feb 1956	From Frank L. Stanley	118
2 Feb 1956	Notes on MIA Executive Board Meeting, by Donald T. Ferron	119
4 Feb 1956	Interview by Donald T. Ferron	123
4 Feb 1956	From Julian O. Grayson	126
5 Feb 1956	From Milton Britton	126
7 Feb 1956	To Fred Drake	127
11 Feb 1956	From Samuel D. Proctor	128
16 Feb 1956	From Marcus Garvey Wood	129
17 Feb 1956	From Sankey L. Blanton	130
20 Feb 1956	From George W. Davis	131
21 Feb 1956	Indictment, *State of Alabama v. M. L. King, Jr., et al.* (facsimile)	132
22 Feb 1956	From Ralph J. Bunche	134
22 Feb 1956	From Roy Wilkins	134
24 Feb 1956	"Negroes Pledge to Keep Boycott," by Wayne Phillips	135
24 Feb 1956	From Charles R. Lawrence	136
24 Feb 1956	From Ella J. Baker	139
24 Feb 1956	From Archibald James Carey, Jr.	139
24 Feb 1956	From William D. Jones	140
24 Feb 1956	From Wade H. McKinney	141
24 Feb 1956	From Peter A. Bertocci	142
25 Feb 1956	From Kelly Miller Smith	143
27 Feb 1956	Notes on MIA Mass Meeting at Holt Street Baptist Church, by Donald T. Ferron	144
28 Feb 1956	To William H. Gray, Jr.	145
28 Feb 1956	From George D. Kelsey	146
28 Feb 1956	From William Jones	147
29 Feb 1956	From Alice Neal	147
29 Feb 1956	From Jesse Jai McNeil	149
1 Mar 1956	Notes on MIA Mass Meeting at Hutchinson Street Baptist Church, by Donald T. Ferron	150
3 Mar 1956	To Roy Wilkins	151
3 Mar 1956	To Archibald James Carey, Jr.	152
4 Mar 1956	From S. Paul Schilling	153
5 Mar 1956	From J. H. Jackson	154
5 Mar 1956	From Leonard G. Carr	156
5 Mar 1956	From Eunice Guy	157
6 Mar 1956	From William Robert Miller	158
6 Mar 1956	From Earline Browning	160
7 Mar 1956	From Thomas G. Kilgore, Jr.	160
7 Mar 1956	To J. H. Jackson	162
8 Mar 1956	From Bayard Rustin	163
8 Mar 1956	To George D. Kelsey	164

8 Mar 1956	From Roy Wilkins 165
9 Mar 1956	From William J. Faulkner 167
10 Mar 1956	From Lillian Eugenia Smith 168
13 Mar 1956	From John Dockery 170
13 Mar 1956	To J. Pius Barbour 171
14 Mar 1956	From Allan Knight Chalmers 173
14 Mar 1956	From Howard Thurman 174
15 Mar 1956	To Dwight D. Eisenhower 175
16 Mar 1956	To Howard Thurman 177
16 Mar 1956	From Homer Alexander Jack 178
18 Mar 1956	From Thelma Austin Rice 179
19 Mar 1956	To W. E. B. Du Bois 180
21 Mar 1956	From St. Clair Drake 181
21 Mar 1956	From William Stuart Nelson 182
22 Mar 1956	Testimony in *State of Alabama v. M. L. King, Jr.* 183
22 Mar 1956	Judgment and Sentence of the Court, *State of Alabama v. M. L. King, Jr.* (facsimile) 197
22 Mar 1956	Reactions to Conviction 198
22 Mar 1956	Address to MIA Mass Meeting at Holt Street Baptist Church 199
22 Mar 1956	From Frank L. Stanley 201
23 Mar 1956	Interview by Joe Azbell 202
23 Mar 1956	From Samuel DuBois Cook 203
23 Mar 1956	From William H. Gray, Jr. 205
23 Mar 1956	From Norman Thomas 206
29 Mar 1956	"When Peace Becomes Obnoxious," Sermon Delivered on 18 March 1956 at Dexter Avenue Baptist Church 207
31 Mar 1956	"Quotable Quotes from Rev. King" 209
2 Apr 1956	From Worth Littlejohn Barbour 210
2 Apr 1956	From Richard Bartlett Gregg 211
12 Apr 1956	From James H. Davis 212
13 Apr 1956	From Glenn E. Smiley 213
14 Apr 1956	From Jewelle Taylor 215
19 Apr 1956	From A. Philip Randolph 216
20 Apr 1956	From Charles C. Diggs, Jr. 218
23 Apr 1956	From Dorothy Canfield Fisher 219
23 Apr 1956	From James P. Coleman 220
24 Apr 1956	To James P. Coleman 221
24 Apr 1956	To Benjamin Elijah Mays 222
24 Apr 1956	To Wayne D. McMurray 223
25 Apr 1956	To William Peters 224
25 Apr 1956	From Harris Wofford 225
25 Apr 1956	From Percival Leroy Prattis 227
26 Apr 1956	From Jeanne Martin Brayboy 228
26 Apr 1956	To William E. Newgent 229

26 Apr 1956   Address to MIA Mass Meeting at Day Street Baptist Church   230

29 Apr 1956   From J. Martin England   232

29 Apr 1956   From Hazel E. Foster   233

30 Apr 1956   From Vivian C. Mason   235

Apr 1956   "Our Struggle"   236

May 1956   To Jewelle Taylor   242

1 May 1956   From Earl E. Nance   242

1 May 1956   To Roy Wilkins   243

1 May 1956   To Richard Bartlett Gregg   244

1 May 1956   To Percival Leroy Prattis   245

2 May 1956   From Sadie Bradford   246

6 May 1956   To Benjamin F. McLaurin   246

7 May 1956   From A. Philip Randolph   247

8 May 1956   To William Robert Miller   249

8 May 1956   To Jesse Hill, Jr.   250

8 May 1956   To Shelby Rooks   251

9 May 1956   From Ernest C. Dillard   252

10 May 1956   To A. Philip Randolph   252

10 May 1956   To Harris Wofford   254

11 May 1956   From Henri Varin de la Brunelière   254

17 May 1956   From Charles S. Johnson   255

17 May 1956   "The Death of Evil upon the Seashore," Sermon Delivered at the Service of Prayer and Thanksgiving, Cathedral of St. John the Divine   256

17 May 1956   Announcement for Speech at Service of Prayer and Thanksgiving, Cathedral of St. John the Divine (facsimile)   257

18 May 1956   From William Robert Miller   262

18 May 1956   "Mother's Day in Montgomery," by Almena Lomax   263

20 May 1956   From Richard Bartlett Gregg   267

22 May 1956   To James E. Huger   269

23 May 1956   To Hobson R. Reynolds   270

24 May 1956   "Recommendations to MIA Executive Board"   271

24 May 1956   To Lillian Eugenia Smith   273

24 May 1956   From Myles Horton   274

29 May 1956   Martin Luther King, Sr., to Dexter Avenue Baptist Church   275

31 May 1956   To E. T. Sandberg   276

May 1956   "Walk for Freedom"   277

June 1956   "The 'New Negro' of the South: Behind the Montgomery Story"   280

1 June 1956   To Arthur R. James   286

1 June 1956   From James Peck   288

1 June 1956	To J. Raymond Henderson	289
4 June 1956	To Ross Allen Weston	290
4 June 1956	To George Lawrence	291
4 June 1956	To William J. Faulkner	292
4 June 1956	To Myles Horton	292
4 June 1956	From Helen M. Hiller	293
5 June 1956	To Charles E. Batten	294
13 June 1956	From Archie L. Weaver	294
15 June 1956	From George Lawrence	296
19 June 1956	To Jimmy and Ellen Hawley	297
20 June 1956	To Annemarie Schader	298
27 June 1956	"The Montgomery Story," Address Delivered at the Forty-seventh Annual NAACP Convention	299
3 July 1956	To W. T. Handy, Jr.	310
5 July 1956	To Glenn E. Smiley	311
5 July 1956	To Almena Lomax	313
5 July 1956	To John Oliver Killens	314
6 July 1956	To Helen M. Hiller	315
10 July 1956	To A. J. Muste	316
10 July 1956	To Lovie M. Rainbow	317
10 July 1956	To Homer Greene	317
10 July 1956	To J. Raymond Henderson	318
12 July 1956	From John Patterson	319
18 July 1956	"From the Pastor's Desk"	320
23 July 1956	"Non-Aggression Procedures to Interracial Harmony," Address Delivered at the American Baptist Assembly and American Home Mission Agencies Conference	321
30 July 1956	From Septima Poinsette Clark	328
31 July 1956	From Medgar Wiley Evers	329
1 Aug 1956	To W. H. Jernagin	331
1 Aug 1956	To Rae Brandstein	332
1 Aug 1956	To Clair M. Cook	333
1 Aug 1956	From E. S. Hope	334
11 Aug 1956	Testimony to the Democratic National Convention, Committee on Platform and Resolutions	335
1956	"The Birth of a New Age," Address Delivered on 11 August 1956 at the Fiftieth Anniversary of Alpha Phi Alpha in Buffalo	339
15 Aug 1956	From Ernest Morgan	347
16 Aug 1956	To O. Clay Maxwell, Sr.	348
16 Aug 1956	To Septima Poinsette Clark	349
20 Aug 1956	To Homer Alexander Jack	350
21 Aug 1956	To Marian and Nelson Fuson	351
21 Aug 1956	To Joffre Stewart	352

21 Aug 1956   To Glenn E. Smiley   353

24 Aug 1956   To Warren J. Bunn   354

27 Aug 1956   To Ernest Morgan   355

27 Aug 1956   From W. H. Jernagin   355

27 Aug 1956   To Dwight D. Eisenhower   357

28 Aug 1956   From Cecil A. Thomas   358

28 Aug 1956   From Nannie H. Burroughs   361

29 Aug 1956   From Kivie Kaplan   362

30 Aug 1956   From L. Harold DeWolf   363

7 Sept 1956   From Warren Olney III   364

8 Sept 1956   From C. W. Kelly   365

14 Sept 1956   To L. M. Terrill   367

17 Sept 1956   To Warren Olney III   368

18 Sept 1956   Minutes of MIA Executive Board Meeting,
               by W. J. Powell   369

18 Sept 1956   To Nannie H. Burroughs   370

18 Sept 1956   To William Cooper Cumming   371

18 Sept 1956   To Vernon Johns   372

19 Sept 1956   To Sally Canada   373

19 Sept 1956   To Manuel D. Talley   373

19 Sept 1956   To Lafayette Dudley   374

20 Sept 1956   To Bayard Rustin   375

24 Sept 1956   To Wilbert J. Johnson   378

25 Sept 1956   From Harold Edward Pinkston   379

25 Sept 1956   From Samuel S. Thomas   380

26 Sept 1956   From Bayard Rustin   381

28 Sept 1956   From Alma John   382

1 Oct 1956   To Viva O. Sloan   383

2 Oct 1956   To Cecil A. Thomas   385

2 Oct 1956   From Warren Olney III   386

3 Oct 1956   To Walter George Muelder   387

3 Oct 1956   Robert L. Cannon to Alfred Hassler
             and Glenn E. Smiley   388

3 Oct 1956   To Sylvester S. Robinson   391

3 Oct 1956   From Douglas E. Moore   393

9 Oct 1956   To Samuel S. Thomas   397

11 Oct 1956   To Charles S. Johnson   398

15 Oct 1956   To Raleigh A. Bryant   399

17 Oct 1956   From Eleanor Roosevelt   400

21 Oct 1956   From T. J. Jemison   402

23 Oct 1956   To L. Harold DeWolf   403

23 Oct 1956   From C. Kenzie Steele   404

25 Oct 1956   From Maxwell M. Rabb   405

26 Oct 1956   From B. J. Simms   405

29 Oct 1956 From Walter R. McCall 406

30 Oct 1956 To George Lawrence 407

30 Oct 1956 To Earl Kennedy 408

31 Oct 1956 Annual Report, Dexter Avenue Baptist Church 409

31 Oct 1956 To Alfred Daniel King 413

31 Oct 1956 To Benjamin F. McLaurin 413

4 Nov 1956 "Paul's Letter to American Christians," Sermon Delivered at Dexter Avenue Baptist Church 414

5 Nov 1956 To Eleanor Roosevelt 420

8 Nov 1956 To Richard H. Dixon 421

9 Nov 1956 From Julius Waties Waring 422

9 Nov 1956 From L. Harold DeWolf 423

14 Nov 1956 Address to MIA Mass Meeting at Holt Street Baptist Church 424

14 Nov 1956 From Benjamin Elijah Mays 433

14 Nov 1956 From John M. Swomley 434

14 Nov 1956 To Ella J. Baker 434

14 Nov 1956 From Ella J. Baker 435

20 Nov 1956 From Glenn E. Smiley 435

21 Nov 1956 From Ralph J. Bunche 436

23 Nov 1956 To Ruth Bunche and Aminda Wilkins 437

24 Nov 1956 To Albert S. Bigelow 438

25 Nov 1956 From William Lusk, Marjorie Gettleman, Naomi Friedman, and Sheila Navarick 439

27 Nov 1956 From Michael J. Quill and Matthew Guinan 440

27 Nov 1956 From Roland E. Haynes 441

27 Nov 1956 To Supporter 442

28 Nov 1956 From Gil B. Lloyd 443

28 Nov 1956 To Lottie Mae Pugh 444

Dec 1956 "We Are Still Walking" 445

3 Dec 1956 "Facing the Challenge of a New Age," Address Delivered at the First Annual Institute on Nonviolence and Social Change 451

5 Dec 1956 To Charles Walker 463

5 Dec 1956 From Charles Walker 464

5 Dec 1956 To Dorothy S. Bowles 466

10 Dec 1956 Sworn Deposition on Station Incident 467

10 Dec 1956 From L. Harold DeWolf 468

10 Dec 1956 From Robert E. Hughes 468

10 Dec 1956 From Joel Lawrence King 469

11 Dec 1956 To Medgar Wiley Evers 470

15 Dec 1956 "Desegregation and the Future," Address Delivered at the Annual Luncheon of the National Committee for Rural Schools 471

17 Dec 1956   To Roland E. Haynes   479
17 Dec 1956   To Benjamin Elijah Mays   480
19 Dec 1956   "Integrated Bus Suggestions"   481
19 Dec 1956   To W. A. Gayle   483
19 Dec 1956   From William Holmes Borders   484
20 Dec 1956   Statement on Ending the Bus Boycott   485
20 Dec 1956   To Wyatt Tee Walker   487
20 Dec 1956   To Eugene Walton   488
20 Dec 1956   To Daniel G. Hill   490
23 Dec 1956   From Bayard Rustin   491
24 Dec 1956   "New Fields Await Negroes, King Tells Mass Meeting"   494
26 Dec 1956   To Fred L. Shuttlesworth   495
27 Dec 1956   From Homer Alexander Jack   496

ILLUSTRATIONS

DRAWINGS

1. Protesters marching
2. Protesters
3. Protester giving the victory sign
4. Martin Luther King, Jr., and attorney
5. E. D. Nixon
6. Jo Ann Gibson Robinson
7. Martin Luther King, Jr.
8. Rosa Parks
9. Protester

PHOTOGRAPHS

1. Mass meeting at Holt Street Baptist Church
2. Rosa Parks, E. D. Nixon, and Fred D. Gray in Montgomery's Police Court
3. County officials with King, Jr., outside King's bombed home
4. Fred D. Gray, Ralph David Abernathy, Robert Graetz, and U. J. Fields after a mass meeting
5. Police Lieutenant D. H. Lackey fingerprints Rosa Parks
6. King and other boycott leaders outside Alabama State Capitol
7. King after his arrest
8. Boycott leaders after press conference
9. D. H. Lackey books King and Abernathy
10. Parks and Nixon attending King's trial
11. King and supporters during trial recess
12. King greets supporters on second day of his trial
13. Coretta Scott King kisses her husband after guilty verdict
14. King at Holt Street Baptist Church
15. King family at Dexter Avenue Baptist Church
16. King speaks to MIA executive board
17. King at Day Street Baptist Church
18. Three women exit from MIA car pool station wagon
19. King family at Dexter baby contest
20. King at Fisk University Race Relations Institute
21. King and others at Alpha Phi Alpha anniversary banquet
22. King at Hampton Institute
23. Abernathy, King, Glen E. Smiley, and others on city bus
24. Two men at front of city bus

The Martin Luther King, Jr., Papers Project is a collective endeavor that depends on the generosity and talent of many people. This comprehensive edition of King's papers builds on the long-term efforts of individuals and institutions involved in assembling and preserving the documentary legacy of King's life. The present volume is the result of the continued commitment of old and new friends who have assisted the Project in large and small ways that sometimes defy adequate description. Suffice it to say that the King Papers Project's effort to document the Montgomery bus boycott was almost as much a collective effort as the movement itself (and required a longer time to complete). The following acknowledgments are a grateful project director's expression of appreciation rather than a definitive apportioning of credit.

Institutional Support

The Project's sponsor, the Martin Luther King, Jr., Center for Nonviolent Social Change, Inc., has undergone substantial changes during recent years that have altered its relationship with the Project. I continue to benefit from the support and advice of the King Center's founding president and former chief executive officer, Mrs. Coretta Scott King. This edition would not have been possible without her determination to preserve the documentary records of her husband's life or her recognition that this project was necessary. Despite pressing official and family obligations, she has devoted many hours to Project matters during the past few years. Her assistants at the King Center—Lynn Cothren, Doris Ford, and especially Delores Harmon—have also been helpful to me.

In April 1994 Mrs. King relinquished her administrative duties at the King Center to her son, Dexter Scott King, who now serves as president and chief executive officer. As head of the King Center, Mr. King has devoted considerable time and energy to the Project, meeting with me on numerous occasions. Even before his assumption of this role, he took on increasing responsibility for the King estate, discussing with me matters of mutual concern regarding the commercial aspects of King's literary property. From the beginning of our relationship I have been aware that he sees the King Center and the King Papers Project in different terms than his mother. Although both Kings recognize the importance of the Project as a means of preserving Martin Luther King, Jr.'s legacy, he has emphasized the importance of reinvigorating that legacy. We share a strong commitment to preserving King's ideas and expanding their influence, especially among young people, in a new era of electronic communication.

My discussions with Mr. King about King estate matters have often involved Phillip Jones, president of Intellectual Properties Management. I have come to appreciate the enthusiasm that he brings to his task of representing and furthering the interests of the King estate. In addition to working with Mr. Jones to resolve issues relating to the estate's proprietary interests, I have secured his sup-

Acknowledgments port for several projects designed to convey King's ideas and our research to a
wider popular audience.

Other members of the King Center administration have devoted considerable
energy to our affairs. I have appreciated the professionalism and warm support
of the Center's chief administrative officer, Johnny Mack, who, in a variety of
financial administrative roles, has always supported the Project and worked with
me to manage the expenditure of grant funds. The King Center's senior vice
president and treasurer, Mrs. Christine King Farris, has likewise continued to offer vital support to the Project. She met with me on several occasions over the
last few years to discuss Project issues, and I consulted with her about her own
and her family's activities during the Montgomery bus boycott. I appreciate also
the help of her assistant, Barbara Williams. Other staff members of the financial office helped to resolve financial matters as well, particularly Isaac Clark,
who went out of his way to expedite arrangements for grant expenditures and
reimbursements.

Director of Archives Cynthia Lewis is a dedicated professional who has consistently lent her support to the Project. I also wish to thank former members of the
King Library and Archives staff Danny Bellinger and Bruce Keys.

The King Papers Project is conducted in association with Stanford University
and Emory University and benefits enormously from the scholarly resources and
administrative support of both institutions. At Stanford during recent years the
Project has been very fortunate to enjoy the continuing support of President Ger-
hard Casper and Provost Condoleezza Rice. Operating under the auspices of the
School of Humanities and Sciences, the Project has also benefited from the counsel and support of its former dean, Ewart Thomas, and its current dean, John
Shoven. I initially reported on Project matters to former Associate Dean Albert
Camarillo, an old friend and colleague from Stanford's history department; I now
report to Vice Provost Ramon Saldívar, who has been equally encouraging. Former Associate Dean of Graduate Studies Cecilia Burciaga offered steady assistance during the time she supervised the Project's grant from the Irvine Foundation, as did Irvine Program Coordinator Daniel Ramirez. Joan Minor, Assistant
Dean of Human Resources, provided vital assistance on personnel matters, as did
Nancy Padgett, Associate Dean and Director of Finance, who has helped the Project with budgetary concerns. Katherine Key, Edgar Chicas, and Victor Sosa of
Sponsored Projects supervised and provided assistance for the Lilly Foundation
grant. Stanley Bo Parker, Norman M. Roth, J. Lynn Sinclair, and Charles M. Stewart of Information Technology Systems and Services (ITSS) have provided consistent expertise, guidance, and support for the Project's computer database systems. Stuart K. Snydman, a former student researcher who now works for ITSS,
has also been extremely helpful regarding computer networking issues and designed the Project's initial World Wide Web site. Development officers Michael
Britt, Evelyn Kelsey, and Henry Organ have assisted the Project's never-ending
pursuit of additional funding. Rev. Floyd Thompkins, former Associate Dean of
Memorial Chapel, not only was unstinting in his general support for the project
but also played the leading role in a theatrical docudrama, *Passages of Martin Luther King*, produced by the King Papers Project.

At Emory, the King Papers Project office has continued to strengthen its
operations under the direction of Volume IV editor Virginia Shadron and Con-

tributing Editors Rosemary Hynes and Penny A. Russell. The Project has received crucial support from Emory administrators at every level, including President William M. Chace, Provost Billy E. Frye, Vice President for Arts and Sciences David F. Bright, Dean of the School of Arts and Sciences and Vice President for Research George Jones, Associate Vice President of Graduate Studies Eleanor Main, Associate Dean Alice Benston, Graduate School Business Manager Tom Stitt, and Administrative Assistant Carl Reid. History Department Chair James Roark was consistently helpful to Virginia Shadron as she has expanded the Project's activities at Emory. The following Emory faculty members have served on the Project's informal faculty advisory committee: Delores Aldridge, Rudolph Byrd, Dan T. Carter, Leroy Davis, Robert M. Franklin, Theophus Smith, and Margaret Spencer.

The Project has also relied on its publisher, the University of California Press, particularly Director James Clark and Associate Director Lynne Withey. Other UC Press staff with whom we have enjoyed working include Erika Büky, Kim Darwin, Fran Mitchell, and copyeditor Anne Canright.

As the Project has progressed, the involvement of its Advisory Board in the editorial process has declined but nevertheless remains important. I have deeply appreciated the useful guidance I have received from this extraordinary group of distinguished scholars and former associates of Dr. King, who are listed on the volume's opening pages. In addition to Mrs. King and Mrs. Farris, I wish to acknowledge in particular the productive discussions of Volume III concerns that I have had with several of the board's members. The sage counsel and friendship of John Hope Franklin and Vincent Harding helped me weather some difficult periods during my time as Project Director. David J. Garrow has always been willing to share his documentary resources and exceptional expertise. I would also like to acknowledge the valuable advice I've received from Louis R. Harlan, Robert A. Hill, Darlene Clark Hine, Otis Moss, Jr., Preston N. Williams, Harris Wofford, and Andrew J. Young.

Financial Supporters

The King Papers Project could not have survived without funding from numerous generous and enlightened donors. Major contributors to this volume include the Division of Research and Education Programs of the National Endowment for the Humanities (NEH); Emory University; the James Irvine Foundation; Peter Kovler; Judith L. Lansing; the Lilly Endowment; the National Historical Publications and Records Commission (NHPRC); the Nordson Corporation Foundation; the David and Lucile Packard Foundation; the John T. Rockefeller Foundation; Stanford University; and the H. W. Wilson Foundation. Individuals at these institutions have often demonstrated a concern for the Project far outside the bounds of their professional responsibilities. I acknowledge in particular NEH staff members who have worked with the project, including former Program Officer Douglas M. Arnold, Grants Administrator Steven F. Veneziani, and current Program Officer Daniel P. Jones. NHPRC Executive Director Gerald George, Deputy Executive Director Roger Bruns, Program Director Nancy Sahli, Assistant Program Director Richard Sheldon, and Archivist Donald L. Singer have been generous in their assistance to the Project. In addition, I have appreciated the

Acknowledgments support of Irvine Foundation President Dennis Collins and Lilly Endowment Program Director Jacqui Burton. Carolyn Gibson and Constance Haqq of the Nordson Corporation Foundation were also very helpful.

Since early 1992, many individuals have taken the opportunity to join the Stanford University Associates of the Martin Luther King, Jr., Papers Project, a fundraising support group for our Stanford office. Associates in the Patron category include the Ruth M. Batson Educational Foundation; Diane F. and James A. Geocaris, Jr.; William P. Madar; the *San Jose Mercury News;* and Elizabeth Traugott.

Donors include Ann Appleman; Keith Archuleta; Big Apple Films; Taylor Branch; Wayne Duckworth; Mary McKinney Edmonds; Ernst and Young, Northern California Division; the First Hebrew Congregation of Oakland, Temple Sinai; George M. Fredrickson; Granite Broadcasting Corporation; Ronne and Donald Hess; L. Tyrone Holt; Benson Kanemoto; Lydia Kennard; KNTV Radio and Television, San Jose; Lockheed Missiles and Space Corporation, Inc.; Leanne MacDougall; the Martin Luther King, Jr., Association of Santa Clara Valley; Woodrow A. and Debra J. Myers, Jr.; Jerry Nightingale; George Ow, Jr.; University National Bank and Trust Co.; the University of Newcastle upon Tyne; and Wyse Technology.

Sustainers and members include Carolyn Barnes; Gracia Bell; Julian Bond; Michael R. and Rosalyn M. Britt; Roger and Ora Clay; Harvey L. and Fannie L. Cole; John A. Dittmer; Richard B. Fields; James and Eva Goodwin; Gloria Guth; Tom Hayden; Virginia M. Henderson; Lisa Hoyos; Gerald Jackson; Michael Kazin; the Links, Inc. (Peninsula Chapter); Doug J. McAdam; Marsha Meinel; Thomas J. Mikelson; Robert S. Moorehead; Henry Organ; Pamela Petty; Beverly P. Ryder; Sun Microsystems, Inc.; Temple Beth El; Bill Walsh; Shelly Weintraub; Rosalind Wolf; and Richard Wylie.

Staff Members

This volume is the result of a long-term collaboration involving student and postgraduate researchers in which academic credentials counted for less than demonstrated ability and dedication. From its inception, the mission of the King Papers Project has been not only to produce a definitive edition of King's papers but also to provide an opportunity for able and dedicated students to acquire research skills and to increase their understanding of the modern African-American freedom struggle. The availability of such learning opportunities has reinforced the project's strong ties to Stanford and Emory. As the project has evolved, a few veteran staff members have provided an essential degree of stability amid the continual turnover of student and professional researchers. The editors listed on the title page have each made vital, and in some instances unanticipated, contributions.

Stewart Burns, the associate editor originally assigned to supervise research on this volume, remained associated with the Project until funding for his position expired in September 1994. Stewart's knowledge of the civil rights movement and his commitment to King's ideals made him an effective mentor for the Stanford students and summer interns assigned to work with him. He personally selected documents for the volume, supervised document transcriptions, and prepared early drafts of the introduction and annotations. Since leaving the Project he

xxviii

has continued to volunteer useful suggestions on the manuscript as it neared completion.

After Stewart's departure, the remaining staff began an intense period of work on the behind-schedule manuscript. A major contributor to this extraordinary effort was Susan Carson, who moved from her position as the Project's librarian and archivist to that of managing editor, coordinating the daily activities of other staff members and many of the student researchers. Having designed the document database, she possessed unparalleled knowledge of the diverse activities associated with the Project, from preparation of grant proposals and document acquisition to cataloging and manuscript preparation.

Editorial Assistant Dana L. H. Powell, whom I recruited upon her graduation from Howard University, worked closely with Stewart before his departure. Her high level of conscientiousness, dedication, and willingness to take on additional responsibilities made it possible for us to complete the volume. During her year and eight months as a staff member, Dana's quick mastery of the necessary documentary editing skills allowed her to make a major contribution both to this volume and to Volume II.

Contributing Editor Peter Holloran has been involved in the Project ever since he joined the staff as a Stanford sophomore in 1985. After contributing heavily to the first two volumes, Pete has made his remarkable editorial skills available to us on a part-time basis during the past two years. It has been a singular pleasure to work with him and to observe his coming-of-age as a scholar and as a person.

In addition to those acknowledged on the title page, many other staff members made essential contributions to this volume. When Dana returned to Washington, D.C., in the spring of 1995, she was replaced by Katrina Nusum, a Stanford graduate who had previously worked at the Project as a research assistant. Katrina assumed primary responsibility for the final preparation of this volume, coordinating its progress through to publication. She participated in hundreds of editorial discussions and managed to stay on top of thousands of details. I have greatly appreciated her patience and persistence.

Since fall 1995 Assistant Archivist Jodie Medeiros, a former summer intern, has made an important contribution to the volume, supervising student researchers and handling the countless details that are required for a documentary edition. Other staff members who assisted on this volume include former Assistant Archivist Elizabeth Báez, who has continued to assist the project while pursuing medical studies in Atlanta, and research assistants Michelle Walsh, Amy Whitcomb, and Judy Wu.

Former volume editor Ralph E. Luker graciously agreed to return to the Project on a temporary basis during 1995. His broad and extended experience with the King Papers Project contributed greatly to the editing of this manuscript during its final stages.

Although not directly involved in the research or writing of this volume, other individuals have contributed to its completion. Project Administrator Karl Knapper has handled the daily management of the Project's financial affairs as well as my own scheduling and travel arrangements. I have appreciated the calm and good cheer with which he has carried out a difficult job. Aylin Altan served the Project well during her year as the Project's consultant on fund-raising. Carolyn Barnes volunteered to assist the Project's fund-raising efforts. In addition, the fol-

Acknowledgments   lowing assistants have undertaken the difficult and sometimes unrewarding task of bringing order to my office: Temera Carson, Mary Anne M. Morgan, Haleema J. Quraishi, and Heather D. Williams.

Student Researchers: Stanford Office

The Project has always depended on the skills, dedication, and exceptional talents of Stanford students. These students, working as interns, volunteers, or for academic credit, have contributed enormous energy and enthusiasm. Undergraduate researchers who worked on Volume III or whose work was not acknowledged in previous volumes include Stephanie Baca-Delancey, Sarah Bacon, Prithika Balakrishnan, Denise Barrett, Lily Batchelder, Kristin Beattie, Alaina C. Beverly, Kofi Bruce, Cherie Burgess, Alan Burnce, Kimberly Burton, Alice Chang, Danielle Colding, Lisa Dawe, Daniel P. K. Diffenbaugh, Theo Emery, Alice Feng, Claudine Gay, Emily Haines, Malcolm Hanson, Sanjiv Harpavat, Louis Jackson, Mark Jeter, Lisa Kohn, Julia Lanoff, Kaira Lingo, Annie Luetkemeyer, Michael MacKenzie, Jennifer Marcus, Anthony Marsh, Tasha McNeil, Hope Mohr, Mary Anne Morgan, Olivia Ongpin, Aresa Pecot, Haleema J. Quraishi, Urmila Rajagopal, Matthew Scelza, Carmella Schaecher, Michelle R. Scott, Chloe Sladden, Stephanie Soler, Ryan Tacorda, Wesley Watkins, Heather D. Williams, Nikki Williams, Thomas Earl Williams, Jr., Michael Winnick, and Zachary V. Wright. Graduate students who contributed to the Project's research efforts include Stephanie Brookins, Angela Brown, Bernard Butcher, Leslie Harris, Kevin Mumford, Lennora Redmond, Renee Romano, Tselane Sheppard-Williams, Stuart K. Snydman, and Michael Whamond. Researchers Robert S. Moorehead and William Tucker also provided indispensable assistance in this area. 'Alim J. Beveridge, Ismael Medrano, Marcus Treviño, and Huma Waheed supplied the Project with invaluable computer expertise that helped to maintain our electronic databases and computers. The Project's World Wide Web site has been upgraded and maintained by Michael MacKenzie, Joshua Jacobson, and Carmella Schaecher.

The Project has also benefited from the participation of a number of graduate and undergraduate students from other colleges and universities who were able to work at our Stanford offices through the auspices of an internship funded by the Irvine Foundation. They include Erica Armstrong (University of Pennsylvania), Crystal Feimster (University of North Carolina–Chapel Hill), Matthew Gladue (University of Michigan), Martha Jones (Columbia University), Jodie Medeiros (Clark University), Hasson Perkins (Emory University), Janet Scott (Spelman College), A. Benjamin Spencer (Morehouse College), and E. Stephen Thompson (Morehouse College). Andre Namphy (Harvard University), Jamie N. Saunders (University of California, Berkeley), and Fawzia Topan (University of Newcastle upon Tyne) also participated as volunteers in the Project's research.

Acquisition and Research Assistance

Volume III, like the volumes that preceded it, would not have been possible without the King-related documents that have been provided to us by numerous individuals and institutions. The King collection at the King Center has been at the
xxx   core of our selection. In addition, the King collection at Boston University, which

is the largest existing archive of pre-1962 King materials, has been critically important to this volume. We are especially grateful for the generous assistance
of Special Collections Director Howard Gotlieb and Assistant Director Margaret
Goostray.

In addition to documents obtained from the King Center and Boston University, we identified more than seventy-five manuscript collections with King-related
material important for this volume. Institutions, archives, and libraries that assisted us in locating documents for this volume include the Alabama Department
of Archives and History; the American Baptist Historical Society; the Amistad
Research Center, Tulane University; the Andover-Harvard Theological Library,
Harvard University; the A. Philip Randolph Institute; the Archives of Labor and
Urban Affairs, Wayne State University; the Chicago Historical Society; the Dwight
D. Eisenhower Library; Fisk University; the University of Georgia; GRM Associates; the John F. Kennedy Library; the Library of Congress; the Linn-Henley Research Library, Birmingham Public Library; the University of Massachusetts, Am-
herst; the Montgomery County Court House; the Moorland-Spingarn Research
Center, Howard University; Morehouse College; the National Archive for Black
Women's History; the National Archives Library; the National Broadcasting Company, Inc.; the Presbyterian Department of History; Princeton University; the Bayard Rustin Fund; the Schlesinger Library on the History of Women in America, Radcliffe College; the Schomburg Collection, New York Public Library; the
Southern Baptist Convention Historical Commission; the Stanford University Libraries; the State Historical Society of Wisconsin; the Swarthmore College Peace
Collection; the Levi Watkins Learning Center, Alabama State University; the Robert W. Woodruff Library Archives and Special Collections, Atlanta University Center; Vanderbilt University; and Yale University.

Dr. King's acquaintances and colleagues have been among the most important
sources of King-related documents. Of those whom we were able to contact, many
assisted us immeasurably in our research, and some graciously allowed us to make
photocopies of the documents in their possession, which until now have not been
published. These individuals include T. M. Alexander, Leonard Ballou, Worth
Littlejohn Barbour, Jeanne M. Brayboy, Raleigh Bryant, Thomasina Burke, Johnnie R. Carr, Samuel DuBois Cook, Charles C. Diggs, Jr., Ernest C. Dillard, Mary
McKinney Edmonds, John England, John D. Erb, Pinkie Smith Franklin, Edgar N.
French, F. Beatrice French, Overa B. Glasco, R. J. Glasco, Robert S. Graetz, Ju-
lian O. Grayson, Hazel Gregory, W. T. Handy, Jr., Roland E. Haynes, R. W. Hilson,
Robert E. Hughes, Homer A. Jack, M. J. Jones, George D. Kelsey, Thomas Kilgore,
Jr., Joel Lawrence King, Sr., Gil B. Lloyd, William Robert Miller, Ernest Morgan,
Walter G. Muelder, Earl E. Nance, Sr., L. Michelle Odom, H. J. Palmer, John
Patterson, Harold E. Pinkston, Sr., Samuel D. Proctor, Maxwell M. Rabb, Thelma
Austin Rice, S. Paul Schilling, Vivian C. Stanley, Francis S. Thomas, Charles
Walker, Eunice Guy Weston, H. Edward Whitaker, and Harris Wofford.

Individuals who gave permission for publication of the documents of relatives
include Ann Muste Baker, Worth Littlejohn Barbour, Sylvia W. Bigelow, Mary E.
Britton, Marie Faulkner Brown, Yvonne Shade Clark, Thomas Allen Coleman II,
Mildred J. Davis, Madeleine DeWolf, Zera L. Dockery, Elizabeth Johns Drake,
Mary McKinney Edmonds, Myrlie Evers-Williams, JoAnne Grant, Hazel Y. Gray,
Mrs. J. Raymond Henderson, Eldredge Hiller, R. Louise Hope, Thorsten W. Hor-

Acknowledgments ton, Howard E. Jernagin, Edward K. Kaplan, Margaret Morgan Lawrence, Martha H. Lorraine, Maurice Marie-Sainte, William T. Mason, Jr., Lovelle A. Maxwell, Diane Dickerson Montgomery, Elizabeth Olney, Janet L. S. Brown Page, Charles L. Peck, Helen M. Smiley, Alice Smith, Esther Smith, Vivian C. Stanley, John M. Swomley, Jr., Fran Thomas, Sue Bailey Thurman, Elizabeth Chalmers Todrank, Joan Blanton Tucker, Aminda Wilkins, Aubrey Williams, Jr., and J. B. Wood.

Dexter Avenue King Memorial Baptist Church and Ebenezer Baptist Church have generously made available to us important documents from King's life as pastor of these churches.

The following institutions and individuals assisted the Project's audiovisual acquisitions and research for this volume: AP World Wide Photos; the Archival and Museum Collection, Hampton University; the Bettman Archives; the CBS News Archives; Harvey Dinnerstein; Magnum Photos, Inc.; Burt Silverman; Vivian C. Stanley; Time, Inc.; and Sandra Weiner.

Permissions were obtained with the assistance of Thomas Battle, the Moorland-Spingarn Research Center; Barbara B. Coolidge, Shawmut Bank Connecticut; Wayne Furman, the Norman Thomas Papers, New York Public Library; Norman Hill, the A. Philip Randolph Institute; Beth M. Howse, the Fisk University Library; Karen L. Jefferson, the Moorland-Spingarn Research Center; Wallace Liverance, Jr., Burke and Burke Law Firm; Jeffrey D. Marshall, the Bailey-Howe Memorial Library, University of Vermont; Mary Lou Morell, Shawmut Bank Connecticut; Archie Motley, the Chicago Historical Society; Clifford L. Muse, Jr., the Moorland-Spingarn Research Center; Walter Naegle, the Bayard Rustin Fund; Tim O'Brien, Curtis Brown Ltd.; Mattie A. Robinson, the Worker at Nannie Helen Burroughs School, Inc.; Brian E. Urquhart, the Ford Foundation; Dr. Kenny J. Williams, Department of English, Duke University; and Joseph Wilson, Department of Political Science, Brooklyn College.

Several scholars without official ties to the Project also provided invaluable assistance. These include Taylor Branch; Steven M. Millner, Santa Clara University; J. Mills Thornton III, the University of Michigan; and Joseph Wilson, Brooklyn College.

The following individuals kindly consented to interviews in connection with this volume: Maude L. Ballou, Mary Fair Burks, Harvey Cole, Virginia Foster Durr, and Glenn E. Smiley.

A few individuals have greatly enhanced the work of the Project simply by visiting us and talking about their involvement with King and the civil rights movement. Dorothy Cotton, Myrlie Evers-Williams, Vincent Harding, Jesse Jackson, Cornel West, and Harris Wofford have been among the Project's recent invited guests.

Certainly there are other individuals and organizations that participated in and contributed to the success of the King Papers Project. Failure to mention them simply reflects the limits of my memory rather than of my gratitude.

CLAYBORNE CARSON
15 JUNE 1996

*I neither started the protest nor suggested it. I simply responded to the call of the
people for a spokesman.*

Martin Luther King, Jr.
Stride Toward Freedom: The Montgomery Story (1958)

During the days after Montgomery police arrested Rosa Parks for refusing to give
her bus seat to a white man, Martin Luther King, Jr., emerged as the acknowledged leader of a major mass protest. King's formative experiences had prepared
him well for this unexpected calling, but his abilities would be tested repeatedly
as he offered guidance to a movement he had not initiated and could not control. Although the yearlong bus boycott in Montgomery was not the first collective protest against the southern Jim Crow system, it attained unique historical
significance by demonstrating that an African-American community could remain united and resolute in its determination to overcome segregation. The
Montgomery struggle marked the beginning of a new era in African-American
history; it also enabled King to begin a new phase of his ministry.

When Parks's solitary protest occurred on 1 December 1955, King was a twenty-
six-year-old minister, serving in only his second year as pastor of Dexter Avenue
Baptist Church. Nevertheless, he already embodied an African-American social-
gospel tradition to which his father and maternal grandfather had contributed.
King's prophetic vision, politically engaged preaching, and expansive pastoral
leadership derived from his experiences at Ebenezer Baptist Church, where admiration for his father's "noble example" had moved him to "serve humanity"
as a minister himself. Martin Luther King, Sr.'s, decades of successful church
management served as a model for the younger King as he asserted control over
the Dexter congregation. His first annual report had insisted that the pastor's
"authority is not merely humanly conferred, but divinely sanctioned." King reminded church members that this implied an "unconditional willingness of the
people to accept the pastor's leadership. This means that leadership never as-
cends from the pew to the pulpit, but it invariably descends from the pulpit to
the pew."

Even as he advocated pastoral authority, however, King was also aware that
effective leadership required enthusiastic lay participation. He urged members
of the congregation to participate in various church committees in order to "assume an equal responsibility" for implementing his plans. Among King's first

1

actions after ascending to Dexter's pulpit was to establish a Social and Political Action Committee that would remind the congregation of the need to "unite with" the NAACP and the "necessity of being registered voters."[1] By the time of Parks's arrest, King had confidently set forth ambitious expectations for the congregation: "Let each of us go out at this moment with grim and bold determination to extend the horizons of Dexter to new boundaries, and lift the spire of her influence to new heights, so that we will be able to inject new spiritual blood into the veins of this community."[2]

King could not have anticipated the unprecedented unity and militancy of Montgomery's black residents as they protested Parks's arrest; nevertheless, he brought singular assets to his new role as a movement leader. During the boycott he received support and advice from an extensive network of relatives, family friends, former classmates, and fellow ministers. Although the extant correspondence from this period understates the significance in King's life of those close to him—Coretta Scott King and Ralph David Abernathy, for example—the letters he wrote and received illuminate the extent to which King relied on established relationships. In addition, even as he acquired a more sophisticated understanding of Gandhian principles, King's public statements continued to reiterate the Christian and democratic values he had affirmed in high school oratory, academic writings, and earlier sermons. He drew upon African-American preaching traditions, transforming familiar Christian principles into rationales for collective protest against injustice. The contemporaneous documents relating to King's involvement in the Montgomery bus boycott reveal the evolution of his religious leadership in the context of a sustained protest movement. These primary sources reveal history as it unfolded, correcting and supplementing the numerous memoirs and recorded recollections of participants and the published accounts of biographers and historians.[3]

Before he learned of Parks's arrest, King had already established connections with Montgomery's network of civil rights activists. Earlier in the year he had

---

1. Quotations from King, "An Autobiography of Religious Development," 22 November 1950, in *The Papers of Martin Luther King, Jr.*, vol. 1: *Called to Serve, January 1929–June 1951*, ed. Clayborne Carson, Ralph E. Luker, and Penny A. Russell (Berkeley and Los Angeles: University of California Press, 1992), p. 363; King, "Recommendations to the Dexter Avenue Baptist Church for the Fiscal Year 1954–1955," 5 September 1954, in *The Papers of Martin Luther King, Jr.*, vol. 2: *Rediscovering Precious Values, July 1951–November 1955*, ed. Clayborne Carson, Ralph E. Luker, Penny A. Russell, and Peter Holloran (Berkeley and Los Angeles: University of California Press, 1994), pp. 287, 290.

2. King, "Annual Report, Dexter Avenue Baptist Church," 31 October 1955, in *Papers* 2:580.

3. Memoirs of participants include: King, *Stride Toward Freedom: The Montgomery Story* (New York: Harper & Row, 1958); Coretta Scott King, *My Life with Martin Luther King, Jr.* (New York: Holt, Rinehart & Winston, 1969); Ralph David Abernathy, *And the Walls Came Tumbling Down: An Autobiography* (New York: Harper & Row, 1989); Jo Ann Gibson Robinson, *The Montgomery Bus Boycott and the Women Who Started It: The Memoir of Jo Ann Gibson Robinson*, ed. David J. Garrow (Knoxville: University of Tennessee Press, 1987). Among the secondary accounts of the bus boycott movement, the following recent studies have been the most useful in the preparation of this volume: Taylor Branch, *Parting the Waters: America in the King Years, 1954–63* (New York: Simon & Schuster, 1988); and David J. Garrow, *Bearing the Cross: Martin Luther King, Jr., and the Southern Christian Leadership Conference* (New York: William Morrow, 1986). Also of value are the primary and secondary sources assembled in David J. Garrow, ed., *The Walking City: The Montgomery Bus Boycott, 1955–1956* (Brooklyn, N.Y.: Carlson, 1989).

given a well-received talk to the Montgomery branch of the NAACP. That talk impressed former branch president E. D. Nixon, the most active and outspoken of Montgomery black progressives, who in the late 1930s founded the Montgomery division of the Brotherhood of Sleeping Car Porters and then promoted voting rights as head of the Montgomery chapter of the Alabama Progressive Democratic Association. King's talk led to an invitation—signed by Parks in her role as branch secretary—to join the executive committee of the local NAACP.[4] King also became involved in the interracial Alabama Council on Human Relations, where he interacted with the few white liberals in the state willing to oppose segregation's worst excesses.[5] Clifford Durr, for example, provided legal advice as well as friendly encouragement to Montgomery's progressive black leadership. His wife, Virginia Foster Durr, had arranged for her friend Parks to attend a school desegregation workshop in August 1955 at interracial Highlander Folk School in Tennessee, an experience that helped inspire her subsequent challenge to Montgomery's bus segregation.[6]

The morning after Nixon, with the Durrs' assistance, gained Parks's release from jail and secured her approval to use her arrest as a test case to challenge bus seating policies, he called King and other black leaders to inform them of the effort, already under way, to boycott Montgomery's buses. By this time Jo Ann Robinson, a leader of Montgomery's Women's Political Council (WPC) and of Dexter's Social and Political Action Committee, had already drafted, mimeographed, and begun circulating thousands of leaflets urging a one-day bus boycott.[7] With the WPC actively mobilizing support for a boycott, Nixon, King, and Ralph Abernathy, pastor of Montgomery's First Baptist Church and a close friend of King's since his arrival in the city, invited black leaders to discuss the situation at a Friday evening meeting in Dexter's basement.

Although King hosted the initial planning meeting, the several dozen ministers and community leaders who gathered at Dexter did not see him as the obvious choice to direct the boycott effort. King recalled that Nixon would have presided at the Friday evening meeting if he had not had to leave town because of his work as a Pullman porter. In Nixon's absence, Rev. L. Roy Bennett, president of

---

4. Parks to King, 26 August 1955, in *Papers* 2:572.

5. Introduction to *Papers* 2:34.

6. See Virginia Foster Durr, *Outside the Magic Circle,* ed. Hollinger F. Barnard (New York: Simon & Schuster, 1985), p. 279.

7. See Robinson, Leaflet, "Another Negro Woman Has Been Arrested," 2 December 1955. (For the complete citation, including archival location, of this and other primary documents, see the Calendar of Documents. King and Abernathy's revision of her leaflet is published on p. 67 in this volume.) After herself being ordered to give up her seat on a Montgomery bus, Robinson had taken over leadership of the WPC in 1950, replacing Mary Fair Burks, the chair of Alabama State's English department, who had founded the political activist group in 1949. During the two years before Rosa Parks's arrest, Robinson, along with other black leaders, had contacted white officials on several occasions to convey complaints about bus company practices. During the spring of 1954 she informed Mayor W. A. Gayle that a protest boycott of buses was being considered (see Robinson to Gayle, 21 May 1954). The WPC again briefly considered calling for a boycott after the arrest on 2 March 1955 of high school student Claudette Colvin for refusing to relinquish her seat to a white person. See Robinson, *Montgomery Bus Boycott and the Women Who Started It.*

Montgomery's Interdenominational Ministerial Alliance, chaired the discussions. Agreeing "that no one should be identified as *the* leader," ministers attending the meeting generally supported a one-day protest but were uncertain whether the boycott should be extended or whether a protest group should be established.[8] King and Abernathy stayed at Dexter afterward to revise Robinson's leaflet, adding a call to attend a mass meeting Monday evening at Holt Street Baptist Church. Along with other black ministers, they announced the proposed action from their pulpits on Sunday morning. The planned protest also received unexpected publicity from a front-page article in Sunday's *Montgomery Advertiser* and from radio and television reports.[9]

African Americans in Montgomery gave overwhelming support to the one-day boycott on Monday morning, 5 December. Montgomery City Lines manager J. H. Bagley estimated that 90 percent of the city's blacks refused to ride the buses, and King later recalled seeing "no more than eight Negro passengers" on the morning buses and insisted that black support for the protest "reached almost 100 per cent." Despite inflammatory statements by Police Commissioner Clyde Sellers about "Negro 'goon squads,'" the first day of the boycott was peaceful, with only one arrest.[10] Meanwhile, Judge John B. Scott convicted Rosa Parks of violating a state law requiring segregation on city buses and fined her ten dollars plus four dollars in court costs. Parks's lawyer, Fred D. Gray, announced that he would appeal the verdict to the Circuit Court of Montgomery.

That afternoon, eighteen black leaders met to plan the evening's mass meeting; to further their effort they decided to form the Montgomery Improvement Association (MIA), a name suggested by Abernathy.[11] After approving an agenda for the later meeting, they unanimously elected King to head the new group. Although King did not seek the position, his selection reflected the reputation he had swiftly built as a congenial and articulate civil rights proponent. The motion to elect King came from Rufus Lewis, a businessman, Dexter stalwart, and voter registration activist, who served as president of the Montgomery Citizens Steering Committee. The minutes of the meeting give little sense of the discussions, but the later recollections of participants offered a variety of reasons for King's selection, with several participants, including Lewis, Nixon, and Abernathy, taking credit for pushing King forward as the best candidate to head the MIA.[12] King recalled that events "happened so quickly that I did not even have

---

8. A. W. Wilson, interview by Donald T. Ferron, 27 January 1956.

9. Joe Azbell, "Negro Groups Ready Boycott of City Lines," *Montgomery Advertiser,* 4 December 1955.

10. King, *Stride Toward Freedom,* p. 54; Joe Azbell, "Extra Police Set for Patrol Work in Trolley Boycott," *Montgomery Advertiser,* 5 December 1955.

11. Abernathy, interview by Donald T. Ferron, 3 February 1956.

12. See U. J. Fields, Minutes of Montgomery Improvement Association Founding Meeting, 5 December 1955, pp. 68–70 in this volume. At the meeting Nixon reportedly chastised the group for considering operating the new organization in secrecy: "Am I to tell our people that you are cowards?" he later remembered saying. King "raised his hand to signify that he was not. Before you know it, he was nominated, seconded and became president" (Nixon, 28 March 1956 speech, reported in *WRL News* 78 [May–June 1956]: 1). Abernathy recalled that he expected Lewis and Nixon to be nominated and was surprised when Lewis nominated King: "Opposed to Nixon, [Lewis] wasn't sure whether or not he himself had the votes, so he proposed a compromise candidate" (Abernathy, *And the Walls Came Tumbling Down,* p. 148).

time to think it through"; he also suggested that he "would have declined the nomination" if he had considered its implications.[13]

That evening King delivered his first address as a protest leader to an audience of several thousand people that spilled out of Holt Street Baptist Church into the street. With only twenty minutes to prepare his remarks, he later recalled praying for divine guidance to resolve a "sobering dilemma": "How could I make a speech that would be militant enough to keep my people aroused to positive action and yet moderate enough to keep this fervor within controllable and Christian bounds?"[14] King's dilemma reflected his characteristic desire to find a middle course between conflicting alternatives;[15] though tactically restrained, his speech was nonetheless a stirring call to action. King depicted the bus boycott as resulting from an accumulation of racial injustices—the "many occasions" when African Americans were "intimidated and humiliated and . . . oppressed, because of the sheer fact that they were Negroes."[16]

King referred only obliquely to prior indignities, but his audience was familiar with them. In particular, a protest had been considered the previous March in response to the arrest of a black teenager, Claudette Colvin, who had refused to give up her seat to a white passenger.[17] Although the Colvin case did not prompt a legal challenge to segregation policies, the failure of the bus company and city officials to make even minor concessions had contributed to festering feelings of resentment among the black residents of Montgomery. As King saw matters, the buildup of such grievances had finally driven the black community to resist: "There comes a time when people get tired of being trampled over by the iron feet of oppression." King concluded his speech with an admonition, drawing a phrase from his Dexter annual report, to transform resentment into resistance rooted in Christian principles:

> As we stand and sit here this evening, and as we prepare ourselves for what lies ahead, let us go out with a grim and bold determination that we are going to stick together. We are going to work together. Right here in Montgomery, when the history books are written in the future, somebody will have to say, "There lived a race

---

13. King, *Stride Toward Freedom*, p. 56.

14. Ibid., pp. 59–60.

15. For example, while addressing the Birmingham NAACP branch earlier in 1955, King had rejected both extreme optimism and extreme pessimism, recommending instead a "realistic approach" that acknowledged that African Americans had "come a long long way but we have a long, long way to go" (quoted in "Apathy Among Church Leaders Hit in Talk by Rev. M. L. King," 25 January 1955, in *Papers* 2:330).

16. King, MIA Mass Meeting at Holt Street Baptist Church, 5 December 1955, p. 72 in this volume. In certain instances King's quotations from this recorded speech are somewhat different from the version found in *Stride Toward Freedom*.

17. The Colvin arrest led black leaders, including King, to meet with white officials of the city and the bus company, who rejected requests for even modest changes in seating policies. On 18 March 1955 Colvin was placed on probation after being convicted of violating the state segregation law and of assaulting a policeman who was removing her from the bus. The conviction was appealed to the circuit court, which on 6 May affirmed the assault conviction while dismissing the segregation code violation. Thus Colvin's lawyers were unable to use her conviction as a test case to challenge the state segregation law.

of people, a *black* people, 'fleecy locks and black complexion,' a people who had the moral courage to stand up for their rights. And thereby they injected a new meaning into the veins of history and of civilization." [18]

King's address responded to immediate events, but it also set forth the main themes of his subsequent public ministry: social-gospel Christianity and democratic idealism, combined with resolute advocacy of nonviolent protest. His interpretation of the Christian mission recalled his father's insistence that clergymen should become "part of every movement for the betterment of our people," as well as his own admonition to an NAACP audience in Birmingham that black Americans "must do more than pray and read the Bible" in order to secure civil rights.[19] Now, speaking in a church to an audience that largely shared his religious reference points, King merged New Testament notions of transformative love with Old Testament prophetic imagery—"until justice runs down like water." While identifying nonviolent tactics with the teachings of Jesus, King also reminded his audience that "it is not enough for us to talk about love." He explained: "There is another side called justice. And justice is really love in calculation. Justice is love correcting that which revolts against love." In order to achieve justice, King argued, black residents must be prepared to use not only "the tools of persuasion" but also those of "coercion." [20]

In addition to identifying the boycott as an expression of Christian principles, King identified it with older American traditions of dissent and protest. Perhaps sensing that some members of his audience feared the consequences of opposing political authorities, King reminded them that "there is never a time in our American democracy that we must ever think we're wrong when we protest. We reserve that right." He cited the example of workers who saw themselves "trampled over by capitalistic power" and recognized that there "was nothing wrong with . . . getting together and organizing and protesting for [their] rights." Speaking during the Cold War era, when leftist dissent was generally suppressed, he justified his call for militancy by insisting that protest was consistent with American political traditions: "If we were dropped in the dungeon of a totalitarian regime we couldn't do this," King explained. "But the great glory of American democracy is the right to protest for right." The boycott, he argued, reflected the nation's fundamental ideals. "If we are wrong, the Supreme Court of this nation is wrong. If we are wrong, the Constitution of the United States is wrong. If we are wrong, God Almighty is wrong. If we are wrong, Jesus of Nazareth was

---

18. King, MIA Mass Meeting at Holt Street Baptist Church, 5 December 1955, p. 74 in this volume.

19. King, Sr., Moderator's Annual Address, Atlanta Missionary Baptist Association, 17 October 1940 (quoted in *Papers* 1:34); King, quoted in "Apathy Among Church Leaders Hit in Talk by Rev. M. L. King," 25 January 1955, in *Papers* 2:330.

20. King, MIA Mass Meeting at Holt Street Baptist Church, 5 December, pp. 73–74 in this volume. King used similar language to describe both Reinhold Niebuhr's and Paul Tillich's conceptions of love and justice. King noted in his dissertation that, for Tillich, "justice is dependent on love. Justice," he continued, "is really an act of love protesting against that which violates love" (King, "A Comparison of the Conceptions of God in the Thinking of Paul Tillich and Henry Nelson Wieman," 15 April 1955, in *Papers* 2:442). See also King, "Reinhold Niebuhr's Ethical Dualism," 9 May 1952, in *Papers* 2:145.

merely a utopian dreamer that never came down to earth. If we are wrong, justice
is a lie." [21]

Inspired by King's address, the several thousand residents attending the mass meeting voted unanimously to continue boycotting the city's buses. During subsequent days and weeks, support for the bus boycott remained strong. Car owners volunteered to pick up riders, and black taxi drivers charged passengers the same ten-cent fare as Montgomery's buses, rather than the required minimum charge of forty-five cents. On 8 December, King and other black leaders met with city and bus company officials and proposed that patrons be seated on a "first-come, first-served basis," with black passengers seated from the rear and whites from the front. King also delivered two other conditions for ending the boycott: more courteous treatment of black passengers and the hiring of black drivers on "predominantly Negro" routes.[22] The meeting, however, ended in an impasse. Although Montgomery's municipal code required segregated seating while leaving implementation largely in the hands of bus drivers, local white leaders were unwilling to modify segregation practices.[23] Most believed that the boycott would be short-lived. "The Mayor's attitude," King wrote, "was made clear when he said, 'Comes the first rainy day and the Negroes will be back on the busses.' " [24] Seeking ideas for extending the boycott, King contacted T. J. Jemison, who had organized an efficient car pool during a 1953 bus boycott in Baton Rouge. By 13 December Rufus Lewis, chairman of the MIA transportation committee, and R. J. Glasco, chairman of the financial committee, had coordinated drivers for forty-eight "dispatch" and forty-two "pick-up" stations.[25]

Encouraged by the boycott's effectiveness, King and other black leaders began to reconsider their goal: was better treatment for black bus riders sufficient, or might an end to bus segregation be called for? King's personal opposition to segregation had been evident early in the year when he told the Birmingham NAACP branch that segregation was "wrong" and even constituted "a form of slavery." [26] He later claimed that boycott participants knew from the start "that the ultimate solution was total integration," but they were at first willing to accept "a temporary alleviation of the problem" while desegregation litigation pro-

---

21. King, MIA Mass Meeting at Holt Street Baptist Church, 5 December 1955, pp. 73 in this volume.

22. The demands were also presented to officials at the bus company's headquarters in Chicago (see King to the National City Lines, Inc., 8 December 1955, p. 81 in this volume). For King's account of this meeting, see Interview by Ferron, 4 February 1956, p. 123 in this volume.

23. Chapter 6 of the 1952 edition of the code read: "Every person operating a bus line in the city shall provide equal but separate accommodations for white people and Negroes on his buses by requiring the employees in charge thereof to assign passenger seats on the vehicles under the charge in such a manner as to separate the white people from the Negroes." The code allowed "Negro nurses having charge of white children [or a] sick or infirm person" to be seated with whites.

24. King, "Our Struggle," April 1956, p. 240 in this volume.

25. King, *Stride Toward Freedom*, pp. 75–77.

26. Quoted in "Apathy Among Church Leaders Hit in Talk by Rev. M. L. King," 25 January 1955, in *Papers* 2:330. During the boycott King was quoted by Tom Johnson, in "The Rev. King Is Boycott Boss," *Montgomery Advertiser*, 19 January 1956, as supporting "immediate integration," although he later claimed that his statement referred to the policy of the NAACP (see Ferron, Notes on MIA Executive Board Meeting, 23 January 1956, p. 104 in this volume).

ceeded.[27] During the initial weeks of the protest, however, he and other MIA leaders continued to claim publicly that their goal was merely better treatment. A newspaper account during the first week of the boycott noted that King spoke "with no little authority" as he assured reporters that black residents were simply seeking fairness, not desegregation: "We don't like the idea of Negroes having to stand where there are vacant seats. We are demanding justice on that point."[28] After a committee appointed by Mayor Gayle failed to arrive at a settlement during December, and white leaders continued to insist that they could not compromise under existing law, the stances of the two sides stiffened. At a crowded public meeting in late January, the city commissioners revealed that they had joined the local Citizens Council, part of a southwide organization to defend segregation.

Recognizing that an acceptable compromise settlement was unlikely, King and other black leaders moved gradually toward a public acknowledgment that their goal was ending segregation, although, as late as 27 January, the MIA's public stance was to seek only "a calm and fair consideration of the situation which has developed as a result of dissatisfaction over Bus policies."[29] MIA leaders were forced to clarify their objectives after city commissioners tried to settle the dispute by arranging a meeting with three black ministers who did not represent the MIA. On Saturday evening, 21 January, King learned from reporter Carl Rowan that city officials had announced that they had secured an agreement to end the boycott in return for a promise to designate sections that black bus riders would not have to relinquish to white passengers. King and other MIA leaders quickly announced that reports of a settlement were erroneous and that the boycott would continue.[30]

King later wrote that during this period white leaders spread false rumors about MIA leaders: "Negro workers were told by their white employers that their leaders were only concerned with making money out of the movement." According to King, some older black ministers were encouraged by whites to believe that they, rather than their younger counterparts, should be leading the protests. "I almost broke down under the continual battering of this argument," he recalled.[31] At the 23 January meeting of the MIA executive board, King responded deftly to the efforts of the white establishment to undermine his leadership, denying allegations that he had personally profited from fund-raising activities on behalf of the MIA. He also strongly condemned ministers who were willing to arrange unauthorized compromises with white officials, though he recommended against retaliation. At the end of the meeting he reminded the board that he had been made president by a unanimous vote, which prompted

27. King, "The Montgomery Story," 27 June 1956, p. 303 in this volume.

28. "Some Observations on the Boycott," *Montgomery Advertiser,* 8 December 1955.

29. See King et al. to the Citizens of Montgomery, 27 January 1956, p. 107 in this volume. See also King et al. to the Commissioners of the City of Montgomery, 9 January 1956, pp. 97–98 in this volume.

30. See MIA Press Release: The Bus Protest Is Still On, 22 January 1956, pp. 100–101 in this volume. See also King, *Stride Toward Freedom,* pp. 124–126; and L. D. Reddick, "The Bus Boycott in Montgomery," *Dissent* 3 (Spring 1956): 1–11.

31. King, *Stride Toward Freedom,* pp. 122–123.

that body's affirmation of confidence in their president. In addition, board members decided that only King could make statements to the press at his discretion; all other press releases would require approval of the MIA executive board.[32]

Seeking to undermine the MIA's resolve, city officials embarked on a "get-tough" campaign. After the city commissioners disclosed their membership in the Citizens Council, police increased harassment of drivers in the MIA car pool, issuing tickets and making arrests for alleged traffic violations. On 26 January, King himself was stopped for speeding. Ordinarily such infractions warranted just a citation, but King was arrested. "As we drove off," he later wrote, "a feeling of panic began to come over me." Uncertain whether the officers were taking him to the city jail or to a waiting mob, he found himself "trembling within and without." To his relief, he was delivered to the jail, where he remained for a short while before being released to a crowd of well-wishers that had gathered outside. Returning home to friends and family, King regained his courage: "I knew that I did not stand alone." That night, responding to widespread concern about his arrest, the MIA held seven mass meetings.[33]

Even before the city government had embarked on its official campaign of intimidation, King had received numerous threats against himself and his family over the telephone and by mail.[34] By mid-January, he found himself "faltering and growing in fear." After "a white friend" informed him of threats against his life, he announced at a mass meeting: "If one day you find me sprawled out dead, I do not want you to retaliate with a single act of violence." Late in the evening of 27 January, a day after his trip to the city jail, a particularly threatening call triggered a spiritual crisis. King recalled in *Stride Toward Freedom* that he sat alone in his kitchen, "ready to give up. With my cup of coffee sitting untouched before me I tried to think of a way to move out of the picture without appearing a coward." He turned to God for support. "The people are looking to me for leadership," he recalled saying in the still room, "and if I stand before them without strength and courage, they too will falter." King wrote that his prayers were answered when he

> experienced the presence of the Divine as I had never experienced Him before. It seemed as though I could hear the quiet assurance of an inner voice saying: "Stand up for righteousness, stand up for truth; and God will be at your side forever." Al-

32. See Ferron, Notes on MIA Executive Board Meeting, 23 January 1956, pp. 101–104 in this volume. In his memoir King recalled that he offered his resignation to the board, telling them that he did not "want to stand in the way of a solution to the problem which plagued our community, and that maybe a more mature person could bring about a speedier conclusion." He recalled that board members quickly urged him "to forget the idea of resignation," then gave him a unanimous vote of confidence (King, *Stride Toward Freedom*, p. 123).

33. See Complaint, *City of Montgomery v. Martin L. King*, 26 January 1956, p. 106 in this volume; "Dr. M. L. King Jr. Arrested, Released on Speeding Charges," *Birmingham World*, 31 January 1956; and King, *Stride Toward Freedom*, pp. 128 and 130–131.

34. "Montgomery Negroes Still Refuse to Ride Busses; Leaders Receive Threats," *Birmingham World*, 17 January 1956; and Ferron, Notes on MIA Executive Board Meeting, 2 February 1956, p. 120 in this volume. See also files of "hate" mail in MLKP-MBU.

most at once my fears began to go. My uncertainty disappeared. I was ready to face anything.[35]

Although King would depict this incident in his memoir as a crucial turning point in his spiritual life, he did not mention it publicly until a year later, when he confronted another wave of segregationist violence in Montgomery.[36]

Increasingly aware of his own importance to the movement, King also appreciated its grass-roots character. One of many individuals responsible for sustaining the bus boycott, he recognized that his influence was important but not always decisive. On 30 January he remarked at an MIA mass meeting, "I want you to know that if M. L. King had never been born this movement would have taken place. I just happened to be here."[37] He became the movement's preeminent spokesperson, but he consulted regularly with other local leaders, synthesized conflicting positions, delegated considerable responsibility, and moderated as well as stimulated mass militancy. He admitted to a friend at the end of January that the situation in Montgomery kept him "so busy that I hardly have time to breathe."[38] King also insisted that the movement's foot soldiers were determined to persevere, even if some leaders had grown weary. "From my limited contact," he remarked at an executive board meeting on 30 January, "if we went tonight and asked the people to get back on the bus, we would be ostracized. They wouldn't get back." He added that the threats against him were "a small price to pay if victory can be won."[39]

Just a few hours later, during a mass meeting at First Baptist Church, King learned that his house had been bombed. After being reassured of the safety of his wife and child, who had been in the parsonage when dynamite exploded on the front porch, King arrived home to find a large crowd of enraged black residents confronting police and city officials. Although Mayor Gayle and Police Commissioner Sellers were there to express their concern, King insisted that the incident was an outgrowth of the city's harassment efforts. In an impromptu address to the angry residents, he said that violence directed at him would not end the movement because he was not indispensable: "If I am stopped our work will not stop." His remarks as quoted in the *Montgomery Advertiser* reaffirmed his commitment to nonviolence and Christian principles: "He who lives by the sword will perish by the sword. Remember that is what God said. We are not advocating

---

35. King, *Stride Toward Freedom,* pp. 133–135.

36. After an unexploded bomb was found on his porch in January 1957, King was quoted as telling his congregation that he had had "a vision" the previous year in which he was told to "stand up for the truth, stand up for the righteousness." He also reportedly insisted: "If I had to die tomorrow morning I would die happy because I've been to the mountain top and I've seen the Promised Land and it's going to be here in Montgomery" (quoted in " 'Montgomery Dangerous' Negro Warns After Week-End of Violence," *New York Post,* 28 January 1957).

37. Willie Mae Lee, Notes on MIA Mass Meeting at First Baptist Church, 30 January 1956, pp. 113–114 in this volume. King later recalled, "The Montgomery story would have taken place if the leaders of the protest had never been born" (*Stride Toward Freedom,* p. 69).

38. King to H. Edward Whitaker, 30 January 1956, p. 113 in this volume.

39. Ferron, Notes on MIA Executive Board Meeting, 30 January 1956, pp. 109–112 in this volume.

violence. We want to love our enemies."[40] Hours later Coretta Scott King's father,
Obadiah (Obie) Scott, and King, Sr., along with his daughter Christine and son
A. D., arrived to find everyone safe. King, Sr., later reported that after the bombing his wife, Alberta Williams King, "wanted M. L. out of the movement right
then," but that their son was "determined to continue his work."[41]

By now, the MIA leadership was no longer expecting a quick settlement; the
boycott movement, they concluded, should directly confront segregated bus seating. This shift in strategy was prompted by the stalemate and encouraged by discussions with NAACP officials, who were eager to provide legal support for the
Montgomery movement once local leaders showed themselves willing to attack
segregation forthrightly.[42] At the 30 January executive board meeting, MIA
leaders decided to accept the NAACP's legal help in a federal lawsuit, *Aurelia S.
Browder et al. v. William A. Gayle,* in which four Montgomery women challenged
the constitutionality of the city and state bus segregation statutes. After debating
the issue, board members voted to continue the bus boycott even as they pursued
desegregation through litigation.[43] At an executive board meeting three days
later, King reaffirmed the MIA's determination to proceed with both the boycott
and the legal challenge despite segregationist intimidation. "We're not going to
give up; they can drop bombs in my house every day, I'm firmer now than ever,"
he reportedly remarked.[44]

King's success as a protest leader derived largely from his understanding of the
religious culture that pervaded the local movement and his ability to express familiar ideas cogently, utilizing concepts drawn from his theological studies. Although ostensibly a secular organization, the MIA was dominated by ministers.
Its mass meetings, held in churches on Mondays and Thursdays, at times re-
sembled evangelical services with the leaders' oratory enlivened by call-and-
response exchanges, congregational singing, scripture reading, and personal testimonials.[45] King and other ministers, especially Abernathy, shared responsibility
for the morale-building "pep talks," but King's frequent addresses were exceptional in their merging of inspirational oratory with thoughtful explications of
the larger philosophical and historical significance of the boycott movement.
King retained some of his ingrained skepticism regarding religious emotionalism, remarking, "If we, as a people, had as much religion in our hearts and souls

40. Quoted in Joe Azbell, "Blast Rocks Residence of Bus Boycott Leader," 31 January 1956, p. 115 in
this volume.

41. Martin Luther King, Sr., with Clayton Riley, *Daddy King: An Autobiography* (New York: William
Morrow, 1980), p. 169. Coretta Scott King's memoir mentions that King, Sr., and her father came to
Montgomery soon after the bombing in an unsuccessful attempt to convince his son to return with
his family to Atlanta (see *My Life with Martin Luther King, Jr.,* pp. 131–132).

42. See Roy Wilkins to W. C. Patton, 27 December 1955.

43. Ferron, Notes on MIA Executive Board Meeting, 30 January 1956, pp. 109–112 in this volume.
See also Wilkins to King, 8 March 1956, pp. 165–167 in this volume.

44. Ferron, Notes on MIA Executive Board Meeting, 2 February 1956, pp. 119–122 in this volume.

45. See, for example, Mass Meeting at the Holt Street Baptist Church, 5 December 1955, pp. 71–79
in this volume; and King's description of meetings in *Stride Toward Freedom,* pp. 85–87.

as we have in our legs and feet, we could change the world."[46] Nevertheless, he delivered compelling addresses to emotionally responsive and staid congregations alike. (He fondly recalled his father's expressive congregation, advising a preacher friend that, when compared to Dexter, Ebenezer had "some of the 'masses' in it," adding that "you can get in an occasional amen there.")[47] Although King's doctoral training set him apart from other ministers, his familiarity with African-American preaching traditions enabled him to display erudition without losing the attention of those with less formal education.

King's effectiveness was enhanced by his "closest associate and most trusted friend," Ralph Abernathy. The two had met briefly in Atlanta during the early 1950s, and after King's arrival in Montgomery they dined together almost nightly, engaging in extended conversations that included Coretta and Abernathy's wife, Juanita. The two men's personalities and abilities complemented each other. Abernathy later wrote that from the beginning of the friendship, "Martin expounded philosophy, [while] I saw its practical application on the local level."[48] King later described his fellow Baptist minister as a "persuasive and dynamic" speaker "with the gift of laughing people into positive action. When things became languid around mass meetings, Ralph Abernathy infused his audiences with new life and ardor."[49] King's and Abernathy's skills and abilities were complementary. One observer of the mass meetings recalled that King's discourses on *agape* and other philosophical concepts were sometimes brought down to earth by Abernathy: "Now, let me tell you what that means for tomorrow morning."[50] They were constant companions in Montgomery, as well as on speaking trips and family vacations. "It was mighty good to see you and Brother Abernathy yesterday," one friend wrote King. "To see one is to see the other now. You are sworn buddies in religion and the missionary journey akin to Paul's of old."[51] King remembered that they "prayed together and made important decisions together. His ready good humor lightened many tense moments. Whenever I went out of town I always left him in charge of the important business of the association, knowing that it was in safe hands."[52]

As in African-American churches, initiative and direction within the MIA came not only from male ministers but also from less visible leaders, especially women. Because they were largely excluded from the ministerial ranks that had traditionally provided leadership in black communities, female leaders stayed out of the spotlight and rarely served as speakers at MIA mass meetings or out-of-town support rallies. Black women played crucial roles, however, in sustaining the MIA's

---

46. Quoted in William Peters, "Our Weapon Is Love," *Redbook*, August 1956, p. 72.

47. King to John Thomas Porter, 30 September 1955. (Although this document predates the volume time period, it is included in the Calendar of Documents because it was among the Dexter Avenue Baptist Church papers discovered after the second volume of this edition was published.)

48. King, *Stride Toward Freedom*, p. 74. Abernathy, *And the Walls Came Tumbling Down*, p. 129.

49. King, *Stride Toward Freedom*, p. 74.

50. Quoted by Bayard Rustin, interview with Howell Raines, *My Soul Is Rested* (New York: G. P. Putnam's Sons, 1977), p. 54.

51. C. W. Kelly to King, 18 July 1956.

52. King, *Stride Toward Freedom*, p. 74.

ongoing committees and volunteer networks. King later conceded that, "more than any other person," Jo Ann Robinson "was active on every level of the protest."[53] Besides assuming an influential role as a strategist on the executive board and several committees, Robinson served as a key MIA negotiator because of her extensive experience lobbying white officials. Other women, such as Euretta Adair, Johnnie Carr, Irene West, and King's secretary Maude L. Ballou, were responsible for most of the daily activities that kept the boycott going, especially the car pool. African-American working women, having once been the primary users of the buses as they commuted to domestic jobs in white homes, were the mainstays of the bus boycott.

Coretta King herself played an active role in the boycott movement, firmly supporting her husband's decision to accept a leadership position in the MIA and, despite caring for an infant daughter, often joining him at movement events. "All along I have supported my husband in this cause," she said in March, "and at this point I feel even stronger about the cause, and whatever happens to him [. . .] happens to me." She became more involved as the boycott progressed, speaking publicly on behalf of the protest and singing at concerts.[54]

Members of the Dexter congregation also gave King vital support as he struggled to handle the physical and psychological demands of his rigorous speaking schedule and the basic operations of the MIA. Coretta King confided to a reporter that her husband "never has a minute to himself. When he isn't in court, he is attending meetings of the Association. When he is home, he is always on the phone." She depended on the help of others, particularly the women of Dexter, who "rallied around" her and her husband. "The ladies of the church and ladies of other churches and women in general have been extremely kind to us," she recalled. "All day long they come to my home. They clean our home, wash the baby, and bring food."[55]

King regretted that his responsibilities as a leader often took him away from Dexter. "For months," he later recalled, "my day-to-day contact with my parishioners had almost ceased. I had become no more than a Sunday preacher."[56] (Even then, sixteen of his Sundays during 1956 were spent preaching elsewhere.) In his end-of-the-year report, King apologized for his absences and thanked the congregation for its support. "Due to the multiplicity of duties that have come to me as a result of my involvement in the protest, I have often lagged behind in my pastoral duties." He expressed appreciation to those who had stepped in for him and "given words of encouragement when I needed them most. Even

---

53. Ibid., p. 78. In a January 1956 interview Rufus A. Lewis commented: "I sense that in addition to Reverend King, there is another leader, tho unknown to the public, of perhaps equal significance. The public recognizes Reverend King as the leader, but I wonder if Mrs. Robinson may be of equal importance" (Lewis, Interview by Donald T. Ferron, 20 January 1956).

54. Reactions to Conviction, 22 March 1956, pp. 198–199 in this volume. See Olivet Baptist Church, Announcement, "Coretta Scott King in Recital," 19 October 1956; and In Friendship, Program, Montgomery Anniversary Concert, 5 December 1956.

55. "Physical Wear and Tear Gets You, Mrs. King Says," *Baltimore Afro-American,* 31 March 1956. See also Coretta Scott King, *My Life with Martin Luther King, Jr.,* pp. 138–139.

56. King, *Stride Toward Freedom,* p. 141.

when my life and the life of my family were in personal jeopardy, you were at my side." [57]

Trusted Dexter members acted as King's personal bodyguards as threats mounted. Bob Williams, a friend from Morehouse and a professor of music at Alabama State, accompanied him nearly everywhere. He was in the car when King was arrested in January and later helped staff the twenty-four-hour protection that the MIA provided the Dexter parsonage after the bombing. "From the moment the protest started," King later wrote, Williams was "seldom far from my side or Coretta's." [58] Coretta King remembered that Williams "came to sleep there every night—not that he slept much." According to her account, Williams had apparently "slipped his shotgun into the house without Martin's knowledge of it and sat up most of the night with his gun beside him." [59] In the tense days following the bombing, King had unsuccessfully sought gun permits for his bodyguards, but he eventually decided to get rid of all guns, including his own, after discussing with his wife and others the inconsistency of leading a nonviolent movement while permitting the use of weapons for protection. "We tried to satisfy our friends by having floodlights mounted around the house, and hiring unarmed watchmen around the clock." [60]

On 21 February white Alabama officials initiated their most concerted effort to defeat the MIA by indicting eighty-nine boycott leaders for violating a 1921 state law barring conspiracies that interfered with lawful businesses. [61] King was in Nashville when he learned that he, Nixon, Parks, and many others had been charged. On his way home he stopped in Atlanta, where his parents sought to dissuade him from returning to Montgomery. That evening King, Sr., tried to convince his son to leave the Montgomery movement by convening a group of black leaders close to the family, including Morehouse College president Benjamin Mays and Atlanta University president Rufus E. Clement, to discuss the matter. Mays supported King's view that he should not abandon the movement. "I would rather be in jail ten years than desert my people now," King recalled telling the group. "I have begun the struggle, and I can't turn back. I have reached the

---

57. King, Annual Report, Dexter Avenue Baptist Church, 31 October 1956, p. 411 in this volume. Anticipating the demands on his time to remain undiminished, King asked the congregation to provide funds for an assistant.

58. King, *Stride Toward Freedom*, p. 141. Williams was later removed from his Alabama State position because of his involvement in the MIA.

59. Coretta Scott King, *My Life with Martin Luther King, Jr.*, p. 122. Williams arranged his first choral work, "Lord, I Can't Turn Back," when he found himself unable to sleep on the night of King's arrest for speeding. It was first sung in New York by Coretta Scott King at the Montgomery Anniversary Concert on 5 December 1956.

60. See Ferron, Notes on MIA Executive Board Meeting, 2 February 1956, p. 120 in this volume; King, *Stride Toward Freedom*, p. 141. Despite King's subsequent insistence that he had banned weapons in the parsonage, even in late February a visitor reported that King's bodyguards possessed "an arsenal" (Glenn E. Smiley to John Swomley and Al Hassler, 29 February 1956). Another visitor in late February remembered nearly sitting on a gun left lying on a chair in the Dexter parsonage (Bayard Rustin, interview by T. H. Baker, 17 June 1969, Lyndon Baines Johnson Presidential Library, Austin, Texas).

61. See Indictment, *State of Alabama v. M. L. King, Jr., et al.*, 21 February 1956, p. 133 in this volume.

point of no return."[62] Finally forced to acquiesce, King, Sr., drove to Montgomery with his son and accompanied him to the courthouse, where the indicted pastor surrendered to the sheriff on 23 February. He was released on bond after being fingerprinted and photographed.[63]

Although the indictment of boycott leaders was intended to weaken the resolve of the MIA activists, in fact it only strengthened the movement, securing extensive national press coverage for King's advocacy of nonviolent resistance to segregation. The indictments attracted numerous expressions of support from sympathizers outside Montgomery.[64] When King spoke at a mass meeting after his arrest, the *New York Times* provided front-page coverage, quoting King's comment that the boycott was "not a war between the white and the Negro but a conflict between justice and injustice." The reporter highlighted King's admonition against violence. "We must use the weapon of love," King was quoted as telling several thousand supporters at First Baptist Church. "We must have compassion and understanding for those who hate us."[65] Even more than the bombing of King's home three weeks before, the prosecution transformed King and the MIA into national symbols of civil rights protest. Afterward the volume of supportive correspondence, speaking requests, and contributions increased dramatically.

King's trial, which began on March 19, became a forum for the bus boycott movement, drawing many prominent spectators, including Detroit congressman Charles C. Diggs, Jr. The legal strategy of the MIA attorneys asserted two main points: first, that the MIA was conducting a constitutional protest rather than an economic boycott, and second, that MIA leaders had only advised local citizens, encouraging them to decide for themselves whether to stay off the buses. Witnesses supported the latter contention. As MIA recording secretary U. J. Fields insisted before the trial, "The people themselves have made up their own minds, their minds have not been made up for them."[66] Mrs. A. W. West similarly commented, "The leaders could do nothing by themselves. They are only the voice of thousands of colored workers."[67] (At a February mass meeting, Abernathy had expressed a widely held view when he announced to the audience, "This is your movement; we don't have any leaders in the movement; you are the leaders." When the audience shouted their approval, Abernathy added, "We tell Rev. King

---

62. King, *Stride Toward Freedom*, p. 145. See also King, Sr., *Daddy King*, pp. 170–172.

63. This photograph appears in the section following p. 33 in this volume. Once he realized that his son was committed to the struggle despite its dangers, King, Sr., joined in himself with characteristic vigor. Speaking at a mass meeting in Montgomery a week later, he reportedly set the meeting on fire with a short presentation, declaring that "I am no outsider, I have vested interest here . . . and if things get too hot I shall move in" (quoted in J. Harold Jones, Notes on MIA Mass Meeting at Hutchinson Street Baptist Church, 1 March 1956). During the year King, Sr., and Alberta Williams King traveled with their son to National Baptist Convention gatherings and attended several of King's addresses, including speeches in Denver and New York; see, for example, King to Anna C. Frank, 7 May 1956.

64. See, for example, letters from Wilkins and Ralph J. Bunche to King, 22 February 1956, pp. 134–135 in this volume; and A. Philip Randolph to Nixon, 23 February 1956.

65. Quoted in Wayne Phillips, "Negroes Pledge to Keep Boycott," *New York Times*, 24 February 1956, p. 136 in this volume.

66. Fields, interview by Ferron, 28 January 1956.

67. West, interview by Lee, 23 January 1956.

what to say and he says what we want him to say.") [68] Gladys Moore reflected the same sentiments when she testified at the trial, "Wasn't no one man started it. We all started it over night." [69]

Despite such protestations, however, the boycott could not have been sustained without effective leadership. Well before the trial, King's role as the MIA's main spokesperson and administrator was evident. Moreover, once Judge Eugene Carter and the prosecutors agreed to a defense request that all defendants be tried separately, with King to be tried first, journalists focused on him. Although the prosecution suggested that the MIA leaders did in fact hold authority in the movement, King temporized on the witness stand, understating the extent to which he had influenced the course of the movement. Rather than using the trial as a public forum to proclaim his willingness to risk jail in order to achieve a worthy goal, King insisted that he had only told MIA members "to let your conscience be your guide, if you want to ride that is all right." Asked if he had ever advocated violence, King was adamant: "My motivation has been the exact converse of that; I urged nonviolence at all points." [70] ✎

After King testified, Judge Carter found him guilty of conducting an illegal boycott against Montgomery City Lines and fined him $500 plus court costs. When he refused to pay, the judge converted the fine into a sentence of 386 days of labor in the Montgomery County Jail. King's attorneys indicated that they would appeal the conviction to the Alabama Court of Appeals; Carter then suspended the sentence and postponed the remaining boycott cases until King's appeal was resolved. MIA supporters attending the trial had been quiet and composed for much of it and showed little emotion as the verdict was read. When King emerged from the courthouse, however, the waiting crowd cheered and vowed to continue the boycott until they achieved their goal. [71]

King's signal contribution to the Montgomery movement was to infuse it with a Christian ethos of nonviolence and explicitly Gandhian precepts of nonviolent action. He undoubtedly learned about the Gandhian independence movement while attending Morehouse, where Benjamin Mays occasionally spoke of his travels in India during his Tuesday morning lectures to the student body. King remembered that his first extensive exposure to Gandhian ideas came during his years at Crozer, when, inspired by a lecture at Philadelphia's Friendship House by Howard University president Mordecai Johnson, he bought "a half-dozen books on Gandhi's life and works." [72] J. Pius Barbour, King's friend and mentor during his Crozer years, recalled King arguing for Gandhian methods during his seminary years. "Mike has always contended that no minority can afford to adopt

68. Abernathy quoted in J. Harold Jones, Notes on MIA Mass Meeting at Holt Street Baptist Church, 27 February 1956. See also Ferron, Notes on MIA Mass Meeting at Holt Street Baptist Church, 27 February 1956, p. 144 in this volume.

69. Transcript, *State of Alabama v. M. L. King, Jr.*, 22 March 1956.

70. King, Testimony, *State of Alabama v. M. L. King, Jr.*, 22 March 1956, p. 186 in this volume.

71. See Reactions to Conviction, 22 March 1956, pp. 198–199 in this volume.

72. King, *Stride Toward Freedom*, p. 96.

a policy of violence," Barbour wrote. King would explain, "Just a matter of [arithmetic], Dr." [73]

In the years before the bus boycott, King had argued that Christians had a duty to bear witness for love and justice and against evil. The redemptive power of love was at the core of his Holt Street address and some of his most powerful early sermons.[74] Early in February 1956 a parishioner at a Boston church wrote to King recalling "the great sermon" he had given during his graduate school days. In the sermon "Loving Your Enemies"—also given at Dexter Avenue Baptist Church—King had preached from a passage in the Book of Matthew to which he would often return during 1956: "But I say unto You, Love your enemies, bless them that curse you, do good to them that hate you, and pray for them which despitefully use you, and persecute you." [75]

During the course of the boycott King was able to merge biblical admonitions with Gandhian principles, but his unwavering advocacy of nonviolent tactics derived mainly from his religious convictions. Even as the Montgomery movement attracted the involvement of veteran proponents of Gandhian activism from outside the South, King understood that "it was the Sermon on the Mount, rather than a doctrine of passive resistance, that initially inspired the Negroes of Montgomery to dignified social action." [76] These ideals would remain central to his rhetoric, but as his familiarity with Gandhi increased, so too did his adherence to the philosophical assumptions underlying Gandhian nonviolence. A week after the boycott began a white sympathizer, Juliette Morgan, had made the Gandhian connection explicit when she wrote to the *Montgomery Advertiser* comparing the boycott to the Indian independence campaign.[77] A week later an Alpha Phi Alpha brother again noted the parallel, adding that the Montgomery movement's sound basis "in good Christian doctrine . . . makes it all the more difficult for the conscience of the white South to rationalize its opposition to it." [78] At about the same time, King reportedly referred to Gandhi's independence campaign as evidence that "love will win." [79]

During 1956 King's understanding of Gandhian ideas expanded following the arrival in Montgomery of Bayard Rustin and Glenn E. Smiley, two veteran pacif-

73. J. Pius Barbour, "Meditations on Rev. M. L. King, Jr., of Montgomery, Ala.," *National Baptist Voice*, March 1956.

74. In a sermon the previous year King decried ethical relativism and asked Christians to bear witness, to "stand up for right and be opposed to wrong, wherever it is" (King, "Rediscovering Lost Values," 28 February 1954, in *Papers* 2:252).

75. Milton Britton to King, 5 February 1956, p. 127 in this volume.

76. King, *Stride Toward Freedom*, p. 84.

77. Juliette Morgan, "Lesson from Gandhi," *Montgomery Advertiser*, 12 December 1955. In an interview two months later Morgan reported that she had received mostly encouraging comments about her published letter (Morgan, interview by Anna Holden, 7 February 1956). Not long afterward she lost her job as a city librarian because of her public stands against segregation. King later wrote that although Morgan "did not long survive the rejection and condemnation of the white community, . . . long before she died in the summer of 1957 the name of Mahatma Gandhi was well-known in Montgomery" (*Stride Toward Freedom*, p. 85).

78. Walter C. Carrington to King, 21 December 1955, p. 89 in this volume.

79. Emory O. Jackson, "The Tip-off," *Birmingham World*, 23 December 1955.

ists who had pioneered in the application of Gandhian techniques to American race relations. Rustin, who arrived about the time the indictments were issued against MIA leaders, was one of the most experienced proponents of Gandhian-style mass protest, having been a race relations secretary for the Fellowship of Reconciliation (FOR) during the 1940s. He had worked closely with A. Philip Randolph in the March on Washington Movement of the early 1940s and participated in Congress of Racial Equality antisegregation protests. He was a controversial figure because of his involvement during the 1930s in the Young Communist League and his 1953 arrest in Pasadena, California, for homosexual activity, which led to his resignation from FOR. Affiliated with the War Resisters League when he came to Montgomery, Rustin quickly recognized the significance of the bus boycott as a demonstration of the potential effectiveness of nonviolent tactics. King, Nixon, and Abernathy welcomed Rustin's expertise in nonviolent theory and practice and invited him to join MIA strategy meetings. Some local black leaders, however, resented him as an outsider whose presence would be harmful to the boycott movement, particularly when a reporter alleged that Rustin had misrepresented himself as a correspondent for *Le Figaro* and the *Manchester Guardian*.[80] After spending just a week in Montgomery, Rustin departed at the behest of both Montgomery leaders and his colleagues in New York.[81] Shortly after meeting with King in Birmingham on 7 March 1956, Rustin reported that, although King was eager to receive help, he was concerned that white southerners wanted to believe that "New Yorkers, northern agitators, and communists are in reality leading the fight." King decided that any ideas or programs developed by northerners would be directed through himself or Nixon. "Strategically, [the MIA] must give the appearance of developing all of the ideas and strategies used in the struggle."[82]

Even after returning to New York, Rustin remained in touch with King and continued to assist the boycott movement. He joined with A. J. Muste, James Farmer, and other activists to form the Committee for Nonviolent Integration (CNI), which offered support to the Montgomery struggle and other grass-roots

---

80. See Rustin to King, 8 March 1956, p. 164 in this volume.

81. On 29 February 1956, after receiving reports of Rustin's Montgomery activities and the controversy they provoked, A. Philip Randolph called a meeting of Rustin's New York associates, including Norman Thomas, James Farmer, and Charles Lawrence. The group identified some "very serious elements of danger to the movement there for Bayard to be present" and asked him to return home, despite having initially encouraged him to make contact with King and the other MIA leaders (Swomley to Smiley, 29 February 1956). Randolph noted at the meeting that "the Montgomery leaders had managed thus far more successfully than 'any of our so-called non-violence experts' a mass resistance campaign and we should learn from them rather than assume that we know it all" (Randolph, quoted in another letter from Swomley to Smiley, also from 29 February 1956). Writing from Montgomery, Smiley disagreed with Randolph's analysis and argued that the movement there had been "petering out" until the indictments and until King began using explicitly Gandhian rhetoric. He argued that FOR had significantly influenced King's apparent turn to principled nonviolence. "For being so new at this, King runs out of ideas quickly and does the old things again & again. He wants help" (Smiley to Swomley, 2 March 1956).

82. Rustin, "Notes of a Conference: How Outsiders Can Strengthen the Montgomery Nonviolent Protest," 7 March 1956.

movements in the South.[83] The short-lived organization complemented another
New York–based group, In Friendship, founded in January by Ella Baker, the
local NAACP branch president, and other activists to "provide economic [assistance] to those suffering economic reprisals in the efforts to secure civil rights."[84]
Besides giving financial and logistical aid, Rustin and other members of King's
expanding support network helped convey his ideas and beliefs to prospective
allies among liberals, labor activists, and the religious left. Rustin also prepared
an article on the bus boycott, to be published under King's name.[85]

Leaders of the Fellowship of Reconciliation, aware of Rustin's meetings with
King, hoped to establish their own direct contact with the MIA. FOR's national
chair, Charles R. Lawrence, wrote in late February to applaud the MIA's accomplishments and to urge King to become "one of us, for you have talked and acted
more like we should like to than many of us could hope to do under similar
pressure." Lawrence, a pioneering black sociologist and, like King, a Morehouse
graduate, stated that FOR did not want "to do anything which your group would
feel unwise or ill-timed. You are doing too good a job to have it unwittingly
harmed by even the best-meaning groups."[86] Lawrence informed King of the
pending Montgomery visit of FOR's national field secretary, Rev. Glenn Smiley.

Smiley, who arrived in Montgomery a few days after Rustin, was a white southerner who had served with FOR for about fifteen years, part of which, like Rustin,
he spent in prison as a wartime conscientious objector. While committed to racial
justice, he was sensitive to southern whites' concerns about "outsiders." In contrast to Rustin, who perceived his role as helping to launch a nonviolent rebellion
against the Jim Crow system, Smiley saw himself as a troubleshooter seeking nonviolent solutions to racial disputes and stressed racial reconciliation.

Hours after first meeting King, Smiley wrote several colleagues that he had
"just had one of the most glorious, yet tragic interviews I have ever had." He
described the youthful King as a potential "Negro Gandhi, or he can be made
into an unfortunate [demagogue] destined to swing from a lynch mob's tree."[87]
Unimpressed by King's understanding of Gandhi (although King told him that
he "had Gandhi in mind when this thing started"), Smiley gave King several
books on Gandhian nonviolence, including *The Power of Nonviolence* by Richard
Gregg, who soon corresponded with King.[88] Writing to FOR colleagues soon after
arriving in Montgomery, Smiley depicted King as a man who

83. King met with CNI members in March. See Muste to Mays, 13 April 1956.

84. Baker to King, 24 February 1956, p. 139 in this volume.

85. Rustin sent King a draft of "Our Struggle," which appeared under King's name in the second
issue of *Liberation,* a radical pacifist journal edited in New York by Rustin, David Dellinger, Paul Goodman, and others that would serve as a vital organ for the black movement and the New Left in the
1960s. See Rustin to King, 8 March 1956, p. 164 in this volume; and King, "Our Struggle," April 1956,
pp. 236–241 in this volume.

86. Lawrence to King, 24 February 1956, p. 138 in this volume.

87. Smiley to Muriel Lester, 28 February 1956. Smiley also sent this letter to Howard Thurman and
others.

88. See Gregg to King, 2 April 1956; King to Gregg, 1 May 1956; and Gregg to King, 20 May 1956;
pp. 211–212, 244–245, and 267–269, respectively, in this volume.

wants to do it right, but is too young and some of his close help is violent. King accepts, as an example, a body guard, and asked for [a] permit for them to carry guns. This was denied by the police, but nevertheless, the place is an arsenal. King sees the inconsistency, but not enough. He believes and yet he doesn't believe. The whole movement is armed in a sense, and this is what I must convince him to see as the greatest evil. . . . If he can *really* be won to a faith in non-violence there is no end to what he can do.[89]

Rustin and Smiley agreed that King's role as the spokesperson of a major non-violent campaign made him a crucial convert to the Gandhian movement but that his grasp of Gandhian principles was tenuous. Rustin, for example, reported to his associates in the War Resisters League that King and other MIA leaders eschewed violence but that there was "considerable confusion on the question as to whether violence is justified in retaliation to violence directed against the Negro community." Nevertheless, he concluded that King was "developing a decidedly Gandhi-like view and recognizes there is a tremendous educational job to be done within the Negro community."[90]

After his meetings with Rustin and Smiley, King's public statements increasingly reflected the views of the network of Gandhian advocates in the United States. In March the *Baltimore Afro-American* depicted him as "Alabama's Gandhi."[91] During the spring he met or corresponded with a number of leading Gandhians, including Muste, head of the Fellowship of Reconciliation; William Robert Miller, assistant editor of FOR's journal, *Fellowship;* Unitarian minister Homer Jack, editor of the *Gandhi Reader* (1956); Howard University dean William Stuart Nelson; Harris Wofford, who with Clare Wofford wrote *India Afire* (1951); theologian Howard Thurman; CORE activist James Peck; and journalist William Worthy.[92] Jack, Nelson, Peck, and Worthy had joined Rustin in the 1947 CORE-sponsored "Journey of Reconciliation," in which an integrated group rode buses to test a Supreme Court decision banning segregation in interstate public transportation. Southern white novelist Lillian Smith, who had traveled in India, also urged King to deepen his commitment to Gandhian nonviolence but warned against depending on northerners. "It would break my heart were so-called 'outsiders' to ruin it all," she advised. "The white South is irrational about this business of 'outsiders.' "[93]

---

89. Smiley to Swomley and Hassler, 29 February 1956.

90. Rustin, "Report on Montgomery, Alabama," 21 March 1956.

91. Al Sweeny, " 'Not Worried' Says Alabama's Gandhi," *Baltimore Afro-American,* 3 March 1956, p. 9.

92. See Muste, "The Magnolia Curtain?" 14 May 1956; King to Muste, 10 July 1956, p. 316 in this volume; King to William Robert Miller, 8 May 1956, and Miller to King, 18 May 1956, pp. 249 and 262–263 in this volume; Harris Wofford to King et al., 25 April 1956, and King to Wofford, 10 May 1956, pp. 225–226 and 254 in this volume; Howard Thurman to King, 14 March 1956, and King to Thurman, 16 March 1956, pp. 174–175 and 177 in this volume; and James Peck to King, 1 June 1956, pp. 288–289 in this volume. See also J. Martin England to King, 29 April 1956, and Hazel E. Foster to King, 29 April 1956, pp. 232–233 and 233–234 in this volume.

93. Smith to King, 10 March 1956, p. 170 in this volume. In the same letter Smith praised Howard Thurman as " a truly great religious leader" who could be helpful to the Montgomery movement. She recommended Rustin as a "fine man" who might be able to provide the "quiet advice" she thought the MIA could use. Rustin later remembered that it was a telegram from Smith that prompted him to visit Montgomery in February 1956; see Rustin, quoted in Raines, *My Soul Is Rested,* p. 53.

Absorbing ideas from proponents of nonviolent direct action, King crafted his own synthesis of Gandhian principles and what he termed the "regulating ideal" of Christian love. Although he continued to assert, particularly at MIA mass meetings, that nonviolence stemmed from the African-American social-gospel tradition, after meeting with Rustin and Smiley he became more likely to refer explicitly to Gandhi's teaching. In late March, when he addressed an interracial audience in Brooklyn, he combined the two sources of his nonviolent strategy in a way that became characteristic: "Christ showed us the way, and Gandhi in India showed it could work." By this time he had become an articulate advocate of Gandhian methods and saw the Montgomery movement as a model for all African Americans. "We in Montgomery have discovered a method that can be used by the Negroes in their fight for political and economical equality," he told the Brooklyn audience. Gandhi—the "little brown man in India"—had used nonviolence "to break loose from the political and economical domination by the British and brought the British Empire to its knees. Let's now use this method in the United States."[94] At the end of May he told a correspondent that "the [Gandhian] influence has been at the center of our movement." He added that the "weapon of passive resistance might be just as effective" in fighting against segregation as it had been in the Indian independence movement.[95]

King's article in the May issue of FOR's *Fellowship* revealed both his firm commitment to Gandhian nonviolence and the extent to which his vocabulary derived from social-gospel Christianity. He had already begun to see the Montgomery struggle as more than simply an African-American movement for racial advancement; it had become a demonstration of the power of Christian love to overcome injustice and evil. "Love *must* be at the forefront of our movement if it is to be a successful movement," King insisted.

> And when we speak of love, we speak of understanding, good will toward *all* men. We speak of a creative, a redemptive sort of love, so that as we look at the problem, we see that the real tension is not between the Negro citizens and the white citizens of Montgomery, but it is a conflict between justice and injustice, between the forces of light and the forces of darkness, and if there is a victory—and there *will* be a victory—the victory will not be merely for the Negro citizens and a defeat for the white citizens, but it will be a victory for justice and a defeat of injustice. It will be a victory for goodness in its long struggle with the forces of evil.[96]

King would later depict his "pilgrimage to nonviolence" as an intellectual journey that brought together his theological studies with his ingrained social-gospel beliefs, but his acceptance of Gandhian principles was more the result of his involvement in a social movement that demonstrated the power of Gandhian ideas. More than in any subsequent stage of the African-American freedom struggle,

---

94. Quoted by Stanley Rowland, Jr., in "2,500 Here Hail Boycott Leader," *New York Times,* 26 March 1956; and "King Speaks at Big Rally in Brooklyn," *Montgomery Advertiser,* 26 March 1956. See also King, "Quotable Quotes from Rev. King," *New York Amsterdam News,* 31 March 1956, pp. 209–210 in this volume.

95. King to E. T. Sandberg, 31 May 1956, p. 276 in this volume.

96. King, "Walk for Freedom," May 1956, p. 278 in this volume.

these principles attracted support in the Montgomery movement. "Living through the actual experience of the protest," King wrote in *Stride Toward Freedom,* "nonviolence became more than a method to which I gave intellectual assent; it became a commitment to a way of life. Many of the things that I had not cleared up intellectually concerning nonviolence were now solved in the sphere of practical action." [97]

In King's speeches, particularly those given outside Montgomery, he linked the African-American freedom struggle to international struggles against colonialism and imperialism, particularly the Indian independence movement. King made two major addresses in New York on 17 May that set a pattern for many of his later speeches by deftly blending a firsthand account of the boycott, social-gospel idealism, anticolonial sentiment, and fervent admonitions against hate, violence, and complacency. Although King's sermon at New York's Cathedral of St. John the Divine contrasted with the secular ethos of his dinner address on behalf of the NAACP Legal Defense and Educational Fund, both allowed him to elaborate on the larger historical significance of the Montgomery movement.

In the NAACP speech, King explained that the Montgomery bus boycott marked a new stage in an ongoing African-American freedom struggle that had left "Old Man Segregation on his death bed." He identified himself with the "maladjusted" who never intended to adapt to "the viciousness of lynch-mobs," "the evils of segregation and discrimination," or "the tragic inequalities of an economic system which takes necessities from the masses to give luxuries to the classes." [98] King's sermon situated Montgomery in a global context: "The great struggle of the Twentieth Century has been between these exploited masses questing for freedom and the colonial powers seeking to maintain their domination." [99]

King's advocacy of mass protest and his expressions of empathy for anticolonial movements defied the Cold War political climate. Nevertheless, despite having identified himself as an "anticapitalist" during his Crozer years, King played down his unconventional beliefs during the boycott, even as he cautiously expanded the boundaries of mainstream political discourse. [100] His skill at presenting himself as a militant but not subversive religious leader helped him to avoid the political repression suffered by leftist black leaders such as W. E. B. Du Bois and Paul Robeson. Fearful that the Montgomery movement might be harmed by suggestions of communist influence, he was circumspect even in his relationship with the now-anticommunist ex-communist Bayard Rustin. King's defensiveness about the possibility of communist influence within the civil rights movement surfaced when he wrote to a white soldier who expressed concern after Rosa Parks was interviewed on a leftist radio program. "One of the things that we have

---

97. King, *Stride Toward Freedom,* p. 101.

98. See the article derived from this speech, King, "The 'New Negro' of the South: Behind the Montgomery Story," June 1956, pp. 283 and 286 in this volume.

99. King, "The Death of Evil upon the Seashore," 17 May 1956, p. 261 in this volume.

100. See King, "Autobiography of Religious Development," 22 November 1950, in *Papers* 1:359.

insisted on throughout the protest is that we steer clear of any communistic in-filtration," King assured him.[101] King also believed, however, that communism posed a constructive challenge to Christianity, and on a number of occasions he used anticommunism as leverage, as when he warned that "if America doesn't wake up, she will discover that the uncommitted peoples of the world are in the hands of a communist ideology."[102]

Along with the publicity surrounding his trial, King's speeches outside Montgomery were decisive in building national support for the MIA and enhancing his status as the nation's foremost protest leader. Having guided the boycott movement for several months, he had overcome earlier doubts and grown more self-assured regarding his ability and authority. Drawing lessons from his father's leadership of one of Atlanta's most prosperous black churches, King inspired followers and influenced overall policymaking through oratory and example while delegating most day-to-day responsibilities. He also understood that the MIA, like a Baptist church, was a financially self-sustaining institution that could survive only through effective fund-raising. In addition to building enthusiasm for the boycott, therefore, he appealed to northern sympathizers to send con-tributions. The MIA's fund-raising efforts succeeded in attracting considerably more funds than were needed to cover its expenses, which had risen to more than $8,000 per week by the summer of 1956.[103] Clearly pleased with the MIA's success, King noted regretfully that "most organizations of goodwill" faced "a serious problem" because their fund-raising efforts suffered from "lack of proper organization."[104]

The management abilities of King and other MIA leaders were severely tested during the spring when reports of a resolution of the boycott proved premature and it became clear that the protest would have to go on indefinitely. After a Supreme Court ruling on 23 April against bus segregation in South Carolina, the Montgomery City Lines announced that it would end segregation but quickly reversed its stand under pressure from city officials.[105] In early June, just as King was preparing to leave for a weeklong preaching mission at a Los Angeles church headed by one of his father's oldest friends, a federal district court panel delivered a ruling in *Browder v. Gayle,* overturning both the Montgomery and the Ala-

---

101. King to Homer Greene, 10 July 1956, p. 318 in this volume.

102. King, "The Montgomery Story," 27 June 1956, p. 308 in this volume. See also the comments on King's sermon "The Challenge of Communism to Christianity" in Melvin H. Watson to King, 14 August 1952, in *Papers* 2:156–157.

103. Franklyn W. Taylor, Jr., "MIA Audit Report, 1 March to 31 May 1956," 25 June 1956. According to this report, the MIA raised the bulk of its funds during the period immediately after the indictments of the MIA leaders. Beginning with a balance of $6,444.07 on 1 March, the MIA received contributions of $220,848.87 by 31 May. Income for these three months greatly exceeded the group's expenses, which were $104,312.41 for the period. Contributions declined after the end of May, but the MIA's surplus was adequate to cover expenses for the remainder of the boycott. At the end of the boycott, the group retained a balance of $87,960.54 (see R. J. Glasco, "MIA Financial Report, 1 November through 15 December 1956," 19 December 1956).

104. King to Eugene Walton, 20 December 1956, p. 489 in this volume.

105. See accounts in "Montgomery Lines End Seating Bias," *New York Times,* 24 April 1956; and Steve Lesher, "Negroes Will Continue Boycott of City Lines," *Montgomery Advertiser,* 25 April 1956.

bama bus segregation statutes.[106] Realizing that the ruling would be appealed, King applauded the legal victory but also announced that the boycott would continue. By this time he had restructured the MIA in order to improve the efficiency of its decision making and to provide more reliable management of boycott operations. Mass meetings were scaled back from two to one per week, and the association began distributing a newsletter with Jo Ann Robinson as editor.[107]

In addition to initiating MIA reorganization efforts, King worked to resolve internal conflicts and to maintain unity within the MIA. The group faced its most serious internal crisis when U. J. Fields resigned on 11 June, announcing, with regard to the handling of MIA finances, that he could "no longer identify . . . with a movement in which the many are exploited by the few." [108] King heard word of Fields's resignation while on his California trip, which would include a speech at the NAACP annual convention in San Francisco. Although he saw "no truth in Fields's charges," he recognized that they might hurt MIA fund-raising efforts and canceled several engagements to return to Montgomery. Lax financial oversight may have encouraged some MIA representatives to divert contributions or honoraria to private use or allowed car pool drivers to charge the MIA for unauthorized expenses. When pressed for details, however, Fields was unable or unwilling to make more specific allegations. Enduring several days of hostile criticism, he issued a retraction on 18 June, claiming that he had made the original charges in "anger and passion"—perhaps fueled by resentment over having been removed as the executive committee's recording secretary. He conceded that he had no evidence that MIA funds had been misused: "To my knowledge money sent to the organization has been used only for the purpose of transportation." [109] Fields then apologized at a mass meeting, admitting that his initial charge "was not a statement of truth." King asked the crowd to forgive Fields, saying, "Let he who is without sin cast the first stone." [110] Confronting the potentially damaging episode with firmness and magnanimity, King emerged from the controversy with his reputation enhanced. "Things are going very well here in

---

106. In the 5 June ruling, Judges Frank M. Johnson, Jr., and Richard Rives determined that, by overturning the *Plessy* doctrine of "separate but equal," the *Brown* decision applied not only to public schools but to other forms of legalized racial segregation. In his dissent Judge Seybourn Lynne argued that it did not.

107. King, "Recommendations to MIA Executive Board," 24 May 1956, pp. 271–273 in this volume.

108. Al McConagha, "MIA Secretary Quits: Boycott Official Hits Funds Use," *Montgomery Advertiser,* 12 June 1956. Fields later elaborated on the reasons for his resignation: "Subsequently, as time moved on, exploitation and misuse of money became so great that I could no longer hold my peace. I had, prior to my public statement, asserted my disapproval of the manner in which the organization was operated. Some of my colleagues admonished me to overlook what was going on. Others said, 'Do the same thing yourself'; and still others said that it is to be expected in this kind of situation" (Fields, *The Montgomery Story: The Unhappy Effects of the Montgomery Bus Boycott* [New York: Exposition Press, 1959], pp. 39–40). See also *National Baptist Voice,* July 1956.

109. King, *Stride Toward Freedom,* p. 154; U. J. Fields, Press Release, "Reverend Fields's Retraction," 18 June 1956.

110. Paul Thompson, "Negro Cleric Retracts Charges of Bus Boycott Fund Misuse," *Montgomery Advertiser,* 19 June 1956.

Montgomery now," he wrote a friend in July. "Rev. Fields seems to be in line, and the internal structure of our organization is as strong as ever." [111]

~~~~~~

As the MIA's preeminent spokesperson, King formed generally cordial relationships with established civil rights leaders, who saw the Montgomery boycott as a significant advance for their cause. Even so, the interactions between King and older leaders of his father's generation, such as A. Philip Randolph, founder of the Brotherhood of Sleeping Car Porters, and Roy Wilkins, executive secretary of the NAACP, also contained elements of tension. In his contacts with Randolph, King acted respectfully but not always deferentially toward the labor leader, who had been engaged in the struggle for racial advancement since well before King's birth. He valued Randolph's support, which was secured with the help of E. D. Nixon, because it opened the door to backing by several national labor unions. [112] Despite Randolph's repeated appeals, however, King did not find time in his hectic schedule to participate in Randolph's 24 April State of the Race Conference in Washington, D.C., in which seventy-five African-American leaders responded to segregationist attacks and charted future civil rights strategy. In May King again cited pressing obligations in Montgomery in declining to address a major civil rights rally organized with Randolph's help at New York's Madison Square Garden. [113]

King's relations with Wilkins were even more complex, given Wilkins's increasing concern that NAACP supporters would contribute directly to the MIA instead of helping the NAACP cover the protest's legal costs. As a board member of the Montgomery NAACP and as the son and grandson of Atlanta NAACP leaders, King consistently supported the nation's oldest civil rights organization. Nonetheless, the overwhelming support among African Americans for the MIA-led boycott undermined the NAACP's dominance in the civil rights arena. In addition, the successful efforts of Alabama authorities to suppress the NAACP encouraged King and other state civil rights leaders to act autonomously. In a 3 March letter to Wilkins, King asked if NAACP fund-raising in the name of the bus boycott would be used to "support us in our local struggle." This brought a quick response from Wilkins, who assured King that the NAACP would continue to handle the MIA's legal expenses and those associated with the *Browder v. Gayle* lawsuit but warned that "it would be fatal for there to develop any hint of disagreement as to the raising and allocating of funds." While insisting that the NAACP had a right to claim a portion of the funds raised on behalf of the Montgomery struggle, he assured King that in cases where "local ministers or local

---

111. King to J. Raymond Henderson, 10 July 1956, p. 319 in this volume. See also King, *Stride Toward Freedom*, pp. 156–157.

112. Randolph told Nixon that he had "followed with great pride and inspiration the great fight for respect and human dignity you and your fellow citizens are waging. . . . The Brotherhood of Sleeping Car Porters and all the negro and white people who love justice and human liberty will never forsake you" (Randolph to Nixon, 23 February 1956).

113. King to Benjamin F. McLaurin, 6 May 1956, and Randolph to King, 7 May 1956, pp. 246–247 and 247–248 in this volume.

committees . . . feel strongly that every dollar should go to Montgomery," his group would comply.[114] This agreement did not end tensions between the two men, however, for Wilkins remained unconvinced that mass protest should be emphasized over litigation. Even following King's address at the NAACP's annual meeting in June, the organization refrained from explicitly endorsing the Montgomery boycott.[115]

King used his NAACP address to continue portraying himself as an activist who was more militant than the established leaders of national civil rights organizations. He deftly appealed for the support of the NAACP membership, while being careful not to offend its more cautious officials. King noted that "the problem of obtaining full citizenship is a problem for which the Negro himself must assume the primary responsibility. Integration will not be some lavish dish that will be passed out by the white man on a silver platter, while the Negro merely furnishes the appetite." He suggested that passive resistance involved a willingness to go to jail or even risk death: "But if physical death is the price that some must pay to free our children from a permanent life of psychological death, then nothing could be more honorable." He criticized those who advised "that we must slow up," explaining that although "wise restraint and calm reasonableness" can be virtues, "if moderation means slowing up in the move for freedom and capitulating to the whims and caprices of the guardians of a deadening status-quo, then moderation is a tragic vice which all people of good will must condemn."[116]

Even as King sought to maintain cordial relations with Wilkins and Randolph, he used his considerable church and fraternal contacts outside Montgomery to develop a fund-raising network independent of existing civil rights organizations. His fellow Alpha Phi Alpha brothers sent encouraging notes and financial contributions during the early months of the bus boycott, and they were joined by other black fraternities as the campaign lengthened.[117] African-American churches and their congregations throughout the country offered substantial donations to the MIA. In many instances, the pastors were men with ties to King or his family, including Thomas Kilgore, O. Clay Maxwell, and Gardner Taylor in New York;

114. Wilkins to King, 8 March 1956, p. 166 in this volume. See also King to Wilkins, 3 March 1956 and King to Wilkins, 1 May 1956, pp. 151–152 and 243–244 in this volume.

115. Responding to a veteran pacifist's complaint that the NAACP had failed to support the Montgomery protest, Wilkins explained: "The resolution of the San Francisco convention did not condemn or criticize the Montgomery type of protest. It simply stated that at this time it was not ready to recommend this type of protest as a national project" (Wilkins to James Peck, 19 July 1956; see also Paul Peck to Wilkins, 22 February 1956). Thurgood Marshall of the NAACP firmly rejected King's suggestion, delivered at a press conference shortly before his NAACP speech, that school boycotts similar to the Montgomery protest might be used to achieve school desegregation. Marshall remarked, "I don't approve of using children to do men's work" ("King Proposal Would Boycott Dixie Schools," *Montgomery Advertiser,* 27 June 1956).

116. King, "The Montgomery Story," 27 June 1956, pp. 307 and 308 in this volume.

117. See, for example, Carrington to King, 21 December 1955, and Frank L. Stanley to King, 2 February 1956, pp. 88–89 and 118–119 in this volume. King also received numerous awards from both local and national fraternal groups, including his own.

Jesse Jai McNeil and A. A. Banks in Detroit; and J. Raymond Henderson in Los Angeles.[118]

King's ability to garner substantial support from black churches was strengthened by his roots not only in Atlanta's Ebenezer Baptist Church but also in the nation's largest black organization, the National Baptist Convention, U.S.A., Inc., with its thousands of preachers, several million lay members, and its profusion of national, state, and citywide bodies, missions, services, training programs, and seminaries. His leadership of the bus boycott accelerated his rise to prominence in this vast, unwieldy organization in which both his father and grandfather had played prominent roles. Before the boycott began he had been active in the convention's Alabama state conference and its Montgomery affiliate. As a spokesman for the MIA he soon expanded his influence within the Baptist ministerial network, speaking before congregations in New York, Chicago, Detroit, and other cities. His many speaking invitations and other correspondence during 1956 reveal his emergence as a symbol of social-gospel activism and a figure who stimulated clergy and laypersons to push for civil rights in their own communities. King was in touch with fellow Baptist minister C. K. Steele, who began boycotting the Tallahassee bus system in May using tactics similar to those of the MIA, including a car pool and weekly mass meetings.[119] In June, after Alabama officials outlawed NAACP operations in that state, Rev. Fred Shuttlesworth and other Birmingham ministers formed the Alabama Christian Movement for Human Rights, which espoused nonviolent resistance.

The national impact of the upsurge in southern civil rights activism was apparent when the ten thousand delegates to the National Baptist Convention's 1956 annual assembly in September heard speeches not only from King but also from Steele, Jemison, and Kilgore.[120] Before his speech King thanked convention president J. H. Jackson for his support of the MIA, which totaled $2,000 in donations from the convention and from Jackson's own church.[121]

King stirred the convention assembly with his sermon, "Paul's Letter to American Christians," an imaginary epistle from the apostle Paul denouncing the excesses of capitalism, materialism, and sectarianism in twentieth-century America. He urged listeners "to get rid of every aspect of segregation," insisting that "the underlying philosophy of Christianity is diametrically opposed" to segregation.

---

118. See McNeil to King, 29 February 1956; Kilgore to King, 7 March 1956; and King to Henderson, 1 June 1956; pp. 149–150, 160–162, and 289–290 in this volume. See also A. A. Banks to King, 15 May 1956, and O. Clay Maxwell to King, 7 June 1956.

119. During the October protest Steele had scheduled King to speak at one of their mass meetings, but an emergency in Montgomery prevented King's visit; see Steele to King, 23 October 1956, p. 404 in this volume.

120. These three participated in a panel discussion titled "National Baptists Facing Integration: Shall Gradualism be Applied?"; see National Baptist Convention, Program of the 76th Annual Session, 4–9 September 1956.

121. Jackson's relations with King stayed cordial during this period, despite the fact that at least two ministers had begun promoting King as a candidate to unseat Jackson, who faced open but unsuccessful opposition at the Denver meeting from ministers who wished to place limits on the president's tenure. See also Leroy Fitts, *A History of Black Baptists* (Nashville: Broadman Press, 1985), pp. 98–100.

Without explicitly referring to Gandhian nonviolence, he advised those struggling against oppression to use "Christian methods and Christian weapons," especially the weapon of love. King found solace in Paul's exemplary optimism in
the face of persecution, identifying his own tribulations with those of the apostle:

> Don't worry about persecution America; you are going to have that if you stand up
> for a great principle. I can say this with some authority, because my life was a con-
> tinual round of persecutions. After my conversion I was rejected by the disciples at
> Jerusalem. Later I was tried for heresy at Jerusalem. I was jailed at Philippi, beaten
> at Thessalonica, mobbed at Ephesus, and depressed at Athens. And yet I am still
> going.[122]

His "calm dispassionate" delivery, one friend told him, created an "everlasting" impression. "You will never be forgotten."[123] J. Pius Barbour expressed
pride that the young Crozer student he had known in the late 1940s had "grown
TWENTY YEARS in about five." He proclaimed King as "the greatest orator on the
American platform," effusing that King was "the first Ph.D. I have heard that can
make uneducated people throw their hats in the air over philosophy."[124]

As he grew in stature, King sought to bring his militant message to the national
debate about the slow pace at which the integration decisions of the Supreme
Court were being implemented. In an August appearance partly arranged by
Randolph, King testified before the platform committee of the Democratic National Convention to urge a strong civil rights plank.[125] Despite his testimony,
however, white southern Democrats kept the party from endorsing the 1954
Brown decision. In late August, in their first effort to contact President Eisenhower since the bus boycott began, King and other Montgomery civic leaders
decried intimidation by city officials and the bombings of MIA leaders' homes,
including that of executive board member Robert Graetz, a white Lutheran pastor of a black congregation who had been harassed since the early months of the
protest. King and his colleagues called for Eisenhower to order a "proper investigation" of events that "have tended to deprive Negroes of their civil rights and

---

122. King, "Paul's Letter to American Christians," 4 November 1956 (when King delivered the same
sermon at Dexter), pp. 418 and 419 in this volume. For Paul's own account of his tribulations, see 2 Corinthians 11:22–29. King would adopt the apostle Paul's persona in later sermons and speeches as well.

123. C. W. Kelly to King, 8 September 1956, p. 366 in this volume.

124. J. Pius Barbour, "Sermons and Addresses at the Convention," *National Baptist Voice,* September
1956. According to a later account, King's father "strode with pride at the back of the auditorium"
while listening to the sermon; "his pride in his son would not allow him to sit down" (Charles H. King,
"The Untold Story of the Power Struggle Between King and Jackson," *Negro Digest,* May 1967, pp. 6–
10, 71–79). Henry H. Mitchell, who was sitting in the balcony with Gardner Taylor that day, later remembered being moved to tears. King's reading "started slowly and never gained speed or volume,
but it gripped and held this audience of ten thousand or more. . . . We hung over the balcony rail and
wept unashamedly. When he quietly announced the pro forma, 'I must close now,' the sea of black
Baptists arose as one and protested" (Mitchell, "The Awesome Meek," *Pulpit Digest,* January–February
1991, pp. 23–26).

125. King, Testimony to the Democratic National Convention, Committee on Platform and Resolutions, 11 August 1956, p. 335–338 in this volume.

have left them without protection of the law." [126] Two Department of Justice representatives responded that such harassment "does not appear to indicate violations of federal criminal statutes"; they did express willingness, however, to look into potential violations of voter registration laws.[127] Finding neither party responsive to his entreaties, King chose not to take a partisan stance in the 1956 election, explaining that "the Negro has been betrayed by both the Democratic and Republican Party." [128]

Montgomery authorities grew increasingly intransigent toward the MIA during the fall, suggesting even that the protesters had bombed Graetz's home as "a publicity stunt." [129] At about the same time, city and state officials asked the Supreme Court to reverse the 5 June federal district court ruling in *Browder v. Gayle.* On 1 November, after Florida officials successfully shut down the car pool operated by Tallahassee bus protesters, the Montgomery city commission sought an injunction in the circuit court suspending the MIA's own car pool operations. Judge Carter granted the circuit court injunction on 13 November, but news arrived during the hearing that the Supreme Court had unanimously affirmed *Browder v. Gayle,* declaring unconstitutional both the Montgomery and the Alabama bus segregation statutes. The following evening, King shared the joy of victory with several thousand supporters at two concurrent mass meetings: "Our feet have often been tired . . . , but we have kept going with the faith that in our struggle we have cosmic companionship, and that, at bottom, the universe is on the side of justice." Yet even though the boycott was nearing its end, MIA leaders agreed to continue the protest until the Supreme Court decision was actually implemented.[130] Delayed by appeals, the court order did not arrive in Montgomery until 20 December. After spirited mass meetings that evening, at which King called on supporters to remain nonviolent and Christian in victory, African Americans returned to the buses.[131] Early in the morning of 21 December 1956, King, joined by Abernathy, Nixon, and Smiley, boarded Montgomery's first integrated bus.

Even as he celebrated the end of the bus boycott movement, King saw it as the beginning of a larger movement. Just days after achieving victory, he and the MIA began to expand the organization's perspective beyond the circumscribed issue of segregated bus seating. King's previous speeches had provided hints of his readiness to focus on broader civil rights concerns. At Dexter he had consistently called on members of the congregation to register to vote, and by May he was urging that the MIA's committee on voting, as well as its committee to establish a

---

126. King et al. to Eisenhower, 27 August 1956, p. 357 in this volume.

127. See Warren Olney III to King, 7 September 1956, and Maxwell M. Rabb to King, 25 October 1956, pp. 365 and 405 in this volume.

128. King to Earl Kennedy, 30 October 1956, p. 409 in this volume.

129. Gayle, quoted in "Mayor Sees 'Publicity Stunt'; Graetz Denies Bomb Hoax," *Montgomery Advertiser,* 26 August 1956.

130. See King, Address to MIA Mass Meeting at Holt Street Baptist Church, 14 November 1956, p. 425 in this volume. King incorrectly predicted that the Supreme Court mandate would come to Montgomery "in a matter of just a few days."

131. King, Statement on Ending the Bus Boycott, 20 December 1956, pp. 485–487 in this volume.

credit union, be given more time at mass meetings "for purposes of getting the idea over to people."[132] In June he had asked those attending an MIA mass meeting to patronize African-American businesses. "Until we as a race learn to develop our power, we will get nowhere. We've got to get political power and economic power for our race."[133] In December, determined to direct the energies of MIA members toward new objectives, he identified voter registration and desegregation of educational and recreational facilities as future projects. "We must work within our race to raise economic, health and intellectual standings. . . . We cannot rest in Montgomery until every public school is integrated," he asserted at a mass meeting.[134]

By late December King began to consider the possibility of creating a new regional organization that would offer tactical and strategic assistance to such grassroots protest movements in the South. Plans for such a coordinating organization had been discussed by a number of activists in the months following King's trial. In May King had met with eighteen leaders, including his father and Abernathy, at a conference on the Morehouse campus organized by Glenn Smiley and FOR to discuss the future of nonviolence in the South. The conference, which A. J. Muste deemed "one of the most moving . . . and important" he had attended in his fifty years of Christian ministry, led to two training workshops on nonviolence in July, bringing together other leaders from around the South.[135] These meetings and workshops prompted King and the other participants to recognize the need for a "South-wide strategy" to develop nonviolent resistance to segregation.[136] Although Smiley and FOR played an important role in promoting such a strategy, those involved understood that a regional movement had to be led by black southerners. Randolph, for his part, had given approval to a plan for a "national passive resistance conference," with the proviso that it would be "called by Reverend King or Reverend Abernathy."[137]

King and other southern black leaders took the first step toward building on the Montgomery movement when, in early December, the MIA hosted an Institute on Nonviolence and Social Change, which brought together African-American religious leaders and veteran nonviolent activists for a week of lectures and workshops. The institute served not only as a fund-raising event marking the MIA's first anniversary but also as an opportunity, in King's words, "to rededicate the community and the nation to the principle of non-violence in the struggle for freedom and justice."[138] African-American Baptist ministers such as Jemison, Steele, and Shuttlesworth shared the stage with white ministers Smiley and Homer A. Jack.[139]

---

132. King, "Recommendations to MIA Executive Board," 24 May 1956, p. 272 in this volume.

133. Quoted in Ted Poston, "The Negroes of Montgomery," *New York Post,* 15 June 1956.

134. Quoted in "New Fields Await Negroes, King Tells Mass Meeting," *Montgomery Advertiser,* 24 December 1956, p. 495 in this volume.

135. Muste, "The Magnolia Curtain?" 14 May 1956. See also Smiley, "Report from the South, II," 15 August 1956.

136. Smiley, Minutes, Atlanta Conference, 12 May 1956.

137. Randolph to George D. Cannon, 21 June 1956.

138. King and Abernathy to Supporter, 27 November 1956, p. 442 in this volume.

139. Program, MIA Institute on Nonviolence and Social Change, 3–9 December 1956.

In his own address King reflected on the achievements of the previous year and set forth an ambitious agenda for future action. When the Montgomery bus boycott had begun a year earlier, King noted, participants could not have predicted its impact. "Little did we know on that night that we were starting a movement that would rise to international proportions." King depicted the Montgomery movement "as the proving ground for the struggle and triumph of freedom and justice in America." African Americans throughout the nation had learned from the Montgomery protest that racial unity was possible, that "leaders do not have to sell out," that violence could not "intimidate those who are sufficiently aroused and non-violent," and that the "church [was] becoming militant." Convinced that "a new social order [was] being born" in the United States and among the nonwhite colonized peoples of the world, King called on his listeners to continue in nonviolent struggle and thereby participate in "the creation of the beloved community." Returning to a theme of his earlier speeches, King argued that the "new age" required "intelligent, courageous and dedicated" leadership. . . . In this period of transition and growing social change, there is a dire need for leaders who are calm and yet positive; leaders who avoid the extremes of 'hot-head[ed]ness' and 'Uncle Tomism.' " [140]

Not long after King outlined his vision for the future, civil rights protests took place in several southern cities. On 24 December, three days after the Montgomery buses were desegregated, Steele and other Tallahassee activists attempted to ride the city buses on a desegregated basis and were arrested. A few days later, Birmingham protesters, led by Shuttlesworth, were also arrested for a similar action. On the day of the Birmingham arrests—one day after Fred Shuttlesworth's home was bombed—King telegraphed the protesters asking that they continue their nonviolent protest and, "if necessary, fill up the jails of Birmingham" before accepting segregation. [141]

As it became evident that the nonviolent methods of the Montgomery movement were applicable to the broader struggle for racial justice in the South, King worked closely during December with several northern activists to develop concrete plans for a new regional protest group. Rustin in particular stressed that King should build on the success in Montgomery. On 23 December he sent King a proposal outlining a "Southern Leadership Conference on Transportation" that would bring together regional leaders to "develop forms of local organization leading to an alliance of groups capable of creating a Congress of organizations." Assessing the historical importance of the bus boycott, Rustin's memorandum identified features, such as the involvement of "all social strata," that set the Montgomery protest apart from earlier integration efforts. "The achievement of unity, the intelligence in planning, the creation of a competent, complex system of transportation, the high level of moral and ethical motivation, all combined to give the closed mind of the white southerner an airing it has never before had," Rustin wrote. The new protest group, he predicted, would bring together

---

140. King, "Facing the Challenge of a New Age," 3 December 1956, pp. 452, 453, 458, and 461 in this volume. Cf. similar remarks on the meaning of the Montgomery struggle in "Our Struggle," April 1956, pp. 236–241 in this volume.

141. King to Shuttlesworth, 26 December 1956, p. 496 in this volume.

leaders "able to guide spontaneous manifestations into organized channels. They will be able to analyze where concentration of effort will be fruitful and . . . be mobile enough to throw reserves and support to areas where a breakthrough is achievable." [142] A few weeks later King, joined by Shuttlesworth and Steele, issued a call for an Atlanta conference that would lead to the creation of the Southern Christian Leadership Conference.[143]

At the end of 1956 King looked confidently toward the future, but he questioned his ability to meet the enormous responsibilities that had been thrust upon him. Still rejecting the notion that he was essential to the bus boycott movement, he occasionally expressed a longing to leave his MIA leadership position. When Stanley Levison, an MIA supporter in New York, met with King in person for the first time at the end of December, he recalled that King presented himself as a reluctant protest leader and that he appeared to be shy rather than "charismatic"—not "the type to be a mass leader." [144] Whatever his preferences, King could not ignore the fact that he had acquired a devoted and demanding following as the movement's preeminent leader. Already some followers and journalists had begun to see him as a prophetic figure—a "Moses" of the African-American freedom struggle. After learning of the bombing of his home, one churchgoer had told him that "for years, we Negro Mothers of the Southland have prayed that God would send us a leader such as you are." She thanked God that "the Almighty has regarded our lowly estate and has raised *you* up among us." [145]

Numerous prominent black leaders acknowledged King as a religious and political leader of national importance. When the *Baltimore Afro-American* polled, among others, NAACP board chairman Channing Tobias, educator Nannie H. Burroughs, and college presidents Benjamin Mays and Horace Mann Bond, the respondents were nearly unanimous in nominating King as the outstanding American of the year and the bus boycott as the outstanding event. Mays extolled King for doing "something for America which had not been done before," while Bond considered the boycott movement "the grandest, most significant thing ever to happen in these United States." [146] William Holmes Borders, an Atlanta minister who had known King since childhood, also predicted an "unlimited" future for King: "There is no position in any church, religious body, University and etc. which you could not fill." [147] Responding to such admiration, King routinely noted, as he did in a letter to someone who had voted for him for president of the United States, that such support gave him "a deep feeling of humility and a new dedication to the cause of freedom." [148]

As he began a new year, King reflected on the rapid transformation of his life

---

142. Rustin to King, 23 December 1956, pp. 492–493 in this volume.

143. See Press Release, "Bus Protesters Call Southern Negro Leaders Conference on Transportation and Nonviolent Integration," 7 January 1957, BRP-DLC.

144. Levison, interview with James Mosby, 13 February 1970, Ralph J. Bunche Oral History Collection, Moorland-Spingarn Research Center, Howard University.

145. Pinkie S. Franklin to King, 31 January 1956, p. 116 in this volume. See also King, Address to Mass Meeting at Holt Street Baptist Church, 22 March 1956, p. 199 in this volume.

146. "Rev. King Picked '56 Top American," *Baltimore Afro-American,* 5 January 1957.

147. Borders to King, 19 December 1956, p. 485 in this volume.

148. King to Albert S. Bigelow, 24 November 1956, p. 438 in this volume.

since the start of the bus boycott. Although he was uncertain about the precise nature of his future role, he was determined to build on the Montgomery triumph. During the fall he had told acquaintances that he intended to write a book about the Montgomery movement, but discussions with New York publishers were unresolved. Other opportunities piled up on his desk. Scores of churches and organizations inquired about his availability to speak or serve on advisory boards. He received appeals from National Baptist Convention members to challenge J. H. Jackson for the group's presidency. His dissertation advisor, L. Harold DeWolf, asked if he would consider a faculty appointment. King turned down such offers, pleading unfinished business in Montgomery. To DeWolf he wrote, "I have had a great deal of satisfaction in the pastorate, and have almost come to the point of feeling that I can best render my service in this area."[149] He felt obligated to remain in Montgomery. "I feel that the confidence that the people have in me and their readiness to follow my leadership have thrust upon me a responsibility that I must follow through with," he explained to a fellow minister.[150]

When King spoke to *New York Post* writer Ted Poston shortly after the boycott ended, he reaffirmed his decision to remain a pastor while engaging in the struggle for racial justice. "I do have a great desire to serve humanity," he told Poston, "but at this particular point, the pulpit gives me an opportunity and a freedom that I wouldn't have in any other sphere of activity." Recalling a conversation with J. Pius Barbour the previous April when his mentor teased him about his national fame, King expressed concern about the expectations he would encounter in the future. "Frankly, I'm worried to death," he recalled telling Barbour. "A man who hits the peak at 27 has a tough job ahead. People will be expecting me to pull rabbits out of the hat for the rest of my life."[151]

---

149. See King to DeWolf, 4 January 1957, MLKP-MBU: Box 15; and DeWolf to King, 10 December 1956, p. 468 in this volume.

150. King to W. H. Jernagin, 1 August 1956, p. 331 in this volume. Jernagin had asked King to consider becoming executive secretary of the National Fraternal Council of Churches (Jernagin to King, 21 July 1956). See also Gil Lloyd to King, 28 November 1956, pp. 443–444 in this volume; and King to Lloyd, 7 January 1957, MLKP-MBU: Box 61A. King repeated to Lloyd what he had written Jernagin about his responsibilities in Montgomery.

151. King, quoted in Ted Poston, "Martin Luther King: Where Does He Go from Here?" *New York Post,* 14 April 1957.

1955

2 Mar   Claudette Colvin, 15, is arrested for allegedly violating Montgomery's ordinance requiring segregation on the city's buses. Martin Luther King, Jr., Jo Ann Robinson of the Women's Political Council (WPC), Rosa Parks of the Montgomery NAACP, and others later meet with city and bus company officials.

14 July   In *Sarah Mae Flemming v. South Carolina Electric and Gas Company,* the U.S. Fourth Circuit Court of Appeals rules that the recent *Brown v. Board of Education* decision applies to segregation on municipal buses.

15 Oct   Montgomery resident Mary Louise Smith is arrested and fined for refusing to yield her seat to a white passenger.

7 Nov   The Interstate Commerce Commission rules that segregation on interstate trains and buses and in waiting rooms used by interstate travelers is in violation of the Interstate Commerce Act.

1 Dec   Rosa Parks refuses to vacate her seat and move to the rear of a Montgomery city bus to make way for a white passenger. The driver notifies the police, who arrest Parks for violating city and state ordinances. Parks is released on $100 bond.

2 Dec   Robinson and other WPC members distribute thousands of leaflets calling for a one-day boycott of the city's buses on Monday, 5 December, the day Parks is to be tried. E. D. Nixon calls King to discuss the arrest of Parks and to arrange for a meeting of black leaders at Dexter that evening. Those present agree to call a citywide meeting on 5 December at Holt Street Baptist Church. King and Ralph Abernathy remain at Dexter after the meeting to mimeograph a redrafted leaflet publicizing the bus boycott and the upcoming mass meeting.

3 Dec   Boycott leaflets are distributed to black residents. Television and radio stations report plans for the Monday boycott and mass meeting at Holt Street Baptist Church.

4 Dec   Joe Azbell reports on the plans for a boycott in a front-page article, "Negro Groups Ready Boycott of City Lines," in the *Montgomery Advertiser.* The city's black ministers announce the one-day boycott from their pulpits on Sunday morning. King preaches at Dexter on "Why Does God Hide Himself?"

5 Dec   In the morning, King watches empty buses pass by his home, indicating a successful first day of the boycott. Parks pleads not guilty but is convicted and fined $14. Fred D. Gray, her lawyer, appeals the conviction. In the afternoon, eighteen black leaders meet to plan the evening mass meeting. The

35

group organizes itself as the Montgomery Improvement Association (MIA), agrees to an agenda for the mass meeting, and elects its officers, including King as president. Later, several thousand people gather at Holt Street Baptist Church. King gives the main address. Abernathy presents resolutions, which are adopted resoundingly, recommending that the boycott continue indefinitely. King leaves the mass meeting early to speak at a YMCA father-and-son banquet.

6 Dec   King meets with reporters to discuss the MIA demands.

7 Dec   The MIA executive board assembles for the first time to organize its committees. The Alabama Council on Human Relations (ACHR) offers to bring together the opposing factions, including the bus company, city officials, and MIA leaders.

8 Dec   King and other members of the MIA executive board meet for four hours with city officials, representatives of the Montgomery City Lines, and members of the ACHR. The MIA proposes courteous treatment by bus drivers; seating on a first-come, first-served basis, with Negroes seated rear to front, whites front to rear; and employment of Negro bus drivers on predominantly Negro lines. These requests are not approved. King calls Rev. T. J. Jemison of Baton Rouge, leader of a brief bus boycott in 1953, to ask for advice on transportation alternatives. That night the MIA's second mass meeting, held at St. John AME Church, approves the establishment of a car pool system as a temporary alternative to the buses.

9 Dec   Montgomery City Lines announces that it will cut bus service to "most Negro districts" effective at 6 P.M. on 10 December. A conference of MIA leaders and bus officials fails to reach a compromise as bus company officials insist that state and city laws require them to enforce segregation.

10 Dec   King and the MIA release a "Statement of Negroes on Bus Situation" suggesting that the bus company could accept MIA's seating proposal and remain within the law if it so desired.

11 Dec   Ralph W. Riley, president of the American Baptist Theological Seminary in Nashville, is the guest speaker at Dexter's seventy-eighth anniversary services.

12 Dec   At the third MIA mass meeting, held at Bethel Baptist Church, leaders announce that an organized car pool will begin the following day. A letter to the editor, "Lesson from Gandhi," in the *Montgomery Advertiser* from a white city librarian, Juliette Morgan, compares the bus boycott to Gandhi's famous "salt march."

13 Dec   King, Gray, and Parks meet with W. C. Patton, state field secretary for the NAACP. After a special meeting of the Montgomery NAACP executive committee, Parks authorizes the NAACP to take charge of the legal aspects of her case. In a statement to the press, King suggests that the boycott could last for a year.

15 Dec   Amid reports that Montgomery black taxicab drivers are charging only ten cents per passenger, city officials remind cab operators that the minimum fare is forty-five cents. Montgomery police chief G. J. Ruppenthal orders strict enforcement of a city law prohibiting more than three people in the front seat of passenger cars. King gives a progress report at an MIA mass meeting at First Baptist Church.

16 Dec   K. E. Totten, vice president of National City Lines in Chicago, parent company of Montgomery City Lines, meets with Mayor W. A. Gayle, City Commissioner Frank Parks, and Police Commissioner Clyde Sellers.

17 Dec   During a meeting with the city commission and MIA leaders, Totten leaves it up to the citizens of Montgomery to resolve the question of segregation. After the meeting, Mayor Gayle appoints a committee composed of eight black leaders, including King, and eight white leaders to resolve the crisis. The committee deadlocks on a resolution offered by the white members to postpone the boycott until 15 January but agrees to a resolution requesting more courtesy from the bus drivers. The car pool reportedly involves two hundred private cars, more than one hundred taxis, and eight gas stations.

18 Dec   King preaches at Dexter.

19 Dec   After a contentious two-hour meeting, the mayor's committee adjourns when Luther Ingalls, secretary of the local Citizens Council, joins the group. King charges that certain white members come to the meetings with "preconceived ideas." King presides at and addresses an MIA mass meeting at Hutchinson Street Baptist Church.

22 Dec   The MIA executive board agrees to make no concessions on its three basic demands and to hold no further conferences with the city commission and the bus company until they recognize the legitimacy of these demands. An evening MIA mass meeting is held at Mt. Zion AME Zion Church.

25 Dec   The black ministers of Montgomery and their congregations place an advertisement titled "To the Montgomery Public" explaining the boycott in the Sunday edition of the *Montgomery Advertiser* and the *Alabama Journal*. King preaches at Dexter on "The Light That Shineth amid Darkness."

26 Dec   An MIA mass meeting is held at Beulah Baptist Church.

29 Dec   An MIA mass meeting is held at Day Street Baptist Church.

30 Dec   Mayor Gayle urges Montgomery citizens to patronize city buses or risk losing the bus company's business.

1956

1 Jan   King preaches "Our God Is Able" at Dexter.

3 Jan   The Montgomery City Lines tells the city commission that unless fares are doubled it will have to shut down, because it is

losing as much as twenty-two cents a mile. The fare increase is approved the following day.

5 Jan   King presides at an MIA mass meeting held at St. John AME Church.

6 Jan   More than one thousand people attend a meeting of the Central Alabama Citizens Council. Police Commissioner Sellers appears at the meeting and announces that he will join the council.

8 Jan   King, Sr., preaches at Dexter, while King, Jr., preaches a sermon titled "The Death of Evil upon the Seashore" at Ebenezer Baptist Church in Atlanta.

9 Jan   King and other MIA leaders meet with the city commission for two hours but resolve nothing. King speaks at an MIA mass meeting at Bethel Baptist Church.

10 Jan   Complying with an Interstate Commerce Commission order to end segregation in airline, railroad, and bus terminals serving interstate passengers, the Louisville and Nashville Railroad removes signs enforcing segregation from all of its Alabama terminals.

11 Jan   At the request of Circuit Solicitor William F. Thetford, Police Commissioner Sellers initiates an investigation of the Montgomery movement. Police Chief Ruppenthal delivers copies of Montgomery city ordinances requiring segregated facilities to managers of bus and train stations.

12 Jan   In response to the city's rejection of its most recent offer to end the boycott, the MIA executive board decides to boycott the buses indefinitely.

14 Jan   *Montgomery Advertiser* reporter Thomas Johnson interviews King at Dexter for an article scheduled to appear on 19 January.

15 Jan   King preaches at Dexter on "How Do We Believe in a Good God in the Face of Glaring Evil?"

16 Jan   At a mass meeting, King announces that the MIA will hold a general mass meeting every Monday and five meetings every Thursday night in different areas of the city. He reports that he has received threats by telephone.

17 Jan   King leaves Montgomery to attend a session of the National Baptist Convention in Hot Springs, Arkansas, with his parents. Police Commissioner Sellers asserts that 85 to 90 percent of Montgomery blacks want to ride the buses but are afraid of violence.

18 Jan   The white members of the biracial mayor's committee insist that state and local law require segregation but recommend reserved sections for white and black passengers in proportion to the average number of riders of each race. King and other black committee members reject the recommendation.

19 Jan   A *Montgomery Advertiser* article entitled "The Rev. King Is Boycott Boss" reports that, although King agrees with the NAACP

position on the abolishment of segregation, the bus boycott seeks only a "better form of segregation." An MIA mass meeting is held at King Hill Baptist Church.

21 Jan   After meeting with "a group of prominent Negro ministers," the city commission announces that the bus situation is resolved. King calls an emergency meeting of the MIA executive board and charges that the statement is unfounded because no MIA leaders were at the meeting. On Saturday night and Sunday morning King and other members of the MIA board announce that the boycott is still on.

22 Jan   King preaches at Dexter on "Redirecting Our Missionary Zeal."

23 Jan   Mayor Gayle declares that there will be no more discussions with black leaders until the MIA is willing to end the boycott. All three members of the city commission announce that they have joined the local Citizens Council. At a meeting of the MIA executive board King offers his resignation, but it is not accepted. A large crowd attending a mass meeting at Beulah Baptist Church affirms support for the boycott.

24 Jan   Mayor Gayle urges whites to stop offering rides to blacks who work for them. Commissioner Parks receives "dozens" of telephone calls from businessmen who report that they will fire blacks who boycott the buses.

26 Jan   Rufus A. Lewis and four other Montgomery blacks organize a transit company and petition the city commission for a franchise to operate it. King leaves Dexter in his car with a friend and the church secretary. After picking up three others at an MIA station, King is stopped for traveling 30 mph in a 25 mph zone. He is arrested, fingerprinted, photographed, and jailed. Abernathy arrives to bail him out; as a crowd gathers at the jail, prison officials escort King out of the jail and drive him back to town. According to King, on this day and the previous two more than one hundred traffic citations are issued to car pool drivers. Later that evening, a group of King's friends decide to organize protection for him. Seven MIA mass meetings are held to accommodate black residents interested in hearing the story of King's arrest.

27 Jan   The MIA and other black civic and ministerial organizations publish a statement, "To the Citizens of Montgomery," in the *Montgomery Advertiser* declaring that they do not seek to challenge segregation laws but to express dissatisfaction with treatment on city buses. The MIA holds an executive board meeting. According to King's later account in *Stride Toward Freedom*, King receives a threatening phone call late in the evening, prompting a spiritual revelation that fills him with strength to carry on in spite of persecution.

28 Jan   King is fined $14 by recorder's court judge Luther H. Waller for speeding.

29 Jan   King speaks at Dexter's Youth Day Service.

30 Jan   The MIA executive board authorizes Fred D. Gray to file a federal suit challenging segregation on Montgomery buses. At 9:15 P.M., while King is speaking before two thousand congregants at a mass meeting at First Baptist Church, his home is bombed. Coretta Scott King and their daughter, Yolanda Denise, are not injured. King addresses a large crowd that gathers outside the house, pleading for nonviolence. The city commission promises police protection for King and offers a $500 reward for the capture and conviction of the persons responsible for the bombing. The Kings stay at the home of Dexter deacon J. T. Brooks. Late that night King, Sr., his daughter Christine, son A. D., and Coretta's father, Obadiah Scott, arrive hoping to convince King and his family to return to Atlanta, but he refuses.

31 Jan   King and four other leaders meet with Alabama governor James E. Folsom to express their lack of confidence in the protection offered by the Montgomery city police.

1 Feb   Gray and Charles D. Langford file a federal district court petition (which becomes *Aurelia S. Browder v. William A. Gayle*) on behalf of five Montgomery women to enjoin the city commissioners from enforcing segregation on city buses. At the county sheriff's office, King, Abernathy, and Rev. H. H. Hubbard apply for a permit to allow a night watchman at King's home to carry a gun. Sheriff Butler denies the permit. A bomb explodes in the yard of Nixon, the MIA treasurer.

2 Feb   King and the MIA executive board approve a security patrol at mass meetings and agree to move MIA headquarters from the Alabama Negro Baptist Center to Abernathy's First Baptist Church. Jeanatta Reese withdraws from the suit filed by Gray and Langford, explaining that she and her husband have been threatened with economic retaliation and violence. King presides at an MIA-NAACP meeting at the Baptist Center.

5 Feb   King preaches at Dexter on "It's Hard to Be a Christian."

6 Feb   After several days of demonstrations, white citizens and students riot at the University of Alabama against the court-ordered admission of Autherine Lucy, the first black student in the school's history. The university's board of trustees responds by barring Lucy from attending classes. King speaks at an MIA mass meeting at Day Street Baptist Church. The local Selective Service Board changes Gray's draft classification from 4-D, an exempt status, to 1-A.

8 Feb   In a *Montgomery Advertiser* article, "Group to Study Possibility of Ending Boycott of Buses," which reported that the MIA executive board will consider ending the boycott, King says that any recommendations agreed upon by the board would be voted on by a full meeting of the MIA at the next mass meeting.

The MIA executive board meets. King denies that the meeting had been called to discuss the end of the boycott. The Men of Montgomery, a civic group of white businessmen, releases a statement calling for an end to racial tension.

9 Feb   In a telegram to President Eisenhower, AFL-CIO president George Meany urges an FBI investigation of violence in Montgomery and elsewhere in Alabama. Abernathy speaks at an MIA mass meeting in King's absence.

10 Feb   Eleven thousand people attending a Citizens Council rally in Montgomery cheer Mayor Gayle and Police Commissioner Sellers for their support of segregation on Montgomery buses.

11 Feb   King arrives in Chicago for a speaking engagement.

12 Feb   King preaches the anniversary sermon at Shiloh Baptist Church in Chicago.

13 Feb   Judge Eugene Carter directs the Montgomery County grand jury to determine whether the boycott of Montgomery buses violates Alabama's antiboycott law. While in Chicago, King and Rev. Owen D. Pelt meet with officials of the United Packinghouse Workers Union to discuss lobbying the Chicago-based parent company of the Montgomery City Lines, the National City Lines.

14 Feb   In a Chicago news conference, King reports that a grand jury is investigating the "legality" of the bus boycott and predicts that several leaders of the Montgomery movement will be indicted. King leaves Chicago by train for Atlanta.

16 Feb   King returns to Montgomery and addresses an MIA mass meeting at First Baptist Church.

18 Feb   Gray is charged by the Montgomery grand jury with "unlawful appearance as an attorney" for representing Reese after she had withdrawn from the suit. King drives to Atlanta, where he releases a statement condemning the grand jury's actions. King then travels to Nashville for a series of speaking engagements.

19 Feb   At 11 A.M., King gives a sermon entitled "What Is Man?" at Fisk Memorial Chapel in Nashville as part of Fisk University's Religious Emphasis Week. While in Nashville, King visits Vanderbilt University and concludes that 90 percent of the white students he speaks with are willing to accept integration.

20 Feb   At 11 A.M., King speaks at Nashville's Public Health Lecture Hall of Meharry Medical College on the "Three Dimensions of a Complete Life." The bus company and the city commission endorse a proposal by the Men of Montgomery that does not meet the MIA's demands. Abernathy reports that the congregants at a mass meeting vote down the proposal by a margin of 3,998 to 2.

21 Feb   At 9:40 A.M., King speaks at Tennessee State University in Nashville on "Going Forward by Going Backward." The Montgomery grand jury indicts 115 leaders (later reduced to 89) of

41

the Montgomery movement on misdemeanor charges of violating Alabama's antiboycott law. Bayard Rustin arrives in Montgomery and speaks with Abernathy and Nixon. Late in the evening, King speaks on the telephone with Abernathy about the indictments.

22 Feb   Seventy-five indicted boycott leaders appear at the county jail; they are arrested and released on bond. King flies to Atlanta, where a group of family friends convened by his father fails to dissuade him from returning to Montgomery. In Montgomery, Judge Carter upholds the conviction of Parks by the recorder's court. City attorneys move to dismiss the suit that Gray and Langford have taken to federal district court.

23 Feb   King, his father, and family drive to Montgomery. King goes to the county jail, where he is arrested and released on bond. He agrees to plead guilty to the speeding charge filed against him in January. King and other leaders meet with Arthur D. Shores and Peter Hall, Birmingham attorneys sent to Montgomery by the NAACP to assist in defending the indicted leaders. About five thousand people hear King address an evening MIA mass meeting at First Baptist Church.

24 Feb   King and other indicted leaders are arraigned in circuit court and plead not guilty to boycott-related charges. Judge Carter assigns a trial date for the week of 19 March. King and the MIA board designate this day as Montgomery's Prayer and Pilgrimage Day, on which all supporters walk to work. King and other leaders gather in the evening to discuss nonviolence with Rustin.

26 Feb   King preaches at Dexter on "Faith in Man." Rustin attends the services and meets with the Kings in the evening.

27 Feb   King addresses an MIA meeting at Holt Street Baptist Church.

28 Feb   Fellowship of Reconciliation (FOR) field secretary Glenn E. Smiley arrives in Montgomery and interviews King.

29 Feb   King and other indicted leaders agree to forgo a trial by jury, allowing Judge Carter to hear their case. In Friendship, a northern group coordinating economic aid for those involved in the southern fight for integration, holds its founding conference in New York.

1 Mar   Gray files a bill of demurrer in Montgomery Circuit Court charging that the 1921 Alabama antiboycott law used to arrest the bus boycott leaders is unconstitutional. King presides at and gives opening remarks at an MIA meeting at the Hutchinson Street Baptist Church.

5 Mar   King speaks at an MIA meeting at Bethel Baptist Church.

6 Mar   Alabama state legislators introduce strict new racial segregation bills, including one that strengthens segregation on buses and at public events. The Alabama lower house also unanimously approves a resolution urging the Supreme Court to modify its school desegregation decision.

7 Mar	King, Rustin, and William Worthy meet in Birmingham to discuss MIA tactics and strategy.
8 Mar	Gray and Langford amend *Browder v. Gayle,* removing Reese from the list of plaintiffs.
11 Mar	Kelly Miller Smith, pastor of First Baptist Church in Nashville, is Youth Day speaker at Dexter.
12 Mar	Ninety-six U.S. congressmen from eleven southern states issue a "Southern Manifesto," which declares the *Brown* decision an abuse of judicial power and pledges to use all lawful means to resist its implementation.
13 Mar	Governor Folsom publicly denounces "mobocracy" and urges Montgomery city officials and black leaders to reach a settlement of the bus boycott.
14 Mar	Eisenhower states at his weekly news conference that he wants a congressional joint commission established to facilitate a meeting of black and white leaders from the South.
18 Mar	King preaches at Dexter on "When Peace Becomes Obnoxious." On the eve of the trial against boycott leaders, eight thousand people attend prayer meetings in Montgomery to demonstrate their continued support for the boycott.
19 Mar	King, the first of eighty-nine leaders to be tried, appears in a Montgomery courtroom for his four-day trial. In opening remarks at an evening mass meeting at St. John AME Church, King urges the protesters to maintain their morale and declares that "we want no cowards in our crowd."
20 Mar	The prosecution continues its case against King.
21 Mar	Defense attorneys for King begin their presentation. In a press conference, President Eisenhower urges the South to "show progress" but calls for moderation on both sides of the segregation issue.
22 Mar	King testifies at his trial in his own defense. Judge Carter finds him guilty of leading an illegal boycott and sentences him to pay a $500 fine plus court costs or to serve 386 days in jail. The sentence is suspended when King files an appeal and is released on $1,000 bond. Judge Carter orders a continuance in the other cases until final appeals are completed in King's case. At an evening mass meeting at Holt Street Baptist Church, King announces that the boycott will continue and that his conviction has not lessened his determination.
23 Mar	King's attorneys begin the formal appeals process. Gray, speaking in King's place at the Union Methodist Church in Boston, tells the crowd that Montgomery blacks will not give up.
25 Mar	King addresses a congregation of 2,500 people at the Concord Baptist Church in Brooklyn, New York. The rally, sponsored by the Brooklyn Chapter of the National Association of Business and Professional Women's Clubs, raises more than $4,000 for the MIA.

27 Mar	Alabama attorney general John Patterson files a motion urging dismissal of the *Browder v. Gayle* federal suit against Montgomery and Alabama transportation segregation laws on the grounds that the case should be heard in a state court first.
28 Mar	The National Deliverance Day of Prayer is observed in cities nationwide as churches and synagogues keep their doors open all day and urge boycott supporters to donate one hour's worth of pay to the MIA. The Massachusetts legislature suspends activities for an hour in support of the bus boycott.
29 Mar	King presents the opening remarks at an MIA meeting at Hutchinson Street Baptist Church. The *Louisville Defender* publishes King's 18 March sermon "When Peace Becomes Obnoxious."
30 Mar	King announces that the MIA is planning a block-by-block voter registration campaign among Montgomery blacks.
Apr	*Liberation* publishes King's article "Our Struggle."
1 Apr	King preaches at Dexter's Easter Sunday services.
2 Apr	The Montgomery city commissioners deny the MIA's request for permission to establish and operate a black-operated bus company. King presents the opening remarks at an evening MIA mass meeting at Beulah Baptist Church.
3 Apr	Montgomery City Lines receives permission from the city commissioners to reduce its bus service by another 135 miles.
10 Apr	In Birmingham, King speaks to the Baptist Ministers Conference in the morning and to the Birmingham Hungry Club at the YMCA in the afternoon. In the evening, King speaks on "The Negro's Re-evaluation of his Nature and Destiny" at the Pan-Community Council Annual Forum at Mt. Zion Baptist Church.
11 Apr	The Chicago NAACP sponsors an "Hour of Prayer" and rally. Abernathy and Roy Wilkins speak to a Chicago Coliseum audience of five thousand that contributes $2,500 for the MIA.
13 Apr	King speaks before 1,600 people on "The Declaration of Independence and the Negro" at the Chicago Area Conference of Religious Liberals' Jefferson Day Rally at the University of Chicago's Rockefeller Memorial Chapel.
14 Apr	At the Ohio NAACP's banquet in Columbus, King criticizes William Faulkner's call for gradualism in the South.
15 Apr	J. Pius Barbour preaches on "Can You Change a Social Order without Violence?" at Dexter. Over the next three days, Barbour gives the Spring Lecture Series in the evenings at Dexter.
16 Apr	King delivers the opening remarks at an MIA meeting at First Baptist Church.
17 Apr	Black citizens in Capetown, South Africa, boycott the city's bus lines after the National Transport Commission orders all blacks to sit upstairs on double-decker buses.

20 Apr	King speaks at a mass meeting at Detroit's Bethel AME Church organized by Jesse Jai McNeil.
22 Apr	King gives the Youth Day sermon at Good Street Baptist Church in Dallas, Texas.
23 Apr	In *Flemming v. South Carolina Electric and Gas Company,* the Supreme Court affirms a federal appellate court ruling striking down segregated seating on buses in Columbia, South Carolina, and making segregation on any public transportation illegal. Montgomery City Lines informs its drivers that they can no longer enforce segregation on the city buses, but Mayor Gayle announces that Montgomery will continue to enforce state and city segregation laws. Government officials throughout the South denounce the court's decision, and C. C. Owen, president of the Alabama Public Service Commission, claims that the ruling does not apply to Alabama. In the evening, King presents the opening remarks at an MIA mass meeting at Dexter. He tells reporters that the boycott will continue until the MIA decides how to react to the court's ruling.
24 Apr	Bus lines in thirteen southern cities, including Dallas and Richmond, discontinue segregation in response to the Supreme Court ruling, but officials in Alabama and Georgia pledge to resist the ruling. In Montgomery, Police Commissioner Sellers announces that drivers who permit desegregation on their buses will be arrested. After a meeting of the MIA executive board, King announces that there will be no immediate change in strategy and the boycott will continue. In Washington, D.C., seventy-five black leaders convene at a State of the Race Conference to discuss rising racial tensions in the South. A Louisiana judge orders a permanent halt of all NAACP activities in that state.
25 Apr	B. W. Franklin, vice president of National City Lines, announces that the company will stand behind any of its drivers who are arrested for refusing to enforce segregation. Mayor Gayle and Commissioner Sellers imply that they might revoke the franchise or seek a court injunction against Montgomery City Lines if it violates local segregation statutes. Officials at National City Lines inform the MIA that union contract stipulations make it nearly impossible for them to hire black drivers.
26 Apr	King presides and gives a speech at a mass meeting at Day Street Baptist Church, and more than three thousand people vote unanimously to continue the boycott until the city "withdraws its threats to arrest drivers and passengers who violate segregation laws."
27 Apr	A meeting between Montgomery officials and bus line representatives fails to produce a solution.
29 Apr	King preaches the Sunday service at Dexter on "Fleeing from

God." In the afternoon, he is the Men's Day speaker at the Hunter's Chapel AME Zion Church in Tuscaloosa.

30 Apr   King delivers the opening remarks at an MIA mass meeting held at Holt Street Baptist Church.

May   FOR's journal, *Fellowship,* publishes King's article "Walk for Freedom."

1 May   Montgomery city officials file suit in Montgomery Circuit Court asking for a temporary injunction to restrain the bus company from implementing its desegregation policy.

2 May   Attorneys for the Montgomery City Lines file a demurrer in circuit court requesting dismissal of the city's bill of complaint against the bus company.

9 May   Judge Walter B. Jones of the circuit court rules that Montgomery and Alabama segregation laws are constitutional and orders Montgomery City Lines to abandon its new policy of not enforcing segregation. Spokesmen for the bus company announce that the company will comply with the court order.

10 May   At an MIA mass meeting leaders circulate a questionnaire assessing community interest in the establishment of an MIA bank.

11 May   A three-judge U.S. District Court panel hears *Browder v. Gayle.* Judges Richard Rives, Seybourn Lynne, and Frank M. Johnson, Jr., hear testimony by city and state officials, employees of the bus company, and the four black women plaintiffs.

12 May   King, King, Sr., and Abernathy attend a meeting of eighteen leaders of the southern desegregation movement organized by Smiley and FOR on the Morehouse College campus in Atlanta. The U.S. District Court hearing in the case of *Browder v. Gayle* ends.

13 May   King delivers the Mother's Day sermon at Dexter, speaking on "The Role of the Negro Mother in Preparing Youth for Integration."

14 May   Eleanor Roosevelt, in her "My Day" column, reports on her meeting with Rosa Parks.

15 May   King is in Berkeley, California, to receive a book of recognition and remembrance from the Stiles Hall University YMCA.

17 May   King delivers the sermon "The Death of Evil upon the Seashore" to an audience of ten thousand in New York's Cathedral of St. John the Divine in observance of the National Day of Prayer and Thanksgiving. Later that evening, he speaks on "A Realistic Look at Race Relations" at an NAACP Legal Defense and Educational Fund banquet at the Waldorf-Astoria celebrating the second anniversary of *Brown v. Board of Education of Topeka.*

18 May   The Unitarian Fellowship for Social Justice awards King, in absentia, its John Haynes Holmes–Arthur L. Weatherly Prize for Outstanding Leadership in Social Justice.

19 May	At a Harlem reception organized by the Committee for Better Human Relations, King announces that Montgomery blacks plan to apply for a license to operate an African-American bank.
20 May	King gives the Youth Emphasis Day sermon at Ebenezer Baptist Church in Pittsburgh. He remains in that city through 23 May to participate in various activities at the church.
24 May	Twenty thousand people attend a civil rights rally in Madison Square Garden to hear Eleanor Roosevelt, Roy Wilkins, A. Philip Randolph, Rabbi Israel Goldstein, Adam Clayton Powell, Jr., and Autherine Lucy. Nixon and Parks represent the MIA at the rally.
26 May	Parks addresses a National Council of Negro Women conference in Washington, D.C.
27 May	King preaches at Ebenezer Baptist Church in Atlanta for the dedication of its new religious education building.
28 May	King attends the Fisk University commencement, where he receives the first annual Fisk Alumni Award for Distinguished Service. Students at Florida A&M launch a bus boycott in response to the arrest of two female students on 26 May.
29 May	The Florida A&M bus boycott spreads to the city of Tallahassee.
30 May	C. K. Steele and Tallahassee's Inter-Civic Council confer with the city manager, call for first-come, first-served seating on buses, more courteous treatment, and the hiring of black drivers. Despite the decision by city officials not to prosecute the two Florida A&M students, the bus boycott in Tallahassee gains momentum.
31 May	King offers his "Recommendations" at an MIA executive board meeting.
1 June	Attorney General Patterson obtains a court order banning most NAACP activities in Alabama. The injunction, issued by Judge Jones of the Montgomery Circuit Court, forbids the Alabama NAACP from engaging in fund-raising, collecting dues, and recruiting new members. The NAACP denies Patterson's charges that it organized the Montgomery bus boycott or employed Lucy to integrate the University of Alabama but says it will abide by the injunction.
4 June	King presides at an MIA mass meeting at Holt Street Baptist Church, now held only once a week. The Tallahassee City Transit Lines suspends service in the black districts of the city in response to the continuing boycott.
5 June	The three-judge U.S. District Court panel rules two-to-one in the case of *Browder v. Gayle* that segregation on Alabama's intrastate buses is unconstitutional and gives lawyers for each side two weeks to submit written suggestions on how the formal antisegregation order should be entered. President Owen

of the Alabama Public Service Commission announces that the state will appeal the decision. King says the boycott will continue until the antisegregation ruling is implemented. Blacks in Birmingham react to the banning of the NAACP in Alabama by organizing the Alabama Christian Movement for Human Rights, led by Fred Shuttlesworth. In Tallahassee, boycott leaders announce that their goal is now desegregation of the city buses.

6 June   The Kings and the Abernathys leave Montgomery by automobile for a vacation in California, stopping first in Los Angeles.

10 June   King preaches a guest sermon, the first of several, at the Second Baptist Church in Los Angeles.

11 June   After publicly charging that MIA leaders have misappropriated funds from the MIA treasury, Fields resigns from his position as secretary of the MIA. The NAACP announces that the organization will take legal steps to dissolve the injunction that bans its operation in Alabama.

12 June   The MIA, denying any misuse of organization funds, dismisses Fields's charges as false.

17 June   King cancels a scheduled speaking engagement at the Ward AME Church in Los Angeles in order to return to Montgomery to deal with the Fields crisis. The congregation of Bell Street Baptist Church votes unanimously to remove Fields from its pulpit.

18 June   At a mass meeting at Beulah Baptist Church, Fields retracts his allegations about the MIA's misappropriation of money and apologizes for his attack on MIA leaders. King asks the crowd to forgive Fields for the false charges.

19 June   Attorneys for Alabama respond to the antisegregation ruling. Hours later, the federal three-judge panel issues a permanent injunction against segregation on Montgomery city buses, subsequently suspending it for ten days in order to allow appeal to the U.S. Supreme Court. The Tallahassee City Transit Lines announces that it will cease operation by 1 July if the bus boycott does not end.

21 June   The Montgomery city commission announces that it will appeal the federal court decision to the Supreme Court.

23 June   The first issue of the *MIA Newsletter* is released, with Robinson as editor.

26 June   At a press conference before the opening of the annual NAACP convention in San Francisco, King proposes a student boycott of segregated schools to force compliance with the *Brown* decision.

27 June   King addresses the forty-seventh annual NAACP convention in San Francisco on "The Montgomery Story."

28 June   The Alabama Public Service Commission formally asks the U.S. Supreme Court to reverse the federal district court's 5

	June decision to ban segregation on Alabama buses. Montgomery city attorneys join the state's appeal the following day.
29 June	Montgomery City Lines lays off twenty-one drivers.
30 June	King returns to Montgomery.
July	*Ebony* publishes an article entitled "The King Plan for Freedom."
1 July	King receives an Honorable Merit Award in absentia at Detroit's Panorama of Progress, sponsored by Diggs Enterprises, Inc.
3 July	King receives a Citation for Distinguished Christian Service from the National Fraternity Council of Churches, U.S.A., Inc., in Birmingham.
8 July	Samuel D. Proctor, president of Virginia Union University, is Men's Day speaker at Dexter.
11 July	A white policeman initially refuses to allow King, his wife, and Robert Williams to pass through the whites-only waiting room of the Montgomery railroad station so they can board their train.
12 July	King tells a Race Relations Institute meeting at Fisk University that bus boycotts in Birmingham or Miami are likely to fail for demographic reasons. Attorney General Patterson subpoenas King to appear as a witness in *State of Alabama v. NAACP.*
17–18 July	King, King, Sr., Abernathy, Steele, and Smiley attend a two-day FOR-sponsored workshop stressing nonviolent social protest tactics at Tuskegee Institute.
20 July	King addresses an NAACP mass meeting in Washington, D.C. King's appeal of his conviction is submitted to the Alabama Court of Appeals.
22 July	King is the guest speaker for Men's Day at New Hope Baptist Church in Niagara Falls, New York.
23 July	King addresses executives at the American Baptist Assembly/ American Home Mission Agencies Conference in Green Lake, Wisconsin, on the subject of "Non-Aggression Procedures to Interracial Harmony."
25 July	Judge Jones of the Montgomery Circuit Court fines the Alabama NAACP $10,000 and orders the organization to make its records available or face higher fines and suspension of its operations in Alabama.
26 July	With King presiding, the MIA executive board concurs with its legal counsel and agrees to wait until the Supreme Court reconvenes in the fall to consider its case challenging Alabama segregation laws, instead of approaching a single Supreme Court justice for an immediate decision.
Aug	*Redbook* publishes the article by William Peters about King entitled "Our Weapon Is Love."
3 Aug	*U.S. News and World Report* publishes King's speech made to the annual NAACP convention in San Francisco on 27 June.

5 Aug	King gives the main address at the British-American Association of Colored Brothers in Windsor, Ontario.
7 Aug	King addresses the National Negro Funeral Directors Association in Cleveland.
11 Aug	King testifies before the platform committee of the Democratic National Convention in Chicago, recommending a strong civil rights plank in the party platform. That evening, he speaks in Buffalo to the Alpha Phi Alpha fraternity on "The Birth of a New Age" and receives an Award of Honor.
12 Aug	King preaches on "Rediscovering Lost Values" at Mount Olivet Baptist Church in New York City. Homer Alexander Jack delivers an address titled "From Gandhi to Montgomery: The Life and Teachings of Mahatma Gandhi" at Dexter.
13 Aug	The Alabama NAACP asks the Alabama Supreme Court to lift the ban on its operations and to revoke the fine placed upon it. The request is denied.
23 Aug	King addresses the Montgomery chapter of the ACHR.
25 Aug	The home of Robert Graetz, the white minister of Trinity Lutheran Church and an MIA executive board member, is bombed.
27 Aug	King addresses the Improved Benevolent Protective Order of Elks in Los Angeles and receives the fraternal order's Elijah P. Lovejoy Award. He and leaders of other black Montgomery civic organizations ask President Eisenhower for a federal investigation of racial violence in Montgomery.
7 Sept	King preaches at the seventy-sixth annual National Baptist Convention meeting in Denver on "Paul's Letter to American Christians." Coretta Scott King sings and Alberta Williams King plays the organ at the convention. Later, King speaks at a Build Negro Business meeting at Denver's Zion Baptist Church.
8 Sept	Insurance policies on seventeen MIA station wagons are canceled.
9 Sept	King preaches the guest sermon at Macedonia Baptist Church in Denver.
12 Sept	King accepts an award in absentia from New York's Afro Arts Theatre.
13 Sept	King presides as the MIA executive board creates a special committee to work toward changing "the bitterness or unfavorable attitude" of white citizens.
17 Sept	King presents the opening remarks at an MIA mass meeting at First Baptist Church.
18 Sept	King and the MIA executive board meet and agree to contact the U. S. Justice Department and the FBI for assistance and protection. King, Graetz, and Robinson are assigned to contact Governor Folsom. Lloyd's of London's liability insurance for Christian churches of Montgomery, at $11,000 per car, becomes effective.

25 Sept	The MIA's special committee meets to consider how to create more "wholesome" attitudes among the city's whites. King says, "We should move from protest to reconciliation."
27 Sept	En route to Hampton, Virginia, King is denied service in the dining room of the Dobbs House restaurant at the Atlanta airport. King then delivers a speech entitled "The Montgomery Story" at Hampton Institute.
30 Sept	Coretta Scott King gives a concert at Dexter.
1 Oct	King presides at an MIA mass meeting at Hutchinson Street Baptist Church. This meeting includes a training session in nonviolence led by King as well as the premiere of the FOR-produced film about the bus boycott, *Walking for Freedom*.
5 Oct	King addresses the twenty-first annual convention of the Virginia State NAACP at Petersburg on "Desegregation in the Future." He stays at the home of Wyatt Tee Walker, pastor of Gillfield Baptist Church.
14 Oct	Arenia C. Mallory of Lexington, Mississippi, speaks at Dexter's Women's Day service.
15 Oct	King speaks at the Annual Trade Week Rally of the Durham, North Carolina, Business and Professional Chain.
16 Oct	King consults with Bayard Rustin at New York's LaGuardia Airport. Later, he delivers an address on "Non-Aggression Procedures to Interracial Harmony" to the New York State Convention of Universalists in Cortland.
18 Oct	King addresses the Pennsylvania State Baptist Convention in Harrisburg.
19 Oct	Coretta Scott King gives a concert at Chicago's Olivet Baptist Church.
20 Oct	The Tallahassee Inter-Civic Council and twenty-one individual defendants are found guilty of operating a car pool for boycotters.
21 Oct	King preaches at Dexter.
24 Oct	After attending an executive board meeting, King presents the year-end report at the Dexter annual business meeting.
28 Oct	After dinner with former advisor L. Harold DeWolf and his wife in Boston, King delivers "A Realistic Look at Race Relations" at the Ford Hall Forum.
29 Oct	King rushes back to Montgomery from Boston after learning of a possible court injunction against the MIA's car pool and announces that the bus boycott is continuing. The MIA holds simultaneous mass meetings at Mt. Zion and St. John AME Churches.
1 Nov	Boycott leaders submit a petition in U.S. District Court for an injunction and a restraining order to block the city commissioners' move for an injunction against the car pool. Later that night Montgomery city authorities deliver a petition asking Judge Carter of the Montgomery Circuit Court for an injunction to halt the MIA car pool.

2 Nov	King delivers an address to the Virginia Teachers Association convention at Virginia Union University in Richmond. In Montgomery, Judge Carter sets a hearing for 13 November. Meanwhile, Judge Johnson of the federal district court denies the motion by MIA legal representatives for an emergency restraining order to prevent city interference with car pool activity and schedules a hearing on the injunction for 14 November.
4 Nov	King preaches "Paul's Letter to American Christians" at Dexter.
5 Nov	King gives the opening remarks at an MIA mass meeting at First Baptist Church.
8 Nov	Coretta Scott King gives a concert in Mobile, Alabama.
11 Nov	King is the guest speaker at the Tuskegee Institute Chapel.
13 Nov	The U.S. Supreme Court affirms the lower court opinion in *Browder v. Gayle* declaring Montgomery and Alabama bus segregation laws unconstitutional. Judge Carter grants a temporary injunction halting the MIA car pools.
14 Nov	Judge Johnson refuses to forestall enforcement of the state court injunction halting car pool operations. That evening, King speaks at MIA mass meetings at Hutchinson Street Baptist Church and Holt Street Baptist Church, where eight thousand attendees vote unanimously to end the boycott when the court mandate arrives.
17 Nov	Thurgood Marshall and three other attorneys ask Supreme Court justice Hugo Black to hasten delivery of the mandate implementing the Supreme Court's 13 November decision. On 19 November, Black refuses to expedite the order.
18 Nov	King is awarded in absentia the Sigma Phi chapter of the Omega Psi Phi fraternity's Citizen of the Year award at Dexter. King delivers a Men's Day sermon at Mt. Zion First Baptist Church in Baton Rouge, Louisiana.
19 Nov	King delivers the opening remarks at an MIA mass meeting at Beulah Baptist Church.
1 Dec	*Liberation* publishes "We Are Still Walking."
3 Dec	At Holt Street Baptist Church, King delivers the opening address, titled "Facing the Challenge of the New Age," at the MIA's weeklong Institute on Nonviolence and Social Change.
4 Dec	King offers remarks at a public forum held at Bethel Baptist Church, part of the weeklong Institute on Nonviolence.
5 Dec	On the first anniversary of the bus boycott, King presides over an institute seminar on "Nonviolence and the Social Gospel." Coretta Scott King speaks and sings at a "Salute to Montgomery" concert in New York City, sponsored by In Friendship to benefit the MIA and other struggles in the South.
6 Dec	In Washington, D.C., King attends an Alpha Phi Alpha executive board meeting and delivers three speeches: "Remember

Who You Are," at a Day of Prayer service at Howard University's Andrew Rankin Chapel; "The Three Dimensions of a Complete Life," at the annual Student Christian Association dinner; and "Facing the Challenge of a New Age," at an NAACP gathering at Vermont Avenue Baptist Church.

7 Dec The Dorie Miller Memorial Foundation in Chicago awards its annual achievement award to King in absentia.

9 Dec King presides and J. H. Jackson gives the address at the closing mass meeting of the Institute on Nonviolence and Social Change at First Baptist Church. Vernon H. Johns preaches at the seventy-ninth anniversary of Dexter.

10 Dec King gives a deposition on an 11 July train station incident with a Montgomery police officer. U.S. Attorney General Herbert Brownell, Jr., meets with thirty-three U.S. district attorneys in a daylong conference at which he calls for "voluntary compliance" by carriers with the Supreme Court's 13 November ruling. The Supreme Court delays hearing petitions from Birmingham and the state of Alabama contesting the ruling.

11 Dec King speaks at a United Negro College Fund symposium, "The Negro Southerner Speaks," at the Hunter College Assembly Hall in New York. He later appears on the NBC radio show "Tex and Jinx" with Carl Rowan.

15 Dec King speaks on "Desegregation and the Future" at the annual meeting of the National Committee for Rural Schools in New York.

17 Dec The U.S. Supreme Court rejects Alabama's final appeal.

19 Dec Anonymous leaflets are distributed throughout Montgomery's black community asking residents to rebel against the leadership of the boycott.

20 Dec The Supreme Court bus desegregation mandate arrives at Judge Johnson's office. U.S. marshals deliver writs of injunction to Montgomery city officials. Judge Jones dissolves his injunction against Montgomery bus integration and rebukes the Supreme Court. Later that day, King presides over MIA meetings at Holt Street Baptist and St. John AME Churches during which attendees vote to end the boycott.

21 Dec Montgomery City Lines resumes full service on all routes. King, Abernathy, Nixon, and Smiley are among the first passengers to seat themselves in the section formerly reserved for whites. The first act of violence involves a black woman who is slapped by a white youth as she leaves a bus.

23 Dec A shotgun blast is fired into the King home. King informs his congregants of the incident at morning services and later speaks at an MIA mass meeting at Hutchinson Street Baptist Church.

24 Dec Several white men beat a fifteen-year-old black woman at a bus stop. Tallahassee's Inter-Civic Council suspends its bus

boycott and attempts to desegregate the city buses. Tallahassee's city commission directs the bus company to enforce segregation on its buses.

25 Dec In Birmingham, the home of Shuttlesworth is bombed.

26 Dec Two Montgomery buses are targeted by snipers. In Birmingham, Shuttlesworth integrates white sections of buses with two hundred participants. Police arrest more than twenty people for violating segregation laws. At a mass meeting that evening, Birmingham bus protesters vote to continue their activities after Shuttlesworth reads a telegram from King. The Alabama Christian Movement for Human Rights files a suit in federal court to desegregate Birmingham's buses. Tallahassee suspends the bus company's franchise after Steele and others attempt to integrate buses.

28 Dec King is the guest speaker at a town meeting held at the Delta Sigma Theta sorority's annual national convention in Detroit. He also appears on the United Auto Worker television program "Telescope." Rosa Jordan, a pregnant black Montgomery resident, is shot while riding a bus. Police Commissioner Sellers orders all bus runs suspended for the rest of the night.

29 Dec King delivers a speech at the Omega Psi Phi fraternity annual convention at Morgan State College in Baltimore and receives its Citizen of the Year award. While there, King meets with Harris Wofford, Stanley Levison, and Rustin. Following four shooting incidents, the Montgomery city commission orders a halt to after-dark bus service for the remainder of the holiday weekend.

31 Dec A Montgomery bus is the target of another sniper attack. Police Commissioner Sellers announces the addition of twenty new officers to the police force.

The central goal of the Martin Luther King, Jr., Papers Project is to produce an authoritative, multivolume edition of King's works. These chronologically arranged volumes contain accurate, annotated transcriptions of King's most important sermons, speeches, correspondence, published writings, unpublished manuscripts, and other papers. For this volume we have examined more than five thousand King-related documents and recordings and selected those that are the most biographically or historically significant to King's life, thought, and leadership.

King's writings and statements were assigned highest priority for inclusion. Most of King's publications, sermons, and speeches were included, although a few were excluded because of their similarity to others from the period. When a public address was available in different formats, we preferred the recorded version or, when alternative texts are available, the version that had greatest public impact. Correspondence containing significant information about King's thought or activities and incoming letters that illuminated relationships with or impact on others were also included. Unsolicited mail and routine or office-generated reply letters were usually excluded.

This volume also contains documents that do not fit within the categories mentioned above but are nevertheless useful sources of information regarding King's attitudes, activities, and associations. These include transcripts of meetings, newspaper articles, interviews with King, and correspondence about King. Notes taken by contemporary observers of MIA mass meetings and executive board gatherings, for example, reveal King's leadership role. It should be noted, however, that this volume, which focuses on King's involvement in the boycott, includes only a small proportion of the total material available on the protest movement.

In addition, this volume contains sections designed to provide information useful to lay and scholarly readers alike. The Chronology lists King's significant activities as well as local and national events that may have affected him. The Introduction is a narrative essay based on the documentary records assembled by the King Papers Project and on the memoirs of participants. It is not intended to substitute for a thorough biography of King or a history of the Montgomery movement. Finally, to assist scholars and others seeking further information regarding King-related primary documents, this volume includes a Calendar of Documents that provides full citations for items chosen for publication or referred to in annotations. It also lists a selection of other significant King-related documents. King Papers Project descriptions of archival collections related to King are available in an electronic database of the Research Libraries Information Network (RLIN).

Documents are introduced by a title, date, and place of origin. Existing titles are used when available and are designated by quotation marks. For untitled items, we have created descriptive titles reflecting their content (e.g., Martin Luther King, Sr., to Dexter Avenue Baptist Church Members), with errors or irregularities in punctuation, capitalization, and spelling silently corrected and names standardized. Speech or sermon titles indicate the occasion of the address. In King's correspondence, the title contains the author or recipient (e.g., To Roy Wilkins), leaving King's participation implied. When the date was not specified in the document but has been determined through research, it is rendered in italics and enclosed in square brackets. When a specific date was not available, we have provided a range date. If the place of origin appears on the document, it is included; if not, and it could be determined through research, it is provided for King-authored documents only. (A more detailed explanation of procedures for assigning titles, dates, and other cataloging information appears at the end of the volume in the Calendar of Documents.)

Annotations are intended to enhance readers' understanding of the documents. Headnotes preceding documents explain the context of their creation; in the case of longer documents, a brief summary may be offered. Headnotes and editorial footnotes also identify individuals, organizations, events, literary quotations, biblical allusions, and other references in the document, as well as relevant correspondence or related documents. Biographical sketches describe the background and relationship to King of individuals who corresponded with him or are mentioned prominently in documents. We have not included such sketches for individuals described in previous volumes, nor have we annotated theological ideas and persons likely to be discussed in standard reference works. Editorial footnotes on occasion refer to alternative accounts of events and to variations among versions (e.g., sentences altered or added by King when he published a previously given speech or sermon). Marginal notes on the document, particularly those written by King, are also noted. Annotations may contain implicit or abbreviated references to documents (e.g., "King replied on 8 March 1956"); full bibliographic information for such documents can be found in the Calendar of Documents.

The source note following each document provides information on the characteristics of the original document and its provenance. Codes are used to describe the document's format, type, version, and form of signature. The code "TLS," for example, identifies the letter as a typed letter with a signature. The location of the original document is described next, using standard abbreviations from *Symbols of American Libraries*. (See List of Abbreviations for all codes used.)

TRANSCRIPTION PRACTICES

Transcriptions are intended to reproduce the source document accurately, adhering to the exact wording and punctuation of the original. In general, errors in spelling, punctuation, and grammar, which may offer important insights into the author's state of mind and conditions under which the document was composed, have been neither corrected nor indicated by *sic*. Capitalization, boldface,

To Benjamin Elijah Mays — Title

24 April 1956 — Date
[*Montgomery, Ala.*] — Place of origin

King declines Mays's invitation of 21 April to speak at Morehouse morning chapel services before the end of the school year in May. King explains that he is "preparing the outline and manuscript for a forthcoming book" and hence cannot accept any more engagements. King expressed interest in working on such a manuscript for many months before finally undertaking the project that became Stride Toward Freedom, *published in 1958.[1]* — Headnote

Dr. Benjamin E. Mays, Pres.
Morehouse College
Atlanta, Georgia

Dear Dr. Mays:

Thanks for your very kind letter inviting me to speak at Morehouse College.
I am in the process of preparing the outline and manuscript for a forthcoming book. Due to the time that must be put into such a venture, I have promised myself that I would accept no further speaking engagements for the month of May. It is my aim to devote this whole month to the necessary research involved in such an undertaking. I am sure that you understand this because of your long experience as a writer. But for this, I would be very happy to come. Please feel free to call on me some other time. — Document

With every good wish, I am

Sincerely yours,
M. L. King, Jr.,
President

MLK:b

TLc. MLKP-MBU: Box 62. — Document description

———
1. King held discussions with several collaborators and publishers, including Doubleday, before choosing Harper and Row in early 1957 (see Clement Alexandre to King; 1 June 1956; and King to Alexandre, 18 June 1956). In April 1956 he contemplated a collaboration with Edith Gilmore, an associate of Bayard Rustin in New York, to write the Montgomery story for publication, but nothing resulted (see Edith Gilmore to King, 9 April 1956).

— Editors' footnote

Brief references; full citation in Calendar of Documents

subscripts, abbreviations, hyphenation, strikeouts, ellipses, and symbols are likewise replicated. This rule has certain exceptions, however. In printed documents, obvious spelling or grammatical errors have been corrected. In typescripts, malformed and superimposed characters and single-letter corrections by the author have also been corrected. In cases where an earlier draft revealed the author's intention, the more correct alternative has been reproduced.

In some instances formatting practices such as outlining, underlining, paragraph indentation, and spacing between words or lines of text have been regularized to maintain consistency within the edition. For example, we use continuous rather than discontinuous underscoring; and em dashes, which appeared in several styles in the original manuscripts, have been regularized. Some aspects of the source document—such as line breaks, pagination, vertical and horizontal spacing, and end-of-line hyphenation—have not been replicated. Other features, such as letterheads and typographic variations, that could not be readily reproduced are described in the annotations (in a few cases, visually interesting documents such as legal indictments or arrest records have been reproduced in facsimile). The internal address, salutation, and complimentary closing of letters are presented left-aligned, regardless of the original format. Insertions in the text by the author (usually handwritten) are indicated by curly braces ({ }) and placed as precisely as possible. Telegrams are rendered using small capital letters.

Editorial explanations are rendered in italics and enclosed by square brackets. Conjectural renderings of text are set in italic type followed by a question mark and placed within brackets: [*there's?*]. Instances of illegible text are indicated: e.g., [*strikeout illegible*]. If a strikeout was by someone other than the author, it has not been replicated but is described in a footnote. If part of a document is lost, the condition is described: [*remainder missing*]. In some instances, long documents have been excerpted to highlight passages that were most significant with respect to King. Editorial deletions to eliminate repetitive or extraneous segments are indicated by ellipses or by explanatory comment: e.g., [. . .] or [*prayer by Rev. Alford*]. Signatures that are identical with the typed name are reproduced as follows:

> Sincerely,
> [*signed*]
> Benjamin E. Mays

The King Papers Project's transcriptions of audio recordings are intended to replicate, to the extent possible, King's public statements as they were delivered, excluding only those utterings that do not convey significant meaning (e.g., unintentional stutters and pause words, such as "uh"). Certain sharply stressed phrases are rendered in italics to indicate the speaker's emphasis. When available, King's written text is used to clarify ambiguous phrases and as a guide to delineating sentences, paragraphs, and punctuation. In cases where the written text is not available, we have supplied punctuation for clarity. Transcriptions also attempt to convey some of the quality of the speech event, particularly the interplay between speaker and audience. When practical, audience responses to King's orations are enclosed in parentheses and placed appropriately within King's text. Editorial descriptions of audience participation are enclosed in square brackets. The first instance of audience response to a speech is indicated as follows: [*Audience:*] (*Amen*). Subsequent audience interjections are enclosed, as is appropriate, in brackets—[*applause*] or [*singing*] or [*laughter*]—or in parentheses: (*Yes*) or (*Lord help him*). Multiple audience responses are indicated in order of occurrence, separated by commas: (*Tell it, Don't stop*). In addition, transcriptions occasionally suggest the loudness or duration of audience responses: [*sustained applause*]. In cases where a recording or its transcription is incomplete or unintelligible, that status is indicated within the text proper: e.g., [*gap in tape*] or [*words inaudible*].

ABBREVIATIONS

COLLECTIONS AND REPOSITORIES

AAGR-A-Ar	Alabama Attorney General Records, Alabama Department of Archives and History, Montgomery, Ala.
ABAC-ABHSP	American Baptist Archives Center, American Baptist Historical Society, Valley Forge, Pa.
ACHRP-GAU	Alabama Council on Human Relations Papers, Robert W. Woodruff Library Archives and Special Collections, Atlanta University Center, Atlanta, Ga.
ACLUC-NjP	American Civil Liberties Union Collection, Princeton University, Princeton, N.J.
AJC-ICHi	Archibald James Carey Collection, Chicago Historical Society, Chicago, Ill.
APRC-DLC	A. Philip Randolph Collection, Library of Congress, Washington, D.C.
APWW	A.P. World Wide Photos, New York, N.Y.
ASRC-GAU	Archives of the Southern Regional Council, Robert W. Woodruff Library Archives and Special Collections, Atlanta University Center, Atlanta, Ga.
BEMP-DHU	Benjamin E. Mays Papers, Moorland-Spingarn Research Center, Howard University, Washington, D.C.
BRP-DLC	Bayard Rustin Papers, Library of Congress, Washington, D.C.
CB-CtY	Chester Bowles Collection, Yale University, New Haven, Conn.
CBSNA-CBSN	CBS News Archives, CBS News, New York, N.Y.
CCDP-DHU	Charles C. Diggs Papers, Moorland-Spingarn Research Center, Howard University, Washington, D.C.
CMCR-AMC	Circuit Court, Montgomery County Records, Montgomery County Court House, Montgomery, Ala.
CSJP-TNF	Charles S. Johnson Papers, Fisk University, Nashville, Tenn.
CSKC	Coretta Scott King Collection (in private hands)
DABCC	Dexter Avenue King Memorial Baptist Church Collection (in private hands)
DDEP-KAbE	Dwight D. Eisenhower Miscellaneous Papers, Dwight D. Eisenhower Library, Abilene, Kans.
DJG	David J. Garrow Collection (in private hands)
EBCR	Ebenezer Baptist Church Miscellaneous Records (in private hands)
ERC-NHyF	Eleanor Roosevelt Collection, Franklin D. Roosevelt Library, Hyde Park, N.Y.

FHP-WHi	Fred Halstead Papers, State Historical Society of Wisconsin, Madison, Wis.
FORP-PSC-P	Fellowship of Reconciliation Papers, Swarthmore College Peace Collection, Swarthmore, Pa.
FSTC	Francis S. Thomas Collection (in private hands)
GDKP	George D. Kelsey Papers (in private hands)
GEpFAR	Federal Archives and Records Center, General Services Administration, Atlanta Region, East Point, Ga.
GESP	Glenn E. Smiley Collection (in private hands)
HDBSD	Harvey Dinnerstein and Burt Silverman Drawings (in private hands)
HG-GAMK	Hazel Gregory Papers, Martin Luther King, Jr., Center for Nonviolent Social Change, Inc., Atlanta, Ga.
HJP-GAMK	H. J. Palmer Papers, Martin Luther King, Jr., Center for Nonviolent Social Change, Inc., Atlanta, Ga.
HRECR-WHi	Highlander Research and Education Center Records, State Historical Society of Wisconsin, Madison, Wis.
HTC-MBU	Howard Thurman Papers, Boston University, Boston, Mass.
JEFAF-A-Ar	Governor James E. Folsom Administration Files, Alabama Department of Archives and History, Montgomery, Ala.
JMEC	J. Martin England Collection (in private hands)
JNS-PSC-P	John Nevin Sayre Papers, Swarthmore College Peace Collection, Swarthmore, Pa.
JOG	Julian O. Grayson Papers (in private hands)
JRC	Johnnie R. Carr Papers (in private hands)
LSP-GU	Lillian Smith Papers, University of Georgia, Athens, Ga.
MAGPC	Magnum Photos, Inc., Collection (in private hands)
MCDA-AMC	Montgomery County District Attorney's Files, Montgomery County Court House, Montgomery, Ala.
MIAFBI-DJ	Montgomery Improvement Association–FBI files, Department of Justice, Washington, D.C.
MLK/BP-ViHaI	Martin Luther King, Jr., Box and Picture Collection, Hampton University Archives and University Museum, Hampton, Va.
MLKJRP-GAMK	Martin Luther King, Jr., Papers, 1950–1968, Martin Luther King, Jr., Center for Nonviolent Social Change, Inc., Atlanta, Ga.
MLKP-MBU	Martin Luther King, Jr., Papers, 1954–1968, Boston University, Boston, Mass.
MMFR	Montgomery to Memphis Film Research Files, Coretta Scott King Collection (in private hands)
MNAACP-NN-Sc	Montgomery Branch, National Association for the Advancement of Colored People Minutes, 1954–55, New York Public Library, Schomburg Collection, New York, N.Y.
NAACPP-DLC	National Association for the Advancement of Colored People Papers, Library of Congress, Washington, D.C.

NBCC-NNNBC	NBC Collection, National Broadcasting Company, Inc., General Library, New York, N.Y.
NCCP-PPPrHi	National Council of the Churches of Christ in the United States of America Papers, Presbyterian Department of History, Philadelphia, Pa.
NCNWR-DABW	National Council of Negro Women Records, National Archive for Black Women's History, Washington, D.C.
NHBP-DLC	Nannie H. Burroughs Papers, Library of Congress, Washington, D.C.
NTC-NN	Norman Thomas Collection, New York Public Library, New York, N.Y.
NULR-DLC	National Urban League Records, Library of Congress, Washington, D.C.
PDNC-MWalK	Proceedings of the Democratic National Convention, John F. Kennedy Library, Waltham, Mass.
PLPC-DHU	Percival Leroy Prattis Collection, Moorland-Spingarn Research Center, Howard University, Washington, D.C.
PV-ARC-LNT	Preston Valien Collection, Amistad Research Center, Tulane University, New Orleans, La.
RGP	Robert Graetz Papers (in private hands)
RJGC	R. J. Glasco Collection (in private hands)
RPC-MiDW	Rosa Parks Collection, Archives of Labor and Urban Affairs, Wayne State University, Detroit, Mich.
RR-ARC-LNT	Race Relations Department of the United Church Board for Home Ministries, Amistad Research Center, Tulane University, New Orleans, La.
RWH	R. W. Hilson Papers (in private hands)
RWP-DLC	Roy Wilkins Papers, Library of Congress, Washington, D.C.
SBHL-TNSB	Southern Baptist Historical Library and Archives, Southern Baptist Convention Historical Commission, Nashville, Tenn.
TMA	T. M. Alexander Papers (in private hands)
UNCFR-GAU	United Negro College Fund Records, Robert W. Woodruff Library Archives and Special Collections, Atlanta University Center, Atlanta, Ga.
UPW-WHi	United Packing House Workers, State Historical Society of Wisconsin, Madison, Wis.
URPh-BETT	U.P.I. and Reuters Photo Collection, Bettman Archives, New York
UUAR-MH-AH	Unitarian Universalist Association Records, Harvard University, Andover-Harvard Theological Library, Cambridge, Mass.
VFDP-MCR-S	Virginia Foster Durr Papers, Radcliffe College, Schlesinger Library on the History of Women in America, Cambridge, Mass.
VSC	Vivian Stanley Collection (in private hands)
WCFG-KAbE	White House Central Files (General Files), Dwight D. Eisenhower Library, Abilene, Kans.

Abbreviations   WCFO-KAbE   White House Central Files (Official File), Dwight D. Eisenhower Library, Abilene, Kans.

WEBD-MU   W. E. B. Du Bois Papers, University of Massachusetts, Amherst, Mass.

WMP-MBU   Walter Muelder Papers, Boston University, Boston, Mass.

WRMP-GAMK   William Robert Miller Papers, 1955–1968, Martin Luther King, Jr., Center for Nonviolent Social Change, Inc., Atlanta, Ga.

WTH   W. T. Handy Collection (in private hands)

ABBREVIATIONS USED IN SOURCE NOTES

The following symbols are used to describe the original documents:

Format
A   Autograph—author's hand
H   Handwritten—other than author's hand
P   Printed
T   Typed

Type
At   Audio tape
Aw   Art work
D   Document
Fm   Form
L   Letter or memo
Ph   Photo
Vt   Video tape
W   Wire or telegram

Version
c   Copy
d   Draft
f   Fragment

Signature
I   Initialed
S   Signed
Sr   Signed with representation of author

DRAWINGS

In 1956 Manhattan artists Burton Silverman and Harvey Dinnerstein traveled to Alabama to record their impressions of the bus boycott and the trial of the boycott leaders. The resulting drawings appeared in such publications as the *New York Times* and *Life.* The drawings here appear courtesy of the artists. The drawing above, by Harvey Dinnerstein, shows protesters marching.

(*Right*) Protesters. Drawing by Burton Silverman.

B. Silverman

(*Left*) Protester giving the victory sign. Drawing by
Burton Silverman.

(*Above*) Martin Luther King, Jr., and attorney listening
to testimony. Drawing by Burton Silverman.

(*Left*) E. D. Nixon. Drawing by Burton Silverman.

(*Above*) Jo Ann Gibson Robinson. Drawing by Burton
Silverman.

(*Above*) Martin Luther King, Jr. Drawing by
Burton Silverman.

(*Right*) Rosa Parks. Drawing by Harvey Dinnerstein.

Mrs. Rosa Parks   1956

Montgomery, Alabama 1956

Protester. Drawing by Harvey Dinnerstein.

PHOTOGRAPHS

(*Above*) Supporters attend the first mass meeting held at Holt Street Baptist Church on 5 December 1955. Photo and permission courtesy of the *Montgomery Advertiser.*

(*Right*) Rosa Parks, E. D. Nixon, and Fred D. Gray in Montgomery's Police Court after Parks's conviction on 5 December 1955. Gray is filing a notice of appeal. Photo and permission courtesy of Associated Press/Wide World Photos.

Mayor W. A. Gayle, Fire Chief
R. L. Lampley, Martin Luther King, Jr., and Police
Commissioner Clyde Sellers outside King's home after
it was bombed on 30 January 1956. Photo and permission courtesy of Associated Press/ Wide World Photos.

(*Top*) Fred D. Gray, Ralph David Abernathy, Robert Graetz, and U. J. Fields on 21 February 1956 after a mass meeting at which MIA supporters decided to continue the boycott. Photo and permission courtesy of Associated Press/ Wide World Photos.

(*Bottom*) On 22 February 1956, Police Lieutenant D. H. Lackey fingerprints Rosa Parks, who was indicted for conspiracy to boycott. Photo and permission courtesy of Associated Press/ Wide World Photos.

(*Left*) King and other indicted boycott leaders in front of the Alabama State Capitol. Photo and permission courtesy of Don Cravens, *Life*. © Time, Inc.

(*Above*) Martin Luther King, Jr., after his arrest on 23 February 1956. Photo and permission courtesy of Don Cravens, *Life*. © Time, Inc.

(*Left*) Fred D. Gray, Orzell Billingsley, Jr., Charles D. Langford, Arthur D. Shores, and Peter A. Hall outside Circuit Solicitor William Thetford's office after a press conference on 23 February 1956. Photo and permission courtesy of Associated Press / Wide World Photos.

(*Bottom left*) D. H. Lackey books Martin Luther King, Jr., and Ralph David Abernathy on 23 February 1956. Photo and permission courtesy of Associated Press / Wide World Photos.

(*Above*) Rosa Parks and E. D. Nixon climb Montgomery's county courthouse stairs to attend the beginning of King's trial on 19 March 1956. Photo and permission courtesy of Associated Press / Wide World Photos.

(*Top left*) King and supporters gather at trial during a recess on 19 March 1956. Photo and permission courtesy of Associated Press/Wide World Photos.

(*Bottom left*) King greets supporters before the second day of his trial on 20 March 1956. Photo and permission courtesy of Associated Press/Wide World Photos.

(*Above*) Coretta Scott King kisses Martin Luther King, Jr., on 22 March 1956 after he was found guilty of conspiracy to boycott. Photo and permission courtesy of Associated Press/Wide World Photos.

(*Above*) King announces that the boycott will
continue at the Holt Street Baptist Church mass
meeting on 22 March 1956, the day of his conviction.
Photo and permission courtesy of Associated Press/
Wide World Photos.

(*Top right*) Coretta Scott King, Yolanda Denise King,
and Martin Luther King, Jr., stand on the stairs of
Dexter Avenue Baptist Church in spring 1956.Photo
and permission courtesy of Sandra Weiner. Photo by
Dan Weiner.

(*Bottom right*) King speaks to MIA executive board on
24 April 1956 after National City Lines orders Montgomery's buses to desegregate. Photo and permission
courtesy of Associated Press/Wide World Photos.

(*Top left*) King at a mass meeting at Day Street Baptist Church on 26 April 1956. Photo and permission courtesy of Associated Press/Wide World Photos.

(*Bottom left*) Three women exit a station wagon used in the MIA car pool on 31 May 1956. Photo and permission courtesy of Associated Press/Wide World Photos.

(*Above*) Martin Luther King, Jr., Coretta Scott King, and Yolanda Denise King at a baby contest at Dexter in July 1956. Photo courtesy of Boston University.

(*Top left*) King speaks at Fisk University's annual Race Relations Institute on 12 July 1956. Photo and permission courtesy of the Amistad Research Center, Tulane University, New Orleans.

(*Bottom left*) James Huger, Frank Stanley, Raymond Pace Alexander, and Martin Luther King, Jr., at the Alpha Phi Alpha fiftieth anniversary convention banquet on 11 August 1956. King was the featured speaker at the event and received the Alpha Award of Honor. Photo and permission courtesy of Vivian Stanley.

(*Above*) King signs autographs at the Hampton Institute in Virginia after his speech on 27 September 1956. Photo and permission courtesy of Hampton University Archival and Museum Collection.

On 21 December 1956, the day after the Supreme
Court's integration order arrived in Montgomery,
Ralph Abernathy, Martin Luther King, Jr., Glenn E.
Smiley, and others ride a Montgomery City Lines bus.
Photo and permission courtesy of Associated Press/
Wide World Photos.

Two men sit at the front of a Montgomery City Lines
bus on 22 December 1956. Photo and permission courtesy of Associated Press/Wide World Photos.

The Papers

> Don't ride the bus to work, to town, to school, or any place Monday, December 5.
>
> Another Negro Woman has been arrested and put in jail because she refused to give up her bus seat.
>
> Don't ride the buses to work to town, to school, or any where on Monday. . If you work, take a cab, or share a ride, or walk.
>
> Come to a mass meeting, Monday at 7:00 P. M. at the Holt Street Baptist Church for further instruction.

On 2 December 1955, the day after the arrest of Rosa Parks, Jo Ann Robinson and the members of the Women's Political Council (WPC) wrote and distributed a leaflet calling for a one-day boycott of buses on Monday, 5 December. That evening, African-American religious and civic leaders met at Dexter Avenue Baptist Church and planned the boycott. A committee that included Martin Luther King, Jr., and Ralph Abernathy edited the leaflet and added a call for a mass meeting Monday evening. It was reproduced on the Dexter mimeograph machine and distributed by volunteers over the weekend.

Minutes of Montgomery Improvement
Association Founding Meeting, by U. J. Fields

5 December 1955
Montgomery, Ala.

The one-day bus boycott on Monday, 5 December, exceeded the organizers' expectations. Only a few black passengers rode the buses. That morning, after her brief trial at the city recorder's court, Judge John B. Scott found Rosa Parks guilty of violating the state segregation law and fined her fourteen dollars. Attorney Fred D. Gray appealed the verdict to the state's court of appeals.[1] That afternoon, Montgomery's black leaders gathered at Rev. L. Roy Bennett's Mt. Zion AME Zion Church to plan the evening mass meeting at Holt Street Baptist Church. A smaller group withdrew to Bennett's study and, as these minutes by Rev. U. J. Fields indicate, created an organization called the Montgomery Improvement Association (MIA).[2] Rufus A. Lewis, a businessman and active member of Dexter Avenue Baptist Church, moved that his pastor become chairman,[3] and King was elected without opposition. After choosing other officers and forming committees, the group "agreed that the protest be continued until conditions are improved" and decided on the agenda for that evening's mass meeting.

---

1. Fred David Gray (1930–), a native of Montgomery, was one of two black lawyers in the city. He earned his B.A. from Alabama State College (1951) and his LL.B. (1954) from Ohio's Case Western Reserve University. Ordained as a teenager, Gray ministered to the Holt Street Church of Christ during the boycott. After he filed a federal suit challenging the constitutionality of the bus segregation laws, the local draft board reclassified Gray's exempt status as a minister and ordered him to report for induction into the armed services. The situation was resolved only after the director of the Selective Service intervened, indefinitely postponing Gray's induction. Gray served as a lawyer for both the local branch and the state conference of the NAACP and for the Montgomery Progressive Democratic Association. Gray later wrote an account of the boycott titled *Bus Ride to Justice* (1994).

2. L. Roy Bennett, pastor of Mt. Zion AME Zion Church, was president of Montgomery's black Interdenominational Ministerial Alliance. On the day after Parks's arrest he had chaired a meeting of ministers and other leaders at Dexter Avenue Baptist Church to plan the one-day boycott. He was also among the ministers indicted for participating in the boycott. During the boycott Bennett was called to the First AME Zion Church in San Francisco, where he served until 1965.

Uriah J. Fields (1930–), born in Sunflower, Alabama, served as a chaplain's assistant in the army during the Korean War. He received his B.A. (1955) and M.Ed. (1956) from Alabama State College and his M.Div. (1959) from Atlanta's Interdenominational Theological Center. Inspired by Montgomery leader E. D. Nixon's campaign for a local office, Fields ran successfully for student body president of Alabama State in 1954. When the boycott began Fields was interim pastor of Bell Street Baptist Church. He later published *The Montgomery Story: The Unhappy Effects of the Montgomery Bus Boycott* (1959).

3. Rufus Andrews Lewis (1906–), born in Montgomery, graduated from Fisk University. A librarian and athletic coach at Alabama State College from the mid-1930s to 1941, he later taught World War II veterans in night school. In 1958, after his wife's death, Rufus began operating her family's company, Montgomery's largest black funeral business. A member of Alpha Phi Alpha fraternity and the NAACP, Lewis organized the Citizens Club, a social club that provided voter registration assistance and required members to be registered voters. Lewis also headed the Citizens Education Committee and traveled throughout Alabama, Georgia, and Mississippi training voter registration workers. During the Montgomery bus boycott he headed the MIA's transportation committee and co-chaired its committee on registration and voting.

A group of 18 persons met at the Mt. Zion A.M.E. Zion Church at 3 P.M.
Officers were elected:

Chairman—Rev. M. L. King
Vice Chairman—Rev. Roy Bennett
Recording Sec.—Rev. U. J. Fields
Corresponding Sec.—Rev. E. N. French [4]
Financial Sec.—Mrs. Erna Dungee [5]
Treasurer—E. D. Nixon [6]

NAME
The Montgomery Improvement Association
Moved and second that the 16 persons here and a suggestion that 9 names be brought in making 25 which constitute the Executive Committee
It was recommended that resolutions would be drawned up.
Resolution Committee & Recommendations

Rev. Abernathy [7] Chairman
Rev Alford
Mr Gray

4. Edgar Nathaniel French (1921–1979), born in Mount Gilead, North Carolina, received his B.A. from Livingstone College, M.Div. from Hood Theological Seminary, and M.A. from Columbia University. During the bus boycott French served as pastor of Hilliard Chapel AME Zion Church in Montgomery and was a member of the NAACP. He was indicted for his participation in the boycott. He later served as dean of Livingstone College and pastor of Trinity AME Zion Church in Greensboro, North Carolina.

5. Erna A. Dungee (ca. 1909–1984) was born in rural Alabama. She moved to Montgomery in the 1920s and graduated from the Montgomery Industrial Schools and Alabama State College. After teaching for several years in rural black schools she married Dr. A. C. Dungee, participated in voter registration efforts in the 1930s and 1940s, and helped found the Women's Political Council. A member of the local NAACP, she served on the MIA's finance committee.

6. Edgar Daniel Nixon (1899–1987) was born in Lowndes County, Alabama. As a Pullman porter (1923–1964) based in Montgomery, Nixon organized the Brotherhood of Sleeping Car Porters' local union and served for many years as its president. His union experience, his involvement in the March on Washington movement of the 1940s, and his observations of nonsegregated facilities inspired his fight for racial equality in Montgomery. He served terms as president of both the state and Montgomery NAACP and organized voting drives. After bailing Rosa Parks out of jail on 1 December, Nixon organized the meeting the next day of the city's black leadership that endorsed the one-day boycott. His union contacts and organizing ability helped the MIA raise thousands of dollars in support of the boycott. Nixon was among the black leaders indicted for violating Alabama's antiboycott law.

7. Ralph David Abernathy (1926–1990), born in Linden, Alabama, was chair of the MIA executive committee and was among the ministers indicted for their role in the boycott. He also chaired the MIA's program and public relations committees, co-chaired the committee to establish a bank and savings association, and was a member of the strategy committee. He assumed leadership of the MIA (1960–1961) when King became co-pastor of Atlanta's Ebenezer Baptist Church. Abernathy served as pastor of Montgomery's First Baptist Church (1952–1961) and then of Atlanta's West Hunter Street Baptist Church (1961–1990). Upon the formation of the Southern Christian Leadership Conference (SCLC) in 1957 Abernathy became secretary-treasurer and took over as president following King's death in 1968, in which capacity he served until 1977. He later wrote an autobiography, *And the Walls Came Tumbling Down* (1989).

Mr. Nixon
Rev. Glasco [8]

The president, Rev. M. L. King, attorney Gray and attorney Langford is on the committee.[9] The program would be tape recorded at its Holt Street Baptist Church.

It was agreed that the protest be continued until conditions are improved.

Transportation Committee

Finance

It was passed that the recommendations from the committee be given to the citizens at the night meeting.

AGENDA

1. Opening Hymn   Onward Christian Soldier
2. Prayer—Rev Alford [10]
3. Scripture   Rev. Fields
4. Occassion—Rev. King

   Presentation of Mrs. Parks—Rev. French
   Fred [*Daniels*]

5. Resolutions—Rev. Abernathy

   Vote on Recomendations

6. Offering—Rev Bonner [11]
7. Closing Hymn—My Country Tis of Thee
8. Benediction—Rev. Roy Bennett

TD. AAGR-A-Ar: Box SG 8423.

---

8. Roseby James Glasco, Sr. (1916–1986), born in Muskogee, Oklahoma, earned his B.S. (1939) from Tuskegee Institute, B.D. (1941) from American Baptist Theological Seminary, and M.Th. (1951) from Central Baptist Theological Seminary. A member of the NAACP, Glasco served as director of the Alabama Negro Baptist Center (1951–1957) and as pastor of First Baptist Church in Jacksonville, Alabama (1953–1957). During the boycott he was an officer of the transportation committee, chaired the MIA's finance committee, served as secretary of its housing committee, and was a member of the committee on registration and voting. When the MIA hired a staff to run the office, Glasco became King's executive secretary. He was also among the indicted boycott leaders. He left Montgomery in 1957 to continue his work in religious education at churches in Kansas City and St. Louis. He was pastor of Mount Bethel Baptist Church in St. Louis from 1967 until his death.

9. Charles D. Langford (1922–), born in Montgomery, received his B.A. (1948) from Tennessee State University and his LL.B. (1952) and J.D. (1967) from Catholic University of America. Langford and Fred D. Gray provided legal services to King and the MIA until 1960. In 1968 Langford joined Gray's legal firm as a partner.

10. Willie Frank Alford (1915–1989), born in Florala, Alabama, had served several churches in Alabama before becoming pastor of Montgomery's Beulah Baptist Church in 1953, where he remained until his death. An underwriter with the Atlanta Life Insurance Company and a public school teacher, Alford was a member of the MIA's committees on resolutions and on relief. An indicted boycott participant, he advocated an early end to the boycott and later resigned from the MIA because of disagreements over tactics.

11. J. W. Bonner was pastor of the First CME Church of Montgomery. A member of the MIA's executive board, he also chaired its speakers' bureau and served on the committee charged with drafting the MIA's constitution. He was among those indicted for participating in the boycott.

MIA Mass Meeting at Holt Street Baptist Church

[*5 December 1955*]
Montgomery, Ala.

*The first mass meeting of the Montgomery Improvement Association attracted several
thousand people to the spacious Holt Street Baptist Church, in a black working-class
section of Montgomery. Both the sanctuary and the basement auditorium were filled
well before the proceedings began, and an audience outside listened via loudspeakers.
In addition to reporters, photographers, and two television crews, black leaders from
other Alabama cities such as Birmingham, Mobile, and Tuscaloosa were among those
in attendance. The meeting opened with two hymns, "Onward Christian Soldiers" and
"Leaning on the Everlasting Arms," a prayer by Rev. W. F. Alford, and a Scripture
reading (Psalm 34) by Rev. U. J. Fields.*

*King then delivered an address that he had quickly composed before the meeting.
He later recalled the questions in his mind as he considered what to say: "How could
I make a speech that would be militant enough to keep my people aroused to positive
action and yet moderate enough to keep this fervor within controllable and Christian
bounds? I knew that many of the Negro people were victims of bitterness that could
easily rise to flood proportions. What could I say to keep them courageous and prepared
for positive action and yet devoid of hate and resentment? Could the militant and the
moderate be combined in a single speech?"* [1]

*In his speech, King described the mistreatment of black bus passengers and the civil
disobedience of Rosa Parks, and then justified the nonviolent protest by appealing to
African-American Christian faith in love and justice and the American democratic
tradition of legal protest.*

*A quiet pause followed King's address, then great applause. Rev. Edgar N. French
of the Hilliard Chapel AME Zion Church introduced Rosa Parks and Fred Daniel, a
student at Alabama State College who had been arrested that morning on a disorderly
conduct charge (later dismissed) for allegedly preventing a woman from getting on a bus.
Rev. Abernathy read the resolutions that he, King, and others on the resolution committee had drafted. The assembly voted overwhelmingly in favor, resolving "to refrain
from riding buses . . . until some arrangement has been worked out" with the bus company. King appealed for funds, then left to speak at a YMCA fathers and sons banquet.*

[*King:*] My friends, we are certainly very happy to see each of you out this evening. We are here this evening for serious business. [*Audience:*] (*Yes*) We are here ●
in a general sense because first and foremost we are American citizens (*That's
right*) and we are determined to apply our citizenship to the fullness of its meaning. (*Yeah, That's right*) We are here also because of our love for democracy (*Yes*),
because of our deep-seated belief that democracy transformed from thin paper
to thick action (*Yes*) is the greatest form of government on earth. (*That's right*)

But we are here in a specific sense, because of the bus situation in Montgomery.
(*Yes*) We are here because we are determined to get the situation corrected. This
situation is not at all new. The problem has existed over endless years. (*That's
right*) For many years now Negroes in Montgomery and so many other areas have

---

1. King, *Stride Toward Freedom: The Montgomery Story* (New York: Harper & Row, 1958), pp. 59–60.
King's quotations from the speech in *Stride* (pp. 61–63) differ somewhat from his actual remarks.

been inflicted with the paralysis of crippling fears (*Yes*) on buses in our community. (*That's right*) On so many occasions, Negroes have been intimidated and humiliated and impressed—oppressed—because of the sheer fact that they were Negroes. (*That's right*) I don't have time this evening to go into the history of these numerous cases. Many of them now are lost in the thick fog of oblivion (*Yes*), but at least one stands before us now with glaring dimensions. (*Yes*)

Just the other day, just last Thursday to be exact, one of the finest citizens in Montgomery (*Amen*)—not one of the finest Negro citizens (*That's right*), but one of the finest citizens in Montgomery—was taken from a bus (*Yes*) and carried to jail and arrested (*Yes*) because she refused to get up to give her seat to a white person. (*Yes, That's right*) Now the press would have us believe that she refused to leave a reserved section for Negroes (*Yes*), but I want you to know this evening that there is no reserved section. (*All right*) The law has never been clarified at that point. (*Hell no*) Now I think I speak with, with legal authority—not that I have any legal authority, but I think I speak with legal authority behind me (*All right*)—that the law, the ordinance, the city ordinance has never been totally clarified.[2] (*That's right*)

Mrs. Rosa Parks is a fine person. (*Well, well said*) And, since it had to happen, I'm happy that it happened to a person like Mrs. Parks, for nobody can doubt the boundless outreach of her integrity. (*Sure enough*) Nobody can doubt the height of her character (*Yes*), nobody can doubt the depth of her Christian commitment and devotion to the teachings of Jesus. (*All right*) And I'm happy since it had to happen, it happened to a person that nobody can call a disturbing factor in the community. (*All right*) Mrs. Parks is a fine Christian person, unassuming, and yet there is integrity and character there. And just because she refused to get up, she was arrested.

And you know, my friends, there comes a time when people get tired of being trampled over by the iron feet of oppression. [*thundering applause*] There comes a time, my friends, when people get tired of being plunged across the abyss of humiliation, where they experience the bleakness of nagging despair. (*Keep talking*) There comes a time when people get tired of being pushed out of the glittering sunlight of life's July and left standing amid the piercing chill of an alpine November. (*That's right*) [*applause*] There comes a time. (*Yes sir, Teach*) [*applause continues*]

We are here, we are here this evening because we're tired now. (*Yes*) [*applause*] And I want to say that we are not here advocating violence. (*No*) We have never done that. (*Repeat that, Repeat that*) [*applause*] I want it to be known throughout Montgomery and throughout this nation (*Well*) that we are Christian people. (*Yes*) [*applause*] We believe in the Christian religion. We believe in the teachings of Jesus. (*Well*) The only weapon that we have in our hands this evening is the weapon of protest. (*Yes*) [*applause*] That's all.

And certainly, certainly, this is the glory of America, with all of its faults. (*Yeah*) This is the glory of our democracy. If we were incarcerated behind the iron cur-

---

2. By custom bus drivers could request that black passengers move to the rear, one row at a time, when the forward white section was filled and additional white passengers had to be accommodated. See discussion of segregation ordinance in "Statement of Negro Citizens on Bus Situation," 10 December 1955, pp. 81–83 in this volume.

tains of a Communistic nation we couldn't do this. If we were dropped in the dungeon of a totalitarian regime we couldn't do this. (*All right*) But the great glory of American democracy is the right to protest for right. (*That's right*) [*applause*] My friends, don't let anybody make us feel that we are to be compared in our actions with the Ku Klux Klan or with the White Citizens Council. [*applause*] There will be no crosses burned at any bus stops in Montgomery. (*Well, That's right*) There will be no white persons pulled out of their homes and taken out on some distant road and lynched for not cooperating. [*applause*] There will be nobody amid, among us who will stand up and defy the Constitution of this nation. [*applause*] We only assemble here because of our desire to see right exist. [*applause*] My friends, I want it to be known that we're going to work with grim and bold determination to gain justice on the buses in this city. [*applause*]

And we are not wrong, we are not wrong in what we are doing. (*Well*) If we are wrong, the Supreme Court of this nation is wrong. (*Yes sir*) [*applause*] If we are wrong, the Constitution of the United States is wrong. (*Yes*) [*applause*] If we are wrong, God Almighty is wrong. (*That's right*) [*applause*] If we are wrong, Jesus of Nazareth was merely a utopian dreamer that never came down to earth. (*Yes*) [*applause*] If we are wrong, justice is a lie (*Yes*). Love has no meaning. [*applause*] And we are determined here in Montgomery to work and fight until justice runs down like water (*Yes*) [*applause*], and righteousness like a mighty stream.[3] (*Keep talking*) [*applause*]

I want to say that in all of our actions we must stick together. (*That's right*) [*applause*] Unity is the great need of the hour (*Well, That's right*), and if we are united we can get many of the things that we not only desire but which we justly deserve. (*Yeah*) And don't let anybody frighten you. (*Yeah*) We are not afraid of what we are doing (*Oh no*), because we are doing it within the law. (*All right*) There is never a time in our American democracy that we must ever think we're wrong when we protest. (*Yes sir*) We reserve that right. When labor all over this nation came to see that it would be trampled over by capitalistic power, it was nothing wrong with labor getting together and organizing and protesting for its rights. (*That's right*)

We, the disinherited of this land, we who have been oppressed so long, are tired of going through the long night of captivity. And now we are reaching out for the daybreak of freedom and justice and equality. [*applause*] May I say to you my friends, as I come to a close, and just giving some idea of why we are assembled here, that we must keep—and I want to stress this, in all of our doings, in all of our deliberations here this evening and all of the week and while—whatever we do, we must keep God in the forefront. (*Yeah*) Let us be Christian in all of our actions. (*That's right*) But I want to tell you this evening that it is not enough for us to talk about love, love is one of the pivotal points of the Christian face, faith. There is another side called justice. And justice is really love in calculation. (*All right*) Justice is love correcting that which revolts against love. (*Well*)

The Almighty God himself is not the only, not the, not the God just standing out saying through Hosea, "I love you, Israel." He's also the God that stands up before the nations and said: "Be still and know that I'm God (*Yeah*), that if you

---

3. Amos 5:24.

don't obey me I will break the backbone of your power (*Yeah*) and slap you out of the orbits of your international and national relationships."⁴ (*That's right*) Standing beside love is always justice, and we are only using the tools of justice. Not only are we using the tools of persuasion, but we've come to see that we've got to use the tools of coercion. Not only is this thing a process of education, but it is also a process of legislation. [*applause*]

As we stand and sit here this evening and as we prepare ourselves for what lies ahead, let us go out with a grim and bold determination that we are going to stick together. [*applause*] We are going to work together. [*applause*] Right here in Montgomery, when the history books are written in the future (*Yes*), somebody will have to say, "There lived a race of people (*Well*), a *black* people (*Yes sir*), 'fleecy locks and black complexion' (*Yes*), a people who had the moral courage to stand up for their rights.⁵ [*applause*] And thereby they injected a new meaning into the veins of history and of civilization." And we're gonna do that. God grant that we will do it before it is too late. (*Oh yeah*) As we proceed with our program let us think of these things. (*Yes*) [*applause*]

[*recording interrupted*] . . . Mrs. Parks and Mr. Fred Daniel. He will tell you why they're being, you know why Mrs. Parks is being presented, and also Mr. Fred Daniel will be presented. Reverend French will make the presentation.

[*French:*] Fellow American citizens. I say "American citizens" because I believe tonight more than any other time in my whole life that we have arrived at the point in life where we can see for ourselves a new destiny. (*Yes*) Our horizons are broader. I think the record of our racial group speaks with various languages attesting to the fact that we have been, since the lifting of the bonds of slavery, law-abiding, honest, tax-paying citizens of America. (*Yeah*) [*applause*] And we believe that our record warrants for us (*All right*) the recognition of citizens of America. (*Yes*) We don't mean Negro citizens. We don't mean second-rate citizens. We simply mean citizens of America. (*That's right*) [*applause*] I have a responsibility to and for a group of students. Like possibly many of you out there before me, I have the responsibility of teaching them democracy. I don't have to remind you that when occurrences like these take place and many of the other things that have happened occur, and when they begin firing questions away at you, you feel just a little unequal to the task of formulating them into real citizens of America. (*Yes*) But that's our solemn responsibility. And each of us, I'm sure, has accepted that responsibility, and we are going to do our best with molding these [*recording interrupted*] . . . active in civic and social affairs in the community. [*applause*] An upstanding, law-abiding citizen, one who would deprive no one of rights that belong to them. (*All right*) [*applause*] It has already been pointed out to you time and again that she was ordered from her seat on the bus, a public conveyance for which she had paid the legal fare. (*Well*) [*applause*] What dif-

---

4. King refers to Hosea 11:1 ("When Israel was a child, I loved him"). He may also refer to Psalm 46:10 ("Be still, and know that I am God; I will be exalted among the nations, I will be exalted in the earth!").

5. The phrase "fleecy locks and black complexion" is from a poem, "The Negro's Complaint" (1788), by British poet William Cowper. In later speeches King included longer quotations from this poem (see note 5, "The 'New Negro' of the South: Behind the Montgomery Story," June 1956, p. 283 in this volume).

ference does it make even if the president of the United States—and [*he's?*]
the greatest individual in these United States of America that I know about [*ap-*
plause]—if he had gotten on the bus? Mrs. Parks was a lady, and any gentleman
would allow a lady to have a seat. (*Speak up*) [*applause*] But because other passengers came after she was seated, she was ordered to leave her seat, and because
she refused, she was put in jail. I have the responsibility, and it's not an easy task,
to present to you the victim of this gross injustice, almost inhumanity, and absolute undemocratic principle: Mrs. Rosa Parks.[6] [*applause*] [*recording interrupted*]

You know, during my life I've heard tell of a number of false alarms, but I have
a responsibility of presenting another victim. President, late President Franklin
Delano Roosevelt said some years ago, in one of his fireside chats to the people
of this nation, that there is nothing to fear but fear itself. (*All right*) [*applause*]
When we become victims of fear, it is hard indeed to explain our actions. (*All
right*) Thank God I feel that I can say this evening that we are moving sanely and
soberly. We are not allowing our emotions to control us. We are guiding and
channeling our emotions to the extent that we feel that God shall give us the
victory. [*applause*]

The press would have us believe that someone has organized some goon
squads, whatever that is [*laughter*], whose purpose it was to molest and intimidate
those who attempted to board the city buses this morning. But if that kind of
thing happened, thank God I don't know anything about it. (*That's right*) But
somebody became a victim of that kind of fear and notion. And you know, the
psychologists have a way of saying that if you begin thinking of things strong
enough, you can become such a victim of that kind of thing until it becomes a
reality to you. [*applause*] Somebody saw a young man, a citizen of America, attending the courtesies that any young man would attend a lady walking down the
street. And he was so engrossed with the idea of intimidation and violence that
even the light, gentle touch of the hand appeared to be an act of molesting to
this individual. (*That's right, Speak up*)

Now the press again would have you believe that here was a young man who
latched on to a lady who was attempting to board the bus and wrestled her away
from the door, saying, "You can't ride this bus. I won't allow you to do it." (*Yes*)
[*applause*] But I have the responsibility of presenting to you the gentleman that
is so erroneously accused. Again we present a young man, an American citizen,
one who is preparing himself for greater service to this country, a student at Alabama State College [*applause*], a member of the First Baptist Church of the city
of Montgomery [*applause*], a young man who is so industrious and zealous about
his undertaking and his studies, until he gets up early hours in the morning and
carries a paper route before he goes to school and makes good grades in the
classroom. I have the responsibility of presenting Mr. Fred Daniel. (*Yes*) [*ap-*
plause] [*recording interrupted*]

They have the moral courage to stand. But these alone cannot win this victory

---

6. Two months later Parks commented, "I wasn't then and [have] not since then been asked to
speak at any of the meetings. I appreciate the fact of not having to make speeches[,] for other people
have suffered indignities, and it is really our fight rather than mine" (Parks, interview by Willie Mae
Lee, 5 February 1956). (The complete citation, including archival location, for all documents referenced in the notes may be found in the Calendar of Documents.)

that inevitably must be ours. (*All right*) [*applause*] Each of us here, and those who are not here tonight, have a responsibility in this great task. (*Yes*) And I'm pleading to you, this evening, to let every one of us, under God, join our hands and hearts together in this great concerted effort. And let each of us go out from here resolved as never before in our lives, to never give back one inch until we shall be accorded the full respect and rights. [*applause*] [*recording interrupted*]

[*King:*] I think we are moving on with a great deal of enthusiasm this evening, the type of thing that we need in our efforts. And we are certainly very happy to see that, indeed. We at least see that you are with this cause and you are with our struggle. It is a struggle for all of us, not just one, but all (*Yeah*), and we're gonna stick with it. I'd like to say just before we move to the next point that I'm very happy to see all over this audience some of the outstanding figures from over the state. (*Right*) Montgomery is not only here but I see folk here from Mobile and Birmingham and Tuscaloosa and some of our other points in Alabama. [*applause*] I see Reverend Ware here from Birmingham, one of the outstanding ministers of our state and a great champion of civil rights; and then that stalwart, militant Christian gentleman, Emory Jackson of the *Birmingham World,* we're certainly happy to see him here, one of the greats in our struggle for democracy and first-class citizenship; and many others that I will not take our time to mention.[7] I'm very happy to see them here.

Now at this point, Reverend Abernathy, pastor of the First Baptist Church of Montgomery, will come to us and read the resolutions and recommendations. I want you to listen to this, and be very careful in listening to it. Listen with a great deal of interest so that you will know everything he said, because we want you to vote on it after it's over. Reverend Abernathy of the First Baptist Church.

[*Abernathy*]: Thank you, Dr. King. All of you who know me, know very well that I would love to make a speech now. [*laughter, applause*] I, whenever you start talking about freedom and start talking about justice, you know I have something to say about it. (*Well*) And you further know, those of you who heard me on this past Sunday morning by radio, beyond a shadow of doubt I stand for integration in this American society. (*Amen*) [*applause*] But I have been asked to read these resolutions and I want to read them carefully to you in order that you might understand them. I've only received them a few moments ago, and it may be that I'll read slow. I'm sorry that some members of the press have dismissed themselves, because there are some things in here I'd really want them to have. [*applause*] I certainly hope, I certainly hope that the television man will come back. (*Well*) [*applause*] You know, it isn't fair to get part of it. I want you to get all of it. [*applause*] I guess I better read. (*Read*) [*laughter, applause*] Resolution:

Whereas, there are thousands of Negroes in the city and county of Montgom-

---

7. James Lowell Ware (1899–1975) was born in Wetumpka, Alabama. He became pastor of the Trinity Baptist Church in 1941 and remained there for the next thirty years. He was president of the Birmingham Baptist Ministers Conference for twenty-five years and the first African American to run for council in Birmingham, in 1963. He was secretary of the Alabama Baptist State Convention for many years. Emory Overton Jackson (1908–1975), born in Buena Vista, Georgia, edited the *Birmingham World,* Alabama's leading black newspaper.

ery who ride buses owned and operated by the Montgomery City Lines, Incorporated, and

Whereas, said citizens have been riding buses owned and operated by said company over a number of years, and

Whereas, said citizens, over a number of years, and on many occasions, have been insulted, embarrassed (*Yeah*), and have been made to suffer great fear of bodily harm (*That's right*) by drivers of buses owned and operated by said bus company (*Yeah*), and

Whereas, the drivers of said buses have never requested a white passenger riding on any of its buses to relinquish his seat and to stand so that a Negro may take his seat. [*applause*] However, said drivers have on many occasions, too numerous to mention, requested Negro passengers on said buses to relinquish their seats and to stand so that white passengers may take their seats [*applause*], and

Whereas, said citizens of Montgomery city and county pay their fares just as all other persons who are passengers on said buses (*All right*) and are entitled to fair and equal treatment (*Yeah*) [*applause*], and

Whereas, there has been any number of arrests of Negroes caused by drivers of said buses, and they are constantly put in jail for refusing to give white passengers their seats and to stand. (*All right*) [*applause*]

Whereas, in March of 1955, a committee of citizens did have a conference with one of the officials of the said bus line, at which time said officials arranged a meeting between attorneys representing the Negro citizens of this city and attorneys representing the Montgomery City Lines, Incorporated, and the city of Montgomery, and

Whereas, the official of the bus line promised that as a result of the meeting between said attorneys he would issue a statement of policy clarifying the law with reference to the seating of Negro passengers on the buses, and

Whereas, said attorneys did have a meeting and did discuss the matter of clarifying the law; however, the official of said bus lines did not make public the statement as to its policy with reference to the seating of passengers on its buses, and

Whereas, since that time, at least two ladies have been arrested for an alleged violation of the city segregation law with reference to bus travel, and

Whereas, said citizens of Montgomery city and county believe that they have been grossly mistreated as passengers on the buses owned and operated by said bus company (*All right*) in spite of the fact that they are in the majority with reference to the number of passengers riding the said buses. [*applause*]

In light of these observations, be it therefore resolved as follows:

Number One. That the citizens of Montgomery are requesting that every citizen in Montgomery, regardless of race, color, or creed, to refrain from riding buses owned and operated in the city of Montgomery by the Montgomery Lines, Incorporated [*applause*], until some arrangement has been worked out [*applause*] between said citizens and the Montgomery City Lines, Incorporated.

Now I'm reading it slow and I want you to hear every word of it.

Number Two. That every person owning or who has access to an automobile will use their automobiles in assisting other persons to get to work without charge. [*applause*]

Number Three. That the employees, I repeat, that the employers of persons whose employees live a great distance from them, as much as possible, afford transportation for your own employees. [*applause*]

That the Negro citizens of Montgomery are ready and willing to send a delegation of citizens to the Montgomery City Lines, Incorporated, to discuss their grievances and to work out a solution for the same. (*All right*) [*applause*]

Be it further resolved that we have not—I said, we have not, we are not, and we have no intentions of—using any unlawful means or any intimidation (*Go ahead*) to persuade persons not to ride the Montgomery City Lines buses. [*applause*] However, we call upon your conscience (*All right*), both moral and spiritual, to give your wholehearted support (*That's right*) to this worthy undertaking. [*applause*] We believe we have a just complaint, and we are willing to discuss this matter with the proper authorities. (*Yes*) [*applause*]

Thus ends the resolution.[8] [*applause*] Dr. King, prayerfully, spiritually, sincerely, I wish to offer a motion. I move that this resolution shall be adopted. (*Dr. King, I second the motion*) [*applause*]

[*King:*] It has been moved, it has been moved, and seconded that these recommendations and these resolutions would be accepted and adopted by the citizens of Montgomery. Are you ready for the question? (*Yes*) [*thundering response*]

All in favor, stand on your feet. [*enthusiastic applause*] Opposers do likewise. Opposers do likewise. [*laughter*] There is a prevailing majority.

I certainly want to thank you, my friends, for this tremendous response. [*pause*] My friends, in order that nothing, that we will not be misquoted, and particularly with the resolutions, copies are prepared for the press; so that if the press would like to secure copies, they may do that, so that we will not be misquoted. [*enthusiastic applause*] [*recording interrupted*]

. . . said here this evening because everything is being recorded. Reverend Glasco is here on hand recording everything that is being said, so that we're not doing anything in the dark here. Everything is recorded. [*applause*] Now my friends, I just want to say once more to you. I've got to leave, I have presided to this point. It so happens that we have a group of very fine men who can do a much better job than I've done, and we're gonna let them do it. You know, we preachers have many engagements sometime. And I've got to go speak to the fathers and sons of this city; so that I'm gonna have to leave.

But just before leaving I want to say this. I want to urge you. You have voted, and you have done it with a great deal of enthusiasm, and I want to express my appreciation to you, on behalf of everybody here. Now let us go out to stick together and stay with this thing until the end. [*applause*] Now it means sacrificing, yes, it

---

8. A mimeographed version of these resolutions also included, in King's handwriting, the three demands the MIA presented to the bus company and city commissioners at an 8 December 1955 meeting arranged by the Alabama Council on Human Relations: "Better treatment and more courteous actions"; "That the seating arrangements be changed to a first come-first serve basis"; "That Negro Bus drivers be employed, especially on predominately Negro lines. Since about 75 percent of the income for the bus company come from Negroes, some of that money should come back to them." On the verso of the document King added, "Bus drivers to complement Negro Police in Colored district. There are times that Negro Policemen serve whites"; "On the predominately Negro routes, run every other bus special for Negroes" (MIA, Resolution with Proposals, 8 December 1955). On 9 December 1955 the *Montgomery Advertiser* reported that Jack Crenshaw, counsel for Montgomery City Lines, suggested having an exclusively Negro bus (see Tom Johnson, "4-Hour Huddle; Bus Boycott Conference Fails to Find Solution," *Montgomery Advertiser*, 9 December 1955).

means sacrificing at points. But there are some things that we've got to learn to sacrifice for. (*Yeah*) And we've got to come to the point that we are determined not to accept a lot of things that we have been accepting in the past.

So I'm urging you now. We have the facilities for you to get to your jobs, and we are putting, we have the cabs there at your service. Automobiles will be at your service, and don't be afraid to use up any of the gas. If you have it, if you are fortunate enough to have a little money, use it for a good cause. Now my automobile is gonna be in it, it has been in it, and I'm not concerned about how much gas I'm gonna use. (*That's right*) I want to see this thing work.

And we will not be content until oppression is wiped out of Montgomery, and really out of America. We won't be content until that is done. We are merely insisting on the dignity and worth of every human personality. And I don't stand here, I'm not arguing for any selfish person. I've never been on a bus in Montgomery. But I would be less than a Christian if I stood back and said, because I don't ride the bus, I don't have to ride a bus, that it doesn't concern me. [*applause*] I will not be content. I can hear a voice saying, "If you do it unto the least of these, my brother, you do it unto me." [9] [*applause*]

And I won't rest, I will face intimidation, and everything else, along with these other stalwart fighters for democracy and for citizenship. We don't mind it, so long as justice comes out of it. And I've come to see now that as we struggle for our rights, maybe some of them will have to die. But somebody said, if a man doesn't have something that he'll die for, he isn't fit to live. [*enthusiastic applause*]

Now, let me tell you this. You know, it takes money to do what we're about to do. We can't do it clapping hands now and we can't do it saying "Amen." (*That's right*) That's not enough. That is, that encourages the speaker to go on, but that isn't enough. We need money to do this and we're gonna have to get ourselves some money tonight. And we're gonna ask everybody here, that's everybody outside and inside, to get ready to make a contribution to this cause. (*That's right*) And the money will be well used. And the committee will tell you, someone will tell you what it will be used for. Now, we're asking Reverend Bonner to come here, from the First CME Church, to come and take this offering. I'm gonna ask Brother Nixon to assist him and we're gonna, I'm gonna ask—huh?—Brother Matthews, also. Where's Brother Matthews? Yeah. Brother Matthews here, the president of our NAACP, to come here and assist. [10] Now I want to say this. We're gonna need somebody to go outside and collect money. So that I'm gonna ask about, we'd say about ten people, I'm gonna ask ten of the ministers of the city to assist us in taking this offering. [*Rev. Bonner begins calling out names*] My friends, let me say this. Just a moment, Reverend Bonner, we don't want anybody to leave until this is over. I'm gonna leave mine as I leave, and this will continue. Reverend Bennett will continue in presiding. I'm sorry I have to leave, but I'm certainly happy to see your enthusiasm.

At. MLKJrP-GAMK: Box 107.

---

9. King quotes from Matthew 25:40: "And the King will answer and say to them, 'Assuredly, I say to you, inasmuch as you did it to one of the least of these My brethren, you did it to Me.'"

10. Robert L. Matthews, president of the Montgomery NAACP branch, would serve on the MIA executive board.

To the National City Lines, Inc.

[*8 December 1955*]
[*Montgomery, Ala.*]

King and the MIA leaders—including Abernathy, Jo Ann Robinson,[1] *and attorney*
Fred D. Gray—wired this letter to National City Lines in Chicago, owner of the
Montgomery bus franchise, after an unsuccessful meeting with city commissioners and
local bus company officials. The officials had refused to change bus segregation policies,
insisting they were required by law; King countered that they could be modified within
the existing segregation laws. National City Lines vice president Kenneth E. Totten
arrived in Montgomery the following week.

To The National City Lines, Inc.
6I6 South Michigan Ave., Chicago, Ill.

Over a period of years the Negro passengers on the Montgomery City Lines,
Inc. have been subjected to humiliation, threats, intimidation, and death through
bus driver action.

The Negro has been inconvenienced in the use of the city bus lines by the
operators in all instances in which the bus has been crowded. He has been forced
to give up his seat if a white person has been standing.

Repeated conferences with the bus officials have met with failure. Today a
meeting was held with Mr. J. H. Bagley and Attorney Jack Crenshaw as representatives of the bus company, and Mayor W. A. Gayle and Associate Commissioners
Frank Parks and Clyde Sellers.[2] At which time as an attempt to end the Monday
through Thursday protest, the following three proposals were made:

---

1. Jo Ann Gibson Robinson (1912–), born in Culloden, Georgia, earned her B.S. at Georgia State
College and taught in Macon's public schools for five years. She received her M.A. (1948) at Atlanta
University and became chair of the English department at Mary Ann College in Crockett, Texas. In
1949 Robinson joined the faculty of Alabama State College. That year an experience on a Montgomery
bus provoked her to lead the Women's Political Council (WPC) in demanding that city officials provide better bus service for African Americans. She became president of the WPC in 1950. After Rosa
Parks's arrest, Robinson utilized elements of a plan for a bus boycott drawn up by the WPC months
before. An MIA executive board member, Robinson served on all the MIA's major committees and
edited the monthly newsletter. She was also indicted for her role in the bus boycott. For Robinson's
account of the boycott, see *The Montgomery Bus Boycott and the Women Who Started It: The Memoir of
Jo Ann Gibson Robinson*, ed. David J. Garrow (1987).

2. See also Minutes, meeting between contact committee of MIA and city and bus officials, 8 December 1955. James H. Bagley, a Harvard Law School graduate, was manager of the Montgomery City
Lines. Jack Crenshaw (1905–), a former president of the Montgomery Bar Association, served as legal
representative of the Montgomery City Lines during the Montgomery bus boycott. William A. "Tacky"
Gayle (1895–1965), born in Montgomery, was commissioner for public works from 1935 until 1951,
when he became mayor; he was defeated in 1959 after serving two terms in office. Franklin Warren
Parks (1898–1966), owner of a decorating business, was Montgomery's public works commissioner
from 1955 until his death. Clyde Chapman Sellers (1908–1976) had been director of the state highway patrol and a Alabama state legislator before serving one term as Montgomery's public safety
commissioner.

1. Courteous treatment by bus drivers.

2. Seating of Negro passengers from rear to front of bus, and white passengers from front to rear on "first-come-first-serve basis with no seats reserved for any race.

3. Employment of Negro bus operators in predominantly Negro residential sections.

The above proposals, and the resolutions which will follow, were drafted and adopted in a mass meeting of more than 5,000 regular bus riders.[3] These proposals were denied in the meeting with the city officials and representatives of the bus company.

Since 44% of the city's population is Negro, and since 75% of the bus riders are Negro, we urge you to send a representative to Montgomery to arbitrate.

The Montgomery Improvement Association
The Rev. M. L. King, Pres.
The Rev. U. J. Fields, Sec'y.

TLc. MLKP-MBU: Box 6.

---

3. The resolutions ratified on 5 December 1955 did not specifically approve the three demands.

"Statement of Negro Citizens on Bus Situation"

[*10 December 1955*]
[*Montgomery, Ala.*]

Two days after the deadlocked talks on 8 December, King and the MIA submitted this statement to their adversaries and the press. The next day the Montgomery Advertiser *quoted portions of it, attributed to King, in a front-page article. The bus company had argued that Alabama law required segregation; King and the MIA, however, cite the relevant statute and argue that it authorized such a policy but did not require it. They also point out that Rosa Parks was charged with violating the state law because the Montgomery City Code did not require a black person to relinquish a seat unless another one was available in the part of the bus reserved for African Americans. The MIA argues that the state law was flexible enough to permit the group's proposed seating arrangement, which would not eliminate bus segregation.*

We have heretofore stated the position of the Negro Citizens of Montgomery with reference to the local bus situation. As good citizens we want to comply with the law until the law is changed or is over-ruled. However, we feel that we have the right to insist that the law be fairly administered.

In answer to our request that the Montgomery City Lines adopt a policy of loading busses from rear to front with colored passengers and from front to rear with white passengers and that all passengers be permitted to retain their seats on a "first come—first served" basis, without reservation of seats for any particular race, the bus company contends that such an arrangement would be in violation of the law and particularly the Act of July 18, 1947, (General Acts of Alabama, 1947, #130, Page 40).

In answer to this contention we would like to call attention to the pertinent provision of Section 1, of this Act, which reads as follows:

> "Section 1. All passenger stations in this state operated by or for the use of any motor transportation company shall be authorized to provide separate waiting rooms, facilities, or space, or separate ticket windows, for the white and colored races but such accommodations for the races shall be equal. All motor transportation companies and operators of vehicles, carrying passengers for hire in this state, whether intrastate or interstate passengers, are authorized and empowered to provide separate accommodations on each vehicle for the white and colored races. Any officer or agent of such motor transportation company or operator, in charge of any vehicle, is authorized to assign or reassign each passenger or person to a division, section or seat on the vehicle designated by such company or operator or by such officer or agent for the race to which the passenger or person belongs . . . " (italics supplied).

We believe that this Act was not intended to apply to busses operating within a single municipality, but only to those under the jurisdiction of the Alabama Public Service Commission. However, it should be noted that under the provisions quoted the method of handling the seating of passengers is left entirely to the transportation companies themselves. They are authorized and empowered to provide separate accommodations but are not directed or required to take any action whatsoever.

The Legislature, it seems clear, wisely left it up to the transportation companies to work out the seating problem in a reasonable and practical way, subject to the limitations of reasonableness and equality of treatment to all passengers, regardless of race.

It should be further noted that even under the City Code of Montgomery (Chapter 6, Section 10 and 11) no person, white or colored, can be required to give up a seat unless there is a vacant seat in the portion of the bus to which the passenger is assigned.[1]

---

1. Section 604 of the Montgomery City Code reads: "All operators and other employees while in charge of busses are hereby invested with the police power of a police officer of said City, to carry out said provisions, and any passenger refusing or failing to take a seat among those assigned to the race to which he belongs—if there is such seat vacant—at the request of the conductor or employee in charge of said bus, shall, upon conviction, be fined not less than one nor more than one hundred dollars" (*The Code of Ordinances of the City of Montgomery* [Montgomery: Wilson Printing Co., 1938], p. 217).

We feel that there is no issue between the Negro citizens and the Montgomery 12 Dec
City Lines that cannot be solved by negotiations between people of good will and 1955
we submit that there is no legal barrier to such negotiations.

Respectfully submitted,
THE MONTGOMERY IMPROVEMENT ASSOCIATION
M. L. King, President

TD. RGP.

From H. Edward Whitaker

12 December 1955
Niagara Falls, N.Y.

*On 30 November King had written his Crozer classmate a letter praising Whitaker's
newly constructed New Hope Baptist Church and announcing the birth of his
daughter, Yolanda Denise.[1] In his reply Whitaker says that he hopes King will visit in
spring 1956. King wrote "Answered" on the letter and replied affirmatively on 28
December.[2]*

Dear Mike,

Thanks a lot for your letter a few days ago. I am glad you feel that our building
is satisfactory. It is certainly one that was badly needed in our city. And so far
things are going quite well. But we have some hard folk to work with from the
point of understanding what Church work is all about. But they are gradually
coming around.

We are now in the process of building a 6 room house for the pastor. Since we
have been here, we have lived in an apartment. Of course this house will be personal property. I have been able to swing a ~~mortage~~ morgtage for $13,000 with no
money in my pocket, merely on community standing as a result of the building
of the church. The Lord is certainly with us. If all goes well, we hope to be in it
by the time we hope to have you up here just before Easter. So far I have not
discussed to any great extent with any of the Church officials the matter of a
spring preaching mission, but I am sure it will find no opposition. Therefore I
would appreciate it very much if you could put in on your calendar for the whole
week just before Easter. I don't know how this would work out with your own
program in view of the fact that you would not have much time to get back to
your Church by Easter Sunday morning. But I guess I am going too far. That's

---

1. See *The Papers of Martin Luther King, Jr.*, vol. 2: *Rediscovering Precious Values, July 1951–November
1955*, ed. Clayborne Carson, Ralph E. Luker, Penny A. Russell, and Peter Holloran (Berkeley and Los
Angeles: University of California Press, 1994), pp. 592–593.

2. The Calendar of Documents provides complete citations for documents referenced in
headnotes.

for you to decide, isn't true. Well anyway, you let me know definitely what you can do.

May I say many congratulations to you and Mrs King in the blessing of the Lord of a daughter. I think her name is really beautiful. Many happy returns. But you must remember that you have just begun walking the floor. But I can assure you that they will be pleasant.

Things here in New York are going fairly well. The Baptist in New York is really a disorganized group. Frankly we are not doing much as a group, but churches indivually are really moving forward. When you see Mac give him my best regards.

Sincerely,
[*signed*] Whit

{over}

Dr. Boddie is leaving Rochester to become Assistant Secretary of the Foreign Mission Boards of American Baptist Convention.[3] I don't know much about the set-up, but if you are interested in coming north, it might bear investigation. It looks like it might be a good opportunity for the right man. I feel that you might be the right man.

TAHLS. DABCC.

---

3. Charles Emerson Boddie (1911–), born in New Rochelle, New York, was pastor of Mt. Olivet Baptist Church in Rochester. He left in 1956 to join the staff of the American Baptist Convention, remaining until 1963, when he became president of the American Baptist Theological Seminary in Nashville. Boddie and his brother, J. Timothy Boddie, were friends of the King family. See also Barbour to King, 2 April 1956, pp. 210–211 in this volume.

Program for MIA Mass Meeting at First Baptist Church

15 December 1955
Montgomery, Ala.

This is King's copy of an agenda for the MIA's fourth mass meeting, which was held at Rev. Ralph Abernathy's First Baptist Church. At the bottom King wrote notes for his "Progress Report and instructions." In his talk he sharply distinguished between the boycott tactics of the MIA and those of the Citizens Council, probably responding to a 13 December Montgomery Advertiser *editorial, titled "The 2-Edged Sword," that equated the two. Rufus A. Lewis, head of the transportation committee, reported that the three-day-old car pool system had been successful, with 215 volunteer drivers participating.*

Mass Meeting of Montgomery Improvement Association
First Baptist Church—December 15, 1955—7:00 P.M.
Presiding Officer—Roy Bennett (Speaks of the importance of following the program)
Hymn—"Lift Him Up."

Reading of Scripture—Rev. H. H. Johnson[1]

Invocation—Rev. R. W. Hilson

Song—"Joy to the World"

Report of Transportation Committee—~~Rev. W. J. Powell~~[2] {Mr. Rufus Lewis}

Acknowledgment of Visitors—Mr. J. ~~Peirce~~ {Pierce}[3]

Progress Report and instructions—Rev. M. L. King

Appeal for Funds—and Collection of Funds—Rev. R. J. Glascoe

Closing Remarks—Rev. M. L. King

Closing Hymn—[*strikeout illegible*] "Bless~~ed~~ Be the Tide"

Benediction—Rev. ~~J. T. Thomas~~ {E. H. Mason}

Next Meeting—Hutchinson Street Baptist Church—Rev. H. H. Johnson

Time—7:00, Monday night.

{1,954.60[4]

1. Thanks for presence

2. The papers reveal that we have many white with us[5]

3. Again we are not to be compared to the Citizen's Councils

4. We are still getting cooperation (we walk if necessary)

5. We are waiting to hear from Chicago[6]

Annocement: The new Headquarters[7]

Patronize Negro Business   All drivers meet at Dexter tomorrow}

THD. MLKP-MBU: Box 6.

---

1. H. H. Johnson was pastor of Hutchinson Street Baptist Church from 1934 to 1971 and was among the ministers indicted for his role in the boycott.

2. William J. Powell (1908–1982) was pastor of Old Ship AME Zion Church from 1953 to 1964. He served on the original executive board of the MIA and was among the indicted ministers.

3. James E. Pierce (1895–1982), born in Lowndes County, Alabama, was an active leader in the Montgomery black community before and during the Montgomery bus boycott. Pierce received his B.S. from the University of Toledo and his M.S. from Ohio State University. In the early 1930s he became a professor of political science at Alabama State College and later chair of the department. As secretary of the Civic League and board member of other organizations, Pierce championed the cause of voter registration. He was a member of the MIA's executive board and negotiating committee and was among those indicted for their role in the bus boycott. He wrote, with Ralph H. Hines, "Negro Leadership after the Social Crisis: An Analysis of Leadership Changes in Montgomery, Alabama," *Phylon* 26 (1965): 162–172.

4. This is the amount of money collected at the preceding mass meeting, at Bethel Baptist Church, on 12 December 1955.

5. King refers to the extent of white support for the protest as indicated by letters to the editor— for example, city librarian Juliette Morgan's letter, titled "Lesson from Gandhi," in the *Montgomery Advertiser* on 12 December 1955.

6. See King et al. to the National City Lines, Inc., 8 December 1955, p. 80–81 in this volume. On 16 December 1955 Vice President Totten of National City Lines in Chicago came to Montgomery to confer with the local bus company and city officials; he contacted the MIA the following day.

7. King announced the transfer of the MIA's office from the Alabama Negro Baptist Center to Lewis's Citizens Club. The MIA left its first headquarters after the white Montgomery Baptist Association pressured the center's trustees. In late January the organization had to relocate again when city officials threatened to revoke the club's license. After temporary lodging in the basement of Abernathy's First Baptist Church, the MIA found a permanent office in the building owned by the Bricklayers Union at 530 South Union Street.

PROGRAM

Mass Meeting of Montgomery Improvement Association

First Baptist Church-- December 15, 1955 -- 7:00P. M.

Presiding Officer -- Roy Bennett (Speaks of the importance of following the program)

Hymn -- "Lift Him Up."

Reading of Scripture-- Rev. H. H. Johnson

Invocation -- Rev. R. W. Hilson

Song -- "Joy to the World" *Mr. Rufus Lewis*

Report of Transportation Committee -- ~~Rev. W. J. Powell~~

Acknowledgment of Visitors -- Mr. J. ~~Peirce~~ *Pierce*

Progress Report and instructions -- Rev. M. L. King

Appeal for Funds -- and Collection of Funds --Rev. R. J. Glascoe

Closing Remarks -- Rev. M. L. King

Closing Hymn -- ~~xxxxxxxxxxxx~~ "Blessed Be the Tide"

Benediction -- Rev. ~~E. D. Thomas~~ *E. H. Musan*

Next Meeting -- Hutchinson Street Baptist Church -- Rev. H. H. Johnson

Time -- 7:00, Monday night.

1, 954.60

1. Thanks for presence

2. The papers reveal that we have many white with us

3. Again we are not to be compared to the Citizen's Council

4. We are still getting cooperation (we walk if necessary)

5. We are waiting to hear from Chicago

Announcement: The new Headquarters

Patronize Negro Business   All Drivers meet at [illegible]

To M. C. Ballenger

15 December 1955
[*Montgomery, Ala.*]

*King declines a position at Shurtleff College, a coeducational Baptist liberal arts college
in southern Illinois.*

Dean M. C. Ballenger[1]
Shurtleff College
Alton, Illinois

Dear Dean Ballenger:

Thanks for your very kind letter of December 6.

I am quite interested in the work that is being done at Shurtleff College, but at
present my pastorate at Dexter Avenue Baptist Church is of such a nature that I
would not like to consider moving. I feel that the job that I am attempting to do
here will take a few more years to be completed. I am deeply grateful to you and
the institution for being willing to consider me for this very significant position.

With every good wish, I am

Sincerely yours,
M. L. King, Jr.

MLK:lmt

TLc. DABCC.

---

1. Milton Cornelius Ballenger (1918–) was a Baptist minister with a Ph.D. (1954) from Yale. He
served as an educator and administrator at Shurtleff College from 1952 until 1970. Ballenger's letter to
King has not been located.

To Ralph W. Riley

21 December 1955
[*Montgomery, Ala.*]

*Riley, president of the American Baptist Theological Seminary and a former pastor of
Dexter Avenue Baptist Church, spoke at Dexter's seventy-eighth anniversary program
on 11 December. On 22 December Riley thanked King "for the pleasure of having been
with you at Dexter."*

Dr. Ralph W. Riley, President
American Baptist Theological Seminary
Nashville 7, Tennessee

Dear Dr. Riley:

This is just a note to again express my appreciation to you for your rich contribution in making our Anniversary occasion a successful one. Your presence as well as your message meant so much to the people of Dexter. Remember you have a standing invitation to come to Dexter.

With every good wish, I am

Sincerely yours,
M. L. King, Jr.

MLK:lmt

TLc. DABCC.

From Walter C. Carrington

21 December 1955

After reading about King in Jet *magazine, a fraternity brother applauds the use of Gandhian methods, asserting that "the possibilities of large scale, well disciplined, non-violent civil disobedience to segregation laws are enormous."* [1]

Dear Martin,

I've just finished reading with a great deal of fascination and admiration about the clear headed and in many respects, unique type of fight you've been leading in Montgomery against bus Jim Crow. May I extend my heartiest congratulations and best wishes for success in your endeavor.

When I first saw the quotes in "Jet" of one Rev. M. L. King Jr. the name failed to ring a bell. Then when I saw your picture I exclaimed, "why there's my good Alpha brother, Martin King!"

---

1. "Negroes Stop Riding Montgomery Buses in Protest over Jim Crow," *Jet*, 22 December 1955, pp. 12–15. Walter C. Carrington (1930–), born in New York City, earned his B.A. (1952) and J.D. (1955) from Harvard University. Carrington was the founding president of the college's NAACP branch, and in 1952 he became the first student and the youngest person elected to the NAACP National Board of Directors. After graduation, Carrington served with the U.S. Army for two years. He was named to the Massachusetts Commission Against Discrimination in 1957 but resigned in 1961 to serve in Sierra Leone, Tunisia, and Senegal as a Peace Corps administrator, becoming director of the Peace Corps in Africa in 1969. Two years later Carrington joined the African American Institute as executive vice president and publisher of its magazine, *Africa Report*. After serving in a variety of political, academic, and consulting positions, Carrington was appointed ambassador to Nigeria in 1993.

It seems to me that the possibilities of large scale, well disciplined, non-violent civil disobedience to segregation laws are enormous. It gives more people a sense of participating in a cause than any other technique I know of. And seated as it is in good Christian doctrine it makes it all the more difficult for the conscience of the white South to rationalize its opposition to it. In the hands of Gandhi civil disobedience proved to be a potent political weapon. It may also prove to be such in the hands of the Southern Negro.

I guess I'll have to sit on the sidelines a while and let you fellows down there carry the ball. Uncle Sam has his hands on me and it's next to fatal to practice a little civil disobedience on a sergeant.

Well, here's wishing you a Merry Christmas and a New Year undimmed by the spectre of bus segregation.

Fraternally yours,
[*signed*] Wally Carrington

ALS. DABCC.

"To the Montgomery Public"

25 December 1955
Montgomery, Ala.

This half-page paid advertisement, signed by "The Negro Ministers of Montgomery and Their Congregations," appeared in the Sunday Advertiser *and* Alabama Journal. *All of the ministers, with the exception of Joseph C. Parker, Sr., were members of the MIA executive board. After detailing eight areas of complaint, including the history of unsuccessful efforts at redress, they explain that the bus protest "is the culmination of a series of unpleasant incidents over a period of years. It is an upsurging of a ground swell which has been going on for a long time. Our cup of tolerance has run over."*

We, the Negro citizens of Montgomery, feel that the public has a right to know our complaints and grievances which have resulted in the protest against the Montgomery City Lines and our refusal to ride city busses. We, therefore, set forth here some of the many bitter experiences of our people, who have, at various times, been pushed around, embarrassed, threatened, intimidated and abused in a manner that has caused the meekest to rise in resentment:

COMPLAINTS:
1. Courtesy:
   The use of abusive language, name calling and threats have been the common practices among many of the bus operators. We are ordered to move from seats to standing space under the threat of arrest, or other serious consequences. No regard for sex or age is considered in exercising this authority by the bus operator.

2. Seating:

The bus operators have not been fair in this respect. Negroes, old, young, men and women, mothers with babes in their arms, sick, afflicted, pregnant women, must relinquish their seats, even to school children, if the bus is crowded. On lines serving predominantly Negro sections, the ten front seats must remain vacant, even though no white passenger boards the bus. At all times the Negro is asked to give up his seat, though there is not standing room in the back. One white person, desiring a seat, will cause nine Negroes to relinquish their seats for the accommodation of this one person.

3. Arrests:

Numerous arrests have been made even though the person arrested is observing the policy as given us. This year the following persons have been arrested and convicted, although they were seated according to the policy given us by the bus company. They are Claudette Colvin, Alberta "Coote" Smith, and Mrs. Rosa Parks. Among others arrested at other times are Mrs. Viola White, Miss Mary Wingfield, two children from New Jersey, and a Mr. Brooks, who was killed by the policeman.[1]

4. Two Fares:

Many house-servants are required to pay an additional fare if the bus is late getting to town, causing them to miss a bus going to Cloverdale or other distant points. Some of these have complained that on returning from work similar incidents have occurred necessitating the payment of double fares.

5. Making Change:

We understand that correct change should be given the operator, but there are times that such is not possible. Several bus operators have refused to make change for passengers and threatened to put them off for not having the exact amount. On one occasion a fellow-passenger paid the fare of one such passenger to prevent her from being put off.

6. Passing Up Passengers:

In many instances the bus operators have passed up passengers standing at the stop to board the bus. They have also collected fares at the front door and, after commanding Negro passengers to enter from the back door, they have driven off, leaving them standing.

7. Physical Torture:

One Negro mother, with two small children in her arm, put them on the front seat while she opened her purse for her fare. The driver ordered her to take the

---

1. Claudette Colvin, a fifteen-year-old high school student, was arrested on 2 March 1955 and charged with violation of city and state segregation laws, disorderly conduct, and assault. Alberta Smith may refer to Mary Louise Smith, who was arrested on 21 October 1955 and, like Colvin, was later a plaintiff in *Aurelia S. Browder v. William A. Gayle*. Viola White had been arrested in the 1940s for refusing to give up her seat when asked by the bus driver, whom she fought with after he assaulted her. According to Jo Ann Robinson's memoir, Mary Wingfield and two children from New Jersey were also arrested for sitting in the front section reserved for whites (see Robinson, *The Montgomery Bus Boycott and the Women Who Started It*, pp. 20–22). Hilliard Brooks was killed by Montgomery police on 12 August 1950 after an argument with a bus driver over the ten-cent fare. His widow, Estella Brooks, testified for the defense during King's trial in March 1956 (Transcript, *State of Alabama v. M. L. King, Jr.*, 22 March 1956).

children from the seat, and without giving her the chance to place the children elsewhere, lunged the vehicle forward, causing the small children to be thrown into the aisle of the bus.

8. Acknowledgement:

Not all operators are guilty of these accusations. There are some who are most cordial and tolerant. They will go to the extent of their authority to see that justice and fair play prevail. To those we are grateful and sympathetic.

9. Adjudication:

Every effort has been used to get the bus company to remove the causes of these complaints. Time and time again complaints have been registered with the bus company, the City Commission and the manager of the bus company. Committees of both sexes have been conferred but to no avail. Protests have been filed with the mayor, but no improvement has been made.

In March we held a conference with the Manager of the Montgomery City Lines and made a very modest request: (1) that the bus company attorney meet with our attorneys and give an interpretation to laws regulating passengers and (2) that the policy of the bus on seating be published so that all bus riders would be well-informed on the policy of the bus. To this date this has not been done.

The manager read to us the city code and informed us that this is in the hands of every bus driver. At this meeting, the arresting officers of the Claudette Colvin case were there along with the Police Commissioner. The bus operator, who caused the arrest of Claudette Colvin, was requested to be present. But did not come.

A committee met with the Mayor and Associate Commissioner when the bus company requested a raise in fare. No protest was made against the raise, but only against seating and courteous treatment of passengers. Nothing came of this and Negroes were treated worse after the increase in bus fare than before.

The Great Decision:

The bus protest is not merely in protest of the arrest of Mrs. Rosa Parks, but is the culmination of a series of unpleasant incidents over a period of years. It is an upsurging of a ground swell which has been going on for a long time. Our cup of tolerance has run over. Thousands of our people, who have had unhappy experiences, prefer to walk rather than endure more. No better evidence can be given that the fact that a large percent of the Negro bus riders are now walking or getting a ride whenever and wherever they can.

Our Proposal:

The duly elected representatives of the people have the approval of the bus riders to present three proposals:

1. That assurance of more courtesy be extended the bus-riders. That the bus operators refrain from name calling, abusive language and threats.

2. That the seating of passengers will be on a "First-come, First-Served" basis. This means that the Negro passengers will begin seating from the rear of the bus toward the front and white passengers from the front toward the rear, until all seats are taken. Once seated, no passenger will be compelled to relinquish his seat to a member of another race when there is no available seat. When seats become vacant in the rear Negro passengers will voluntarily move to these vacant seats and by the same token white passengers will move to vacant seats in the front of the bus. This will eliminate the problem of passengers being compelled to

stand when there are unoccupied seats. At no time, on the basis of this proposal, will both races occupy the same seat. We are convinced by the opinions of competent legal authorities that this proposal does not necessitate a change in the city, or state laws. This proposal is not new in Alabama, for it has worked for a number of years in Mobile and many other Southern cities.

3. That Negro bus drivers be employed on the bus lines serving predominately Negro areas. This is a fair request and we believe that men of good will, will readily accept it and admit that it is fair.

Nature of Movement:

1. Non violence—

At no time have the participants of this movement advocated or anticipated violence. We stand willing and ready to report and give any assistance in exposing persons who resort to violence. This is a movement of passive resistance, depending on moral and spiritual forces. We, the oppressed, have no hate in our hearts for the oppressors, but we are, nevertheless, determined to resist until the cause of justice triumphs.

2. Coercion—

There has not been any coercion on the part of any leader to force any one to stay off the busses. The rising tide of resentment has come to fruition. This resentment has resulted in a vast majority of the people staying off the busses willingly and voluntarily.

3. Arbitration—

We are willing to arbitrate. We feel that this can be done with men and women of good will. However, we find it rather difficult to arbitrate in good faith with those whose public pronouncements are anti-Negro and whose only desire seems to be that of maintaining the status quo. We call upon men of good-will, who will be willing to treat this issue in the spirit of Him whose birth we celebrate at this season, to meet with us. We stand for Christian teachings and the concepts of democracy for which men and women of all races have fought and died.

THE NEGRO MINISTERS
of Montgomery and Their Congregations

THE METHODIST MINISTERIAL ALLIANCE,
The Rev. J. W. Hayes, President[2]

THE BAPTIST MINISTERS' CONFERENCE
The Rev. H. H. Hubbard, President[3]
The Rev. R. D. Abernathy, Secretary

---

2. Joshua William Hayes (1905–1969), a native of Lowndes County, Alabama, earned his B.A. (1944) from Livingstone College. The presiding elder of the West Montgomery District of the AME Zion Church from 1954 to 1958, Hayes chaired the MIA's membership committee and served on its transportation and programs committees. He was also indicted for his role in the bus boycott. After leaving Montgomery he pastored Trinity AME Zion Church in Birmingham and participated in that city's 1963 civil rights campaign.

3. Hillman H. Hubbard (ca. 1892–1967), pastor of Bethel Baptist Church, served as an MIA negotiator and a member of the committees for relief, programming, and establishing a bank and savings association. He was among the indicted boycott leaders.

THE INTER-DENOMINATIONAL MINISTERIAL ALLIANCE
The Rev. L. Roy Bennett, President
The Rev. J. C. Parker, Secretary[4]

THE MONTGOMERY IMPROVEMENT ASSOCIATION
Dr. M. L. King, Jr., President
The Rev. U. J. Fields, Secretary

PD. *Montgomery Advertiser–Alabama Journal,* 25 December 1955.

---

4. Joseph C. Parker, Sr. (1920–1987), was pastor of Hall Street Baptist Church from 1953 to 1957.

To Archibald James Carey, Jr.

27 December 1955
Montgomery, Ala.

*King and Rev. E. N. French request that Carey, pastor of Chicago's Quinn Chapel
AME Church, chair a committee of religious and civic leaders to lobby Chicago-based
National City Lines, Inc., owner of the Montgomery bus company. The enclosure was
sent to all the members of the suggested committee, which included Congressman
William L. Dawson and J. H. Jackson, president of the National Baptist Convention.
Carey did not reply until 24 February 1956.[1]*

Dr. Archibald Carey
188 West Randolph Street
Suite 1501
Chicago, Illinois

Dear Dr. Carey:

We are sending to you under separate cover information which will inform,
and bring you up to date on the matter of the Negro protest of the Montgomery
City Lines busses here in Montgomery, Alabama.[2]

Having practically exhausted all means by which we hoped to have found a
solution to our problem here, we are asking you, and other outstanding persons
in your City, to present our cause to the National City Lines, Inc., 616 South Michigan Avenue, Chicago, Illinois, which Corporation owns the Bus Lines here in
Montgomery.

Our Organization, The Montgomery Improvement Association, named you as

---

1. See p. 139–140 in this volume.

2. See "Legal Requirements Concerning the Segregation of Races on City Buses," 27 December
1955.

Chairman of a Committee we are asking to represent us. We are asking you to please call the Committee at your earliest convenience and share the information we are sending to you with them. The attached letter will give you the names of others asked to serve on the Committee. We are leaving it up to you to add any others you deem necessary.

A copy of the attached letter has been mailed to each person on the Committee. They will be expecting a call from you.

We are sure that you are able to realize how meaningful this will be to the Negro Citizens of Montgomery, as well as how much we will appreciate your help.

With sincere appreciations for your cooperation, we are,

Sincerely yours,
Montgomery Improvement Association

[*signed*] M. L. King/n
(Rev.) M. L. King, President

[*signed*] E. N. French
(Rev) E. N. French, Corresponding Secretary

[*enclosure*]
A ground swell of social unrest has gripped Montgomery, Alabama, the seat of the Confederacy! The long overdue protest on the part of Negro citizens against the methods and manners of the Transit Lines of this City has come to fruition. The protest that started on December 5th. continues. Until this time no negotiations have been successful. The protest is almost one hundred per cent effective.

You surely must know that the struggle is terrific. But on the other hand the determination on the part of people on all social levels, all ages, and conditions is most heartening. How long this will continue depends, to some extent, upon how much help we can get from others.

The City Bus Lines here are controlled by the National City Lines, Inc., 616 South Michigan Avenue, Chicago, Illinois. Although the Vice President of the Company has been here, we are asking you, with others herein named, to take our cause directly to the Official Staff there. We are sending to the Chairman materials which will explain, not only our objectives, but a number of the long standing grievances which are the motovating forces of our action at this time.

Two things we seek in you: 1. Put on the hearts and minds of the officials of the Bus Company that they have a responsibility in the human aspect of their business, especially where more than seventy-five per cent of their profits come from people who are treated inhuman in the operation of said business. 2. If you have a suggestion or advice to give us we shall be glad to hear from you.

We are calling upon you for your prestige, great influence, and human interest. Please do not fail us.

COMMITTEE HEREIN NAMED:

Dr. Archibald Carey, Chr., 188 W. Randolph St.
Bishop W. J. Wells, 4736 South Parkway

Dr. J. H. Jackson, 3101 South Parkway   3 Jan
Dr. J. W. Eichelberger, 128 East 58th. Street   1956
Hon. William L. Dawson

Att. Earl Dickerson, 35 and South Parkway c/o Liberty Life Ins.
Company[3]

Very truly yours,
Montgomery Improvement Association
[*signed*] M. L. King
(Rev.) M. L. King, President

P.S. Please answer the call of the Chairman of the Committee.

TLSr. AJC-ICHi: Box 29.

---

3. William Jacob Walls (1885–1975) was consecrated as a bishop of the AME Zion Church in 1924 and became a senior bishop in 1951. Joseph Harrison Jackson (1900–1990) served as president of the National Baptist Convention from 1953 to 1982. James William Eichelberger, Jr. (1886–1967), became secretary of the Department of Christian Education for the AME Zion Church in 1932 and served there until his death. William L. Dawson (1886–1970) was a Chicago lawyer and city alderman before being elected to Congress, where he served from 1942 until 1970. Earl Burrus Dickerson was president of Supreme Liberty Life Insurance (see Dickerson to King, 11 January 1956, pp. 98–99 in this volume).

From Aubrey Willis Williams

3 January 1956
Montgomery, Ala.

Williams, publisher of Southern Farmer *magazine, was one of the small group of white liberals in Montgomery who supported the bus boycott.*[1]

Dear Rev. King:

I never did tell you and the other brave men who joined you in making it how fine I thought the published statement was.[2]

It now appears, what Gayle & Co are hawking on is that the Negro people will

---

1. Aubrey Willis Williams (1890–1965), born in Springville, Alabama, received his B.A. (1920) from the University of Cincinnati. During the New Deal he held several posts, including executive director of the National Youth Administration. In 1945 Williams moved to Montgomery and became publisher of *Southern Farmer,* the South's leading liberal magazine until it folded in 1959. From 1948 to 1963 he was president of the Southern Conference Education Fund, also serving as president of the National Committee to Abolish the House Un-American Activities Committee from 1960 to 1963.

2. See "To the Montgomery Public," 25 December 1955, pp. 89–93 in this volume.

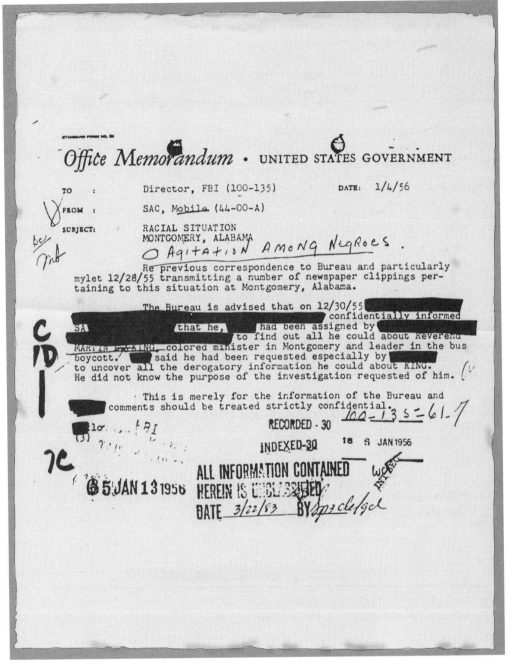

Office Memorandum · UNITED STATES GOVERNMENT

TO : Director, FBI (100-135)   DATE: 1/4/56

FROM : SAC, Mobile (44-00-A)

SUBJECT: RACIAL SITUATION
MONTGOMERY, ALABAMA
○ Agitation Among Negroes .

Re previous correspondence to Bureau and particularly
mylet 12/28/55 transmitting a number of newspaper clippings pertaining to this situation at Montgomery, Alabama.

The Bureau is advised that on 12/30/55 ▓▓▓▓▓▓▓▓▓
▓▓▓▓▓▓▓▓▓▓▓▓▓▓▓ confidentially informed
SA ▓▓▓▓▓▓ that he, ▓▓ had been assigned by ▓▓▓▓▓
▓▓▓▓▓ to find out all he could about Reverend
MARTIN ▓▓▓▓▓, colored minister in Montgomery and leader in the bus
boycott. ▓▓▓▓ said he had been requested especially by ▓▓▓▓
to uncover all the derogatory information he could about KING.
He did not know the purpose of the investigation requested of him.

· This is merely for the information of the Bureau and
comments should be treated strictly confidential.

100-135-61-7

RECORDED - 30

INDEXED-30   18   S   JAN 1956

ALL INFORMATION CONTAINED
HEREIN IS UNCLASSIFIED
DATE 3/22/83 BY ▓▓▓▓▓

5 JAN 13 1956

On 7 December 1955 the FBI's Mobile office began forwarding information on the bus boycott to
FBI director J. Edgar Hoover. The special agent in charge of the office reports that someone, probably a member of the Montgomery police department, had been assigned to find "derogatory information" about King.

finally get tired of walking etc and give in. I saw 3 Negroes on an Oak Park bus 9 Jan
this morning. Thats the most Ive seen on one bus since the Protest was launched. 1956
We have probably reached the critical period.

With every good wish,
[*signed*] Aubrey Williams

ALS. MLKP-MBU: Box 107.

To the Commissioners of the
City of Montgomery

[*9 January 1956*]
[*Montgomery, Ala.*]

At the fourth meeting between Montgomery black leaders and city officials, attorney
Fred Gray presented the following resolution, explaining that it was "not a request for
the abolition of segregation on buses but for a fair and reasonable seating of passengers
to assure all passengers equal treatment."[1] *City officials, however, refused to alter*
existing bus seating arrangements. Mayor Gayle later announced, "we are going to
carry out the law as we see it, and state law and city law call for segregation on
buses."[2]

TO: The Honorable Commissioners of the City of Montgomery
FROM: The Negro Ministers of the City of Montgomery and their
            congregations (The Methodist Ministerial Alliance, The Baptist
            Ministers' Conference, and The Inter-Denominational
            Ministerial Alliance) and The Montgomery Improvement
            Association
SUBJECT: The Negro Protest Against The Montgomery City Lines

The organizations named above, in their recent mass meeting, appointed this
committee and requested that this committee present to you the following resolution for your consideration:

WHEREAS, there are thousands of Negroes in the city and county of Montgomery who have refrained from riding busses owned and operated by the
Montgomery City Lines, Incorporated since December 5, 1955, and

WHEREAS, we have made known previously to the City Commissioners of the
City of Montgomery, The Montgomery City Lines, Incorporated, and the public

---

1. Quoted by Emory O. Jackson in "Seating May Bring End to Montgomery Bus Refuse to Ride,"
Birmingham World, 10 January 1956.
2. Quoted in "Bus Request Denied 'Boycott' Spokesmen,'" *Montgomery Advertiser,* 10 January 1956. 97

in general our reasons for refraining from riding busses owned and operated by said company, and

WHEREAS, one of our reasons for refraining from riding the busses is because of the present seating arrangment, and

WHEREAS, our request is not a request for the abolition of segregation on busses but for a fair and reasonable seating of passengers so as to assure all passengers equal treatment, and

WHEREAS, similar cities in the South and in Alabama have similar seating arrangements to that which we are requesting, namely Mobile, Alabama; Dothan, Alabama; Huntsville, Alabama; Macon, Georgia; Nashville, Tennessee and other southern cities, and

WHEREAS, The Montgomery City Lines, Incorporated through its attorney has stated that it "is willing to reinstate bus service into every district of the City and operate under {any} arrangement of seating the races that will meet with the approval of the City Commission . . . "

BE IT THEREFORE RESOLVED, The Negro Ministers of Montgomery and their Congregations, (The Methodist Ministerial Alliance, The Baptist Ministers' Conference, The Inter-Denominational Ministerial Alliance) and The Montgomery Improvement Association, representing approximately 50,000 Negroes in the city and county of Montgomery, in meeting jointly called upon the City Commission of the City of Montgomery to adopt the following seating arrangement on busses operated within its jurisdiction:

> That the seating of passengers will be on a "first come-first served" basis. This means that the Negro passengers will began seating from the rear of the bus toward the front, and the white passengers from the front toward the rear until all the seats are taken.

TD. MLKP-MBU: Box 6.

From Earl B. Dickerson

11 January 1956
Chicago, Ill.

Dickerson, president of Supreme Liberty Life Insurance, agrees to join the committee of Chicago African-American leaders to lobby National City Lines.[1] *He applauds King*

---

1. Earl Burrus Dickerson (1891–1986), born in Canton, Mississippi, earned his B.A. (1914) at the University of Illinois and his J.D. (1920) at the University of Chicago. After serving as general counsel for Supreme Life Insurance Company for more than thirty years, Dickerson presided over the company from 1955 to 1971. In 1940 he successfully argued before the U.S. Supreme Court the landmark case *Hansberry v. Lee* (1940), which affirmed the unconstitutionality of racially restricted real estate covenants. He was a national board member of the NAACP (1941–1980) and served terms as president of the Chicago Urban League (1939–1947, 1951–1955) and the National Lawyers Guild.

Rev. M. L. King, President
Montgomery Improvement Association
309 South Jackson Street
Montgomery, Alabama

Dear Rev. King:

I have your communication addressed to me under date of December 27, 1955 regarding the matter of your citizens with the Transit Lines of Montgomery. I shall be happy to sit down and confer with Dr. Archibald Carey, the Chairman whom we designated, when, and as soon as he makes the request for a meeting of the committee.

Meanwhile, let me congratulate you and your associates for the fine work you are doing in protesting the unfair treatment of the Transit Lines of Montgomery. It seems to me that unless the Negro people are prepared to boycott companies and organizations which discriminate against them, we shall never be able to solve the problems involved in segregation and discrimination. Economic pressure is a weapon which we must now use as a means of obtaining complete equality in our great American Democracy. And I congratulate you again and trust that you will hold steadfast to the end in your opposition to the unfair and unchristian-like practices of this company.

Very truly yours,
[*signed*]
Earl B. Dickerson
President

khm

TLS. MLKP-MBU: Box 107.

From H. Edward Whitaker

18 January 1956
Niagara Falls, N.Y.

Whitaker discusses plans for King's visit, scheduled for 25 March but later rescheduled to 22 July. King noted "to be answered soon" on the letter and responded on 30 January.[1]

---

1. See p. 113 in this volume.

Dr. M. L. King Jr
Dexter Avenue Baptist Church
Dexter Avenue at Decatur St
Montgomery, Ala.

Dear Mike:

Sometime ago I wrote to you concerning your coming here for a of services. Well we have finally set the date, which I hope you will find it convenient. We should like to begin the services on the evening of Palm Sunday, March 25 and conclude with a Maundy Thursday Communion service. This arrangement would give you ample time to get back home for Easter Sunday. This is a venture for us in our attempt to spiritualize the church to a greater degree. This you will understand when you get here. Some people call such series of services Religious emphasis Week, others call them Revivals. You may take your choice.

We shall be glad to pay your expenses and give an honorarium commensurate with all that's involved.

It was quite pleasant to talk with your wife the other day while you were out of town. And as I said to her, you people are doing a nice job in the bus situation. It is getting nationwide publicity. I hope and pray that every thing it will work out satisfactory, because if it can be done there it can be done elsewhere in the south. If there is anything we can do, don't hesitate to let us know. We have a good many people from Alabama and from conversations with them they are quite interested in what's going on there now. I am sure they will be glad to go further if their support is needed.

If for any reason you will not be able to accept these services let me know at once. With kind regards and best wishes to the family, I remain

Sincerely,
[*signed*] Whit
H. Edward Whitaker

THLS. DABCC.

MIA Press Release,
The Bus Protest Is Still On

[*22 January 1956*]
[*Montgomery, Ala.*]

On Saturday night, 21 January, King received word from Minneapolis reporter Carl T. Rowan of an Associated Press wire story stating that an agreement to end the bus boycott had been reached between the city commissioners and a "group of prominent Negro ministers."[1] Earlier that day the commissioners had indeed arranged a meeting with three ministers not associated with the MIA and apparently persuaded them to accept a settlement preserving designated sections for white and black bus riders. King

---

1. Quotation from "City Commission States Position on Bus Services," *Montgomery Advertiser,* 22 January 1956. Carl Thomas Rowan (1925–), born in Ravenscroft, Tennessee, earned his B.A. (1947) from Oberlin College and his M.A. (1948) from the University of Minnesota. The *Minneapolis Tribune*

*and other MIA leaders quickly spread word throughout the black community that the
three pastors did not represent the MIA and that the boycott was continuing. This is
King's handwritten draft of the MIA's response, portions of which were quoted in the*
Montgomery Advertiser *on 24 January.*[2]

You have probably received a ~~statement~~ release from Commissioner Clyde Sellers
stating that the Montgomery bus protest is nearing an end as a result of a meeting
with a group of Negro ministers, city bus line officials, and the city Commission.
If this release gives the impression that [*strikeout illegible*] an agreement has been
reached, it is totally erroneous. ~~The city has~~ If there were any ministers in a meeting with the city Commission on Saturday, I assure you that they do not represent
even a modicum of the Negro bus riders. {More than 99 percent of the} The
Negro citizens of Mont have stated their position and it remains the same. The
bus protest is still on and it will last until our proposals are given sympathetic
consideration through our appointed leaders.

The Montgomery Improvement Ass.
Rev. M. L. King Jr., Pres.
Rev. U. J. Fields, Secr

ALdS. MLKP-MBU: Box 6.

---

hired Rowan in 1948 as its first black reporter. Three years later Rowan won the first of many awards
for a series of eighteen articles entitled "How Far from Slavery?" His first profile of the boycott appeared as "Jim Crow Rides on Buses, So 60,000 Walk" in the *Minneapolis Tribune* on 22 January 1956.
In 1961, Rowan became deputy assistant secretary of state for public affairs and was named ambassador
to Finland in 1963. In 1964 he was appointed head of the United States Information Agency. The
following year Rowan became the first black syndicated columnist, writing for the *Chicago Daily News.*
Rowan discussed his involvement in the Montgomery movement in his memoir, *Breaking Ground*
(1991).
  2. Joe Azbell, "Mayor Stops Boycott Talk," *Montgomery Advertiser,* 24 January 1956.

Notes on MIA Executive Board Meeting,
by Donald T. Ferron

23 January 1956
Montgomery, Ala.

*Two days after the reported settlement of the bus boycott, King gives a full account of
the weekend's events, including his conversation with one of the pastors who met with
city officials, to an MIA executive board meeting. He then shifts to a discussion of the
boycott's goals in light of earlier negotiations with city officials. To avoid a "split
within the ranks," the MIA president refutes several accusations that had appeared in
a recent* Advertiser *profile, after which the board members give him a "unanimous
rising vote of confidence."*[1] *The following was recorded by Ferron, a member of a team*

---

  1. See Tom Johnson, "The Rev. King Is Boycott Boss," *Montgomery Advertiser,* 19 January 1956.

of Fisk University researchers that was conducting a study of the bus boycott in its early months.[2] (Errors in the typed version have been corrected according to Ferron's handwritten draft.)

In the section of the notes not included here, the board listened to committee reports and recommended filing an application for the MIA to operate its own transportation franchise. "If our franchise is not granted," they resolved, "the MIA will get a court injunction and attack the segregation law itself." The board empowered King, but no other officer, to release press statements without prior approval. It also decided to hold simultaneous mass meetings and to appoint a membership card committee.

DATE:	Monday, January 23, 1956	Observed by:	Donald T. Ferron
TIME:	11:00 a.m.–2:45 p.m.	Presiding:	Rev. M. L. King
PLACE:	Baptist Center	Secretary:	Mrs. Dungee

Meeting of the Executive Board

Rev. King describing his first knowledge that the protest had "ended". Carl Rowan is doing a series of articles for the "Minneapolis Tribune" on the protest here. His first article was to have appeared on Sunday morning, January 22. Mr. Rowin in the interim before publishing his article received an Association Press dispatch stating that the protest had ended. He immediately phoned (Rev. King) because he was disturbed over this, for he didn't want a compromise. He was told that this was the first that he (Rev. King) had known about it, and that none of the members of the M.I.A. had been to any meeting with the City Commissioners. Rowan called Commissioner Sellers, and while Sellers wouldn't give the names of the men, he did say that they were three Negro Ministers and gave their denominations. In the mean time, Rev. King called Mr. Brennan of the A. P. to have the release modified by stating that none of the members of the M.I.A. were present at the meeting.[3] This was done in order that the public wouldn't get the impression that the protest had ended, so that money contributions wouldn't be blocked. Rowin called Rev. King and gave him the information that he had received from Sellers. Att. Gray, through a process of elimination found the men to have been Rev. Mosely, Bishop Rice, and Rev. Kynes.[4]

---

2. Led by sociologist Preston Valien, this biracial research team, including Ferron, Willie Mae Lee, and Anna Holden, produced dozens of eyewitness reports of executive board meetings and mass meetings and conducted interviews with boycott participants and leaders from both the white and the black communities. See Valien's report "The Montgomery Bus Protest as a Social Movement," in *Race Relations: Problems and Theory*, ed. Jitsuichi Masuoka and Preston Valien (Chapel Hill: University of North Carolina Press, 1961), pp. 112–127; and several boxes of archival material in Valien's collection at Amistad Research Center, Tulane University.

3. King apparently succeeded. The Associated Press story, "Alabama City Asks End of Bus Boycott," as published in the *New York Times* on 22 January, reported that "Mr. King said tonight that his group had not been reached. He added that he did not believe the Negroes were ready 'to go back on the buses.'"

4. Benjamin F. Mosely was pastor of First Presbyterian Church. He released a statement denying his complicity in any agreement to end the boycott ("Mayor Stops Boycott Talk," *Montgomery Advertiser*, 24 January 1956). Doc C. Rice and William K. Kinds were pastors of Oak Street Holiness Church and Jackson Street Baptist Church, respectively.

In giving the possible reasons for the newspaper article, Rev. King suggested that the Mayor wanted it to appear that there are two factions within the Negro community; that we're split up, divided, to confuse the people into thinking that the leader did this.

Rev. King describes a talk with later with Rev. Kynes:

Kynes said that the Mayor called (Phoned—at least the person said he was the mayor) him to come to the Chamber of Commerce Building to discuss an insurance plan that was trying to be adopted in the city. When he entered the room the only person he recognized was Bishop Rice. The group talked for about three minutes, about insurance, and then the Mayor said that they couldn't arrive at suitable arrangements until the bus situation is straightened out first. Where upon Rev. Kynes asked why the members of the M.I.A. weren't called. The Mayor answered by saying that they wouldn't compromise, and the Commissioners just couldn't work with them; wanted people with sense. The meeting ended with no agreement. Rev. Kynes said he didn't know why the Mayor called him. (Rev. King told the Executive Board that he didn't know how true Rev. Kynes' statement was).

(At this point there resulted general disorder for about two minutes, with on the other hand, most if not all of those present (there were approximately. 22 members there) voicing disapproval and resentment over the fact that the three ministers had even attended the meeting, and, on the other hand, the President trying to achieve order) He said, in effect, that there are some violent Negroes (smiling) who would like nothing better than to get their hands on those ministers (their names had not officially been made known to the public), and he stated further that at one of the night clubs where it was announced that the newspapers on the following day would carry the story that a compromise had been reached, while in reality the protest was still on, someone shouted: "Just let us know who they were, we'll hang 'em". Rev. King smiled as he said it. Then quickly, changing to a serious, solemn, and determined attitude, he said that we cannot over estimate the importance of non-violence. We must be <u>sane</u> and unemotional. We must not be accused of intimidation. "We can't hurt Uncle Tom's by violence, but only by mass action."

All agreed that this <u>must</u> be the policy.

Rev. King at this point turned to a brief discussion of the goals in which he stated that on last Monday there was a meeting with some whites with Rev. Bennett, Rev. Abernathy, Rev. Hubbard, and Rev. King present. When the meeting was over, he said, without detail, they felt the M.I.A. would compromise, although representatives of the M.I.A. made no definite commitments. (the nature of the arrangement for the meeting was not given) Someone (my vision was blocked) raised the question if the Executive Board would "relinquish Number 3 goal (Negro drivers) if No. 2. (seating) is accepted. The discussion ranged from the suggestion that if any goal is given up it should be number three, to the suggestion that the M.I.A. should hold out for number three at the loss of the others if there should be a compromise on the goals. Rev. Young[5] stated that firmly if we com-

5. Ferron mistakenly notes that Ronald R. Young (1919–) is a minister. An Alpha Phi Alpha member, Young received his B.S. (1947) and M.Ed. (1958) from Alabama State College. He was in the U.S. Marine Corps before becoming a coach for St. Jude's Educational Institution, where he taught from 1947 to 1958. He was also among the indicted boycott leaders.

promise on any, it should be on the first two rather than number three, otherwise I'm not for it; I'm sticking for the whole!" Because bus drivers have police powers we can as a result get the other two, he said. Atty. Gray suggested that perhaps the best strategy would be to give the impression that concession might be made on goal number 3 if the first two goals are accepted, but without making a definite commitment. In this way the M.I.A. would not be commiting itself first, so that in reality the whites would be making the first commitment and the M.I.A. can then commit itself on the white's commitment. Before any definite compromise is reached the conditions of it should be presented first to the Negroes in a mass meeting for their decision which would be final.

The truth of the editorial by Johnson in the "Montgomery Advertiser" concerning Rev. King was then refuted. This was in the form of what amounted to a "pep talk", aimed at preventing a "split within the ranks". It was denied that there was any discussion of Deacons in his church, or that his was a "professional church". It was further denied that he knew anything about transferal of $5,017 to the Citizens Trust Bank of Atlanta, as he was out of the city at the time (at conference of Baptist Ministers in Hot Springs, Arkansas) It was verified that the transferal was made without his consent or knowledge, that it (the money) was drawn in a check made to "cash", Rev Hubbard suggestion and sent in form of money orders to the Atlanta bank; it was denied that he has a cadillac car and his wife a new station wagon. [6] Rev. King had been interviewed by Johnson but when he was asked about the policy of the NAACP, Rev. King said that all he said was that "the policy of the NAACP doesn't allow compromise on segregation", and that if he wanted more information to see the President of the local branch, Mr. Matthews. All of the above statements were printed in order that there would be a split in the ranks. Rev. King emphasized the importance of unity, that he was made president of the M.I.A. by unanimous vote. Rev. Young asked for a vote of confidence—there was loud approval and a unanimous rising vote of confidence.

TD. PV-ARC-LNT.

---

6. Later in the meeting several board members noted that the decision to transfer funds out of state was taken on the advice of the MIA's attorneys, who were worried about legal proceedings against the organization and the boycott.

26 January 1956

*King's father reports on church-related activities in Atlanta. He encloses a check sent to
him by Hampton Z. Barker, an organist and director of music at Morris College in
South Carolina. In his letter thanking Barker, King, Sr., wrote: "Altho we need it
badly on our building Fund here at Ebenezer, but I agree fully with you, Negroes out of
Alabama should contribute something to this protest."* [1]

Dr. M. L. King, Jr.
309 South Jackson St
Montgomery, Ala.

Dear M. L.:

Glad to say that this leaves us all well at this time and theings are moving on in
a very fine way around the church. When you visit again you will hardly know the
place. They have gutted the upstairs, and are now roughing in the new work. If
the weather is pretty for another two weeks, they will have the top on the new
building.

Dr. Henderson preached at the Union yesterday and he did a marvelous job.
It was thought provoking and yet spirit filled. I introduced him. He told them
that you woruld be with him one week preceeding the Congress in June. [2] He had
some very nice things to say about you.

I am enclosing the check from Hampton be sure and drop him a line of
thanks — Professor Hampton Z. Barker Morris College, Sumter, S.C.

Love to Coretta and Yolanda.

Yours,
Daddy.

MLK/ w

TLc. EBCR.

---

1. Martin Luther King, Sr., to Hampton Z. Barker, 25 January 1956.

2. J. Raymond Henderson, pastor of Second Baptist Church in Los Angeles, had delivered a sermon entitled "Immortal Lips of Human Kind" to a gathering of the Atlanta Baptist Ministers Union,
which King, Sr., moderated for many years. King, Jr., gave several sermons at Henderson's church in
mid-June 1956, just prior to the annual session of the National Baptist Sunday School and Baptist
Training Union Congress that met in Los Angeles from 18 to 24 June.

King drove home on Thursday afternoon with church secretary Lilie Thomas and a Morehouse friend, Robert Williams. On the way King picked up a few passengers at a car pool station and was questioned by the police. Two motorcycle policemen followed as he drove away and stopped him for driving thirty miles per hour in a twenty-five zone. King was arrested and taken to Montgomery City Jail, where he spent some time before being released. That night the MIA held seven mass meetings to inform the crowds interested in King's arrest.

"To the Citizens of Montgomery"

27 January 1956
Montgomery, Ala.

After the settlement was exposed as having been contrived, the city commissioners
toughened their stance against the boycott by refusing to negotiate and initiating a
campaign of police harassment. On 23 January, after announcing that all three
commissioners had joined the pro-segregation Citizens Council, Mayor Gayle accused
the MIA and the boycotters of stirring up "racial strife."[1] *A few days later, responding*
to the heated rhetoric, the MIA and several other organizations published this
conciliatory advertisement in the Montgomery Advertiser.

On December 25, 1955, there was released through these columns a document
from the Negro Citizens of Montgomery explaining the reasons the protest had
been staged.[2]

Since recent public pronouncements have attempted to cloud and distort issues in the protest, we feel that further explanation is needed.

Negroes want the entire citizenry of Montgomery to know that at no time have
we raised the race issue in this movement, nor have we directed our aim at the
segregation laws. We are interested in a calm and fair consideration of the situation which has developed as a result of dissatisfaction over Bus policies.

The protest, which has been a non-violent method of bargaining, has been
used in a democratic society to secure redress of grievances. This technique, however, has caused some of the leaders of the city to reject unrelated issues—such
as "destruction of the social fabric" or "the southern tradition," which we feel is
an effort to evade the real issues involved.

**1. RACE RELATIONS: We have used the non-violent approach and have
sought relief for our complaints within the frame-work of the law. We de-
plore any attempt to pit one race against the other. And we are amazed that
there are among us those who could impute any sinister motive other than
the request submitted to the Bus Officials and the City Commission. We
believe that our proposals, if considered fairly, will help to improve race
relations in Montgomery.**

**2. DEMOCRACY: As we interpret the democratic way of life, we are con-
vinced that it gives to each Citizen equal opportunities and privileges to
enjoy the benefits of what ever service he is able to pay for, so long as he
does not infringe upon the rights of others. Under the present policies of
the bus company the rights of Negroes have been infringed upon repeatedly. Up until now our proposals have not been given fair consideration. We
have no alternative, therefore, but to continue the bus protest until something fair, just and honorable has been done in our behalf.**

---

1. Quoted in "Mayor Stops Boycott Talks," *Montgomery Advertiser,* 24 January 1956.
2. "To the Montgomery Public," 25 December 1955, pp. 89–93 in this volume.

3. THE CHRISTIAN WAY: We live in a Christian community in which brotherhood and neighborliness should prevail among all the people. We can only rely upon these principles to guide those in authority and other people of influence to see that the Christian way is the only way of reaching a satisfactory solution to the problem.

We submit this to all the Citizens of Montgomery in the name of Him who brought Peace on Earth and Good Will to All Men.

**RESPECTFULLY SUBMITTED,
NEGRO MINISTERS AND CONGREGATIONS**

**BAPTIST MINISTER'S CONFERENCE
THE REV. H. H. HUBBARD, PRES.**

**METHODIST MINISTERIAL ALLIANCE
THE REV. W. J. HAYES**

**INTERDENOMINATIONAL MINISTERIAL ALLIANCE
THE REV. L. R. BENNETT**

**MONTGOMERY IMPROVEMENT ASSOCIATION
DR. M. L. KING, PRES.**

**CITIZENS COORDINATING COMMITTEE
RUFUS LEWIS**

PD. *Montgomery Advertiser*, 27 January 1956.

To Roy Wilkins

28 January 1956
Montgomery, Ala.

King sends Wilkins, executive secretary of the NAACP, this form letter of appreciation. Wilkins had sent a $500 contribution from the NAACP to the MIA.[1]

---

1. Someone in the NAACP office noted on King's letter that $500 had been sent to him on 17 January 1956 via Ruby Hurley, the NAACP regional secretary based in Birmingham. Roy Ottaway Wilkins (1901–1981) was born in St. Louis, Missouri, and raised in St. Paul, Minnesota. While earning his B.A. (1923) at the University of Minnesota, Wilkins joined the NAACP. After graduating Wilkins spent

Mr. Roy Wilkins, Executive Secretary,
National Association for Advancement of Colored People,
20 West 40th Street,
New York 18, N.Y.

Dear Mr. Wilkins:

   This is just a note to express our deepest gratitude to you for your very fine contribution. I assure you that we will long remember your coming to our aid in this momentous struggle. Such contributions from friends and organizations sympathetic with our struggle give us renewed courage and vigor to carry on.
   With every good wish, I am

Cordially yours,
[*signed*]
M. L. King, Jr.,
President.

MLK/ehr

THLS. RWP-DLC.

————————

several years as a journalist at the *Call,* a leading black weekly in Kansas City, Missouri, and was elected secretary of the local NAACP. He became assistant executive secretary of the NAACP's national branch in 1931. He succeeded W. E. B. Du Bois as editor of the NAACP's journal, *The Crisis,* holding that position from 1934 to 1949. Wilkins also served as an advisor to the War Department in 1941 and a consultant for the American delegation to the United Nations in 1945. From 1955 until his retirement in 1977 he served as executive secretary of the NAACP.

Notes on MIA Executive Board Meeting,
by Donald T. Ferron

30 January 1956

> *At this specially called meeting of the MIA executive board, King and the other leaders discuss two important matters: a bus seating compromise that falls short of their initial demands and the filing of a lawsuit challenging the constitutionality of the city and state bus segregation laws. King notes that "some of the ministers are getting weary," but after Rev. W. F. Alford expresses a desire to compromise, King warns, "if we went tonight and asked the people to get back on the bus, we would be ostracized. They wouldn't get back." He also reminds the board of their earlier decision to take legal action if the city renewed the bus company franchise and denied their own application for an MIA-sponsored jitney service. He and Fred D. Gray then explain the two lawsuits about to be filed in Montgomery federal district court.*

Executive Board "Call" Meeting
Monday, January 30, 1956
11:00 A.M.–2:35 P.M.
Rev. M. L. King, presiding

—prayer

This meeting was called because there are some "important issues to discuss rather than to hold off until Thursday."

Rev. Alford—Said that he had been pondering over a proposal which was made to Rev. Binion by some of his "white friends" some weeks back. (apparently the exec. board rejected it then). Rev. Alford feels that it is "worthy of our studying it." I think we should go back under those conditions."

Rev. Binion[1]—to the question ~~as to~~ of the nature of the proposal:

Mr. Nacrosie (his "white friend") explained the proposal to him before the three N. ministers had been "hoodwinked" into a "compromise". The City had decided that if N. would give W. the first two seats on the Jackson, Day and Cleveland St. routes, and on the rest of the routes give the first six seats to the W.—an agreement could be reached.[2]

Mr. E. D. Nixon—Did the proposal of two seats mean the long seat plus the next two seats? Mr. Binion—"I don't know."

Mr. Nixon—If you talk about the first two seats, then that's the same as before. We would be returning to the same conditions, and if we accept it we are "going to run into trouble" with the people who had been riding the bus. "If that's what you're doing to do, I don't want to be here when you tell the people."

Mr White—"This morning was the test." The rain was pouring and "they still walked." "If they don't want to go back, I don't see why we should decide otherwise. Folk just made too much sacrifice. I hold that we should go on to the end. I think we should stay just where we're at."

Rev. King—"I've seen along the way where some of the ministers are getting weary." Says he won't call names. "If you have that impression (that N. should go back {under same conditions} to the buses), we won't ostracize you. We should "iron it out here" (exec. meetings) and "show wherein we shouldn't go back."

Rev. Alford—"There's a time in the life of any crisis when you ~~go~~ ought to be reasonable; The parties concerned ought to "give and take". If we can get two out of the three demands (Alford called them "concessions"), I think we ought to accept. We have no protection to give those people—our wives and daughters[3] are not out there. We can arrive at some type of agreement that is pleasing even to us."

Rev. King—"From my limited contact, if we went tonight and asked the people to get back on the bus, we would be ostracized. They wouldn't get back." We

---

1. R. B. Binion served on the MIA's finance committee and was a trustee of the MIA. He was one of the ministers indicted during the boycott.

2. Ferron placed an asterisk after Cleveland and noted at the bottom of the page that Jackson, Day, and Cleveland Streets "are predominantly Negro used routes."

3. Ferron placed an asterisk here and noted at the bottom of the page: "Rev. Bennett has referred to the masses of Negroes, those who had once ridden the buses, but who are now walking, as 'those in the gutter.'"

"shouldn't give people the illusion that there are no sacrifices involved, that it could be ended soon. My intimidations are a small price to pay if victory can be won." We "shouldn't make the illusion that they won't have to walk. I believe to the bottom of my heart that the majority of Negroes would ostracize us. They are willing" to walk.

Rev. King (changing the subject), "I think this is a basic point."

We agreed that in the event the Chicago franchise was renewed and ours was rejected, we would go to court. Attorney Gray went to New York last week for a few days to discuss this whole problem with Thurgood Marshall and another lawyer.[4] Att. Gray has drawn up two suits: 1) demanding that the segregation law of the City is null and void because it is unconstitutional; 2) in the process of litigation, all intimidation be outlawed. This joint suit is to be filed in the Federal Court this afternoon or tomorrow. We are in the process of drawing up a list of plaintiffs (those who can stand up under intimidation and who are not susceptible to losing their jobs). So far we have Miss Colving, Miss Smith, Mrs. Reese, Mrs. Hamilton, and Mrs. McDonald.[5] This suit on the City of Montgomery would go directly to the Federal Courts, but it would not be filed in the name of the Naacp.

Rev. King What are we to do for the people in the process of litigation? The court has 20 days to answer—don't know how long the litigation would take.

Mr. Saye[6]—Number 1, "issue an ultimatim {—giving a time limit} (leaving out goal 3) to the Commission stating our position to see what they would do; 2, we need to do that to have a point from which to prepare people to return to the buses. We need to train people to go back to the bus. "We would disgrace ourselves before the world if we give up now."

Mr. Nixon—Hold people off the bus for the end of the 20 days, instructing them about going back to the bus. At least for the first 20 days from tomorrow keep them off the bus.

Rev. King—It is <u>very</u> important that this information does not leak out about the Naacp and the court action until its printed in the newspaper. We want to surprise the whites. Don't mention the 20 days. Some liberal whites say that because of the stigma that has been put on the Naacp, its part in this should not be

---

4. Thurgood Marshall (1908–1993), born in Baltimore, Maryland, earned his B.A. (1930) at Pennsylvania's Lincoln University and his LL.B. (1933) at Howard University. In 1938 he became special counsel to the NAACP, and in 1950 he was named director of the NAACP's Legal Defense and Educational Fund. He headed the legal team that successfully argued the NAACP's case in *Brown v. Board of Education* in 1954. In 1961 President Kennedy appointed him to the U.S. District Court for the Second Judicial Circuit. He was later appointed solicitor general before joining the Supreme Court in 1967.

5. The plaintiffs were Aurelia S. Browder, Susie McDonald, Claudette Colvin, and Mary Louise Smith. Jeanatta Reese withdrew as a plaintiff, apparently out of fear. The successful lawsuit (*Aurelia S. Browder v. William A. Gayle*) challenging bus segregation was filed in U. S. District Court on 1 February, decided on 5 June, and upheld by the U.S. Supreme Court on 13 November 1956.

6. Solomon S. Seay, Sr. (1889–1988), was raised in Macon County, Alabama, and studied at Alabama State College and Talladega College. He served AME Zion churches in Alabama, Mississippi, North Carolina, and Tennessee before becoming pastor of Montgomery's Mt. Zion AME Zion Church (1947–1962). Seay was a member of the MIA's negotiating committee and, after King and Abernathy left Montgomery, served as the third president of the MIA. He was among those indicted for their role in the boycott. He also became a Southern Christian Leadership Conference (SCLC) executive board member. His autobiography, *I Was There by the Grace of God,* was published in 1990.

mentioned because of its effect on public sentiment. We should use the "legal structure of the Naacp," but refer to the participants as "legal citizenry."

Dr. Saye—Because we can't settle this within the framework of the law, we should state publicly that we're taking it to the Federal Court.

Rev. King—By the way, I've found out that the {N.} lady who was beat up by a N. man a few ~~weeks~~ {days} ago is the cook for the Mayor; she attends the mass meetings and tells the mayor what happened the next morning. We also found out that Sellers has let 3 N. prisoners attend the mass meetings so that they can tell him what has happened.

Att. Gray—about selection of plaintiffs:

I think it's good strategy to have at least one minster, people of different ages, and people with different grievances. It's not good strategy to have Rev. King because he's too much in the "limelight."

Rev. King—I think its very important in throwing sentiment our way if we have a minister as a plaintiff. Who (of 25 present) will volunteer? After discussion {of about 10 minutes} in which Rev. King said that he knew of many in the meeting who had been fined and otherwise intimidated, still no one would volunteer. Rev. King reiterated their stand on a policy of non-violence. It was suggested in this connection that we go "on record not to come to the rescue of people arrested for carrying concealed weapons."

Rev. King—about lawyers fees.

Att. Gray (A. H. Langford not present)[7] The branch Naacp made an agreement with me about a figure for my work for the Mrs. Parks Case. Explains that the retaining fee ($50/wk for each lawyer) covers anything that comes up other that court cases.

Rev. King I would ask this question even if A. H. Langford was here: Is it necessary to retain two lawyers?

Att. Gray—"I'll leave while you discuss it." (he leaves the room)

Dr. Saye—"I never did see the wisdom of hiring two lawyers."

——" ——

It was agreed that the lawyers be paid $500 (the figure the two lawyers had submitted) for their work from Dec. 11 to Jan. 4, and from that time retain the two lawyers at $50/wk. each until the case is filed in the Federal Court. They will then be paid a "general fee" which will be added to that fee paid by the branch Naacp (this money will come from collections at the meetings).

Each lawyer will ~~be paid~~ submit a bill for "services rendered" to get away from having to pay the retainer fee during or after court action. Announcement: Mass meeting tonight at 7:00 p.m. at First Baptist Church.

Meeting ends with prayer.

AD. PV-ARC-LNT.

_____

7. Ferron refers to attorney Charles D. Langford.

30 January 1956
[*Montgomery, Ala.*]

The Reverend H. Edward Whittaker
1122 Buffalo Avenue
Niagara Falls, New York

Dear Horace:

This is just a note to say that I will be very happy to preach for you on the dates that you have designated. I have already placed this engagement on my calendar.

Please feel free to contact me concerning necessary details. I am looking forward with great anticipation to a rich fellowship with you and your fine members.

With every good wish, I am

Sincerely yours,
M. L. King, Jr.

MLK:lmt

P.S. The bus situation here in Montgomery is keeping me so busy that I hardly have time to breathe.

TLc. DABCC.

Notes on MIA Mass Meeting at First Baptist Church, by Willie Mae Lee

30 January 1956
Montgomery, Ala.

In a stirring address to more than 2,000 boycotters at an MIA mass meeting at Rev. Ralph Abernathy's First Baptist Church, King links the city's "get-tough" policy with his recent arrest and imprisonment for speeding but insists that "we still hold steadfast."[1] "I want you to know that if M. L. King had never been born this movement would have taken place. I just happened to be here." Lee, a member of the Fisk University research team, also took notes on speeches (omitted here) by Abernathy, Rufus Lewis, and S. S. Seay that evening. She did not record King's announcement during the meeting that his house had been bombed. According to another source, he told the gathering to "be calm and quiet. Don't do anything that will not be for justice, for God is with us."[2]

---

1. See Complaint, *City of Montgomery v. Martin L. King*, 26 January 1956, p. 106 in this volume.

2. Quoted in Joe Azbell, "Blast Rocks Residence of Bus Boycott Leader," *Montgomery Advertiser*, 31 January 1956.

"Some of our good white citizens told me today that the relationships between white and colored use to be good, that the whites have never let us down and that the outsiders came in and upset this relationship. But I want you to know that if M. L. King had never been born this movement would have taken place. I just happened to be here. You know there comes a time when time itself is ready for change. That time has come in Montgomery, and I had nothing to do with it.

"Our opponents, I hate to think of our governmental officials as opponents, but they are, have tried all sorts of things to break us, but we still hold steadfast. Their first strategy was to negotiate into a compromise and that failed. Secondly, they tried to conquer by dividing and that failed. And now they are trying to intimidate us by a get-tough-policy and that's going to fail too because a man's language is courage when his back is against the wall.

"We don't advocate violence. WE WILL STAY WITHIN THE LAW. When we are RIGHT, WE DON'T MIND GOING TO JAIL! (The applause rang out like a great clasp of thunder) If all I have to pay is going to jail a few times and getting about 20 threatening calls a day, I think that is a very small price to pay for what we are fighting for. (applause very loud and long).

"We are a chain. We are linked together, and I cannot be what I ought to unless you are what you ought to be.

"This good white citizen I was talking to said that I should devote more time to preaching the gospel and leave other things alone. I told him that it's not enough to stand in the pulpit on Sunday and preach about honesty, to tell people to be honest and don't think about their economic conditions which may be conducive to their being dishonest. It's not enough to tell them to be truthful and forget about the social environment which may necessitate their telling untruths. All of these are a minister's job. You see God didn't make us with just soul alone so we could float about in space without care or worry. He made a body to put around a soul. When the body was made in flesh, there became a material connection between man and his environment and this connection means a material well being of the body as well as the spiritual well being of the soul is to be sought. And it is my job as a minister to aid in both of these." (roaring applaud)

TD. PV-ARC-LNT.

"Blast Rocks Residence of Bus Boycott Leader," by Joe Azbell

31 January 1956
Montgomery, Ala.

At 9:30 P.M., 30 January, a single stick of dynamite exploded on the King family's porch; Coretta Scott King and a friend, Dexter member Mary Lucy Williams, had been in the living room when they heard an object land on the front porch. They bolted to the back room, where Yolanda was sleeping, just as the dynamite exploded, ripping a hole in the porch floor, shattering four windows, and damaging a porch column. King arrived home about fifteen minutes later to find a large and boisterous crowd—many apparently armed—gathered outside and refusing to obey police orders to disperse. When he walked onto the porch, one onlooker reported, "the people let out with cheers that could be heard blocks away. With the raising of his hand they became quiet to hear what he had to say."[1] In his remarks, King asked the crowd to go home peacefully. Police Commissioner Clyde Sellers and Mayor W. A. Gayle addressed the crowd next, promising to investigate the bombing and to defend the King family against future attacks. King spoke to the gathering again, urging them to be calm. The crowd then broke into spontaneous song, including hymns and "My Country, 'Tis of Thee," before finally dispersing at 10:45 P.M." The following comments by King were quoted in the Montgomery Advertiser *article by Joe Azbell published the next day.*

"We believe in law and order. Don't get panicky. Don't do anything panicky at all. Don't get your weapons. He who lives by the sword will perish by the sword. Remember that is what God said.[2] We are not advocating violence. We want to love our enemies. I want you to love our enemies. Be good to them. Love them and let them know you love them.[3] I did not start this boycott. I was asked by you to serve as your spokesman. I want it to be known the length and breadth of this land that if I am stopped this movement will not stop. If I am stopped our work will not stop. For what we are doing is right. What we are doing is just. And God is with us." [*quotations from Gayle, Sellers, and Sheriff Mac Sim Butler omitted*]

The Rev. King addressed the crowd again saying "go home and sleep calm. Go home and don't worry. Be calm as I and my family are. We are not hurt and remember that if anything happens to me, there will be others to take my place."

PD. *Montgomery Advertiser*, 31 January 1956.

---

1. Willie Mae Lee, "The Bombing Episode," 31 January 1956.
2. Matthew 26:52 and Revelations 13:10.
3. Matthew 5:44.

From Pinkie S. Franklin

31 January 1956
Birmingham, Ala.

King received scores of sympathetic letters after the bombing, from both friends and strangers. Franklin wrote this letter of solace while unable to sleep.[1] She later became

---

1. Pinkie Smith Franklin (1915–) was born in Selma and graduated from Alabama State College in 1938. She taught in Alabama schools before opening a grocery store in Birmingham with her husband in 1946. She was a member of the Alabama Christian Movement for Human Rights and the Southern Christian Leadership Conference (SCLC). As a participant in the Birmingham civil rights protests of 1963 she was jailed for two days.

active in the Birmingham civil rights movement. Her own church, Sixteenth Street Baptist Church, was bombed in 1963, killing four young girls.

Dear Rev. King,

For years, we Negro Mothers of the Southland have prayed that God would send us a leader such as you are. Now that the Almighty has regarded our lowly estate and has raised you up among us, I am indeed grateful. Be asured that day and night without ceasing I shall be praying for your safety and that of your family's. The Arm of God is everlastingly strong and Sufficient to keep you and yours. There shall no harm come to you, and the Comforting Spirit of God shall guide you.

A fellow Suffer
(Mrs.) Pinkie S. Franklin

of the Sixteenth Street Baptist Church

ALS. MLKP-MBU: Box 17.

From J. Pius Barbour

31 January 1956
Chester, Pa.

Barbour, pastor of Calvary Baptist Church in Chester, Pennsylvania, became a mentor to King when the latter studied at Crozer Theological Seminary.

REV M L KING
280 SO JACKSON ST MONTGOMERY ALA

STAND YOUR GROUND WE ARE PRAYING FOR YOU
CALVARY BAPTIST CHURCH CROZER SEMINARY BOYS

J. PIUS BARBOUR

PWSr. MLKP-MBU: Box 14.

From Major J. Jones

1 February 1956
Nashville, Tenn.

Jones, dean of the chapel at Fisk University, had been a close friend of King's since they were fellow graduate students at Boston University. Several weeks before King's scheduled lecture at Fisk, Jones conveys his concern and that of his wife, Mattie Parker Jones, about the bombing.

Dr. Martin Luther King   1 Feb
309 South Jackson Street   1956
Montgomery Alabama

Dear Martin:

    Mattie and I were very concerned upon learning that your house was bombed Monday evening. We were relieved, however, to hear later that no one was injured.

    I tried to reach you yesterday by phone but after thinking it through, I thought probably it would not have been the best method of communication anyway under the circumstances. I am very concerned, as you know, about the implications of this and its weight upon you personally but the issues are of such that I can not give you any personal advice but only hope that you will take every precaution and be careful in what you do and say.

    Please accept my prayers in all that you do.

Sincerely yours,
[*signed*]
M. J. Jones
Dean of Chapel

MJJ
a
r
p

{Give my regards to all
Major}

TALS. MLKP-MBU: Box 119.

From Walter R. McCall

1 February 1956
Fort Valley, Ga.

King's classmate at Morehouse and Crozer offers encouragement and advice. McCall's letter included the notation "Reverend King c/o Dr. Trenholm," a reference to H. Councill Trenholm, president of Alabama State College and a deacon of Dexter.

Dear Mike,

    It was good to get first hand information as to how you are getting on the strife involving so many people.

    Needless to say that {the} momentous task under which you and others have gone is a well worthy one. That in itself should give you all the encouragement necessary. But more than that THE PEOPLE ARE WITH YOU. So, be not afraid in as much as they are with you. . . . God is even more on your side. DO NOT BACK DOWN, DO NOT SWERVE. KEEP THE COURAGE. KEEP THE PA-TIENCE. THE task must be met head-on which well merits your stand.

I may add that it will be a good thing if you would, as the occasion arises, leave town for a rest. The task takes strength. So, as often as possible, go away for a rest, prayer and meditate that you may build up a reservoir of strength. . . . Re-turn. Above all, ONLY ENTER THE SCENE WHEN NECESSARY, AND WITH SOMEONES. This will enable witnesses to speak if when necessary. Have your home protected as much as possible.

Dr. and Mrs. Troup and a host of others sent their best regards and wishes to you but I did not think to pass it on to you.[1]

AGAIN, DO NOT DESPAIR. THIS IS YOUR TASK! FACE WITH IT COUR-AGE. THE STORM WILL BREAK!

Call me or drop me a line to let me know how things are working out. I did not have much interest in Tabernacle before now, but I can say with truth that I am interested in the psatorate.[2]

Remember I shall ever pray for you during these crises days . . . and not for you only but all those faced with the momentous task!

[*strikeout illegible*]

Your pal,
Mac.

TAHL. DABCC.

---

1. McCall refers to Cornelius V. Troup, president of Fort Valley State College, and Katie Troup.
2. On 28 October 1955 McCall asked King to "use his influence in trying to get an appointment" at Tabernacle Baptist Church in Birmingham, but McCall remained at Fort Valley State College.

From Frank L. Stanley

2 February 1956
Louisville, Ky.

Stanley, editor of the Louisville Defender *and general president of Alpha Phi Alpha, pledges the support of the oldest African-American college fraternity, which King had joined in 1952 at Boston University.*[1] *King's response to this letter has not been located, but the notation "answered" appears on it.*

---

1. Frank Leslie Stanley, Sr. (1906–1974), born in Chicago and raised in Kentucky, received his B.A. (1929) from Atlanta University. Stanley joined the staff of the *Louisville Defender* in 1933, becoming editor and general manager in 1936. He was editor and publisher until his death. He served as general president of Alpha Phi Alpha from 1955 to 1957.

Reverend M. L. King   2 Feb
309 South Jackson   1956
Montgomery, Alabama

Dear Brother King:

Alpha is proud of the leadership that you have given to the bus segregation protest movement in your city.

We realize the trying hours you are experiencing as the object of a white council-controlled police department, and bombwielding segregationists. But by the grace of God, you have been spared to continue the fight.

Twenty-four thousand Alphas and millions of other Negroes fight with you, even though removed from the immediate scene of your battlefront. You have but to call on us, your Brothers, if we can be of any material assistance. We are already with you spiritually. At least, I personally and officially want to keep in close touch with you in this period of peril.

I know you cannot communicate afar too easily, but your story should be kept alive, at least until victory is won over those who would still deny you full and unsegregated access to your city transportation facilities.

Saturday, February 4, I shall be meeting in Buffalo, New York, with the Central Committee of the Executive Council. If there is any information you think should be given Alpha, call me at the Statler Hotel. Further, I will arrange to come to Montgomery, if you desire.[2]

May God keep you as you vigorously endeavor to demonstrate that the brotherhood of man was intended for practical application here on earth—even in Montgomery, Alabama.

Fraternally and sincerely,
[*signed*]
Frank L. Stanley, General President

THLS. MLKP-MBU: Box 67.

---

2. After King and several other Alphas were indicted for their role in the bus boycott, Stanley, general secretary James Huger, and southern vice president Lewis O. Swingler traveled to Montgomery to offer moral and financial support (see Stanley to King, 22 March 1956, pp. 201–202 in this volume).

Notes on MIA Executive Board Meeting,
by Donald T. Ferron

2 February 1956
Montgomery, Ala.

*A day after E. D. Nixon's home was bombed, King and the MIA executive board
discuss the need to protect mass meetings and leaders from violent reprisals. After
appointing a committee to organize church patrols, the executive board discusses the*

ongoing federal lawsuit, particularly the role of the local NAACP branch. They also decide to move the MIA office from the Alabama Negro Baptist Center to Ralph Abernathy's First Baptist Church.

DATE:	February 2, 1956	Observed by:	Donald T. Ferron
TIME:	11:00 a.m.–2:00 p.m.	Presiding:	Rev. M. L. King
PLACE:	Baptist Center		

Executive Board Meeting

Prayer: Rev. Palmer [1]

Rev. King: "We got to decide how the suit will be handled". There has been an "increase in the amount of violence in recent days". "Fortunately no one was injured; that was <u>very</u> fortunate. I don't know the motives, whether along line of fear tactics, or attempts at bodily harm. They may become more desperate with the suit on. We need right now a comittee of 50 people who will volunteer to patrol all of the churches where mass meetings are being held (before and during). Look for time bombs and the like. Now this mustn't get to the people, because it may panic them and they may not come. I'm not saying that these things will happen, but it's well to take precautionary measures. The minute that it was announced that the Commissioners had joined the white Citizens Council, we received 20–25–30 threatening calls each day. We're not going to give up; they can drop bombs in my house every day, I'm firmer now than ever. I went to the sherrif to get a permit for those people who are guarding me. "Couldn't get one". In substance he was saying 'you are at the disposal of the hoodlums. [2]

"Mrs Reese agreed to be plaintiff last night, but I heard that she had been to the Mayor's office and withdrew. How will that affect the case?" [3]

Atty. Gray: "It won't effect the case, but the whites will use it as a propaganda technique."

Mr. Binion: "Her husband received a call this morning from a man with a rough voice who asked for Julia Reese." He said she was "not home."

1. Hustis James Palmer (1907–1971), a native of Evergreen, Alabama, was pastor of Rock Elvin Baptist Church in Troy, Alabama, and an upholstery shop owner. He served on the MIA's membership and transportation committees and also as a driver in the car pool. He was among the indicted boycott leaders. Palmer was later secretary of the MIA.

2. On 31 January 1956 King met with Governor James Folsom to discuss the MIA's doubts about the protection offered by the Montgomery police department (see Cliff Mackay, "Ala. Bus Boycotters Sing 'My Country 'Tis of Thee,'" *Baltimore Afro-American*, 11 February 1956). The next day King (along with two other ministers, Ralph Abernathy and H. H. Hubbard) applied for a weapons permit, but the local sheriff denied the application (see "Negro Leader Fails to Get Pistol Permit," *Montgomery Advertiser*, 4 February 1956).

3. Jeanatta Reese had decided that day to withdraw from the *Browder v. Gayle* lawsuit ("Negro Woman Withdraws Action on Segregation," *Montgomery Advertiser*, 3 February 1956). Although Fred Gray disputed her contention that she "didn't know" what she was signing when she agreed to participate, he was later arrested for unauthorized legal representation and released on bond. The charges were dropped once Reese's name was withdrawn from the list of plaintiffs. See "Boycott Attorney Indicted by Grand Jury," *Montgomery Advertiser*, 19 February 1956; and *MIA Newsletter* 1 (7 June 1956).

"Is she in town?"

"Yes".

"Better tell her not to be in town tonight!"

Dr. Seay: "I don't pose to be a wise man, but there's one thing I'm deadsure of—you had better turn over every leaf. Make sure you know the husband, for God's sake. We have to use precautions every step of the way."

Rev. King: suggestion that two committees be formed immediately:

1. "To talk with plaintiffs"—to give them "assurance", let them know "we're behind them".

[*Appointment of committee members is omitted.*]

2. To see that the churches are patrolled.

[*Appointment of committee members and a suggestion concerning its function are omitted.*]

Rev. King: "You are to contact the ministers, keep secret, they are not to let anybody know that they are doing this. We don't want it to get out because it will hurt our mass meetings. You should start out immediately."

Rev. Glasco: "There was a meeting held yesterday concerned with the use of the Baptist Center by the Association. 3:45 p.m. Baptist Association. office. Dr. Davison, Sup't of Missions decided that due to the lengthy run of the movement, and since it has taken on a political angle, you might say; it has been suggested by the Committee yesterday that they (M.I.A.) should seek other quarters for their organizations or operations. Up until now, any decision made concerning the Center's operation was made by the colored trustees—the "whites" would go along with it."

[*Discussion of Glasco's comment is omitted.*]

Rev. King: "What is the latest that we can move out—without jeoparadizing the Center, and Rev. Glasco's position? I think the position of the white Baptists is that they're just against it. I don't want to accept anything from them—that's just my feeling about it."

[*After some discussion the board decided to move MIA headquarters to First Baptist Church.*]

Rev. King: "As you know the suit is before us. So the question is, what is our role now? Whether or not the name of the NAACP might create emotional disturbance (tension on part of "whites"), if not otherwise mentioned."

Mr. Matthews: "Dr. Berry called me and asked for a meeting. He advanced this thought—whether the local branch will take the responsibility, or Mrs. Hurley—Regional Director of the 7 states." [4]

[*Rev. Bennett: "Would the Naacp stay in the background?"*] [5]

---

4. Robert L. Matthews, Montgomery NAACP president, refers to the organization's southeastern regional secretary, Ruby Hurley (1909–1980), who studied at Washington, D.C.'s Miners Teachers College and Robert H. Terrell Law School. Hurley was the NAACP's national youth secretary before becoming its first southeastern regional secretary in 1951. She investigated the racial murders of Emmett Till and George Lee and was with Autherine Lucy when University of Alabama students physically attempted to keep her from the campus. After Alabama attorney general John Patterson obtained an injunction against NAACP activity in June 1956, she moved her office to Atlanta, where she continued to investigate racial injustices.

5. From Ferron's handwritten notes of this meeting.

Mr. Matthews: "I firmly believes this—that if it remains local, they would. I'm not saying they would. When the case is appealed to a high court, I'm sure that the National NAACP would step in then. If the NAACP takes over the case, Atty. Gray would have the assistance of the staff of the National NAACP. Any pay would go to lawyer Gray, and not to anyone else."

Atty. Langford: "If the case goes to a higher court" there will be "another lawyer".

Rev. Hubbard: "All of us belong to the Naacp, or should." I say bring the whole thing out "in the open." "Turn over the whole thing to the NAACP, and let the Association support the NAACP financially".

Rev. King: "What about transportation?"

Atty. Langford: "Continue the protest until the hearing of the district court. they must answer the charges within 20 days or we win by default."

Rev. Palmer: "Will we be able to make enough money to support the NAACP and the protest at the same time? The NAACP says it won't work in the background. Would we get any help from the state office?"

Rev. King: "I understand that they've been raising money for the Rosa Parks's case."

Mr. Matthew: "The only expenses you have are the expenses of the two lawyers, if the NAACP takes the case."

Rev. Seay: "To me it doesn't matter who handles this case, this is still our case (Negroes of Montgomery). I don't think we should go out for saying we're raising money in the name of the NAACP."

Rev. Palmer: "Since Mrs. Hurley will be here at 5:30, I move that we table the discussion until then". (Motion carried.)[6]

Moved that Association assume the responsibility for paying fees for night watchmen out of Sunday offerings to the movement.—homes of key individual leaders.

Mrs. P[arks]: "Some strange men have been coming in my neighborhood inquiring about the woman who caused all of this trouble. I'm not worried about myself, but it does upset my mother quite a bit."[7]

Motion (by Rev. Bennett) carried that the Association assume responsibility for giving Mrs. Parks protection at night.

TD. PV-ARC-LNT.

---

6. King and other MIA leaders met with Hurley and Alabama field secretary W. C. Patton later that day, deciding that the *Browder v. Gayle* federal lawsuit would be "turned over to the local branch of the NAACP." King had argued that "we need the Naacp in an advisory capacity, the machinery they have set up over a period of years." The MIA promised to provide "necessary contributions" for legal costs (Ferron, Notes, Joint MIA and NAACP Meeting, 2 February 1956). On the handling of legal costs, see also King to Wilkins, 3 March 1956, pp. 151–152 in this volume, and their subsequent correspondence.

7. One of the indicted boycott leaders, Rosa Parks recalled in her autobiography that her family was threatened and harassed during the boycott. Her husband kept a gun by his bed, while her mother would occasionally call a friend and "talk for long periods just to jam the lines so the hate calls couldn't get through for a while." The Parks family left Montgomery in 1957. See Rosa Parks, with Jim Haskins, *Rosa Parks: My Story* (New York: Dial Books, 1992), p. 161.

4 February 1956
Montgomery, Ala.

*Interviewed at his home on a Saturday afternoon, King recounts the bus boycott's
history following the arrests of Claudette Colvin and Rosa Parks, explains the MIA's
negotiations with city and bus officials, and reflects on the potential for nonviolent
racial reform in Mississippi.*

DATE: February 4, 1956   INTERVIEWER: Donald T. Ferron
TIME: 1:30–3:45   RESPONDENT: Rev. M. L. King
PLACE: 309 S Jackson Street

Interviewer: . . . . I would like to know how all of this came about.

Respondent: "Mrs. P. arrest was a precipitating factor rather than causal. There
have been a series of incidents." When Miss Colving was arrested a "boycott was
threatened." "We went down and talked with the bus officials" and "promises"
were made. "We waited for policy and it never came." [1]

Interviewer: Was the bus company threatened with a "boycott" as such?

Respondent: "I don't remember whether the word "boycott" was used."
(phone 15 minutes)

Interviewer: I am interested in negotiations. . . . how they came about and what
happened during the meetings?

Respondent: "I would say that the first negotiation took place about 5 days
after the boycott. It was called by the Alabama Council on Human Relations. It
served as a mediating committee. We met in the City Commissioner's room. We
had a committee of about 10 men which met with the city officials. Atty. Gray set
forth our greviances, and told them why we were off the buses. We told them the
3 proposals in that meeting. We discussed it pro and con. We were fighting for
our position. Bus officials said it could not be done under the law. We said it
could. . . . under the law. Finally, the mayor decided to appoint a smaller group
of 4 to see if we couldn't come to an agreement. The lawyer for the bus company
was very recalcitrant about Negro drivers, and said 'first come first served' was
out of their domain. All of this was on the same day. They finally saw that we
weren't going to give in. "It ended in a stalemate. All attempts at settlement were
ended; nothing concrete was affirmed." [2]

In the second meeting, the mayor appointed a committee of whites to confer

---

1. King refers to the arrest on 2 March 1955 of Claudette Colvin (see Jo Ann Robinson to W. A.
Gayle, 21 May 1954).

2. For the MIA proposals, see King to the National City Lines, Inc., 8 December 1955, pp. 80–81 in
this volume.

with our group. I think we had six or seven, maybe eight. The mayor said that he was appointing a cross-section of the white citizenry of Montgomery. On this committee he appointed two men whom we knew were rabid segregationists. One was a white businessman—Ingalls, an attorney—who was a member of the white Citzens Councils; the other was Rev. Frazer—a known pro-segregationist. I wondered then why he would appoint such people whose attitudes were definitely anti-Negro. But we went on with the meeting. Mr. G. Totin was present; we invited him down. He was brainwashed with the Mayor. He just echoed what Crenshaw had said earlier. The committee was dismissed at 11:00. The Mayor did the same thing that day—he decided to make the group smaller. Seven from each group (bus officials and M.I.A.) stayed over for 1/2 hr. for "mediation". Somebody made the motion that we stop the boycott and negotiate without its pressure. They voted solid for; the Negroes voted solid against." It was decided to postpone that meeting until three days later.[3]

"The third meeting was just a confirmation of the last meetings. I started out that the proposal of seating be accepted. Rev. Frazer offered a substitute motion—buses be divided on the basis of patronage in the various areas /i.e./ the relative number of patrons on the various lines, and that signs be placed separating the sections. There was a heated discussion. I told the presiding officer that he may as well dismiss the meeting because the whites were here with preconceived notions.[4] Finally we decided to dismiss the meeting. I think Ingalls made the motion. They (Dr. Parker was chairman, presiding officer) were to have called another meeting, but it never was.[5] We had decided that we wouldn't go anyway. The only other meeting we had was with the bus company then to accept our seatings proposal. That was the last time we had any meeting or contact with them at any time."

Interviewer: Suppose the second proposal had been granted, what about your third demand, drivers—would you have gone back to the buses?

Respondent: "If they had accepted this proposal, the City Commissioners said

---

3. This meeting occurred on 17 December 1956. King refers to Luther Ingalls, chair of the Central Alabama Citizens Council; G. Stanley Frazer, pastor of St. James Methodist Church; Kenneth E. Totten, vice president of National City Lines, Inc.; and Jack Crenshaw, an attorney who represented the bus company in Montgomery. Ingalls did not attend the meeting, and King challenged his presence on the mayor's committee at the following meeting on 19 December (see "Committee Fails to Reach Settlement in Bus Boycott" and "Mayor's Committee Stalls in Hunt for Transit Truce," *Montgomery Advertiser*, 18 and 20 December 1955).

4. This meeting occurred on 19 December 1956. On that occasion King objected to Ingalls's involvement in the negotiations. Claiming that some of the white members brought "preconceived ideas" to the discussion, King moved for adjournment. Several whites countered that King held preconceived notions of his own. King later recalled, "For a moment it appeared that I was alone. Nobody came to my rescue, until suddenly Ralph Abernathy was on the floor in my defense. He insisted that I spoke for the whole Negro delegation. . . . As he continued, one could see obvious disappointment on the faces of the white committee members. By trying to convince the Negroes that I was the main obstacle to a solution they had hoped to divide us among ourselves. But Ralph's statement left no doubt" ("Mayor's Committee Stalls in Hunt for Transit Truce," *Montgomery Advertiser*, 20 December 1955; and *Stride Toward Freedom*, p. 120).

5. King refers to Henry Parker, pastor of Montgomery's other First Baptist Church; Ralph Abernathy was pastor of a predominantly black church with the same name.

that they (city) had nothing to do with the third proposal." . . . it would be up to the bus company. Respondent stands up and peers out of the window, saying "I thought somebody was putting something on the porch"

Interviewer: When did you hear about Mrs. P. arrest?

Respondent: "I heard about it on Friday, the next day. I was called . . . " I can give "no names up to Monday (day of first mass meeting) because the City Commissioners said they would indict /the leaders/ on the basis of the anti-boycott law. I don't like to use the word 'boycott', because "boycott gives the connotation that we're placing an economic squeeze on an enterprise. It's more in the lines of non-cooperation. The economic factor is just incidental. The fact that it hurts the company economically is just incidental; this is a movement of passive resistance to a system that has perpetuated for so many years."

Interviewer: To what do you attribute the relative inactivity of the police at the downtown car pools?

Respondent: "There are probably two or three factors: 1) it didn't break down the transportation system." They couldn't "frighten the folk", 2) "the court injunction—maybe." [6]

Interviewer: Have you or has anyone in the Association contacted the Governor?

Respondents: (Hesitates)—"I've talked with the Governor twice . . . he came down once. I promised him I wouldn't say anything" about his part in this. "He promised us protection and said he would talk to the Mayor." He is very "liberal" and "sympathetic with our cause." He wants the reapprotioning bill to go through because it would provide for "more senators and representatives from North Alabama" who are "in accord with his views". [7]

Interviewer: How effective do you think this sort of movement would be in Mississippi?

Respondent: "It wouldn't work! I'm for "peaceful evolution" rather than "damaging revolution." If you've noticed, when a chicken's head is cut off, it struggles most when it's about to die. Somebody told me that a whale puts up its biggest fight after it has been harpooned. It's the same thing with the Southern white man. Maybe its good to shed a little blood. What needs to be done is for a couple of those white men to lose some blood; then the Federal Government will step in. No matter how they feel, they respect the law. Legislation (is an) effective weapon. [8]

---

6. As part of the federal lawsuit filed by Fred Gray and Charles Langford, the NAACP and the MIA asked the federal court to enjoin the city of Montgomery from violating the protesters' civil rights. The injunction was not granted.

7. James Elisha Folsom (1908–1991) was governor of Alabama for two terms, 1947–1951 and 1955–1959. On King's meeting with Folsom, see Cliff Mackay, "Ala. Bus Boycotters Sing 'My Country 'Tis of Thee,'" *Baltimore Afro-American,* 11 February 1956.

8. In *Stride Toward Freedom,* p. 88, King attributed similar statements to a member of his congregation: "It would be to our advantage to 'kill off' eight or ten white people. 'This is the only language these white folks will understand. . . . If we fail to do this they will think we're afraid. We must show them we're not afraid any longer.' Besides, he thought, if a few white persons were killed the federal government would inevitably intervene and this, he was certain, would benefit us."

Came to Montgomery in 1954. Called to the Church on March 1. Came once a month until September 1954 when he came for full time.

Organizations:

President—Montgomery Improvement Association

Vice President—Montgomery Branch of Alabama Council[9]

Executive Board of NAACP

TD. PV-ARC-LNT.

---

9. King was vice president of the Montgomery branch of the Alabama Council for Human Relations.

From Julian O. Grayson

4 February 1956
Washington, D.C.

Crozer classmate Grayson wires King after the bombing, likening him to an Old Testament prophet.[1]

DR M L KING

309 SOUTH JACKSON ST MONTGOMERY ALA

FIGHT ON AMOS GOD IS WITH YOU

J O GRAYSON

PWSr. MLKP-MBU: Box 91.

---

1. Julian O. Grayson (1916–) was born in Alexandria, Virginia. A World War II veteran, he received his B.A. (1947) from Virginia Union and M.Div. (1950) from Crozer Theological Seminary. After serving as a Methodist minister (1952–1957), Grayson was ordained an elder in the Methodist Church. The churches and charges to which he ministered included Carrol Chapel (1955), Chicamuxen (1957–1960), and the Colesville Circuit (1964–1966), all in Maryland.

From Milton Britton

[*5 February 1956*]
Roxbury, Mass.

This letter of support came from a member of Twelfth Baptist Church in Roxbury, where King had occasionally served as a guest preacher while a student in Boston.

Rev. King

How are you and family. We are well.

I am writing because of the recent incident that took place last week to your home. It takes great spiritual courage to brave the trail of equal liberty. I pray that God is with your (and others) every move. With God as your guidon you are bound to succeed.

Since I heard of your crusade, and {others} there in Montgomery, remind me of the great sermon you preached at 12th/. It was taken from the 5th/ chapter of St Matthew, and the 44th/ verse: But I say unto You, Love your enemies, bless them that curse you, do good to them that hate you, and pray for them which despitefully use you, and presecute you; (45) That ye may be the children of your Father which is in Heaven;

May God bless all of you Your efforts of great works will be a blessing to generations to come.

Yours in Christ
[*signed*] Milton Britton

ALS. MLKP-MBU: Box 15.

---

1. King, *Strength to Love* (New York: Harper & Row, 1963), pp. 34–41. "Loving Your Enemies" was King's first sermon as pastor of Dexter Avenue Baptist Church in 1954. Milton Britton (1922–1984), born in Alabama, graduated from West Virginia's Dunbar High School in 1941. A factory worker from the early 1950s to the late 1970s, Britton served as a deacon and Sunday school superintendent for Twelfth Baptist Church for many years.

To Fred Drake

7 February 1956
[*Montgomery, Ala.*]

On 10 January Drake invited King to be the guest speaker at the annual Negro History Week observance in Tuscaloosa.[1] *In this letter to the high school teacher, King cancels his mid-February appearance, citing the "mounting tension" in Alabama. Two bombings had occurred in Montgomery just the week before, while students rioted at the*

---

1. Fred Drake (1914–1987), born in Greensboro, Alabama, earned his B.S. from Alabama State College and his M.Ed. from Wayne State University. An Alabama high school teacher from 1937 to 1976, Drake was active in local Baptist and community service organizations.

Mr. Fred Drake
Druid High School
Tuscaloosa, Alabama

Dear Mr. Drake:

I regret very deeply to say at this late date that I will have to cancel my speaking engagement with you. In the light of recent happenings my closest advisors have insisted that I cancel all speaking engagements in Alabama until the mounting tension dies down. I hope that this will not seriously interfere with your program. Please know that I desire to be with you very much, but my present position of leadership in Montgomery demands that I take all precaution possible. Give all of the people at Tuscaloosa my best regards, and give them the assurance that in our struggle for justice here in Montgomery we do not intend to retreat one inch.

With every good wish, I am

Sincerely yours,
M. L. King, Jr.

MLK:lmt

TLc. DABCC.

---

2. Autherine Lucy (1929–), raised near Shiloh, Alabama, graduated from Miles College in Fairfield, Alabama (1952). After Lucy unsuccessfully applied in 1955 to the University of Alabama in Tuscaloosa for graduate studies, the NAACP appealed her case to the U.S. Supreme Court, which ordered her enrollment. A student-led mob rocked the campus in early February and physically harassed Lucy as she attended classes. The university suspended her—for her safety, it claimed. Although the university was court-ordered to reinstate her, it expelled her on disciplinary grounds for making conspiracy accusations against school officials. The court that had ordered Lucy's reinstatement later upheld the university's action. Lucy ended her fight in April 1956, becoming a part-time English teacher in Shreveport, Louisiana.

From Samuel D. Proctor

11 February 1956
Richmond, Va.

Proctor, who received graduate degrees from Crozer Seminary and Boston University, became president of Virginia Union University in 1955. Proctor had considered appointing King to replace him as dean of the university's school of religion but apparently changed his mind after talking with King's friend and advisor, Morehouse president Benjamin Mays.

Rev. M. L. King, Jr.   16 Feb
193 Boulevard, N.E.   1956
Atlanta, Georgia

Dear Rev. King:

I telephoned your home shortly after the news report. I was sorry to hear what happened, but I am glad that there is a person of your calibre in town who cannot be intimidated and whose character is so unassailable that they have to attack your porch. Your mother expressed some anxiety about this when I talked with her.

After my conversation with Dr. Mays a few weeks ago in Atlanta, I think that I had better fix my hopes somewhere else for a Dean of our Seminary. I'll discuss this with you when I see you in June.[1]

Warmest personal regards to you and the family.

Sincerely yours,
[*signed*] Samuel D. Proctor/m
Samuel D. Proctor,
President

SDP:mem

TLSr. MLKP-MBU: Box 91.

---

1. Proctor was Men's Day speaker at Dexter Avenue Baptist Church in July (see King to Whitaker, 30 April 1956).

From Marcus Garvey Wood

16 February 1956
Baltimore, Md.

Wood, pastor of Baltimore's Providence Baptist Church, affirms the righteousness of the struggle in Montgomery using biblical allusions and calls his Crozer classmate "Lion King."[1] He also compares King to Davy Crockett, the nineteenth-century American pioneer.

Dear Dr. King or Dr. David Croket:

It was one of the happiest moments of my life when I read a few weeks ago of the wonderful work you are doing for your people in the South. I wish I were there to help you. You are becoming as a prophet of this day and age and I hope

---

1. Marcus Garvey Wood (1920–), born in Gloucester, Virginia, earned his B.A. (1948) from Storer College and his B.D. (1951) from Crozer Theological Seminary. He served as pastor of Wainwright

you will see it through. Be like Isaiah of old walk the streets barefooted until the waters of hate roll back to the ocean of eternity. [2] Fight on till the stars shall reach dwon and take in their nimble hands the slivery clouds and wipe the tears from the face of the moon tilling it to weep no more for Lion King is on the march. Fight on and if necessary ask God to stop the sun or close up the heavens and let no rain or dew fall on the soil of Alabama until judgment shall come to town with righteousness in his suitcase. Fight on till the hills of Alabama skip and dance like a fairy just waking from a long winter nap.

The Ministers here in Baltimore and in other communities across the country are with you. You were the topic at our conference last monday. They ask me to write you to let you know they are praying for you and know of the hardship through which you are passing.

I know you are preaching like mad now. You have thrown Crozer aside and you have found the real God and you can tell the world now that he is a God who moves in a mysterious way. That he will be your battle ax in the time of war and preserve you from your enemy. He will send his angles to camp around you and none shall come neigh unto you. Go on son in the name of Jesus you will conquor.

Kind regards to Mrs. King. Together you all are writing history.

Yours truly,
[*signed*]
M. G. Wood

TLS. MLKP-MBU: Box 91.

Baptist Church in Charles Town, West Virginia (1945–1948); Bethlehem Baptist Church in Woodbury, New Jersey (1948–1952); and Providence Baptist Church in Baltimore, Maryland (1952–). Since 1952 he has been a member of the NAACP and the Baptist Ministers Conference of Baltimore and Vicinity.
   2. Isaiah 20:1–3.

From Sankey L. Blanton

17 February 1956
Chester, Pa.

Blanton, president of Crozer Theological Seminary, expresses pride in King's leadership of the bus boycott.

Dr. Martin Luther King
First Baptist Church
Montgomery, Alabama

Dear Dr. King:

I had hoped to come by to see you before this time but a series of mishaps on the road when we started that way, forced us to curtail our visit and return to the campus much earlier than we had intended.

I just wanted you to know that we at Crozer are proud of you and your outstanding leadership in your part of the world.

Bring Mrs. King and the baby and come to see us when you can. We are looking forward with pleasure to having Mr. Carter as our guest at the annual Conference on the Ministry.[1] You may be sure that we will be glad to have anyone in this student body whom you can endorse.

Yours cordially,
[*signed*]
Sankey L. Blanton

SLB/hd

TLS. MLKP-MBU: Box 91.

---

1. King had written a letter of recommendation for Harold Carter, whom he had known for "well-nigh two years," for admission to Crozer (King to Lucille B. Knapp, 21 December 1955).

From George W. Davis

20 February 1956
Chester, Pa.

King hears from his most important mentor at Crozer, a Baptist who taught seven of his courses at the seminary. Davis and his wife, Mildred J. Davis, convey their concern for King and his family following the bombing.

The Rev. Martin L. King, Ph.D.,
309 S. Jackson St.,
Montgomery, Ala.

Dear Martin:

This letter has been in my mind for days, but it is only now getting to penpoint. You and yours have been very close in our hearts and minds since the violence experienced upon your home a few weeks ago. We were dismayed, of course, by this manifestation of ill-will, but rejoiced that no harm came to those you love. We have heard of your stand for a life of equal privilege and opportunity for your people and admire you for your willingness to take such a stand.

Mrs. Davis and I thought you would like to know of our concern for you and yours and also for this cause in which we stand with you. We trust that the strain of these days will soon be but an unhappy memory and that the day of our equality before men as before God may not be far away.

As ever,
[*signed*] George W. Davis

ALS. MLKP-MBU: Box 91.

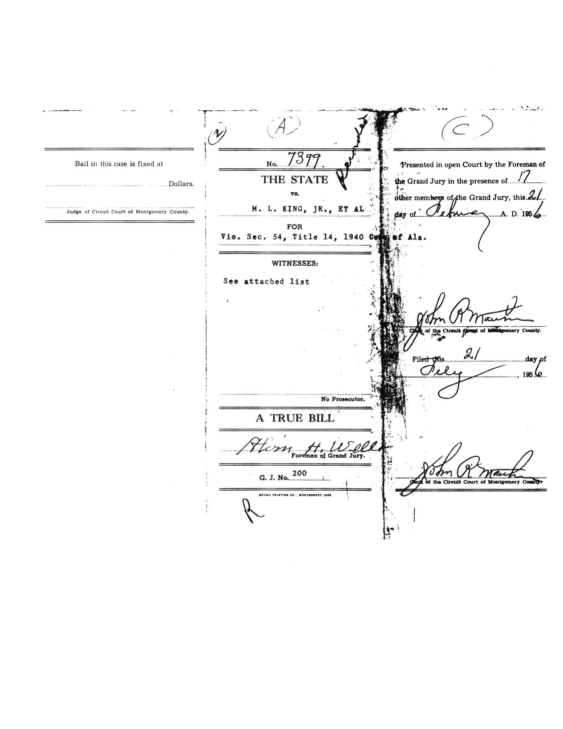

Bail in this case is fixed at

....Dollars.

_____
Judge of Circuit Court of Montgomery County.

(2)   (A)   (C)

No. 7399.

THE STATE

vs.

M. L. KING, JR., ET AL

FOR

Vio. Sec. 54, Title 14, 1940 Code of Ala.

WITNESSES:

See attached list

No Prosecutor.

A TRUE BILL

_____
Foreman of Grand Jury.

G. J. No. 200

BROWN PRINTING CO., MONTGOMERY 1955

R

Presented in open Court by the Foreman of
the Grand Jury in the presence of 17
other members of the Grand Jury, this 21
day of February A. D. 1956

John R Mauter
Clerk of the Circuit Court of Montgomery County.

Filed this 21 day of
July 1956

John R Mauter
Clerk of the Circuit Court of Montgomery County.

While in Nashville for a series of lectures, King received a telephone call from Ralph Abernathy informing him that the Montgomery County grand jury had indicted 115 (later reduced to 89) participants in the bus boycott for violating Alabama's 1921 statute against conspiracies that interfered with lawful business. King canceled several lectures and flew home via Atlanta. On 23 February King, accompanied by his wife and other family members, voluntarily reported to the county courthouse for arrest. He was released on bond after being fingerprinted and photographed.

From Ralph J. Bunche

22 February 1956
Kew Gardens, N.Y.

*This telegram of support is the first known communication to King from the prominent
African-American diplomat and winner of the 1950 Nobel Peace Prize.*[1]

REVEREND M L KING JR
309 SOUTH JACKSON STR MONTGOMERY ALA

I GREET YOU AS A FELLOW AMERICAN AND A FELLOW NEGRO STOP YOU AND OUR FELLOW
NEGRO CITIZENS OF MONTGOMERY ARE DOING HEROIC WORK IN THE VINEYARDS OF
DEMOCRACY STOP YOUR PATIENT DETERMINATION YOUR WISDOM AND QUIET COURAGE ARE
CONSTITUTING AN INSPIRING CHAPTER IN THE HISTORY OF HUMAN DIGNITY STOP YOU HAVE
STEADFASTLY REFUSED TO BARTER AWAY YOUR DIGNITY AND MAY GOD BLESS YOU FOR THAT
STOP YOU ARE GOOD AMERICANS AND YOU ARE ACTING IN THE SPIRIT OF THE FINEST
AMERICAN TRADITION AND IN THE BEST INTERESTS OF OUR COUNTRY YOU MAY BE
CONFIDENT THAT IN THE END JUSTICE AND DECENCY WILL PREVAIL STOP I GREATLY ADMIRE
AND WARMLY CONGRATULATE YOU ALL I KNOW THAT YOU WILL CONTINUE STRONG IN SPIRIT
AND THAT YOU WILL STAND FIRM AND UNITED IN THE FACE OF THREATS AND RESORTS TO
POLICE STATE METHODS OF INTIMIDATION STOP RIGHT IS ON YOUR SIDE AND ALL THE WORLD
KNOWS IT STOP

RALPH J BUNCHE

PHWSr. MLKP-MBU: Box 14.

---

1. Ralph Johnson Bunche (1904–1971), born in Detroit, Michigan, earned his B.A. (1927) from the
University of California, Los Angeles, and his M.A. (1928) and Ph.D. (1934) from Harvard University.
While teaching at Howard University (1929–1950), Bunche assisted Swedish sociologist Gunnar Myrdal
in writing *An American Dilemma* (1944), a study of the United States' black and white race relations.
During World War II Bunche became a War Department analyst of African and Far Eastern affairs;
by 1944 he headed the State Department's Division of Dependent Area Affairs. That same year he
composed the trusteeship sections of the United Nations Charter. In 1947 Bunche joined the UN
Secretariat, where he developed the guidelines under which many territories gained nationhood. In
1950 Bunche became the first African-American Nobel Peace Prize winner after heading a UN peace-
seeking commission that negotiated a 1949 armistice between the new state of Israel and the Arab
nations. Bunche continued to direct UN peace-keeping efforts until just before his death in 1971.

From Roy Wilkins

22 February 1956
Jamaica, N.Y.

*While meeting on 22 February in Atlanta with King, his father, and other black
leaders, attorney A. T. Walden telephoned two NAACP lawyers, Thurgood Marshall*

and Arthur Shores, who promised him that King would have the NAACP's full legal
support.[1] *Wilkins conveys a similar message in this telegram sent the same afternoon.*
In a statement released the next day, Wilkins derided the indictments as the actions of
a "police state," while Marshall promised that "we have agreed to use all of the
resources of the NAACP" in defending the indicted leaders.[2]

24 Feb
1956

REV M L KING

309 SOUTH JACKSON MONTGOMERY ALA

ALL OUR PEOPLE OVER THE NATION AND MILLIONS OF FRIENDS STAND WITH YOU AND YOUR
COURAGEOUS FELLOW CITIZENS AS YOU ANSWER THE INDICTMENT OF THE GRAND JURY. WE
WILL CONTINUE TO OFFER LEGAL ADVICE UPON YOUR REQUEST. PLEASE DO NOT HESITATE
TO CALL UPON US.

ROY WILKINS

PHWSr. MLKP-MBU: Box 67.

---

1. King, *Stride Toward Freedom*, pp. 145–146. Arthur Davis Shores (1904–), a native of Birmingham, received his B.A. (1927) from Talladega College and his LL.B. (1935) from Lasalle Extension University. He joined the NAACP legal staff in 1944 and devoted his legal career to civil rights law in Alabama, including Autherine Lucy's desegregation case against the University of Alabama.

2. NAACP press release, "NAACP Support Pledged to Bus Protest Victims," 23 February. When the bus boycott began, Roy Wilkins noted privately that the NAACP "will not officially enter the [Rosa Parks] case or use its legal staff on any other basis than the abolition of segregated seating on the city buses. . . . We could not enter an Alabama case asking merely for more polite segregation" (Roy Wilkins to W. C. Patton, 27 December 1955).

"Negroes Pledge to Keep Boycott,"
by Wayne Phillips

24 February 1956
New York, N.Y.

At a prayer meeting on 23 February, King reflected on his arrest that day and promised to continue using the weapons of love and protest to effect change. Several thousand people attended the mass meeting at Ralph Abernathy's First Baptist Church, including many reporters. The following quotations from King's speech appeared in a New York Times *article the next day, its first front-page article on the bus boycott.*

Rev. Martin Luther King Jr., head of the Montgomery Improvement Association, which has directed the eighty-day boycott, told the gathering that the protest was not against a single incident but over things that "go deep down into the archives of history."

"We have known humiliation, we have known abusive language, we have been plunged into the abyss of oppression," he told them. "And we decided to rise up only with the weapon of protest. It is one of the greatest glories of America that we have the right of protest." [1]

"There are those who would try to make of this a hate campaign," the Atlanta-born, Boston-educated Baptist minister said. "This is not war between the white and the Negro but a conflict between justice and injustice. This is bigger than the Negro race revolting against the white. We are seeking to improve not the Negro of Montgomery but the whole of Montgomery. [2]

"If we are arrested every day, if we are exploited every day, if we are trampled over every day, don't ever let anyone pull you so low as to hate them. We must use the weapon of love. We must have compassion and understanding for those who hate us. We must realize so many people are taught to hate us that they are not totally reponsible for their hate. But we stand in life at midnight, we are always on the threshold of a new dawn."

PD. *New York Times*, 24 February 1956.

---

1. Another account extends King's remarks ("Boycotters Plan Passive Battle," *Montgomery Advertiser*, 24 February 1956): "[King] told the audience that the bus boycott began because Negroes in Montgomery 'were tired of the conditions they had experienced over a number of years.' 'We are using the weapon of protest. We are using the weapon of love. For ours is a protest for right,' he said. He added that in a democracy a man 'could protest but that behind the Communist Iron Curtain a man could not protest. That is the glory of democracy. We are free men and we can protest.'"

2. Ibid.: "'There is not a tension between the Negro and whites. There is only a conflict between justice and injustice. If our victory is won—and it will be won—it will be a victory for Negroes, a victory for justice, a victory for free people, and a victory for democracy. This is bigger than Negroes revolting against whites. We are not just trying to improve Negro Montgomery but we are trying to improve the whole of Montgomery,' he declared. 'There are some who like to use the word boycott. The word is too small. The word can be interpreted as economic reprisal or economic squeeze. This movement is more than an economic squeeze. It is a moral and spiritual movement. We are using moral and spiritual force. That is all we have. We are using the weapon of love.'"

From Charles R. Lawrence

24 February 1956
Pomona, N.Y.

Prompted by news articles on the bus boycott, Lawrence, national chair of the Fellowship of Reconciliation (FOR) and a Morehouse alumnus, expresses his enthusiasm for King's emphasis on love and nonviolent protest.[1] Lawrence notes

---

1. Charles Radford Lawrence II (1915–1986) was born in Boston and graduated from Morehouse College in 1936. He received his master's degree (1938) from Atlanta University and his Ph.D. (1952) from Columbia University. From 1936 to 1939 he taught in Atlanta public schools. He then served with the YMCA before becoming an instructor and research associate at Fisk University in 1943. In 1948 he joined the faculty at Brooklyn College, City College of New York. He served as national chairman of the Fellowship of Reconciliation from 1955 to 1963.

that while FOR, a Christian-based pacifist organization founded in 1914, was "very
anxious to 'do something,'" it was aware of the problems "outsiders" could create.
"You are doing too good a job," he writes, "to have it unwittingly harmed by even the
best-meaning groups." Nevertheless, Lawrence and others in FOR decided to send
national field secretary Glenn E. Smiley to Montgomery and other southern towns to
"find out what is happening and what the possibilities" are for nonviolence training
workshops.[2] Lawrence indicates that Smiley would be arriving in Montgomery shortly.
Former FOR activist Bayard Rustin, who was dedicated to furthering social justice and
peace issues, had also recently decided to visit Montgomery. A few days before this letter
was written, Lawrence and others in FOR decided not to "compete with or collaborate
with Bayard," but to send Smiley on a fact-finding mission to Montgomery.[3]

Dr. M. L. King, Jr.
Dexter Avenue Baptist Church
Montgomery, Alabama

Dear Doctor King:

The accounts which I have read of the work which you and others are doing in Montgomery have been most gratifying. The TIMES and HERALD TRIBUNE stories of last night's meeting I found among the most thrilling documents that I have ever read. It has been particularly good to read your own statements in which you have urged unwavering militancy in a spirit of love and non-violence. I was so impressed by the excerpts of your last night's speech in this morning's New York TIMES that I read it to my family at dinner this evening.

The solidarity of the Montgomery Negro population, their quiet dignity, and dogged determination have undoubtedly gained the admiration of millions of people throughout the world. During the past three months they have given the lie to those—often including ourselves—who have so often said that, "Negroes won't stick together." And they are blessed with leaders of courage and imagination.

You and other leaders of this movement have been very right in insisting upon the peaceful, non-violent and loving nature of the struggle. You are especially right to point out that this is not a Negro-White conflict but rather a struggle against injustice and for human dignity. Who knows? Providence may have given the Negroes of Montgomery the historic mission of demonstrating to the world

---

2. John M. Swomley, FOR's national secretary, reported this decision in a 21 February 1956 letter to Wilson Riles. See also Swomley's letter of support to King on 24 February 1956. Glenn E. Smiley (1910–1993), born in Loraine, Texas, was educated at McMurry College, Southwestern University, the University of Redlands, and the University of Arizona. He joined FOR in 1942 and two years later was jailed for conscientious objection to World War II. He later worked with King on the Poor People's Campaign of 1968 and helped found the Martin Luther King, Jr., Center for Nonviolence in Los Angeles.

3. Swomley to Wilson Riles, 21 February 1956. Swomley added that "Charles Lawrence feels strongly that it were better if Bayard did not go South, that it would be easy for the police to frame him with his record in L.A. and New York, and set back the whole cause there"—a reference to Rustin's 1954 arrest for homosexual behavior and his past ties to the Young Communist League. For more information on Rustin and Smiley's relationship with King, see Introduction, pp. 17–20 in this volume.

the practical power of Christianity, the unmatched vitality of a non-violent, loving approach to social protest.

I know that the struggle has only begun, that there are many days and maybe years ahead of rough going for those who battle for human dignity in American race relations; but, even if the specific matter of Montgomery's buses should remain unchanged for awhile, you have shown an image of religiously inspired, passive resistence which is bound to be a landmark in American human relations.

I am the National Chairman of the Fellowship of Reconciliation (FOR) whose statement of purpose I enclose. (The statement was printed several years ago, before I became chairman.) I wish very much that you were one of us, for you have talked and acted more like we should like to than many of us could hope to do under similar pressure. Our National Field Secretary, the Reverend Glenn Smiley, will be coming to Montgomery the early part of next week. His mission will be primarily that of finding out what those of you who are involved directly would have those of us who are "on the outside" do. Glenn was born in the South, was ordained in what was then the Southern Methodist Church, and has been on the FOR staff for about fifteen years—a period of which he spent in prison as a conscientious objector. He is a person in whom you can have complete confidence. I hope that you can find time in your busy round of activities to have a good, long talk with him. While our organization is very anxious to "do something", we do not wish to do anything which your group would feel unwise or ill-timed. You are doing too good a job to have it unwittingly harmed by even the best-meaning groups.

The enclosed check from Margaret Lawrence and me is to be used in whatever way will aid the cause, wither through the Montgomery Improvement Association or through whatever legal defense fund is set up. We wish that it could be more; and will certainly contribute to other efforts, such as the one being organized by A. Philip Randolph.[4]

May you continue to have strong local and national support and, above all, God's guidance.

Cordially yours,
[*signed*] Charles R. Lawrence
(Morehouse, '36
Assistant Professor of Sociology-Anthropology, Brooklyn College)

TLS. MLKP-MBU: Box 91.

---

4. Lawrence refers to In Friendship, a New York–based civil rights support group organized by Randolph and Ella Baker.

From Ella J. Baker

24 February 1956
New York, N.Y.

Ella Baker, veteran civil rights organizer and an NAACP branch president in New York City, was the driving force behind In Friendship, a coordinating group created to aid victims of racial terrorism in the South.[1] Baker enlisted support for the new venture from more than twenty-five political, labor, and religious organizations. During its first year In Friendship not only gave funds to beleaguered activists such as Mississippi NAACP leader Amzie Moore but also organized a New York civil rights support rally in May and a December benefit concert for the bus boycott featuring Coretta Scott King, Harry Belafonte, and Duke Ellington. King noted at the top of the telegram that it was "to be answered," but his response has not been located. King was unable to attend In Friendship's 29 February founding conference to which Baker invites him.

REVEREND MARTIN LUTHER KING JR
309 SOUTH JACKSON AVE OR ST MONTGOMERY ALA

A LARGE NUMBER OF ORGANIZATIONS AND DISTINGUISHED INDIVIDUALS ARE ORGANIZING TO PROVIDE ECONOMIC ASSISTENCE TO THOSE SUFFERING ECONOMIC REPRISALS IN THE EFFORTS TO SECURE CIVIL RIGHTS. MR A PHILIP RANDOLPH IS CHAIRMAN AND LEADING CLERGYMAN OF PROTESTANT CATHOLIC AND JEWISH FAITHS ARE SPONSORS. ON WEDNESDAY FEB 29 A CONFERANCE TO LAUNCH THE ORGANIZATION IS TAKING PLACE. WE WOULD BE HONORED IF YOU COULD ATTEND AT OUR EXPENSE SO THAT WE MAY EXPRESS OUR DEEP RESPECT FOR YOU AND YOUR FELLOW WORKERS. PLEASE WIRE COLLECT ELLA J BAKER 452 ST NICHOLAS AVE NEW YORK CITY

ELLA J BAKER

PHWSr. MLKP-MBU: Box 14.

---

1. Ella Josephine Baker (1903–1986) was raised in Littleton, North Carolina. After graduating as valedictorian from Shaw University in 1927, Baker moved to Harlem, where, as national director of the Young Negroes Cooperative League, she helped organize African-American consumer cooperatives during the depression. She joined the staff of the NAACP as a field secretary in 1938 and served as national director of branches from 1943 to 1946. As NAACP branch president from 1954 to 1958, Baker advocated a decentralized leadership structure. She emphasized job training for African-American workers and led campaigns for school desegregation. Baker would later move to Atlanta at King's request to set up SCLC's headquarters.

From Archibald James Carey, Jr.

24 February 1956

Three weeks after the boycott began, King had written Carey, pastor of Quinn Chapel AME Church, and other Chicago leaders asking them to lobby the Chicago-based National City Lines. By mid-February, after receiving few responses from Chicago,

King expressed disappointment that the MIA "requested support from some of our
Chicago leaders and did not [receive] an answer or support."[1] A day after King's
arrest, Carey asks how he and others in the North can assist the bus boycott.

Reverend M. L. King, Jr.
309 Jackson
Montgomery, Alabama

Dear Brother King:

I have watched with intense interest and admiration the performance of Ne-
gro-Americans in the Montgomery bus strike. I certainly want to salute your own
magnificent leadership in it. Be comforted by knowing that there are tens of
thousands who are giving you their support and their prayers. May God bless and
keep you through these trying hours.

Now, I would like to know what we, particularly in the North, can do to help. I
have thought of taking a collection at Quinn Chapel and perhaps stimulating
some others around here to raise money. On the other hand, I do not wish to do
anything that would in any way jeopardize or upset your own program. I know
the damage that could be done to your cause by any proof that your effort was
either being financed by northern money or directed by outside influence. That
is why I am consulting you first.

If you will kindly indicate to me that it's all right, I will take such an offering
and I will send it directly to you for you to use in any way you, personally, see fit.
I saw your father in Atlanta (I think it was) a few weeks ago but it was before all
of this business had developed. Again, God bless you and let me know what either
I or others that I may contact may do to help you.

Kind regards to your wife and little one.

Very sincerely,

AJC:gt

TLc. AJC-ICHi: Box 27.

---

1. Quoted in Frances Jett, Proceedings of the Montgomery, Alabama Bus Boycott Conference,
13 February 1956. See also King to Carey, 27 December 1955, pp. 93–95 in this volume.

From William D. Jones

24 February 1956
Birmingham, Ala.

Jones, a student at Miles College in Birmingham, sends a telegram to King
announcing his participation in Montgomery's Prayer and Pilgrimage Day. The MIA
designated 24 February as a day for car owners and carpoolers to walk to work in
solidarity with those protesters who walked every day.

I LIVE IN BIRMINGHAM BUT I AM GOING TO WALK THE 20 MILES ROUND TRIP FROM MY HOME
TO SCHOOL WITH THE PEOPLE OF MONTGOMERY. CONTINUE THE FIGHT. DON'T GIVE UP
BECAUSE WE ARE WITH YOU

WILLIAM D JONES

PWSr. MLKP-MBU: Box 60A.

From Wade H. McKinney

24 February 1956
Cleveland, Ohio

*McKinney, a family friend and pastor of Antioch Baptist Church, offers financial
support to the bus boycotters and invites King to preach the Youth Day service at his
church.[1] On 29 February King thanked McKinney for the financial contribution but
declined the invitation because of scheduling conflicts.*

Rev. M. L. King Jr.
309 S. Jackson Street
Montgomery, Ala.

Dear Rev. King:

I am sending you this letter for two main reasons. First, to extend to you and
the other ministers of Montgomery my sincere congratulations for the Christ-like
manner {with} which you are conducting the protest against the social injustices
of your city. Further, I have seen you at least three times on television and was
deeply moved by your courage, composure, and profound analyses about the
significance of the fight in which you are engaged.

Among the many things of which I am sure are these:

1. Prayer changes things.

2. Money talks.

You have my prayers, but how can we get some money to you without violating
the laws of your state? Should it come directly to you or should we send it to the
Yew York office of the NAACP? Kindly let me know by return mail.[2]

---

1. Wade Hampton McKinney (1892–1963), born in White County, Georgia, graduated from Morehouse College (1920) and Colgate-Rochester Theological Seminary (1923). In 1923 he became pastor
of Mount Olive Baptist Church in Flint, Michigan, though he left after five years to become pastor of
Antioch Baptist Church in Cleveland, Ohio, where he served until his death. He also served as president of the Cleveland Baptist Association and the Cuyahoga Interdenominational Ministerial
Alliance.

2. On 26 February 1956 McKinney wired King with the news that his church had raised "more than
$631 for your [cause]" and asked once again for instructions.

The second reason for this letter is this, I would like to have you for our Annual Youth Day speaker on June 17, 1956. My twin daughters, Ruth and May, have been urging me for several weeks to extend to you this invitation.[3] For years we have had some of the most outstanding men of the nation, such as Dr. Samuel D. Proctor, President of Virginia Union University and others. I sincerely hope you will see your way clear to accept our invitation.

I wish to assure you that the honorarium will be worthwhile, all expenses ambly taken care of, plus a generous donation to be used as you see fit.

Your father and I have been friends over the years, and your mother and my wife were at Spelman together. I believe also, that you and my son Samuel, who is now pastoring in Providence, Rhode Island, were in Morehouse College at the same time.[4] Kindly let me hear from you by return mail.

Yours in Christ,
[*signed*]
W. H. McKinney, Pastor

WHM/lr

TLS. MLKP-MBU: Box 116.

---

3. Virginia Ruth McKinney (Henderson), a graduate of Spelman College, studied for her M.A. at Boston University during the same time King was completing his doctoral work. She and Mary McKinney (Edmonds), also a Spelman graduate, had been impressed by the sermons they heard when King served as an occasional guest preacher at Morehouse Chapel between 1949 and 1953.

4. Samuel Berry McKinney (1926–), born in Flint, Michigan, earned his B.A. (1949) at Morehouse College and his B.D. from Colgate-Rochester Divinity School. As pastor of Olney Street Baptist Church in Providence, Rhode Island, McKinney invited King to address a mass rally on 27 May 1956. King declined owing to a previous commitment. In 1958 McKinney became pastor of Seattle's Mount Zion Baptist Church, where he still serves. See McKinney to King, 9 April 1956 and 25 April 1956; and King to McKinney, 28 April 1956.

From Peter A. Bertocci

24 February 1956
Boston, Mass.

Bertocci, Borden Parker Bowne Professor of Philosophy at Boston University, commends his former student's "fight for greater justice."

Dear Martin,

Paul Deats has been telling me about the kind of witness you have been giving to your conviction[1]—of which I have been reading also in the newspapers. I was

---

1. Paul Deats, Jr. (1918–), was an assistant professor of social ethics and religious higher education at Boston University, having just received his Ph.D. at the university in 1954.

so glad to see that someone was speaking to destroy bitterness at the very moment when it can be allowed to swell beyond any possible good purpose. I have just returned from a student conference in Mississippi and am distressed by the way in which the attempt to do good can destroy good and discourage steps toward improvement. Because I realize more than ever how difficult it is for the Christian to witness most effectively, I want to tell you how humble I feel about even writing this note—which is simply to say that I pray that you may continue to know the best way to take in your situation as you try to guide in the fight for greater justice.

Cordially,
[*signed*] Peter A. Bertocci

ALS. DABCC.

From Kelly Miller Smith

25 February 1956
Nashville, Tenn.

Smith, pastor of Nashville's First Baptist Church, praises King's leadership and encloses a biographical sketch for his appearance as Youth Day speaker at Dexter on 11 March.

Dr. M. L. King
454 Dexter Avenue
Montgomery, Alabama

Dear "Mike,"

Although I can't for the life of me see how you will have time to do anything with it, here is the "immodest" sketch you requested.

Your contribution to our fare in America is rare. Not as an NAACP executive but as a Gospel minister you are doing these things. The mantle of the prophets rests well upon your shoulders.

We are trying to have an affair at our NAACP Branch meeting Tuesday night to help out the cause there in Montgomery. You will be hearing from us soon.

We bid you God's speed.

Yours sincerely,
[*signed*]
Kelly Miller Smith

KMS:meb

TLS. MLKP-MBU: Box 119.

Notes on MIA Mass Meeting at Holt Street
Baptist Church, by Donald T. Ferron

27 February 1956
Montgomery, Ala.

King and other MIA leaders sought to maintain morale at a prayer service and mass meeting at Holt Street Baptist Church. The capacious sanctuary was filled by 5 P.M. for the prayer service; informal singing continued until King and the other ministers began the program two hours later. In Ferron's notes that are not printed here, Rufus Lewis, head of the transportation committee, expressed concern about the effect of the mass arrests on the car pool and called for more cars, drivers, and dispatchers. Ralph Abernathy then reminded the audience that by arresting the leaders, the grand jury wouldn't stop the movement: "This is your movement," he said, "you are the leaders." Abernathy clarified King's role as president: "There are too many people to talk at once. We tell Rev. King what to say and he says what we want him to say." According to another account of the same meeting, another clergyman identified King as the preeminent spokesperson for the MIA: "He is our elected leader, no other individual is authorized to speak for us, unless specifically designated by him (King) to do so."[1] In the following portion of Ferron's notes, King observes that the Montgomery struggle has become an "international" one, but "wherever there's progress, there is the pulling back force of retrogression."

Rev. M. L. King — "Presiding officer, platform associates and friends," Good Evening! We have "new zeal, new stamina to carry on. When we saw this protest many, many weeks, ago, we thought it would last but a short time." It has "reached out beyond Montgomery", it has become an "international problem". "We have the prayer and support of men an women all over the nation. They're saying one thing—'You've gone too far; you can't turn back now'.[2] Altho confronted with splinters, we're going to keep going. Wherever there's progress, there is the pulling back force of retrogression; where there's burden there is pain. Therefore, we're using Christian "principles". Out of progress may come "damaging revolution" as set forth by "Karl Marx and communism", or "passive resistence with love as ammunition and a breast plate of rightousness". Negroes have suffered "economic reprisal", have been "segregated", and have suffered "humility", Rev. King concluded, but if in spite of these obstacles we continue to carry on with a policy of non-violence, a "voice from high heaven will say, 'well done'." This is the way we'll carry on. God bless you." [. . .]

---

1. J. Harold Jones, Notes, MIA Mass Meeting at Holt Street Baptist Church, 27 February 1956.

2. According to Jones's account of the mass meeting, King mentioned that "eight or ten hours would be required to read the telegrams and letters" of support. He added: "The method has not changed, it is the same as at the beginning. Whenever there is a surge toward the new, there is a resurge toward the old. The method comes from Judeo-Christian principles as opposed to Karl Marx's damaging revolutionary methods. Ours is a spiritual movement. We are protesting segregation with passive resistance."

1. Keep your "sense of dignity"

2. Vote to stop protest—Rev. Bennett was exercising his "democratic right" to vote the way he did. We should "admire him for his courage". He is as much with us as he was in the beginning.[3]

3. Continue your policy of "non-violence"

4. Mrs. Reese withdrew her name as a plaintiff. Stop bothering her with "phone call threats." [4]

AD. PV-ARC-LNT.

---

3. On 20 February 1956, amid growing rumors that boycott leaders were about to be indicted, MIA members overwhelmingly voted down a compromise seating proposal mediated by the Men of Montgomery, a white business group. Rev. L. Roy Bennett and his assistant pastor were the only dissenting votes out of four thousand. The compromise would have preserved segregated sections in the front and rear of city buses while eliminating several humiliating practices and granting amnesty to protesters (see Ralph Abernathy, Memo to the Men of Montgomery, 20 February 1956; and Men of Montgomery, Outline of Suggestions to End Montgomery Bus Boycott, 13 February 1956).

4. Fearing the personal consequences, Jeanatta Reese had withdrawn as a plaintiff in the *Browder v. Gayle* federal lawsuit.

To William H. Gray, Jr.

28 February 1956
[*Montgomery, Ala.*]

On 16 February Gray, a prominent religious leader and family friend, inquired about preaching at Dexter on 11 March if King thought "that a northern Yankee like me could have a message for your courageous people in Montgomery." Because Kelly Miller Smith was already scheduled to preach that day, King arranges for Gray to preach at Ralph Abernathy's church. On 27 February Gray appealed to fellow members of the Baptist Ministers Conference of Philadelphia to support the boycott, securing contributions of over $1,500 for the MIA.[1]

Dr. William H. Gray, Pastor
Bright Hope Baptist Church
Twelfth and Oxford Street
Philadelphia 2, Pennsylvania

Dear Dr. Gray:

I have made arrangements for you to preach at the First Baptist Church on Sunday morning, March 11. As you know, the church is pastored by the Rev. Ralph

---

1. See Gray to King, 29 February 1956.

D. Abernathy. I am sure that Montgomery will be expecting you with great anticipation. Please let me know when you will be arriving.

With every good wish, I am

Sincerely yours,
M. L. King, Jr.

MLK:lmt

TLc. DABCC.

From George D. Kelsey

[*28 February 1956*]

*Kelsey, professor of religion at Drew University in Madison, New Jersey, had taught
King at Morehouse College in an undergraduate course on the Bible, focusing on the
ethical teachings of Jesus. King replied on 8 March.*[1]

Dr. M. L. King
Dexter Avenue Baptist Church
Montgomery, Alabama.

Dear M. L.,

Congratulations on the great leadership which you are providing our deprived
people in Montgomery

You are taking your stand and conducting activities in the finest Mosaic and
prophetic tradition. You are quite correct when you say the struggle in Montgomery is for justice, humanity decency, and democracy.

Many of us are proud of the high plane on which you are waging the fight, and
are deeply moved by the effectiveness with which you keep love as the regulating
ideal in a situation which calls for resistance as the chief instrument.

I have always been proud of you as one of my students and as a friend. You
surely can imagine my present feelings.

Please find enclosed a small check to assist in the car pool.

Our prayers are continuously with you.

AHLd. GDKP.

---

1. See pp. 164–165 in this volume.

From William Jones

28 February 1956
San Francisco, Calif.

In a manner typical of the support the boycott movement received from labor union members, the International Longshoremen's and Warehousemen's Union donated about $1,500 to the MIA during the first six months of the boycott.

REV MARTIN L KING

DEXTER AVENUE BAPTIST CHURCH

MONTGOMERY ALA

NEGRO AND WHITE WAREHOUSEMEN IN SAN FRANCISCO BACK YOU IN COURAGEOUS FIGHT
FOR DEMOCRACY IN SOUTH. KEEP SPIRITS UP AND STAY UNITED

WM JONES JR. STEWARD INTL LONGSHOREMEN'S AND WAREHOUSEMENS UNION

PHWSr. DABCC.

From Alice Neal

29 February 1956
Oakland, Calif.

Hundreds of telegrams and letters arrived in King's office from grass-roots groups around the country, including this one from an interracial club in Oakland. Neal refers to the National Deliverance Day of Prayer planned for 28 March and initiated by Congressman Adam Clayton Powell, Jr., pastor of Harlem's Abyssinian Baptist Church. Powell denied press claims that he had called for a work stoppage to support the Montgomery boycott; instead, as Neal suggests, many participants supported the cause by donating an hour's pay.[1] King noted on the bottom of the telegram that "we deeply appreciate your concern for our situation here in Montgomery," but his actual reply has not been located.

---

1. Adam Clayton Powell, Jr. (1908–1972), born in New Haven, Connecticut, and raised in New York City, received his B.A. (1930) from Colgate University and his M.A. (1932) from Columbia University. While serving as pastor of Abyssinian Baptist Church (1937–1972) Powell was elected to the New York City Council in 1941, remaining a member of that body until his election to Congress in 1944. He represented Harlem in the House of Representatives until 1970. On 28 March Powell addressed more than five thousand persons attending a National Deliverance Day observance in New York to display support for the Montgomery boycott and to mark the anniversary of congressional approval of the Fifteenth Amendment. National Deliverance Day was officially endorsed by the Massachusetts legislature and California's governor (see NAACP press release, Powell Prayer Plan Supported by NAACP, 1 March 1956).

WESTERN UNION
TELEGRAM
W. P. MARSHALL, PRESIDENT

1201

The filing time shown in the date line on domestic telegrams is STANDARD TIME at point of origin. Time of receipt is STANDARD TIME at point of destination

NSA293 OA169   (26)

O FKA035 NLPD=FK SAN FRANCISCO CALIF 28= FEB 28 PM 2 39

REV MARTIN L KING =

    DEXTER AVE BAPTIST CHURCH MONTGOMERY ALA=

NEGRO AND WHITE WAREHOUSEMEN IN SAN FRANCISCO BACK
YOU IN COURAGEOUS FIGHT FOR DEMOCRACY IN SOUTH.
KEEP SPIRITS UP AND STAY UNITED=

    WM JONES JR STEWARD INTL LONGSHOREMEN'S AND

    WAREHOUSEMENS UNION

WE'RE MEETING TONIGHT BOTH WHITE AND COLORED IN OUR CLUB TO MAP A PLAN TO
RAISE ONE MILLION DOLLARS TO GIVE YOU PEOPLE FREE BUS SERVICE. BUT FIRST WE WOULD
LIKE TO KNOW IF YOU WANT US TO HELP. INSTEAD OF STOPPING WORK ONE HOUR AS
PRESIDENT POWELL SAID WE WILL GIVE UP ONE HOURS PAY AND MAKE UP THE MONEY. THIS
IS BETTER THAN STOPPING WORK. WE WILL STILL PRAY AND THIS MONEY WILL HELP MORE.
DONT FIGHT OR CAUSE ANYBODY HARM BUT HOLD OUT AND PRAY. OUR PRAYERS ARE WITH
YOU. WAITING ON AN ANSWER FROM PRESIDENT POWELL AND YOU. WE WILL START OUR
WORK AS SOON AS AS WE GET AN ANSWER

ALICE NEAL

PHWSr. MLKP-MBU: Box 91.

From Jesse Jai McNeil

29 February 1956
Detroit, Mich.

*McNeil, pastor of Detroit's Tabernacle Baptist Church, arranged for members of
the Baptist Ministers Conference of Detroit and Vicinity to solicit support for the
Montgomery protesters during the first three weeks of March. Writing to his friend,
McNeil reports that a delegation of ministers would present their contribution to the
MIA during King's trial. On 22 March, the day King was convicted for leading the
bus boycott, McNeil and the delegation turned over $4,554 to the MIA and promised
further contributions. At a mass meeting that evening McNeil declared that he had
"never seen such emancipated people as the Negroes of Montgomery."[1] King wrote
"answered" on McNeil's letter, but his reply has not been located.*

The Reverend Dr. M. L. King, Jr.
Minister, Dexter Avenue Baptist Church
309 South Jackson Street
Montgomery, Alabama

Dear M. L.:

Please find herewith for your information a copy of recommendations unanimously approved by our Baptist Ministers Conference.[2]

Our delegation plans to arrive in Montgomery the evening of 21 March and to
depart late the evening of 22 March, if such schedules are possible. I hope you
can procure reservations for us at the hotel you suggested.

---

1. Anna Holden, Notes, MIA Mass Meeting at Holt Street Baptist Church, 22 March 1956.
2. The conference asked local ministers not only to collect funds for the MIA but also to "write to
their white minister friends and other white friends in Alabama urging them to give support to our
Montgomery brethren in their present struggle" ("Recommendations Approved by the Baptist Ministers Conference of Detroit and Vicinity," 28 February 1956).

The Ministers Conference has appointed a delegation to bring our contribution to your Improvement Association. Many men have expressed their intentions of being there for the trial. But we have all agreed that we shall be as inconspicuous and as silent as possible. And any word that is to be said will be left to the head of our delegation. We have even suggested to our men to use the train instead of their automobiles for obvious reasons.

If you have any words of instruction for me and our men who will be coming to Montgomery I shall be pleased to receive them and to abide by them.

With warm personal regards, I am

Sincerely yours,
[*signed*]
Jesse Jai McNeil, Minister

P.S.: Arthur Johnson is arranging for me to meet Abernathy after the rally Friday night since other committments will preclude my being present at the meeting.[3]

JJM/alj
Enclosure: 1

THLS. MLKP-MBU: Box 91.

---

3. On 2 March 1956 Abernathy spoke for the MIA at a Detroit mass meeting in St. John's CME Church.

Notes on MIA Mass Meeting at Hutchinson Street Baptist Church, by Donald T. Ferron

1 March 1956
Montgomery, Ala.

After hours of prayer and song by early arrivals, the mass meeting began at 7:00 P.M. when King and Abernathy entered the church as the crowd sang "When the Saints Go Marching In." Members of the executive board led prayers and hymns, and then King introduced out-of-town visitors, including his father. Following the pattern of previous meetings, the visitors presented large donations to the MIA and made a few remarks. Transportation coordinator R. J. Glasco asked bus boycotters traveling short distances to walk because of a shortage of cars and drivers. King's remarks appear below.

Prayer—Rev. B. D. Lambert[1]—It was during the prayer that two, interesting developments took place. Rev. Lambert impresses me as one who resorts to emotionalism to capture his congregation. This was evinced by his mannerisms, his shouting presentation which ~~latter~~ later flowed into a type of "singing prayer."

---

1. Lambert was pastor of Maggie Street Baptist Church, a local religious radio personality, and was among the indicted boycott participants.

It was at this point that the audience began to complain (but not so loudly) by making such comments as "oh! oh!", "oh, my!", "Not again!", and "Why doesn't he shut up?" The second development was what appeared to me to be a state of discomfort, uneasiness, restlessness on the part of Rev. King. I was in the balcony facing Rev. King and observed him crossing and uncrossing his legs, placing first one and then the other hand over his face. Unless I'm greatly mistaken, {he} mustered all of his resources to prevent his ~~laug~~ smiles from leading to open laughter. It was comical to me to see him "fighting" with himself and to note his definite relief once the prayer had ended.

Hymn—"What A Friend We Have in Jesus"

Rev. King—We have among us tonight a number of "distinguished Guests." [2] "I must decrease that they might increase. God is using Montgomery as a proving ground." He will "cause democratic conditions to stand where they should stand." We have now "new dignity" and "awareness." "We are God's children." "We're walking because we're tired of" being suppressed "politically." "We're walking because we're tired of" being suppressed "economically;" "we're walking because we're tired of being segregated and discriminated. Freedom is the just claim of all men. As we walk we're going to walk with love in our hearts. Somebody has to have sense enough to cut off the hate." The "power of love" is very strong; "love your enimies." The "whole armour of God" is the "weapon of love" and the "breastplate of righteousness." There is "something about love that transforms; we're going to keep on in the same spirit."

AD. PV-ARC-LNT.

---

2. The guests included Owen D. Pelt, pastor of Shiloh Baptist Church in Chicago, where King had delivered a sermon on 12 February 1956; A. Saunders, representing the United Auto Workers in Chicago; Thomas Kilgore, pastor of Friendship Baptist Church in New York; a representative of Cleveland ministers; Sandy F. Ray, pastor of Cornerstone Baptist Church in Brooklyn; Glenn E. Smiley, national field secretary for the Fellowship of Reconciliation; and King, Sr. More than $12,000 was collected by the end of the meeting. One observer noted that "a high point in the meeting" was King, Sr.'s, presentation. "I am no outsider," King, Sr., reportedly said; "I have vested interest here . . . and if things get too hot I shall move in" (J. Harold Jones, Notes, MIA Mass Meeting at Hutchinson Street Baptist Church, 1 March 1956). Except for three reporters, Smiley was the only white person in attendance. He wrote in a letter to his wife that evening, "When I made my first point the house almost came apart. . . . You see, there are so few if any white ministers who will come out and speak at all" (Smiley to Helen Smiley, 1 March 1956).

To Roy Wilkins

3 March 1956
[*Montgomery, Ala.*]

King explains the MIA's legal needs and asks Wilkins to clarify what financial assistance the MIA will receive from the NAACP. He is particularly concerned that the MIA receive funds raised by the NAACP "in the name of our movement."

Mr. Roy Wilkins
Executive Secretary
N.A.A.C.P.
20 West 40th Street
New York 18, New York

Dear Mr. Wilkins:

After consulting with Attorney Shores and his associates, our association decided to have Attorney Shores represent us in the pending case in which some 90 persons have been indicted on a so-called anti-boycott law. The fees involved are $100 per person. I am sure that Attorney Shores will contact you concerning the details.

Before we can make final arrangements with these attorneys, however, we will need to know how much financial assistance will be given by the National Office of the N.A.A.C.P.

It is our understanding that the National Office will lend us financial assistance. One of the problems which we are confronting in raising funds is that so many people are giving through mass meetings sponsored by the N.A.A.C.P. with the impression that the total legal expense is being defrayed by the National Office. Since this money is being raised in the name of our movement, we are hoping that the bulk of it will come to support us in our legal struggle. With the coming of this court case our expenses have risen to astronomical proportions. Our car pool is still in operation which along with a well-staffed office will run at least $3,000 per week. And of course there is the present court case which will run approximately $10,000. And there is also the case in the federal courts which will be of tremendous expense. With all of these expenses it is vitally important that we have the support of persons and organizations over the nation.

We will appreciate all of the support that you can possibly give and we are more than grateful to the National Office for the cooperation and encouragement that it has already given to our movement.

With every good wish, I am

Cordially Yours,
M. L. King, Jr.,
President

MLK/ehr

TLc. MLKP-MBU: Box 64.

To Archibald James Carey, Jr.

3 March 1956
Montgomery, Ala.

Responding to Carey's 24 February inquiry, King notes that the MIA's "most pressing need is for additional finances." On 5 March Carey reported that Bishop George W.

*Baber had requested donations from Michigan AME churches, but advised, "I do not
know where he plans to send [the donations]." Carey indicated that he would use his
influence to have funds sent where King wished, "and I will treat your opinion as a
confidential communication, if you so indicate." With help from the NAACP's Chicago
branch Carey organized an April prayer meeting at the Chicago Coliseum featuring
Ralph Abernathy and Roy Wilkins that generated $2,500 for the MIA.*[1]

Mr. Archibald J. Carey, Jr.
188 West Randolph Street
Chicago, Illinois

Dear Mr. Carey:

Thanks for your very kind letter of February 24, making inquiry concerning
what our needs are at this particular time. Our most pressing need is for additional finances. Our car pool is still in operation, plus the need for a well staffed
office. At present we are in the process of revamping our transportation system.
With this new system our transportation will run approximately $3,000.00 a week.
Along with these responsibilities, we confront a court case, in which some 100
persons have been indicted for giving assistance in the present non-violent protest against injustice. In order to fight this in the courts, we will need unlimited
funds. Whatever you can do to assist us at this point will be highly appreciated.

May I close by saying we are always in need of your prayers.

Cordially yours,
[*signed*]
M. L. King, Jr.,
President.

MLK/ds

TLS. AJC-ICHi: Box 27.

---

1. See Carey to King, 10 April 1956; and Abernathy to Carey, 17 April 1956.

From S. Paul Schilling

4 March 1956
Boston, Mass.

*Schilling, professor of systematic theology at Boston University and second reader of
King's doctoral dissertation, responds to news accounts of the bus boycott movement.
"I thank God for what you are doing," he writes, "and the emphasis you are laying on
Christian love."*

Dear Martin Luther,

Ever since first learning of your courageous leadership in the cause of justice in Montgomery I have been wanting to write. Only the annual pressure—greater this year because of the absence of Dr. DeWolf on sabbatical leave in Southern Rhodesia—of reading and evaluating dissertations has prevented my writing earlier.[1] (I have seven dissertations to evaluate, and from your experience with one you will know that that can't be done in five minutes!)

It is hard for some of us to realize how tense the situation is becoming in some areas. Yet the sheer complexity and tenseness of it makes me all the more grateful for the quality of the contribution you are rendering. The AP dispatches have quoted you on several occasions, and every time I read such statements I thank God for what you are doing and the emphasis you are laying on Christian love, extending even to those who are opposing you with such an absence of love.

Please know that multitudes of us here are with you heart and soul in your struggle. We deeply regret that the things which you must do as a conscientious Christian and minister are bringing so much suffering upon you, yet know that you are finding spiritual resources which are more than equal to your need. You don't need me to tell you that in enduring arrest in a cause like yours you are joining the ranks of some of the greatest persons of all time. That number which appears so boldly across your chest in the picture in LIFE is a badge of honor.[2]

May God strengthen and sustain you in your efforts for both fair treatment and equal, unsegregated opportunity and the maintenance of order and sanity on both sides in the midst of the struggle. Sooner or later, victory is sure.

You are much in my thoughts and prayers in these trying days. Are there further concrete ways in which friends here can help?

Most cordially,
[*signed*] S. Paul Schilling

TLS. MLKP-MBU: Box 91.

---

1. L. Harold DeWolf was King's advisor at Boston University and first reader of his dissertation.
2. "A Bold Boycott Goes On," *Life*, 5 March 1956, pp. 40–43; see photograph following p. 33 in this volume.

From J. H. Jackson

5 March 1956
Chicago, Ill.

Jackson had served as president of the National Baptist Convention since 1953 and pastor of Chicago's Olivet Baptist Church for twenty-five years. On 23 February, immediately after the indictments, Jackson telegraphed his support for King and the movement: "We are deeply moved over recent developments there . . . and pledge *ourselves to you and your cause." He encloses with this letter two checks for $1,000, one from the National Baptist Convention and another from his church. According to King, Sr., Jackson had contacted King, Jr., in January, offering to purchase a bus for the car pool. "At that time," King, Sr., reported to a friend, "M. L. thought it not wise." Jackson reportedly "kept in constant contact with M. L." since then.[1] King replied to Jackson on 7 March.[2]*

Montgomery Improvement Association
Dexter Avenue Baptist Church
Rev. M. L. King, Jr.
309 S. Jackson Street
Montgomery, Alabama

My dear Co-Workers In The Struggle of
Human Freedom:

I salute your heroic deeds, and the Christian spirit in which they have been performed. My interest in your cause is depened every time I hear by radio, television or press, the sacrifices you are making, and the determination with which you face the difficulties of the hour.

As president of our National Baptist Convention, I have sent the message both by telephone and by telegram, to every state in the union, asking that your cause will be supported. You will find enclosed two checks; one from the treasury of the National Baptist Convention, Inc., for one thousand dollars ($1,000); and the other, from the Olivet Baptist Church of which I am minister, for one thousand dollars ($1,000). And, I hope others have sent their funds directly to you as we have requested. For this and any other effort that I might put forth, I seek and deserve no credit; for I am one among thousands who believe that all men are the children of God, and deserve to live within the framework of justice, self-respect and goodwill.

And now, may our floating flag wave over you, and the Federal Constitution sustain you, and the laws of justice and fair play protect you; and may the God of heaven smile upon you, breaking every chain, removing every barrier, and giving unto you the life of comfort and of solace, in the darkest hour of your heroic struggles.

Sincerely yours,
[*signed*]
J. H. Jackson, President
National Baptist Convention, Inc.

JHJ:nb
Enc. 2

THLS. MLKP-MBU: Box 91.

---

1. King, Sr., to J. Timothy Boddie, 3 March 1956.
2. See pp. 162–163 in this volume.

From Leonard G. Carr

5 March 1956
Philadelphia, Pa.

*Carr, treasurer of the National Baptist Convention, compliments King for his
leadership in the bus boycott but warns him against associating with "subversive"
organizations. He also invites King back to Philadelphia's Vine Memorial Baptist
Church, where King had preached in April 1954. King wrote "answered" on Carr's
letter, but the reply has not been located. King did not speak at the church during 1956.*

Rev. M. L. King Jr.
309 South Jackson Street
Montgomery, Alamaba

Dear Rev. King:

This letter comes to congratulate you for the stand you have taken in sphere
of leadership in the Montgomery Bus Boycott. I want you to know that millions
are standing at your back because of the thing that you are doing in fighting for
the rights of all of us.

I am this day, turning over $151.00 to the Baptist Ministers Conference in Phil-
adelphia that will be forwarded to you sometimes this week.

Your stand has been so perfect that I trust that there will be nothing done to
mar it. So whenever you are invited to speak for civic movements, be sure that
they are not on the subversive list. It was called to my attention that the Rev.
Ralph D. Abernathy is to speak for the Civil Rights Congress in these parts.[1] If I
recall correctly, they have been placed on the subversive list. You can check at the
Montgomery Courthouse and see if that checks. If so, then I would counsel with
him to withdraw because it might bring bad repercussion.

As my pulpit has been opened to you before, it is now. I would like for you to
come and be my guest speaker on the 4th Sunday in April or any Sunday that it
is convenient. With best wishes, I remain,

Sincerely yours,
[*signed*]
Leonard G. Carr

LGC:bb

THLS. MLKP-MBU: Box 91.

---

1. The Civil Rights Congress (CRC), founded in 1946 and headed by William L. Patterson, used
legal strategies and mass protest to combat racism and defend leftists from prosecution. In 1953 the
CRC was the first of twelve organizations to be cited as a communist front by Attorney General Herbert
Brownell, Jr. The Subversive Activities Control Board ordered the CRC in December 1955 to register
with the attorney general and submit information about its membership, finances, and activities.

5 March 1956
Marshall, Texas

*Guy, an English teacher at Wiley College, visited the King family often while attending
Spelman College.*[1]

Dear M. L.,

Just a few lines to let you know that I am among the millions of well-wishers
who watch with pride and interest the up-heaval in Montgomery and pray earnestly for your personal safety and for the cause you champion. One can't pick
up a national magazine or paper, nor listen to a news report or watch a telecast
without your name being mentioned.[2]

I would have written much sooner, but didn't have your address nor the name
of the church you pastor. Then it occurred to me that you would get mail addressed simply: M. L. King, U.S.A. (SMILE)

Remember how I used to tease you about playing the girls so cool? Never did I
dream that God could use that particular talent of yours. You certainly got plenty
practice.

Seriously though, that calmness & coolness of yours, that ability to control your
emotions effectively has kept the whole boycott from breaking into violence.

I saw the picture of you & your family that appeared in Jet a couple of weeks
ago.[3] You must have a very brave little wife. Frankly, I believe I would have taken
suitcase in hand and baby in arms and made a 100 yard dash for the hills long
ago.

We have a little girl now—she's almost fourteen months old.

Did you know that Perry's sister (La Verne Weston) and David Briddell were
married last July? He is pastoring in Cristfield, Maryland. They were all set to
move into the apartment in Boston for a long stay when the offer came.[4]

Did you ever meet my sister, Clarie? She's living in Atlanta & is librarian at

---

1. Eunice Guy (1930–), born in Little Rock, Arkansas, earned her B.A. from Spelman in 1949. After
finishing her M.A. (1951) at Atlanta University she taught for several years at Wiley College in Marshall,
Texas, before moving on to Texas Southern University in Houston in 1956, where she has continued
her teaching career.

2. On 24 April she informed King of a lecture given at Wiley College by Shaun Herron, editor of
the *British Weekly*, who had said, "There is not a newspaper reader in the civilized world that does not
know about this man King."

3. "How Alabama Negroes Are Winning the Bus Fight: Bombing, Harassment Don't Stop," *Jet*,
16 February 1956, pp. 8–12.

4. David W. Briddell (1931–), born in Berlin, Maryland, received his B.A. (1952) from Morgan State
University and his M.S.T. (1955) from Boston University, where he participated in the Dialectical Society with King. He later served as pastor of Methodist churches in Maryland and Pennsylvania. La-
Verne Weston (1930–), born in Houston, studied at Texas Southern University and at the New England Conservatory of Music, where she was Coretta Scott King's classmate.

Carver Vocational. She married Wendell Whalum from Memphis (Harold's brother).[5]

My brother, Fred married Altoise Chennault. They're in Nashville now; this is his second year at Meharry Dental School.

My younger brother William received a grant for a year's study abroad & is now in France. He says Frenchmen find it very difficult to believe that over a hundred people can be arrested for staging a peaceful boycott!!

I find it hard to believe that anybody could get so many Negroes to cooperate for so long!!

Sincerely,
[*signed*] Eunice

P.S. My regards to your parents & sister when you see or write them.[6] We were in Atlanta for two days in September. I went out to the house but picked a time when no one was at home. So, I didn't get a chance to see any of the Kings.

ALS. MLKP-MBU: Box 91.

---

5. Wendell Whalum (1931–1987), born in Memphis, Tennessee, received his B.A. (1952) from Morehouse, his M.A. (1953) from Columbia University, and his Ph.D. (1965) from the University of Iowa. He joined the Morehouse faculty in 1953 as a professor of music and served as director of the music department from 1961 until his death in 1987.

6. Willie Christine King Farris (1927–), born in Atlanta, Georgia, earned her B.A. (1948) from Spelman College. After receiving her M.A. (1950) in the social foundations of education from Columbia University, she taught elementary school in Atlanta. During the summers she returned to Columbia, studying for a master's in special education, which was awarded in 1958. An associate professor of education at Spelman College since 1958, she currently directs its Learning Resource Center. She is a member of the Martin Luther King, Jr., Papers Project Advisory Board and the vice chair and treasurer of the Martin Luther King, Jr., Center for Nonviolent Social Change, Inc.

From William Robert Miller

6 March 1956

Miller, assistant editor of the New York–based FOR journal Fellowship, *explains that his experiences as a soldier stationed in the South during World War II led him to express "heartfelt solidarity" with the bus boycott.*[1]

---

1. William Robert Miller (1927–1970), a native of Waterloo, New York, served in the U.S. Air Force from 1945 to 1947. He received his B.A. (1964) at the New School for Social Research. After several jobs as a journalist, he served as managing editor of *Fellowship* from 1956 to 1961. Among his writings are *Nonviolence: A Christian Interpretation* (1964) and *Martin Luther King, Jr.: His Life, Martyrdom, and Meaning for the World* (1968).

Rev. Martin Luther King, Jr.   6 Mar
309 So. Jackson Street   1956
Montgomery, Alabama

Dear Mr. King:

Since I first heard of the nonviolent protest for human rights which you and
your courageous friends are leading, I have taken every opportunity in personal
conversation and otherwise to make your inspiring activities better known. Somehow it did not occur to me until now, that I was indeed remiss in not communicating to you my heartfelt solidarity with your cause.

As a soldier stationed in Mississippi and North Carolina during World War II, I
got my first awareness that our country was not wholly free. I was appalled by jim
crow, and to the best of my adolescent ability refused to abide by the segregation
laws. I made it a particular point to sit behind the color line on busses in New
Orleans, Mobile and elsewhere, and though I was greeted by hostile looks from
other white passengers, I was never ousted—perhaps because I was pretty big, or
because it was wartime and I was obviously a yankee. At any rate, these experiences I had when I was only eighteen and had gone out into the world for the
first time made me respond instantly when I heard of the refusal of Negroes to
be jimcrowed on the Montgomery buses.

I was impressed to learn that you are a year younger than I am. I have a pretty
strong ego, and that knowledge really puts me in the shade. For me, friendship is
something I am not able (though as a professing Christian I wish it) to give
easily—and admiration comes even harder. But I want you to know, Mr. King,
that I admire you deeply for your steadfast adherence to the nonviolent teachings
of Our Lord in this time of crisis. If I can ever approximate in my life the sterling
standard of conduct you have set, I shall really think my life had meaning and
value. May God bless you and yours, and may my daily prayers for you soften the
hard hearts of sinful men and bring victory for your cause not only in Montgomery but everywhere in the United States and in the world.

In fellowship,
William Robert Miller
Assistant Editor,
Fellowship

TLc. WRMP-GAMK: Box 1.

From Earline Browning

6 March 1956
Boise, Idaho

Rev. M. L. King Jr.
Dexter Ave. Baptist Church

Dear Sir.

I'm a reader of The [*Pittsburgh*] Courier and get it also. Seeing where you were asking for help in order to Keep up the fight. Sorry I can't send no money I were hurt year before last and haven't been able to work since. But I'm sending 2 pairs of Shoes some of my better ones to two of the ladies who can wear them and tell them may God bless all of you and I'm with you even if I'm so far off The prayers of the ones who are pure in heart are heard by the lord.

I've been able to send money each time the Naacp ask for it but once. And maybe I'll be able to send some later on. I do pray So.

May God bless all of you and whatever you do keep up the fight, and let them know God is Mighter than Man.

Please let me know when you get them.

From one of the race
Mrs Earline Browning

AHLS. MLKP-MBU: Box 91.

From Thomas G. Kilgore, Jr.

7 March 1956
New York, N.Y.

Kilgore, pastor of New York's Friendship Baptist Church, where King had preached in 1954, announced a large contribution from New York area churches at an MIA mass meeting on 1 March.

Reverend Martin L. King
309 South Jackson Street
Montgomery, Alabama

Dear Reverend King:

This letter comes bearing another report. I will have to write you, when I have more time, about my reaction to the visit there. I simply state this time, 'More power to you and the people of Montgomery as you go forward'.

Boise Idaho
March 6 - 56
Rev. M. L. King Jr.
Dexter Ave. Baptist Church
Dear Sir.

I'm a reader of the Courier
and get it also. Seeing where
you were asking for help in
order to keep up the fight-
Sorry I can't send no money
I and haven't been able to work
and haven't been able to work
since. But I'm sending 2 pair
of shoes some of my better ones
to two of the ladies who can
wear them and tell them may
god bless all of you and find
with if you ever if I'm so far off
the prayers of the ones who

are pure in heart are heard
by the lord.
I've been able to send some
each time the N.A.A.C.P. ask of
for it but once. And maybe
I'll be able to send some late
on. I do pray so.
May God bless all of you
and what ever you do keep
up the fight, and let them
know his blood is mightier than
Man.
Please let me know
when you get them.
From one of the race.
Mrs Earline Browning
508 - So. 14th St.
Boise Idaho.

I would like to make two statements. One in the form of a request. First, the check for $267.67 that was to complete the report I left seemed to have been lost in the mail. The Baptist State Convention has agreed to issue another in the next two days. I will send it as soon as I receive it. Secondly, the conference has asked me to request from you a photostat copy or a verified typed copy of the letter you received last week from Reverend Richard Lowe.[1] (If you remember this is the letter which expressed doubt about our contribution being sent to Montgomery.) It would help us a great deal if you would get this letter to me by Monday, March the 12th.

I am enclosing an additional report of $1,227.82. There will be more next week.

Sincerely yours,
[*signed*]
Thomas Kilgore, Jr.

TK:ac
Enc.

THLS. MLKP-MBU: Box 91.

---

1. Kilgore refers to a 27 February 1956 letter from Lowe, a minister at Mount Zion Baptist Church in Newark, New Jersey, in which he expressed concern that the funds raised in New York for the MIA would not be received by the group. Lowe asked King to confirm the legitimacy of the MIA and account for its expenses. In response to a second letter from Lowe, King's secretary, Maude Ballou, explained that "the tremendous pressure of the present situation" prevented a prompt reply from King. King's response to Kilgore or Lowe, if any, has not been located. See Richard A. Lowe to King, 27 February and 7 April 1956; and Ballou to Lowe, 13 April 1956.

To J. H. Jackson

7 March 1956
[*Montgomery, Ala.*]

Reverend J. H. Jackson, Pastor
Olivet Baptist Church
3101 South Parkway
Chicago 16, Illinois

Dear Reverend Jackson:

This is just a note to express our deepest gratitude to you and to the members of your congregation for your very fine contribution. I assure you that we will ⟨
long remember your coming to our aid in this momentous struggle for justice.

Such contributions from friends and organizations sympathetic with our struggle give us renewed courage and vigor to carry on.

    With every good wish, I am

Cordially yours,
M. L. King, Jr.,
President.

MLK/ds

THLc. MLKP-MBU: Box 91.

From Bayard Rustin

8 March 1956
New York, N.Y.

Rustin, executive secretary of the New York–based War Resisters League and former Fellowship of Reconciliation activist, had arrived in Montgomery on 21 February to offer his help as an expert on nonviolent direct action.[1] Rustin departed a week later, fearing that controversy over his presence would hurt the movement, but King, E. D. Nixon, and other MIA leaders continued to value his advice. One Alabama journalist alleged that Rustin had misrepresented himself as a correspondent for two European newspapers, Le Figaro *and the* Manchester Guardian. *Rustin clarifies the matter in this letter written the day after he met with King in Birmingham and discussed the appropriate role for outsiders in the movement. According to Rustin's notes from the meeting, King was "very happy to receive outside help." They agreed, however, that any ideas or programs developed by northerners would be directed through King or Nixon, to avoid the appearance of interference by "northern agitators."[2] Rustin asks King to review a draft of an article on the bus boycott, which would be published under King's name. "Our Struggle" appeared in the April issue of* Liberation, *a new pacifist journal published in New York.[3]*

---

1. Bayard Rustin (1912–1987), born in West Chester, Pennsylvania, studied at Wilberforce University, Cheyney State Teachers College, and City College of New York. In 1941, after a stint as an organizer with the Young Communist League, Rustin joined the FOR staff, first as a field secretary and then as race relations director. A devout Quaker, Rustin was sentenced to twenty-eight months in prison in 1942 as a conscientious objector to World War II. He directed the Free India Campaign and led sit-ins at the British Embassy in Washington in 1945. A founder of the Congress of Racial Equality (CORE), Rustin coordinated the organization's first Freedom Ride (then known as the Journey of Reconciliation) in 1947. In 1953 he resigned from FOR and joined the staff of the War Resisters League as its executive secretary, serving there until 1964. Rustin remained an important advisor to King after the bus boycott and organized the March on Washington in 1963.

2. Rustin, "How Outsiders Can Strengthen the Montgomery Nonviolent Protest," 7 March 1956. His suggestions included encouraging northern pacifists to visit Montgomery for a few days; providing "ghostwriters" for King, who was too busy to write himself; developing sympathetic protests in other parts of the country; and establishing a revolving bail fund for arrested protesters.

3. King, "Our Struggle," April 1956, pp. 236–241 in this volume.

Reverend Martin Luther King
309 Jackson
Montgomery, Alabama

Dear Reverend King:

I called your wife today and told her that I had gotten the matter cleared up with the Manchester Guardian. Actually, they had never offered any reward for my identification. In regard to Le Figaro, we are in process of getting that cleared up. For the record, at no time did I say that I was a correspondent for either of these papers. I did say that I was writing articles which were to be submitted to them and this is now in the process of being done.

Enclosed you will find an article which I should like you to revise and to give permission for being printed under your name in the April issue of Liberation. Also enclosed is a copy of Liberation so that you may know the nature of the magazine. This magazine is being widely distributed to the kind of moral leadership who are intensely interested in non-violence and many important leaders of the church. For this reason I emphasized the moral aspects of the problem. I hope you can see your way clear to give us permission to publish it, to revise it where you wish, and to get it back to me as soon as possible. I am working on a couple of other things for you for wider distribution.

Let me hear from you as soon as possible.

Sincerely yours,
[*signed*]
Bayard Rustin

BR/ms
Encl: cc of article and Liberation

TLS. MLKP-MBU: Box 5.

To George D. Kelsey

8 March 1956
Montgomery, Ala.

King enclosed a receipt for ten dollars in this thank-you letter to his former teacher at Morehouse.

Mr. George D. Kelsey
Drew University
Madison, New Jersey

Dear Mr. Kelsey:

This is just a note to express our deepest gratitude to you for your very fine contribution. I assure you that we will long remember your coming to our aid in this momentous struggle for justice. Such contributions from friends and organizations sympathetic with our struggle give us renewed courage and vigor to carry on.

With every good wish, I am

Cordially yours,
[*signed*] M. L.
M. L. King, Jr.,
President

MLK:ovg

{P.S. It was really good hearing from you. Your words were very encouraging. Please give my regards to the family. M. L.}

TALS. GDKP.

From Roy Wilkins

8 March 1956
New York, N.Y.

> *The NAACP executive secretary responds to King's 3 March letter expressing concern about funds raised by the NAACP on behalf of the bus boycott. Wilkins pledges that the NAACP will pay for most of the MIA's legal expenses and bear the full cost of the* Browder v. Gayle *federal lawsuit challenging the bus segregation laws. Wilkins adds that "it would be fatal for there to develop any hint of disagreement as to the raising and allocating of funds." In subsequent telephone conversations, the two leaders apparently finalized an agreement regarding fund-raising.*[1]

Rev. M. L. King, Jr., President
The Montgomery Improvement Association
725 Dorsey Street
Montgomery 8, Alabama

Dear Reverend King:

Upon my return from the Civil Rights Assembly in Washington I find your letter of March 3, which arrived here March 5.[2]

We certainly wish to continue our support in every way to the magnificent effort being carried forward in Montgomery.

It was our intention from the first news of the indictments and mass arrests to assume the entire cost of the defense for those persons arrested and indicted and thus to relieve the Montgomery Improvement Association of any burden in that respect. Mr. Marshall stated that our legal staff would be one hundred percent

---

1. See Wilkins to King, 12 April 1956; and King to Wilkins, 1 May 1956, pp. 243–244 in this volume.

2. On 4 March Wilkins was the keynote speaker at a three-day conference of the Delegate Assembly for Civil Rights, a coalition of civic groups that sponsored an eight-point program of national civil rights legislation.

for the indicted persons. I stated in several speeches and numerous letters that the NAACP would undertake the defense of the persons indicted.

On the strength of that we made appeals to our branches to raise money, to cooperate with local ministers in their cities and to send funds either to the national office or to Montgomery, or send some to each. We stated that you needed funds in Montgomery to keep up the protest and that we needed funds for the legal defense. We have tried to be absolutely fair in the presentation. As evidence that we have been, at least one of our branches, Jersey City, New Jersey, sent us a check made out to you which we forwarded to you last week. I am sure there will be other contributions. In the meantime, we will be receiving funds which we will use to defray the expenses in the legal proceedings in connection with the persons indicted.

In addition to those legal expenses, we expect also to bear the major part, if not the entire cost, of the bus segregation case challenging the state law. This will be an expensive proceeding which undoubtedly will go to the Supreme Court. I say we will bear the major part because in such cases in the past arising in other localities local citizens have raised some part of the cost.

In addition to the above two legal actions I am advised by our legal department that they are committed to most, if not all, of the expenses in connection with the case of Mrs. Parks as an individual.

We have in mind at all times that you need a sum of money each week to maintain the car pool and related activities. We feel confident that the churches of the nation and the NAACP branches will continue to send you contributions adequate for this expense. We assure you, also, that the national office of the NAACP, in addition to the legal expenses which it will undertake to bear, stands ready in any emergency to help with the weekly expenses. I cannot promise to do this regularly or indefinitely, but I do pledge that any time you reach an emergency point where funds are needed and are not at once forthcoming you have but to call upon us.

I am certain I do not need to stress that at this time it would be fatal for there to develop any hint of disagreement as to the raising and allocating of funds. We wish to avoid any semblance of this, and I am cautioning our chapters to give full cooperation to the churches in their localities and while setting forth the claim of the NAACP to some of the funds collected—because of our legal activity—to enter into no public dispute with such local ministers or local committees who are unable to see our point and who feel strongly that every dollar should go to Montgomery.[3] I am confident that if it should develop that funds in excess of actual needs should be accumulated in Montgomery your organization would volunteer financial assistance in the legal cases. What I have tried to say to you above is similarly that we stand ready to contribute, over and above the legal expenses, to the car pool effort if we should receive here monies in excess of the requirements of the legal activity insofar as we can estimate them.

---

3. On the same day this letter was written, Wilkins sent a telegram to the NAACP's West Coast Regional Office asking that on 28 March, the National Deliverance Day of Prayer, branches "cooperate fully with churches and their leaders in a day of prayer and fund raising" for the MIA. He explained that although money is needed for other cases, the NAACP "will not quarrel with Montgomery Improvement Association over who gets funds" (see Wilkins to Franklin H. Williams, 8 March 1956).

I would be happy to hear from you again so that we may have a clear understanding on this matter.

With kind personal regards,
Very sincerely yours,
[*signed*]
Roy Wilkins
Executive Secretary

RW:erb

TLS. MLKP-MBU: Box 67.

From William J. Faulkner

9 March 1956
Chicago, Ill.

The Congregational Church of Park Manor in Chicago was one of many northern churches that raised funds to support the bus protest. Its minister, William J. Faulkner, had worked with King's grandfather, A. D. Williams, at Ebenezer Baptist Church in Atlanta.[1] Faulkner refers to Williams's "tremendous fight" for passage of a 1921 school bond issue, which resulted in the building of eighteen new schools, including four black elementary schools and Atlanta's first secondary school for blacks.[2] King replied on 4 June.[3]

The Reverend M. L. King,
Montgomery Improvement Association,
309 South Jackson Street,
Montgomery, Alabama.

Dear Mr. King:

A few days ago our church sent to your organization, a check for $286.05, in response to my appeal that we contribute generously in support of the worthy cause which you and other courageous leaders are fighting for in Montgomery. We are not only willing to give of our money, but we are also praying that your protest against injustice may succeed.

---

1. William J. Faulkner (1891–1987), born in Society Hill, South Carolina, earned a B.H. (1914) from Springfield College and an M.A. (1935) from the University of Chicago. In 1934 he joined Fisk University's staff as minister and dean of men, becoming dean of the chapel in 1942. That year he also served as president of Nashville's NAACP. He left Fisk in 1953 to become the first pastor of the Park Manor Congregational Church in Chicago. Faulkner was a member of the executive committee of the Fellowship of Reconciliation.

2. See Introduction to *The Papers of Martin Luther King, Jr.*, vol. 1: *Called to Serve, January 1929–June 1951*, ed. Clayborne Carson, Ralph E. Luker, and Penny A. Russell (Berkeley and Los Angeles: University of California Press, 1992), p. 17.

3. See p. 292 in this volume.

I think the whole world is amazed and gratified over your non-violent but firm crusade to correct some age-old social evils, and to remove man's brutal indignities to his brothers. More power to you, my friend! And may the mantle of your fearless and distinguished grandfather fall heavily upon your shoulders.

It was my joy and privilege to serve in the Sunday School and church of the Reverend A. D. Williams, back in the early twenties. And I know something of the tremendous fight which he put up ~~to~~ {with} the NAACP to get decent schools for colored children in the city of Atlanta. He and his colleagues won in that struggle, and I am convinced that you and yours will win out in Montgomery.

Faithfully and cordially yours,

[*signed*]

W. J. Faulkner,
Minister.

WJF: elc {Mrs. Faulkner and I hold your father and mother in very high esteem.}

TAHLS. MLKP-MBU: Box 15.

From Lillian Eugenia Smith

10 March 1956
Neptune Beach, Fla.

Smith was a white novelist, journalist, and civil rights activist from Georgia. Her controversial 1944 novel Strange Fruit, *about an interracial love affair in the Deep South, was banned in Boston and Detroit but became a best-seller.[1] After commending King for leading the bus boycott "wisely and well," she offers "just a spoonful of advice: don't let outsiders come in and ruin your movement," particularly "northern do-gooders." Having received no response to her letter, Smith wrote again on 3 April, telling King that "I am urging the white southerners who believe in your way to let you know they do; that it is important for them to take a stand within their own hearts as well as for your group in Montgomery." On 24 May King finally replied, thanking Smith for her encouragement and financial support.[2]*

Dear Dr. King:

I have with a profound sense of fellowship and admiration been watching your work in Montgomery. I cannot begin to tell you how effective it seems to me, although I must confess I have watched it only at long distance.

It is the right way. Only through persuasion, love, goodwill, and firm nonviolent resistance can the change take place in our South. Perhaps in a northern city

---

1. Lillian Eugenia Smith (1897–1966), born in Jasper, Florida, briefly attended Piedmont College in Georgia and studied music at Peabody Conservatory in Baltimore. She taught at a missionary school in China from 1922 to 1925. After returning to the United States she assumed leadership of Laurel Falls Camp, the elite girls' school her parents founded in Georgia. Committed to nonviolent racial reform, she was active in the Congress of Racial Equality (CORE) and the Southern Conference for Human Welfare.

2. See pp. 273–274 in this volume.

this kind of nonviolent, persuasive resistance would either be totally misinter-
preted or else find nothing in the whites which could be appealed to. But in our
South, the whites, too, share the profoundly religious symbols you are using and
respond to them on a deep level of their hearts and minds. Their imaginations
are stirred: the waters are troubled.

You seem to be going at it in such a wise way. I want to come down as soon as I
can and talk quietly with you about it. For I have nothing to go on except television reports and newspaper reports. But these have been surprisingly sympathetic to the 40,000 Negroes in Montegomery who are taking part in this resistance movement. But I have been in India twice; I followed the Gandhian
movement long before it became popular in this country. I, myself, being a Deep
South white, reared in a religious home and the Methodist church realize the
deep ties of common songs, common prayer, common symbols that bind our two
races together on a religio-mystical level, even as another brutally mythic idea,
the concept of White Supremacy, tears our two people apart.

Ten years ago, I wrote Dr. Benjamin Mays in Atlanta suggesting that the Negroes begin a non-violent religious movement. But the time had not come for it,
I suppose. Now it is here; now it has found you and others perhaps, too, in Montgomery who seem to be steering it wisely and well.

I want to help you with money just as soon as I can; I cannot, just now; I have
had cancer for three years and have been unable to make much of a living during
this time; also have found it an expensive illness. My home, also, was burned this
winter by two young white boys; and this fire destroyed all my writings, manuscripts, work in progress, books, records, 7000 letters on race relations etc. etc.
But I will have a turn of luck soon, I hope, and just as soon as I do I shall send
your group some money.

In lieu of money, I send my encouragement and just a spoonful of advice: don't
let outsiders come in and ruin your movement. This kind of thing has to be in-
digenous; it has to be kept within the boundaries of the local situation. You know
the fury a northern accent arouses in the confused South—especially if that accent goes along with a white face. Keep the northernern do-gooders {sincere and
honest as they may be} out; tell them to help you with their publicity in the North,
giving you a sympathetic and honest press; tell them to send money if they are
able to do so; tell them to try to use some of these methods in their northern
communities. But don't, please, my friend, let them come down and ruin what
you are doing so well. It will then seem to the country a "conspiracy" instead of
a spontaneous religio-social movement. It has had a tremendous effect on the
conscience of the people everywhere. But it won't have, if these people come in.

Dr. Homer Jack has written a most sympathetic news-letter about his visit. I was
glad he wrote it. But I think his advice for northern "experts" in non-violence to
go down and help is unwise. You can't be an expert in non-violence; it is like being
a saint or an artist: each person grows his own skill and expertness. I think Howard Thurmond could be of help, perhaps, to you. He is truly a great man; warm,
deeply religious. Bayard Rustin is a fine man, too.[3] Whoever comes should come

---

3. In his 9 March newsletter to "those interested in the non-violent resistance aspects of the Montgomery, Alabama protest against segregation on the city buses," Jack suggested that "certain well-

only on invitation and should give only quiet advice. Except Howard Thurman. Mr Thurman, as I said, is a truly great religious leader. Your congregation and that of other ministers in Montgomery would respond to him. He would encourage them in numerous ways and his advice would be wise and skilled. I think, instead of coming, if these leaders of CORE (with whom I have worked for years) would write you letters; send messages of encouragement to your group that that would in the end help more than anything else. You have the awe and respect of many southern whites at present; they are genuinely touched and amazed at the discipline, the self-control, the dignity, the sweetness and goodness and courage and firmness of your group. It would break my heart were so-called "outsiders" to ruin it all. The white South is irrational about this business of "outsiders." ~~It can turn itself~~

But please give your group a message from me: Tell them that Lillian Smith respects and admires what they are doing. Tell them, please, that I am deeply humbled by the goodwill, the self discipline, the courage, the wisdom of this group of Montgomery Negroes. Tell them that I, too, am working as hard as I can to bring insight to the white group; to try to open their hearts to the great harm that segregation inflicts not only on Negroes but on white people too. Tell them, that I hope and pray that they will keep their resistance on a high spiritual level of love and quiet courage; for these are the only way that a real change of heart and mind can come to our South.

Sincerely,
[*signed*] Lillian Smith

TALS. MLKP-MBU: Box 65.

---

known Gandhians," such as Amiya Chakravarty, Richard Gregg, George Houser, Ralph Templin, and Howard Thurman, counsel MIA leaders "on Gandhian philosophy and techniques." Jack noted that Rustin had already been to Montgomery and seemed "especially effective in counseling the leader of the protest during the crucial 2 weeks after the mass arrests. . . . His contribution to interpreting the Gandhian approach to the leadership cannot be overestimated." King referred to Smith's advice in a subsequent letter to Thurman (see King to Thurman, 16 March 1956, p. 177 in this volume).

From John Dockery

13 March 1956
Stockton, Calif.

Dockery, president of his local NAACP, informs King of a sympathy boycott of Stockton City Lines, a subsidiary of National City Lines.[1] The Stockton Deliverance Day

---

1. John Isaac Dockery (1919–1977), president of the Stockton NAACP branch until 1975, was born in Hawkins, Texas, and attended Jarvis College. After serving in the Navy (1942–1945) he settled in Stockton and became the proprietor of a well-known eatery, Doc's Bar-B-Q.

*Committee, formed by the NAACP branch and the Interdenominational Ministers
Union, planned a one-day boycott and an evening prayer meeting as part of the
National Deliverance Day of Prayer on 28 March (the date in the telegram is a
typographic error). The committee raised $450 for the MIA at the prayer meeting but
called off the sympathy boycott after local bus officials agreed to hire a black driver.*[2]

REV. M L KING JR

309 SOUTH JACKSON ST MONTGOMERY ALA

STOCKTON CITY BUS LINES SUBSIDIARY NATIONAL CITY LINES WILL BE BOYCOTTED MARCH 18
BY STOCKTON NEGROES UNLESS THE COMPANY MEETS WITH NEGRO LEADERS OF
MONTGOMERY ALABAMA PRIOR TO THE 28TH TO DISCUSS DIFFERENCES

JOHN DOCKERY,
PRESIDENT NAACP BRANCH STOCKTON CALIFORNIA

PWSr. MLKP-MBU: Box 91.

---

2. See "Bus Boycott Proposal to Be Studied," 16 March 1956; "Stockton Negro Groups Prepare for
Deliverance Day Ceremonies," 27 March 1956; and "Prayer Day Observed to Aid Negroes," 29 March
1956; all in the *Stockton Record*.

To J. Pius Barbour

13 March 1956
[*Montgomery, Ala.*]

*Commenting that the bus boycott's demands "have worked me overtime," King confirms
a guest appearance at Dexter for Barbour, editor of the* National Baptist Voice.
*Barbour had drawn attention to his long-standing ties to King in a March article for
the* Voice: *"King, Jr., practically lived in my home and preached at my Church very
often while a student at Crozer." Barbour recounted intense discussions with King over
social issues: "I have heard Mike argue dearly all night about Gandhi and his
methods against my thesis of coercion." Despite his own skepticism about nonviolence,
Barbour applauded King's commitment. "I was thrilled when I read your remarks: 'We
must not fall so low as to allow our enemies to make us hate.' I have heard you say that
many a time. I thought you were just carrying on an intellectual argument. BUT YOU
REALLY MEANT IT."*[1]

*Barbour was reluctant to accept King's earlier invitations to preach at Dexter,
remarking in a December 1954 letter to King that "Montgomery always reminds*

---

1. J. Pius Barbour, "Meditations on Rev. M. L. King, Jr., of Montgomery, Ala.," *National Baptist Voice*,
March 1956. Barbour may refer to a King quotation in the *New York Times* on 24 February 1956: "Don't
ever let anyone pull you so low as to hate them" (see excerpt from Wayne Phillips, "Negroes Pledge
to Keep Boycott," 24 February 1956, pp. 135–136 in this volume).

*me of my failure," a reference to Barbour's troubled years as a young preacher in the
city.[2] Barbour responded to a 19 July 1955 invitation by musing, "I wonder if I am your
man. I am distinctly a 'preacher's preacher' and a college lecture man. I can preach
'Mob-sermons' but I cant lecture to mobs."[3] In his 15 April sermon at Dexter— "Can
You Change a Social Order Without Violence?"—Barbour contended that "the New
Testament has no social strategy and the doctrine of non-resistance is strictly a personal
ethic and has nothing to do with social strategy." After the sermon, several listeners
argued with Barbour, prompting him to write that, in all his decades of preaching, no
church had surpassed Dexter "in intellectual alertness and keen insight."[4]*

Dr. J. Pious Barbour
1614 West Second Street
Chester, Pennsylvania

Dear Dr. Barbour:

Dexter Avenue Baptist Church and the Montgomery Community are looking
forward to your coming to us with great anticipation. As you know, the Spring
Lectures Series begins April 15. We will expect you to preach that Sunday morning and the three lectures will be Sunday evening, Monday evening and Tuesday
evening.

Please forward to me immediately a biographical sketch and at least two mats.
I would also appreciate it if you would send your subjects and the suggestion of a
general theme. All of this is very vital for publicity purposes. I intended writing
for this information long before now, but the pressing demands of the bus situation have worked me overtime. Consequently, I have gotten behind in my correspondence. However, I would highly appreciate it if you would get this information to me within the next week.

I hope things are going well with you. Give my best regards to the family. Coretta and the baby are fine.

With every good wish, I am

Sincerely yours,
M. L. King, Jr.

MLK:lmt

TLc. DABCC.

---

2. Barbour to King, 21 December 1954, in *Papers* 2:324.
3. Barbour to King, 21 July 1955, in *Papers* 2:564.
4. Barbour, "Religion in Montgomery, Alabama," *National Baptist Voice,* May 1956. When one listener asked Barbour about his distinction between social and personal interpretations of Scripture,
Barbour acknowledged that he was "pinned against the wall when King came to my rescue by saying
that any interpretation of Scripture that did violence to the known character of Jesus was to be
avoided."

14 March 1956
Boston, Mass.

*King viewed Chalmers, professor of preaching and applied Christianity at Boston
University's School of Theology, as an activist theologian with a "passion for social
justice."[1] As treasurer of the NAACP, Chalmers assures King that the organization
"will back you at the national level without any questions." He also invites King, who
was scheduled to speak in Boston on 23 March, to meet with students; King canceled
the speech, however, after his 22 March conviction. Fred Gray spoke in his place at
Boston's Union Methodist Church.*

Reverend Martin Luther King
309 Jackson Street
Montgomery, Alabama

Dear Martin:

In one sense I hate to add another letter to that pile on your bed and desk. I
have a feeling that sometime your lovely wife is going to put a special delivery on
the baby instead of a change of diapers.

Nevertheless, I do want to get in touch with you about a couple of things. In
the first place, as you know, we will back you at the national level without any
question. I talked with Roy Wilkins about it the other day, and he says that he had
written you to that effect.[2] We don't want to throw any money away unnecessarily,
but neither do we want to skimp on it when it is going to be of value for you. We
are very much pleased with the way in which you are handling this whole matter
from your end. We will work in cooperation with you in any way that seems to be
necessary.

I had a very interesting time in Tuscaloosa and in Birmingham after I left you,
and will be down the first week in April to work on the same situation which has
been opened up by my previous visit. The white churches are, in all probability,
going to give some leadership, which, to me, was somewhat unexpected. I have,
in addition to that, some very good contacts, both with the state administration
and with the University of Alabama, so that we can look forward with some confidence on this whole area of development.

I am hoping to see you when you are up here on Friday the 23rd (if, by that

---

1. King, *Stride Toward Freedom*, p. 100. Allan Knight Chalmers (1897–1972), a native of Cleveland,
Ohio, received his B.A. (1917) from Johns Hopkins University and his B.D. (1922) from Yale University.
Chalmers was minister of New York's Broadway Tabernacle Congregational Church from 1930 to 1948,
when he joined the faculty at Boston University; he remained at Boston University until his retirement
in 1962. His positions in the service of social justice movements included chair, Scottsboro Defense
Committee; co-chair, Fair Employment Practices Committee; president, NAACP Legal Defense and
Education Fund; and executive committee member of the Federal Council of Churches, FOR, ACLU,
and the Religion and Labor Foundation.

2. See Wilkins to King, 8 March 1956, pp. 165–167 in this volume.   173

time, you are out of custody in the courts, as I hope you will be), and you may be interested to know that I shall be the speaker for the Boston area in the sympathy meeting we are holding at noon on the 28th in Old North Church.

When you are here on the 23rd, our students at Boston University would be very grateful if they had a chance to meet with you. I have several alternatives in mind—one is that you might meet with the group where I could set it up for you in the period of one to three or any portion of that you want. A second alternative would be that you could come in to my seminar from eleven to one, and I would allow visitors to come in for the general forum conference with you, if that would be at all congenial. The first alternative is preferable, but this second would be o.k., if that would fit your schedule better.

A third alternative would be arranging in some way for them to meet with you, either at Union Church, where, I assume, you are to speak, or to have you come up here afterwards for those men who could be present for a late Friday meeting.

Of course, any of these alternatives may not be in the picture at all because of other engagements you may already have, only we are eager to be in touch with the situation, both for whatever help we can give and for the men here as a part of their involvement in this whole matter which has moved so strongly in your area.

Drop me a note about the alternatives, and remember that one of them is that you can't be with us at all, and we would understand that if that is true.

My best to you and your wife and your dear baby. I hope all things are working along well for you, and appreciate the calm and sturdy way in which you are doing your job.

As ever,
[*signed*] "Doc"

AKC:IH

{P.S. Don't forget you were going to send me a couple of copies (an original if you can get it) of that Citizens Council leaflet we discussed.[3] I'm in touch with the administration at Washington, and such things help build real sympathy with our "cause."}

TALS. MLKP-MBU: Box 91.

---

3. Chalmers refers to a leaflet entitled "A Preview of the Declaration of Segregation" that was distributed at a Citizens Council meeting in Montgomery. The anonymous author advocated using violence to halt the end of segregation, reviled African Americans, and expressed fear that King would become president of the United States (see "Preview," 10 February 1956).

From Howard Thurman

14 March 1956
Boston, Mass.

Thurman, a family friend and an influential theologian and pacifist who served as dean of Boston University's Marsh Chapel, had known King during the latter's graduate student years. The previous November he had declined King's invitation to preach Dexter's Men's Day sermon in July 1956.[1]

Dr. Martin Luther King
309 S. Jackson Street
Montgomery, Alabama

Dear King:

I have not communicated with you before, because I wanted to be sure of my Tuskegee dates. I shall be in Tuskegee for the weekend of March 24. I arrive Saturday morning.

I would like very much to sit down and have two or three hours talk with you and one or two of your close associates. I prefer doing it in private at Tuskegee. Would you be interested in such a possibility and, if so, would it be possible for you to drive over to Tuskegee any time of Saturday afternoon, March 24? Please let me know as soon as possible.

Mrs. [*Sue Bailey*] Thurman wants you to use the enclosed to do something personal in nature for Mrs. King.

Sincerely yours,
[*signed*]
Howard Thurman
Dean
enc.

TLS. MLKP-MBU: Box 91.

---

1. See King to Thurman, 31 October 1955, and Thurman to King, 14 November 1955; in *Papers* 2: 583–584 and 588, respectively.

To Dwight D. Eisenhower

[*8 March–15 March 1956*]
[*Montgomery, Ala.*]

On 14 March at Eisenhower's weekly news conference a reporter asked the president if a meeting at the White House of local black and white leaders would help ease tensions about integration. Eisenhower suggested a congressional joint commission as an alternative. "I would like to have that body organized, bipartisan, and with every point of view represented on it, and as quickly as possible," he said. The following week, when questioned about the Montgomery bus boycott, Eisenhower answered: "As I understand [it] there is a state law about boycotts, and it is under that kind of thing that these people are being brought to trial."[1]

---

1. *Public Papers of the President of the United States: Dwight D. Eisenhower* (Washington: GPO, 1960–1961), pp. 305 and 335. During this period congressmen Adam Clayton Powell, Jr., and Charles C.

In this drafted telegram, which may have been written in response to Eisenhower's 14 March comment, King urges the president to intervene in the boycott: "We are convinced, Mr. President, that by taking a direct interest in this stalemated situation you and you alone can tap fountainheads of goodwill." He asks that Eisenhower host a meeting between bus boycott leaders, owners of Montgomery City Lines, and "other universally respected persons." A press release announcing the dispatch of the telegram was also drafted.[2] Neither the telegram nor the press statement was released.

(Suggestion: if the President is to receive the telegram on, say, Friday morning, the text could be given to the press for release in the Friday <u>afternoon</u> papers.

<u>As a rule</u>, a story receives better press coverage if released for the afternoon papers. The reason is that, on the following day, the morning papers will usually pick it up as well.)

For fourteen weeks a united Negro community, led by the clergy, has stayed off the Montgomery busses in a peaceful protest against injustice.

With dignity and with the power of the human spirit we have sought to implement the American tradition of fair play. Our threefold demands are simple and moderate: courtesy from the bus drivers, seating on a first-come first-served basis, and employment of Negro drivers on busses transversing predominantly Negro neighborhoods.

Throughout these past three months our approach has been non-violent and our language non-inflammatory. Nevertheless bombs have been thrown at two Negro homes, clergymen and laymen have been arrested en masse under an obsolete "conspiracy" statute, and the wild charges of pro-segregation extremists have set the tone of the criticism that our white brothers have directed toward our spiritual movement.

Although fear has silenced many tongues we know that not all white citizens are against us. By no means do we seek to divide Montgomery along color lines. We merely say that, despite hardship and persecution and in the face of pressure and inconvenience, we shall not ride again on the busses under the humiliating conditions that have so long prevailed. Every Negro in our city who has been arrested faces the prospect of imprisonment with equanimity and with a readiness to sacrifice for our cause.

We are convinced, Mr. President, that by taking a direct interest in this stalemated situation you and you alone can tap fountainheads of goodwill and activate "white corpuscles" of brotherhood.

Therefore we appeal to you to summon to the White House the leaders of the Negro community, the owners of the Montgomery City Line and several universally respected persons.

Diggs, Jr., joined others, including AFL-CIO president George Meany, in calling on Eisenhower to convene a meeting of southern leaders to ease tensions in the region. Administration officials refused to respond, contending that Eisenhower had already asked Congress to create a commission on racial matters and that therefore "it is not the President's present intention to abrogate in effect his recommendation by now proceeding without regard to the Congress in the establishment of such a commission" (see Powell to Eisenhower, 2 March 1956; Diggs to Eisenhower, 9 March 1956; Meany to Eisenhower, 9 February 1956; and Bryce N. Harlow to Diggs, 12 March 1956).

2. Press release, "King Urges Exploratory White House Conference," 8–15 March 1956.

Faced with the great prestiage of your office and confronted by world public opinion, the participants in such an exploratory conference ought to be able to come to a meeting of minds out of which an amicable settlement could then spring.

Even if no immediately tangible results were achieved, the very meeting itself would stimulate the intangible forces that reduce anxiety, fear and tension.

16 Mar
1956

Rev. Martin Luther King Jr., President
Montgomery Improvement Association
309 Jackson Street Montgomery
telephone: 35179

TWd. MLKP-MBU: Box 78.

To Howard Thurman

16 March 1956
Montgomery, Ala.

King informs Thurman that he will be unable to meet with him in Tuskegee because he had already scheduled speaking engagements in Boston (later canceled) and New York.

Dr. Howard Thurman
Boston University
Marsh Chapel
300 Bay Street Road
Boston 15, Mass.

Dear Dr. Thurman:

Thanks for your very kind letter of March 14. I am very happy to know of your interest in our cause. I just received a letter from Lillian Smith, and she mentioned your name as a person who could give us real advice in this situation.

Unfortunately, I will have to be out of the city on the weekend of March 24. But for this, I would be more than happy to talk with you concerning this whole situation. I will be back in town sometime Monday morning, March 26. Do you plan to be in Tuskegee that long? If not, I hope it will be possible to talk with you some time in the near future.

Mrs. King sends her best regards and wants Mrs. Thurman to know how deeply grateful she is to her for her thoughtfulness. She plans to write soon.

With warm personal regards, I am

Sincerely yours,
[*signed*] M. L.
M. L. King, Jr.
President

MLK/b

TLS. HTC-MBU: Box 43.

From Homer Alexander Jack

16 March 1956
Evanston, Ill.

*Unitarian minister Homer Jack, together with Albert A. Harkins, former president of
the Universalist Ministers Association of America, and David H. Cole, current
president of the organization, visited Montgomery for four days in early March. On 9
March Jack wrote a newsletter to "those interested in the non-violent resistance aspects
of the Montgomery, Alabama protest against segregation on the city buses." In it he
listed "surface" similarities and differences between the Montgomery struggle and other
Gandhian movements, noting that although "the Gandhian flavor was not apparent
at the beginning" of the boycott, it had not been "imported by outsiders."* [1]

Dr. and Mrs. Martin Luther King, Jr.
309 S. Jackson
Montgomery, Alabama

Dear Friends,

I want to thank you again for your kindness toward myself and my associates in
our recent visit to Montgomery. In two days we were able to get the feel of your
wonderful protest movement—The Montgomery Advertiser to the contrary. [2]

What you are leading is a very heartening movement with the greatest of im-
port for the future of race relations in the nation as a whole. Last weekend I had
a good talk with Howard Thurman about your protest and a few days ago with
Archibald Carey.

I understand one of my colleagues telephoned you and urged you to come
here to address a meeting. He did not speak for me, certainly, for I feel you have
much more important work to do in Montgomery just now, and all speaking can
wait.

---

1. Homer Alexander Jack (1916–1993), born in Rochester, New York, earned his B.S. (1936) and
Ph.D. (1940) from Cornell University and his B.D. (1944) from Meadville Theological School in Chicago. He was pastor of the Unitarian Church of Evanston from 1948 to 1959. A founder of the Congress
on Racial Equality, Jack also served as executive secretary of the Chicago Council Against Racial and
Religious Discrimination (1944–1948) and vice chair of the Illinois ACLU (1950–1959). He would later
become active in the American Committee on Africa and the peace movement. Jack edited *The Wit
and Wisdom of Gandhi* (1951) and *The Gandhi Reader: A Source Book of His Life and Writings* (1956). In his
newsletter, Jack compared the Montgomery movement to other nonviolent resistance campaigns that
he had observed. Among the differences Jack noted were the Montgomery movement's lack of a charismatic leader, "although Dr. King may soon fill that need"; the lack of preparation "for non-violence
in an extreme situation"; the absence of "careful organizational machinery"; and no "communist
party participation . . . as in South Africa and Goa."

2. On 9 March 1956 the *Montgomery Advertiser* published a critical article, "Boycott Experts from
North Plan Full Report for Public," about their visit to Montgomery.

If we in the North can, with circumspection, be of specific help, please let us know. In the meantime, our thoughts and prayers will be with you, especially as the trials begin.

Cordially,
[*signed*]
Homer A. Jack

HAJ:blm

TLS. MLKP-MBU: Box 91.

From Thelma Austin Rice

18 March 1956
Montgomery, Ala.

As King awaited trial, expressions of support came not only from around the country but from within his own congregation. As part of his reorganization of Dexter during his first months as pastor, King had asked parishioners to join one of twelve fund-raising clubs according to their month of birth. Rice, president of the January Club, expresses concern for King and encloses a collection of poems and biblical quotations that members selected for him, entitled "Comforting Sense of Direction—Tidbits for Our Pastor and Club Member." [1]

TO: The Reverend M. L. King, Jr.
FROM: The January Club
ON: The Eve of the March 19th Trials

It comes a time in the life of each individual when he or she faces trying moments. At such times, it often happens that solace as well as sense of direction come through a spoken or unspoken word.

Realizing these circumstances, we, the members of the January Club share with you our favorite sources of comfort, hope and sense of direction, whether or not these sources are poems, quotes from the Bible, a printed prayer or words out of the creations of our own thinking. Whatever the case, these that we share have sustained and offered us a sense of direction, and we share them with you that

---

1. Thelma Austin Rice (1917–) was born in Montgomery and earned her B.S. (1937) and M.Ed. (1946) from Alabama State College. Rice taught in Mobile public schools from 1937 to 1945 and then, from 1945 to 1952, at the Mobile campus of Alabama State. In 1945 she organized the Metropolitan Council of the National Council of Negro Women, serving as its president until 1952. She returned to Montgomery in 1954 to head Alabama State's math department, where she remained until 1962. She was also an active member of the Women's Political Council, the NAACP, the Business and Professional Women's Club of Montgomery, and the Mobile Non-Partisan Voters League.

you may find in them a spark to comfort and sustain you as you face a trial situation made by man and all that such an experience could mean.

We are joined in this bond of expression of our concern for you.

Very sincerely yours,
THE JANUARY CLUB
[*signed*]
Thelma Austin Rice, President

Enclosures: In alphabetical order of the members.

TALS. MLKP-MBU: Box 119.

To W. E. B. Du Bois

19 March 1956
Montgomery, Ala.

Earlier in March Du Bois had sent King the first stanza of the poem Battle Hymn, *written by Gustavus Adolphus in 1630: "Fear not, O little flock the foe / That madly seeks thine overthrow / Dread not [h]is rage and power / What through thy courage sometime faints? / Its seeming power o'er God's saints / Lasts but a little hour." King may not have seen the verse; his office sent Du Bois this form letter of thanks.[1]*

Dear Friends:

This is a note to express my deepest gratitude to you for your kind letter. Such letters from friends sympathetic with our momentous struggle for justice give us renewed vigor and courage to carry on.

With every good wish, I am

Cordially yours,
[*signed*]
M. L. King, Jr.,
President

MLK/ehr

TLSr. WEBD-MU.

---

1. Du Bois to King, March 1956. William Edward Burghardt Du Bois (1868–1963), born in Great Barrington, Massachusetts, earned his B.A. (1888) from Fisk Uuniversity and his B.A. (1890), M.A. (1891), and Ph.D. (1895) from Harvard University. He taught at Wilberforce University (1894–1896), the University of Pennsylvania (1896–1897), and Atlanta University (1897–1910). A founder of the NAACP, Du Bois was the director of publications and the editor of *The Crisis* magazine from 1910 to 1934. He rejoined Atlanta University as head of its sociology department in 1933, returning briefly to the NAACP in 1944 to head the special research department (to 1948). Du Bois also served as editor of *Phylon* (1940–1944). In 1961 Du Bois joined the Communist Party and moved to Ghana to become editor in chief of *Encyclopedia Africana*. Du Bois contributed numerous articles to magazines and journals and authored many books on American race relations, most notably the classic *Souls of Black Folk* (1903).

21 March 1956
Chicago, Ill.

Drake, professor of sociology and anthropology at Roosevelt University, was a pioneer in the study of African-American life.[1] He applauds King as "among that small group of prophetic figures who have tried to teach the world how to fight for justice with weapons of the spirit."[2]

Dr. Martin Luther King
Dexter Ave. Baptist Church
Montgomery, Alabama

My dear Dr. King:

I am enclosing a page from one of our Chicago dailies. I thought, perhaps, you would like to have it for your archives. Whatever the outcome of the boycott and the attendant trials, you and your colleagues—and the Negro people of Montgomery—now belong to history. And you, particularly, will find your place among that small group of prophetic figures who have tried to teach the world how to fight for justice with weapons of the spirit. Toynbee, in A Study of History predicted that the Negro in America would eventually open up new dimensions of spiritual insight. Destiny has called you to participate in that process. How fortunate our people are that a man with your insight and training was "raised up" in the fullness of time.

In 1932, as a young man fresh out of Hampton, I attended a Quaker school in Pennsylvania, Pendle Hill. We spent a great deal of time studying Gandhi's philosophy. We used to dream of the day when someone would arise in our country to lead us in a similar fashion. Then Reinhold Niebuhr, in Moral Man and Immoral Society, threw out a few ideas as to the possibilites of non-violent direct action among Negro Americans. But the time was not ripe. The day has now come. When you held your great prayer meeting, I wired both the American Friends Service Committee and Reinhold Niebuhr, pointing out that what they had talked of in the Thirties had now come into being—quite independently of them, and that they should wire their support. I was very happy to receive communications from both sources indicating that they had acted. I shall send on

---

1. John Gibbs St. Clair Drake (1911–1990), born in Suffolk, Virginia, received his B.S. (1931) from Hampton Institute and his Ph.D. (1954) from the University of Chicago. In 1945 Drake co-authored a landmark study of African Americans in Chicago, *Black Metropolis*. While teaching at Roosevelt University in Chicago from 1946 to 1969, Drake also served as a Peace Corps consultant and an advisor to a number of postcolonial governments in Africa. In 1969 Drake became the first director of Stanford University's African and Afro-American studies program.

2. Drake enclosed a published poem he had written, "Freedom Fighters," dedicated to Charles Houston, Carter Woodson, and Charles Drew, with this notation typed above it: "I wrote this bit of verse many years ago, and held it, waiting for an event which I felt was worthy of dedicating it to. Time passed. When the three men named died during a single year, I sent it on to PHYLON where it was published. Now, I should like to rededicate it—to you and your colleagues, and the Negro people of Montgomery." The poem's last three lines are: "We focus Freedom's rays into a beam, / Illuminate the destined hour, / And justify the dreamer's dream" (*Phylon* 11, no. 3 [1950]: 222).

their letters for your files. I burned up the phone wires and telegraph wires the day before your meeting, trying, in my limited way, to mobilize financial and moral support. As one who had dreamed for twenty years of that day, I was stirred to the very core of my being. Having grown up in a Baptist parsonage, I took special pride in the fact that it was the Negro ministers who were in the vanguard.

Please accept these expressions of gratitude for your courage in fighting the battle for us all—as Negroes, as Christians, as Americans, as human beings. You fight not for us alone, but for all mankind. "Walk together children, Don't get weary, There's a great camp meeting in the promised land." [3]

Sincerely,
[*signed*]
St. Clair Drake,
Professor of Sociology and Anthropology;
co-author of Black Metropolis; Ford
Foundation Traveling Fellow in West
Africa, 1954–55.

TALS. MLKP-MBU: Box 91.

———————

3. This line is from the spiritual "There Is a Great Meeting in the Promised Land."

From William Stuart Nelson

21 March 1956
Washington, D.C.

Nelson, dean of Howard University, was an advocate of nonviolent resistance who had marched with Gandhi in 1946 to promote friendship between Hindus and Muslims in the Indian state of Bengal.[1]

The Reverend Martin Luther King
309 South Jackson Street
Montgomery, Alabama

Dear Mr. King:

This is just a line to wish you well in your present trials and to assure you that in the end right will prevail. I have followed the course of affairs in Montgomery

———————

1. William Stuart Nelson (1895–1977), a native of Paris, Kentucky, received his B.A. (1920) from Howard University and his B.D. (1924) from Yale University. After teaching philosophy and religion at Howard, Nelson served as the first black president of Shaw University (1931–1936) and the first black president of Dillard University (1936–1940). While dean of Howard University's School of Religion (1940–1948) he founded the *Journal of Religious Thought* and taught a pioneering course on the philosophy of nonviolence. Nelson marched with Gandhi in 1946 as a representative of the American Friends Service Committee.

with the deepest interest and concern and always with the hope that your cause would triumph.

As a fellow Negro and a fellow minister, I am naturally interested in what you are doing. In addition, your methods have made a deep impression upon me because of my associations with Mahatma Gandhi and my study of his great ideals. Once I asked him whether his method of non-violent non-cooperation might prove successful in the struggle here for our rights. Now it appears that you are are experimenting in that direction. My hope is that in the near future I might find it possible to visit Montgomery and discuss with you and your courageous fellow ministers and friends the inner forces and the events which have moved and sustained you. I wish somehow I had the power to help you.

With many thousands everywhere I join in prayer and assurance that your cause and our cause will triumph over every difficulty.

Sincerely yours,
[*signed*]
Wm. Stuart Nelson
Dean

TLS. MLKP-MBU: Box 28.

Testimony in *State of Alabama v. M. L. King, Jr.*

22 March 1956
Montgomery, Ala.

King's trial before Judge Eugene Carter attracted enormous press attention, including front-page coverage in the New York Times. *Several dozen reporters, including writers from England, France, India, and most of the major African-American newspapers, attended the four-day proceedings. More than five hundred African Americans waited outside the courthouse on Monday morning, 19 March, the first day of the trial. They were unable to get into the segregated courtroom, which seated about 230 people, because most of the seats were reserved for the defendants and for the seventy-odd witnesses.*[1] *King was accompanied by his wife and parents, as well as by out-of-state visitors including Michigan congressman Charles Diggs, Jr., and Alpha Phi Alpha general president Frank Stanley. Responding to a letter sent by the Fellowship of Reconciliation, more than two hundred clergymen announced "their own willingness to go personally to Montgomery to supply the pulpits of any of the defending ministers who were jailed."*[2] *At a meeting that night attended by several thousand, King declared that "this is the year God's gonna set his people free, and we want no cowards in our crowd."*[3] *To maintain movement morale and keep supporters informed, the*

1. Wayne Phillips, "First Negro Tried in Bus Boycotting," *New York Times,* 20 March 1956. See also Anna Holden, Notes on Trial, 19 March 1956.

2. See Fellowship of Reconciliation press release, "Four Hundred Clergymen Express Support for Montgomery Pastors," 18 March 1956. See also "Negro Congressman Attending Trial Here; Raps Segregation," *Montgomery Advertiser,* 20 March 1956.

3. Quoted in James Booker, " 'God Will Find Way,' Boycotters," *New York Amsterdam News,* 24 March 1956.

*MIA held two mass meetings on Tuesday night, the eve of King's testimony, attracting
nearly eight thousand people.*

*During two days of prosecution testimony, Circuit Solicitor William F. Thetford
called twenty-seven witnesses in an effort to prove that King was the primary leader of
the boycott, responsible for formulating demands, presiding at meetings, authorizing
financial expenditures, and representing the MIA in negotiations. His witnesses,
however, many of whom were King's associates and fellow officers in the MIA, resisted
his attempts to link the boycott to King. Thetford also argued that the boycott involved
intimidation and violence. Nine bus drivers testified that shots had been fired and
bricks thrown through bus windows, and three black witnesses claimed to have been
pulled off buses or threatened with violence for riding. King's defense counsel objected,
arguing that King's connections to these events could not be established.*

*After an unsuccessful motion to exclude the state's evidence, King's defense began
its presentation on Wednesday, 21 March. Led by local attorneys Fred D. Gray and
Charles D. Langford, King's legal team also included Alabama NAACP lawyers
Arthur D. Shores, Orzell Billingsley, Jr., Peter Hall, and NAACP general counsel
Robert L. Carter, who was unable to participate in the courtroom proceedings because
he was not a member of the Alabama Bar.[4] The cornerstone of their defense was an
attack on the evils of bus segregation and the abuse that Montgomery blacks had
suffered for years from Montgomery bus drivers, thus establishing under the 1921 anti-
boycott law a "just cause" or "legal excuse" for the boycott. Thirty-one of thirty-five
defense witnesses were bus patrons who described personal experiences of abuse by bus
drivers and their own motivations for boycotting the buses. Many testified that bus
drivers routinely called them derogatory names and often refused to give them change
or forced them to enter the bus from the back door. Georgia Gilmore, for example, said
that once a bus driver had told her, after she paid for her fare, "Nigger, get out that
door and go around to the back door"; he then sped away. Martha Walker recalled
helping her blind husband off a bus when the driver slammed the door shut on her
husband's right foot and dragged him some distance before he managed to get free.*

*Most black witnesses testified that their decision to boycott the buses was spontaneous
and that King was a representative of the community, not its leader. "Wasn't no one
man started it," Gladys Moore insisted. "We all started it over night." Robert S.
Graetz, pastor of the Trinity Lutheran Church and the most visible white MIA leader,
remarked that King had not asked people to boycott the buses; rather, he urged them to
decide for themselves. Graetz also quoted King and other MIA leaders as saying, "If
someone wants to ride the busses, let them ride, we are not suggesting to threaten them,
coerce them, or intimidate them, or anything else."[5]*

*As the final defense witness on the concluding day of the trial, King testifies in his
own defense. Addressing a packed courtroom as the crowd outside presses to get in,
King defends the Montgomery protest movement while denying responsibility for*

---

4. Orzell Billingsley, Jr. (1924–), a native of Birmingham, Alabama, earned his B.A. (1946) from
Talladega College and his LL.B. (1950) from Howard University. He joined the firm of Arthur Shores
and Peter Hall in 1951. An NAACP legal advisor, he was active in voter registration and, along with
Peter Hall, repeatedly challenged the exclusion of African Americans from Alabama's juries. Peter A.
Hall (1912–), born in Birmingham, graduated from Johnson C. Smith University and earned his J.D.
and LL.B. (1946) degrees from DePaul University. Robert Carter (1917–), born in Caryville, Florida,
earned a B.A. (1937) from Lincoln University, an LL.B. (1940) from Howard University, and an LL.M.
(1941) from Columbia University. He served as Thurgood Marshall's legal assistant at the NAACP and
worked on many desegregation cases, including *Brown v. Board of Education,* before becoming the
group's general counsel.

5. Transcript, *State of Alabama v. M. L. King, Jr.*

leading an illegal boycott. King's occasionally evasive testimony downplays his own role in the MIA's decision-making processes. "My exposition has always been 'to let your conscience be your guide,'" King insists. Asked if he had ever advocated violence, King replies, "My motivation has been the exact converse of that; I urged non-violence at all points."

After the prosecution called several bus drivers forward as rebuttal witnesses, who asserted that they treated black and white passengers alike with courtesy, each side presented closing arguments.

Judge Carter brought the four-day trial to a close that afternoon, finding King guilty of conducting an illegal boycott against Montgomery City Lines. Carter fined King $500 plus court costs but later suspended the sentence and postponed the remaining boycott cases while King's lawyers appealed the judgment. On 30 April 1957 the Court of Appeals rejected King's appeal, stating that his lawyers had filed it after the sixty-day deadline.

The following testimony by King is from the official transcript of his trial prepared for his appeal.

M. L. KING, JR., having been duly sworn, was examined and testified as follows:

Direct Examination

BY LAWYER SHORES:

Q   Will you state your full name?

A   Martin Luther King, Jr.

Q   What is your occupation?

A   I am a minister.

Q   You are the minister of one of the local churches here in Montgomery, Alabama?

A   Yes, I am minister of the Dexter Avenue Baptist Church.

Q   Are you a member of the Montgomery Improvement Association?

A   Yes, I am.

Q   Are you an official of this organization?

A   I am.

Q   Are you one of the organizers of the Montgomery Improvement Association?

A   Yes, I was in the meeting when it was organized.

Q   For what purpose was this organization formulated?

A   Well, the name itself covers the basic purposes of the organization, to improve the general status of Montgomery, to improve race relations, and to uplift the general tenor of the community.

Q   How does one become a member of the Montgomery Improvement Association?

A   Well, any citizen who is interested in becoming a member of the Montgomery Improvement Association can become a member—there are no dues—it is just a matter of being interested in improving Montgomery, thereby one can become a member.

Q   There are no joining fees or dues?

A   No.

Q   From what source is the Association receiving its funds?

A   Well, the funds have been received from free-will offerings, individuals who have given freely for the fund.

Q   Have you any idea about how much this Association has received?

A   I don't know the exact figures on that. I don't have them. That is in the hands of the Finance Committee.

Q   Are members of the Montgomery Improvement Association restricted by race or to any particular race?

A   No, not at all, anyone.

Q   Have there been mass meetings held by the Montgomery Improvement Association?

A   Yes.

Q   Have you attended those meetings?

A   Yes, I have.

Q   Have you presided at those meetings?

A   Some of them.

Q   Have you spoken at those meetings?

A   Yes, I have.

Q   During the course of your speeches have you urged any of the listeners or members of the M.I.A. to refrain from riding the busses of the Montgomery City Lines?

A   No, I have not. My exposition has always been "to let your conscience be your guide, if you want to ride that is all right."

Q   Have those meetings always been open to anybody, the members, as well as to all citizens?

A   Yes, they have.

Q   Have you urged any violence, or any of these violent acts that have been testified about here in Court, have you urged any of the members to perform any of those acts?

A   No, I have not. My motivation has been the exact converse of that; I urged non-violence at all points.

Q   Do you know if any members urged anybody to do acts of violence or perpetrate acts of violence?

A   No, sir, I do not. I never heard that mentioned.

Q   I believe there have been several proposals mentioned. Have you attended any of the meetings called by the Mayor or other groups who tried to solve the bus situation?

A   Yes, I have.

Q   And have you carried proposals back to the organization for presentation to its members?

A   Yes, I have.

Q   And what was the reaction, or what action was taken on these proposals?

A   Well, they were always rejected by the people. We made it clear we couldn't make any final statement on any of the proposals and they had to be taken back to the people, and we did that through the mass meetings, and when they were rejected I would make the contact and let the officials know what happened.

Q   Do you know what these proposals were?

A   Well, to the best of my recollection, the main proposal was, or the main one we took back was the proposal to reserve ten seats in the front for the negro passengers and ten seats in the back for white passengers. Also included in that was a guarantee of courtesy. Now, that is about the substance of that proposal.[6]

Q   Did you say ten seats in front for negroes or white?

A   I mean white passengers, ten in front for white passengers and ten in the rear for negro passengers.

Q   What proposals did your group present for the bus company's consideration?

A   We presented three proposals. The first dealt with the question of courtesy; that is, more courteous treatment from the bus drivers themselves. The second proposal dealt with the whole question of seating; that we requested a seating arrangement based on a first come first served basis, negro passengers seating from the rear of the bus to the front, and white passengers from the front to the rear with no reserved seats for anybody. And the third proposal was a request to hire negro bus drivers on predominantly negro lines.[7]

Q   And what was the reaction to those proposals by the bus company and the City officials?

A   On their part those proposals were rejected. There was some concession on the first proposal—that is the question of courtesy—the others were rejected outright at every meeting we attended.

Q   Did the Montgomery Improvement Association organize this car pool?

A   Yes.

Q   Will you describe the operation of this car pool?

A   Well, the car pool is just a matter of individuals volunteering to give their cars for the purpose of transporting persons to and from their jobs and their business. These persons volunteered to place their cars in the pool from the pick-up stations and dispatch stations, and these cars will be there at certain hours for the purpose of transporting people to various places.

Q   Are the persons charged any fees for being transported?

A   No, they are not.

Q   Are the persons paid for operating their cars?

A   No.

Q   Is there any payment made to persons who own cars?

A   No.

Q   To operate them in the pool? Or anything?

A   Well, there is a payment which is for the purpose of upkeep—that is for the wear and tear on the cars. We have all day drivers, about twenty all day drivers that start at six o'clock in the morning and work throughout the day, and there is a bonus given for the purpose of wear and tear on the car, and no one is paid a salary for driving.

Q   Are you paid a salary by the Montgomery Improvement Association?

A   No, I am not.

---

6. On 13 February 1956 an organization formed by local white businessmen submitted a proposal to the MIA that preserved segregated bus seating while also promising that "there will be no retaliation whatsoever resulting from the boycott." At a 20 February 1956 mass meeting the MIA overwhelmingly rejected this proposal (see Ralph Abernathy to the Men of Montgomery, 20 February 1956).

  7. See "To the National City Lines," 8 December 1955, pp. 80–81 in this volume.

Q Is anyone paid a salary?

A No.

Q Do you know anything about these incidents of vandalism or unrest that were testified to here by the witnesses on the Stand?

A No, other than reading about them, and I don't know anything else about them. I just heard about them.

Q Do you know whether or not any one in your organization has ever resorted to any acts of vandalism?

A No, I don't. I am sure I know of no one in the organization has anything to do with it or responsible for it.

Q Have any acts of vandalism, or acts of intimidation or worrisome nature, been perpetrated against you?

A Yes, very definitely.

Q What act of violence was perpetrated against you or your home?

A Well, my home has been bombed on one occasion, and I have received numerous threats. I couldn't really give the number. I received numerous threats.

Q And at the time your house was bombed did you or any member of your organization to your knowledge urge any member of your organization or anybody else to commit violence?

A No, just the opposite.

Q I believe some statement was made about a telephone conversation between you and the Mayor where terms of the proposal was accepted by you and later rejected. Did you receive any proposal from the Mayor with respect to the settlement of this controversy over the telephone? And later rejected?

A No, I did not. I have never received a proposal that I accepted. I have always contended I could only take it up with the people, and that is what I said to Mayor Gayle, when he offered the proposal over the phone, I would take it up with the people, and that is as far as I would go. And he was to call me back on Friday to discuss it, but he never called back.

Q And have you always taken the proposals to the people to have them decide whether or not the proposal would be accepted?

A Yes, sir, I have.

Q And what has been the results of taking the proposals back to the people?

A Well, to this point all of the proposals I took to the people and put before them they felt were not satisfactory so they have rejected the proposals to this point.

Q Have you any concern for the status of negroes in Montgomery?

THE SOLICITOR: We object to that.

THE COURT: If you connect it up with the Montgomery Improvement Association as a member.

BY LAWYER SHORES:

Q Does everyone connected with the Montgomery Improvement Association?

A Yes, they do have concern for the general status of negroes here.

Q Is it, or not, a fact your activities in connection with the Montgomery Improvement Association constitute a part of your effort to improve the negro status in Montgomery?

A That is right, quite right.

Q	In connection with the transportation was Rev. Glasco paid any amount in connection with transportation?
A	Yes.
Q	Do you recall what amount was paid?
A	No, I don't remember the exact amount off hand.
Q	The finances are not handled by you, are they?
A	No.
Q	You have a finance committee?
A	That is right.
Q	Is there an office worker that receives any pay?
A	Office worker?
Q	Yes.
A	Yes.
Q	How many office workers that you pay a salary?
A	I think it is seven.
Q	Seven?
A	Yes, that is right.

Cross Examination

BY THE SOLICITOR:

Q	This bus boycott or bus protest, whatever you choose to call it, was called for the 5th of December through a series of little pamphlets—you are familiar with what I am talking about?
A	Yes, I am familiar.
Q	It is true they appeared on the streets a day or two before the protest meeting concerning alleged grievances?
A	I really couldn't say. I don't know if the pamphlets were put out for more than one day. I just don't recall what the pamphlet said concerning the time.
Q	Those pamphlets were pretty well distributed over Montgomery?
A	Yes.
Q	Starting about Thursday or Friday before the 5th of December; is that true?
A	That is true, yes.
Q	Did you see any of these pamphlets?
A	Yes, I remember seeing one of them.
Q	I believe you and a group of other men met on Monday afternoon?
A	That is true, yes.
Q	And formed the Montgomery Improvement Association?
A	That is right.
Q	How many of you were there? If you like to, we have the Minutes of the meeting here for the purpose of refreshing your recollection.[8] This is just a photostatic copy of them.
A	All of these persons were present. (Indicating)
Q	Did you personally know all of them?

---

8. See Fields, Minutes of Montgomery Improvement Association Founding Meeting, 5 December 1955, pp. 68–70 in this volume.

A	Oh, yes, sir.
Q	Refreshing your recollection, how many of them?
A	According to the Minutes, eighteen.
Q	After refreshing your recollection would you say there were substantially that number?
A	That is right.
Q	Where did this meeting take place?
A	It was held at the Mt. Zion A.M.E. Church.
Q	Around three P.M. on December the 5th?
A	That is right.
Q	At that time you formed the Montgomery Improvement Association?
A	Yes, we did.
Q	You elected your officers?
A	Yes.
Q	Elected an Executive Committee too, I believe? Refreshing your recollection, "Moved and second that the sixteen persons here"—the Minutes up here show eighteen present—"And a suggestion that nine names be brought in making twenty-five which constitutes the Executive Committee." Do you remember the Executive Committee of twenty-five with nine others to be named?
A	Yes, that is right. I remember that.
Q	Now, I believe your transportation committee was set up at that time, and your finance committee; is that true?
A	No. My best judgment, they were not. Maybe I am wrong.
Q	Was it agreed at that time to set up the transportation and finance committee, names to be supplied later?
A	I don't know.
Q	Refresh your recollection with this. I don't know exactly what it means myself. On page 3 of these Minutes it simply shows transportation committee and finance. Can you explain what that means?
A	I don't know, and that really isn't clear enough for me to make any statement concerning it. I really don't remember about these committees.
Q	Let me ask you this. Did you have anything to do with what I will refer to as the first boycott, the boycott called for December the 5th?
A	No. Do you mean if I had anything to do with calling it?
Q	That is right.
A	No, I didn't.
Q	Do you know who did?
A	No, I don't. It was a spontaneous beginning, one of those things which just had been smoldering.
Q	Do you know who printed those pamphlets?[9]

---

9. King was not involved with the first leaflets, produced and distributed by the Women's Political Council on Friday, 2 December 1955, which encouraged Montgomery's African Americans not to ride the buses. That evening, however, King and other black leaders met to plan the one-day boycott and decided that another leaflet should be prepared for distribution on Saturday. King and Abernathy mimeographed the second set of leaflets (see Leaflet, "Don't Ride the Bus," 2 December 1955, p. 67 in this volume).

A	No, I don't.	22 Mar 1956

Q   Do you know that the Montgomery Improvement Association according to all the testimony we have had here up to now has spent of this money it collected some $30,000 in supporting the boycott or protest; is that correct?

A   That would be impossible to say. I don't know enough about it.

Q   Do you know any other money that has been spent, you sign all the checks, don't you?

A   Yes, I do. I would say most of it has been used for that.

Q   And you couldn't give us any amount or in which manner it has been spent other than on the boycott or protest?

A   Well, I don't have it before me. I don't remember of any.

Q   I note in your Minutes of that first meeting "It was recommended that Resolutions would be drawn up," and a Resolutions Committee was appointed?

A   Yes.

Q   You were on that committee, I take it?

A   I don't believe I worked on the Resolutions Committee. That committee was appointed.

Q   Your Minutes show "The President, Rev. M. L. King, Attorney Gray and Attorney Langford is on the committee." Is that true? They are your Minutes, aren't they?

A   It might be true I was on the committee and I had worked with the committee.

Q   Who drew up that Resolution?

A   This committee, this Resolutions Committee.

Q   Who was on the Resolutions Committee at that time?

A   I don't remember.

Q   When was the Resolution drawn up?

A   Sometime during the meeting at the Holt Street Baptist Church.

Q   You are telling the Court that the Resolution wasn't drawn up at the afternoon meeting, but it was drawn up that night; is that what you are telling us?

A   That is right.

Q   And it was also agreed at the afternoon meeting that the protest would be continued; is that correct?

A   I don't know.

Q   Let me read it to refresh your recollection, or you can read it.

A   Well, that is true according to the Minutes, according to the Minutes here. I don't remember the discussion at this point.

Q   You are familiar with that Resolution I take it?

A   Well, I have seen it.

Q   You have seen it?

A   Yes, I have.

Q   You stated you have never asked anybody not to ride the busses. Let me read you what the Resolution says. It says: "That the citizens of Montgomery are requesting that every citizen in Montgomery, regardless of race, color or creed, to refrain from riding busses owned and operated in the City of Montgomery by the Montgomery City Lines, Incorporated until some arrangement has been worked out between said citizens and the Montgomery City Lines,

Incorporated." You say this was made up on that night. That is what the Resolution says.[10]

A   I didn't read the Resolution.

Q   You heard the Resolution read?

A   This was done by the committee. Oh, yes.

Q   You were there?

A   Oh, yes, sir.

Q   Who read the Resolution?

A   My best recollection, Rev. Abernathy read the Resolution.

Q   Rev. Abernathy?

A   Yes, sir.

Q   This is the Resolution the Montgomery Improvement Association presented at that mass meeting; is that correct?

A   Yes, it was presented at that meeting.

Q   In other words, what the Montgomery Improvement Association did, as I unooderstand it, is to back an existing one day boycott and by this the protest, or whatever you want to call it, has extended over a period of several months and it is still in existence; is that substantially true?

A   Yes and no. The last part is true, it is still in existence. Now, as to the first part I would say the Montgomery Improvement Association came into being in an attempt to improve the general status of the city plus the—

Q   That is not in response to my question at all.

A   I was fixing to give the other part of it.

Q   That wasn't responsive to my question.

THE COURT: Ask it again.

BY THE SOLICITOR:

Q   I ask you this. I said the Montgomery Improvement Association, as I understand it, backed an existing one day boycott and has through its transportation committee and others urged people not to ride the busses, and that situation is still existing today?

A   No, I wouldn't say so.

Q   Isn't that the way it came about?

A   No.

Q   When did you come here to Montgomery?

A   I came to Montgomery in 1954.

Q   You have been here about a year and a half, two years?

A   That is right.

Q   Since you have been here how many times have you ridden busses?

A   Only one.

Q   How many white members have you at this time in the Montgomery Improvement Association, to your knowledge?

A   I really don't know. We don't keep records of those by race. I couldn't say how many white members we have.

---

10. See MIA Mass Meeting at Holt Street Baptist Church, 5 December 1955, pp. 71–79 in this volume.

Q How many do you think that are members of the Montgomery Improvement Association that are white?

A Well, I don't know. I know Rev. Graetz is a member, and we probably have some other. I know we have some other.[11]

Q Do you know of any.

A I know we have some others.

Q Who are they?

A I don't recall at this point.

Q How many members do you have?

A I don't know. We don't keep a record of that.

Q Coming back to the Minutes of your first meeting: "It was passed that the recommendations from the committee be given to the citizens at the night meeting." That is right, isn't it?

A That is right.

Q The recommendation they are referring to there was the recommendation that the protest or boycott be continued; is that correct?

A I don't think I quite caught your question.

Q You testified that "It was passed that the recommendations from the committee be given to the citizens at the night meeting." You say that is right?

A What Resolutions does that refer to?

Q "It was passed that the recommendations," as you see this here. (Indicating)

A What recommendation does that refer to?

Q I don't know. I wasn't at the meeting.

A This don't say about what. I really don't remember what transpired about that there.

Q Don't know what it means?

A No, I really don't.

Q As a matter of fact, you remember being at this organizational meeting on the afternoon of the 5th?

A Yes, sir.

Q Did you draw up this agenda for the meeting that night on the afternoon of December the 5th?

A I don't remember for sure when that was drawn up.

Q Look at this right there and you read that. (Indicating)

A I imagine so, that it was drawn up there.

Q Were you at a meeting of the Montgomery Improvement Association on December the 8th, 1955?

A I don't remember. What was the nature of the meeting?

---

11. Robert S. Graetz (1928–), born in Clarksburg, West Virginia, and educated in Columbus, Ohio, graduated from Capital University (1950) and received his B.D. (1955) from Evangelical Lutheran Theological Seminary. Graetz was assigned from 1955 to 1958 to the Trinity Lutheran Church in Montgomery. Graetz and his family were ostracized by other whites for his involvement in the MIA, and, on 25 August 1956, while the family was out of town, three dynamite sticks exploded in their front yard. Mayor Gayle accused Graetz of bombing his own home in order to stimulate out-of-state contributions to the MIA. Later Graetz's car tires were slashed and sugar was placed in his gasoline tank. The harassment continued, and Graetz finally left Montgomery to become pastor of St. Philip Lutheran Church in Columbus, Ohio, where he served until 1967. See *Montgomery: A White Preacher's Memoir* (1991) for his account of the boycott.

Q I am referring to the Minutes of the meeting and it says "The contact committee of the Montgomery Improvement Association."

A The contact committee?

Q The contact committee.

A I don't see anything about a contact committee. I don't know about it.

Q I am reading from your Minutes.

LAWYER SHORES:	We object to that. From whose Minutes?
THE SOLICITOR:	They are the Montgomery Improvement Association Minutes that are in evidence.
THE WITNESS:	I didn't write these.
THE SOLICITOR:	Take a look at your Minutes and see what they say.
LAWYER BILLINGSLEY:	You are using "your" and "we" sometimes. "Your." You are using your organization.
THE SOLICITOR:	I take it it is his organization.

BY THE SOLICITOR:

Q Look at it and see what it relates to and give an answer to my question.

A I am not familiar with that name. I guess that is the name the secretary used.
However, that committee was appointed by the Executive Board.

Q By the Executive Board?

A Yes, sir.

Q That is the Executive Board of the Montgomery Improvement Association?

A That is right.

Q That is the committee that met with Mr. Thrasher, Rev. Hughes, the bus officials and the City Commission? [12]

A That is right.

Q On December the 8th?

A Yes, I think that is the date.

Q How was contact made with the Executive Committee to attend that meeting?

A The Alabama Council on Human Relations made the contact.

Q Who did they contact?

A They contacted the City Commission first, I think, and they contacted the
Montgomery Improvement Association.

Q Who of the Montgomery Improvement Association?

A Well, they contacted me as President of the Association.

Q They contacted you as President of the Association?

---

12. Thomas R. Thrasher was rector of the Episcopal Church of the Ascension in Montgomery and
a leader of the Alabama Council on Human Relations (ACHR). Mayor Gayle was a member of his
congregation. Robert E. Hughes (1928–), a Methodist preacher, received his B.A. (1949) from the
University of Alabama, his M.Div. (1952) from Emory University, and his M.S.T. (1967) from Boston
University. He became pastor of the Rockford Circuit (Methodist Church) in Alabama in 1953 but left
the next year to serve as executive director of the ACHR. On 7 December 1955 Hughes contacted the
city commission and helped organize the first negotiating session between the MIA and the city commissioners (see Minutes, Meeting Between Contact Committee of MIA and City and Bus Officials, 8
December 1955). After leaving the ACHR in 1961, Hughes worked on human rights issues in Southern
Rhodesia until 1964, when the government expelled him because of his support for that nation's liberation movement.

A	That is right.	22 Mar
Q	Then what action did you take?	1956

A   Well, at that time just talked to the Executive Board.

Q   Did you call a meeting of the Executive Board?

A   Oh, yes.

Q   Where was that meeting held?

A   I don't remember.

Q   Do you remember who was there?

A   The whole Board was present—I think most of the members of the Board were present.

Q   Approximately how many were there?

A   I don't know exactly. It must have been about twenty or more.

Q   You say that the contact committee, of which you were a member, was appointed by the Executive Committee?

A   That is right.

Q   Did the Executive Committee at that time formulate the demands that would be made upon the bus company?

A   I don't remember; I couldn't say.

Q   When were those demands formulated, and who formulated them?

A   I think that was done at the Holt Street Church, as I recall. I wouldn't like to make a definite statement because I really don't remember, as I said, the people made these demands.

Q   What people?

A   More than four thousand people at the Holt Street Baptist Church.

Q   Those four thousand people formulated these three specific demands; is that what you are telling us?

A   Well, it is according to how you interpret the word formulate, if you mean they wrote them?

Q   That is right.

A   Well, no, not four thousand people.

Q   Who did write them?

A   I don't know; I don't remember who wrote them.

Q   When is the first you ever heard of the three demands?

A   Well, as I stated, I believe it was at the Holt Street meeting. I don't remember. I don't like to go to that extent.

Q   Anyone ever tell you the three requests that were going to be made to the bus company?

A   Who told me, I cannot recall. I think I heard them at the mass meeting. There were so many speakers at that meeting I don't know who mentioned them.

Q   Who was it got up and said, "These are the demands we are going to make on the City or the bus company?"

A   It was one speaker.

Q   That is what I am trying to get at. Who worked out these demands?

A   I don't know.

Q   You just don't know?

A   I don't know.

Q	How much money have you in your bank account over in Atlanta now?	195
A	I really don't know.	

LAWYER SHORES: We object to the wording of the question "In your bank account."

THE COURT: He has already said he don't know.

BY THE SOLICITOR:

Q   Let me change that. You have a bank account in the name of the Montgomery Improvement Association in the Citizens Trust of Atlanta?

A   That is right, we do.

Q   Now, I believe that $5000 was deposited in that bank in Atlanta, the same $5000 you drew out of the Alabama National Bank?

A   That is right.

Q   Did you take it over there or send it over there?

A   No, it was sent over.

Q   It was sent over by mail?

A   That is right.

Q   On February 21st do you know what the amount was you had put into bank?

LAWYER SHORES: We object to that. It has nothing to do with this case.

THE COURT: Overrule your objection. The reason I am going to let it in, this is money spent by the Montgomery Improvement Association and collected for the purpose of helping out with the so-called boycott. For that reason I will let it in.

LAWYER SHORES: The amount wouldn't make any difference.

THE COURT: Show how much they collected at that time. He said voluntary contributions were given for the purpose of aiding the boycott.

LAWYER SHORES: We concede money was collected and put in the account.

THE SOLICITOR: We would like to know the amount.

LAWYER SHORES: This is fishing.

THE COURT: Overrule your objection.

LAWYER SHORES: We take an exception.

(Exception noted for the defendant.)

BY THE SOLICITOR:

Q   Do you know?

A   No, I don't know.

Q   I believe that you have stated that the Montgomery Improvement Association is being run on a budget of about $3000 a week?

A   Well, approximately that.

Q   The Montgomery Improvement Association is spending approximately $400 a day?

A   I wouldn't say exactly, but it might be in that area.

Q   And whatever is being spent by the Montgomery Improvement Association, so far as you know, is being spent for the continuance of the protest or boycott?

A   Well, I don't know exactly what you mean by the continuance of it. When you say continuance, I don't exactly know. [*King's testimony concludes*]

196   TD. Transcript, *State of Alabama v. M. L. King, Jr.*, No. 7399 (Court of Appeals of Alabama, 1956), pp. 482–507; copy in AAGR-A-Ar: SG 8423.

JUDGMENT AND SENTENCE OF THE COURT
THURSDAY, MARCH 22nd, A.D.1956
COURT MET PURSUANT TO ADJOURNMENT
PRESENT THE HONORABLE EUGENE W. CARTER, JUDGE PRESIDING.

THE STATE   XXXXXXXXXXXXXXXX
#7399   INDICTMENT FOR VIO. SECTION 54 TITLE 14 CODE
M. L. KING, JUNIOR OF ALABAMA 1940.

This day came the State by its Solicitor and came also the
defendant in his own proper person and by attorney; and the said defendant
being duly arraigned upon the indictment for his plea thereto says he is
not guilty.

And after taking of testimony on behalf of the State and
after the State had rested its case; the defendant filed a motion to
exclude all of the evidence introduced by the State; and said motion
being xxxxxxxxx argued by counsel and understood by the Court, it is
considered and ordered by the Court that said motion to exclude be and
the same is hereby overruled.

And after the completion of all testimony in said cause; and
after hearing xxxxxxxx (hearing) said testimony, and after hearing arguments
of counsel, xxxxxx the Court being of opinion, it is considered and
ordered by the Court, and it is the judgment of the Court that judxxxxx
the said defendant is guilty as charged in the complaint and a fine of
five hundred ($500.00) dollars xxxx was assessed against him by the Court.

And said fine and cost not being paid; and the said defendant
being asked by the Court if he had anything to say why the sentence of the
law should not now be pronounced upon him says nothing. It is therefore
considered and adjudged by the Court that the said defendant perform hard
labor for Montgomery County for one hundred forty days for the fine; and
the cost of this prosecution not being presently paid or otherwise
secured, and the same being now ascertained and amount gxx to _____;
it is further considered and adjudged by the Court, and it is the
judgment and sentence of the Court that the said defendant perform
hard labor for Montgomery County for an additional term of 246 days
in payment of said costs at the rate of 75cents per diem, making in all
_386_ days during which said defendant is to perform hard labor for
Montgomery County beginning from this day and ending on the _12_ day
of _April_, 19_57_.

And questions of law arising in this case for the decision
of the Court of Appeals of Alabama, the defendant xx gives notice of
appeal and requests a suspension of sentence pending said appeal;
it is therefore considered and ordered by the Court that pending said
appeal to said Court of Alabama this sentence be and the same is hereby
suspended and that pending said appeal the defendant may be admitted
to bail in the sum of $1,000.00 to be made and approved as required by law.

[*22 March 1956*]
[*Montgomery, Ala.*]

Moments after Judge Eugene W. Carter fined King $500 for violating an antiboycott law, a crowd of three hundred cheering supporters greeted King and his wife outside the courthouse. In an impromptu curbside press conference King expresses his faith that the verdict would be overturned on appeal and that the boycott would continue in the same spirit of nonviolent resistance. Crowd noises can be heard in the background of the recording, including an exchange reported the next day in the New York Times: *after someone shouted, "You gonna ride the buses?" the crowd roared back, "No!"*[1] *The Martin Luther King, Jr., Film Project assembled the following recordings for use in the film* Montgomery to Memphis *(1969).*[2]

[*King:*] . . . we are right and that we have a legitimate complaint, and also we feel that one of the great glories of America is the right to protest for right, and I feel that the courts will substantiate our contention at that point, that along the way we will be justified. [*recording interrupted*]

[*Coretta Scott King:*] Do you want me to talk now to, the statement that I have to say, or you just want to get my voice in? [*recording interrupted*] All along I have supported my husband in this cause and at this point I feel even stronger about the cause, and whatever happens to him it happens to me. [*recording interrupted*]

[*King:*] The court reached its verdict a few minutes ago and I was convicted. The fine was five hundred dollars. Of course we are appealing the case and it will come up next in the court of appeals, and I have faith to believe that as the case is appealed and as it goes up through the higher courts, the decision will be reversed. We feel and we have felt all along that we stand under the aegis of the constitution, we feel that this protest which we are involved in is constitutional, and to deny us that right would be to deny our constitutional right as citizens of the United States of America. [*recording interrupted*] [*noise from the crowd*]

I don't know exactly what pertinent subject would apply. [*recording interrupted*] We still feel that we are right and that we stand within our constitutional rights in the protest. And we still advocate nonviolence and passive resistance and still determine to use the weapon of love. Now I can say that there is no bitterness on my part as a result of the decision and I'm sure that I voice the sentiment of the more than forty thousand Negro citizens of Montgomery. We still have the attitude of love, we still have the method of passive resistance and we are still insist-

---

1. Wayne Phillips, "Negro Minister Convicted of Directing Bus Boycott," *New York Times*, 23 March 1956. See also Anna Holden, Notes, Statements After Decision, *State of Alabama v. M. L. King, Jr.*, 22 March 1956; Tom Johnson and Frank McArdle, "Court Fines King $500 on Boycott Law Charge," *Montgomery Advertiser*, 23 March 1956; and "Boycott Leader Convicted, Vows Integration Fight," *Atlanta Constitution*, 22 March 1956.

2. These "sync sound" recordings, originally made by Twentieth Century–Fox Movietone News and Hearst Metrotone News, are owned by the Martin Luther King, Jr., Estate. They are quarter-inch single-track tapes and consist of audio material intended to be synchronized with motion picture footage.

ing, emphatically, that violence is self-defeating, that he who lives by the sword will perish by the sword.

At. MMFR: Sync Sound 103.

Address to MIA Mass Meeting at Holt Street Baptist Church

22 March 1956
Montgomery, Ala.

Hours after his conviction for violating Alabama's antiboycott law, King declares that "the protest is still on" to the thousands gathered at Holt Street Baptist Church. As hymns such as "We Shall Not Be Moved," "Go, Send Me Oh Lord," and "Walk Together, Children" filled the church, a participant remarked, "We all wanted to be together tonight and we [wanted] to be here, because this is where we started."[1] As King entered amid thundering cheers, a platform speaker declared that "he who [was] nailed to the cross for us this afternoon approaches," while several audience members commented "He's next to Jesus himself," "We are sure with him," [and] "He's my darling."[2] During his speech King discusses his trial and expresses confidence that he will win the appeal. "You don't get to the promised land without going through the wilderness," he concludes. "Though we may not get to see the promised land, we know it's coming because God is for it." Coretta Scott King sent an audiotape recording of King's remarks to Cecil and Fran Thomas, her former teachers, who transcribed excerpts of it as follows.

"As I look at it, I guess I have committed three sins. The first sin I have committed is being born a Negro. The second sin that I have committed, along with all of us, is being subjected to the battering rams of segregation and oppression. The third and more basic sin which all of us have committed is the sin of having the moral courage to stand up and express our weariness of this oppression. . . . Thank God we are no longer content to accept second-class citizenship, but we are determined to struggle for justice and equality."

"Today the judge handed down a decision which said in substance that I am guilty of dis-obeying the anti-boycott law. The fine was $500. As you know, the penalty could have been six months in prison and $1,000, but I was very happy to hear Judge Carter say that he was a little lenient because I had enough religion in me to at least preach non-violence.[3] We must not totally condemn Judge Carter. He was in a tragic dilemma. Maybe he did the best he could under the expedient method. As you know, men in political positions allow themselves to suc-

---

1. Quoted in Anna Holden, Notes, MIA Mass Meeting at Holt Street Baptist Church, 22 March 1956.
2. Ibid.
3. According to Holden, King also said: "I think we were aware of the consequences before the cases came up. I think we knew when we started that this might happen. I [was] enough of an optimist to expect the best, but enough of a realist to also expect the worst."

cumb to the expedient rather than reaching out for the moral that might be eternally corrective and true."

"We are not bitter. We are still preaching non-violence. We are still using the weapon of love. We are still using the method of passive resistance. I feel confident that as this case moves up through the higher courts, somewhere along the way the decision will be reversed."

"And let us not lose faith in democracy. For with all of its weaknesses, there is a ground and a basis of hope in our democratic creed. If we have the courage in America to transform democracy from thin paper to thick action, we will find that we are involved in the greatest form of government that the mind has ever conceived. So we're not to lose faith in democracy. We feel that democracy gives us this right to protest."

"We have never and we do not intend to engage in any acts of violence. There was no evidence in the court to point out that we have participated in violence. Five or six cases were brought out, but never on any occasion did they prove that these acts of violence were carried out by Negroes. So we can say and we can be true to ourselves and we can say honestly that we have not advocated violence and we have not participated in violence, but that we have gone courageously with the Christian movement."

"This is a spiritual movement and we are depending on moral and spiritual forces. That is the only weapon we have."

"The protest is still on.[4] And we want it known throughout the length and breadth of this land—to Asia and Africa—let the world know—that we are standing up for justice. Christianity has always insisted that in the perennial struggle between good and evil, the forces of light will eventually emerge as the victor. God is speaking to his children today and saying, 'Don't play with me! For if you keep playing with me, I'll break the backbone of your power and knock you out of the orbits of your international and national prestige. I am going to be God in this universe.' We want the world to know that we believe in God, and we believe that God controls the destiny of the universe, and Evil can't triumph in this universe. This is our hope. This is the thing that keeps us going."

"Freedom doesn't come on a silver platter. Whenever there is any great movement toward freedom, there will inevitably be some tension. Somebody will have to have the courage to sacrifice. You don't get to the promised land without going through the wilderness. Though we may not get to see the promised land, we know it's coming because God is for it. So don't worry about some of the things we have to go through. They are just a necessary part of the great movement that we are making toward freedom. There can never be growth without growing pains. Let us continue with the same spirit, with the same orderliness, with the

---

4. Holden recorded more of King's speech: "I want you to know that for the last two months I have had a grea[*t*] rende[*z*]vous with the jail house. I was arrested for driving 35 miles an hour and put in a cell. I went to court and was convicted and fined. I [went] to jail again with some of the finest citizens of Montgomery when we [were] arrested for breaking the anti-boycott law. I [had] to go to court this week and now I will have to go again. I might have to go four or five times more. This past conviction, the one before it, and all they can heap upon us will not diminish our determination one iota. (two rounds of applause) I'm going to stand in the morning, stand in the afternoon and stand in the evening."

same discipline, with the same Christian approach. I believe that God is using Montgomery as his proving ground. It may be that here in the capital of the Confederacy, the birth of the ideal of freedom in America and in the Southland can be born. God be praised for you, for your loyalty, for your determination. God bless you and keep you, and may God be with us as we go on." [5]

TTa. MLKP-MBU: Box 80.

---

5. Holden noted that following King's address and testimonials from other MIA leaders, he returned to the podium: "'I want to ask you all a question. I want to ask you because they said in court that I started the protest. They said that a selfish, power-seeking group who wanted to get publicity started it. Who started the protest?' Audience—'We did.' 'The bus drivers'. 'The bus company'. King—I heard that you are tired of it. Are you tired? Audience—'No, No.' 'We're going to keep on.'"

From Frank L. Stanley

22 March 1956
Louisville, Ky.

The editor of the Louisville Defender *informs King that his 18 March sermon at Dexter Avenue Baptist Church will be published in his newspaper.*[1] *Stanley was in Montgomery to cover the trial for the newspaper and convey Alpha Phil Alpha's support for its fellow member. Stanley, fraternity general secretary James Huger, and southern vice president Lewis O. Swingler presented a check for $1,000 to the MIA at a 20 March mass meeting.*[2]

Reverend M. L. King, Jr.
Dexter Avenue Baptist Church
Montgomery, Alabama

Dear Brother King:

Here is a copy of your sermon as copied by me. I plan to use it in a feature I am doing on Montgomery.

If at all convenient, send me by return air mail special a photo of you and wife or alone, or in a group. I am assuming that you have prints of some of the many photos made of you. I want to use them to help raise some money for the cause that you are so nobly fighting.

It was a source of unlimited inspiration to be with you during the beginning days of your trial. Your father and I journed back to Louisville together and I had the opportunity of meeting your fine mother in the Atlanta airport.

Alpha will be sending you additional sums. The least we can do is to supply

---

1. See King, "When Peace Becomes Obnoxious," 29 March 1956, pp. 207–208 in this volume.
2. Alpha Phi Alpha Fraternity *Newsletter* 5, no. 4 (23 March 1956).

financial and moral support to you, our champion of human decency. I know that your conviction by Judge Carter neither surprised nor unnerved you. If you have made any public statement on the outcome of the trial, please send me a copy immediately.

What you are doing is not only a tribute to your great leadership in Montgomery, but it will forever remain the outstanding example of the most intelligent and effective resistance to bigotry known to our people.

May God keep you erect as you carry out His work where it counts the most.

Fraternally,
[*signed*] Frank
Frank L. Stanley,
General President

b
Enclosure

TLS. MLKP-MBU: Box 13A.

Interview by Joe Azbell

[*23 March 1956*]
[*Montgomery, Ala.*]

> *Joe Azbell of the* Montgomery Advertiser *interviewed King the day after his conviction. According to Azbell, King stated during the interview: "We don't want to be unreasonable. We would end the boycott tomorrow if we could get some type of give. But we're not getting any give. We're being treated like we're down there to cause trouble."* [1]

[*King:*] I feel that there will be a victory and it will be greater than any particular race. It will be for the improvement of the whole of Montgomery, and I think that is so because this is a spiritual movement depending on moral and spiritual forces.

[*Azbell:*] You've had some rather personal trying experiences yourself. Are you afraid?

[*King:*] No I'm not. My attitude is that this is a great cause, it is a great issue that we are confronted with and that the consequences for my personal life are not particularly important. It is the triumph of the cause that I am concerned about. And I have always felt that ultimately along the way of life an individual must stand up and be counted and be willing to face the consequences whatever they are. And if he is filled with fear he cannot do it. My great prayer is always for God to save me from the paralysis of crippling fear, because I think when a per-

---

1. Quoted in "Awakenings (1954–1956)," rough-cut script for episode in the documentary series *Eyes on the Prize: America's Civil Rights Years,* 1986, Blackside, Inc.

son lives with the fears of the consequences for his personal life he can never do anything in terms of lifting the whole of humanity and solving many of the social problems which we confront in every age and every generation.

At. MMFR: Sync Sound 48.

From Samuel DuBois Cook

23 March 1956
Baton Rouge, La.

Cook, a philosophy professor at Southern University in Baton Rouge, had been King's classmate at Morehouse, serving as student body president as well as a founder of the campus NAACP branch.[1] After remarking on their similar training in philosophical theology, Cook declares that King had "achieved that rare combination of social action and love."

Dear M. L.,

It has been a long time, much too long in fact, since we have conversed. When you spoke at Southern, I had returned to the Army for discharge; hence I missed seeing you. From a variety of sources, however, I understand you were really great—which, of course, is precisely what I expected.[2]

Congratulations on your many accomplishments since you left the "house." Especially do I want to congratulate you for having won your doctorate in a most difficult area, philosophical theology. Since I have read considerably the works of Brunner, Barth, Niebuhr, Buber, Ferre, and Tillich, I have some appreciation of the dimensions, depth, and wonder of philosophical theology.[3] Incidentally, my dissertation deals with ethics and democracy. I have chapters in it on "Christianity and Democracy," "The Neo-Orthodoxy of Reinhold Niebuhr," and "The Neo-Thomism of Jacques Maritain." [4] Hence there is a parallel element in our inquiries subsequent to our graduation from Morehouse.

Busy people seem always to emit excuses or at least explanations for writing as

---

1. Samuel DuBois Cook (1928–), born in Griffin, Georgia, received his B.A. (1948) from Morehouse College and his Ph.D. (1955) from Ohio State University. Cook taught at Southern University (1955–1956), Atlanta University (1956–1966), and Duke University (1966–1974) before assuming the presidency of Dillard University (1975–). He has served on the board of trustees for the Martin Luther King, Jr., Center for Social Change, Inc., since its founding in 1969.

2. King preached "The Three Dimensions of a Complete Life" at Southern University on 16 October 1955.

3. Cook refers to religious philosophers Emil Brunner (1899–1966), Karl Barth (1886–1968), Reinhold Niebuhr (1892–1971), Martin Buber (1878–1965), Nels Ferré (1908–1971), and Paul Tillich (1886–1965). See *Papers*, vol. 2, for King's graduate school writings on these philosophers.

4. Cook's 1955 dissertation was entitled "An Inquiry into the Ethical Foundations of Democracy."

well as for failures to write. Mine is the immediate social context of the sequence of events in Montgomery. Hence this is a letter of the spirit.

My mind, heart and spirit go out to you and to all the others for heroic efforts in behalf of human dignity and freedom. Freedom is not a gift but an achievement. Historically and morally speaking, it is the fruit of struggles, tragic failures, tears, sacrifices, and sorrow. Likewise, social changes, if more than accidental occurences, if constitutive of moral goodness, are products of imaginative constructions and presuppose the will to make the "is" conform to the "ought." Morris R. Cohen, in <u>The Meaning of Human History</u>, notes, with great truth, that one of the tragic lessons of history discloses that "good causes are more often defeated by negligence in the pursuit of the right than by positive forces of evil." [5] The tragic lesson of American Negro history is not so much rooted in the activity of evil spirits but the inactivity of men of goodwill—in their willingness to yield instead of fulfill. Your activity and that of others similarly located reveal a radical departure, a new orientation.

I have read with avidity the newpaper accounts of happenings. Your indictment and conviction depress me greatly. Yet your moral heroism offers deep and sustaining consolation. Moreover, I am confident that the federal courts will, without hesitation, nullify the conviction. Ultimately, the state of Alabama is trying to tell free men in a free society (ideally) that they must be slaves, that they must negate rather than affirm their essence. You have inserted, if I may use a phrase of Emil Brunner, a big "No" in the state's "Yes."

The history of human freedom is the history of human struggles. You have achieved that rare combination of social action and love. When one acts on the presupposition of love, who can condemn, who can fail to admire? History knows of many who have traveled your present journey. Witness Socrates, the Christians under the pagan Roman Empire, Ghandi, or Thoreau in America. This is noble company, noble indeed. They attest to the gruesome conquest of freedom.

You know, I am teaching political philosophy. I read the other day anew the Aristotelian dictum that the cause of our love is dearer to us that the object of our love. Our cause is certainly just and it is closer to our hearts than integration. For our cause is grounded in the secret cravings of the human spirit.

Please give my best regards to Mrs. King, and, when you see them, your father, mother, sister and brother.

Your pal,
[*signed*] Sam
Samuel DuBois Cook

TLS. MLKP-MBU: Box 91.

---

5. Morris R. Cohen, *The Meaning of History* (LaSalle, Illinois: Open Court Publishing Company, 1947).

23 March 1956
Philadelphia, Pa.

Gray invites King to preach at Bright Hope Baptist Church in Philadelphia. King was unable to appear.

Reverend M. L. King
309 South Jackson Street
Montgomery, Alabama

Dear Mike:

I would like very much to have you preach for me here on one of the three following Sundays: April 15, 22 or May 6. I would prefer having you Sunday, April 15 since I would like to have you for both morning and evening services. However, if one of the other dates would be more convenient, I am sure we could work it out.

I think you acquitted yourself most excellently throughout the trial. Naturally the papers here have carried the story as front page news.

Sincerely yours,
[*signed*] Bill
William H. Gray, Jr.

WHG:mih

P.S. We will give you enough to take care of your fare by freight train and to purchase hot dogs on the way.[1]

THLS. MLKP-MBU: Box 16.

---

1. After the postscript someone identified as "JRB" wrote, "Tell him don't be so expensive. For me."

23 March 1956
New York, N.Y.

*Norman Thomas, leader of the American Socialist Party and six times its presidential
candidate, had long advocated social and racial justice.[1] After the bus boycott began he
cautioned colleagues that the presence of northern activists in Montgomery, white
or black, would tend to discredit the local movement and further alienate the white
community.[2] As this letter indicates, he believed their proper role was to build
support and raise funds in the North. King responded with a brief note on 27 April,
apologizing for his "long delay in answering" and expressing gratitude "for your
wonderful spirit in the situation we are presently facing."*

Rev. Martin L. King
Dexter Avenue Baptist Church
Montgomery, Alabama

Dear Mr. King:

I am not surprised to read that you were convicted in that court. It seems to me
that your lawyers are pursuing all the way the proper tactics and I want you to
know my very deep admiration for the great service the Negroes in Montgomery
are rendering to liberty in America and the world, not only by standing for the
rights of human beings but by the method which you have adopted.

I am of the opinion that the intrusion of Northerners in Montgomery will do
more harm than good but if there is any help that I can give in the country, I
should like to know it. What is the financial situation of the movement? I assume
the NAACP has funds in hand for the strictly legal work. I speak for a great many
whom you do not know in telling you how earnestly we hope for the triumph of
your cause which is the cause of justice and fraternity.

Sincerely yours,
[*signed*] Norman Thomas
NT:S

TLS. MLKP-MBU: Box 66.

---

1. Norman Mattoon Thomas (1884–1968), a native of Marion, Ohio, received his B.A. (1905) from
Princeton University and his B.D. (1911) from Union Theological Seminary. A former Presbyterian
minister (1911–1918), he joined the Fellowship of Reconciliation in 1917, founding and editing the
organization's magazine, *The World Tomorrow,* from 1918 to 1921. In 1917 he helped establish the organization that became known as the American Civil Liberties Union. After joining the Socialist Party in
1918, Thomas headed its national ticket in every presidential election from 1928 to 1948. He also co-
directed the League for Industrial Democracy (1922–1937). In 1957 he was a founder of the Committee
for a Sane Nuclear Policy.

2. Thomas, for example, disagreed with Homer Jack's call for northerners to visit Montgomery: "I
do not think it good from all I have heard to send Northerners into that Montgomery situation especially as on your own showing the Southern Negroes are handling it so well" (Thomas to Jack, 12
March 1956).

"When Peace Becomes Obnoxious,"
Sermon Delivered on 18 March 1956
at Dexter Avenue Baptist Church

29 March 1956
Louisville, Ky.

*Preaching from Dexter's pulpit the morning before facing trial, King condemns the
false, "obnoxious" peace that was restored to the University of Alabama campus after it
barred Autherine Lucy from attending classes. Quoting Jesus—"I come not to bring
peace but a sword"—King insists that peace "is not merely the absence of some
negative force—war, tension, confusion, but it is the presence of some positive force—
justice, goodwill, the power of the kingdom of God."* Louisville Defender *editor
Frank L. Stanley transcribed the sermon while in Montgomery covering the trial and
sent a copy to King for his review before publication on 29 March. On 3 April King
thanked Stanley for his "fine" coverage of the Montgomery movement and expressed
his "deepest appreciation for your interest in our cause and for the interest you have
stimulated in Alpha men all over the country."*

A few weeks ago, a Federal Judge handed down an edict which stated in substance that the University of Alabama could no longer deny admission to persons
because of their race. With the handing down of this decision, a brave young lady
by the name of Autherine Lucy was accepted as the first Negro student to be
admitted in the history of the University of Alabama. This was a great moment
and a great decision. But with the announcement of this decision, "the van-
guards of the old order began to surge." The forces of evil began to congeal. As
soon as Autherine Lucy walked on the campus, a group of spoiled students led
by Leonard Wilson and a vicious group of outsiders began threatening her on
every hand.[1] Crosses were burned; eggs and bricks were thrown at her. The mob
jumped on top of the car in which she was riding. Finally, the president and
trustees of the University of Alabama asked Autherine to leave for her own safety
and the safety of the University. The next day after Autherine was dismissed, the
paper came out with this headline: "Things are quiet in Tuscaloosa today. There
is peace on the campus of the University of Alabama."

Yes, things are quiet in Tuscaloosa. Yes, there was peace on the campus, but it
was peace at a great price: it was peace that had been purchased at the exorbitant
price of an inept trustee board succumbing to the whims and caprices of a vicious
mob. It was peace that had been purchased at the price of allowing mobocracy to
reign supreme over democracy. It was peace that had been purchased at the price
of capitulating to the force of darkness. This is the type of peace that all men of
goodwill hate. It is the type of peace that is obnoxious. It is the type of peace that
stinks in the nostrils of the Almighty God.

---

1. Leonard Wilson, head of the Citizens Council of West Alabama and a sophomore at the University of Alabama, was expelled after his major role in fomenting the university's riots was revealed (see
"Segregation: That Defiant Sophomore," *Newsweek*, 26 March 1956, p. 25).

Now let me hasten to say that this is not a concession to or a justification for physical war. I can see no moral justification for that type of war. I believe absolutely and positively that violence is self-defeating. War is devastating and we know now that if we continue to use these weapons of destruction, our civilization will be plunged across the abyss of destruction.

However, this is a type of war that every Christian is involved in. It is a spiritual war. It is a war of ideas. Every true Christian is a fighting pacifist.

In a very profound passage which has been often misunderstood, Jesus utters this: He says, "Think not that I am come to bring peace. I come not to bring peace but a sword." [2] Certainly, He is not saying that He comes not to bring peace in the higher sense. What He is saying is: "I come not to bring this peace of escapism, this peace that fails to confront the real issues of life, the peace that makes for stagnant complacency." Then He says, "I come to bring a sword" not a physical sword. Whenever I come, a conflict is precipitated between the old and the new, between justice and injustice, between the forces of light and the forces of darkness. I come to declare war over injustice. I come to declare war on evil. Peace is not merely the absence of some negative force—war, tension, confusion, but it is the presence of some positive force—justice, goodwill, the power of the kingdom of God. [3]

I had a long talk with a man the other day about this bus situation. He discussed the peace being destroyed in the community, the destroying of good race relations. I agree that it is more tension now. But peace is not merely the absence of this tension, but the presence of justice. And even if we didn't have this tension, we still wouldn't have positive peace. Yes, it is true that if the Negro accepts his place, accepts exploitation and injustice, there will be peace. But it would be a peace boiled down to stagnant complacency, deadening passivity, and if peace means this, I don't want peace.

1) If peace means accepting second-class citizenship, I don't want it.

2) If peace means keeping my mouth shut in the midst of injustice and evil, I don't want it.

3) If peace means being complacently adjusted to a deadening status quo, I don't want peace.

4) If peace means a willingness to be exploited economically, dominated politically, humiliated and segregated, I don't want peace. So in a passive, non-violent manner, we must revolt against this peace.

Jesus says in substance, I will not be content until justice, goodwill, brotherhood, love, yes, the Kingdom of God are established upon the earth. This is real peace—a peace embodied with the presence of positive good. The inner peace that comes as a result of doing God's will.

PD. *Louisville Defender*, 29 March 1956.

---

2. Matthew 10:34.

3. In subsequent speeches King often returned to this theme. See, for example, "The 'New Negro' of the South: Behind the Montgomery Story," June 1956, p. 282 in this volume.

31 March 1956
New York, N.Y.

In one of his first speeches in the North since the beginning of the boycott, King
addressed an enthusiastic capacity crowd of 2,500 at Concord Baptist Church in
Brooklyn. Sponsored by the Brooklyn chapter of the National Association of Business
and Professional Women's Clubs, the 25 March mass meeting featured brief remarks by
a Catholic priest, a Jewish rabbi, and the president of the city council. In his speech
King noted his long friendship with a leader of Brooklyn's religious community: "I'm
glad to see Rev. Sandy Ray out there," he said. "You know, for years he was 'Uncle
Sandy' to me. In fact, I did not know he was not related to me by blood until I was 12
years old." [1] *(Ray was a college friend of King, Sr.'s, and pastor of Bedford-*
Stuyvesant's Cornerstone Baptist Church.) King also argued against William
Faulkner's admonition that integrationists "stop now for a moment." [2] *"We can't slow*
up," he declared, "and have our dignity and self-respect." At the end of the meeting
Rev. Gardner Taylor, pastor of the church, asked for the collection, which "was taken
up in waste baskets, cake boxes, cartons, cooking utensils, and other containers,"
yielding more than $4,000 for the MIA. [3]

Here are some quotable quotes from the address delivered by Rev. Martin Luther King in Brooklyn Sunday:

"I do not come here with a message of bitterness, hate or despair." "I come with a message of love and a message of hope." [4]

"Press on and keep pressing. If you can't fly, run; if you can't run, walk; if you can't walk—'CRAWL.'"

"We can't slow up." "We can't slow up and have our dignity and self respect. "We can't slow up because of our love for democracy and our love for America. Someone should tell Faulkner that the vast majority of the people on this globe are colored."

"In our generation something has happened to the Negro. He has decided to reevaluate himself and he is coming to see that he is somebody.

"He has come to realize that every man, from a bass black to a treble white is significant on God's keyboard."

"There comes a time when people get tired of being plunged across the abyss of frustration. Today's expression in Montgomery is the expression of 50,000 people who are tired of being pushed around."

---

1. Cholly Herndon, "Sidelights of a 'Kingly' Meeting in Brooklyn," *New York Amsterdam News*, 31 March 1956.

2. William Faulkner, "A Letter to the North," *Life*, 5 March 1956, pp. 51–52.

3. Stanley Rowland, Jr., "2,500 Here Hail Boycott Leader," *New York Times*, 26 March 1956.

4. Another reporter noted that King quoted Jesus, "I come not to bring peace but a sword," explaining that "the sword was one of nonviolent revolt against 'narrow and oppressive traditions.' . . . 'We will not resort to violence, we will not degrade ourselves with hatred. We will return good for evil, we will love our enemies—not the way you love your wife, but the mighty, transcendent, God-given love for our brother men, white and dark. Christ showed us the way and Gandhi in India showed it could work'" (ibid.).

"Yes, there are tensions in the South. But the tension we experience there is due to the revolutionary reevaluation of the Negro by himself.

"You can't understand the Montgomery situation unless you understand that the Negro has a new sense of dignity, a new realization of his own worth." [5]

"Dixie has a heart all right. But it's having a little heart trouble right now."

"Montgomery is known as the Cradle of the Confederacy. It has been a quiet cradle for a long, long time, but now the cradle is rocking."

PD. *New York Amsterdam News*, 31 March 1956.

---

5. King continued: "We in Montgomery have discovered a method that can be used by the Negroes in their fight for political and economical equality. . . . We fight injustice with passive resistance. And it works. . . . The little brown man in India—Mohandas Gandhi—used it to topple the British military machine. Gandhi was able to break loose from the political and economical domination by the British and brought the British Empire to its knees. Let's now use this method in the United States" ("King Speaks at Big Rally in Brooklyn," *Montgomery Advertiser*, 26 March 1956).

From Worth Littlejohn Barbour

2 April 1956
Minneapolis, Minn.

In 1950 King had recommended Barbour, pastor of Minneapolis's Bethesda Baptist Church and the son of J. Pius Barbour, for admission to Crozer.[1] Barbour forwards several hundred dollars to the MIA from his church and congregation; his handwritten list of donors is not reprinted here.

Dr. Martin Luther King, Jr.
309 South Jackson Street
Montgomery, Alabama

Dear Mike:

Man never knows his destiny. It was almost inconceivable a few years ago that you, "Mike" King, would have been the chosen one to lead the redemption of the Southland. The Un-finished Task is your lot.

---

1. King to Charles E. Batten, 30 October 1950, in *Papers* 1:333. Worth Littlejohn Barbour (1929–), born in Spartanburg, South Carolina, received his B.A. (1951) from Shaw University and his B.D. (1954) from Crozer Theological Seminary. Barbour later worked as a lecturer, social worker, and NAACP field representative before pursuing a career as an equal employment opportunity specialist in Colorado.

I could spend much time elaborating the whole Mission, but I, like my father, believe in "less words and more deeds." Therefore, enclosed is $264.68 (two hundred and sixty-four dollars and sixty-eight cents) for the Association. Our church is small Mike, but tried our best and believe me the people here, white and black, in Minnesota {are} prayerfully concerned about the whole issue. If you need more, don't fail to call on us.

How is the baby? Like you, God forbid, more like beautiful Coretta is my hope. How is Coretta, and how is she facing the situation? Without her, you couldn't make it Mike. Give my best regards to her.

Incidentally, McCall and I both were candidates for Chuck Boddie's church in Rochester.[2] I hope it's his call; for Mc really wants to be a pastor and I think he would fit in that church very nicely.

Well, write a LONG letter when you find the time and continue to pray to stay in God's grace. We will pray with and for you Mike.

Sincerely yours,
[*signed*] Littlejohn
Worth Littlejohn Barbour

TAHLS. MLKP-MBU: Box 14.

---

2. Neither Walter R. McCall, King's Morehouse and Crozer classmate, nor Barbour succeeded Charles Emerson Boddie as pastor of Mt. Olivet Baptist Church in Rochester, New York.

From Richard Bartlett Gregg

2 April 1956
Jamaica, Vt.

Gregg's book The Power of Nonviolence, *first published in 1935 and informed by Gregg's personal witness of Gandhian* satyagraha *campaigns in India, was a major treatise on nonviolent resistance.[1] It was one of several books on the subject that Glenn Smiley gave King when they met in February. Gregg concludes his letter of support by suggesting that King and the MIA undertake a program of "constructive work," which Gandhi considered crucial to a successful nonviolent campaign. King answered the letter on 1 May.[2]*

---

1. Richard Bartlett Gregg (1885–1974), born in Colorado Springs, Colorado, earned his B.A. (1907) and his law degree (1911) at Harvard University. Increasingly intrigued with nonviolent conflict resolution, Gregg left his job as a lawyer in 1925 to embark on a four-year sojourn in India that led to the publication of *The Power of Nonviolence* (1935). Gregg was an influential member of FOR.

2. See pp. 244–245 in this volume.

Dear Dr. King:

Let me assure you and your associates of the moral support of not only myself but of many, many people not only here in New England but wherever the news of your protest against injustice has gone. It is support not only of your efforts to attain justice and sound human relations but also, and perhaps specially, of the method which you have chosen,—non-violent loving resistance.

Though you do not know me personally, let me introduce myself as the author of "The Power of Non-violence", a copy of which, Glenn Smiley tells me, you have. For seven months of the four years I lived in India I was with Gandhi in his ashram, and I can tell you he would mightily rejoice to know you have chosen this way. As you know, the Negroes of the Gold Coast in Africa recently won their freedom by this method. Even though it may take several years and be experience in terms of suffering, the price is far less than when violence is used; the chances of success are greatly increased, and happy relations arising afterward between the contestants is a great future blessing. Though the unity of the human race may be denied by prejudice, pride or other mistakes, it is a spiritual, social, moral and biological fact upon which every man can bet his very life. If pressured with non-violent love persistently, it is a truth which will win. May God bless your efforts.

May I suggest that as a part of it you try to get going among your community some constructive work, after the fashion of Gandhi's hand spinning. Offhand I would think some sort of campaign of clean-up, paint-up, tidy-up, creation of sanitation and good physical order might do. It would add to people's self respect, increase their solidity, use their emotions and energy on permanent constructive self-help as well as the effort of protest. Choose active leaders, good organizers, people who can see the value of such a thing. In India it was the districts where much work went on constantly which offered the strongest, purest and most enduring non-violent resistance to the British rule.

God's blessing on you and your efforts. Remember the 13th chapter of I Corinthians.

Yours sincerely,
[*signed*] Richard B. Gregg
Don't bother to answer this.

ALS. MLKP-MBU: Box 17.

From James H. Davis

12 April 1956
Newark, N.J.

Probably inspired by the National Deliverance Day of Prayer on 28 March, Davis forwards a contribution from members of Skycap Local 297 of the United Transport Service Employees, AFL-CIO. The skycaps were among many workers around the country who donated an hour's wage to the bus boycott. On 25 April King thanked Davis, the local shop steward: "Such moral support and christian generosity from you, our friends, in this momentous struggle, is of inestimable value in the continuance of our humble efforts."

13 Apr
1956

Rev. M. L. King,
725 Dorsey St.
Montgomery, Ala.

Dear Sir:

Enclosed you will find a check for twenty six dollars, this represents one hour pay from the Skycap personnel of Newark Airport, N.J.
 We hope that this will help all of you in your great cause.

Respectfully yours,
Newark Airport Skycaps
[*signed*] James H. Davis, Shop Chr.

AHLS. MLKP-MBU: Box 66A.

From Glenn E. Smiley

13 April 1956
New York, N.Y.

Unable to meet with King during a five-day visit to Montgomery, Smiley writes of his efforts to promote reconciliation among white and black clergy. He describes a successful 6 April meeting of seventy white ministers from all over Alabama who agreed to meet again to release a public statement encouraging a "liberal approach" to racial conflict. The meeting, he writes, "could very easily be the most significant thing I have done, in that it stands a good chance of being the beginning of a rebuilt 'middle ground' in Alabama." Smiley also mentions his conversations with Rev. Thomas Thrasher and Rev. Ralph Abernathy exploring the possibility of interracial prayer meetings in Montgomery.[1]

Dr. Martin Luther King
309 S. Jackson
Montgomery, Ala.

Dear Martin:

 We are sorry to hve missed you while we were in Montgomery and I am especially sorry that our secretary from Los Angeles did not have the privilege of a

---

 1. For more on Thrasher's pleas for dialogue, see Thrasher, "Alabama's Bus Boycott," *Reporter,* 8 March 1956 (also excerpted in the *Montgomery Advertiser* as "Fear, the Only Common Bond" on 3 March 1956).

213

conversation with you, as it would have enhanced his usefulness in securing support on the west coast.[2] We did do a good deal of thinking on the problem and did hold the meeting of ministers of which I spoke. Seventy ministers from all over the state and the northern tip of Florida attended the meeting at the YMCA camp near Montgomery, and discussed all day from 10:00 a.m. to 4,00 p.m. what could be done. Everyone was surprised at the turnout, as it was by invitation rather than by publicity, and strictly on the basis of a liberal approach to the problems in the state. I feel that this could very easily be the most significant thing I have done, in that it stands a good chance of being the beginning of a rebuilt "middle ground" in Alabama. The ministers agreed that although they had met with the promise of no publicity and no statements, that they would meet again sometime during the first two weeks of May in a <u>publicized</u> meeting and would make a statement then. This latter part should be held confidentially until they have had the opportunity to make the first move, but I believe that it will occur. There was a good deal of talk about reestablishing communications between the groups in the south, and a good deal of feeling of guilt and repentance that they had done so little and had allowed the church to be pushed about so much.

I also talked with Thrasher and some others about the possibility of establishing some prayer groups between a few of you in Montgomery and I hope that I was not too far wrong when I intimated to them that I felt you would be interested in getting together regularly with some members of the white ministerial group to pray for illumination and guidance in the problems that face the Christian church in the south. I mentioned this to Ralph and he thought it probably was a good idea.

I also mentioned to Ralph the fact that we are now preparing a 15-minute documentary film on nonviolence in the race question, about 7 minutes of it dealing with the Montgomery situation and the rest of it being devoted to experiences in South Africa and India, and the growing unrest of the world. If it turns out as good as we think it will—and it should be ready in about three weeks to a month from now—I was wondering if there is a possibility that we might show it first for one of the mass meetings in Montgomery.[3] This is just a suggestion and would certainly appreciate your reaction to it. I suspect that we could arrange it from our end, although I have not talked with the man who is doing the picture. Also Wilson Riles and I were discussing the matter the other night, and wondered if there would not be some value in a boycott, if you would want to call it that, of the humiliating experience you suffer, in that the local Advertiser has a Negro sheet which is not sent to the white community and therefore it does nothing to forward the communication between the two groups, except to spread the poison of the rascists among the Negro people. {What a sentence!} We were wondering if there is any value in casually suggesting that there is really no service to the Negro people, and further suggesting to some private capital that a sheet, or even

---

2. Wilson Riles, FOR's southwest regional secretary, accompanied Smiley in Montgomery.

3. *Walk to Freedom,* produced by the Fellowship of Reconciliation, was first shown at an MIA mass meeting on 1 October 1956. See Robert L. Cannon to Alfred Hassler and Glenn E. Smiley, 3 October 1956, pp. 388–391 in this volume.

a daily paper in Montgomery for Negro people might really serve the community 14 Apr
more adequately than the Advertiser can do. Just to continue with our thinking, 1956
we thought that there might be a possibility that the Atlanta Daily World might
issue a Montgomery daily edition, or that they would publish a daily sheet for you
and airmail it to Montgomery for distribution. It does seem that Negro people
are paying for being discriminated against in the Advertiser paper. I am not sure
that this would serve as much pressure on the white community, although it
would undoubtedly affect the advertising rates of the Advertiser, itself. Another
possibility might be to have the paper printed at the Negro publishing house in
Birmingham. Anyway, it is an idea presented for your consideration, and shall
leave it with you.

Blessings upon you, and our prayers continue to be with you.

Sincerely,
[*signed*] Glenn
Glenn E. Smiley
National Field Sec.
cc to Ralph Abernathy

GES/hs

TAHLS. MLKP-MBU: Box 16.

From Jewelle Taylor

14 April 1956
Washington, D.C.

*Taylor, a 1955 graduate of Radcliffe College, was acquainted with King when he
attended Boston University.[1] King replied in early May.[2]*

Dear Martin,

It was only a few years ago that we were all enjoying the casual pace of college
life in Boston. In my Ivory Tower at Radcliffe I never envisioned the problems I
would face as a Negro in the South and still in many areas in the North. Would
you have known or even anticipated four years ago that the leadership of such an
historic protest as the Montgomery boycott would devolve upon you?

None of the articles and the publicity have captured the essence of your unique

---

1. Jewelle Taylor (Gibbs) (1933–), born in Stratford, Connecticut, received her B.A. (1955) from
Radcliffe College and her M.S.W. (1970), M.A. (1976), and Ph.D. (1980) from the University of California at Berkeley. During the early 1960s she served as co-chair of the Minnesota Women's Committee
on Civil Rights and member of the Governor's Commission on the Status of Women.

2. See p. 242 in this volume. 215

personality, although they have won many heretofore lukewarm Negroes to the cause of civil rights. You and Coretta are living examples of the new generation of Negro leaders who, through perseverance and intelligent methods, are effectively tearing down the last vestiges of separate and unequal facilities.

Those of us who were in school with you in Boston have not yet ceased to wonder at the steadfastness and charismatic leadership that you have consistently exemplified through this movement. Your actions and your courage have belied your youth. Reports from some of my personal friends in that area indicate that you have been doing a wonderful job in your church and your community ever since you settled there.

A series of civil rights issues, climaxed by the Montgomery Boycott, pricked my conscience about my own apathy. As a result, I joined the local NAACP and am now working on a drive to get contributions and memberships from the businessmen. Enclosed is an item in this week's Afro-American describing the project. Like a pebble thrown into the water, your efforts in Montgomery have produced many waves of action in other communities throughout the nation.

After I graduated from Radcliffe last June I accepted an appointment with the U.S Department of Labor as a Junior Management Trainee. My present training assignment is with the Foreign Labor Division of the Women's Bureau. The training program is interesting but I'm going to give it up to be married in August to Jim Gibbs who is at Harvard now.

May you and you associates continue this wonderful work in Montgomery and throughout the South. You are living your faith and it is inspiring countless millions of darker people all over the world. Please give my sincerest regards to your wife and a kiss for your beautiful baby.

{With most affectionate regards,
[*signed*] Jewelle Taylor
"Sister in the Baptist Brotherhood"}

TALS. MLKP-MBU: Box 66.

From A. Philip Randolph

19 April 1956
New York, N.Y.

Randolph, president of the Brotherhood of Sleeping Car Porters, urges King to attend the "State of the Race" Conference in Washington, D.C., on 24 April.[1] *Randolph*

---

1. Asa Philip Randolph (1889–1968), born in Crescent City, Florida, graduated from Cookman Institute in 1911. In 1917 he co-founded the *Messenger,* an African-American socialist journal that was critical of American involvement in World War I. He founded the Brotherhood of Sleeping Car Porters in 1925. In 1937 Randolph gained national prominence when he successfully battled the Pullman Palace Car Company for recognition of the union. In 1941, after Randolph threatened to organize

called the conference, a closed meeting of black leaders from across the country, to
coordinate civil rights efforts nationwide; to support the NAACP and its efforts to
enforce desegregation; and to respond to the "Southern Manifesto," a resolution by 100
southern members of Congress that denounced the Supreme Court's school desegregation
ruling. Having appointed King as chairman of the Montgomery boycott panel,
Randolph requests that he prepare a brief presentation. King wrote "answered" on the
telegram, but his reply has not been located. Because of a crucial MIA executive board
meeting, he did not attend the gathering of about seventy-five black leaders, who met at
the headquarters of the National Council of Negro Women.[2]

REV MARTIN KING

MONTGOMERY IMPROVEMENT ASSOC 647 CLINTON AVE

MONTGOMERY ALA

AM LOOKING FOWARD TO RECEIVING YOUR ACCEPTANCE OF MY INVITATION TO ATTEND
"STATE OF THE RACE" CONFERENCE IN WASHINGTON DC APRIL 24TH HAVE ARRANGED
SEVERAL PANEL DISCUSSION GROUPS IN ORDER TO EXPEDITE AND FACILITATE ACTION ON
THE QUESTIONS BEFORE US HAVE TAKEN THE LIBERTY OF APPOINTING YOU CHAIRMAN OF
THE "MONTGOMERY BOYCOTT": PRESENT AND FUTURE PLANS PANEL EXPECT YOUR FULL
PARTICIPATION IN THE ENTIRE DAYS PROCEEDINGS BUT WISH YOU TO REPARE BRIEF SALIENT
POINTS IN REGARD TO THE ABOVE TOPIC TO PRESENT AT THE PANEL DISCUSSION

A PHILIP RANDOLPH

PHWSr. MLKP-MBU: Box 64A.

---

a march on Washington demanding equal hiring practices in the war industry, President Roosevelt
issued an executive order banning racial discrimination in federal employment and established the
Fair Employment Practices Committee. Randolph helped form the League for Nonviolent Civil Disobedience Against Military Segregation and influenced President Truman to desegregate the armed
services in 1948. Following the merger of the American Federation of Labor with the Congress of
Industrial Organizations, Randolph was appointed to the AFL-CIO executive council in 1955; two years
later he became vice president of the new organization. For Randolph's early response to the boycott,
see Randolph to E. D. Nixon, 23 February 1956.

2. The executive board met to discuss Montgomery City Lines' stated intention to comply with the
recent U.S. Supreme Court decision upholding a July 1955 ruling by the federal appeals court in Richmond, Virginia, that declared segregation in intrastate public transportation unconstitutional (*Sara
Mae Flemming v. South Carolina Electric & Gas Company*, 351 U.S. 901 [1956]). Faced with state and city
resistance to bus integration, however, King announced that the boycott would continue, a decision
affirmed at a mass meeting on 26 April (see King, Address to MIA Mass Meeting at Day Street Baptist
Church, pp. 230–232 in this volume).

From Charles C. Diggs, Jr.

20 April 1956
Washington, D.C.

*Congressman Diggs had attended King's trial in March and raised funds for the
Montgomery struggle on his weekly radio show.[1] This message was sent to King in
Detroit, where he was speaking at a civil rights rally organized by a group of ministers
that included Jesse Jai McNeil. On 26 April King thanked Diggs and those in Detroit
for their contribution. He also acknowledged Diggs's role in focusing national
attention on Montgomery: "I cannot adequately express our gratitude to you and other
friends who are responsible for the tremendous interest shown in our behalf."*

THE REVEREND MARTIN L KING, CARE BETHEL AME CHURCH
585 FREDRICK STDET=DELIVER 730 PME

YESTERDAY I SENT TO YOUR OFFICE IN MONTGOMERY $1,836.12 WHICH REPRESENTS THE
BALANCE OF MONIES COLLECTED THROUGH APPEALS OVER THE HOUSE OF DIGGS RADIO
PROGRAM.[2] THIS MAKES A TOTAL OF $4,436.12 WHICH WE HAVE COLLECTED AND TURNED
OVER TO YOU TO AID THE CAUSE OF THE NEGRO PEOPLE OF YOUR CITY.

I DEEPLY REGRET THAT PRESSURE OF ACTIVITIES HERE IN WASHINGTON PREVENTS ME
FROM BEING AT THE RALLY AND PERSONALLY WELCOMING YOU TO DETROIT. YOUR
CHERISHED LEADERSHIP IN THE FIGHT FOR EQUALITY FOR ALL PEOPLE IS AN
INDESTRUCTIBLE MONUMENT WHICH WILL DEFY THE RAVAGES OF TIME. MAY GOD KEEP YOU
AND YOUR DISCIPLES IN MONTGOMERY FOREVER STRONG

CHARLES C DIGGS JR MEMBER OF CONGRESS

PWSr. MLKP-MBU: Box 16.

---

1. Charles C. Diggs, Jr. (1922–), attended the University of Michigan (1940–1942) and Fisk University (1942–1943) before receiving a degree from Wayne State University's School of Mortuary Science (1946). In 1952 he graduated from the Detroit College of Law. During his first year of law school Diggs won a seat in the Michigan state senate, and in 1954 he became Michigan's first African-American member of the House of Representatives, a seat he held until 1980. Diggs Enterprises, Inc., gave King an award for outstanding contributions in the field of religion at its "Panorama of Progress" held 30 June–4 July 1956, although King was unable to attend (Charles C. Diggs, Sr., et al., to King, 8 May 1956; King to Diggs, Jr., 10 April 1956; and Diggs Enterprises, Inc., Program, Panorama of Progress, 4 July 1956.)
2. See Diggs to King, 19 April 1956.

23 April 1956
Arlington, Vt.

*Fisher (1879–1958), a noted novelist and short story writer, expresses support for the
bus boycott and encloses contributions from members of her Quaker meeting. King
acknowledged the contributions on 25 May with a form letter.*

Dear Mr. King:

I am writing you as representative of the members of a small, informally organized Quaker Meeting in our Vermont village. Like all Quakers—like thoughtful
and conscientious Americans everywhere—we have a deep and anxious concern
about the troubles in the South over the question of obeying the Supreme Court
decision against racial segregation.

We hear so much about the possibility of doing more harm than good by well-
intentioned efforts, from outside the South, to help find an equitable, democratic solution to this difficulty, that we hardly know which is the wise manner to
help those in the South who are, we feel, following the best American principles
by their actions. We have written to Miss Lillian Smith, [whose name is well-
known to us as an ardent supporter of equality before the law of all American
citizens] for advice and she has given us your name and address suggesting that
the legal expenses of your group are high and that a contribution to those expenses may be a good way for us to help an effort to obey the decision of the
Supreme Court in regard to segregation based on color. We are few in number,
and without large financial resources, but the checks I enclose represents our
sympathy for your efforts and our great admiration for the fully Christian and
peaceable manner in which your group is carrying on your resistance to illegal
(against the Supreme Court) practice of the bus company of your city.

{P.S. The radio news-bulletin has <u>just</u> brought in the news—news in which the
whole nation is interested—that the Montgomery bus lines are giving up segregation, following on a decision of the Supreme Court on this precise question An
enormous relief to all of us, (outside the South!) [1] But we know that this is only
one step forward. You have plenty of difficulties ahead of you. You can't imagine
how we trust in your fine, non-violent, Christian spirit to carry you through. And
when <u>you</u> surmount obstacles, you raise the moral plane for all of us who follow
the doings of your group with such sympathy.

I have just been shown by a Quaker friend, the enclosed clipping from The

---

1. Fisher refers to the Montgomery City Lines' decision to honor the Supreme Court's decision in
the case *Sara Mae Flemming v. South Carolina Electric & Gas Company.*

Times. Clarence Pickett is one of our Quaker heroes, and I rejoice that you are to see him.[2]

With friendly and [*word illegible*] admiring greetings}
[*signed*] Dorothy Canfield Fisher

TAHLS. MLKP-MBU: Box 17.

---

2. An 8 April 1956 article in the *New York Times,* "Quakers Will Send Mission to Alabama," reported that Clarence Evan Pickett (1884–1965), executive secretary emeritus of the American Friends Service Committee, would visit Montgomery. Pickett and his two Quaker colleagues, Dorothy M. Steere and George C. Hardin, spent three days meeting with representatives of both sides in an effort to "express Friends' concern that the controversy should be nonviolent and that those belonging to each side should be led to a deeper search for their responsibility in the light of their religious faith" (quoted in *Friends Journal,* 5 May 1956).

From James P. Coleman

[*23 April 1956*]
Jackson, Miss.

After newspapers announced that King would be a featured speaker, along with Congressman Adam Clayton Powell, Jr., at the fifth annual meeting of the Mississippi Regional Council of Negro Leadership in Jackson on 27 April, Mississippi governor James P. Coleman announced that "it would be a tragedy to have professional agitators like Powell and King come to our state and fan the fires anew."[1] The meeting was expected to draw an audience of thousands, which prompted Coleman to urge King (and Powell) to "reconsider and indefinitely postpone your visit."

REVEREND MARTIN LUTHER KING
MONTGOMERY ALA

THE PRESS REPORTS THAT YOU ARE SCHEDULED TO ADDRESS A PUBLIC MEETING IN JACKSON MISSISSIPPI ON FRIDAY OF THIS WEEK STOP MISSISSIPPI HAS NO INTENTION NOW OR HEREAFTER OF INTERFERING WITH THE CONSTITUTIONAL RIGHTS OF FREEDOM OF ASSEMBLY AND FREEDOM OF SPEECH YET I FEEL IT MY DUTY AS GOVERNOR OF MISSISSIPPI TO INFORM YOU THAT CONDITIONS IN OUR STATE ARE NOW MORE TRANQUIL THAN AT ANY TIME IN RECENT MONTHS AND IN VIEW OF YOUR RECORD YOUR APPEARNACE HERE WILL BE A GREAT

---

1. "NAACP Maps Court Battle in Mississippi," *Montgomery Advertiser,* 24 April 1956. James Plemon Coleman (1914–1991), born in Ackerman, Mississippi, graduated from the University of Mississippi in 1935. He served as the state's attorney general from 1950 to 1956 and was governor from 1956 to 1960. President Johnson later appointed him to the Fifth Circuit Court of Appeals.

DISSERVICE TO OUR NEGRO PEOPLE STOP I TRUST YOU WILL RECONSIDER AND INDEFNITELY   24 Apr
POSTPONE YOUR VISIT   1956

J P COLEMAN GOVERNOR OF MISSISSIPPI

PWSr. MLKP-MBU: Box 15.

To James P. Coleman

[*24 April 1956*]
Montgomery, Ala.

HON J P COLEMAN
GOVENOR OF MISSISSIPPI
JACKSON MISS

YOUR TELEGRAM WAS RECEIVED, AND CONTENTS HAVE BEEN NOTICED VERY SCRUTINIZINGLY
FIRST, I MUST SAY THAT I AM NOT SCHEDULED TO SPEAK IN JACKSON MISSISSIPPI. WHEN THE
INVITATION WAS EXTENDED SOME MONTHS AGO I MADE IT CLEAR THAT I COULD NOT ACCEPT
THE INVITATION BECAUSE OF A PREVIOUS COMMITTMENT.[1] HOWEVER, IF I HAD ACCEPTED
THE INVITATION I WOULD FEEL IT MY MORAL RESPONSIBILITY TO COME TO MISSISSIPPI IN
SPITE OF YOUR MOST CAUTIOUS WARNING. YOU STATED THAT IN VIEW OF MY RECORD MY
COMING TO MISSISSIPPI WOULD BE A GREAT INJUSTICE TO THE NEGRO PEOPLE. I THINK IF
YOU WOULD OBSERVE MY RECORD VERY CAREFULLY YOU WOULD DISCOVER THAT {IT.} IS
MORE THE RECORD OF A PEACE MAKER THAN A PEACE BREAKER. THE MOST GLARING THING
APPEARING IN MY RECORD IS THAT I AM CONCERNED ABOUT ACHIEVING JUSTICE FAIR PLAY
AND EQUALITY FOR ALL PEOPLE THROUGH LEGAL AND NON VIOLENT METHODS. THE
PHILOSOPHY UNDERGIRDING MY STAND IS DEEPLY ROUTED IN THE CHRISTIAN FAITH. I HAVE
STATED MORE THAN ONCE THAT IN OUR STRUGGLE FOR JUSTICE THAT OUR WEAPON MUST BE
THE WEAPON OF LOVE. CERTAINLY I THINK THE STATE OF MISSISSIPPI COULD WELL PROFIT
FROM A GOSPEL OF LOVE. THAT IS THE PIVOTAL POINT AROUND WHICH MY WHOLE
PHILOSOPHY REVOLVES AND IF I WERE COMING TO MISSISSIPPI I WOULD BE PREACHING SUCH
A GOSPEL. I AM QUITE GRATIFIED TO LEARN, ACCORDING TO YOUR TELEGRAM, THAT RACIAL
CONDITIONS ARE MORE PEACEFUL IN MISSISSIPPI THAN EVER BEFORE. I WOULD ASK YOU TO
CONSIDER, HOWEVER, THAT PEACE IS NOT NEARLY THE ABSENCE OF SOME NEGATIVE
FORCE——TENSION, CONFUSION, THE MURDERING OF EMMETT TILL, AND THE REVEREND
GEORGE LEE——BUT THE PRESENCE OF SOME POSITIVE FORCE——LOVE, JUSTICE, AND
GOODWILL.[2]

SINCERELY
MARTIN LUTHER KING JR

THWc. MLKP-MBU: Box 15.

----

1. See J. F. Redmon to King, 14 March 1956; and King to Redmon, 27 March 1956.
2. Emmett Till, a fourteen-year-old Chicagoan visiting his uncle, was murdered on 28 August 1955, purportedly for acting disrespectfully toward a white woman. George Lee, an African-American minister and voting rights activist in Mississippi, was shot and killed on 7 May 1955.

24 April 1956
[*Montgomery, Ala.*]

*King declines Mays's invitation of 21 April to speak at Morehouse morning chapel
services before the end of the school year in May. King explains that he is "preparing
the outline and manuscript for a forthcoming book" and hence cannot accept any more
engagements. King expressed interest in working on such a manuscript for many
months before finally undertaking the project that became* Stride Toward Freedom,
published in 1958.[1]

Dr. Benjamin E. Mays, Pres.
Morehouse College
Atlanta, Georgia

Dear Dr. Mays:

Thanks for your very kind letter inviting me to speak at Morehouse College.

I am in the process of preparing the outline and manuscript for a forthcoming
book. Due to the time that must be put into such a venture, I have promised
myself that I would accept no further speaking engagements for the month of
May. It is my aim to devote this whole month to the necessary research involved
in such an undertaking. I am sure that you understand this because of your long
experience as a writer. But for this, I would be very happy to come. Please feel
free to call on me some other time.

With every good wish, I am

Sincerely yours,
M. L. King, Jr.,
President

MLK:b

TLc. MLKP-MBU: Box 62.

---

1. King held discussions with several collaborators and publishers, including Doubleday, before
choosing Harper and Row in early 1957 (see Clement Alexandre to King, 1 June 1956; and King to
Alexandre, 18 June 1956). In April 1956 he contemplated a collaboration with Edith Gilmore, an associate of Bayard Rustin in New York, to write the Montgomery story for publication, but nothing resulted (see Edith Gilmore to King, 9 April 1956).

24 April 1956
[*Montgomery, Ala.*]

McMurray (1897–1974), editor of the Asbury Park Press, *had informed King on 12
April that his newspaper had "conducted a campaign to raise funds to assist you with
your legal expenses."*

Mr. Wayne D. McMurray
Asbury Park Press
Asbury Park, N.J.

Dear Mr. McMurray:

First, let me apologize for being somewhat tardy in answering your letter. Absence from the city for several days delayed my reply.

Words can never adequately express my appreciation to you for your interest in my behalf. The two thousand dollars ($2,000.00) which was raised through the strong appeal of your paper will go a long, long way in helping the total situation. I assure you that this type of christian generosity gives us renewed courage to carry on. Ultimately the thing that keeps the true fires of democracy burning is the existence of people of good will who are able to keep at the forefront of their thoughts the noble and sublime affirmations of our democratic creed. Your spirit gives new hope to those of us who are forced by sectional necessity to stand under the battering rams of segregation and discrimination. Our struggle here is not merely a struggle for Montgomery but it is really a struggle for the whole of America.

The check may be sent to our headquarters here at 530 South Union Street. Please make the check payable to The Montgomery Improvement Association. Please extend my thanks and best regards to all those noble persons who are associated with you and who made contributions through your paper.

Cordially yours,
M. L. King, Jr.,
President

MLK:b

TLc. MLKP-MBU: Box 14.

To William Peters

25 April 1956
[*Montgomery, Ala.*]

King offers corrections to a draft profile by Peters, a freelance journalist, to be published in Redbook. *King explains to Peters, "I did not say that the economic boycott can never be used as a weapon by the Negro . . . [but] it can be used if the proper conditions bring it about and the community situation is taken into consideration." Peters incorporated the majority of King's comments but chose to retain King's earlier characterization of the boycott as a religious movement, not an economic one. Peters's article remains an important source for tracing King's intellectual development. King explained to Peters, for example, that "the spirit of passive resistance came to me from the Bible, from the teachings of Jesus. The techniques came from Gandhi."*[1]

Mr. William Peters
921 Grant Avenue
Pelham Manor, New York

Dear Mr. Peters:

Thanks so much for your thoughtfulness in sending a carbon copy of your article for Red Book. Absence from the city has delayed my reply. I see you work very fast. The article is certainly an excellent one and I am sure that it will be welcomed by the American public. It is set forth in a very lucid style and the contents reveal a real grasp of the total situation.

I have noticed just a few minor things that need to be worked. The first is found on page thirteen. I feel that this paragraph should be deleted because it doesn't adequately express my feelings at this point. That is to say I don't feel that all white churches follow an empty pattern of ritual. That might be misunderstood by many. The second is found on the bottom of page fourteen. There were six Negro students at Crozier and about eighty whites. The next is found on page twenty. Instead of saying hundreds of Negroes were assembled at the jail, I believe it would be better to say "there were numerous or a large number, because I don't think the number went up into the hundreds. The next is on page twenty-three, the second paragraph. Maybe I didn't clearly express my views on that point. I did not say that the economic boycott can never be used as a weapon by the Negro in the struggle for justice. It seems to me that it can be used if the proper conditions bring it about and the community situation is taken into consideration. I would not, however, advocate the indiscriminate use of the boycott in cases, for instance, where counter boycotts can upset the total economic struc-

---

1. William Peters, "Our Weapon Is Love," *Redbook*, August 1956, pp. 42–43, 71–73; see also Peters to King, 16 April 1956. Peters (1921–), born in San Francisco, received his B.S. (1947) from Northwestern University. After working on the staff of several magazines and as a freelance journalist, Peters produced documentaries on race relations for CBS television during the early 1960s.

ture of the Negro. I would agree that in the South there are not many areas where the boycott can be applied. However, there are communities in the South where the Negro wields a great deal of economic influence and power. In these cases boycotts can be much more effective than in poorer communities.

Thanks again for your thoughtfulness. I'll be looking forward to the publishing of this article with great anticipation. It was a real pleasure meeting you, and I hope that at a very early date we will be able to renew this great fellowship. When I am in New York I will be sure to look you up.

With warm personal regards, I am

Cordially yours,
M. L. King, Jr.,
President

MLK:b

THLc. MLKP-MBU: Box 64.

From Harris Wofford

25 April 1956
Alexandria, Va.

Since visiting India in 1949 Wofford, an attorney in the Washington law firm of Covington and Burling, had promoted Gandhian nonviolence as a strategy for confronting American segregation.[1] On 13 March Wofford sent King a copy of India Afire *(1951), a book he and his wife, Clare Wofford, had written after their visit.[2] In this letter, to protest continued enforcement of segregation laws despite the recent Supreme Court ruling, Wofford urges "some straight Gandhian civil disobedience," suggesting a test bus ride by ministers. Perhaps responding to King's public statement that the bus boycott would continue until the demand to hire black drivers was met, he encourages King to leave out "the employment question in return for the complete end of segregation." King replied on 10 May.[3]*

---

1. Harris Llewellyn Wofford, Jr. (1926–), born in New York City, received his B.A. (1948) from the University of Chicago and received law degrees from both Howard and Yale in 1954. He later served as assistant to the Commission on Civil Rights (1958–1959) and, as President John F. Kennedy's aide, helped forge the Kennedy administration's civil rights policies. Wofford also helped establish the Peace Corps, of which he was associate director from 1964 to 1966.

2. Wofford praised King in the letter that accompanied the gift: "Your venture is improving us all. It is the most significant development I know of anywhere." In addition to the book, he enclosed a booklet on nonviolent resistance and an assignment he had given his law school class ("Opinion Memorandum Assignment for the Howard University School of Law," 1 April 1956) about legal issues facing a hypothetical Shapeless Shoe Company that sought to make a donation to the MIA, noting that the assignment "may amuse you."

3. See p. 254 in this volume.

{Thanks for your letter}[4]

To Messrs. King, Abernathy, Nixon, and Company:

Once again your arm chair strategist presumes to be presumptuous. Rev. Abernathy, however, invited this presumption, saying he wanted all the suggestions and criticisms anyone could give.[5]

Isn't this the time for some straight Gandhian civil disobedience? With the Supreme Court sending the bus case back for trial and the Circuit Opinion thus standing as the highest law of the land, are you not almost invited by the law to ride the buses refusing to suffer segregation?

What if the several score ministers, as a first batch, announced that they intended to ride the buses at a certain time and place, and not submit to segregation, thus defending the Constitution and the law of the land? I would think that at first you would not want to call on all your companions to commit such civil disobedience, although such a stage might arrive. I would also think that since your end would be, as it has been, the persuasion and conversion of your opponents, that you would also announce in advance that you would not sue for private damages, no matter how you are mistreated. Thus you would be on this occasion foregoing the legal possibility of suit for damages for anything done to you while seeking your rights. I should think such a gesture would help make your point.

I also wonder if this isn't the time to compromise on your demands, for the present, leaving out the employment question in return for the complete end of segregation. The latter is more than you sought originally, which is reason for suspending your campaign for something else you sought. One of the best ingredients of Gandhi's campaigns was the willingness to compromise, to make really painful compromises, and then in good time to resume the struggle. Also Gandhi had a knack of knowing when to change the rythm of his campaigns, when to go from struggle to constructive service, from one form of action to another. But of course this is your campaign and not Gandhi's, and you have already proved yourselves master artists of non-violent direct action. It would not be Gandhian at all if you were merely copying Gandhi. He was, like you, a creator, not a copier.

But some jail-going, at least by selected members of your body, would be a wonderful thing for this country and for the world. And I would think if enough of you, in the right cheerful spirit, rode the buses, and went to jail rather than to submit to segregation, the whole silly house of cards might now crumble on bus segregation.

Respectfully yours,
[*signed*]
Harris Wofford, Jr.

TAHLS. MLKP-MBU: Box 67.

---

4. Wofford refers to correspondence that is no longer extant. Maude Ballou, King's secretary, wrote "Please read this!"

5. Ralph Abernathy had met Wofford during a March visit to Washington, D.C.

25 April 1956
Pittsburgh, Pa.

Prattis was executive editor of the Pittsburgh Courier, *an influential African-
American newspaper with a nationwide circulation that claimed to be the "largest
Negro weekly newspaper in the world."* [1] Courier *reporter Evelyn Cunningham had
written extensively on the bus boycott and visited Montgomery for King's trial, but here
Prattis urges King to tell his story "in your own words." King replied on 1 May.* [2]

Dr. Martin Luther King, Jr.,
Dexter Avenue Baptist Church,
Dexter Avenue,
Montgomery, Alabama.

Dear Dr. King:

It has just occurred to us that you have never told your story in connection with
the Montgomery bus situation.

We thought Miss Cunningham did an excellent job when one takes into account the speed with which she had to work. But only you, in your own words,
can tell what this entire "accident of history" has really meant.

We want to offer you the opportunity to point up the significance of the Montgomery story in three articles, each of not more than 1,000 words in length. This
we believe, would give you the chance to tell the public of hitherto untold facets
of the story. It would also provide a device which you could use to give proper
credit to all those persons who have worked with you, colored and white.

The Courier would also like to be the medium through which the Montgomery
Improvement Association expressed its appreciation to the many persons and
agencies, white and colored, throughout the country, who have helped through
moral and financial support. We are not interested in exact figures as to the
amount given, but we are interested in the spread of interest, geographically and
inter-racially.

We hope very much that you will use The Courier as the medium through
which you might accomplish the foregoing objectives of (1) pointing up your own
philosophy in respect to the problem you have faced and the significance of the
action taken as a tactic in race relations; (2) giving due credit to those who have

---

1. Quotation from Prattis's stationery. Percival Leroy Prattis (1895–1980) was born in Philadelphia
and attended Christiansburg Industrial Institute, Hampton Institute, and Ferris Institute. After working as an editor and writer for the *Michigan State News* and the *Chicago Defender,* Prattis joined the
Associated Negro Press in 1923, where he remained for twelve years. After a short stint at the *New York
Amsterdam News* he joined the *Pittsburgh Courier* in 1936, where he served as city editor until 1940,
executive editor until 1956, editor-in-chief until 1961, and finally as associate publisher and treasurer
until 1963.

2. See p. 245 in this volume.

worked with you in the Association, and (3) expressing appreciation for the moral and financial support the Association has received.

Will you do this job? You can choose your own time, but we would like to know at least five weeks in advance if and when you will do it. Thank you.

Yours very truly,
[*signed*]
P. L. Prattis
Executive Editor

PLP/vs

TLS. MLKP-MBU: Box 64.

From Jeanne Martin Brayboy

26 April 1956
Charlotte, N.C.

A friend and fellow graduate student at Boston University congratulates King for his achievements in Montgomery.[1]

Dear Martin

Of course you are surprised to hear from me, but I imagine you are hearing from many old friends now that you are a national figure. I have wanted to write you for a long time to wish you well in the great task you are leading, but only recently found your address in a newspaper.

I am sure there are many like me who are proud to say that we were good friends in school together. It is also true that they, like me, are not surprised at your achievements. Keep at it, Pal, you've got what it takes (I almost feel I shouldn't speak in such undignified terms to you!).

Charlotte seems destined to be my home. You may have heard that I was married in Dec. 1954. This year Jack is working on his doctorate at the U. of Penn. an arrangement we hate, but the year is almost over.[2] I'm still working. Jack's a wonderful guy and I'd love for you two to meet sometime.

---

1. Jeanne Martin Brayboy (1930–), born in Camden, South Carolina, received her undergraduate degree from Bennett College in Greensboro (1951) and her M.A. (1953) from Boston University. She was an elementary school music teacher in Charlotte, North Carolina, at the time she wrote this letter.

2. Jack S. Brayboy (1921–1976) taught at Johnson C. Smith University (1946–1976) in Charlotte, where he later became administrative vice president.

My best wishes to you and Corretta. If ever you should come this way, stop to see us. We can always be located through Johnson C. Smith Univ.

My prayers go with you in your work, in all your endeavors.

Sincerely,
[*signed*] Jeanne Martin Brayboy

Do you see Rev. Crockett?[3] What fun it'd be to reminisce of old times! Pardon bad pen.

ALS. MLKP-MBU: Box 91.

----

3. Brayboy refers to Roosevelt David Crockett (1917–1968), a Dexter deacon and chaplain of Alabama State College who received his Ph.D. from Boston University shortly before King.

To William E. Newgent

26 April 1956
[*Montgomery, Ala.*]

Newgent, a member of the Fellowship of Reconciliation, wrote King on 20 April about a newspaper report that stated that he had been asked to resign as Dexter pastor. "In substance," Newgent said in his letter, "the thought was expressed that some of your members were being influenced by outsiders and they wanted only peaceful living, and had requested your resignation."

Mr. William E. Newgent
17 67th Avenue, S.E.
Washington 27, D.C.

Dear Mr. Newgent:

This is to acknowledge receipt of your very kind letter of April 20, expressing concern about my situation. If a Washington paper carried a report that I was asked to resign as pastor of my church, it has revealed a total erroneous impression. My congregation is with my stand now and has been with it one-hundred per cent. Actually, the mix-up probably came because of some difficulties which developed with a minister on the other side of town by the name of Rev. U. J. Fields. There were three or four members of his church who tried to bring some type of charge against him but they insisted that it had nothing to do with the bus protest. The charges were later dropped. Rev. Fields is Secretary of The Mont-

gomery Improvement Association and is still pastor of The Bell Street Baptist
Church.

With every good wish, I am

Sincerely yours,
M. L. King, Jr.,
President

MLK:b

TLc. MLKP-MBU: Box 63A.

Address to MIA Mass Meeting at Day Street
Baptist Church

[*26 April 1956*]
[*Montgomery, Ala.*]

*At an MIA mass meeting at Day Street Baptist Church King reads the executive board's
recommendation to continue the bus protest after city and state officials contested the
National City Lines' decision to end segregated seating. Despite bus company officials'
unwillingness to meet with MIA leaders during recent negotiations with the city, King
expresses appreciation for their stand, explaining, "Our action now is not aimed at
putting the bus company out of business, but only at putting justice in business." The
crowd of three thousand greeted the resolutions with a "thunderous ovation,"
unanimously approving the decision to continue the boycott.[1] CBS News recorded this
excerpt.*

[*King:*] Thank you very much my friends. That certainly is very kind of you. We
never assemble with a feeling of a sense of bitterness. We always assemble with
deep tones of love in our hearts. [*Audience:*] (*Yeah*) And we always assemble with
great hope and with a feeling of the ultimate triumph of righteousness and justice. (*Yeah*) [*applause*] It is certainly gratifying to— (*Can you turn the mike up? Turn
on the mike*) I don't know if the mike . . . [*recording interrupted*] that to see you in
such large numbers. We are very happy to see you. And I know you are here
because of your interests in this movement and because of your determination
to stand in the same sense of dignity that you've always stood in. (*Yeah*) Whereas
it is unanimously agreed . . . [*recording interrupted*] the adjustment involved in the
emergence of any new order. (*Yeah, That's right*) And we must be willing to confront the onslaught of the recalcitrance of the old order. (*Yeah, That's right*) And
we must stand with the deep spirit of Christian love (*That's right*) as we have always
done. (*That's right, All right*) We started out with. . . . [*recording interrupted*]

Several things have happened since we met together on last Monday evening.
(*Oh yeah*) We had a very fine meeting at the Dexter Avenue Baptist Church and
we discussed in that meeting the decision which had been handed down that day,

---

1. See John N. Popham, "Negroes to Keep Boycotting Buses," *New York Times,* 27 April 1956; and
Steve Lesher, "Negroes Vote to Continue Bus Boycott," *Montgomery Advertiser,* 27 April 1956.

the Supreme Court's decision. But since that time several things have happened, things that are vitally important for our whole movement. And I'm sure that you've been reading about them in the papers, you have been hearing about them on television, and you've been talking about them. We've been thinking about these things, and at every moment and every second, we have this movement on our hearts and in our hearts. (*Oh yeah, Yes*) We are always seeking to do the right thing. (*Yeah, That's right*). We feel that we cannot afford to make mistakes, so we are trying at every point to be wise in our decisions. We are not depending only on our judicious capacities. We are not depending only on our power to speculate. We are not depending only on our knowledge and our supposed wisdom, we are also depending on the guidance of the Almighty God. (*Amen, Amen, All right*) [*applause*] So that everything that we will say today comes not only from what we have thought about, although it comes from that, but also from what we have prayed over. (*Yeah, That's right*) We have thought over it, and we have prayed over it.

I have a resolution that I would like to read to you and I want you to listen to this at every point and notice everything in it. Be very scrutinizing in analyzing it. I want everybody to listen carefully. [*recording interrupted*]

Resolution:

Whereas, a majority of the Negro citizens of Montgomery, Alabama, have refrained from riding city buses since December fifth, 1955, because of mistreatments and because of the unconstitutional seating arrangement. And

Whereas, it was reported that on Monday, April twenty-third, 1956, the United States Supreme Court held that city ordinances and state statutes requiring segregation on public conveyances for hire intra-state are unconstitutional. And

Whereas, National City Lines, Incorporated, parent of the Montgomery City Lines, Incorporated, has issued a statement and instructed its drivers to cease and desist from enforcing city and state laws requiring segregation on city buses. And

Whereas, it has been reported through reliable sources that several southern cities, including Richmond, Virginia; Little Rock, Arkansas; Dallas, Texas; and others, have ended segregation on city buses and white and Negro passengers rode together on front seats without incidents, mishaps, or disturbances. And

Whereas, the public officials of the city of Montgomery and the state of Alabama have indicated both orally and in writing that they intend to and will use all means available, including the arrest of the bus drivers and passengers who refuse to abide by and obey the segregation laws of the city of Montgomery and the state of Alabama requiring segregation of the races on city and state buses [*recording interrupted*]

[*thundering applause*] [*recording interrupted*]

[*B. D. Lambert:*] With the Supreme Court of the United States in our favor.

[*King:*] Let's, let's hear it.

[*Lambert:*] I said, with the Supreme Court of the United States in our favor and the [*federal?*] government on our side, the people of Montgomery will never go back to Jim Crow buses! [*thundering applause*] [*words inaudible*]

[*King:*] Let's hear the motion. Let's hear the motion. Let's hear the motion.

[*Lambert:*] [*words inaudible*] I make a motion that the resolution and the recommendation made by the president be received and adopted! (*I second that*) [*applause*]

[*King:*] It has been moved and seconded that the resolution that was read will be received and adopted. Are you ready for the question? (*Yeah*) All those in favor let it be known by standing on your feet. [*thundering applause*] Opposed. [*recording interrupted*]

Be it therefore resolved that we, the Negro citizens of Montgomery, Alabama, do now and will continue to carry on our mass protest until such time as the matters stated above are clarified and we hereby authorize and direct the officers and board of directors of the Montgomery Improvement Association to do any and all acts that it deems necessary to perfect our desires. (*That's right*) [*applause*]

Now my. . . . [*recording interrupted*]

We are grateful to them and we feel that they acted in all good faith (*That's right*), and they decided to comply with the Supreme Court's decision. And in continuing this protest, we are not attempting to punish the National City Lines. (*That's right*) As I have said to you before, in our movement we are not bogged down in a negative. . . . [*recording interrupted*]

(*That's right, That's right, That's all right*) [*applause*] And we intend to stand up until justice comes our way. (*Yeah*) Now let me urge you to continue in the same spirit that we have carried on for these twenty weeks or more. Let me urge you to be sane and rational. Eventually, segregation in public transportation will pass away (*Yeah*), eventually. And I think we should start now preparing for the inevitable. (*Yeah*) And let us, when that moment comes, go into the situations that we confront with a great deal of dignity, sanity, and reasonableness. (*Yeah*) We never intend to get on the buses kicking people over and trying to show that we had won a victory. (*No*) For when segregation dies it will not be merely a victory for fifty thousand Negroes of Montgomery (*No*), it will not be a victory for sixteen million Negroes of America, but it will be a victory for democracy. (*Yeah*) It will be a victory for justice. (*Yeah*) It will be a victory for the forces of light. (*Yeah*) Not just a victory for one segment but for the whole of the nation. (*All right*) And let us not abuse our new rights and privileges (*That's right*) by overdoing them. (*That's right*) [*recording interrupted*]

Vt. CBSNA-CBSN.

From J. Martin England

29 April 1956
Somerville, N.J.

England, a fellow Baptist minister and graduate of Crozer, praises King's Gandhian approach and advises him to use nonviolence not "to conquer the opponent" but to redeem him.[1] Noting that "it is always good to hear from a Crozer alumnus," King thanked England on 5 June for his "helpful suggestions."

---

1. J. Martin England (1901–1989), born in Seneca, South Carolina, received degrees from Furman University in Greenville, South Carolina, and from Crozer Theological Seminary. From 1933 until 1939

Rev. Martin Luther King   29 Apr
Montgomery   1956
Alabama

Dear Mr. King,

During my last year at Crozer Seminary (1933), I had a little to do, together with my good friend Lee Philip of Union Seminary, in opening the seminary to Negro students. I must confess therefore to a little pride as I have followed the reports of your protest movement.

For the clear and obvious Gandhian aspects of your effort I am thankful, and take courage. However, the absence of one vital part of Gandhi's teaching, as I have read the reports from Montgomery, disturbs me. I hope it means only that the reporters have failed to observe it.

As I understand it, Satyagraha involves not only the refusal to accept violence as a means in one's own struggle. It also goes so far as to accept responsibility for helping the opponent find release for the violence in his nature. Many who use Gandhi's name so glibly seem never to have known that he called off a boycott when his followers acted in such a spirit, albeit "non-violent", as to stimulate violence in their opponents.

Non-violence is such a powerful tool that when its advocates discover its strength they may be tempted to use it for the same ends for which others use violence: to conquer the opponent, rather than redeem him.

Much has been said about love, in the reports of your movement. You must know better than I do how much easier it is to defeat segregationists than to transform them. God grant that you and your associates may have the love that will lead those who now oppose you to cry out, like the Philippian jailer, "Men and brethren, what must we do to be saved?" [2]

Sincerely,
[*signed*] J. Martin England

THLS. MLKP-MBU: Box 16.

---

and again from 1945 to 1950, England and his wife served as Baptist missionaries in Burma. They also helped found Koinonia Farm in Americus, Georgia, in 1942, living there for two years. Later, as a staff member of the American Baptist Church's Ministers and Missionaries Benefit Board, England arranged to provide King with a retirement and death benefit policy (Norman J. Kansfield to King Papers Project, 21 September 1992).

   2. Acts 16:30.

From Hazel E. Foster

29 April 1956
Cleveland, Ohio

On 3 May, Benjamin E. Mays forwarded to King a letter and a British newspaper   233
clipping from Foster, a former Morehouse professor who had met Gandhi while in India

from 1939 to 1941.[1] *Mays had written in his note to King that "it is heart warming that this movement has taken on such world wide significance."*

Rev. Dr. M. L. King
Montgomery
Ala.

Dear Dr. King:

The enclosed clipping sent me by a London friend I am thrilled to feel illustrates the universal significance of the noble effort you are heading. I was in India in 1940–41 when ~~Gand~~ Gandhi was carrying on his "Partial Civil Disobedience Campaign" with non-violent, self-suffering resistance to the great injustice the Indian people were suffering.[2] It was a matter of free speech, free assembly and free press during the Second World War, and Gandhi's folowers insisted on speaking out with the expectation of imprisonment. I visited him just before the Campaign began. The effort looked so futile and so hopeless to outsiders, but all India ultimately won its freedom on such as basis. Complete good will toward everybody, great sufferings received and accepted, but no sufferings inflicted. Love the motivation! I have wondered whether, now Gandhi has died, ~~whether~~ his ideas and ideals had died with him. You prove to me they have not. And as he was earnestly trying to follow the Sermon on the Mount, so you are folowing his grat example—Jesus.

May I also add that I am proud to know your fine parents and gave several talks in their church while I was teaching in the School of Religion at Morehouse College.

Gratefully yours,
[*signed*] Hazel E. Foster
Rev. Hazel E. Foster

TLS. MLKP-MBU: Box 31A.

---

1. Hazel Elora Foster (1885–?), born in Cleveland, Ohio, earned her B.A. (1909) at Ohio Wesleyan University and her M.A. (1929), B.D. (1932), and Ph.D. (1933) at the University of Chicago Divinity School. She served various churches and Christian colleges until she left for India. Upon her return to the United States she was pastor of a Congregational church in Wisconsin before taking teaching positions at Randolph-Macon Woman's College (1946–1947), Spelman College (1947–1950), and Morehouse College (1950–1953). After teaching in the Philippines for a year she became an independent scholar and author.

2. Foster refers to the "Quit India" campaign, the last major *satyagraha* Gandhi launched against the British.

30 April 1956
Washington, D.C.

As president of the National Council of Negro Women (NCNW), Mason informs King
of the upcoming Mary McLeod Bethune Commemoration Week and its culminating
conference of African-American women leaders on 26 May.[1] The NCNW, founded
by Bethune in 1935, was the first national coalition of African-American women's
organizations. Mason requests the names of the women arrested in the bus boycott so
that the council can invite them to the conference as special guests. On 7 May King's
secretary, Maude L. Ballou, replied with the addresses of Rosa Parks, Jo Ann
Robinson, Euretta Adair, Jimmie Lowe, and Irene West; on 26 May Parks spoke at
the conference.[2]

Rev. M. L. King, Jr.
309 South Jackson Street
Montgomery, Alabama

Dear Mr. King:

The National Council of Negro Women will observe Mary McLeod Bethune
Commemoration Week, May 18 to 26, 1956. We believe that Mrs. Bethune's friends
will welcome the opportunity to pay tribute to the creative power and influence
of her life. The climax of this observance will be a One-Day Conference of Negro
women leaders at the Hotel Statler in Washington, D.C. on May 26. The heads of
Negro women's national organizations and individual women leaders in sunday
fields will be invited to participate.

The purpose is to discuss the impact of a changing world on women's organizations politically, socially and economically, with the hope that organizations
and individuals will be challenged to review and reevaluate their programs; adopt

---

1. Vivian Carter Mason (1900–1982), born in Wilkes-Barre, Pennsylvania, received her B.A. (1921)
from the University of Chicago. Mason served on the national board of the YWCA and as president of
the National Council of Negro Women from 1953 to 1957. Mary McLeod Bethune (1875–1955), a pioneering African-American educator, was born in Mayesville, South Carolina, and graduated from the
Moody Bible Institute in Chicago (1895). In 1936 President Roosevelt appointed Bethune director of
the Division of Negro Affairs of the National Youth Administration, the highest federal office then
held by a black woman.

2. National Council of Negro Women, press release, Leaders Conference Held 26 May, May 1956.
Euretta Adair, a prominent member of the Women's Political Council, belonged to the MIA's inner
circle, serving on the finance and strategy committees. Jimmie Lowe was a member of the city's Federation of Colored Women's Clubs. Irene West (1892–1975), a graduate of Alabama State College who
also attended Tuskegee and Hampton Institutes, was, along with her husband, dentist A. W. West,
active in civil rights groups, including the NAACP. She served on the MIA executive board and was a
member of the Federation of Colored Women's Clubs and treasurer of the Women's Political Council.
Adair, Lowe, and West were indicted by the Montgomery court grand jury for participating in the bus
boycott. Adair and Robinson were among those invited to speak on 25 March at an NCNW event in
Washington to raise funds for the MIA (Mason to King, 9 and 15 March 1956).

new objectives, if warranted, and finally to be stimulated to take whatever action is called for to meet the unmet needs of this scientific era. We are distressingly aware of the fact that this one day is scarcely sufficient to explore each topic as thoroughly as it deserves but our hope is that the conference will point the way in providing markers for other such meetings by each organization at gradd root levels.

We would like to invite as our special guests the Negro women who were arrested in the bus boycot in Montgomery and would be pleased if you would furnish the names and addresses of these women. An early reply would be appreciated.

Sincerely yours,
[*signed*] Vivian C. Mason
Mrs. William T. Mason

THLS. MLKP-MBU: Box 63.

"Our Struggle"

April 1956
New York, N.Y.

This report on the Montgomery movement, drafted initially by Bayard Rustin, was the featured article in the second issue of Liberation, *which was devoted to the boycott.[1] A new journal edited by Rustin and other radical pacifists,* Liberation *included several related articles, including Rustin's "Montgomery Diary." King, according to this report, sees a "new Negro" emerging in the South: "The extreme tension in race relations in the South today is explained in part by the revolutionary change in the Negro's evaluation of himself and of his destiny and by his determination to struggle for justice." The movement finds its strength, King argues, in the black community's economic power, the church's militant leadership, and a "new and powerful weapon— ·non-violent resistance." The MIA and the Congress of Racial Equality (CORE) reprinted and distributed King's article.*

THE SEGREGATION of Negroes, with its inevitable discrimination, has thrived on elements of inferiority present in the masses of both white and Negro people. Through forced separation from our African culture, through slavery, poverty, and deprivation, many black men lost self-respect.

In their relations with Negroes, white people discovered that they had rejected the very center of their own ethical professions. They could not face the triumph

---

1. Rustin sent King a draft for his review, but King's changes, if any, are not extant. See Rustin to King, 8 March 1956, p. 163 in this volume. *Liberation's* editorial board included such prominent pacifists as A. J. Muste and Charles Walker.

of their lesser instincts and simultaneously have peace within. And so, to gain it, they rationalized—insisting that the unfortunate Negro, being less than human, deserved and even enjoyed second class status. ♪

They argued that his inferior social, economic and political position was good for him. He was incapable of advancing beyond a fixed position and would therefore be happier if encouraged not to attempt the impossible. He is subjugated by a superior people with an advanced way of life. The "master race" will be able to civilize him to a limited degree, if only he will be true to his inferior nature and stay in his place.

White men soon came to forget that the Southern social culture and all its institutions had been organized to perpetuate this rationalization. They observed a caste system and quickly were conditioned to believe that its social results, which they had created, actually reflected the Negro's innate and true nature.

◊ In time many Negroes lost faith in themselves and came to believe that perhaps they really were what they had been told they were—something less than men. So long as they were prepared to accept this role, racial peace could be maintained. It was an uneasy peace in which the Negro was forced to accept patiently injustice, insult, injury and exploitation. ◊

Gradually the Negro masses in the South began to re-evaluate themselves—a process that was to change the nature of the Negro community and doom the social patterns of the South. We discovered that we had never really smothered our self-respect and that we could not be at one with ourselves without asserting it. From this point on, the South's terrible peace was rapidly undermined by the Negro's new and courageous thinking and his ever-increasing readiness to organize and to act. Conflict and violence were coming to the surface as the white South desperately clung to its old patterns. The extreme tension in race relations in the South today is explained in part by the revolutionary change in the Negro's evaluation of himself and of his destiny and by his determination to struggle for justice. *We Negroes have replaced self-pity with self-respect and self-depreciation with dignity.*

When Mrs. Rosa Parks, the quiet seamstress whose arrest precipitated the non-violent protest in Montgomery, was asked why she had refused to move to the rear of a bus, she said: "It was a matter of dignity; I could not have faced myself and my people if I had moved."

The New Negro

MANY OF THE NEGROES who joined the protest did not expect it to succeed. When asked why, they usually gave one of three answers: "I didn't expect Negroes to stick to it," or, "I never thought we Negroes had the nerve," or, "I thought the pressure from the white folks would kill it before it got started."

In other words, our non-violent protest in Montgomery is important because it is demonstrating to the Negro, North and South, that many of the stereotypes he has held about himself and other Negroes are not valid. Montgomery has broken the spell and is ushering in concrete manifestations of the thinking and action of the new Negro.

We now know that:

WE CAN STICK TOGETHER. In Montgomery, 42,000 of us have refused to ride the city's segregated busses since December 5. Some walk as many as fourteen miles a day.

OUR LEADERS DO NOT HAVE TO SELL OUT. Many of us have been indicted, arrested, and "mugged." Every Monday and Thursday night we stand before the Negro population at the prayer meetings and repeat: "It is an honor to face jail for a just cause."

THREATS AND VIOLENCE DO NOT NECESSARILY INTIMIDATE THOSE WHO ARE SUFFICIENTLY AROUSED AND NON-VIOLENT. The bombing of two of our homes has made us more resolute. When a handbill was circulated at a White Citizens Council meeting stating that Negroes should be "abolished" by "guns, bows and arrows, sling shots and knives," we responded with even greater determination.

OUR CHURCH IS BECOMING MILITANT. Twenty-four ministers were arrested in Montgomery. Each has said publicly that he stands prepared to be arrested again. Even upper-class Negroes who reject the "come to Jesus" gospel are now convinced that the church has no alternative but to provide the non-violent dynamics for social change in the midst of conflict. The $30,000 used for the car pool, which transports over 20,000 Negro workers, school children and housewives, has been raised in the churches. The churches have become the dispatch centers where the people gather to wait for rides.

WE BELIEVE IN OURSELVES. In Montgomery we walk in a new way. We hold our heads in a new way. Even the Negro reporters who converged on Montgomery have a new attitude. One tired reporter, asked at a luncheon in Birmingham to say a few words about Montgomery, stood up, thought for a moment, and uttered one sentence: "Montgomery has made me proud to be a Negro."

ECONOMICS IS PART OF OUR STRUGGLE. We are aware that Montgomery's white businessmen have tried to "talk sense" to the bus company and the city commissioners. We have observed that small Negro shops are thriving as Negroes find it inconvenient to walk downtown to the white stores. We have been getting more polite treatment in the white shops since the protest began. We have a new respect for the proper use of our dollar.

WE HAVE DISCOVERED A NEW AND POWERFUL WEAPON—NON-VIOLENT RESISTANCE. Although law is an important factor in bringing about social change, there are certain conditions in which the very effort to adhere to new legal decisions creates tension and provokes violence. We had hoped to see demonstrated a method that would enable us to continue our struggle while coping with the violence it aroused. Now we see the answer: face violence if necessary, but refuse to return violence. If we respect those who oppose us, they may achieve a new understanding of the human relations involved.

WE NOW KNOW THAT THE SOUTHERN NEGRO HAS COME OF AGE, POLITICALLY AND MORALLY. Montgomery has demonstrated that we will not run from the struggle, and will support the battle for equality. The attitude of many young Negroes a few years ago was reflected in the common expression, "I'd rather be a lamp post in Harlem than Governor of Alabama." Now the idea expressed in our churches, schools, pool rooms, restaurants and homes is:

"Brother, stay here and fight non-violently. 'Cause if you don't let them make you mad, you can win." The official slogan of the Montgomery Improvement Association is "Justice without Violence."

The Issues in Montgomery

THE LEADERS of the old order in Montgomery are not prepared to negotiate a settlement. This is not because of the conditions we have set for returning to the busses. The basic question of segregation in intra-state travel is already before the courts. Meanwhile we ask only for what in Atlanta, Mobile, Charleston and most other cities of the South is considered the Southern pattern. We seek the right, under segregation, to seat ourselves from the rear forward on a first come, first served basis. In addition, we ask for courtesy and the hiring of some Negro bus drivers on predominantly Negro routes.

A prominent judge of Tuscaloosa was asked if he felt there was any connection between Autherine Lucy's effort to enter the University of Alabama and the Montgomery non-violent protest. He replied, "Autherine is just one unfortunate girl who doesn't know what she is doing, but in Montgomery it looks like all the niggers have gone crazy."

Later the judge is reported to have explained that "of course the good niggers had undoubtedly been riled up by outsiders, Communists and agitators." It is apparent that at this historic moment most of the elements of the white South are not prepared to believe that "our Negroes could of themselves act like this."

Miscalculation of the White Leaders

BECAUSE THE MAYOR and city authorities cannot admit to themselves that we have changed, every move they have made has inadvertently increased the protest and united the Negro community.

Dec. 1—They arrested Mrs. Parks, one of the most respected Negro women in Montgomery.

Dec. 3—They attempted to intimidate the Negro population by publishing a report in the daily paper that certain Negroes were calling for a boycott of the busses. They thereby informed the 30,000 Negro readers of the planned protest.

Dec. 5—They found Mrs. Parks guilty and fined her $14. This action increased the number of those who joined the boycott.

Dec. 5—They arrested a Negro college student for "intimidating passengers." Actually, he was helping an elderly woman cross the street. This mistake solidified the college students' support of the protest.

Two policemen on motorcycles followed each bus on its rounds through the Negro community. This attempt at psychological coercion further increased the number of Negroes who joined the protest.

In a news telecast at 6:00 PM a mass meeting planned for that evening was announced. Although we had expected only 500 people at the meeting, over 5,000 attended.

Dec. 6—They began to intimidate Negro taxi drivers. This led to the setting up of a car pool and a resolution to extend indefinitely our protest, which had originally been called for one day only.

Dec. 7—They began to harass Negro motorists. This encouraged the Negro middle class to join the struggle.

Dec. 8—The lawyer for the bus company said, "We have no intention of hiring Negro drivers now or in the foreseeable future." To us this meant never. The slogan then became, "Stay off the busses until we win."

Dec. 9—The Mayor invited Negro leaders to a conference, presumably for negotiation. When we arrived, we discovered that some of the men in the room were white supremacists and members of the White Citizens Council. The Mayor's attitude was made clear when he said, "Comes the first rainy day and the Negroes will be back in the busses." The next day it did rain, but the Negroes did not ride the busses.

At this point over 42,000 Montgomery Negroes had joined the protest. After a period of uneasy quiet, elements in the white community turned to further police intimidation and to violence.

Jan. 26—I was arrested for travelling 30 miles per hour in a 25 mile zone. This arrest occurred just 2 hours before a mass meeting. So, we had to hold seven mass meetings to accommodate the people.

Jan. 30—My home was bombed.

Feb. 1—The home of E. D. Nixon, one of the protest leaders and former State President of the NAACP, was bombed. This brought moral and financial support from all over the state.

Feb. 22—Eighty-nine persons, including the 24 ministers, were arrested for participating in the non-violent protest.

Every attempt to end the protest by intimidation, by encouraging Negroes to inform, by force and violence, further cemented the Negro community and brought sympathy for our cause from men of good will all over the world. The great appeal for the world appears to lie in the fact that we in Montgomery have adopted the method of non-violence. In a world in which most men attempt to defend their highest values by the accumulation of weapons of destruction, it is morally refreshing to hear 5,000 Negroes in Montgomery shout "Amen" and "Halleluh" when they are exhorted to "pray for those who oppose you," or pray "Oh Lord, give us strength of body to keep walking for freedom," and conclude each mass meeting with: "Let us pray that God shall give us strength to remain non-violent though we may face death."

The Liberal Dilemma

AND DEATH there may be. Many white men in the South see themselves as a fearful minority in an ocean of black men. They honestly believe with one side of their minds that Negroes are depraved and disease-ridden. They look upon any effort at equality as leading to "mongrelization." They are convinced that racial equality is a Communist idea and that those who ask for it are subversive. They believe that their caste system is the highest form of social organization.

The enlightened white Southerner, who for years has preached gradualism, now sees that even the slow approach finally has revolutionary implications. Placing straws on a camel's back, no matter how slowly, is dangerous. This realization has immobilized the liberals and most of the white church leaders. They have no answer for dealing with or absorbing violence. They end in begging for retreat, lest "things get out of hand and lead to violence."

Writing in *Life*, William Faulkner, Nobel prize-winning author from Mississippi, recently urged the NAACP to "stop now for a moment." [2] That is to say, he encouraged Negroes to accept injustice, exploitation and indignity for a while longer. It is hardly a moral act to encourage others patiently to accept injustice which he himself does not endure.

In urging delay, which in this dynamic period is tantamount to retreat, Faulkner suggests that those of us who press for change now may not know that violence could break out. He says we are "dealing with a fact: the fact of emotional conditions of such fierce unanimity as to scorn the fact that it is a minority and which will go to any length and against any odds at this moment to justify and, if necessary, defend that condition and its right to it."

We Southern Negroes believe that it is essential to defend the right of equality now. From this position we will not and cannot retreat. Fortunately, we are increasingly aware that we must not try to defend our position by methods that contradict the aim of brotherhood. We in Montgomery believe that the only way to press on is by adopting the philosophy and practice of non-violent resistance.

This method permits a struggle to go on with dignity and without the need to retreat. It is a method that can absorb the violence that is inevitable in social change whenever deep-seated prejudices are challenged.

If, in pressing for justice and equality in Montgomery, we discover that those who reject equality are prepared to use violence, we must not despair, retreat, or fear. Before they make this crucial decision, they must remember: whatever they do, we will not use violence in return. We hope we can act in the struggle in such a way that they will see the error of their approach and will come to respect us. Then we can all live together in peace and equality.

The basic conflict is not really over the busses. Yet we believe that, if the method we use in dealing with equality in the busses can eliminate injustice within ourselves, we shall at the same time be attacking the basis of injustice— man's hostility to man. This can only be done when we challenge the white community to reexamine its assumptions as we are now prepared to reexamine ours.

We do not wish to triumph over the white community. That would only result in transferring those now on the bottom to the top. But, if we can live up to non-violence in thought and deed, there will emerge an interracial society based on freedom for all.

PD. *Liberation* 1 (April 1956): 3–6.

---

2. Faulkner, "A Letter to the North," *Life*, 5 March 1956, pp. 51–52.

[*May 1956*]
[*Montgomery, Ala.*]

Miss Jewelle Taylor
2515 Thirteenth Street, N.W.
Apartment 501
Washington 9, D.C.

Dear Jewelle,

This is just a note to thank you for your very kind letter. It was a real pleasure hearing from you. I can assure you that all of your encouraging words will be long remembered.

We are still involved in the non-violent protest against injustice, and we plan to be in it until the finish. I have been profoundly moved by the discipline, wise restraint and dignity by which our people have carried on this protest. I feel that it has given the Negro a new sense of dignity.

I am very happy to know of your progress since finishing Radcliffe and above all your intentions of being married in August. May I extend my congratulations at this point. Coretta and the baby are doing fine and she sends her best regards.

With warm personal regards.

Very sincerely yours,

TLc. MLKP-MBU: Box 66.

From Earl E. Nance

1 May 1956
St. Louis, Mo.

Nance, pastor of Greater Mt. Carmel Baptist Church in St. Louis, urges King to run for president of the National Baptist Convention.[1] Fearing that the convention would split over the issue of presidential tenure, Nance seeks a strong candidate against J. H. Jackson. King's response, if any, has not been located. He did not pursue the presidency.

---

1. Earl Edward Nance, Sr. (1913–), was born in Alma, Arkansas, and graduated from Morehouse College in 1945. He did graduate work at Gammon Theological Seminary after being ordained as a Baptist minister in 1942. In 1951 he became pastor of Greater Mt. Carmel Baptist Church, where he still serves.

Dexter Avenue Baptist Church   1 May
309 So. Jackson Avenue   1956
Montgomery Alabama

Dr. M. L. King Jr.

Dear M. L.

I am writing you in behalf of an organization that is being formed here, that
will be know as, "KING FOR PRESIDENT OF THE NATL. BAPTIST CONVEN-
TION INC.", If you will accept the same.

If you will accept there is and will not be any strings attached, such as, signing
papers or nothing else. All we want is for you to give us the go signal.

We feel that you are the only one that can or keep the convention from split-
ting. Secondly, you are the type of man that we need to lead us to "VICTORY"
because you depend on God to lead you.

I would like to hear from you at once on this matter for we want to set up such
organizations in every state.

Your Classmate
[*signed*] Rev. Earl E. Nance Sr.
Rev. Earl E. Nance

E.E.N./mw

TLS. MLKP-MBU: Box 91.

To Roy Wilkins

1 May 1956
Montgomery, Ala.

King expresses appreciation for the NAACP's agreement, confirmed in Wilkins's 12
April letter to King, to provide legal and financial support for three court cases: King's
trial and appeal, Rosa Parks's appeal, and the Browder v. Gayle *federal lawsuit.*

Mr. Roy Wilkins
Executive Secretary
National Association for the
Advancement of Colored People
20 West 40th Street
New York 18, New York

Dear Mr. Wilkins:

This is just a note to follow up our recent telephone conversation. As I said to
you the other day, the whole Executive Board of The Montgomery Improvement
Association is deeply gratified to know of the support that the National Office   243

consented to give for our struggle. All of the offers that were made concerning the three legal matters are satisfactory to us. I assure you that this will go a long, long way in lifting the legal burden that we confront. Moreover, this deep spirit of cooperation from the NAACP will give us renewed courage and vigor to carry on.

We are quite conscious of our dependence on the NAACP. I have said to our people all along that the great victories of the Negro have been gained through the assiduous labor of the NAACP. As time goes on, and the problems which we confront move toward some point of solution, you may rest assured that we will turn all of the support that we possibly can to the NAACP. My church has just taken out a life membership in the NAACP, and I am urging other churches in our community to do likewise. Again, let me thank you for this very fine response.

With every good wish, I am

Sincerely yours,
[*signed*]
M. L. King, Jr.,
President

MLK:b
(Dictated by Rev. King but translated and signed in his absence.)

TLSr. NAACPP-DLC: Group III-A177.

To Richard Bartlett Gregg

1 May 1956
[*Montgomery, Ala.*]

King thanks Gregg for his 2 April letter and praises his book, The Power of Nonviolence. *When a second revised edition was published in 1959, King provided the foreword. Gregg responded on 20 May.*[1]

Mr. Richard B. Gregg
Forest Farm
Jamaica, Vermont

Dear Mr. Gregg:

This is just a note to say how happy I was to receive your very kind letter. At present I am in the process of reading your book. I must say that it has been a most stimulating experience. The content is profound, the style very lucid and the general tone filled with lasting spiritual meaning. I don't know when I have

---

1. See pp. 267–269 in this volume.

read anything that has given the idea of non-violence a more realistic and depth- 1 May
ful interpretation. I assure you that it will be a lasting influence in my life. 1956

I hope it will be possible for me to meet you personally some time in the near future. Glenn Smiley speaks of you quite often. He has been quite helpful throughout our situation here. Please feel free to write me at any time.

With every good wish, I am

Sincerely yours,
M. L. King, Jr.,
President

MLK:b

TLc. MLKP-MBU: Box 17.

To Percival Leroy Prattis

1 May 1956
Montgomery, Ala.

Mr. P. L. Prattis
Executive Editor
The Pittsburgh Courier
P.O. Box 1828
Pittsburgh 30, Pa.

Dear Mr. Prattis:

Thanks for your very kind letter of April 25.

I will be more than happy to do a series of articles for The Pittsburgh Courier on the significance of the Montgomery story. At this point, however, I find it rather difficult, because of an extremely busy schedule. As soon as I catch up sufficiently I will contact you and seek to comply with your request.

Let me express my personal appreciation to you and the Pittsburgh Courier staff for the excellent coverage that you have given to our situation here, and also for the many contributions that have come to us through your influence. I am sure that I voice the sentiments of the whole Montgomery community in saying this.

With every good wish, I am

Cordially yours,
[*signed*]
M. L. King, Jr.,
President

MLK:b
(Dictated by Rev. King but signed in his absence.)

TLSr. PLPC-DHU.

From Sadie Bradford

2 May 1956
Gastonia, N.C.

The proprietor of the Sadie Beauty Shop sends her support to King.[1] On 19 June, he thanked her for the donation.

Dear Rev Kings.

We are so proud of our people's, and your pride. Please keep up the good work's. I am taking up a Donation in my Beauty Shop. for you all. We have taken up a Donation in our chuch for you all. Now we are taken up one in my shop. You also have our praye, How can these Devils keep us Down, unless they stay with us,? Please keep us the good work's, I am co-worker. for the NAACP I am working just as hard as you are.

May God Bless you and your menember's also your church and everything that you <u>undertake</u>

I am

[*signed*] Miss Sadie Bradford.

ALS. MLKP-MBU: Box 16.

---

1. Sadie Bradford (1918–) was born in Bowling Green, South Carolina, and graduated from Apex Beauty College in 1942. She opened her beauty shop in 1945. She was also a member of the NAACP and Weeping Mary Baptist Church in Gastonia.

To Benjamin F. McLaurin

6 May 1956
[*Montgomery, Ala.*]

King informs McLaurin, coordinator of a major civil rights rally at Madison Square Garden on 24 May, that he will not be speaking at the event.[1] Believing that King had agreed to speak, McLaurin had written on 1 May requesting publicity photographs.

---

1. Benjamin F. McLaurin (1906–1989) was born in Jacksonville, Florida, and graduated from Edward Waters College. He also studied at Brookwood Labor College. He was a porter and organizer for the Brotherhood of Sleeping Car Porters during its early years. As a union official and one of A. Philip Randolph's closest aides, McLaurin helped orient the brotherhood toward social activism by helping build several civil rights groups. He was secretary of the March on Washington Movement and helped found the National Committee for Rural Schools, which sent donated goods to poor people in the rural South. In 1960 he was a co-founder of the Negro American Labor Council, which fought racial bias in the labor movement.

Mr. B. F. McLaurin, Coordinator 7 May
Madison Square Garden Civil Rights Rally 1956
217 West 125th Street
Room 319
New York 27, New York

Dear Mr. McLaurin:

This is to acknowledge receipt of your letter of May 1. I talked with Bayard Rustin the other day, and stated that I would not be able to accept the invitation to be at the Madison Square Garden Civil Rights Rally May 24. Certainly I regret this very deeply. I also made contact with Rev. Abernathy and found that he would not be able to come. I think that Mrs. Parks is being contacted, and in the event that she cannot come, I believe it will be possible for Mr. E. D. Nixon to come. You may feel free to contact Bayard Rustin for the major details of our telephone conversation.

You have my prayers and best wishes for a most successful program. We will forever be grateful to you and the fine citizens of New York for the real interest you have taken in our struggle.

Sincerely yours,
M. L. King, Jr.,
President

MLK:b

TLc. MLKP-MBU: Box 62.

From A. Philip Randolph

7 May 1956
New York, N.Y.

Randolph asks King to reconsider his decision not to speak at the Madison Square Garden rally, explaining that promotional literature publicizing King's presence had already been distributed. Because King symbolized the Montgomery struggle, Randolph writes, "we can scarcely adequately 'Salute the Heroes of the South' without you." Handwriting on this letter says, "sent telegram," but King responded by letter on 10 May.[1]

Rev. Martin Luther King
309 South Jackson St.
Montgomery, Alabama

Dear Reverend King:

Mr. Benjamin F. McLaurin, who has been responsible for coordinating the historic Madison Square Garden Civil Rights Rally for May 24th, has informed me of

---

1. See pp. 252–253 in this volume.

the embarrassment created for you and for us in relation to your coming to the Rally.

After Mr. Nixon's telegram was received, we naturally proceeded with publicity, including posters and leaflets calling for "Salute and Support of the Heroes of the South—Autherine Lucy, Rev. Martin Luther King, Dr. T. R. M. Howard and Gus Courts." [2] When a day or so later Bayard Rustin reported that there had been some misunderstanding and that you felt you could not come, we saw no way to recall the promotional literature that had gone out to all major religious, labor, and civic organizations in Greater New York and New Jersey. For one thing, the time and cost involved in attempting to do so would have been confusing, if not impossible, and extremely costly.

I know how very busy you are and how much you are urgently needed in Montgomery. Yet, on reflection, I feel I should point out the significance and importance of the Rally in relation to our entire struggle for freedom:

It will command national attention. It will undoubtedly represent the most extensive aggregation of organizational support that any such effort ever has had, including such groups as the National NAACP, The Brotherhood of Sleeping Car Porters, the Catholic Dioceses, Jewish Clergymen, the Protestant Council, and hundreds of other labor and community groups. Finally, we have hopes of raising $100,000 to be divided between the National NAACP, the Montgomery Improvement Association, and the victims of economic boycotts in Mississippi and South Carolina. This alone is the most extensive financial effort yet made.

For these reasons, and because we can scarcely adequately "Salute the Heroes of the South" without you—since you have become in the minds of Americans a symbol of the Montgomery struggle—will you, therefore, reconsider your decision? In this connection, we are prepared to make arrangements by plane that will ensure your spending the shortest possible time away from home.

Needless to say, I know the pressure you are under, and normally I should not urge you to return to New York one week after you have been here on the 17th, but I feel this rally to be of such importance to you in Montgomery and for the entire struggle that I urge you to reconsider coming.

May I hear from you telegraph collect as soon as you have had time for consideration.

Sincerely,
[*signed*]
A. Philip Randolph
City-Wide Chairman

THLS. MLKP-MBU: Box 62.

---

2. E. D. Nixon's telegram has not been located. Theodore Roosevelt Mason Howard (1908–1977), chief medical examiner at Friendship Clinic in Mound Bayou, Mississippi, was co-founder of the National Medical Association and president of the Mississippi Regional Council of Negro Leaders. In November 1955 he spoke at Dexter Avenue Baptist Church about segregation in Mississippi. Gus Courts, a store owner and local leader of the Mississippi NAACP, was harassed and shot in 1955 when he insisted on his right to register to vote. Courts survived the attack but eventually left the state.

8 May 1956
Montgomery, Ala.

After interviewing King on 28 February, Glenn Smiley forwarded a transcript to
Miller, assistant editor of FOR's Fellowship *magazine, who accepted it for publication*
as "Walk for Freedom" in the May issue. Responding to Miller's request that King
expand the article to include his trial and conviction, influences on his belief in
nonviolence, and the positive role of whites in the bus boycott, King asks that the
transcript be published without any changes.[1] He explains that his busy schedule and
the pressing deadline prevented him from revising the piece, but that he hopes to do "a
more painstaking and scholarly article" for Fellowship *in the future. Miller responded*
on 18 May.[2]

Mr. William Robert Miller
Assistant Editor
Fellowship Publications
21 Audubon Avenue
New York 32, New York

Dear Mr. Miller:

This letter is long over due. I have been intending to write you for several days, but absence from the city plus the accumulation of a flood of mail have delayed my reply.

Your letter of April 10, came too late for me to make the addition in the article which you requested. Consequently I had to go on with the third alternative you suggested in your letter of April 16, namely, letting the article go as it was already set up. I hope it will serve some purpose. I am sorry that I did not get an opportunity to put my best literary foot forward. Actually that was just a spontaneous or rather extemporaneous statement that I made on tape for Glenn Smiley. I hope that it will be possible for me to do a more painstaking and scholarly article for your very fine journal in the near future.

With every good wish, I am

Sincerely yours,
[*signed*]
M. L. King, Jr.,
President

MLK:b

THLS. WRMP-GAMK: Box 1.

---

1. See "Walk for Freedom," May 1956, pp. 277–280 in this volume.
2. See pp. 262–263 in this volume.

To Jesse Hill, Jr.

8 May 1956
[*Montgomery, Ala.*]

Hill, an Atlanta Life Insurance Company actuary, collected donations from fellow
workers and sent them to the MIA through his company's Montgomery office.[1]

Mr. Jesse Hill, Jr.
Acting Actuary
Atlanta Life Insurance Company
148 Auburn Avenue, N.E.
Atlanta 1, Georgia

Dear Mr. Hill:

This is to acknowledge the tremendous contribution you and the very fine
people connected with your organization have made.

Mr. McHaney forwarded a total of $1,019.87 to this office to be used in our
struggle for justice in the present situation here in Montgomery. Please know that
we are deeply grateful and will long remember your coming to our aid. We are
enclosing a receipt to cover this amount. Please express our gratitude to all person responsible for this wonderful contribution.

Sincerely yours,
M. L. King, Jr.,
President

MLK:b

enc. 1 receipt for $1,019.87
(Dictated by Rev. King but transcribed in his absence.)

TLc. MLKP-MBU: Box 14.

---

1. On 22 May the company secretary, E. M. Martin, forwarded to King a letter to King, Sr., "con-
gratulating you and Mrs. King on contributing such a noble son to the cause of practical freedom and
Democracy." Jesse Hill, Jr. (1929–), born in St. Louis, Missouri, received his B.S. (1947) from Lincoln
University in Jefferson City and an M.B.A. (1949) from the University of Michigan. He was the second
African American to be licensed as an actuary in the United States. During the 1950s Hill served as
chairman of Atlanta's All-Citizens Registration Committee, and, as a member of the Atlanta Committee for Cooperative Action, he helped integrate Georgia's high schools and universities. Hill chaired
Andrew Young's successful 1972 campaign for Congress and Maynard H. Jackson's successful 1973 campaign for mayor of Atlanta. He later became president of Atlanta Life Insurance Company, one of the
nation's oldest and largest black-owned businesses. Hill also served as chair of the board of directors
of the Martin Luther King, Jr., Center for Social Change, Inc.

8 May 1956
[*Montgomery, Ala.*]

*Rooks, pastor of St. James Presbyterian Church in Harlem, had asked King about the
"extent of your personal responsibility for the proper distribution" of funds donated to
the MIA. After receiving King's response, Rooks sent $500 from his congregation.*[1]

The Rev. Shelby Rooks
St. James Presbyterian Church
St. Nicholas Avenue at 141st Street
New York 31, New York

Dear Rev. Rooks:

This is to acknowledge receipt of your very kind letter of April 30, making inquiry concerning the present status of our situation.

Yes funds are still being received by the association. We still have tremendous
financial obligations. Our operation expenses, including the car pool and the
running of a well staffed office, run upwards of four thousand dollars ($4,000.00)
per week. I can assure you that the money is being properly handled. The finance
committee of the Montgomery Improvement Association is composed of some of
the finest and most respected citizens of Montgomery. So you can rest assured
that whatever contribution you make to our struggle will be properly distributed.

Let me express my personal appreciation to you for your interest in our cause.
Such moral support from friends sympathetic with our struggle give us renewed
vigor and courage to carry on. Although I have never met you personally, I have
long known of the very fine job that you are doing in New York City. You have my
prayers and best wishes for continued success in your pastorate.

Yours sincerely,
M. L. King, Jr.,
President

MLK:b

TLc. MLKP-MBU: Box 65.

---

1. Rooks to King, 30 April and 8 June 1956. Shelby Rooks (1905–), born in North Carolina, earned
his B.A. in 1928 from Lincoln University in Pennsylvania, where he remained to teach English (1929–
1931). He earned an M.Div. in 1934 from Union Seminary in New York. That year Rooks became pastor
at the Nazarene Congregational Church in Brooklyn. He moved to St. James Presbyterian Church in
1943, serving as pastor there until 1976.

From Ernest C. Dillard

9 May 1956
Detroit, Mich.

*Dillard, head of the Detroit-based Committee to Aid the Montgomery, Alabama, Bus
Protest, notifies King of the committee's contribution to the MIA.[1] He urges that the
boycott continue until democracy "exists in living fact and not only in the dusty files of
unimplemented and forgotten laws and court decisions," a phrase that King may have
adapted for use in his address to the NAACP convention on 27 June.*

REV M L KING, PRESIDENT MONTGOMERY IMPROVEMENT ASSN
530-C SOUTH UNION ST MONTGOMERY ALA

I TRUST YOU HAVE RECEIVED BY NOW THE COMMITTEES CONTRIBUTION OF $200.00 WIRED
ON MAY 7TH 1956 OUR COMMITTEE FURTHER CONGRATULATES YOU AND THE COLORED
PEOPLE OF MONTGOMERY FOR YOUR GREAT AND HEARTWARMING DECISION TO CONTINUE
YOUR PROTEST UNTIL DEMOCRACY ON MONTGOMERYS BUS LINES EXISTS IN LIVING FACT AND
NOT ONLY IN THE DUSTY FILES OF UNIMPLEMENTED AND FORGOTTEN LAWS AND COURT
DECISIONS. THE NATION AND THE WORLD CANNOT BUT HAIL YOUR DECISION TO CONTINUE
THIS VALIENT FIGHT. OUR COMMITTEE BELIEVES WITH YOU THAT CONTINUED PROTESTS WILL
CAUSE THE SAGGING WALLS OF BUS SEGREGATION LIKE THOSE OF "JERICHO" TO SURELY COME
TUMBLING DOWN THAT IS WHY OUR COMMITTEE IS MORE THAN HAPPY TO BE ABLE TO MAKE
ITS MODEST CONTRIBUTION TO THIS HISTORIC AND JUST CAUSE OF MAKING DEMOCRACY WORK.
IN ACKNOWLEDGEMENT OF ABOVE CONTRIBUTION PLEASE INCLOSE REMARKS ON THE GENERAL
SITUATION ON THE MONTGOMERY BUS PROTEST FIGHT SUCH INFORMATION WILL AID OUR
COMMITTEE IN THE FORMULATION OF FURTHER PLANS AND PROGRAMS TO AID THE PROTEST

ERNEST C DILLARD CHAIRMAN THE COMMITTEE TO AID THE MONTGOMERY ALABAMA BUS
PROTEST 3830 MCCLELLAN DETROIT 14 MICHIGAN TELEPHONE WALNUT 55269.

PWSr. MLKP-MBU: Box 89.

---

1. Ernest C. Dillard (1915–) graduated from Wayne State University and the University of Michigan
Labor School. He became active in the United Auto Workers (Fleetwood Local #15) in the late 1930s
and eventually joined the UAW staff in 1964 as assistant director of educational activities.

To A. Philip Randolph

10 May 1956
[*Montgomery, Ala.*]

*Replying to Randolph's 7 May letter about the Madison Square Garden rally scheduled
for 24 May, King apologizes for the "mixup." He agrees to do his "very best to be*

present for this momentous occasion" and to send a representative if he is unable to attend. King was in Montgomery on the day of the rally, presiding at an MIA executive board meeting. The crowd of sixteen to twenty thousand at the New York rally gave a standing ovation to Rosa Parks and E. D. Nixon and heard speeches from Randolph, Adam Clayton Powell, Jr., Eleanor Roosevelt, Autherine Lucy, Roy Wilkins, and Rabbi Israel Goldstein, president of the American Jewish Congress.

Mr. A. Philip Randolph
City-Wide Chairman Committee
Madison Square Garden Civil Rights Rally
217 West 125th Street
New York 27, New York

Dear Mr. Randolph:

This is to acknowledge receipt of your letter of May 7. Absence from the city has delayed my reply.

I am very sorry that the mixup in my coming to New York has arisen. As I said to Bayard Rustin a few days ago and later said to Mr. McLaurin through a letter, the pressure of the situation here plus an extremely busy schedule made it impossible for me to accept the invitation. However, I can understand the difficulties which you are confronting. I know it will be almost impossible and certainly confusing to attempt to recall the promotional literature at this point. Since this is the case I would suggest that you continue with your publicity, and I will do my very best to be present for this momentous occasion. If at the last minute, I find that I cannot come I am sure that I can send a representative in my place. This is about the best I can say at this point. I hope it meets your approval.

Please know that I am deeply in accord with what you and the very fine citizens of New York are doing in our behalf. I have always felt that the problems of the South are bigger than the South and that we need the concerted efforts of the whole nation to revolt against the evils of injustice which are so rampant in our society. It is such persons as you that give us grim and bold determination to keep going in our struggle for first class citizenship. We will long remember your coming to our aid in this great struggle for justice.

With every good wish, I am

Sincerely yours,
M. L. King, Jr.,
President

MLK:b

TLc. MLKP-MBU: Box 62.

To Harris Wofford

10 May 1956
[*Montgomery, Ala.*]

Mr. Harris Wofford, Jr.
1226 Rebecca Drive
Alexandria, Virginia

Dear Mr. Wofford:

This is to acknowledge receipt of you very kind letter of April 25. I was very happy to receive your very helpful suggestions. I assure you that I am taking all of them under consideration and using that which is possible. You have mastered both the technique and the spirit of Ghandi, and such wide experience in this area is always helpful in our struggle.

Always feel free to write and to give constructive criticism. I can assure you that they will always be accepted in the same noble and generous spirit they are given.

I have received your book and also the pamphlet that you sent. Please know that I am deeply grateful to you for your thoughtfulness at this time. Unfortunately, I have not had an opportunity to read the book because of the pressure of the present situation. As soon as I am somewhat relieved of this pressure, I will be reading your book.

With every good wish, I am

Sincerely yours,
M. L. King, Jr.,
President

MLK:b

TLc. MLKP-MBU: Box 67.

From Henri Varin de la Brunelière

11 May 1956
Fort-de-France, Martinique

NAACP field secretary Clarence Laws forwarded this letter from Bishop de la Brunelière to King, noting that "the courageous and sacrificial stand of Negro citizens of Montgomery is having a world wide impact on peoples everywhere." [1] *Bishop de la Brunelière had read about the boycott in the Parisian Catholic newspaper* La Croix. *On 10 July King thanked him for his support.*

---

   1. Clarence A. Laws to King, 22 May 1956.

Dear Reverend Pastor,

I am a frenchman and Bishop of Martinique F.W.I. In "La Croix" one of Paris's leading catholic news papers, I read an article written about the injustices inspired by the decision handed down by the Supreme Court condemning segregation. In this article a full account is given of your heroic struggle against these injustices. Your cause is a juste one. You wish to defend it in an excellent way, one truly inspired by the bible: "Conquer evil in doing good". Do not triumph against the white man; triump with him. He is a vitim of the prejudices whose author he is.

I wished to publicize your way of seeing and acting through the enclosed article which appeared in the catholic paper of Martinique. I should like to say that the colored people of the USA and you especially, Reverend dear Pastor, have our deepest sympathy. Perhaps you are aware of the fact that our spirituel leader, Pope Pius XII shortly after his election to the Papacy manifested his deep sympathy for the colored people of your country who deserve it so well because of the long and hard trials which have been inflicted upon them by these injustices.

Further proof of his devotion to the cause of the colored race and his rejection of race discrimination is shown by the fact that he has consecrated thirteen negro bishops of Africa two of them in recent months. I thank God for it.

The cause for which the colored people are fighting is a just one and I pray daily that victory shall be yours. Reverend and dear Sir, please be assured of my continued sympathy and my cordial devotion.

Sincerely Yours in Jesus Christ.
[*signed*] Henri Varin de la Brunelière
bishop of Martinique

TAHLS. MLKP-MBU: Box 16.

From Charles S. Johnson

17 May 1956
Nashville, Tenn.

Fisk University president Johnson tells King that he has been honored with the "Fisk Distinguished Service Award," to be presented at the 28 May Fisk commencement ceremony.[1] King received the award in person and wrote a letter of appreciation on

---

1. Charles Spurgeon Johnson (1893–1956), born in Bristol, Virginia, to a former slave, received B.A.'s from Virginia Union University (1916) and the University of Chicago (1917). He joined the National Urban League in 1921, where he served as director of research and editor of the league's monthly journal. In 1928 he became the first director of the Institute of Social Studies at Fisk University and five years later took over the directorship of the Institute of Race Relations at Swarthmore College. Johnson served on a League of Nations commission investigating allegations of slavery in Liberia in 1930 and was sent to Japan to help reorganize Japan's educational system after World War II. In 1947 Johnson became the first African-American president of Fisk University.

5 June in which he assured Johnson that "such recognition gives me new determination to continue the struggle for freedom and justice."

The Reverend Martin Luther King
309 South Jackson Street
Montgomery, Alabama

Dear Reverend King:

This year, for the first time, Fisk University is presenting a citation with a cash award to the person who, in the judgment of a committee selected from over the country, has contributed most to the cause of race relations, civil liberties and economic justice during the current year. This citation is known as the "Fisk Distinguished Service Award" and carries a cash honorarium of five hundred dollars. This annual award is sponsored by the Fisk General Alumni Association and a special donor, Dr. Jerome Davis, the latter in honor of the memory of his father, Jerome Dean Davis, pioneer missionary to Japan who fought all his life for equality between the races.

The committee has recommended you overwhelmingly for this first award and I should like to ask if you could be present on Commencement Day, May 28 at 11:00 A.M. to receive it. The members of the committee are as follows: Dr. Homer Cooper, Chicago; Judge William Hastie, Philadelphia; Mrs. William Thomas Mason, Washington; Dr. Benjamin E. Mays, Atlanta; Mr. P. L. Prattis, Pittsburgh; Mr. A. Maceo Smith, Dallas; Mr. Willard S. Townsend, Chicago; Dr. Jerome Davis and myself.

It is the wish of the committee to withhold the name of the awardee until the date of presentation.

Sincerely yours,
[*signed*]
Charles S. Johnson

CSJ:aef

TLS. MLKP-MBU: Box 17.

"The Death of Evil upon the Seashore," Sermon Delivered at the Service of Prayer and Thanksgiving, Cathedral of St. John the Divine

17 May 1956
New York, N.Y.

King delivered this sermon at the Cathedral of St. John the Divine, headquarters of the Episcopal diocese of New York State, in an ecumenical program commemorating the second anniversary of the Supreme Court's school desegregation decision in Brown v. Board of Education. *Twelve thousand people attended the event; several other*

Service of Prayer And Thanksgiving

PRINCIPAL SPEAKER

The REVEREND DR.

MARTIN LUTHER KING, JR.

LEADER OF THE MONTGOMERY, ALABAMA,

PASSIVE RESISTANCE MOVEMENT

at THE CATHEDRAL
of ST. JOHN THE DIVINE

112th STREET & AMSTERDAM AVENUE, NEW YORK CITY

THURSDAY, MAY 17th
7:30 P. M.

SPONSORED BY THE GREATER NEW YORK COMMITTEE FOR A NATIONAL DAY OF PRAYER AND THANKSGIVING

Dr. O. Clay Maxwell, Sr.,
National Baptist Leader and
Pastor of Mount Olivet Baptist Church

Co-Chairmen

The Reverend Dan M. Potter,
Executive Director of the Protestant
Council of the City of New York

All Welcome!

Interdenominational
Interracial

(PLEASE POST)

ministers shared the platform with King, including O. Clay Maxwell, Sr., pastor of Mount Olivet Baptist Church, and James A. Pike, dean of the cathedral. Later that evening, with his parents in attendance, King delivered "A Realistic Look at Race Relations" at the annual dinner sponsored by the NAACP Legal Defense and Educational Fund, held to commemorate the Brown *decision.[1]*

King had preached "Death of Evil upon the Seashore" at least twice in the past, including once at Dexter in 1954.[2] King tells the biblical story of the exodus from Egypt, comparing the Israelites' captivity with the plight of African Americans. "Many years ago the Negro was thrown into the Egypt of segregation," he writes, but "through a world shaking decree by the nine justices of the Supreme Court of America . . . the Red Sea was opened and the forces of justice marched through to the other side." King remembered the program as "one of the greatest experiences of my life." His listeners' praise was equally effusive: Dean Pike called King's presentation the "greatest sermon" he had ever heard.[3] The text reprinted here was probably published by the organizing committee, which received King's address several days before the event. The sermon also appeared in the National Baptist Voice *and in a FOR pamphlet.[4]*

"And Israel saw the Egyptians dead upon the seashore."—Exodus 14:30

There is hardly anything more obvious than the fact that evil is present in the universe. It projects its nagging, prehensile tentacles into every level of human existence. We may debate over the origin of evil, but only the person victimized with a superficial optimism will debate over its reality. Evil is with us as a stark, grim, and colossal reality.

The Bible affirms the reality of evil in glaring terms. It symbolically pictures it in the work of a serpent which comes to inject a discord into the beautiful, harmonious symphony of life in a garden. It sees it in nagging tares disrupting the orderly growth of stately wheat. It sees it in a ruthless mob hanging the world's most precious character on a cross between two thieves. The Bible is crystal clear in its perception of evil.

But we need not stop with the glaring examples of the Bible to establish the reality of evil; we need only to look out into the wide arena of everyday life. We have seen evil in tragic lust and inordinate selfishness. We have seen it in high places where men are willing to sacrifice truth on the altars of their self-interest. We have seen it in imperialistic nations trampling over other nations with the iron feet of oppression. We have seen it clothed in the garments of calamitous wars which left battlefields painted with blood, filled nations with widows and orphans, and sent men home physically handicapped and psychologically wrecked. We have seen evil in all of its tragic dimensions.

---

1. An edited version of the speech was reprinted in the *Socialist Call* as "The 'New Negro' of the South: Behind the Montgomery Story," June 1956, pp. 280–286 in this volume.

2. He later expanded and revised the sermon for publication in *Strength to Love,* pp. 76–85.

3. See King to George W. Lawrence, 4 June 1956, and Lawrence to King, 15 June 1956, pp. 291 and 296–297 in this volume.

4. King sent an advance typed version of the sermon to George W. Lawrence for publicity purposes (King to Lawrence, 14 May 1956). It was also published in the *National Baptist Voice,* June 1956.

So in a sense, the whole history of life is the history of a struggle between good and evil. There seems to be a tension at the very core of the universe. All the great religions have seen this tension at the center of life. Hinduism called it a conflict between illusion and reality; Zoroastrianism looked upon it as a tension between the god of light and the god of darkness; Platonism called it a conflict between spirit and matter; traditional Judaism and Christianity called it a conflict between God and Satan.[5] Each of these religions recognized that in the midst of the upward climb of goodness there is the down pull of evil.

The Hebraic Christian tradition is clear, however, in affirming that in the long struggle between good and evil, good eventually emerges as the victor. Evil is ultimately doomed by the powerful, insurgent forces of good. Good Friday may occupy the throne for a day, but ultimately it must give way to the triumphant beat of the drums of Easter. A mythical Satan, through the work of a conniving serpent, may gain the allegiance of man for a period, but ultimately he must give way to the magnetic redemptive power of a humble servant on an uplifted cross. Evil may so shape events that Caesar will occupy a palace and Christ a cross, but one day that same Christ will rise up and split history into A.D. and B.C., so that even the life of Caesar must be dated by his name. Biblical religion recognized long ago what William Cullen Bryant came to see in the modern world: "Truth crushed to earth will rise again;" and what Carlyle came to see: "No lie can live forever." [6]

A graphic example of this truth is found in an incident in the early history of the Hebrew people. You will remember that at a very early stage in her history the children of Israel were reduced to the bondage of physical slavery under the gripping yoke of Egyptian rule. Egypt was the symbol of evil in the form of humiliating oppression, ungodly exploitation and crushing domination. The Israelites symbolized goodness, in the form of devotion and dedication to the God of Abraham, Isaac and Jacob. These two forces were in a continual struggle against each other—Egypt struggling to maintain her oppressive yoke and Israel struggling to gain freedom from this yoke. Finally, however, these Israelites, through the providence of God, were able to cross the Red Sea, and thereby get out of the hands of Egyptian rule. The Egyptians, in a desperate attempt to prevent the Israelites from escaping, had their armies to go in the Red Sea behind them. But as soon as the Egyptians got into the Red Sea the parted waves swept back upon them, and the rushing waters of the sea soon drowned all of them. As the Israelites looked back all they could see was here and there a poor drowned body beaten upon the seashore. For the Israelites, this was a great moment. It was the

---

5. Cf. Harry Emerson Fosdick, "How to Believe in a Good God in a World Like This," in *Living Under Tension* (New York: Harper & Brothers, 1941), p. 216: "All the great religions have so pictured life in terms of conflict. Hinduism called it a conflict between reality and illusion; Zoroastrianism a conflict between light and darkness; Platonism a conflict between spirit and matter; traditional Judaism and Christianity a conflict between God and Satan."

6. William Cullen Bryant, *The Battlefield* (1839), stanza 9. King probably paraphrases Thomas Carlyle's *The French Revolution* (1837); see note 3 to "Rediscovering Lost Values," 28 February 1954, in *Papers* 2:253.

end of a frightful period in their history.[7] It was a joyous daybreak that had come to end the long night of their captivity.

This story symbolizes something basic about the universe. It symbolizes something much deeper than the drowning of a few men, for no one can rejoice at the death or the defeat of a human person. This story, at bottom, symbolizes the death of evil. It was the death of inhuman oppression and ungodly exploitation.

The death of the Egyptians upon the seashore is a glaring symbol of the ultimate doom of evil in its struggle with good. There is something in the very nature of the universe which is on the side of Israel in its struggle with every Egypt. There is something in the very nature of the universe which ultimately comes to the aid of goodness in its perennial struggle with evil. There is something in this universe which justifies James Russell Lowell in saying:

> Truth forever on the scaffold, wrong
> forever on the throne
> yet that scaffold sways the future
> and behind the dim unknown stands God
> within the shadow
> Keeping watch above His own.[8]

Notice how we have seen the truth of this text revealed in the contemporary struggle between good, in the form of freedom and justice, and evil, in the form of oppression and colonialism. Gradually we have seen the forces of freedom and justice emerge victoriously out of some Red Sea, only to look back and see the forces of oppression and colonialism dead upon the seashore. There are approximately 2,400,000,000 people in the world today. The vast majority of these people are found in Africa and Asia. More than 1,400,000,000 of the peoples of the world are found on these two continents. Fifty years ago most of these people were dominated politically, exploited economically, segregated and humiliated by some foreign power. There were 400,000,000 persons in India and Pakistan under the iron feet of British rule. There were 600,000,000 persons in China under the gripping yoke of British, Dutch and French rule. There were 100,000,000 persons in Indonesia under the oppressive hands of Dutch rule. There were 200,000,000

---

7. Cf. Phillips Brooks, "The Egyptians Dead upon the Seashore," in *Selected Sermons*, ed. William Scarlett (New York: E. P. Dutton, 1949), p. 105: "The parted waves had swept back upon the host of the pursuers. The tumult and terror, which had rent the air, had sunk into silence, and all that the escaped people saw was here and there a poor drowned body beaten up upon the bank, where they stood with the great flood between them and the land of their long captivity and oppression. It meant everything to the Israelites. . . . It was the end of a frightful period in their history."

8. James Russell Lowell, *The Present Crisis* (1844), stanza 8. This passage, as well as the two earlier ones from Bryant and Carlyle, became commonplace in King's oratory. Cf. Harry Emerson Fosdick, "Why We Believe in God," in *On Being Fit to Live With: Sermons on Post-war Christianity* (New York: Harper & Brothers, 1946), p. 94: "There is something in this universe besides matter and motion. There is something here that justifies Carlyle in saying, 'No Lie can live for ever'; and Shakespeare in saying, 'There's a divinity that shapes our ends, / Rough-hew them how we will'; and Lowell in saying, 'Truth forever on the scaffold, Wrong forever on the throne,—/ Yet that scaffold sways the future.'" In the version of "Death of Evil" published in *Strength to Love* (p. 77), King corrected and lengthened the quotation from Thomas Carlyle.

persons in Africa dominated and exploited by the British, the Belgium, the French, and the Dutch. The great struggle of the Twentieth Century has been between these exploited masses questing for freedom and the colonial powers seeking to maintain their domination.[9]

What we are seeing now in this struggle is the gradual victory of the forces of freedom and justice. The Red Sea has opened, and today most of these exploited masses have won their freedom from the Egypt of colonialism and are now free to move toward the promised land of economic security and cultural development. As they look back, they clearly see the evils of colonialism and imperialism dead upon the seashore.

In our own struggle for freedom and justice in this country we have gradually seen the death of evil. Many years ago the Negro was thrown into the Egypt of segregation, and his great struggle has been to free himself from the crippling restrictions and paralyzing effects of this vicious system. For years it looked like he would never get out of this Egypt. The closed Red Sea always stood before him with discouraging dimensions. There were always those Pharaohs with hardened hearts, who, despite the cries of many a Moses, refused to let these people go. But one day, through a world shaking decree by the nine justices of the Supreme Court of America and an awakened moral conscience of many White persons of good will, backed up by the Providence of God, the Red Sea was opened, and the forces of justice marched through to the other side. As we look back we see segregation caught in the rushing waters of historical necessity. Evil in the form of injustice and exploitation cannot survive. There is a Red Sea in history that ultimately comes to carry the forces of goodness to victory, and that same Red Sea closes in to bring doom and destruction to the forces of evil.

This is our hope. This is the hope and conviction that all men of goodwill live by. It is at bottom the conviction that all reality hinges on moral foundations and that the whole cosmic universe has spiritual control.[10] It is therefore fitting and proper that we assemble here, just two years after the Supreme Court's momentous decision on desegregation, and praise God for His power and the greatness of His purpose, and pray that we gain the vision and the will to be His co-workers in this struggle.

Let us not despair. Let us not lose faith in man and certainly not in God. We must believe that a prejudiced mind can be changed, and that man, by the grace of God, can be lifted from the valley of hate to the high mountain of love.

Let us remember that as we struggle against Egypt, we must have love, compassion and understanding goodwill for those against whom we struggle, helping them to realize that as we seek to defeat the evils of Egypt we are not seeking to defeat them but to help them, as well as ourselves.

God has a great plan for this world. His purpose is to achieve a world where all

---

9. In subsequent oratory King included similar references to colonialism (see, for example, "The Montgomery Story," 27 June 1956; "Non-Aggression Procedures to Interracial Harmony," 23 July 1956; "The Birth of a New Age," 11 August 1956; and "Facing the Challenge of a New Age," 3 December 1956, pp. 308, 324, 340–341, and 454 in this volume, respectively).

10. These two principles form the basis for King's sermon "Rediscovering Lost Values," 28 February 1954, in *Papers* 2:248–256.

men will live together as brothers, and where every man recognizes the dignity and worth of all human personality. He is seeking at every moment of His existence to lift men from the bondage of some evil Egypt, carrying them through the wilderness of discipline, and finally to the promised land of personal and social integration. May it not be that this is entirely within the realm of possibility? I prefer to live by the faith that the kingdoms of this world shall become the kingdoms of our Lord and His Christ, and He shall reign for ever and ever,[11]

Hallelujah!

Hallelujah!

PD. MLKP-MBU: Box 10.

---

11. Revelations 11:15.

From William Robert Miller

18 May 1956
New York, N.Y.

Miller and his wife, Edith Lorraine, heard King preach "Death of Evil upon the Seashore" at St. John the Divine. Miller praises the sermon and suggests that King publish it along with others in a volume. He also responds to King's 8 May letter.

The Rev. Dr. Martin Luther King, Jr.
The Montgomery Improvement Association
530-C South Union Street
Montgomery 8, Alabama

Dear Dr. King:

You should have been out in the congregation at the Cathedral Church of St John the Divine last night. The service was magnificent, and your sermon was more stirring than you could have imagined from the pulpit.

When we rose to sing Ein' Feste Burg, the ancient hymn had greater power and grandeur than ever I have experienced in it before. In all, the occasion was an experience neither my wife nor I will soon forget.

Listening to your sermon, I wondered if it had ever occurred to you to publish a volume of your sermons. Some of the best and most widely read works of men like Paul Tillich and Harry Emerson Fosdick came before the public in that way, and I am sure that a number of leading publishers—Harper, Scribners, Macmillan, or the religious book houses—might consider you a good bet financially.

My main purpose for writing now, however, is to thank you for your letter of May 8. Our June issue is in page proof now, and the July one is all but made up.

We do not publish in August. The manuscript deadline for the September issue is July 15, so you have almost two months in which to "put your best literary foot forward." Knowing how heavy your commitments must be, I am sure that the amount of leeway this gives you will be welcome.

May I close with a personal note? My wife and I live in rather humble quarters, which were cozy a few months ago and have, since our daughter was born on February 20, become quite cramped. With this warning in advance, I want you to know that we would be very pleased to have you visit us informally any time you happen to come to New York.* We are not important people in any sense, but we would, I am sure, derive great satisfaction from getting to know you and your wife personally. My wife, who is descended from West Indian Negroes, never had much regard for Negroes from the American South until the Montgomery bus protest began. You have radically altered her views in the direction of respect bordering on high enthusiasm.

I shall be looking forward to seeing a draft of your scholarly article when you get to it. Until then, as Dean Pike says, May the Lord bless you and keep you.

In fellowship,
[*signed*]
William Robert Miller

*We live at 23 West 12 St., CH 2–1418

THLS. MLKP-MBU: Box 61.

"Mother's Day in Montgomery,"
by Almena Lomax

18 May 1956
Los Angeles, Calif.

On Sunday, 13 May, Almena Lomax, editor of the weekly black newspaper the Los Angeles Tribune, *attended Dexter's Mother's Day service and took notes on King's sermon.[1] In this excerpt from Lomax's account, King exhorts mothers to prepare their children for life in an integrated society by instilling "a sense of dignity, of self-respect" and an "awareness that they must acquire excellence in everything they do. . . . The Negro must work a little harder than the white man, for he who gets behind must run a little harder or forever remain behind." M. K. Curry, president of Bishop College in*

---

1. Almena Lomax was born in Galveston, Texas, and grew up in Chicago and California. She studied at Los Angeles City College but left in 1941 before graduating to work for the *California Eagle*. In 1943 Lomax and her husband, Lucius, purchased a small black religious weekly and renamed it the *Los Angeles Tribune*. She expanded its coverage to include nonreligious news and served as editor and co-publisher until the paper folded in 1960. Lomax later recalled that many of her readers, eager to receive firsthand information on the boycott, helped finance her fact-finding trip to Montgomery and offered to babysit her six children (interview with King Papers Project staff, 20 February 1995). King thanked Lomax for her articles on the boycott in a 5 July 1956 letter, p. 313 in this volume.

*Marshall, Texas, was a pulpit guest. After the sermon two collections were taken up,
the second being for the MIA; King thanked his congregation for its loyalty to "the
movement," but noted that "we don't take time out in the worship services to go into
it." He advised them to "come out to the twice a week mass meetings" for more
information on the bus protest.*[2]

The Rev. Dr. King preached Sunday morning from the subject, "The Role of
the Negro Mother in Preparing Youth for Integration."

He told his hearers that he doesn't "give much of a Mother's Day sermon,"
noting the "tendency of ministers to exploit certain emotions.

"I assure you," he said, "that I will not play on that theme."

IS LEADER AS WELL AS
PHILOSOPHER, STUDENT

He also expressed the "hope that you will not feel I am being racial or provincial," but with the strong sense of the immediate, which mingled with the philosopher and student that he is, undoubtedly account for his effectiveness as a
leader in these troubled and indeterminate times, he pointed out that the Negro
mother has certain "practical problems" in rearing her children, and he proceeded to give her the benefit of his thoughts on the subject.

◊"The word, integration, is probably one of the best known words in our language now," he said. "It is on the lips of statesmen of all races; it is a big word in
our society. ◊

"If I may make a prediction, integration is as inevitable in America as the rising
of the sun . . . not only because of 9 justices of the Supreme Court . . . not only
because the Negro has a new sense of dignity and destiny, and a determination
to press on to achieve integration. . . . not only because whites, North and South,
have a moral faith in its coming. . . .

"But because the God of the universe is on the side of integration."

He quoted a religious philosopher to the effect that "God is a process of integration," and said he differed only in that, to him, "God is a person of power." [3]
However, he thought this philosopher "getting at something quite vital and true
since part of the activity of God is a movement toward integration.

"God seeks to bring the disintegration of the universe together," he said. "He
is seeking to bring that which is disunited into unity."

"God, himself," is the "final fact of the universe on the side of integration.

---

2. In a letter to a fellow minister a few days later, King reiterated his position that he was "very
reluctant to make a speech on the bus situation at a regular Sunday morning worship hour" (King to
Fred E. Stephens, 23 May 1956).

3. King probably refers to Henry Nelson Wieman, one of the subjects of his dissertation. See King,
"A Comparison of the Conceptions of God in the Thinking of Paul Tillich and Henry Nelson Wieman," 15 April 1955, in *Papers* 2:339–544.

"The individual must be prepared to accept and live with integration," he warned; and he "must inevitably think about being prepared.

"The great question is, are Negroes prepared? . . . For if there was any foolishness on the part of the foolish virgins, it was complacency, and the wisdom of the wise virgins was preparation.[4]

"We have a great responsibility to be prepared not only for the worst, but for the best.

"Every mother has the responsibility to prepare for this great moment of history," he said; and then he proceeded to list three lessons which he said are necessary that mothers teach.

"1. A sense of dignity, of self respect;

"Start teaching your child early that he is somebody. There is a danger of succumbing to a sense of feeling that we are not."

He said all the mechanics first of slavery and then of segregation had been directed at convincing the Negro that he was not fit to be "elevated to . . . the human race."

In the "background of segregation is a theory that there is something inferior about the group segregated," he stated.

He advised that "although you may have to live with segregation a while longer, you must never feel inferior. You are just as significant to God as anybody else." He urged upon them the necessity of "living with a mind that is free . . . reaching out every moment for freedom.

"I must be measured by my soul—the mind is the standard of the man," he said.[5]

DAY OF "GOOD
NEGRO-ANYTHING" PAST

Next he urged parents to instill in their children "awareness that they must acquire excellence in everything they do.

"It is not enough to be prepared to be a good Negro-anything . . . Never let the circumstance of race cause you to be something good only within the framework of race. . . . The need for excellence is a pressing need.

"The great challenge of the Negro is to be prepared. Emerson's lines, 'Make a better mousetrap and the world will beat a path to your door,' hasn't always been

---

4. King refers to the parable of the ten virgins from Matthew 25:1–13.

5. This line is from the eighteenth-century poem "False Greatness" in *Horae Lyricae* (1706) by British poet Isaac Watts. In later speeches King combined passages from Watts's poem and William Cowper's "The Negro's Complaint" (1788). See note 5 to "The 'New Negro' of the South: Behind the Montgomery Story," June 1956, p. 283 in this volume.

true for us; but it will be true.[6] Get the child ready for these opportunities. Stop just getting prepared to get by.

"Everyone is not able to do the so-called great things of life. . . . But if you sweep streets, sweep streets like Michelangelo painted pictures, like Beethoven wrote music . . . so that people will say of you, 'here lives a great street sweeper.' It's not so much what you're doing as how you're doing it."

Perhaps, he conceded, "the Negro must work a little harder than the white man, for he who gets behind must run a little harder or forever remain behind."

"There is a temptation," he said, "as we move toward integration, to be better, to seek to retaliate. . . . That isn't the way. . . ."

"LOVE THE SOLUTION"

"Love is the only solution to the problems of man. There is something about hate that can never solve a problem. Hate destroys the unity of a personality. Hate, like an erosive acid, eats up the best part of our lives."

Cautioning his audience to self-discipline, a theme he returns to frequently in his addresses, he said, "Let's not . . . run wild, boasting that we have done better than the whites. Integration is not a victory for the Negro, but a victory for God and justice . . . Forgiveness means reconciliation, totally blotting out the past."

He quoted Arnold Toynbee, the great British historian, to the effect that the ability of civilizations to survive is measured in terms of "challenge and response" . . . civilizations have died because when the great challenge came, they had not the power to give the proper response."

"The destiny and survival of white civilization depends upon its responses.

"It may well be," he said Toynbee has suggested, that "the Negro may give to white civilization that spiritual revitalization it needs to survive.[7]

"This lack of bitterness; this faith of our fathers—this is a thing we can give at our country's darkest hour. Something beautiful will happen in this universe because we were able to look out into darkness and see the pressing daybreak."

The young preacher paused in his prophecy to look back and pay a tribute to mothers of the race; "There have always been mothers who could see the vision . . . who didn't know the difference between 'you does' and 'you don't,' but

---

6. This familiar quotation, often attributed to Emerson, may have originated as an entry in Emerson's 1855 journal: "If a man has good corn, or wood, or boards, or pigs, to sell, or can make better chairs or knives, crucibles or church organs, than anybody else, you will find a broad hard-beaten road to his house, though it be in the woods" (quoted in *The Journals of Ralph Waldo Emerson*, ed. Robert N. Linscott [New York: Random House, 1960], p. 382).

7. See Arnold Toynbee, *A Study of History*, vol. 2 (New York: Oxford University Press, 1934), pp. 219–220: "With their childlike spiritual intuition and their genius for giving spontaneous aesthetic expression to emotional religious experience, they [American Negroes] may perhaps be capable of rekindling the cold grey ashes of Christianity which have been transmitted to them by us, until in their hearts the divine fire glows again. It is thus, perhaps, if at all, that Christianity may conceivably become the living faith of a dying civilization for the second time." This quotation appeared in a section of the volume entitled "The Range of Challenge-and-Response."

who wanted their offspring to 'get it all' . . . Mothers not only ought to be praised for their greatness, but for keeping on," he said with a particularly appealing perceptiveness; and he recited with a rhapsodic lilt to his voice, Langston Hughes' "Life for me ain't been no crystal stair"—closing with the prophecy that "The kingdoms of this world will be the kingdoms of God—Grant that we will catch the vision of the great city of integration which is the city that has foundations whose builder was God." [8]

PD. "Mother's Day in Montgomery: Boycott Leader Serves His Congregation Toynbee, Langston Hughes, Emerson and Jesus Christ, and Is Received in Complete Consanguinity," *Los Angeles Tribune*, 18 May 1956.

---

8. Langston Hughes's poem "Mother to Son" (1930) was first published in the NAACP's *The Crisis* in December 1922. For other instances where King uses this poem, see "The Montgomery Story," 27 June 1956, p. 310 in this volume; and "Address to MIA Mass Meeting at Holt Street Baptist Church," 14 November 1956, p. 432 in this volume. King weaves together quotations from Hebrews 11:10 and Revelations 11:15.

From Richard Bartlett Gregg

20 May 1956
Chester, N.Y.

Rev. M. L. King, Jr.
530-C South Union St.
Montgomery 8, Ala.

Dear Mr. King:

Your good letter of May 1st was forwarded from Jamaica, Vt. to me here where I will be for the rest of the summer. I am glad to learn that "The Power of Non-violence" is being useful to you.

If you do not mind I would like to pass on to you a few ideas I would like to incorporate in that book if I were to make a revised edition of it. Possibly some of these ideas might also be helpful.

Buddha once said something that is very profound and true and also so neatly and pithily stated. (Please pardon the way my typewriter stutters in the middle of each line.) He said that anger is like spitting against the wind;—it always comes back on the person who feels and expresses it. That is true, I think, of all the divisive emotions such as resentment, suspicion, mistrust, pride, [*strikeout illegible*] fear, etc. In your present situation at Montgomery it holds true of most of the white people, and would also apply to any negroes whose discipline might fail. The spiritual realm is a realm of unity, and whoever puts up a barrier to that unity inevitably suffers himself whether he causes suffering on others or not. If the members of your Association can come to realize that truth {of Buddha's} deeply and steadily, it will help them and the whole situation immensely, I think.

If in the course of the many private and public discussions of the validity of your non-violent actions, anyone asserts that it is undemocratic, you can answer that democracy rests on the principle of consent of the governed. There is no doctrine that the consent can be registered only by voting ballots. ~~Lack of consent~~ Voting is only one way by which consent or refusal of consent can be registered. The refusal to consent to injustice or deceit can be registered by non-violent resistance. And that kind of refusal is effective in many situations where voting is impossible or too slow.

Though I pray that your people may adhere faithfully to the principle and practise of non-violent resistence despite ~~ev~~ every kind of provocation or delay, no matter how long, nevertheless if there should be a failure of discipline and some Negroes under extreme provocation or in despair ~~after~~ at the length of time it may take to change the hearts of the local white population, should break out into violence, do not despair. Accept whatever penalties may come, and then later reform your ranks, develop constructive action among your people as Gandhi did, action which will restore their self-respect and self-confidence, as the village sanitaion and hand spinning did under Indian conditions, preach the principle of non-violence again, and after some years of such renewed discipline, try it again. You will remember that Gandhi did this. In the struggle of 1921 violence broke out at Chauri-Chaura; he suspended the movement, and did not make another big attempt until 1930.[1] But in the interime he carried out a few local satyagrahas on limited grounds. And when he was put in jail with all the other Congress leaders in 1931, he bided his time until when the World War came the British Government had to have Indian cooperation and released the Congress leaders, yet another non-violent movement was begun which finally brought freedom. No failures could daunt Gandhi; let them not daunt you. Keep at it over a long period of years if necessary. Your eventual success will cleanse all of American political and social and economic life. You are doing something big enough to call for all your energy and devotion and endurance. The whole world will be grateful to you. May God give you strength.

This situation clarifies and explains, I think, the meaning of two of the Beatitudes. "Blessed are the meek, for they shall inherit the earth;" and Blessed are ye when men shall revile you and persecute you and shall say all manner of evil against you falsely for my sake".[2] For my sake means, I think, for the sake of spiritual principles. Non-violence and justice are spiritual principles. If you, being persecuted, stick to non-violent resistence for the sake of justice, the conscience of mankind all over the world will be touched and cleansed, and you will be blessed (I believe the Greek word of the New Testament could also be translated as "happy") for thus helping your brothers of all races. The deep and strong

---

1. On 5 February 1922 at Chauri Chaura in the state of Gorakhpur, Indian police violently disrupted a Gandhian noncooperation march; the protesters proceeded to set fire to the town hall and attacked the police trying to escape. Twenty-two people died. Discouraged that his followers had not adhered to nonviolent principles, Gandhi began a fast and halted all direct action, focusing instead on the "constructive programme." See *The Collected Works of Mahatma Gandhi*, vol. 22 (New Delhi: Publications Division, Ministry of Information and Broadcasting, Government of India, 1958), pp. 377–378, 416, 420.

2. Matthew 5:5 and 5:11.

pride of the white man is his greatest moral weakness. He is too weak to get rid 22 May
of it himself. Perhaps he can get rid of it only after he realizes that he was too 1956
weak and had to have the help of Negroes to get it out of himself. The spiritual
realm is where there is neither superioirty nor inferiority, only equality before
God. I hope that Gandhi can help us all to attain that realm.

Remember, many many repetitions of little gentle stimuli will call forth the
smothered spirit of God in you opponents, make it grow, until it takes charge of
them and alters their very being.

You have my best wishes always.

Yours sincerely,
[*signed*]
Richard B. Gregg

TAHLS. MLKP-MBU: Box 17.

To James E. Huger

22 May 1956
[*Montgomery, Ala.*]

> *King agrees to address the anniversary banquet of Alpha Phi Alpha, which had*
> *conferred upon him its Alpha Award of the Year. He chose "The Birth of a New Age"*
> *as his subject for the event held 11 August in Buffalo, New York.*[1]

Mr. James E. Huger
General Secretary
Alpha Phi Alpha Fraternity
4432 South Parkway
Chicago 15, Illinois

Dear Brother Huger:

This is to acknowledge receipt of your very kind letter of May 9, inviting me to
address the 50th Anniversary Banquet of Alpha Phi Alpha Fraternity on Saturday,
August 11, 1956 and informing me that I have been chosen to receive the Alpha
Phi Alpha Award of Honor. I assure you that I am deeply grateful to the fraternity
for choosing me for this great honor. I will accept it with humility and deep
gratitude.

I am arranging to be present at the banquet on August 11, at 8:00 P.M. to deliver
the address and to receive the award.

---

1. See pp. 339–346 in this volume. James E. Huger (1915–) attended Bethune-Cookman College
and the University of Michigan and held several administrative positions at the latter institution before
becoming general secretary of Alpha Phi Alpha.

Again, let me express my sincere appreciation to you and the members of the fraternity. I will be looking forward with great anticipation to receiving this award. Please feel free to contact me concerning further details.

Fraternally yours,
M. L. King, Jr.,
President

MLK:b

TLc. MLKP-MBU: Box 14.

To Hobson R. Reynolds

23 May 1956
[*Montgomery, Ala.*]

On 18 April Reynolds had informed King that he would receive the Lovejoy Award, given annually by the Improved Benevolent Protective Order of Elks of the World to an American citizen "who has made a great contribution towards the advancement of minority groups in America." [1] *Previous recipients included Marian Anderson, Mary McLeod Bethune, Ralph Bunche, and Thurgood Marshall. King attended the award ceremony on 27 August in Los Angeles. In May 1944 he had participated in an Elks oratorical contest in Dublin, Georgia, delivering a speech entitled "The Negro and the Constitution."* [2]

Judge Hobson R. Reynolds
Grand Director
Elks Department of Civil Liberties
I.B.P.O.E.W.
1522 North 16th Street
Philadelphia 21, Pa.

Dear Judge Reynolds:

This is just a note to acknowledge receipt of your letter of May 18, and to state how happy I was to hear from you. It was a real pleasure having you in our city

---

1. Hobson R. Reynolds (1898–1991), born in Winton, North Carolina, opened Reynolds Funeral Home after graduating from Echels College of Mortuary Science. In 1934 he was elected to the Pennsylvania General Assembly. During his two terms he drafted the Reynolds Civil Rights Bill, the first such legislation in Pennsylvania, and served as a family court judge in Philadelphia. President Roosevelt chose Reynolds to be an observer at the formation of the United Nations, and President Eisenhower appointed him as assistant secretary of the Department of Housing and Urban Development. Reynolds joined Elks in the early 1930s and became Grand Director of Civil Liberties in 1939. He was elected Grand Exalted Ruler in 1960, in which capacity he served until 1982.

2. See *Papers* 1:109–111.

and in our home. You were a real inspiration to the whole community in our struggle.

I am looking forward with great anticipation to receiving the "Lovejoy Award." Let me again express my appreciation to you and the members of the committee for choosing me for this great honor. I will accept it with great humility and profound gratitude. Please feel free to contact me concerning further details.

Very sincerely yours,
M. L. King, Jr.,
President

MLK:b

TLc. MLKP-MBU: Box 16.

"Recommendations to MIA Executive Board"

24 May 1956
[*Montgomery, Ala.*]

Recognizing that the bus boycott might continue indefinitely, King makes recommendations for restructuring the MIA to "prepare ourselves for a long struggle." These include reducing the number of mass meetings from two to one each week, streamlining the MIA decision-making process and financial management, and creating newsletter and history committees. To increase economic and political power, King emphasizes the need for voter registration and an MIA-sponsored savings and loan association. On 31 May King presented these recommendations to the executive board, which accepted his suggestions.

1. In order to lessen the pressure that we have worked under for several months and prepare ourselves for a long struggle which might possibly last several more months, our mass meetings will be reduced to once a week beginning the first week in June. This meeting will be held each Monday at 7:00 P.M., and the program committee shall be urged to limit the program to one hour and a half. If necessary situations arise special mass meetings will be called.

2. In order to valuably utilize the present relaxed phase of the bus situation and capitalize on the prevailing enthusiasm and amazing togetherness of the people, a strong emphasis shall be placed on increasing our political power through voting and increasing our economic power through the establishment of a bank. The committee on registration and voting shall seek to implement its program immediately. This committee shall meet weekly to discuss methods, findings and results. The Montgomery Improvement Association shall provide every avenue necessary to make the work of this committee successful. The Banking Committee shall meet immediately and make application for a charter through the Federal Home Loan Bank in Greensboro, North Carolina. If the

charter is denied at this level a committee shall be immediately sent to Washing-ton to appeal for a charter through the head office of all savings and loan banks.[1] The program committee shall be requested to allot more time in the mass meet-ings to the voting and banking committees for purposes of getting the idea over to the people.

3. In order to give our numerous friends over the nation and the various news-papers an accurate account of developments in the bus situation, a bi-monthly newsletter shall be released. The letter shall be edited by Mrs. Jo Ann Robinson, assisted by persons of her choice. Before the letter is released it shall be read and approved by the president, the vice-presidents, and the secretary of the Mont-gomery Improvement Association. Since the job of editor entails such a tre-mendous responsibility plus certain technical skills, a reasonable salary, recom-mended by the finance committee and approved by the Executive Board, shall be offered. It is hoped that this newsletter will very soon be expanded into a newspaper with an official staff, which will become the official organ of the Mont-gomery Improvement Association.[2]

4. In order that there may be a reliable and orderly record of the bus protest plus an accurate record of the origin, growth and future development of the Montgomery Improvement Association, a History Committee shall be organized consisting of the following persons: Dr. L. D. Reddick, Chairman; Mr. N. W. Wal-ton, Mr. J. E. Pierce, and Mrs. Jo Ann Robinson.[3]

5. That an executive committee be established consisting of all officers of the association and all committee heads. The function of this committee shall be to make decisions on minor matters of policy when it is not possible to call the whole executive board. Also this committee shall from time to time make rec-ommendations to the executive board concerning vital matters of policy.

6. In order to maintain good public relations and keep the executive board

---

1. Late in 1956 the MIA abandoned the idea of a charter after learning of the requirement for $400,000 in deposits. MIA leaders decided instead to establish a credit union, but in 1959 the federal government denied the group a charter for such an entity because they lacked a defined membership.

2. The *MIA Newsletter* first appeared in June 1956. It was initially published biweekly, then monthly, and became a quarterly in 1957. It included reports of meetings, educational workshops, fund-raising appeals, and "recent happenings" in the Montgomery struggle and was sent to supporters throughout the country.

3. Lawrence Dunbar Reddick (1910–1995), born in Jacksonville, Florida, received his B.A. (1932) from Fisk University and his Ph.D. (1939) in history from the University of Chicago. Reddick taught at New York City College, the New School for Social Research, and Atlanta University before joining the faculty of Alabama State College in 1956. In 1960 Reddick was fired for his support of student civil rights activists. He helped King draft and edit *Stride Toward Freedom* and accompanied the Kings on their trip to India in 1959. His publications include an article on the boycott in the Spring 1956 issue of *Dissent* and *Crusader Without Violence* (1959), the first biography of King.

Norman W. Walton (1921–) received B.A. (1947) and M.A. (1949) degrees from Tennessee A&I Uni-versity. At the time of the boycott Walton was a professor in the history and political science depart-ment at Alabama State College, which he eventually chaired. Walton wrote a five-part series for the *Negro History Bulletin* in 1956 and 1957 chronicling "The Walking City, a History of the Montgomery Boycott." In 1958 Walton produced *A Short History of Dexter Avenue Baptist Church, in the Eightieth Anni-versary of the Dexter Avenue Baptist Church* (Montgomery: Dexter Avenue Baptist Church, 1958).

well informed on the financial standing of the organization, a financial report of all receipts and disbursements shall be presented bi-monthly by the finance com- mittee to the Executive Board.

TD. HG-GAMK.

To Lillian Eugenia Smith

24 May 1956
Montgomery, Ala.

King belatedly responds to Smith's letters of 10 March and 3 April, thanking the novelist and activist for her encouragement and financial support. Acknowledging her three-year battle with cancer, King accepts her $50 contribution "with more humility and gratitude than any other contribution that I can recall."

Miss Lillian Smith
P. O. Box 352
Neptune Beach, Florida

Dear Miss Smith:

I have written you a thousand times in my mind, but I am just getting to the point of putting it on paper. Absence from the city on several occasions and the accumulation of a flood of mail account for the slowness of my reply.

Both of your letters came as a great consolation to me. For many years I have had the opportunity of knowing you through your books, and now I am happy to know you in a more directly personal sense. I only hope that it will be possible to meet you in person in the near future. We are still in the midst of our non-violence protest against injustice here in Montgomery. It has been gratifying to know how the idea of non-violence has gradually seeped into the hearts and souls of the people. There has been an amazing amount of discipline and wise restraint on the part of our people. I feel that the whole struggle here has given the Negro a new sense of dignity and destiny.

This whole struggle has given me a new awareness of the transforming power of love. I am convinced now more than ever before that we as a race must never succumb to the temptation of becoming bitter or of retaliating with hate. So in our struggle I advocate passive resistance as the instrument and love as the regulating ideal. From this you can see why your very sincere words on the power of love came as such an encouragement to me.

I will long remember your coming to our aid in this struggle for justice. We always accept financial contributions with deep humility and profound gratitude, but knowing your condition the fifty dollars ($50.00) which you sent was accepted with more humility and gratitude than any other contribution that I can recall. You can never know what this meant to us. You will remain in our thoughts so long as the cords of memory shall lengthen.

You have my prayers and best wishes for a speedy recovery. The whole world owes so much to you.

May I close by saying that even though we stand here in Montgomery amid the midnight of injustice I am convinced that God lives. They that stand against Him stand in a tragic and an already declared minority. They that stand with Him stand in the glow of the world's bright tomorrows.

Sincerely yours,

[*signed*]

M. L. King, Jr.,
President

MLK:b

TLS. LSP-GU: Box 65.

From Myles Horton

24 May 1956
Monteagle, Tenn.

Horton was the founder and director of the Highlander Folk School, an important training center for labor and civil rights activists.[1] Rosa Parks had attended a Highlander workshop on school integration in August 1955, four months before her defiance of bus segregation ignited the Montgomery bus boycott.

Rev. M. L. King
Montgomery Improvement Association
Montgomery, Alabama

Dear Mr. King:

It was my privilege recently to speak with Mrs. Rosa Parks at the Church of the Master in New York. There was an offering of $103.63 to be devided between Highlander and the Montgomery Improvement Association. I am enclosing a check for $52.00.

While in New York, I had the opportunity to talk with many people about the wonderful job you folks are doing there. I can't remember when I've been so proud of any activity on the part of my fellow Southerners.

---

1. Myles Horton (1905–1990), born in Savannah, Tennessee, graduated from Cumberland Presbyterian College in 1928 and studied at Union Theological Seminary in New York before founding Highlander in 1932. When postwar anticommunist sentiment caused some unions to sever their ties with the school, Horton and his co-workers, including Septima Clark, focused their organizing and educational work on the southern freedom struggle. After a long fight, Tennessee officials closed the school in 1961. Transferring its citizenship education program to King and SCLC, the institution was reborn the same year in New Market, Tennessee, as the Highlander Research and Education Center.

No doubt Rosa will tell you about some of the greetings she was asked to convey. You will be interested in the enclosed statement from Mrs. Roosevelt's column following our visit in her apartment.[2]

I had hoped by now to have met you. I had dinner with John Thompson in Chicago the day after you spoke in the Chapel there.[3] We hope you will get to Highlander sometime.

Cordially yours,
[*signed*]
Myles Horton

THLS. MLKP-MBU: Box 14A.

---

2. Eleanor Roosevelt reported on meeting with Parks in her 14 May 1956 syndicated newspaper column. Describing Parks as "a very quiet, gentle person," Roosevelt thought it "difficult to imagine how she could ever take such a positive and independent stand." Parks's passive resistance, she wrote, may "save us from war and bloodshed and teach those of us who have to learn that there is a point beyond which human beings will not continue to bear injustice" (David Elmbridge, ed., *Eleanor Roosevelt's "My Day,"* vol. 3: *First Lady of the World* [New York: Phonos Books, 1991], p. 99).

3. After studying with Reinhold Niebuhr at Union Theological Seminary, John B. Thompson went to the newly founded Highlander Folk School in 1933 to teach a seminar on religion and social change. Thompson served as dean of Rockefeller Memorial Chapel at the University of Chicago (1948–1958), where King spoke on 13 April 1956. When King delivered a keynote address on 2 September 1957 at Highlander's twenty-fifth anniversary, Thompson directed a seminar on southern integration.

Martin Luther King, Sr., to Dexter Avenue
Baptist Church

29 May 1956
Atlanta, Ga.

King, Sr., writes to thank Dexter for a donation to Ebenezer's building fund. He also commends his son's 27 May sermon at Ebenezer for the dedication of the Religious Education Building.

Dexter Avenue Baptist Church
Dexter Avenue and Decatur St
Montgomery, Alabama

Dear Friends:

This is exclusively a letter of thanks:

Churches unlike other institutions, depend entirely on the cooperation and fine christian spirit of people like you. So we want to tell you right now how much we appreciate your donation of One hundred dollars, ($100.00) made to our Building Fund. Your generous support is greatly appreciated.

The Dedication Services held on last Sunday will be long remembered. Your Pastor, Dr. Martin L. King Jr., delieverd a great sermon. We only wish that Dexter, in its entirety could have been here.

So thank you again for your part in helping our Church to meet its responsibilities in the task ahead.

Cordially yours,
[*signed*]
M. L. King, Sr.

MLK/w

TLS. DABCC.

To E. T. Sandberg

31 May 1956
[*Montgomery, Ala.*]

Sandberg, a professor at Wartburg College, had asked King about Gandhi's influence in a 23 March letter.[1] *Sandberg suggested that since "your movement and its defense in the present situation seems to depend very largely upon proving that no mob violence was at the root of the so-called bus boycott, I believe that a published statement that the idea of passive resistance was central would do your cause great good."*

Dr. E. T. Sandberg
Wartburg College
Waverly, Iowa

Dear Mr. Sandberg:

First let me apologize for being so tardy in my response to your very kind letter of March 23. Absence from the city on several occasions plus the accumulation of a flood of mail account for the delay. Please know that this was not due to sheer negligence, but to the pressure in the involved situation.

Yes, the Ghandian influence has been at the center of our movement. Many of us have been impressed over the years with the method of passive resistance used so effectively in India by Ghandi. So in our struggle against the evils of segregation in the South we feel that this weapon of passive resistance might be just as effective. We are using passive resistance as the method and love as the regulating ideal.

---

1. Edwin T. Sandberg received his B.S. (1943) from the University of Minnesota, M.A. (1945) from the School of Education at University of Minnesota, and Ph.D. (1951) from the University of Indiana. After teaching at Buena Vista College in Storm Lake, Iowa, he became an English professor at Wartburg College in 1953.

We certainly appreciate your interest in our movement. Your suggestions are certainly helpful. Please feel free to write us any time.

With every good wish, I am

Sincerely yours,
M. L. King, Jr.,
President

MLK:b

TLc. MLKP-MBU: Box 65A.

"Walk for Freedom"

May 1956
New York, N.Y.

King's statement for Fellowship, *the journal of the Fellowship of Reconciliation, is based on a half-hour interview recorded by Glenn Smiley on 28 February. In the article King recounts the bombing of his home on 30 January and his speech to the throng outside. Fearing that "violence was a possibility," he urged the crowd to "manifest love" and to "carry on the struggle with the same dignity and with the same discipline that we had started out with." A photograph of King speaking to the crowd that night graced the cover of the magazine.*

The present protest here in Montgomery on the part of the Negro citizens, grows out of many experiences—experiences that have often been humiliating and have led to deep resentment. The Negro citizens of Montgomery compose about 75% of the bus riders. In riding buses, they have confronted conditions which have made for a great deal of embarrassment, such as having to stand over empty seats, having to pay fares at the front door and going out to the back to get on, and then the very humiliating experience of being arrested for refusing to get up and give a seat to a person of another race.

These conditions and those experiences have now reached the point that the Negro citizens are tired, and this tiredness was expressed on December 5, when more than 99 percent of the Negro bus riders decided not to ride the buses, in a protest against these unjust conditions. This protest has lasted now for many, many weeks and it is still in process.[1]

---

1. The editors omitted King's discussion of the city's response to their demands: "It is still continuing because we have failed to get any consideration from the city officials on our proposals. They were very moderate, they certainly fitted within the framework of the present law, and we insisted, and we still insist, that the city commission could do these things without a lot of trouble, without changing the foundation of the community. We felt however, that if we could be granted these proposals, this would at least be a temporary alleviation of the problem, knowing that the ultimate solution would be in the total eradication of segregation itself. However, we have not received any consideration on these proposals, and we are still involved in the protest" (King, interview by Smiley, 28 February 1956).

From the beginning, we have insisted on nonviolence. This is a protest—a *nonviolent* protest against injustice. We are depending on moral and spiritual forces. To put it another way, this is a movement of passive resistance, and the great instrument is the instrument of love. We feel that this is our chief weapon, and that no matter how long we are involved in the protest, no matter how tragic the experiences are, no matter what sacrifices we have to make, we will not let anybody drag us so low as to hate them.

Love *must* be at the forefront of our movement if it is to be a successful movement. And when we speak of love, we speak of understanding, good will toward *all* men. We speak of a creative, a redemptive sort of love, so that as we look at the problem, we see that the real tension is not between the Negro citizens and the white citizens of Montgomery, but it is a conflict between justice and injustice, between the forces of light and the forces of darkness, and if there is a victory— and there *will* be a victory—the victory will not be merely for the Negro citizens and a defeat for the white citizens, but it will be a victory for justice and a defeat of injustice. It will be a victory for goodness in its long struggle with the forces of evil.

Violence Is Immoral

This is a spiritual movement, and we intend to keep these things in the forefront. We know that violence will defeat our purpose. We know that in our struggle in America and in our specific struggle here in Montgomery, violence will not only be impractical but immoral. We are outnumbered; we do not have access to the instruments of violence. Even more than that, not only is violence impractical, but it is *immoral*; for it is my firm conviction that to seek to retaliate with violence does nothing but intensify the existence of evil and hate in the universe.

Along the way of life, someone must have *sense* enough and morality enough to cut off the chain of hate and evil. The greatest way to do that is through love. I believe firmly that love is a transforming power that can lift a whole community to new horizons of fair play, good will and justice.

Love vs. Bombs

Love is our great instrument and our great weapon, and that alone. On January 30 my home was bombed.[2] My wife and baby were there; I was attending a meeting. I first heard of the bombing at the meeting, when someone came to me and mentioned it, and I tried to accept it in a very calm manner. I first inquired about

---

2. Smiley prompted King's discussion of the bombing: "I understand that on January 30th, your home was bombed. Could you tell us something about this instance, and how it was met by nonviolence?" (King, interview by Smiley).

my wife and daughter; then after I found out that they were all right, I stopped in the midst of the meeting and spoke to the group, and urged them not to be panicky and not to do anything about it because that was not the way.

I immediately came home and, on entering the front of the house, I noticed there were some 500–1000 persons. I came in the house and looked it over and went back to see my wife and to see if the baby was all right, but as I stood in the back of the house, hundreds and hundreds of people were still gathering, and I saw there that violence was a possibility.

It was at that time that I went to the porch [see cover photo] and tried to say to the people that we could not allow ourselves to be panicky. We could not allow ourselves to retaliate with any type of violence, but that we were still to confront the problem with *love*.

One statement that I made—and I believe it very firmly—was: "He who lives by the sword will perish by the sword." [3] I urged the people to continue to manifest love, and to continue to carry on the struggle with the same dignity and with the same discipline that we had started out with. I think at that time the people did decide to go home, things did get quiet, and it ended up with a great deal of calmness and a great deal of discipline, which I think our community should be proud of and which I was very proud to see because our people were determined not to retaliate with violence.

"Stand Up to the Finish"

Some twenty-six of the ministers and almost one hundred of the citizens of the city were indicted in this boycott. But we realized in the beginning that we would confront experiences that make for great sacrifices, experiences that are not altogether pleasant. We decided among ourselves that we would stand up to the finish, and that is what we are determined to do. In the midst of the indictments, we still hold to this nonviolent attitude, and this primacy of love.

Pray For Justice

Even though convicted, we will not retaliate with hate, but will still stand with love in our hearts, and stand resisting injustice, with the same determination with which we started out. We need a great deal of encouragement in this movement. Of course one thing that we are depending on, from not only other communities but from our own community, is prayer. We ask people everywhere to pray that God will guide us, pray that justice will be done and that righteousness will stand. And I think through these prayers we will be strengthened; it will make us feel

---

3. Matthew 26:52.

the unity of the nation and the presence of Almighty God. For as we said all along, this is a spiritual movement.[4]

PD. *Fellowship* 22 (May 1956): 5–7.

---

4. Miller promised King that the article would end with an appeal for funds, but it was omitted in the final copy. King concluded his interview with Smiley with a discussion of the financial situation of the MIA: "Along with [prayers from other communities] there is always a pressing need for funds. This is a very expensive movement, our local operations like the car pool, running of an office, are now running into about $3000.00–$3500.00 a week, and of course we have court cases before us, and we are involved in a great deal of litigation which will be very expensive. We can see now that that will cost with the present indictments and the other suit in the federal court, both will cost some $16,000.00–$18,000.00. So that you can see that our expenses are high and that we need financial assistance at every point. So that through your prayers and your financial assistance, we will be greatly benefited" (King, interview by Smiley). See also Miller to King, 10 April 1956.

"The 'New Negro' of the South: Behind the Montgomery Story"

June 1956
New York, N.Y.

This article, printed in the Socialist Party–sponsored journal, the Socialist Call, *was drawn from an address King delivered on 17 May at the annual dinner of the NAACP Legal Defense and Education Fund, commemorating the second anniversary of the Supreme Court's school desegregation decision. Expounding on three basic attitudes regarding progress in race relations, King dismisses both "extreme optimism" and "extreme pessimism," arguing instead for a "realistic" approach that acknowledges substantial progress but recognizes that "we have a long long way to go." He then discusses the emergence of the "new Negro" in the South, "with a new sense of dignity and destiny," particularly in Montgomery, and urges an interrelated strategy of education, legal reform, and nonviolent resistance to move African Americans toward "the promised land." Significant variations between the article and a typed draft of the speech, containing marginal handwritten comments by King, are noted.[1]*

There are three basic attitudes that one can take toward the question of progress in the area of race relations. The first is the attitude of extreme optimism. The optimist would contend that we have come a long way in race relations. He would point proudly to the marvelous strides that have been made in the area of civil rights over the last few decades. From this he would conclude that the problem is just about solved, and that we can sit comfortably by the wayside and wait for the coming of the inevitable.

---

1. See King, "A Realistic Look at Race Relations," 17 May 1956.

The second attitude that one can take toward the question of progress in the area of race relations is that of extreme pessimism. The pessimist would argue that we have made only minor strides in the area of race relations. He would contend that the present tension which we witness in certain sections of the nation is fit testimony to the fact that we have created more problems than we have solved.

The Taint of Sin

He would turn to the realm of orthodox theology and seek to show that hovering over every man is the tragic taint of original sin, and that at bottom nature cannot be changed.[2] He would turn to the realm of psychology and seek to show the determinative effects of habit structures, and the gripping effect of certain attitudes that are instilled in the child at an early age. Once these attitudes and habits are adapted, he contends, they are permanent and inflexible. So the pessimist would conclude that we can do nothing toward progress in race relations. The extreme pessimist and the extreme optimist have at least one thing in common: they both agree that we must sit down and do nothing in the area of race relations. The optimist says do nothing because integration is inevitable. The pessimist says do nothing because integration is impossible.

The third attitude that one can take toward the question of progress in race relations is the realistic attitude. Like the synthesis of Hegelian philosophy, the realistic attitude seeks to reconcile the truths of two opposites and avoid the extremes of both. So the realist in race relations would agree with the optimist in saying, we have come a long way, but he would balance that by agreeing with the pessimist that we have a long long way to go. It is this realistic position that I would like to set forth: We have come a long long way, and we have a long long way to go.

Let us notice first that we have come a long long way.[3] It was in the year of 1619 that the Negro slaves first landed on the shores of this nation. They were brought here from the soils of Africa, and unlike the Pilgrim fathers who landed at Plymouth a year later, they were brought against their wills. For more than two hundred years Africa was raped and plundered, her native kingdoms disorganized, her people and rulers demoralized, and the whole continent inflicted with pains and burdens unparalleled by any other race in the history of the civilized world.

---

2. In "Realistic Look" King inserted another sentence: "He would argue that we are retrogressing instead of progressing."

3. The following account of African-American history became a standard aspect of King's oratory during this period. See, for example, "The Montgomery Story," 27 June 1956; "Non-Aggression Procedures to Interracial Harmony," 23 July 1956; "The Birth of a New Age," 11 August 1956; and "Facing the Challenge of a New Age," 3 December 1956, pp. 300–301, 322–324, 341–342, and 454–456 in this volume, respectively.

Throughout slavery the Negro was considered a thing to be used, not a person to be respected. He was merely a depersonalized cog in the vast plantation machine. The famous Dred Scott decision of 1857 clearly expressed the status of the Negro during slavery. In this decision the United States Supreme Court affirmed, in substance, that the Negro is not a citizen of the United States; he is merely property subject to the dictates of his owner.

With the growth of slavery it became necessary to give some defense for it. It seems to be a fact of life that human nature cannot continue to do wrong without eventually reaching out for some rationalization which will help to clothe an obvious wrong in the beautiful garments of righteousness. This is exactly what the slave owners did. They fell victim to the danger that forever confronts religion and a too literalistic interpretation of the Bible. There is always the danger that religion and the Bible not properly interpreted can be used as forces to crystallize the status-quo. This is exactly what happened. It was argued from pulpits that Negroes were inferior by nature. There were even pseudo-scientists who sought to prove that in brain size and lung capacity Negroes were inferior to whites.[4]

In time many Negroes lost faith in themselves and came to believe that perhaps they were inferior. The tragedy of physical slavery was that it gradually led to the paralysis of mental slavery; the Negro's mind and soul became enslaved. So long as the Negro was willing to accept this "place" assigned to him, racial peace was maintained. But it was an uneasy peace in which the Negro was forced patiently to accept injustice, insult and exploitation. Truly it was an obnoxious negative peace, for true peace is not merely the absence of some negative force—confusion, tension, war—but the presence of some positive force—justice, good will, brotherhood. For years the Negro accepted this negative peace.

The Negro Masses Revaluated

Then something happened to the Negro. The Negro masses began to re-evaluate themselves. They came to feel that they were somebody. Their religion revealed to them that God loves all of his children, and that the important thing about a man "is not his specificity but his fundamentum," not the texture of his hair or the color of his skin, but the texture and quality of his soul. So he can now cry out with the eloquent poet:

> Fleecy locks and black complexion
> cannot forfeit nature's claim
> Skin may differ, but affection
> Dwells in black and white the same.
> And were I so tall as to reach the pole
> Or to grasp the ocean at a span,

---

4. In "Realistic Look" King marked this paragraph for deletion.

With this new self-respect and new sense of dignity on the part of the Negro, the South's negative peace was rapidly undermined. The tension which we are witnessing in race relations in the South today is to be explained in part by the revolutionary change in the Negro's evaluation of himself and his determination to struggle and sacrifice until the walls of injustice crumble.

The Meaning of Montgomery

This is at bottom the meaning of what is happening in Montgomery. You cannot understand the bus protest in Montgomery without understanding that there is a new Negro in the South, with a new sense of dignity, and destiny. For years the Negroes of Montgomery have suffered abuses, indignities and injustices on the buses. The story of these numerous injustices are too well known to mention. But there comes a time when people get tired of being trampled over by the iron feet of oppression. There comes a time when people get tired of being plunged across the abyss of exploitation where they experience the bleakness of nagging despair. There comes a time when people get tired of being pushed out of the glittering sunlight of life's July and left standing in the piercing chill of an Alpine November.

The story of Montgomery is the story of 50,000 Negroes who are tired of injustices and oppression, and who are willing to substitute tired feet for tired souls, and walk and walk until the walls of injustice are crushed by the battering rams of historical necessity. This is the new Negro. We have come a long way since 1619.

Not only has the Negro come a long way in the recognition of his own intrinsic worth, but he has come a long long way in achieving civil rights. For many years we were forced to live with segregation. In 1896, through the famous Plessy v. Ferguson case, the Supreme Court of this nation established the doctrine of separate-but-equal as the law of the land. Segregation had both legal and moral sanction. But then came May 17, 1951.[6] It was on this date that the Supreme Court gave a death blow to the old Plessy doctrine, insisting that separate facilities are inherently unequal and that to segregate a child because of his race is to deny him the equal protection of the law. If I may speak figuratively, we now see in our generation Old Man Segregation on his death bed. There will be some who will mourn his death, but most of us will be proud to see him pass on. He has been a

---

5. These lines are from two British eighteenth-century poems. The first four lines of this passage are quoted from "The Negro's Complaint" (1788) by William Cowper, and the remaining lines are quoted from *Horae Lyricae*, "False Greatness" (1706), by Isaac Watts. Although King often used this passage in his oratory, he was unaware who its authors were. When asked on one occasion, he concluded after investigation that the author was "unknown" (King to M. B. Powell, 1 August 1956).

6. In "Realistic Look" King correctly dates the Supreme Court decision *Brown v. Board of Education* as 17 May 1954.

problem and burden to the whole community. Yes, we have come a long long way
since 1896.

The Long Road to Travel

But we cannot stop here. To stop here would mean to become victims of an
optimism which would blind our eyes to the true realities of the situation. To stop
here would mean to become victims of an illusion wrapped in superficiality. We
must go on to affirm that we have a long long way to go.

Let's not fool ourselves. We are far from the promised land, both North and
South. In the South we still confront segregation in its glaring and conspicuous
forms. In the North we confront it in its hidden and subtle forms. Segregation is
still a fact. It is true that segregation is on its death bed. But history has proven
that social systems have a great last-minute breathing power. And the guardians
of the status-quo are always on hand with their oxygen tents to preserve the dying
order. But if democracy is to live, segregation must die. The underlying philosophy of democracy is diametrically opposed to the underlying philosophy of segregation, and all the dialectics of the logicians cannot make them lie down together. Segregation is a cancer in the body politic which must be removed before
our democratic health can be realized.

Toward Eliminating Segregation

 So we must work with grim and bold determination to eliminate segregation
from every area of American life. We must continue to struggle through legislation. There are those who contend that integration can come only through education, if for no other reason than that morals cannot be legislated. I choose,
however, to be dialectical at this point. It isn't either legislation or education;
it's both legislation and education. I quite agree that it is impossible to change
a man's internal feeling merely through law. This was never the intention of
the law.

The law does not seek to change one's internal feelings, it seeks to control the
external effects of those internal feelings. For instance, the law cannot make a
man love me — religion and education must do that . . . but it can keep him from
lynching me. The law cannot make an employer have compassion for me, but it
can keep him from refusing to hire me because of the color of my skin. Religion
and education must change one's internal feelings, but it is scarcely a moral act
to encourage others to patiently accept injustice until a man's heart gets right. All
that we seek through legislation is to control the external effects of one's internal
feelings.

Along with this emphasis on legislation, we must have the moral courage to
stand up and protest against injustice wherever we find it. Wherever we find segregation we must have the fortitude to passively resist it.

We must not think in terms of retaliatory violence. To attempt to use the
method of violence in our struggle would be both impractical and immoral. Violence creates many more problems than it solves. There is a voice crying through

the vista of time saying: "He who lives by the sword shall perish by the sword." [7] History is replete with the bleached bones of nations who failed to follow this truth. So we must not seek to fight our battles for freedom with weapons or arms. The method must be that of nonviolent resistance, using love as the regulating ideal. The Negro in his struggle for justice must never succumb to the temptation of becoming bitter.

The Technique of Resistance

We have tried this method in Montgomery, and it has worked amazingly well. It has given the Negro in Montgomery a new sense of dignity, and a new determination to tell the truth. Through this persistent protest the Negro is saying to his oppressors, "I don't like the way I am being treated." The truth of the matter is he never did like it, but he was afraid to say it. Now through passive resistance he says it in vociferous terms.

This method is not at all new. A little brown man in India tried it. For years his people had been trampled over by the iron feet of British rule. He watched the British Empire. He noticed her vast and intricate military machinery. He noticed the boundless outreach of her empire. Yet in the midst of this he decided to use another method. He decided to confront physical force with soul force. Through this method of passive resistance Mahatma Gandhi was able to free his people from the political domination, the economic exploitation and the humiliation inflicted upon them by Britain.

We've come a long long way, but we have a long long way to go. I am mindful that there are those who are urging us to adopt a policy of moderation, still others are preaching the "slow up" gospel. They are telling us we are going too fast, which causes us to wonder, how fast is too fast? But in the midst of all of this both Negro and white persons of goodwill realize that we can't afford to slow up. We have a moral obligation to press on.

Our self respect is at stake: but even more, the prestige of our nation is at stake. The rhythmic beat of the deep rumblings of discontent from Africa and Asia are at bottom expressions of their determination not to follow any power that denies basic human rights to a segment of its citizens. So in order to save the prestige of our nation and prevent the uncommitted peoples of the world from falling into the hands of a communistic idealogy we must press on. We have a long long way to go.

The Cause of the 'Maladjusted'

There are certain technical words in the vocabulary of every academic discipline which tend to become stereotypes and clichés. Psychologists have a word which is probably used more frequently than any other word in modern psychol-

---

7. Cf. Matthew 26:52 and Revelations 13:10.

ogy. It is the word "maladjusted." This word is the ringing cry of the new child psychology. Well, there are some things in our social system to which I am proud to be maladjusted and to which I suggest that we ought to be maladjusted.

I never intend to adjust myself to the viciousness of lynch-mobs. I never intend to become adjusted to the evils of segregation and discrimination. I never intend to adjust myself to the tragic inequalities of an economic system which takes necessities from the masses to give luxuries to the classes. I never intend to become adjusted to the madness of militarism and the self-defeating method of physical violence.

History still has a choice place for those who have the moral courage to be maladjusted. The salvation of the world lies in the hands of the maladjusted. The challenge to you is to be maladjusted; as maladjusted as the prophet Amos, who, in the midst of the injustices of his day, could cry out in words that echo across the centuries, "Let judgement run down like waters and righteousness like a mighty stream";[8] as maladjusted as Lincoln, who, about a century ago, had the vision to see that this nation could not survive half free and half slave. As maladjusted as Jefferson, who, in the midst of an age amazingly adjusted to slavery, was maladjusted enough to cry out in words lifted to cosmic proportions, "All men are created equal and are endowed by their creator with certain inalienable Rights, that among these are Life, Liberty and the pursuit of Happiness."

The world is in desperate need of such maladjusted persons. It is only through such maladjustment that we will emerge from the bleak and desolate midnight of "man's inhumanity to man" to the bright and glittering daybreak of freedom and justice.

PD. *Socialist Call* 24 (June 1956): 16–19; copy in MLKJrP-GAMK: Box 107.

---

8. Amos 5:24.

To Arthur R. James

1 June 1956
[*Montgomery, Ala.*]

King belatedly answers a 29 March letter from James, pastor of Central Baptist Church and president of the United Baptist Convention of Delaware.[1] James had written on

---

1. Arthur R. James (1887–1972), born in Balcarres, Jamaica, did his undergraduate work at McMaster University in Ontario and received his master's degree from Crozer Theological Seminary. In 1931 James became pastor of the Shiloh Baptist Church in Wilmington, Delaware, and also headed the Wilmington branch of the NAACP. He helped found Central Baptist Church in 1943, where he served until 1962. James also presided over the United Baptist Convention of Delaware and served as a trustee of the Delaware Baptist Convention. In 1950 James became the first black city magistrate in Delaware's history.

behalf of the Interdenominational Ministerial Union of Wilmington, Delaware, and Vicinity, which comprised all the black churches in that area, to inquire how they could best aid the MIA. He asked whether the state of Alabama might prevent the MIA from using donations by outside groups and whether boycotters in Montgomery had suffered from economic reprisals and needed special assistance.

The Rev. Arthur R. James, Pastor
Central Baptist Church
1215 Tatnall Street
Wilmington, Delaware

Dear Rev. James:

After going through the stack of mail, I discovered a letter that you wrote to me on March 29, 1956. Please let me apologize for just answering this letter. We have had to move our office four times within the last three months, and I am sure that your letter was misplaced during this period of moving. Please know that my failing to answer your letter immediately was not due to sheer negligence but to the inevitable pressure of an involved situation. I was very happy to know of the interest taken by the Interdenominational Ministerial Union of Wilmington and vicinity in our struggle for justice. I can assure you that such moral support and christian generosity give us renewed vigor and courage to carry on.

Funds are still coming in for our cause and so far we have not had any difficulty in using these funds. The state has not tried to block them to this point. Most of our money is deposited in out-of-state banks and it would be difficult to block that money anyway. So far the economic conditions of Montgomery are holding up very well. We do not have evidence of many reprisals on the part of white employers seeking to undo the economic structure of the Negro community. We have had only minor cases of Negroes losing jobs as a result of the boycott. Most of the funds that we use are for the operation of the transportation system and the office. This local operation runs approximately five thousand dollars ($5,000.00) a week. So you can see that this is a very expensive venture.

I hope that this will answer your questions in some way. We will be getting a newsletter out within the next few days, and I am sure that this will clear up additional questions that you might raise. I will be sure to place your name on the mailing list.

Again let me express my appreciation to you and the brethren for your interest and your sincere concern in the cause of justice.

With every good wish, I am

Yours very truly,
M. L. King, Jr.,
President

MLK:b

TLc. MLKP-MBU: Box 15.

1 June 1956
New York, N.Y.

On behalf of the Committee for Nonviolent Integration, a national support organization for the bus boycott and other southern desegregation efforts, Peck sends the MIA a shipment of matchbooks bearing the slogans "Justice Without Violence" and "Walk for Freedom" to be used for fund-raising.[1]

Martin Luther King, President
Montgomery Improvement Assn.
1903 Myles
Montgomery 8, Ala.

Dear Rev. King,

Within a week or two, you will receive from the Mercury Match Corp. of Zanesville, Ohio, a case of matchbooks bearing the slogans of the protest action and with the name and address of the Montgomery Improvement Association on the inside cover. You will recall that Bayard Rustin consulted with you regarding such matches.

This first case (including shipment) is donated by me through the Committee for Nonviolent Integration, with which I work closely. They come in cartons of 50 matchbooks and may well be sold by the carton, the proceeds going to the Montgomery Improvement Association. On the other hand, you might find it more effective to distribute them free of charge. That is up to you.

Anyway, I would appreciate knowing whether you find this an effective medium for publicizing the protest. This is not the first time I have designed matches to promote just causes and in many instances they have proved more effective than leaflets. If you find them successful, you might want to order more.

Sincerely,
[*signed*]
Jim Peck

---

1. James Peck (1914–1993), born in New York City, was active in the War Resisters League before World War II and was imprisoned for refusing to register for the draft. During his twenty-eight-month prison sentence he led a strike that led to the first desegregation of a federal penitentiary. Peck served as a member of the Congress of Racial Equality's national action committee and was editor of the *CORElator* for seventeen years. He participated in the group's 1947 Journey of Reconciliation and its 1961 Freedom Ride, during which he was badly beaten by a Birmingham mob.

In March King met with several members of the newly formed Committee for Nonviolent Integration (CNI) and agreed to its initial list of projects. A. J. Muste was secretary pro tem of the group; Donald Harrington and William Stuart Nelson served as co-chairs. For a list of proposed CNI projects and committee members, see Muste to Benjamin Mays; Committee for Nonviolent Integration, Nine Initial Projects; and Committee for Nonviolent Integration, Statement of Purpose; all 13 April 1956.

IMPORTANT PS—If you should have occasion to send any of these matches 1 June through the mails, be sure to, first, wrap them in aluminum foil (available at most 1956 dimestores and supermarkets). Failure to do so would be a violation of the postal laws and I'm sure they would be only too eager to harass you over this sort of thing.

TLS. MLKP-MBU: Box 63A.

To J. Raymond Henderson

1 June 1956
[Montgomery, Ala.]

Juanita and Ralph Abernathy accompanied the Kings on a June vacation and speaking trip to Los Angeles. Among other engagements, King was scheduled to speak at the annual preaching mission at Henderson's Second Baptist Church from 10 to 15 June and the Fifty-first National Baptist Sunday School and Baptist Training Union Congress. In this letter King responds to Henderson's 22 May letter (which King received 24 May) confirming the arrangements.

The Rev. J. Raymond Henderson, Minister
Second Baptist Church
Griffith Avenue at Twenty-Fourth Street
Los Angeles 11, California

Dear Rev. Henderson:

Thanks for your kind letter of May 24. Absence from the city delayed my reply.

After talking with Rev. and Mrs. Abernathy I find that they had been invited to stop with Rev. T. M. Chambers. Since this invitation had been extended they felt that it would be expedient to accept it. Therefore, Mrs. King and I will stop with you and the Abernathys will be with Rev. Chambers.

Unfortunately, I will not be able to accept the invitation to a dinner in my honor on June 21. I will have to leave Los Angeles that morning coming back to Montgomery for a few days. (Mrs. King will remain in Los Angeles through Sunday, June 24.) Then I would return to California on the twenty-sixth to join Mrs. King in San Francisco. If the dinner could be arranged earlier than June 21, I would be very happy to participate.

Thanks for the invitation to speak in the Baptist Minister's Union on Tuesday, June 19. I will be indeed honored to accept this invitation.[1]

---

1. King was unable to fulfill his engagements after 17 June because he had to return to Montgomery to deal with U. J. Fields's charges against the MIA. On 27 June King spoke at the forty-seventh annual NAACP convention in San Francisco.

We plan to leave Montgomery Wednesday morning for Los Angeles by auto-mobile. We should arrive in Los Angeles some time Saturday afternoon. We will immediately contact you on our arrival.

Sincerely yours,
M. L. King, Jr.,
President

MLK:b

P.S. Don't worry about our meals. Mrs. King and I will arrange to have all our meals out.

TLc. MLKP-MBU: Box 65.

To Ross Allen Weston

4 June 1956
Montgomery, Ala.

On 18 May the Unitarian Fellowship for Social Justice gave King its John Haynes Holmes–Arthur L. Weatherly Award for "outstanding leadership in the cause for social justice." King was unable to attend the award presentation in Boston. On 11 July King granted the group permission to reprint his letter acknowledging the award in Unitarian Action.[1]

The Rev. Ross Allen Weston, President
Unitarian Fellowship for Social Justice
4444 Arlington Boulevard
Arlington 4, Virginia

Dear Rev. Weston:

This is just a note to express my appreciation to you and the members of the Unitarian Fellowship for Social Justice for so graciously honoring me by present-ing your annual award. I assure you that I will be able at all times to live up to the noble and sublime principles stated therein. I can assure you that such recogni-tion gives me new determination to continue the struggle for freedom and jus-tice. Moreover, it awakens within my mind the fact that there are persons of good will in America who are deeply concerned about justice and freedom for all people, and who are willing to make the noble precepts of democracy living facts lifted out of the dusty files of unimplemented and forgotten court decisions.

Again, let me apologize for not being able to get to Boston in person. I deeply

---

1. See Ross Allen Weston to King, 25 April 1956; and King to Lois McColloch, 11 July 1956.

regret that the conflict arose. Please know that I am greatly in sympathy with the program of The Unitarian Fellowship.

With every good wish, I am

Sincerely yours,
[*signed*]
M. L. King, Jr.,
President

MLK:b

TLS. UUAR-MH-AH.

To George Lawrence

4 June 1956
[*Montgomery, Ala.*]

King thanks Lawrence and the Greater New York Committee for a National Day of Prayer and Thanksgiving for organizing the 17 May service at the Cathedral of St. John the Divine, at which King delivered the sermon.[1]

The Rev. George Lawrence, Minister of Education
Friendship Baptist Church
144 West 131st Street
New York 27, New York

Dear Brother Lawrence:

This is just a note to again express my appreciation to you and your very fine committee from the Protestant Council of New York, for making my stay in New York such a meaningful one. The program at St. John the Divine was one of the greatest experiences of my life. I will long remember it. Give my best regards to Tom Kilgore. I hope I will have the opportunity of seeing you in the near future.

With warm personal regards, I am

Sincerely yours,
M. L. King, Jr.,
President

MLK:b

TLc. MLKP-MBU: Box 17.

---

1. George Lawrence (1927–) was secretary of the committee that organized the program at St. John the Divine and executive chairman of In Friendship. He was minister of education for a short time at Friendship Baptist Church, where King's friend Thomas Kilgore served as pastor. Lawrence became pastor of Brooklyn's Antioch Baptist Church in 1959. Throughout the 1950s and 1960s he held various church leadership positions, including press secretary for the National Baptist Convention and director of communications for the Progressive National Baptist Convention.

To William J. Faulkner

4 June 1956
[*Montgomery, Ala.*]

King responds to Faulkner's letter of 9 March.

The Rev. William J. Faulkner, Minister
The Congregational Church of Park Manor
7000 South Park Avenue
Chicago 37, Illinois

Dear Rev. Faulkner:

This is just a note to say how happy I was to hear from you and to receive the very fine contribution from your church. I assure you that we will long remember your coming to our aid in this great struggle.

We are still involved in the non-violent protest against injustice here in Montgomery. I have been deeply moved by the discipline, wise restraint and dignity by which our people have carried out the protest. I feel that the whole situation has given the Negro a new sense of dignity and destiny.

I was very happy to know of your relationship with my grandfather. I am sure that his spirit still lives on through such a movement. It has been my pleasure to hear you speak on several occasions, and I have always admired the rich contributions that you have made through the christian ministry.

Cordially yours,
M. L. King, Jr.,
President

MLK:b

TLc. MLKP-MBU: Box 15.

To Myles Horton

4 June 1956
[*Montgomery, Ala.*]

Mr. Myles Horton
Highlander Folk School
Monteagle, Tennessee

Dear Mr. Horton:

This is just a note to acknowledge receipt of the very fine contribution of fifty-two dollars ($52.00) taken up at the Church of the Master in New York City. Such moral support and christian generosity are of inestimable value in the continuance of our struggle. Please know that we deeply appreciate this contribution.

I have heard much of the fine work being done at the Highlander Folk School.

I hope it will be possible for me to come there very soon. You have my prayers and best wishes for continued success in such a noble work.

4 June 1956

Cordially yours,
M. L. King, Jr.,
President

MLK:b

enc. Receipt # 455

TLc. MLKP-MBU: Box 14A.

From Helen M. Hiller

4 June 1956
Mattapoisett, Mass.

King responded to Hiller on 6 July.[1]

Rev. Martin Luthur King, Jr.
309 South Jackson St.,
Montgomery, Ala.

Dear Rev. King:

Please forgive me for what I am going to say. You may be the most humble person in the world, but you now hold a position of great responsibility. You are supported by true Christians every{where} You have suddenly (comparatively) become world famous. There must be a temptation to boast—to "put on airs". That would be to the advantage of the opposition and must not be.

The greatest are the humblest. They are the meek and lowly. There is power in simplicity. "The meek shall inherit the earth".[2] One must be neat and clean but not wear showy or expensive clothing. The furnishing of the home and table must sufficient for health and efficiency only. Of course there may be special occasions which are exceptions.

You show great strength in your leadership for non-violence and love. Probably the same is true for humility because you follow your Master. I have no excuse whatever for writing this, but wanted to be sure you drove a Dodge and not a Cadillac.

Very sincerely,
[*signed*] Helen M. Hiller

P.S. I'm glad Clarence Pickett visited you. He is one of our greatest Quakers.

ALS. MLKP-MBU: Box 60.

---

1. See p. 315 in this volume.
2. Matthew 5:5.

To Charles E. Batten

5 June 1956
[*Montgomery, Ala.*]

*King responds to a 10 March letter from his former dean at Crozer.[1] "These must be
terrifically trying as well as challenging days for you," Batten had written, "and
I wanted you to know that one who was always interested in you and had great
confidence in you, still feels that you are 'one of my boys.'"*

The Rev. Charles E. Batten, Rector
Parish of the Epiphany
70 Church Street
Winchester, Mass.

Dear Dean Batten:

Although you are no longer Dean, I would feel strange not calling you "Dean."
It was a real pleasure receiving your letter several weeks ago. I have been intending to drop you a note for quite some time, but an extremely busy schedule plus
the accumulation of a flood of mail delayed my reply.

We are still involved in the non-violent protest against injustice here in Montgomery. I have been deeply moved by the dignity, discipline and wise restraint
that have characterized our people throughout the protest. We have avoided hate
and animosity on every hand. We are using passive resistance as our instrument
and love as the regulating ideal.

I hope everything goes well with you and your family. Please extend my best
regards to Mrs. Batten and the boys.

Cordially yours,
M. L. King, Jr.

MLK:b

TLc. MLKP-MBU: Box 64.

---

1. In 1954 Batten left Crozer to become minister of education at the Parish of the Epiphany in
Winchester, Massachusetts.

From Archie L. Weaver

13 June 1956
Chicago, Ill.

*Weaver, president of Chicago's Second Ward Improvement Association, expresses
concern about Rev. U. J. Fields's recently publicized accusations of malfeasance among
MIA board members. On 20 June King's secretary, Maude Ballou, responded in*

his absence, assuring Weaver that Fields "admitted [that his charges were totally unfounded] at the Mass Meeting the other night and confessed that he had no basis for any of it." To Weaver's query about inconsistent addresses on MIA letterhead, Ballou responded that their office had been moved four times during the past five months.[1]

Mr. Martin Luther King, Jr., President
The Montgomery Improvement Association,
530-C South Union Street,
Montgomery 8, Alabama.

Dear Dr. King:

Thanks for yours of May 2nd and official receipt No. 2865 dated May 3rd acknowledging a previous contribution of mine to a most worthy cause. I am impressed with your business methods. I am attaching my check for another contribution of Five Dollars.

Note enclosed clipping from our Chicago Daily Tribune in connection with The Rev. U. J. Fields. Can you not prevail upon Rev. Fields not to defeat the great purpose and not find fault now? Especially the broadcasting disharmony—playing into the hands of our enemies. You are doing a great job for all the Negroes and citizens of all our nation. "Keep moving" are your words to us in Rockfellow Memorial Chapel University of Chicago.

I have a tape recording of Rev. Abernathy's address in our coliseum here and your address two days later on the campus of the University of Chicago.[2] He spoke to "us" while you spoke to "them." Both are master pieces and I am playing them back all over Chicago upon request—I have many requests. Such is my pleasure.

In the spirit of love, may I offer a suggestion? You have one address on your letter head, another on the official receipt and you include a "C" in the return card on the envelope address. Why not CONSISTENTLY have ONE address and allay confusion and possible suspicion that might support Rev. Fields? I am a Life Member of our N.A.A.C.P. and the only surviving charter member of our Chicago Branch organized in 1910—forty six years ago. I am deeply interested in the success of your movement.

Lovingly and sincerely yours,
[*signed*]
Archie L. Weaver.

THLS. MLKP-MBU: Box 67.

1. Fields made his allegations at a mass meeting after the executive board replaced him as recording secretary. Members of his church then voted unanimously to oust him; Fields appeared before an MIA mass meeting a week later to retract the charges. Urging forgiveness, King introduced him to the crowd and said, "Let he who is without sin cast the first stone" (Job 8:7; Paul Thompson, "Negro Cleric Retracts Charges of Bus Boycott Fund Misuse," *Montgomery Advertiser,* 19 June 1956). See also Press Release, Rev. Fields's Retraction, 18 June 1956.

2. Ralph Abernathy spoke at an 11 April 1956 NAACP rally at the Chicago Coliseum. Two days later King gave a speech entitled "The Declaration of Independence and the Negro" at the Rockefeller Memorial Chapel at the University of Chicago. He ended that speech, as he did others, by urging those who "can't run, walk; if you can't walk, crawl, but keep moving forward!" (quoted in Theodore Silver, "Rev. King: Alabama Moses," *American Negro,* June 1956, p. 15).

15 June 1956
New York, N.Y.

*Lawrence thanks King for his sermon at the Cathedral of St. John the Divine, citing the
enthusiastic response of the congregation to King's "monumental sermon."*

The Reverend Martin Luther King, Jr., D.D.,
President, The Montgomery Improvement Association
530-C South Union Street
Montgomery 8, Alabama

Dear Brother King,

I have been away from the city for a few days, attending the annual session
of the New England Baptist Missionary Convention at Philadelphia. My desk is
stacked high with unanswered correspondence, but I feel so ashamed that I
simply must drop you this note to "atone" in some way for not having officially
thanked you for the monumental sermon you delivered at the Cathedral of St.
John the Divine on May 17.

There are no words to express the most glorious sunrise. It would be folly for
me to attempt to say what is on my heart with reference to "The Death of Evil on
the Seashore." Dean Pike said it was the greatest sermon he has heard in his
entire life. An old soldier of 82 years sent me a note in the mail. He said: "I ain't
never heard nobody like that boy!" Who can add testimony to such expert observations? Officials at the Cathedral said they received more than 200 messages, all
favorable. I have in my files at least 75 letters from folk who were inspired and
moved. So you see, the service of divine worship at the Cathedral was one of the
greatest experiences of our lives, too!

I trust that by this time you have received the check for the Montgomery movement.[1] We could have raised more that night if the accent had been on commer-
cialism. However, the "big payoff" comes to us all in terms of hearts, minds, souls
and spirits which were touched, inspired and renewed May 17 as a direct result of
the God-given message you brought.

I can only say that you must keep us up-to-date on the movement and on what
you need to carry on. You can rest assured that we will do everything in our power
to help you and the great cause for which you are pouring out life's blood.

I am sure that you have seen the reports of the service in the newspapers. If
not, I plan to send you the clippings anyway, in addition to some pictures taken
that evening if I can locate the photographers.

Tom [*Kilgore*] is fine, and still battling! He received an honorary D.D. from

---

1. Someone in King's office wrote "yes" in the margin next to this sentence.

Shaw the other day (after turning it down three times), and then made another of his quiet and famous On-the-spot Investigations of the North Carolina and South Carolina (especially!) situations. He is off today for Los Angeles and the Congress. I will not be going.

I, too, enjoyed the brief but impressive fellowship we had personally during your trip here. Please count me as a close personal friend, and feel free to call on me at any hour to do anything I possibly can to aid you or your great cause. By all means, keep in touch with us constantly. If there are needs, we will try to find the answers.

Remember, above all, there are thousands praying constantly to Almighty God for you and what you are doing. I am proud to stand up and be counted among that number. I hope we can get together in the near future, but I have the feeling that we are as close as brothers in the great Fellowship, and I want you to feel that way too.

Let us hear from you soon. With warm personal regards, I am

Ever sincere,
FRIENDSHIP CHURCH
[*signed*] George
George Lawrence,
Minister of Education

GL:my

THLS. MLKP-MBU: Box 17.

To Jimmy and Ellen Hawley

19 June 1956
[*Montgomery, Ala.*]

On 14 June Peter K. Hawley had written King that his two children, aged twelve and nine, and a nephew were "so impressed with the courage, vitality and determination" of the Montgomery black community that at a family gathering they "put on a little show, and at the conclusion asked those who wished to make a contribution to aid in your tremendous and democratic struggle."

Jimmy and Ellen Hawley
310 E. 75th Street
New York 21, New York

Dear Jimmy and Ellen:

I am deeply grateful to both of you for the very fine contribution of three dollars and thirty-one cents ($3.31) sent me by your father.

It means so much to all of us here to know that there are little folks like you

297

who are genuinely interested in the struggle for justice. Such moral support and christian generosity from you, our friends, in this momentous struggle, are of inestimable value in the continuance of our humble efforts.

Again, may I express my deepest gratitude for your interest and support in our struggle for justice.

Cordially yours,
M. L. King, Jr.,
President

MLK:b

enc. Receipt # 4121

TLc. MLKP-MBU: Box 60.

To Annemarie Schader

20 June 1956
[*Montgomery, Ala.*]

In a 13 June letter to King, Schader decried the lack of concern about the Montgomery boycott among her acquaintances: "They don't feel, how very much more horrible and difficult your situation is, and that there is nothing worse in the whole world but what white people did to you. For me the distance of some thousand kilometres is no excuse— somehow we are all guilty." Enclosing a $500 donation, Schader wrote: "It is nothing but money; yet it is important for me that you get back from white people what you had to pay to white people."

Mrs. Annemarie Schader
Parkring 37
Zurich 2
Switzerland

Dear Mrs. Schader:

Words can never adequately express our appreciation to you for the personal donation of five hundred dollars ($500.00). This is one of the highest personal contributions we have received, and I assure you that it will go a long, long way in helping us in our struggle. It is even more significant because it comes from a person of another country. This reaffirms my conviction in the fact that all humanity is involved in a single process, and that whatever affects one nation directly affects every nation indirectly.

We feel that in our struggle here in Montgomery we have cosmic companionship because of this abiding religous faith we have been able to stand through turbulent periods of our history. We know that although we stand now in the midst of the midnight of injustice we are only a few steps from the daybreak of freedom and equality.

Again, let me express my appreciation to you. You will remain in our thoughts so long as the cords of memory shall lengthen.

Cordially yours,
M. L. King, Jr.,
President

MLK:b
enc. Receipt #4095
(Dictated by Rev. King but signed in his absence.)

TLc. MLKP-MBU: Box 89.

"The Montgomery Story,"
Address Delivered at the
Forty-seventh Annual NAACP Convention

[27 June 1956]
[San Francisco, Calif.]

King and A. Philip Randolph were the featured speakers at the forty-seventh annual NAACP convention, addressing a public session at the San Francisco Civic Auditorium that attracted more than a thousand delegates from thirty-five states. King discusses the historical background of the black freedom struggle and the emergence of "a brand new Negro in the South, with a new sense of dignity and destiny." Despite violence and intimidation, King declares, the "[new] Negro in the South has been freed from the paralysis of crippling fear." He concludes with an appeal for passive resistance to segregation and injustice. Significant variations between this audio transcript and typed or handwritten versions of King's prepared text are noted.[1]

Mr. Chairman, distinguished platform associates, officers and delegates to this great convention, ladies and gentlemen. I need not pause to say how happy I am to be here this evening, and to be a part of this auspicious occasion. It is indeed a privilege and a distinct honor to have the opportunity of sharing the speaking responsibility this evening with that great American, A. Philip Randolph. [*applause*] I am sure we all consider him one of the great men of our generation. It is also great to share the platform with Mrs. Rosa Parks. [*applause*] She too is a great symbol in our struggle. It was suggested to me that I talk this evening about the Montgomery story. I might say that the Montgomery story is only one story and I am sure that some of you, many of you, have already heard the Montgomery story by representatives from Montgomery who have been willing to go all over

---

1. The handwritten version is from King, "The Montgomery Story, Address at 47th Annual NAACP Convention," 27 June 1956. King's typed version appeared as "Alabama's Bus Boycott: What It's All About," *U.S. News and World Report,* 3 August 1956, pp. 82, 87–89.

the nation. Some of you have probably heard it from me. So that those who have already heard it will have the unfortunate burden to bear this evening of being bored with me for a few minutes time to tell the story [*words inaudible*]. It is the story, a dramatic story, of a handsome little city that for years has been known as the cradle of the Confederacy. It is the story of a little town grappling with a new and creative approach to the crisis in race relations. It is impossible, however, to tell the Montgomery story without understanding the larger story of the radical change in the Negro's evaluation of himself. A brief survey of the history of the Negro in America reveals this change in terms that are crystal clear.

It was in the year of 1619 that the Negro [*word inaudible*] slaves first landed on the shores of this nation. They were brought here from the soils of Africa, and unlike the Pilgrim fathers who landed at Plymouth a year later, they were brought here against their wills. For more than two hundred years Africa was raped and plundered, her native kingdoms disorganized, her people and rulers demoralized, and the whole continent inflicted with pains and burdens hardly paralleled by any race of people in the whole history of the civilized world.

Throughout slavery the Negro slave was treated in a very inhuman fashion. They were things to be used, not persons to be respected. They were merely depersonalized cogs in a vast plantation machine. The famous Dred Scott decision of 1857 well illustrates the status of the Negro during slavery. In this decision the Supreme Court of this nation affirmed that the Negro was not a citizen of the United States; he was merely property subject to the dictates of his owner. That was the attitude that prevailed throughout.

With the rise of slavery, it became necessary to justify it. It seems to be a fact of life that human nature cannot continue to do wrong without eventually reaching out for some rationalization with which an obvious evil is covered up in the garments of righteousness. The psychologist William James used to talk a great deal about the stream of consciousness. James says one of the uniquenesses of human nature is that man has the unique capacity of blocking the stream of consciousness temporarily and injecting anything in it that he wants to. That capacity of man temporarily makes him justify the rightness of the wrong.[2] This is what happened to the slave owners. They fell victim to the danger that forever confronts religion and a too literalistic interpretation of the Bible. There is always the danger that religion and the Bible not properly interpreted can be used as instruments to crystallize the status quo. This is exactly what happened. So from pulpits all over the nation it was argued that the Negro was inferior by nature because of Noah's curse upon the children of Ham. Paul's command became a watchword, "Servant, be obedient to your master."[3] Then there was one person who had probably read something of the logic of Aristotle and he could put his argument in a framework that was somewhat similar to an Aristotelian syllogism. He could say all men are made in the image of God. Then the [*word inaudible*] comes out: God, as we know, is not a Negro; then the conclusion: therefore, the Negro is not a man. [*applause*] That was the type of reasoning that prevailed.

---

2. These two sentences do not appear in the prepared text.

3. Ephesians 6:5.

In time the Negro lost faith in himself and then he came to fear that perhaps they were less than human. The tragedy of physical slavery was that it finally led to the paralysis of mental slavery. So long as the Negro accepted this place, this place assigned to him, a sort of peace, a racial peace was maintained. But it was an uneasy peace in which the Negro was forced patiently to accept injustice, insult and exploitation.

But then something happened to the Negro. Negro masses all over began to reevaluate themselves. The Negro came to feel that he was somebody. His religion revealed to him that God loves all of his children, and that every man, from a bass black to a treble white, is significant on God's keyboard. [*applause*] So he could now cry out with the eloquent poet:

> Fleecy locks and black complexion
> Cannot forfeit nature's claim
> Skin may differ, but affection
> Dwells in black and white the same. [*applause*]
> If I were so tall as to reach the pole
> Or to grasp the ocean at a span,
> I must be measured by *my* soul,
> The mind is the standard of the man. [*applause*] [4]

With this new self-respect, this new sense of dignity on the part of the Negro, the South's negative peace was gradually undermined. The tension which we witness in the southland today can be explained by the revolutionary change in the Negro's evaluation of his nature and destiny, by his determination to stand up and struggle until the walls of injustice have crumbled. [*applause*] The Negro [*figures it's?*] clear insanity, that feeling that he is inferior, everything would be alright down in Alabama, Georgia, and Mississippi, but the Negro rightly feels that he is somebody now.[5] [*applause*] [*words inaudible*]

That is at bottom the meaning of what is happening in Montgomery. You can never understand the Montgomery story without understanding that there is a brand new Negro in the South, with a new sense of dignity and destiny. [*applause*] Over the years the bus situation has been one of the sore spots of Montgomery. If a visitor had come to Montgomery prior to last December, he would have heard bus operators referring to Negro passengers as "niggers," "black apes," and "black cows." He would have frequently noticed Negro passengers getting on the front door and paying their fares, and then being forced to get off and go to the back doors to board the bus, and often after paying that fare he would have noticed that before the Negro passenger could get to the back door, the bus rode off with his fare in the box. But even more, that visitor would have noticed Negro passengers standing over empty seats. I am sure that visitor would have wondered what was happening, but soon he would discover that the reserved section, the

---

4. These lines are a composite of passages from William Cowper's "The Negro's Complaint" (1788) and Isaac Watts's "False Greatness" (1706). See note 5 to "The 'New Negro' of the South: Behind the Montgomery Story," June 1956, p. 283 in this volume.

5. The two preceding sentences do not appear in the prepared text.

unoccupied seats, were for "whites only." No matter if a white person never got on the bus, the bus was filled up with Negro passengers, these Negro passengers were prohibited from sitting in the first four seats—which hold about ten persons—because they were only for white passengers. But it even went beyond this. If the reserved section for whites was filled up with white persons, additional white persons boarded the bus, then Negro passengers sitting in the unreserved section were often asked to stand up and give their seats to white persons. If they refused to do this, they were arrested.

On December the first, 1955, Mrs. Rosa Parks refused to move when she was asked to get up and move back by the bus operator. [*applause*] And interestingly enough, Mrs. Parks was not seated in the reserved section for whites as the press has often mistakenly reported; she was sitting in the first seat in the unreserved section. The other interesting thing is that all of the seats were taken, and if Mrs. Parks had followed the command of the bus operator she would have stood up and given up her seat for a *male* white passenger, who had just boarded the bus, would take the seat. In a quiet, calm, dignified manner, so characteristic of the radiant personality of Mrs. Parks, she refused to move.[6] [*applause*]

The trial was set for Monday, December fifth, and almost out of nowhere, leaflets were circulating, saying: "This must be stopped. We must, we should stay off the buses on Monday in protest of this situation. We must stand together and let it be known that we don't like it." The word got around. [*applause*] The word got around the Montgomery community amazingly well that Sunday, December the fourth. All of the ministers went to their pulpits and endorsed it heartily, and so the word was out.

Then came Monday. [*applause*] Then came Monday, December the fifth. The buses were empty. [*applause*] The Negro passengers, who constituted about seventy-five percent of the bus riders, were now united. The bus protest on that day, and even now, has been more than ninety-nine and nine-tenths percent effective. [*applause*]

Feeling the need to give some guidance to the protest, the ministers came together[7]—forgetting about denominations, forgetting about Baptists and Methodists [*applause*] [*words inaudible*], realizing that we strode on in the great struggle—and we came together with civic leaders throughout the community on Monday afternoon, December fifth, and organized what is now known as the Montgomery Improvement Association. [*applause*] This association started out with about twenty-five or [*word inaudible*] persons on the executive board. Now it has a membership that goes way up in the thousands, almost as large as the Negro community.[8] [*applause*] And it has been this organization, under the leadership of some of the finest ministers and laymen of the Montgomery community, that has guided the protest throughout.

On Monday afternoon or Monday evening a mass meeting had been called by the ministers at the Holt Street Baptist Church. That afternoon by three o'clock

---

6. King omits the sentence "The result was her arrest," which is included in the prepared text.
7. In the prepared texts this phrase reads, "ministers of all Protestant faiths."
8. This sentence does not appear in the prepared text.

hundreds of people started assembling in the church. About seven o'clock it was reported that more than five thousand persons were jammed and packed in this church and were overflowing in the street. [*applause*] At this meeting these persons, this vast audience, went on record adopting this resolution: that the Negro passengers would refuse to ride the buses until more courtesy was extended by the bus operators; until the seating arrangement had been changed to a first-come, first-serve basis with no reserved seats for anybody;[9] and until bus, Negro bus operators had been employed on predominantly Negro lines. [*applause*]

Now I might say that in the beginning we were not out to compromise or to sanction segregation. Some people have wondered why we didn't ask for integration in the beginning. We realized that the first-come, first-serve seating arrangement was only a temporary alleviation of the problem. We felt that the ultimate solution to the problem would be integration on the buses, but we knew that we had a case that would come up in court on that so that we were willing to accept this as a temporary alleviation of the problem, knowing full well that the ultimate solution was total integration. As time went on we discovered that the City Commission didn't even want to work within the framework of the present segregation law. So it was necessary for our brilliant young attorney, who is here tonight, attorney Fred Gray, to go into the federal court with the case, and it went into the courts, and as you know the federal court ruled the other day that segregation in public transportation in Alabama is unconstitutional.[10] [*applause*] I talked with Montgomery this morning and I understand that the city, the state is planning to appeal this to the Supreme Court of the United States, which as you know is just a tactic to delay the situation, and that means that we will probably have to be off the buses several months more because we don't intend to go back until segregation is driven back.[11] [*applause*]

But you can now see that the one-day protest moved out into an indefinite protest which has lasted now for more than six months. So it is becoming clear now. The history of injustices on the buses has been a long one. Almost everybody in the community, almost every Negro citizen of the community, can point to an unfortunate incident that he had experienced or that he had seen. But you know there comes a time in this life that people get tired of being trampled over by the iron feet of oppression. There comes a time when people get tired of being plunged across the abyss of exploitation where they experience the bleakness of nagging despair. The story of Montgomery is the story of fifty thousand Negroes who are tired of oppression and injustice and who are willing [*applause*], and who are willing to substitute tired feet for tired souls, and walk and walk and walk until the sagging walls of injustice have been crushed by the battering rams of historical necessity. [*applause*]

One of the first practical problems that the ex–bus riders [*word inaudible*] is

---

9. In the prepared text this second demand reads, "passengers were seated on a first-come, first-served basis—Negroes seated from back of the bus toward the front and whites seated from the front toward the back."

10. The *Browder v. Gayle* decision was rendered on 5 June 1956.

11. This paragraph does not appear in the prepared text.

that in finding some way to get around the city. The first thing that we decided to do was to use a taxi, and they had agreed to transport the people for just ten cents, the same as the buses. Then the police commission stopped this by warning the taxis that they must charge a minimum of forty-five cents a person. Then we immediately got on the job and organized a volunteer car pool, and almost overnight over three hundred cars were out on the streets of Montgomery. [*applause*] They were out on the streets of Montgomery carrying the people to and from work from the various pick-up and dispatch stations. It worked amazingly well. Even Commissioner Sellers had to admit in a White Citizens Council meeting that the system worked with "military precision." [*applause*] It has continued to grow and it is still growing. Since that time we have added more than twenty station wagons to the car pool and they're working every day, all day, transporting the people. It has been an expensive project. Started out about two thousand dollars or more a week, but now it runs more than five thousand dollars a week. We have been able to carry on because of the contributions coming from the local community and nationally, from the great contributions that have come from friends of goodwill all over the nation and all over the world. [*applause*]

From the beginning the city commission, where there's the reactionary element of the white community, attempted to block the protest. And I say reactionary elements of the white community because I never want to give the impression that all of the white people in the South are downright and low in terms of civil rights. [*applause*] I assure you that there are white persons even in Montgomery, Alabama, who are deeply sympathetic with the movement and who have given us great words of encouragement and even contributions.[12] [*applause*] And from the beginning the reactionary element of the community, the white community, sought to block it. They used many methods. First they tried to negotiate us into a compromise. After that didn't work, they tried to conquer by dividing and they spread false rumors throughout the community about the leaders. They had it out that I had purchased a Cadillac car with the money and bought my wife a station wagon.[13] [*laughter*] Everybody in the community, in the Negro community, knew that I was driving around in a humble Pontiac and I'll still be driving it five or six years from now. [*applause*] They tried to divide the leadership. They went to the ministers and, the Negro ministers, and said to them, "Now, it's a pity that you gonna have, you oughta be in the leadership. These young men coming here and running over you like this. It just looks bad on you."[14] That was an attempt to establish petty jealousy, but it didn't work. For after the method of conquering by dividing didn't work, they moved out to what the Commissioner Gayle, Mayor Gayle, called a "get tough" policy. A "get tough" policy was, turned out to be the arrest of persons in the car pool and other persons for minor or imaginary traffic violations. It was in this period when I was arrested, carried down, and put into jail for supposedly going thirty miles an hour in a twenty-five

---

12. The two preceding sentences do not appear in the prepared text.

13. King refuted the charges at an MIA executive board meeting (see Ferron, Notes on MIA Executive Board Meeting, 23 January 1956, pp. 101–104 in this volume).

14. The six preceding sentences do not appear in the prepared text.

mile zone.[15] This was the "get tough" policy. After that didn't stop the movement, then came actual physical violence. It was during this period that my home was bombed, along with the home of a Mr. E. D. Nixon, one of the most outstanding and most progressive leaders in our community. Even physical violence didn't stop us. Then after that didn't work came the method of mass indictment. This time more than a hundred persons were indicted, including all of the members of the executive board of the Montgomery Improvement Association, were indicted on the basis of an old antilabor law of doubtful constitutionality. That law was brought into being in [*word inaudible*]. It was on the basis of this law that I was convicted, and whether you know it or not, a convicted criminal is speaking to you tonight.[16] [*applause*]

But none of this stopped the protest. [*applause*] Instead of blocking it, all of these things merely served to give us greater momentum and to give the people greater determination. It revealed to me at least one thing: that the Negro in the South has been freed from the paralysis of crippling fear. He is no longer afraid. He is willing to stand up now without any fear in his heart.[17] This is a characteristic also of the new Negro. [*applause*]

From the beginning there has been a basic philosophy undergirding our movement. It is a philosophy of nonviolent resistance. It is a philosophy which simply says we will refuse on a nonviolent basis, to cooperate with the evil of segregation. In our struggle in America we cannot fret with the idea of retaliatory violence.[18] To use the method of violence would be both impractical and immoral. We have neither the instruments nor the techniques of violence, and even if we had it, it would be morally wrong.[19] There is the voice crying [*applause*], there is a voice crying through the vista of time, saying: "He who lives by the sword will perish by the sword." [20] [*applause*] History is replete with the bleached bones of nations who failed to hear these words of truth, and so we decided to use the method of nonviolence, feeling that violence would not do the job.

Along with this emphasis on nonviolence goes the emphasis on love as the regulating ideal. We have refused in our struggle to succumb to the temptation of becoming bitter and indulging in a hate campaign. We are not out to defeat or to humiliate the white man. We are out to help him as well as ourselves. [*applause*] [*recording interrupted*][21] The festering sore of segregation debilitates the white man as well as the Negro [*applause*], and so we are not out to win a victory over the white man. And I assure you that the basic struggle in Montgomery after all is not between Negroes and white people. The struggle is at bottom a tension

---

15. This sentence does not appear in the prepared text.

16. The phrase "and whether you know it or not, a convicted criminal is speaking to you tonight" does not appear in the prepared text.

17. The two preceding sentences do not appear in the prepared text.

18. King omits the phrase "we, as a race," which is included in the prepared text.

19. The two preceding sentences do not appear in the prepared text.

20. Matthew 26:52.

21. It is unclear whether this gap means that a portion of King's speech is missing; however, the sequence of the sentences immediately before and after the gap matches that of the sentences in the prepared text.

between justice and injustice. [*applause*] It is a tension between the forces of light and the forces of darkness. And if there is a victory in Montgomery, it will not be a victory merely for fifty thousand Negroes, but it will be a victory for justice [*applause*], a victory for democracy [*applause*], and a victory for good will. This is at bottom the meaning of Christian love, and we are trying to follow that. It is that high type of love that I have talked about so often. The Greeks talked of so many types of love. But we are not talking about *eros* in Montgomery, we are talking about *agape*.[22] We are talking about understanding good will. We are talking about a love which seeks nothing in return. We are talking about a love that loves the person who does the evil deed, while hating the deed that the person does. That is a higher type of love. [*applause*]

Also basic in our philosophy is a deep faith in the future. This is why our movement is often referred to as a spiritual movement. We have the strange feeling down in Montgomery that in our struggle we have cosmic companionship. We feel that the universe is on the side of right and righteousness. This is what keeps us going. Oh, I would admit that, yes, it comes down to us from the long tradition of our Christian faith. We look back to that date, and look down through history, and we see the meaning of it. Good Friday may occupy the throne for a day, but ultimately it must give way to the triumphant beat of the Drums of Easter. Evil may so shape events that Caesar will occupy the palace and Christ the cross. But one day that same Christ will rise up and split history into A.D. and B.C. so that even the life of Caesar must be dated by his name.[23] There is something [*applause*], there is something in this universe that justifies Carlyle in saying: "No lie can live forever." There is something in this universe which justifies William Cullen Bryant in saying: "Truth crushed to earth will rise again." [*applause*] There is something in this universe which justifies James Russell Lowell in saying:

> Truth forever on the scaffold,
> Wrong forever on the throne
> Yet that scaffold sways the future
> And behind the dim unknown stands God
> Within the shadow keeping watch above His own.[24]

We believe that, and that is what keeps us going. That is why we can walk and never get weary because we know that there is a great camp meeting in the promised land of freedom and equality.[25] [*applause*]

This in brief is just an introduction to a story that would take many, many speeches to tell, and even many books. It is the expression of a method. It might well be added to the several methods that we must use to achieve integration in

---

22. The three preceding sentences do not appear in the prepared text. King examined the concept of *agape* in his dissertation (see "A Comparison of the Conceptions of God in the Thinking of Paul Tillich and Henry Nelson Wieman," 15 April 1955, in *Papers* 2:440–442). He presents a more extended discussion in "Non-Aggression Procedures to Interracial Harmony," 23 July 1956; and "Facing the Challenge of a New Age," 3 December 1956, pp. 327 and 458–459 in this volume, respectively.

23. The six preceding sentences do not appear in the prepared text.

24. For a discussion of the above passage see notes 6 and 8 to "The Death of Evil upon the Seashore," 17 May 1956, pp. 259 and 260 in this volume.

25. This line is from the spiritual "There Is a Great Meeting in the Promised Land."

America. Secondly, we must continue the struggle through legislation. No one can underestimate the power of this method. It is an important, valuable method, and we must continue to use it. [*Audience:*] (*Right on*) We must continue to gain the ballot, to urge the executive and the legislative branches of our government to follow the example so courageously set by the judicial branch. We must admit that these other branches have been all too slow in this area; yet we must also depend on the growing group of white liberals, both North and South, who are willing to take a stand together. But in the final analysis, the problem of obtaining full citizenship is a problem for which the Negro himself must assume the primary responsibility. [*applause*] Integration will not be some lavish dish that will be passed out by the white man on a silver platter, while the Negro merely furnishes the appetite. [*laughter*] If we are to achieve integration, we must work for it. We must be willing to sacrifice for it, yes, and even to die for it if necessary. [*applause*]

I have no doubt that by 1963 we will have won the legal battle. On May the four—seventeenth, 1954, the Supreme Court of this nation gave the legal death blow to segregation. Then after the legal battle is won, we must confront the problem of lifting the noble precepts of our Constitution from the dusty files of unimplemented court decisions. This problem of implementation will be carried out mainly by the Negro's refusal to cooperate with segregation.[26] [*applause*]

Wherever segregation exists we must be willing to stand up in mass and courageously and non-violently protest against it. (*That's right*) And I might say that I must admit that this means sacrifice and suffering. Yes, it might even mean going to jail. But if it means going to jail, we must be willing to fill up the jail houses of the South. (*Yes*) [*applause*] Yes, it might even mean physical death. But if physical death is the price that some must pay to free our children from a permanent life of psychological death, then nothing could be more honorable.[27] [*applause*] This is really the meaning of passive resistance. It confronts physical force with an even greater force, namely, soul force.

This method is not at all new. It was tried by a little brown man in India. He looked out at the British empire, with all of the vastness of her empire. He noticed all [*words inaudible*] military machinery. But in the midst of that physical force, he confronted that empire with soul force.[28] Through this method he was able to free his people from the political domination, the economic exploitation, and the humiliation that had been inflicted upon them by Britain. This a powerful force [*applause*] and we must be willing to use it.[29]

---

26. At a press conference the day before, King remarked that strategies of passive resistance such as Montgomery's bus boycott "might become the pattern in many areas of the South." Suggesting that African Americans boycott segregated schools to force local school boards to comply with the Supreme Court's 1954 *Brown* decision, King added that such direct action would lead to legal action against the protesters and that "it i[s] interesting to have legal action from the other side." Thurgood Marshall, the NAACP special counsel, commented on King's suggestion: "I don't approve of using children to do men's work" ("King Proposal Would Boycott Dixie Schools," *Montgomery Advertiser,* 27 June 1956).

27. King later attributed this sentence to Kenneth Clark. See "Desegregation and the Future," 15 December 1956, p. 478 in this volume.

28. The three preceding sentences do not appear in the prepared text.

29. This sentence does not appear in the prepared text.

As I come to a close let me say to you this evening, continue to move on in the struggle for integration. Let's not fool ourselves, we haven't reached the promised land, North or South. [*applause*] We still confront segregation in the South in its glaring and conspicuous forms. We still confront it in the North in its subtle and hidden forms. [*applause*] Segregation is still a fact. Now it might be true that Old Man Segregation is on its deathbed, but history has proven that social systems have a great last-minute breathing power. [*laughter*] And the guardians of the status quo are always on hand with their oxygen tents to keep the old order alive. [*applause*] But if democracy is to live, segregation must die. [*applause*] The underlying philosophy of democracy is diametrically opposed to the underlying philosophy of segregation, and all of the dialectics of the logicians cannot make them lie down together. [*applause*] Segregation is an evil, segregation is a cancer in the body politic which must be removed before our democratic health can be realized. [*applause*]

Now I realize that there are those all over who are telling us that we must slow up. They're telling us to adopt a policy of moderation. Well, if moderation means pressing on for freedom with wise restraint and calm reasonableness, then moderation is a great virtue that all must seek to achieve in this tense period of transition. But if moderation means slowing up in the move for freedom and capitulating to the whims and caprices of the guardians of a deadening status quo, then moderation is a tragic vice which all people of good will must condemn.[30] [*applause*]

We cannot afford to slow up. We have a moral obligation to press on. We have our self-respect to maintain. But even more we can't afford to slow up because of our love for America and our love for the democratic way of life.

Out of the two billion, four hundred million people in this the world, one billion, six hundred million are colored. Most of these colored people of the world have lived under the yoke of colonialism and imperialism. Gradually most and all of these people are gaining their freedom, and they are determined not to follow any nation that will subject [*word inaudible*] citizens to second-class citizenship. [*applause*] And if America doesn't wake up, she will discover that the uncommitted peoples of the world are in the hands of a communist ideology.[31] So because of our love for *America*, we cannot afford to slow up.[32] But even more [*applause*], but we can't stop there. The motive for America giving freedom and justice to the Negro cannot be merely to compete with godless communism. We must do it because it's part of the ethical demands of the universe. We do it not merely because it is diplomatically expedient, but because it is morally compelling. We must do it [*applause*]; it must be done because it is right to do it. We cannot afford to slow up. The motor is now cranked up, we are moving up the highway of freedom toward the city of equality, and we can't afford to slow up

---

30. In this sentence King says "people," though the prepared text employs the word "men."

31. In the prepared text this sentence reads: "If America doesn't press for justice and freedom we will wake up and find the uncommitted peoples of the world in the hands of a communistic ideology."

32. This sentence does not appear in the prepared text.

because we have a date with destiny. We must keep moving. We must keep going.
[*applause*]

May, in closing, I refer to and extend an analogy that was once mentioned by Walter White, the late Walter White.[33] Since the turn of the century we have brought the football of civil rights to about the fifty-yard line. And now we are getting ready to move in the opposition's territory. And the great problem which confronts us, the great path to cross now, is to carry that ball across the goal line. [*applause*] Now let's not fool ourselves, this will not be easy; it will be difficult. The opposition will use all the power, all the force possible to prevent our advance. They will strengthen the line on every hand. My friends, if we would put the proper leaders in the backfield to call the signals and run the ball, leaders who love the cause, leaders who are not in love with publicity but in love with humanity [*applause*], leaders not in love with money but in love with justice [*applause*], leaders who are willing to subject their personal and particular egos to the greatness of the cause. If we would put the proper leaders in the backfield—and we need them all over the nation—and the proper followers on the line to make the way clear, we will be able to make moves which will both stagger and astound the imagination of the opposition.[34] [*applause*] We will make some mistakes, yes, we might even fumble the ball, but for God's sake, recover it! [*laughter, applause*] Teamwork and unity are necessary for the winning of any game. In this area it means that every segment of the Negro race is significant. It means that the backfield must realize that they need the people on the line to make the way clear.[35] So away with our class systems.[36] We have come to see that in this struggle, Aunt Jane who knows not the difference between "you is" and "you are" is just as significant as the Ph.D. in English [37] [*applause*]; that we will come together and work together. I assure you that in the next few years we will be able to carry this ball of civil rights successfully across the goal line.

We [*applause*], we will stand before [*word inaudible*] all the members of [*words inaudible*]. It would be a great team. Let us unite. Let us keep moving on towards the city of freedom and equality. Let nothing stop us, let us keep moving, let no obstacle stand in our way. If we will do that, when the history books are written in future years historians will have to say, there lived a great people, a black people, who injected a new meaning into the veins of our civilization, because they had the courage to stand up and press on for the pressing values of freedom. And when we do that [*applause*], whenever we as a race, whenever men of goodwill

---

33. As national secretary of the NAACP from 1930 until his death, Walter White (1893–1955) directed its campaigns for federal civil rights legislation, including laws banning lynching, poll taxes, and discrimination in the U.S. armed forces and laws guaranteeing voting rights and promoting integration.

34. In the prepared text this sentence reads: "But if we place good leaders in the backfield to call the signals and run the ball, and good followers on the line to make the way clear, we will be able to make moves that will stagger and astound the imagination of the opposition."

35. In this sentence King says "people" instead of "men" as in the prepared text.

36. In the prepared text King adds: " . . . that so easily separate us. Remember the highest will not rise without the lowest."

37. This sentence does not appear in the prepared text.

strive to do that, the immortal God will sing together and the sons of God will shout for joy.[38] [*lengthy applause*]

At. MLKJrP-GAMK.

---

38. Job 38:7. In his prepared text, King closes not with this paragraph, but with a variant of the Langston Hughes poem "Mother to Son": "This is our profound challenge and lasting responsibility. We must continue to move on in the face of every obstacle. 'Mother to Son': 'Well, Son, I'll tell you / Life for me ain't been no crystal stair / It's had tacks in it, / and splinters / And boards torn up / And places with no carpet on the floor—/ Bare / But all the time / I'se been a climbin' on / And reachin' landings / And turnin' corners / And sometimes going in the dark / Where there ain't been no light / So, boy, don't you stop now, / Don't you sit down on the steps / 'Cause you finds it's kinder hard / Don't you fall back / For I'se still goin' boy / I'm still climbin' / And life for me ain't been no crystal stair.'

Well, life for none of us has been a crystal stair. But we must keep moving. If you can't fly, run; if you can't run, walk; if you can't walk, crawl, but by all means keep moving!"

To W. T. Handy, Jr.

3 July 1956
Montgomery, Ala.

King declines his Boston University classmate's invitation to speak at a Louisiana church on 8 November.

The Rev. W. T. Handy, Jr., Pastor
Newman Methodist Church
Corner Fulton & Eighth Streets
Alexandria, Louisiana

Dear W. T.,

This is to acknowledge receipt of your very kind letter of June 8. Absence from the city for several days has delayed my reply.

After checking my schedule I find that I have accepted as many speaking engagements for the next five or six months as my schedule will allow. For this reason I will have to decline your gracious invitation to speak for the Community-wide Fellowship Banquet. Please know that I regret this very deeply. It is even more regretful in the light of our personal friendship and my real concern and respect for the great work you are doing. I certainly hope that it will be possible for me to serve you at some future date.

I hope everything goes well with you and Ruth.[1] It would really be a gratifying

---

1. Ruth Odessa Robinson, a friend of the King family, married Handy on 11 August 1948.

experience to see both of you, since it has been so long since we have seen each other. I hope you will find it possible to stop through Montgomery next time you are in this section.[2] Coretta and I are doing fine. We have a little daughter now, Yolanda Denise, who is a little more than seven months old. She is really the boss of the family.

With warm personal regards.

Sincerely yours,
[*signed*] M. L.
M. L. King, Jr.,
President

MLK:b

TLS. WTH.

---

2. On 18 September Handy wrote King to thank him and Coretta for a wonderful visit during the summer.

To Glenn E. Smiley

5 July 1956
Montgomery, Ala.

King responds to Smiley's letters of 11, 18, and 20 June. In this correspondence Smiley discussed arrangements for King's participation in an upcoming workshop for southern movement leaders in Tuskegee on 17–18 July. In his 20 June letter, Smiley enclosed a suggestion by Alfred Hassler, editor of Fellowship, *urging the MIA to purchase space in the* Montgomery Advertiser *every week in order to explain "the reasons for its actions in the bus situation."[1] Hassler asserted that such a column would "create a wordless but vital understanding between the two communities." Smiley affirmed the idea: "Of all the things that you are doing in the MIA, the weakest seems to be at the point of interpretation to the people whom we eventually want to live with in harmony and love." In September the MIA appointed a special committee, which included King, to explore ways of influencing white attitudes; shortly thereafter, King initiated discussions with the editor of the* Advertiser *about a statement, but it never appeared.[2]*

---

1. Alfred Hassler (1910–1991) was born in Allentown, Pennsylvania, and grew up in New York City. He studied journalism at Columbia University and then worked for American Baptist Publications in Philadelphia. In 1942 he became editor of the FOR journal *Fellowship*. In 1960 he assumed the position of executive secretary of the United States Fellowship, serving until his retirement in 1974. He was also president of the International Confederation for Disarmament and Peace.

2. See W. J. Powell, Minutes of MIA Special Committee, 25 September 1956; Grover C. Hall to King, 10 October 1956; and King to Hall, 29 October 1956.

5 July
1956 The Rev. Glenn E. Smiley, Field Secretary
The Fellowship of Reconciliation
21 Audubon Avenue
New York 32, New York

Dear Glenn,

On my return to the city, after being away for several weeks, I found your three letters. The contents of all have been noted with care. The first letter, I think, deals with the Workshop to be held at Tuskegee Institute July 17 and 18. I think all of the arrangements are very good so far, and the rates are about as good as we can find. Accommodations are always extraordinarily good at Dorothy Hall. I know that this will be a very fruitful workshop. I will look forward to hearing from you concerning the invitation.

The second letter concerns my coming to Chicago to speak for The Fellowship of Reconciliation. Certainly I can see the predicament that you are in at this point. And I assure you that I regret saying no to you almost more than anybody I know, if for no other reason than the fact that you have been so helpful to me in our personal encounters. However, my doctor is insisting that I slow up and stop living such a rushed schedule. I feel that it will be entirely too much of a rush for me to speak Friday night in Denver and leave Saturday morning for Chicago and speak that afternoon in Chicago and then return to Denver to preach the next morning. I do hope you will understand my situation and the strain under which I am working. I am very sorry that this conflict has arisen. I know no organization that I would enjoy speaking to more than the <u>FOR</u>. I hope you will hold a place for me somewhere on the agenda for the next meeting.

The next letter deals with the suggestion of buying space in the Montgomery Advertiser to interpret our point of view to the white community. I have read Mr. Hassler's suggestion very carefully, and I think this is an excellent idea. It is one of the things that has been neglected throughout our movement. I will take up the matter with a few members of the Executive Board immediately. Also, I will contact the Advertiser to see if it is possible to purchase such space. As soon as this is done, I will let you know the outcome.

I hope everything is going well with you. I will look forward to hearing from you in the very near future. I intended writing more in this letter, but my desk is stacked with a pile of mail that must be answered immediately.

Sincerely yours,
[*signed*] Martin
M. L. King, Jr.

MLK:b

TLS. FORP-PSC-P.

5 July 1956
[*Montgomery, Ala.*]

*King thanks Lomax for her newspaper articles on Montgomery and the hospitality that
she and her mother-in-law, Minnie Lomax, had shown during the Kings' visit to Los
Angeles. On 18 July Lomax responded by noting that she had published his letter.[1] "By
now, you should be used to the fact that your every utterance is news, so perhaps you
won't mind." Lomax also reported that she was moved "to become an associate member
of your church" after hearing him preach, even though she had been "indifferently an
agnostic since the age of 12."*

Mrs. Almena Lomax, Editor
The Los Angeles Tribune
2323 W. Jefferson Blvd.
Los Angeles 18, California

Dear Mrs. Lomax:

This is just a note to again express my appreciation to you for the interest that
you have taken in our struggle. The meeting at the Town Club in Los Angeles was
indeed a rich experience with all of us who had the opportunity to attend. We
had the pleasure of meeting many of the influential citizens of the Los Angeles
community. Thanks to you for making these arrangements.

I have been following your articles on Montgomery very closely. They represent
journalism at its best. You have a profound grasp of the situation plus the gift of
presenting it in a very lucid style. I assure you that this series has rendered a great
service for our cause.

I hope everything goes well with you. Mrs. King sends her best regards. Please
give our regards to your very gracious and charming Mother-in-law.

With warm personal regards.

Sincerely yours,
M. L. King, Jr.,
President

MLK:b

THLc. MLKP-MBU: Box 61.

---

1. See "From Rev. King," *Los Angeles Tribune*, 13 July 1956.

To John Oliver Killens

In a 10 June letter Killens remembered sitting on the platform when King spoke at Brooklyn's Concord Baptist Church in March and being "tremendously moved by the experience." He donated $50 to the Montgomery movement and gave "best wishes for the fifty thousand who have shown the rest of us Americans how it can be done." Killens also sent a copy of his first novel, Youngblood, *describing it as "a novel of Negro life in Georgia" that "tries to deal with many of the questions you and your colleagues are presently dealing with so ably in real life."* [1]

Mr. John Oliver Killens
652 Lafayette Avenue
Brooklyn 16, N.Y.

Dear Mr. Killens:

On returning to the city, after being away several weeks, I found your most gracious letter. Since that time I have received the copy of your novel, <u>Youngblood</u>. I assure you that I am deeply grateful to you for your letter and for this autographed copy of your novel. I have known of your work for quite some time, and I have heard of the greatness and depth of <u>Youngblood</u>. I only regret that I have not had time to read it. But since I have a copy directly at my disposal, I will read it at my earliest convenience. From what I have heard about the book, I am sure that it will meet a real need in my life.

May I also express my personal appreciation to you for the fine contribution which you made to our organization. I assure you that such moral support and christian generosity are of inestimable value in the continuance of our humble efforts.

I hope it will be possible to talk with you some time in the near future. I was

---

1. John Oliver Killens (1916–1987), born in Macon, Georgia, attended Edward Waters College and Morris Brown College before graduating from Howard University. Killens founded the Harlem Writers Guild in 1952 and published *Youngblood* two years later. He taught creative writing at several institutions, including Fisk, Howard, and Columbia Universities. Killens later worked in Hollywood on a screenplay about the boycott.

more than happy to know that we are natives of the same state. I notice that you are married and have two children. Please give them my best regards.

  With warm personal regards.

Sincerely yours,
M. L. King, Jr.,
President

MLK:b

P.S. I asked the secretary to clear up the matter with you concerning the check for fifty dollars ($50.00).[2]

TLc. MLKP-MBU: Box 61.

---

2. After realizing that the check had not yet been redeemed, Killens asked King to ensure that it had been deposited by the MIA.

To Helen M. Hiller

6 July 1956
[*Montgomery, Ala.*]

Mrs. Helen M. Hiller
Mattapoisett
Massachusetts

Dear Mrs. Hiller:

  This is just a note to acknowledge receipt of your very helpful letter dated June 4. I am always open for constructive advice and I assure you that the things said in your letter were accepted with all humility. It is my great hope and prayer that I will be able to live up, with a real sense of humility and staggering simplicity, to the tremendous responsibility that has been invested in me as a leader. You are eminently correct in everything that you say. Please know that I am grateful to you for such advice.

  With every good wish, I am

Sincerely yours,
M. L. King, Jr.,
President

MLK:b

P.S. May I say that I am driving an old Pontiac and I never anticipate buying a Cadillac.

TLc. MLKP-MBU: Box 60.

To A. J. Muste

10 July 1956
[*Montgomery, Ala.*]

Muste, of the Fellowship of Reconciliation, heard King describe the Montgomery movement at a Morehouse College gathering of civil rights activists on 12 May, which he reported as "one of the most moving" and "important" events of his long career as a pacifist.[1] On 28 June he sent King a request to host Mishree Lal Jayaswal, a nonviolent activist from India who was on a four-year bicycle journey around the world to champion peace and nonviolence. King responds on the same day to Muste and to Bayard Rustin, telling the latter that he would be "very happy to meet the young man from India, and also provide a place for him to stay."[2]

Mr. A. J. Muste
The Fellowship of Reconciliation
21 Audubon Avenue
New York 32, New York

Dear Mr. Muste:

Thanks for your release concerning your Indian friend, Mishree Lal Jayaswal. I will be anticipating his coming to Montgomery, and I assure you that he will receive every possible courtesy.
With every good wish, I am

Sincerely yours,
M. L. King, Jr.,
President

MLK:b

TLc. MLKP-MBU: Box 17.

---

1. Muste, "The Magnolia Curtain?" 14 May 1956. See also Glenn E. Smiley, Minutes of the Atlanta Conference, 12 May 1956. Abraham Johannes Muste (1885–1967) was born in Holland and became a U.S. citizen at age eleven. After earning his B.A. (1905) and M.A. (1909) from Hope College in Michigan, he became an ordained minister, receiving a degree from Union Theological Seminary in New York in 1913. Muste directed Brookwood Labor College in New York from 1921 to 1933. He joined the Fellowship of Reconciliation in 1916, serving as the group's chair for several years in the late 1920s and becoming its executive secretary in 1940. He retired from that position in 1953 but continued his pacifist work with FOR and the Committee for Nonviolent Action, which he chaired from its founding in 1957. A co-founder and editor of *Liberation,* he was a prolific writer whose publications included *Nonviolence in an Aggressive World* (1940) and *Not by Might* (1947).

2. See Rustin to King, June–July 1956; and King to Rustin, 10 July 1956.

To Lovie M. Rainbow

10 July 1956
[*Montgomery, Ala.*]

*King accepts blues composer and publisher W. C. Handy's offer, conveyed by his
cousin, to donate one hundred printed copies of the song "We Are Americans, Too,"
by Eubie Blake and Andy Razaf, to raise funds for the MIA.*[1]

Mrs. Lovie M. Rainbow
161 East Lorain Street
Oberlin, Ohio

Dear Mrs. Rainbow:

This is just a note to acknowledge receipt of your letter of June 29, as well as the enclosed letter from your cousin W. C. Handy.[2] First, I might mention what a debt of gratitude that we owe him for his interest in our struggle. His offer to give us one hundred copies of the song "We Are Americans, too" is one that will be well accepted. I will be very happy to appoint someone in the organization to dispose of these copies. It can mean a great deal for our organization financially. I will look forward to receiving the music in the very near future. Thanks for your interest and cooperation. Please extend my personal regards to your cousin who has made such a rich contribution to the musical field in America.

Sincerely yours,
M. L. King, Jr.,
President

MLK:b

TLc. MLKP-MBU: Box 64.

---

1. William Christopher Handy (1873–1958), known as the "father of the blues," was most famous for his 1914 composition "St. Louis Blues." He also formed a company to publish blues compositions, including "We Are Americans, Too."
2. Handy's 22 June 1956 letter to Rainbow, which she forwarded to King, noted that Handy would receive an award at a celebration of black achievements at the Panorama of Progress held 30 June–4 July 1956 in Detroit. Singer Nat King Cole recorded "We Are Americans, Too" for the event, where King also received an award. Neither King nor Handy attended the celebration.

To Homer Greene

10 July 1956
[*Montgomery, Ala.*]

*Greene, a white soldier from California, had written King a letter of support in which
he expressed concern about a radio interview with Rosa Parks by Sidney Rogers, a San
Francisco radio commentator who had been accused of having Communist ties by*

*congressional and California state investigating committees.[1] Denied by Rogers, the
allegations were never proven. Greene replied to King's letter on 18 July and apologized
for associating King with Rogers.*

SP2 Homer Greene, RA 32 808 912
Admin. Svc. Company
3d Division
Fort Benning, Georgia

Dear Mr. Greene:

Thanks for your very kind letter of June 25, expressing deep concern for our struggle here in Montgomery. I read your letter very carefully, and was very happy to know of your interest.

I don't know of the Mr. Rogers that you refer to in your letter. I have never spoken over any program sponsored by a Mr. Rogers. It is probable that someone else from Montgomery spoke over the program. One of the things that we have insisted on throughout the protest is that we steer clear of any Communistic infiltration and I think we have succeeded very well to this point. I only hope that we will be able to continue our struggle without anything that borders on Communism.

However, your point is well taken. We must always be on guard for possible exploitation by Communistic forces. Thanks very much for your concern. I will inquire from Mrs. Rosa Parks, the lady whose arrest precipitated the protest, whether or not she spoke on Mr. Rogers' program.

Yours very truly,
M. L. King, Jr.,
President

MLK:b

TLc. MLKP-MBU: Box 17.

---

1. The interview with Rosa Parks had aired on Pacifica Radio stations earlier in 1956 (see Rosa Parks, interview by Sidney Rogers, 1956, Pacifica Radio Archive, Los Angeles).

To J. Raymond Henderson

10 July 1956
[*Montgomery, Ala.*]

*King thanks the Los Angeles minister and his wife, Velva Henderson, for their
hospitality and anticipates their next meeting in Denver at the National Baptist
Convention's annual conference in September.*

Dear Rev. Henderson:

I have written you and your lovely wife a thousand times in my mind but I am just getting to the point of putting it on paper. There is a word in Catholic Theology called "supererogation" which means in substance "more than justice requires." I can assure you that the kind hospitality that you and Mrs. Henderson rendered toward Mrs. King and me was a work of supererogation. Words can never adequately express our appreciation to you. To have been able to preach in your great church for a week was an unsurpassable experience. To have been in your palatial home was living life in all of its abundance. I only hope that some day we will be able to return the kindness in some little way.

We had a very nice trip back to Montgomery. The NAACP Convention went over in a big way. We arrived in Montgomery on Saturday evening, June 30, in time to get plenty of rest for the Sunday morning service. We found our little daughter doing fine and still growing as fast as ever.

Things are going very well here in Montgomery now. Rev. Fields seems to be in line, and the internal structure of our organization is as strong as ever.

I hope things are going well with you and Mrs. Henderson. Be sure to tell the madam that she is one of the most charming and impressive minister's wives that I have ever met. She gets "A" on my book straight down the line. Give my best regards to all of my friends in Los Angeles and to all of the members of your church.

Again, I say I will never forget this experience. And I will never forget your real genuine friendship.

Sincerely yours,
M. L. King, Jr.

MLK:b

P.S. We will look forward to seeing you in Denver.

TLc. MLKP-MBU: Box 65.

From John Patterson

12 July 1956
Montgomery, Ala.

Alabama attorney general Patterson sought King's testimony in the state's attempt to ban NAACP activities, including raising funds, collecting dues, and soliciting new members.[1] Patterson argued that the NAACP was behind the "illegal boycott" in

---

1. John Malcolm Patterson (1921–), born in Goldville, Alabama, received his law degree from the University of Alabama in 1949. Patterson was attorney general of Alabama from 1955 to 1959 and governor from 1959 to 1963.

Montgomery. The NAACP's appeal stretched on for eight years until the U.S. Supreme Court ruled in its favor. King never testified.

REGISTERED MAIL
RETURN RECEIPT REQUESTED

Martin Luther King
309 South Jackson
Montgomery, Alabama

You have heretofore been serve with a subpoena to appear as a witness, at a hearing set for 10:00 A.M., on Tuesday, July 17, 1956, in the case of <u>State of Alabama ex rel. John Patterson, Attorney General v. National Association for the advancement of Colored People.</u>

You are hereby advised that this hearing has been continued until July 25, 1956, and that you must now appear as a witness in this case at 10:00 A.M., on Wednesday, July 25, 1956, before the Circuit Court of Montgomery County, Alabama, in equity, at the Court House on Dexter Avenue, Montgomery, Alabama.

Very truly yours,
JOHN PATTERSON
Attorney General
By—
[*signed*]
EDMON L. RINEHART
Assistant Attorney General

ELR/ar

TLSr. MLKP-MBU: Box 62A.

"From the Pastor's Desk"

18 July 1956
Montgomery, Ala.

In his first column for the Dexter Echo, *the new biweekly church newsletter edited by George W. Jones, King asks each Dexter member to "remember his church responsibilities" for the summer months. He also refers to the baby contest won by his daughter, Yolanda Denise King, in whose name the most funds were raised.*[1]

Since this is my first column in the Dexter ECHO, I might just make a statement concerning the paper itself. Every member will agree that the ECHO will

---

1. See photograph following p. 33 in this volume.

serve to meet a real need in the life of the church. It will be possible now for each member to have the opportunity to keep abreast with all of the activities of the church. Naturally, there are vital things happening in the experiences of members as well as in the church program generally which time will not permit to be mentioned at the regular Sunday service. Such vital information is now released through our official organ. Each of us owes a real debt of gratitude to the very competent editor of the ECHO and the fine staff.

Now, to change the subject a bit. As you know, we are presently in the summer phase of our work and our church life. All too often this is a period in which church activities and church interest fall hopelessly off. This should not be the case. The church must operate in the summer as well as in the winter; so I am urging each member to remember his church responsibilities for the remaining weeks of the summer period. If you find it necessary to be away for a few weeks, remember that the church needs your pledge to continue to meet its financial obligations.

Many commendable thins have already happened in the church this summer. We have just closed a baby contest which proved to be a tremendous success. Once again Dexter proved what power there is in a group of people dedicated to the program of the church. For everything which you did, we are exceedingly grateful.

In a few weeks, each member will be asked to make a pledge toward the fund for the general renovation of the church (downstairs auditorium) and the parsonage. I am sure that we can expect the cooperation of the entire membership in this venture. Each member will be urged to pledge at least ten dollars toward this effort and can extend payments over a three-month period. Let us prove once again the power of a dedicated congregation. I am sure that we can do it, just as we have done it so often before!

TD. *Dexter Echo*, 18 July 1956, pp. 1, 2; copy in MLKP-MBU: Box 77.

"Non-Aggression Procedures to Interracial Harmony," Address Delivered at the American Baptist Assembly and American Home Mission Agencies Conference

[*23 July 1956*]
Green Lake, Wisc.

In this address to executives of the Home Mission Societies of Christian Friends, sponsored by the American Baptist Assembly, King responds to the question "How will the oppressed peoples of the world wage their struggle against the forces of injustice?" Dismissing the use of violence as "both impractical and immoral," he endorses the method of nonviolent protest. This "mentally and spiritually aggressive" technique not only avoids "external physical violence" but also "seeks to avoid internal violence [to the] spirit. He delivered the same speech on 16 October to the 131st Universalist Convention in Courtland, New York; it was edited for publication in the organization's

*journal.[1] Significant variations between the Green Lake speech and the article are
noted.*

Thank you very much for your kindness, Dr. Diamond, executives of the Home Mission Societies of Christian Friends. I need not pause to say how happy I am to be here this evening and to be a part of this very rich fellowship. I consider this a unique privilege as well as a unique honor and I certainly want to express my personal appreciation to the executives of the Home Mission Societies for extending the invitation. I assure you that I am very happy to be here. I didn't know that I would run into so many old friends in coming to Green Lake, so that all of this served to increase my interest and my stay here and to make the fellowship even richer. I am more than happy to be a part of this very rich assembly, and I am very proud to be a Baptist when I can see something like this.

Our subject for the evening, as you will notice it on the programs, is Non-Aggression Procedures to Interracial Harmony. Now what I will be talking about, if I can break that down a little bit, is the technique of nonviolence in bringing about better race relations. Nonviolence as a technique in bringing about better race relations. It is impossible to look out into the broad arena of American life without noticing a real crisis in race relations. This crisis has been precipitated on the one hand by the determined resistance on the part of reactionary elements in the South to the Supreme Court's momentous decision on segregation.[2] It has been precipitated on the other hand by the radical change in the Negro's evaluation of himself. And it is impossible to understand the tension in race relations without understanding this revolutionary change in the Negro's evaluation of his nature and destiny.[3]

A brief survey of the history of the Negro in America reveals this change in terms that are crystal clear. It was in the year 1619 that the first Negro slaves landed on the shores of this nation. They were brought here from the soils of Africa and, unlike the pilgrim fathers who landed at Plymouth a year later, they were brought here against their wills. For more than two hundred years, Africa was raped and plundered, her native kingdoms disorganized, her people and rulers demoralized, and the whole continent inflicted with pains and burdens hardly paralleled by any race of people in the whole history of the civilized world.[4] Throughout slavery the Negro was treated in a very inhuman fashion. He was not a person to be respected but a thing to be used. He was merely a depersonalized cog in a vast plantation machine. The famous Dred Scott decision of 1857 well

---

1. King, "Non-violent Procedures to Inter-Racial Harmony," *Empire State Universalist,* November 1956, pp. 7–10.

2. In the article King added: "This resistance has often risen to [ominous] proportions. Many states have risen up in open defiance. Legislative halls of the South ring loud with such words as 'interposition' and 'nullification.' In many states a modern version of the Ku Klux Klan has arisen in the form of so-called respectable White Citizens Councils. All of these forces have conjoined to make for massive resistance."

3. In the article King added: "It is true to say that there would be no crisis in race relations if the Negro thought of himself in inferior terms and patiently accepted injustice and exploitation. It is at this very point that the change has come."

4. Of these three sentences, the two with references to Africa do not appear in "Non-violent Procedures."

illustrates the status of the Negro during slavery. For it was in this decision that the Supreme Court of this nation said, in substance, that the Negro is not a citizen of the United States, he is merely property subject to the dictates of his owner, and this was the attitude that prevailed throughout slavery. With the growth of slavery it became necessary to give some defense for it. It seems to be a fact of life that human beings cannot continue to do wrong without eventually reaching out for some rationalization and to cover up an obvious wrong with the beautiful garments of righteousness.[5]

William James, a psychologist, used to talk a great deal about the stream of consciousness, and he said one of the uniquenesses of human nature is that man has the capacity and the ability to temporarily block the stream of consciousness and inject anything in it that he wants to. And so man has the unique and tragic power of justifying the rightness of the wrong. This is exactly what happened to the slave owners. They fell victim to the danger that forever confronts religion. That is the danger that religion and the Bible, not properly interpreted, can be used as instruments to crystallize a status quo. This was the thing that often happened, and so from pulpits all over the nation certain ideas went out. It was argued that the Negro was inferior by nature because of Noah's curse upon the children of Ham, and Paul's command became a watchword: "Servants be obedient to your masters." [6] And then one of the brethren had probably read some of the logic of Aristotle, and he could put his argument almost in the form of an Aristotelian syllogism. He could say a man is made in the image of God; and then comes his minor premise: God, as everybody knows, is not a Negro; and then the conclusion: therefore, the Negro is not a man. [*laughter*] Now this was the type of reasoning that prevailed at that time.[7]

With all of this, living under this, the Negro came to the point of losing faith in himself. He came to feel that perhaps he was less than human. The great tragedy of physical slavery was that it led to the paralysis of mental slavery. And so long as the Negro accepted this place assigned to him a sort of racial peace existed, but it was an uneasy peace in which the Negro was forced patiently to accept injustice and oppression and exploitation. It was a negative peace, for real peace is not merely the absence of some negative force—tension, confusion, or law—but real peace is the presence of some positive force—justice, goodwill, and brotherhood. So that this was merely a negative peace.

But then one day something happened to the Negro. He traveled a great deal. He had been to war and he had seen a lot of things. Literacy was fastly coming

---

5. The three preceding sentences do not appear in "Non-violent Procedures"; instead the following statements appear: "After his emancipation in 1863, the Negro still confronted oppression and inequality. It is true that for a time, while the Army of Occupation remained in the South and Reconstruction ruled, the Negro had a brief period of eminence and political power. But he was quickly overwhelmed by the white majority. So in 1896, through the Plessy v. Ferguson Decision, a new kind of slavery came into being covered up with certain [niceties] of complexity. In this decision the Supreme Court of the nation established the doctrine of separate-but-equal as the law of the land. Following this decision there was a strict enforcement of the 'separate' with not the slightest intention to abide by the equal. So the Plessy Doctrine ended up plunging the Negro across the abyss of exploitation where he experienced the bleakness of nagging injustice."

6. Ephesians 6:5.

7. This paragraph does not appear in "Non-violent Procedures."

into being and illiteracy passing away, and all of these things came together and to cause the Negro to take a new look at himself. Negro masses all over began to reevaluate themselves. The Negro came to feel that he was somebody. His religion revealed to him that God loves all of his children, and at bottom, the basic thing about a man is not "his specificity but his fundamentum." And so he came to the point that he could agree with the eloquent poet:

> Fleecy locks and black complexion
> Cannot forfeit Nature's claims
> Skin may differ but affection
> Dwells in black and white the same.
> If I were so tall as to reach the pole
> Or to grasp at the ocean at a span,
> I must be measured by my soul,
> The mind is the standard of the man.[8]

With this new self-respect and this new sense of dignity, the negative peace of the South was gradually undermined. And the tension which we notice the day, today, in the area of race relations can be explained by this revolutionary change in the Negro's evaluation of his nature and destiny and his determination to struggle and sacrifice until the sagging worlds of segregation have been finally crushed by the battering rams of rugged justice. This is the meaning of the whole crisis.

Now this determination on the part of the Negro to struggle and to struggle, until segregation and discrimination have passed away, springs from the same longing for human dignity that motivates oppressed peoples all over the world. This is not only a nation in transition, but this is a world in transition. There are approximately two billion four hundred million people in this world, and the vast majority of these people live in Asia and Africa. More than one billion five hundred million of the people of the world live on these two continents—six hundred million in China, four hundred million in India and Pakistan, two hundred million in Africa, a hundred million in Indonesia, and about eighty-six million in Japan, and all of these people constitute more than one billion five hundred million of the people of the world; and over the years most of these people have lived under the pressing yoke of some foreign power. They have been exploited economically, dominated politically, segregated and humiliated by some other power, but now they are gradually gaining their freedom. And there is a determination on the part of people, oppressed people, all over the world to gain this freedom and this human dignity, so that the struggle of the Negro is a part of this *great* struggle all over the world. It's a struggle on the part of oppressed peoples in general and the Negro in America, in particular. It is not something that will

---

8. These lines are a composite of passages from William Cowper's "The Negro's Complaint" (1788) and Isaac Watts's "False Greatness" (1706). See note 5 to "The 'New Negro' of the South: Behind the Montgomery Story," June 1956, p. 283 in this volume. This passage does not appear in "Non-violent Procedures." King stated instead: "His religion revealed to him that God loves all his children, and that the important thing about a man 'is not his specificity but his fundamentum,' not the texture of his hair or the color of his skin, but the texture and quality of his soul."

suddenly disappear.[9] Realism impels us to admit that the struggle will continue until justice becomes a reality.

But the great question, the basic question, in the face of all of this is this question: How will the struggle be waged? How will the oppressed peoples of the world wage their struggle against the forces of injustice, the forces of oppression? And there are two basic answers to this question. One is to resort to the conventional methods of violence and hatred. We all know the danger of this method. Violence creates many more problems than it solves. And the oppressed peoples of the world cannot afford to flirt with retaliatory violence. And there is a voice crying through the vista of time saying, "He who lives by the sword will perish by the sword." [10] And history is replete with the bleached bones of nations who refused to listen to the words of Jesus at this point. The method of violence would be both impractical and immoral. If this method becomes widespread, it will lead to terrible bloodshed, and that aftermath will be a bitterness that will last for generations. So we must all pray and hope and work that the oppressed peoples of the world will not use the method of violence to stand out against oppression and injustice.

There is another method which can serve as an alternative to the method of violence, and it is a method of nonviolent resistance. This is an important method, a significant method, and it is a method that I would like to recommend, a method that all of the oppressed peoples of the world must use if justice is to be achieved in a proper sense. There are several basic things that we can say about this method of nonviolent resistance, this technique of nonviolence, and these things are basic, these things are important, and understanding this method and this technique in confronting the problems of discrimination and of segregation and standing out against the forces of injustice. The first thing that can be said about this method is that it is not a method of submission or surrender. And there are those who would argue that this method leads to stagnant complacency and deadening passivity, and so it is not a proper method to use. But that is not true of the nonviolent method. The nonviolent resister is just as opposed to the evil that he is protesting against as a violent resister. Now it is true that this method is nonaggressive and passive in the sense that the nonviolent resister does not use physical aggression against his opponent. But at the same time the mind and the emotions are active, actively trying to persuade the opponent to change his ways and to convince him that he is mistaken and to lift him to a higher level of existence. This method is nonaggressive physically, but it is aggressive spiritually. It is passive physically, but it is active mentally and spiritually. So that the first thing about the method of passive resistance, or the method of nonviolent resistance, is that it is not a method of surrender, or a weapon, or a method of submission, but it is a method that is *very* active in seeking to change conditions, and even though it is passive it is still resisting.

---

9. In the article King added: "It is also sociologically true that privileged classes rarely ever give up their privileges without strong resistance. It is also sociologically true that once oppressed people rise up against their oppression there is no stopping point short of victory." He also did not provide the numerical breakdown of the world's colonized population.

10. Matthew 26:52.

There is another basic point about this technique of passive resistance, and it is this: That this method, in this method, the nonviolent resister seeks to lift or rather to change the opponent, to redeem him. He does not seek to defeat him or to humiliate him. And I think this is very important, that the end is never merely to protest but the end is reconciliation. And there is never the purpose behind—this method is never to defeat or to humiliate the opponent. Now the method of violence seeks to humiliate and to defeat the opponents, and therefore it leads to bitterness. The aftermath of the method of violence is bitterness. But the method of nonviolence seeks not to humiliate and not to defeat the oppressor, but it seeks to win his friendship and his understanding, and thereby and therefore the aftermath of this method is reconciliation.[11]

We must come to see, and all of those who struggle against injustice must come to see it, that the tension at bottom is not between races. As I like to say in Montgomery, the tension in Montgomery is not between seventy thousand white people and fifty thousand Negroes. The tension is at bottom a tension between justice and injustice. It is a tension between the forces of light and the forces of darkness. And if there is a victory, it will not be a victory merely for fifty thousand Negroes. If there is a victory for integration in America, it will not be a victory merely for sixteen million Negroes, but it will be a victory for justice, a victory for goodwill, a victory for democracy. And so the aim must always be to defeat injustice and not to defeat the persons who are involved in it. This method of nonviolence seeks to win the friendship and the understanding of the opponent, rather than to defeat him or to humiliate him.

Another basic factor in the method of nonviolent resistance is that this method does not seek merely to avoid external physical violence, but it seeks to avoid internal violence of spirit. And at the center of the method of nonviolence stands the principle of love. Love is always the regulating ideal in the technique, in the method of nonviolence. This is the point at which the nonviolent resister follows the Lord and Savior Jesus Christ, for it is this love ethic that stands at the center of the Christian faith. And this stands as the regulating ideal for any move or for any struggle to change conditions of society.[12]

Now I realize that to talk about love can be something very sentimental. I realize that it can end up as empty words. It's very easy to say, "Love your oppressor." It's very easy to say, "Love your enemy." It's very easy to say, "Pray for those that despitefully use you." But it can be empty talk unless we understand the real meaning of this love.[13] Now we all know, we must be frank enough to admit that you cannot love your enemy or your oppressor like you love your personal friends, or like you love your wife, or your husband. And I don't think it means that. That is not the meaning of love at this point.

---

11. In the article King added: "The aftermath of non-violence is the creation of the beloved community."

12. In "Non-violent Procedures" King replaced these three sentences with: "In struggling for human dignity the Negro must not succumb to the temptation of becoming bitter or indulging in hate campaigns. To retaliate with hate and bitterness would do nothing but intensify the existence of hate in the universe. Along the way of life, someone must have sense enough and morality enough to cut off the chain of hate. This can only be done by projecting the ethics of love to the center of our lives."

13. The four preceding sentences do not appear in "Non-violent Procedures."

The Greek helps us out a great deal. It talks about love in several senses. It talks about *eros*. And *eros* is a significant type of love, *eros* is a sign of aesthetic love. Plato talks about this love a great deal in his dialogue with Phaedrus. It is, it boils down to a romantic love. It is craving for something, and it has with it a bit of affection, an affectionate feeling.

And then there is another type of love that we talk about a great deal, it's a love that we have for personal friends. The Greek talks about it in *philia*. And it is a type of love, it stands on the basis of reciprocity. It has with it that mutual taint; it loves because it is loved. But then the Greek comes out with something higher, something that is strong, something that is more powerful than *eros* or any other type of love. It talks about *agape*, and *agape* is understanding goodwill for all men. *Agape* seeks nothing in return. It is a redemptive love. It is a love of God working within men. And so when men move to the point of *agape*, they love not because the individuals are so wealthful to them, not because it's anything they like so much about the individuals, but they love them because God loves them. They love them because they are wealthful to God, and this is the meaning of *agape*. It is a love that loves a person that does a evil deed, while hating the deed that the person does. And this is the type of love that can redeem. It is a transforming love. And this is the type of love that we talk about, and that we are supposed to live about in this method of nonviolent resistance. It is a love that can change individuals. It can change nations. It can change conditions.

Well I cannot close without mentioning another aspect of the method of non-violence. Another thing that goes along with this method, a basic belief that goes along with it. And it is the belief that the universe is on the side of justice. The nonviolent resister has great faith in the future. And there is a belief that, at bottom, *justice* will triumph in the universe over all of the forces of injustice. People are frequently asking me and people in Montgomery: How is it that we continue to move on and continue to walk after seven or eight months? How is it that we continue to burn out our automobile tires and keep going amid all of the tension? Well, my wife answered the question a few days ago in a matter quite satisfactory to me. One reporter was asking her how it was that she remained so calm in the midst of all of the pressure of the situation, how she was able to keep moving in the midst of all of the tension and constant flux. And I never will forget her words, "We believe we are right, and in believing that we are right, we believe that God is with us." And that is the answer, that is the answer that eventually comes to the aid of the passive resister.

We have the strange feeling down in Montgomery that in our struggle for justice we have cosmic companionship. And so we can walk and never get weary, because we believe and know that there is a great camp meeting in the promised land of freedom and justice.[14] And this belief, and this feeling that God is on the side of truth and justice and love and that they will eventually reign supreme in this universe, this comes down to us from the long tradition of our Christian faith. There is something that stands at the center of our faith. There is a great epic. There is a great event that stands at the center of our faith which reveals to us that God is on the side of truth and love and justice. It says to us that Good Friday

---

14. This line is from the spiritual "There Is a Great Meeting in the Promised Land."

may occupy the throne for a day, but ultimately it must give way to the triumph and beat of the drums of Easter. It says that evil may so shape events that Caesar will occupy the palace and Christ the cross, but one day that same Christ will rise up and split history into A.D. and B.C. so that even the life of Caesar must be dated by his name. There is something in this universe that justifies Carlyle in saying, "No lie can live forever." There is something in this universe that justifies William Cullen Bryant in saying, "Truth crushed to earth will rise again." And there is something in this universe that justifies James Russell Lowell in saying, "Truth forever on the scaffold, wrong forever on the throne, yet that scaffold sways a future, and behind the dim unknown stands God within the shadow keeping watch above his own." [15] And this is what the method of nonviolent resistance says to the individual engaged in the struggle. And this is why the nonviolent resister can suffer and not retaliate, because he has this strong faith in the future. This is a method, this is a technique, and this is a procedure. It is not at all without precedent. A brown man tried it in India. He looked over at the powerful British empire and he noticed all over vast and intricate military machinery. And in the midst of looking at all of this, something said to him—and he said to himself, "We cannot use this method." And so he decided to confront physical force with an even greater force, namely soul force. And this brown man, Mahatma Gandhi, was able to free his people from the political domination and the economic exploitation inflicted upon them by Britain. And so those four hundred million people stand out today with their freedom through the method of nonviolent resistance.

And God grant that we will continue to move on all men of goodwill, and all those who are confronted with oppression in this world will move on with this method. Not with the method of violence, not with the method of retaliatory violence, not with any method that seeks to retaliate, but the method that seeks to redeem. And whenever we decide to do this, we will be able to emerge from the bleak and desolate midnight of man's inhumanity to man and to the bright and glittering daybreak of justice and freedom and brotherhood for all people. God bless you. [*applause*]

At. ABAC-ABHSP.

---

15. See a discussion of these passages in note 8 to "The Death of Evil upon the Seashore," 17 May 1956, p. 260 in this volume.

From Septima Poinsette Clark

30 July 1956
Monteagle, Tenn.

In the spring of 1956 Clark had been fired as a public school teacher in Columbia,
South Carolina, when she refused to resign from the NAACP, as required by a new state

law prohibiting public employees from belonging to the organization.[1] *Determined to
carry on her civil rights activism, she then became director of workshops at Highlander
Folk School. King replied to her letter on 16 August.*[2]

Rev. & Mrs. M. L. King
Dexter Ave. Baptist Church
Montgomery, Alabama

Dear Rev. & Mrs. King:

The staff and director of Highlander Folk School invite you as a guest to spend
a week or two with them.

The mountain top is cool and delightful especially at nights and we feel that
you and your family can relax here in comfort. You deserve this and more for
your courage.

For your information; room, board, and transportation will be furnished you.
You may choose to come in during a workshop and stay on.

The enclosed folder will give you dates to choose from. You may write or call
Monteagle 164 collect.

Sincerely yours,
[*signed*] Mrs. Septima P. Clark
Workshop Director

ALS. MLKP-MBU: Box 14A.

---

1. Septima Poinsette Clark (1898–1987), born in Charleston, received her B.A. (1942) from Bene-
dict College in South Carolina and her M.A. (1945) from Hampton Institute in Virginia. Clark began
teaching in 1916 and four years later campaigned against job discrimination in the teaching profession. Clark later joined the NAACP and participated in a class action suit that in 1945 established
teacher pay equity. Recruited by Myles Horton to work at Highlander, Clark became an influential
leader in the civil rights struggles of the late 1950s and early 1960s. She was instrumental in creating
citizenship schools throughout the South and served as director of education for the SCLC. She was
one of the few women to serve on SCLC's staff and executive board. Her autobiographical publications include *Echo in My Soul* (1962) and *Ready from Within* (1986).

2. See pp. 349–350 in this volume.

From Medgar Wiley Evers

31 July 1956
Jackson, Miss.

*After meeting King at the NAACP national convention in San Francisco in June,
the organization's Mississippi field secretary invites King to speak in Jackson.*[1] *King*

---

1. Medgar Wiley Evers (1925–1963), born in Decatur, Mississippi, graduated from Alcorn A&M College in 1952. He served as the NAACP's first field secretary in Mississippi from 1954 until 1963 and was

declined the invitation on 16 August, prompting Evers to invite him on several other occasions. King would eventually speak in Jackson on 23 September 1959 for a meeting sponsored by the Southern Christian Leadership Conference.

Rev. Martin L. King, Jr.
389 South Jackson Street
Montgomery, Alabama

Dear Rev. King:

I am quite sure you do not remember me, but I managed to shake your hand and introduce myself at the National Convention, as being the field secretary for the NAACP in the State of Mississippi, and, at which time, I asked if it were possible to have you come to Jackson to speak to our branch here. You said that you would consider it. I am therefore, at this time, inviting you to speak to us on the first or second Sunday in October, or <u>on any other date</u> that will be convenient for you.

We, the NAACP here, feel that your presence would do more to bring together our ministers and the people of Jackson than any other person or incident conceivable.

In a recent conversation with Dr. Allan Knight Chalmers, who visited Jackson, he mentioned your having been a ministerial student in his class at Boston University.

Please let me hear from you immediately, and may God bless you.

Respectfully yours,
[*signed*]
Medgar W. Evers
Field Secretary

MWE:mes

TLS. MLKP-MBU: Box 62.

---

a determined advocate of school integration, voter registration, and boycotts of discriminatory businesses. When Emmett Till was lynched in 1955, Evers and other NAACP leaders secured media coverage of the situation, found witnesses, and helped them leave the state after they testified at the trial of Till's murderers. In 1957 Evers became one of the first officers of SCLC but resigned later that year because of an NAACP policy forbidding its staff members from holding positions in other organizations. He was assassinated by a white supremacist on 12 June 1963 outside his Jackson home.

1 August 1956
[*Montgomery, Ala.*]

King responds to Jernagin's 21 July request that King consider becoming executive secretary of the National Fraternal Council of Churches, an alliance of fourteen African-American denominations with eight million members. On 3 July King had received an award for "distinguished Christian service" at the organization's annual meeting in Birmingham. Jernagin, chair of the group's executive committee, thought that King should "not only serve the people in Montgomery, Alabama but serve the entire Negro church in America and bring about a victory for the race such as we have never had."[1]

Dr. W. H. Jernagin, President
National Sunday School and B.T.U. Congress
1728 Webster Street, N.W.
Washington 11, D.C.

Dear Dr. Jernagin:

On returning to Montgomery, I found your letter and I discovered that you had made several calls seeking to contact me. I am very sorry that I missed you. I had to postpone our initial engagement because I received a subpoena to appear in court to serve as a witness for the State in an injunction against the NAACP.[2] At the last minute I was notified that the case was postponed until the following week. So I came on to New York any way. After thinking over the proposition which you have suggested concerning the executive secretaryship for the Fraternal Council of Churches, I have concluded that maybe I have an obligation to stay in Montgomery for a while longer. I feel that the confidence that the people have in me and their readiness to follow my leadership have thrust upon me a responsibility that I must follow through with. If I would leave at this time I am sure that it would not be understandable to a large segment of the group. However, I would be more than happy to discuss it with you, as well as some of the bishops. As you continue to think through it, feel free to contact me, and I am open to suggestions and conferences at any time.

I hope everything goes well with you and Mrs. Jernagin. I am sure that you are

---

1. William H. Jernagin (1869–1958), born in Mashulaville, Mississippi, graduated from Jackson State College. After serving churches in his home state and Oklahoma, he became pastor of Mt. Carmel Baptist Church in Washington, D.C., in 1912. In addition to his work with the National Fraternal Council of Churches, he served as president of the National Baptist Sunday School and Baptist Training Union Congress from 1926 until his death.

2. See John Patterson to King, 12 July 1956, pp. 319–320 in this volume.

having a most profitable vacation. I will look forward to hearing from you soon and to seeing you in the National Baptist Convention in Denver.

Sincerely yours,

M. L. King, Jr.,

Minister

MLK:b

TLc. MLKP-MBU: Box 63A.

To Rae Brandstein

1 August 1956
[*Montgomery, Ala.*]

King turns down an invitation to speak at the annual conference of the National Committee for Rural Schools on 17 November. Brandstein, the organization's executive secretary, rescheduled the conference for 15 December to accommodate King, who accepted the revised invitation on 20 August.[1] Formed in 1948 by Benjamin McLaurin and other members of the Brotherhood of Sleeping Car Porters, the committee sent food, clothing, books, seeds, fertilizer, and other materials to southern blacks suffering economic hardships as a result of their civil rights activism. In this letter King applauds their efforts to establish a cooperative general store in Clarendon County, South Carolina, where the local Citizens Council initiated reprisals against those fighting for school desegregation.[2]

Mrs. Rae Brandstein, Executive Secretary
National Committee for Rural Schools, Inc.
112 East 19th Street
New York 3, New York

Dear Mrs. Brandstein:

I was more than happy to talk with you by phone a few days ago. Your letter and the enclosed check were received within two days after our telephone conversation. Thanks a million for your continued interest in our behalf.

---

1. Rae Brandstein, born in New York City, studied at the University of Berlin, Columbia's School for Journalism, and Rand School for Social Science in New York. Before organizing the National Committee for Rural Schools she was the educational director and an organizer for the Congress of Industrial Organizations, an area coordinator for the Labor League for Human Rights, and a union representative on New York's War Labor Board.

2. The committee sent more than $500,000 worth of materials to Clarendon County blacks during 1956. See remarks by Joe Black, a member of the National Committee for Rural Schools (NCRS), at 15 December NCRS conference, reprinted in Joseph F. Wilson, *Tearing Down the Color Bar: A Documentary History and Analysis of the Brotherhood of Sleeping Car Porters* (New York: Columbia University Press, 1989), pp. 294–295. See also King's conference address, "Desegregation and the Future," 15 December 1956, pp. 471–479 in this volume.

After checking my calendar, I find that I have made a previous commitment
for the same date that you are desirous of my speaking for your annual Confer-
ence-Luncheon. But for this, I would be more than happy to serve you. I had
thought for a while that it would be possible to make both engagements since the
other engagement is in the evening. But after checking plan schedules I find that
it is absolutely impossible. Please know that I regret this very deeply. It is even
more regretable in the light of the fact that you have taken such a personal interest in me and my family. Please feel free to call on me at any other time.

Let me again commend you for the project you are undertaking in Clarendon
County. Such a general store will solve many problems for the Negro community.
More and more this type of thing will have to be done if the Negro is to stand up
amid the economic reprisals that he is confronting in the southland. Such a project is both economically sound and morally praiseworthy. The good will that you
have evinced through the great work that you are doing will long be remembered. Those of us who stand amid the midnight of injustice are able to see signs
of the daybreak of justice and freedom because of the noble and courageous
stands and attitudes that you are taking.

Mrs. King sends her best regards. We are looking forward with great anticipation to meeting you personally. Please give our regards to Kenneth and Mamie
Clark.[3] We were very sorry to hear of the passing of their dear friend.

Sincerely yours,
M. L. King, Jr.,
Minister

MLK:b

TLc. MLKP-MBU: Box 63.

---

3. Kenneth Bancroft Clark (1914–) married Mamie Phipps (1917–1983) in 1938. Clark, born in Ca-
nal Zone, Panama, earned his B.A. (1935) and M.S. (1936) at Howard University and his Ph.D. (1940)
at Columbia University. He taught psychology at City College of New York from 1942 to 1975. A board
member of the National Committee for Rural Schools, he introduced King at its 15 December 1956
conference. He later served as the organization's vice president.

To Clair M. Cook

1 August 1956
[*Montgomery, Ala.*]

*King accepts the annual Social Justice Award from the National Religion and Labor
Foundation, sharing the award with Senator Herbert H. Lehman of New York and
Father John La Farge. Previous recipients included Thurgood Marshall, George
Meany, Walter Reuther, and Eleanor Roosevelt. King received the award on 24 April
1957 in New York.*

Dr. Clair M. Cook, Executive Director[1]
National Religion and Labor Foundation
3494 1/2 North High Street
Columbus 2, Ohio

Dear Dr. Cook:

This is just a note acknowledging receipt of your very kind letter of July 26, informing me that I have been selected to receive the annual award of the National Religion and Labor Foundation. I cannot begin to say how happy I am to know that I have been chosen for such an award. I will gladly accept the award with deep humility and profound gratitude.

I will be looking to hear from you concerning future developments. As soon as the date is set, please inform me so that I can place it on my calendar.

I am very happy to know that you are a fellow alumnus of Boston University. If I remember correctly, I read a portion of your dissertation on "Ethical Relativism in the thinking of Rheinhold Niebuhr." [2]

With kindest regards.

Yours very truly,
M. L. King, Jr.,
Minister

MLK:b

TLc. MLKP-MBU: Box 67.

---

1. Clair M. Cook, born in Hartland, Minnesota, received his B.A. (1932) from Hamline University in St. Paul and his Th.D. (1953) from Boston University. He was ordained as a Methodist minister in 1935 and served churches in the northeast before joining the Religion and Labor Foundation in 1954 as associate director, becoming executive director two years later. Cook also edited *Economic Justice*, the organization's news bulletin.

2. In a 27 August reply Cook informed King that "the dissertation to which you refer was not mine but that of Marvin Cook, who was there at the same time."

From E. S. Hope

1 August 1956

The son of longtime Morehouse president John Hope sends a contribution of $100 and reports that newspapers in Beirut, Lebanon, where he taught at American University, were covering the Montgomery protest.[1]

---

1. Edward Swain Hope (1901–1991), born in Atlanta, Georgia, earned a B.A. from Morehouse College, a B.S. and an M.S. from Massachusetts Institute of Technology, and a Ph.D. from Columbia University. After serving as Howard University's superintendent of building and grounds (1932–1944), Hope became the first African-American lieutenant commander in the U.S. Navy. Hope joined Howard University's faculty as a professor of civil engineering in 1947. In 1951 he was appointed chairman of American University's civil engineering department in Beirut.

Rev. Martin Luther King, Jr.
Dexter Avenue Baptist Church
Montgomery, Ala.
U.S.A.

Dear Rev. King:

There has been considerable mention of the Montgomery strike in the local Arabic press and the fight against segregation and for first class citizenship is being watched with interest in many parts of the world. It is surprizing to see how big a spread is given to such news about the American Negro. The treatment he receives greatly influences the attitude of many people and countries toward the United States.

e have just read in Ebony some of the details of the movement in Montgomery. I was delighted to find that a Morehouse man was leading the fight. I am sure that my father, the late John Hope, former president of Morehouse, would fully approve of your movement. Enclosed is my check for one hundred dollars to assist in it. Best wishes for success.

Enclosed also is a set of reports which we have sent out each year and a reprint on Engineering Education at this university. I think you might be interested in reading a little of our experiences during five years in the Middle East.

I am leaving here on the 17th of this month for my sabbatical leave and will be a guest at the Massachusetts Institute of Technology next year. My address will be 102 Crawford St., Boston, Mass. I hope that I may have the opportunity of seeing you and personally congratulating you for success in a fight that for the sake of the world as well as ourselves, must be won.

Sincerely
[*signed*] ESH
E. S. Hope

TLI. MLKP-MBU: Box 60.

Testimony to the
Democratic National Convention,
Committee on Platform and Resolutions

11 August 1956
Chicago, Ill.

More than three hundred people testified before the platform and resolutions committee during six days of hearings at the 1956 Democratic National Convention in Chicago. Reacting to eventual nominee Adlai Stevenson's casual suggestion that the Democratic platform should endorse the Brown v. Board of Education *decision, southern segregationists argued vehemently in opposition. Roy Wilkins of the NAACP and labor leaders George Meany, Walter Reuther, and A. Philip Randolph were among those who testified in favor of a strong civil rights plank.*

King's testimony, originally scheduled for 10 August, was postponed until the following day. John W. McCormack, chair of the committee and majority leader of the House of Representatives, scheduled King as the day's first witness and asked him to offer a prayer as well. In his testimony, King urges the committee to ensure that "the Federal Government take the necessary executive and legislative action to implement the desegregation decisions of the Supreme Court," perhaps even to the point of withholding federal funds from public schools "where there is willful refusal to comply" with court-ordered desegregation. King left immediately afterward to receive an award that evening in Buffalo from the Alpha Phi Alpha fraternity. The convention adopted a compromise plank that did not specifically support the Supreme Court's rulings but did condemn "the use of force to interfere with the orderly determination of these matters by the courts." [1]

DR. KING: Oh God our Gracious Heavenly Father we thank Thee for the privilege of assembling here this morning.

We thank Thee for all of the opportunities of life and as we stand together today and discuss vital matters confronting our Nation and confronting the world, we ask Thy guidance be with us in all of our deliberations and help us at all times to seek to do those things which are high, noble and good, and to make our Nation a great Nation, a nation that follows all of the noble precepts of the Christian Religion and all of the noble precepts of democracy.

Grant, O God that as we move on we will move toward that city which has foundations whose builder and maker is God. Amen.

CHAIRMAN MCCORMACK: You are now recognized, Dr. King.

DR. KING: Mr. Chairman, Members of the Platform and Resolutions Committee of the Democratic Party:

First I might say that I am very happy to have the opportunity of being here this morning and making this presentation and I want to express my appreciation to the Committee for affording me this opportunity.

As you know, I come from Montgomery, Alabama, and I come representing the Negro citizens of that City as President of the Montgomery Improvement Association. [2]

We, the Negro citizens of Montgomery, Alabama, wish to stress the urgent need for strong federal action in the area of civil rights. There is hardly any issue confronting the nation today more crucial than the question of civil rights. To overlook this issue would mean committing both political and moral suicide. The question of civil rights is one of the supreme moral issues of our time.

Many tragic occurrences have taken place in the South in recent months to place in jeopardy the basic rights guaranteed every citizen by the Constitution. Elements in the South have risen up in open defiance. The legislative halls of the

---

1. Donald Bruce Johnson and Kirk Porter, eds., *National Party Platforms, 1840–1956* (Urbana: University of Illinois Press, 1956), p. 542. King's associates were disappointed with the platform.

2. These introductory comments, as well as the prayer, do not appear in King's prepared text. Otherwise, his testimony as transcribed by the secretary of the committee does not vary significantly from his prepared text. See also "Statement Before the Democratic National Convention, Committee on Platform and Resolutions," 11 August 1956.

South ring loud with such words as "nullification" and "interposition." Methods of defiance range from the economic reprisals of the deep South to the tragic reign of bombings, beatings and mob rule. Many noble citizens are losing jobs because they stand in accord with the decisions of the Supreme Court on desegregation.

But, even more, all types of conniving methods have been used to prevent Negroes from becoming registered voters. Foremost among the civil rights of citizens in a democracy is the right to participate in the government through free exercise of the franchise, yet in the attempt to achieve this basic right of democracy, numerous persons have confronted insuperable difficulties. Some have even been killed because they sought to qualify as registered voters.

Most of these glaring denials of basic freedoms are done in the name of "States' Rights." But States' Rights are only valid as they serve to protect larger human rights. We have no opposition to state government, and we are not at all advocating a centralized government with absolute sovereign powers. But we do feel that the doctrine of States' Rights must not be made an excuse for insurrection. Human rights are prior to and therefore more basic than States' Rights, and whenever human rights are trampled over by States' Rights, the Federal Government is obligated to intervene for the protection.[3]

The Federal Government has a basic responsibility to guarantee to all of its citizens the rights and privileges of full citizenship. The state of affairs in the South has come to such a point that the only agency to which we can turn for protection is the Federal Government. Without this protection we will be plunged across the abyss of mob rule and tragic anarchy. We are sorry that the situation is such that we must mention these unpleasant things. But candor and realism impel us to stress the desparateness of the situation. We face a situation in which the hard facts are that law and order have broken down insofar as the protection of the Negro and the enjoyment of his rights as a citizen are concerned.

The Negro in his efforts to achieve the securing of his rights is determined to employ only the orderly processes of law. We will act within the framework of legal democracy without violence or force. We will not succumb to the temptation of flirting with retaliatory violence or indulging in hate campaigns.

In seeking a strong civil rights plank we are not seeking to defeat or humiliate the white man, but to help him as well as ourselves. The festering sore of segregation debilitates the white man as well as the Negro. We realize that the present tension is not so much between white people and Negro people, but between justice and injustice, between the forces of light and the forces of darkness. And if there is a victory for civil rights, it will be a victory not merely for 16,000,000 Negroes, but a victory for justice and democracy.

We must make it clear that we stand firmly against any form of segregation. Segregation is evil. Segregation is not only rationally inexplicable, but morally scandalous. The underlying philosophy of segregation is diametrically opposed to the underlying philosophy of democracy and all the dialectics of the logi-

---

3. In his prepared text King ended this sentence with the phrase "of all its citizens."

cians cannot make them lie down together. If democracy is to live segregation must die.

We are mindful of the fact that there are those who are calling for a doctrine of moderation. Now, if moderation means pressing on toward the goal of justice with wise restraint and calm reasonableness, then moderation is a great virtue which all men should seek to achieve in this tense period of transition. But if moderation means slowing up in the move toward justice and capitulating to the whims and caprices of the guardians of a deadening status quo, then moderation is a tragic vice which all men of good will must condemn.

In the light of the foregoing, we urge the platform committee to seriously consider including the following recommendations in the Democratic platform:

1. That this party pledge itself to the support of all of the Civil Rights legislation necessary to protect the full citizenship rights of Negroes.

2. That the Federal Government take the necessary steps to insure every qualified citizen the right to vote without threats and intimidation.

3. That the Federal Government take the necessary executive and legislative action to implement the desegregation decisions of the Supreme Court.

4. That the Federal funds be witheld from public schools and public facilities where there is wilful refusal to comply with the Supreme Court's desegregation decisions.

5. That there be a revision of the Senate rule on cloture, thus restoring the rule of the majority and thereby removing the chief stumbling block to passage of civil rights legislation.[4]

In conclusion, I must say once more that the issue of civil rights is one of the supreme moral issues of our time. It is true that a firm stand for civil rights would tremendously increase our prestige in international affairs, and eliminate a convenient tool in the hands of Communistic propaganda. But the motive for making justice a reality in America must not be merely to compete with totalitarian powers. It must be done not merely because it is diplomatically expedient, but because it is morally compelling. The adoption by this Convention of a strong civil rights plank will aid us in emerging from the bleak and desolate midnight of man's inhumanity to man to the bright and glittering daybreak of freedom and justice.

TD. PDNC-MWalK: Box 104.

---

4. A letter to the committee from King and a biracial group, including such southern white liberals as Anna Holden and James McBride Dabbs, made recommendations similar to those in King's testimony but called on the Democratic Party to pledge federal assistance to local officials assigned to bring public schools into compliance with *Brown* (King et al., "Letter to the 1956 Democratic National Convention, Committee on Platform and Resolutions," August 1956). The adopted platform concurred that federal support would be required to combat racial discrimination and urged revision of Senate cloture rules. "While we were expecting a much better civil rights plank," organizer Benjamin McLaurin of the Brotherhood of Sleeping Car Porters told King, "I suppose we will have to make ourselves satisfied with the splinter that we got" (McLaurin to King, 28 August 1956).

"The Birth of A New Age,"
Address Delivered on
11 August 1956 at the Fiftieth
Anniversary of Alpha Phi Alpha in Buffalo

1956
Chicago, Ill.

The evening after testifying at the Democratic National Convention King delivered the featured speech at the fiftieth-anniversary convention banquet of the Alpha Phi Alpha fraternity in Buffalo. He received the Alpha Award of Honor for "Christian leadership in the cause of first class citizenship for all mankind." Other award winners that evening included Autherine Lucy, Thurgood Marshall, and Arthur Shores. In his address King suggests how Alpha men and other African Americans can best prepare for the challenges and responsibilities of the "new order" that is replacing the "old order" of colonialism abroad and segregation at home. Declaring that "we will have to rise up in protest" to usher in this "new age," King envisions "a beloved community . . . where men will live together as brothers." The speech was transcribed for publication in an anniversary booklet published by the fraternity later in 1956.

Thank you so much for your kindness Brother Alexander. Brother Stanley, Brothers of Alpha, Ladies and Gentlemen, I need not pause to say how happy I am to be here this evening and to be a part of this auspicious occasion.[1] I can assure you that this is one of the happiest moments of my life. As I look over the audience I see so many familiar faces and so many dear friends that it is a real pleasure to be here. I only regret that certain responsibilities elsewhere made it impossible for me to be in on the other part of the sessions. My heart was here and I was here in spirit. I am very happy to share the platform with so many distinguished Alpha men and so many distinguished American citizens and I say once more that this is a high moment in my life.

I would like to take just a moment to express my personal appreciation to our General President, Brother Stanley in particular, and to all of the Alpha brothers over the country in general for the moral support and the financial contributions that you have given to those of us who walk the streets of Montgomery. I can assure that these things have given us renewed courage and vigor to carry on. The thing that we are doing in Montgomery we feel is bigger than Montgomery and bigger than 50,000 Negroes, and I assure you that we always appreciate your kind words and your contributions. I can remember those days, very dark days, when many of us confronted a trial in court and I could look out in the court-room and see our very eminent General President. That made me feel very good as an Alpha man and I want to thank you for what you have done all along. But I

---

1. King refers to Raymond Pace Alexander, toastmaster for the evening, and Frank L. Stanley, Alpha Phi Alpha general president.

did not come here tonight to talk about Montgomery and I know it is getting late. I am sure you don't want to be bored with me too long and I am going to try to comply with your silent request.

I want to use as a subject, "The Birth of A New Age." Those of us who lived in the 20th Century are privileged to live in one of the most momentous periods of human history. It is an exciting age, filled with hope. It is an age in which a new world order is being born. We stand today between two worlds—the dying old and the emerging new. I am aware of the fact that there are those who would argue that we live in the most ghastly period of human history. They would contend that the deepest of deep rumblings of the discontent in Asia, and we have risings in Africa, the naturalistic longings of Egypt and the racial tensions of America, are all indicative of the deep and tragic midnight which encounters our civilization. They would argue that we are going backwards instead of forward, that we are retrogressing instead of progressing. But far from representing retrogression or tragic hopelessness, the present tension represents the necessary pains that accompany the birth of anything new. It is both historically and biologically true that there can be no birth or growth without birth and growing pains. Wherever there is the emergence of the new and the fading of the old, that is historically true and so the tensions which we witness in the world today are indicative of the fact that a new world is being born and an old world is passing away.

We are all familiar with this old world that is dying, the old world that is passing away, we have lived with it, we have seen it, we look out and see it in its international proportion and we see it in the form of Colonialism and Imperialism. We realize that there are approximately 2,400,000,000 people on the face of the globe and the vast majority of these peoples in the world are colored. About 1,600,000,000 of these people of the world are colored and most of these people, if not all of the colored people of the world, have lived under the yoke of Colonialism and Imperialism, fifty years ago to twenty-five years ago. All of these people were dominated and controlled by some foreign power. We could look over to China and see the 600,000,000 men and women there under the yoke of the British and the Dutch and the French. We could look to Indonesia we could notice the 100,000,000 there under the pressing yoke of the Dutch. We could turn our eyes to India and Pakistan and notice there are 400,000,000 brown men and women under the pressing yoke of the British. We could turn our eyes to Africa and notice the 200,000,000 black men and women there dominated by the British, the Dutch, the French and the Belgian. All of these people lived for years and centuries under the yoke of foreign power and they were dominated politically, exploited economically, segregated and humiliated. But there comes a time when people grow tired, when the throbbing desires of freedom begin to break forth. There comes a time when people get tired of being trampled over by the iron feet of the tramper. There comes a time when people get tired of being plunged across the abyss of exploitation, where they have experienced the bleakness and madness of despair. There comes a time when people get tired of being pushed out of the glittering sunlight of life's July and left standing in the pitying state of an Alpine November.

So with the coming of this time an uprising started and protest started and
these peoples rose up against Colonialism and Imperialism and as a result, out of

1,600,000,000 colored people in the world today, 1,300,000,000 are free. They have
their own government, their own economic system and their own educational
system. They have broken aloose from the evils of the Colonialism and they are
passing through the wilderness of adjustment, through the promised land of cultural integration, and if we look back we see the old order of Colonialism and
Imperialism thrown upon the seashores of the world and we see the new world
of freedom and justice emerging on the horizon of the universe. But not only
have we seen the emergence of this new order on the international scale, not
only have we seen the old order on the international scale, we have seen the old
order on the national scale. We see it on the national scale in the form of segregation and discrimination—that is the old order that we witness today passing
away. We know the history of this old order in America.

You will remember that it was in the year 1619 that the first Negro slave was
brought to the shores of this nation. They were brought here from the soils of
Africa and unlike the Pilgrim fathers who landed here at Plymouth a year later,
they were brought here against their will. For more than 200 years Africa was
raped and plundered, a native kingdom disorganized, the people and rulers
demoralized and throughout slavery the Negro slaves were treated in a very
[in?]human form. This is expressed very clearly in the Dred Scott Decision in
1857 when the Supreme Court of this nation said in substance that the Negro is
not a citizen of the United States, he is merely property subject to the dictates of
his owner.

Then came 1896 when the same court, the Supreme Court of the nation, in the
famous Plessy vs. Ferguson Case, established the doctrine of "separate but equal"
as the law of the land. Now segregation had moral and legal sanction by the highest court in the land and of course, they were always interested in the separate
aspect but never the equal and this doctrine "separate but equal" made for tragic
inequality. It made for injustice, it made for exploitation, it made for suppression,
and it went a long time but then something happened to the Negro himself. He
had traveled and he was getting more education and getting greater economic
power and he came to feel that he was somebody. He came to the point that he
was now re-evaluating his natural investments and he came to the point of seeing
that the basic thing about an individual is this fundamental, not in the texture or
the quality of his hair, but the texture and quality of his soul, so he could now cry
out with eloquent force. Fleecy locks and black complexion cannot scoff at nature's claim, skin may differ but affection dwells in white and black the same.
"Were I so tall as to reach the pole, or grasp the ocean with my span, It must be
measured by my soul, the mind is the standard of man." [2]

With this new sense of dignity, with this new self respect, the Negro decided to
rise up against this old order of segregation and discrimination. Then came May
17, 1954 in the same Supreme Court of the nation, passed unanimously the decision stating that the old "Separate Doctrine" must go now, that separate facilities

---

2. These lines are a composite of passages from William Cowper's "The Negro's Complaint" (1788)
and Isaac Watts's "False Greatness" (1706). See note 5 to the "The 'New Negro' of the South: Behind
the Montgomery Story," June 1956, p.283 in this volume.

are inherently unequal and that this segregation, therefore, on the basis of his race is to deny him equal protection of the law. With this decision we have been able to see the gradual death of the old order of segregation and discrimination.

We now see the new order of integration emerging on the horizon. Let nobody fool you, all the loud noises we hear today in terms of nullification and interposition are nothing but the death groans of the dying system. The old order is passing away, the new order is coming into being. But whenever there is anything new there are new responsibilities. As we think of this coming new world we must think of the challenge that we confront and the new responsibilities that stand before us. We must prepare to live in a new world.

I would like to suggest some things that we must do to live in this new world, to prepare to live in it, the challenges that confront us. The first thing is this, that we must rise above the narrow confines of our individualistic concerns, with a broader concern for all humanity. You see, this new world is a world of geographical togetherness. No individual can afford to live alone now. The nation cannot live alone for we have been brought together. This has been done certainly by modern man with great scientific insight. Man through his scientific genius has been able to draw distance and save time and space. He has been able to carry highways through the stratosphere. We read just the other day that a rocket plane went 1900 miles in one hour. Twice as fast as the speed of sound. This is the new age. Bob Hope has described this new age, this jet age; it is an age in which planes will be moving so fast that we will have a non-stop flight from New York to Los Angeles, when you start out you might develop the hiccups and you will hic in New York and cup in Los Angeles. This is an age in which it will be possible to leave Tokyo on a Sunday morning and arrive in Seattle, Washington on the preceding Saturday night. When your friends meet you at the airport and ask what time did you leave Tokyo, you will have to say I left tomorrow. That is this new age. We live in one world geographically. We face the great problem of making it one spiritually.

Through our scientific means we have made of the world a neighborhood and now the challenge confronts us through our moral and spiritual means to make of it a brotherhood. We must live together, we are not independent we are interdependent. We are all involved in a single process. Whatever affects one directly affects all indirectly for we are tied together in a single progress. We are all linked in the great chain of humanity. As one man said, that no man is an Island, entirely of himself. Every man is a piece of a continent and a part of a main. I am involved in mankind, therefore we will not send to know for whom the bells toll, they toll for thee.[3] We must discover that and live by it . . . if we are to live meaningfully in this one world that is emerging. But not only that, we must be able to achieve excellency in our various fields of endeavor. In this new world doors will be opening that were not open in the old world. Opportunities will come now that did

---

3. These three sentences are from John Donne's poem "Devotions upon Emergent Occasions" (1624). In later speeches King included longer quotations from the poem. See, for example, "Facing the Challenge of a New Age," 3 December 1956, pp. 456–457 in this volume.

not come in the past and the next challenge confronting us is to be prepared for these opportunities as they come.

We must prepare ourselves in every field of human endeavor. We must extend our interest and we must accomplish a great deal now to be prepared for these doors to be open. There are so many things, so many areas we need to be prepared in. We need more ingenuity. We have been relatively content with the relatively material possessions such as medicine, teaching, and law. All of these are noble and gracious but we must prepare ourselves. Doors will be opening in all of these areas and we need people, we need more kinds who can qualify in the area of engineering, more architects and even more in the medical profession. We need to do more in the area of specialization now because the opportunities are coming and we must be prepared. In this new world we can now compete with people, not Negro people. We must not go out to be a good Negro barber, a good Negro lawyer, a good Negro teacher, we will have to compete with people. We must go out to do the job. Ralph Waldo Emerson said in an Essay back in 1878 that, "If a man can write better books or preach a better sermon or make a better mouse trap than his neighbor, even if he builds his house in the woods, the world will make a beaten path to his door." [4] That will be increasingly true. We must be ready. We must confront the opportunities and we must be ready to go into these doors as they open.

No matter what area and all fields, we should be ready. We need more skilled laborers. We need more people who are competent in all areas and always remember that the important thing is to do a good job. No matter what it is. Whatever you are doing consider it as something having cosmic significance, as it is a part of the uplifting of humanity. No matter what it is, no matter how small you think it is, do it right. As someone said, do it so well that the living, dead, or the unborn could do it no better.[5] If your son grows up to be a street cleaner, sweep streets like Michelangelo painted pictures, sweep streets like Beethoven composed music, sweep streets like Shakespeare wrote poetry, sweep streets so well that all the hosts of heaven and earth will have to pause and say, "here lived a great street sweeper who swept his job well". If you can't be a pine on the top of the hill be a shrub on the side, but be the best shrub on the side of the hill. Be a bush if you can't be a tree, if you can't be a highway be a trail, if you can't be the sun be a star. It isn't by size that you win or you fail. Be the best of whatever you are and that is the second challenge, that we confront the issues of today and prepare to live in this new age.[6]

There is a third and basic challenge. We must prepare to go into this new age without bitterness. That is a temptation that is a danger to all of those of us who have lived for many years under the yoke of oppression and those of us who have

---

4. The source of this quotation, often attributed to Emerson, is uncertain; see note 6 to "Mother's Day in Montgomery," 18 May 1956, p. 266 in this volume.

5. When giving this speech to an Atlanta audience, King attributed the quotation to Benjamin Mays (see King, "Facing the Challenge of a New Age," 1 January 1957, Paul H. Brown Collection, in private hands).

6. King paraphrases the poem "Be the Best of Whatever You Are" (1926) by Douglas Malloch.

been confronted with injustice, those of us who have lived under the evils of segregation and discrimination, will go into the new age with bitterness and indulging in hate campaigns. We cannot do it that way. For if we do it that way, it will be just a perpetuation of the old way. We must conquer the hate of the old age and the love of the new age and go into the new age with the love that is understanding for all men, to have with it a forgiving attitude, it has with it something that will cause you to look deep down within every man and see within him something of Godliness. That something that will cause you to stand up before him and love him.

As we move in this transition from the old age into the new we will have to rise up in protest. We will have to boycott at times, but let us always remember that boycotts are not ends within themselves. A boycott is just a means to an end. A boycott is merely a means to say, "I don't like it." It is merely a means to awaken a sense of shame within the oppressor but the end is reconciliation. The end is the creation of a beloved community.

The end is the creation of a society where men will live together as brothers. An end is not retaliation but redemption. That is the end we are trying to reach. That we would bring these creative forces together we would be able to live in this new age which is destined to come. The old order is dying and the new order is being born. You know, all of this tells us something about the meaning of the universe. It tells something about something that stands in the center of the cosma, it says something to us about this, that justice eventually rules in this world. This reminds us that the forces of darkness cannot permanently conquer the forces of light and this is the thing that we must live by. This is the hope that all men of goodwill live by, the belief that justice will triumph in the universe and the fact that the old order is passing away and a new order is being born is an eternal reminder of that truth that stands at the center of our faith.

It is something there that says this, that iniquity may occupy the throne of force but ultimately it must give way to the triumphant Jesus on the throne of Egypt. It says to us that evil may prevail again and the Caesar will occupy the palace and Christ the cross, but one day that same Christ will rise up and split history into A.D. and B.C. so that even the life of Caesar must be dated by His name. There is something in this universe that justified Carlisle in saying, "No lie can live forever." There is something in the universe that justifies James Russell Lowell in saying, "Truth forever on the scaffold, wrong forever on the throne, yet that scaffold weighs the future and behind the demon, Wrong, stands God within the shadow, keeping watch above his own." There is something in the universe that justified William C. Bryant in saying, "Truth crushed down will rise again." That is the meaning of this new age that is emerging. This is the hope that we can live by.

Now I am about to close, but I cannot close without giving a warning signal. I have talked a great deal about this coming new age, about this age that is passing away and about this age that is now coming into being. There is a danger that after listening to that you will become the victims of an optimism covered with superficiality. An optimism which says in substance we can sit down now and do nothing because this new age is inevitable. We can sit down and wait for the rolling in of the wheels of inevitability, we don't need to do anything, it's coming anyway. We cannot be complacent. We cannot sit idly by and wait for the coming

of the inevitable. I would urge you not to take that attitude for it might be true
that this new age is inevitable but we can speed it up, the coming of the new age.
It might be true that old man segregation is on his deathbed but history has
proven that social systems have a great last minute breathing power. The van-
guards and the guardians of the status quo are always on hand with their obstacles
in an attempt to keep the old order alive. So that we are not to think that segregation will die without an effort and working against it. Segregation is still a reality
in America. We still confront it in the South and it is blaring in conspicuous
forms. We still confront it in the North in its hidden and subtle form. But if democracy is to live, segregation must die. Segregation is evil, segregation is against
the will of the Almighty God, segregation is opposed to everything that democracy stands for, segregation is nothing but slavery covered up with the niceties of
complexities. So we must continue to work against it.

We must continue to stand up, we must gain the ballot—that is important—
we cannot overlook the importance of the ballot. By gaining the ballot we will
gain political power and doing that we will be able to persuade the Executive and
Legislative branches of the government to follow the examples so courageously
set by the Judicial clan. We must continue to get the ballot. We must continue to
work through legislation and that is an important avenue, we can never overlook
that. It may be true that they cannot make them live more moral, that might be
true, I don't know. But that never was the intention of the law anyway. The law
doesn't seek so much to change a man's internal feelings but it seeks to control
the external effect of those internal feelings. So that we must continue to support
the N.A.A.C.P. which has done such a noble and courageous job in this area. They
may try to outlaw this organization in Alabama and Louisiana but it still remains
true that this is the greatest organization in the nation working for the Civil
Rights of our people.

Then, in order to gain this freedom and to move away from the cycles of segregation we have got to go down in our pockets and give some money. I assure
you that integration is not some lavish gift that the white man will pass out on a
silver platter while the Negro merely furnishes the appetite. If we are to gain it
we have got to work for it, we have got to sacrifice for it. We have got to pay for it.
We cannot use the excuse any more that we don't have the money. The national
income of the Negro now is more than 16 billion dollars, more than the national
income of Canada. We have the money, we can do it. We have it for everything
else that we want. We have the biggest and the finest cars in the world and we can
spend it for all those frivolities, now let us use our money for something lasting,
not merely for extravagances. I am not the preacher that would condemn social
life and recreational activities—those are important aspects of life—but I would
urge you not to put any of these things before this pressing and urgent problem
of Civil Rights. We must spend our money not merely for the adolescent and
transitory things, but this eternal, lasting something that we call freedom.

Finally, in order to do this job we have got to have more dedicated, consecrated, intelligent and sincere leadership. This is a tense period through which
we are passing, this period of transition and there is a need all over the nation
for leaders to carry on. Leaders who can somehow sympathize with and calm us
and at the same time have a positive quality. We have got to have leaders of this
sort who will stand by courageously and yet not run off with emotion. We need

leaders not in love with money but in love with justice. Not in love with publicity but in love with humanity. Leaders who can subject their particular egos to the pressing urgencies of the great cause of freedom. God give us leaders. A time like this demands great leaders. Leaders whom the fog of life cannot chill, men whom the lust of office cannot buy. Leaders who have honor, leaders who will not lie. Leaders who will stand before a pagan god and damn his treacherous flattery.[7]

God grant from this noble assembly, this noble assembly of fraternity men some of the leaders of our nation will emerge. God has blessed you, he has blessed you with great intellectual resources and those of you who represent the intellectual powers of our race. God has blessed many of you with great wealth and never forget that those resources came from people in the back doing a little job in a big way. Never forget that you are where you are today because the masses have helped you get there and they stand now out in the wilderness, not being able to speak for themselves, they stand walking the streets in protest just not knowing exactly what to do and the techniques. They are waiting for somebody out in the midst of the wilderness of life to stand up and speak and take a stand for them.

God grant that the resources that you have will be used to do that, the great resources of education, the resources of wealth and that we will be able to move into this new world, a world in which men will live together as brothers; a world in which men will no longer take necessities from the masses to give luxuries to the classes. A world in which men will throw down the sword and live by the higher principle of love. The time when we shall be able to emerge from the bleak and desolate midnight of man's inhumanity to man into the bright and glittering daylight of freedom and justice. That there will be the time we will be able to stand before the universe and say with joy—The kingdom of this world has become the kingdom of our Lord and our Christ! And he shall reign forever and ever! Hallelujah![8]

PD. In *The Golden Anniversary Story of Alpha Phi Alpha Fraternity, 1906–1956,* ed. Charles Wesley (Chicago: Alpha Phi Alpha, 1956), pp. 85–90; copy in MLKP-MBU: Box 10.

---

7. Cf. Josiah Gilbert Holland's "Wanted" (1872), in *Garnered Sheaves: The Complete Poetical Works of J. G. Holland* (New York: Scribner/Armstrong, 1873), p. 377: "God give us men! A time like this demands / Strong minds, great hearts, true faith, and ready hands; / Men whom the lust of office does not kill; / Men whom the spoils of office cannot buy; / Men who possess opinions and a will; / Men who have honor,—men who will not lie; / Men who can stand before a demagogue, / And damn his treacherous flatteries without winking!" In a 3 December 1956 speech that included these lines, King noted that he was paraphrasing Holland (see "Facing the Challenge of a New Age," p. 461 in this volume). See also King's use of Holland's poem in "Desegregation and the Future," 15 December 1956, p. 477 in this volume.

8. Revelations 11:15.

15 August 1956
Yellow Springs, Ohio

Morgan, president of a publishing firm, was a strong supporter of Koinonia Farm,
a Christian cooperative community in Sumter County, Georgia, formed in 1942 by
J. Martin England and Clarence Jordan. The integrated community had long been a
target of racist harassment. In March 1956, after Jordan became involved in an effort
to desegregate his alma mater, the University of Georgia, Koinonia suffered violent
reprisals and the collapse of its local customer base. Its roadside market was destroyed
by an explosion on 23 July, prompting the farm to expand its mail order business.[1]
King replied to Morgan's letter on 27 August.[2]

Rev. M. L. King, Jr., President
Montgomery Improvement Association
530 South Union Street
Montgomery, Alabama

Dear Mr. King:

You may remember our company as the one whose staff, white and colored
alike, chipped in an hour's pay a while back to help the bus boycott.

I am writing this time on an urgent matter in which your organization may be
able to help. You have probably heard of Koinonia Farm, Route 2, Americus,
Georgia. Founded eight years ago by a southern white Baptist minister who was
expelled from his church for preaching racial equality, this farm applies Christianity directly in the form of racial equality and common ownership, and, like
your movement, is dedicated to non-violence. It has grown now to include 1100
acres and about 50 men, women and children. It is an efficient outfit, well
equipped with houses, barns, trucks, tractors and modern irrigation. It has, also,
of course, a nice big mortgage.

As its strength and influence grew and its inter-racial habits became better
known, Koinonia has come under severe attack by southern reactionaries. To
have an operation like this carried on in the deep south, by white southerners,
would badly undermine their position. Not only has Koinonia run an inter-racial
children's camp and accepted a Negro family in membership, but lately one of
the leaders, a graduate of the University of Georgia, sponsored a Negro candidate
for that institution.

This summer an injunction was brought against the camp on phony grounds.

---

1. Ernest Morgan (1905–) did undergraduate work at Antioch College in Yellow Springs, Ohio,
and, while a student there in 1926, founded the Antioch Bookplate Company (later Antioch Publishing). In the 1930s Morgan chaired the Socialist Party in Ohio and campaigned for governor on its
slate. In 1949 he served on a Quaker–United Nations team that administered relief for Palestinian
refugees in the Gaza Strip.

2. See p. 355 in this volume.

The entire camp was then moved to Highlander Folk School (with which you are probably familiar) at Monteagle, Tennessee. Recently the roadside store run by Koinonia was severely bombed, and all the farm's insurance was cancelled. (That complicates the mortgage problem.) Children from Koinonia dare not appear on the streets of Americus without an adult. Tax inspectors go to great lengths to find technical errors in the farm books. Pressure is rising in various ways, but the farm community is standing firm.

One of the most dangerous threats is the gradually tightening boycott against the farm products. While Koinonia has many friends and enjoys a good business reputation, its enemies are slowly but surely cutting off its markets. It is at this point that your organization might help. Your members buy food. Might it not be possible for a special committee to be formed to work out some arrangement with Koinonia? Perhaps wholesale connections might be found, or possible a weekly food market could be set up. That would have to be worked out. It would mean a lot to the spirit of your members to extend fellowship and aid to a group of hard-pressed white southerners who are fighting the same battle. And it would strengthen them {(Koinonia)}, both fiancially and morally. I might mention that my younger son has spent the summer at Koinonia without pay, driving tractors and doing other farm work, to help pull them through.

I hope you will seriously explore the possibility of cooperating with Koinonia,

Sincerely,
[*signed*]
Ernest Morgan, President

jck
copies to Highlander, Koinonia

TALS. MLKP-MBU: Box 14.

To O. Clay Maxwell, Sr.

16 August 1956
[*Montgomery, Ala.*]

On 31 July King informed Maxwell, pastor of Harlem's Mount Olivet Baptist Church, that he would be in New York on 11 August and would be available to preach the following day. In his sermon, delivered to a congregation of 2,500, King mentioned the bus boycott only in passing, Instead he decried the "tragic secularism" and "moral relativism" into which American society had lapsed. Too many people, King asserted, believed that "it's all right to exploit others as long as you're dignified about it." We must "rediscover" two principles, he stated: that "all reality hinges on moral foundations" and that "all reality has spiritual control."[1] In this letter King thanks

---

1. Quoted in "'Slickness' Cited as Modern Evil," *New York Times*, 13 August 1956. This sermon is probably "Rediscovering Lost Values" (see the version in *Papers* 2:248–256).

Dr. O. Clay Maxwell, Minister
Mount Olivet Baptist Church
114 West 120th Street
New York 27, New York

Dear Dr. Maxwell:

There is a word in Catholic Theology called supererogation, which means in substance "more than justice requires. I can assure you that the kind hospitality that you and Mrs. Maxwell rendered to me on my visit to your church was a work of supererogation.

Words can never adequately express my appreciation to you. To have been in this great church was an experience that I will long cherish. The fellowship was rich indeed. The financial contribution was unsurpassable. All of these things added together result in making my visit to Mount Olivet one of the truly great experiences of my life. You will always be remembered for the great contribution that you have made to the christian Ministry and your big-hearted brotherly attitude.

Please give my best wishes to Mrs. Maxwell. I will look forward to seeing both of you in Denver.

Most sincerely,
M. L. King, Jr.,
President

MLK:j

TLc. MLKP-MBU: Box 61A.

---

2. O. Clay Maxwell, Sr. (1885–1973), was pastor of Mount Olivet Baptist Church for forty years. He helped found the Protestant Council of the City of New York in 1943, and in 1957 he became the first African American to receive the group's Distinguished Service Award. He also served as president of the National Baptist Sunday School and Baptist Training Union Congress. Maxwell headed the committee that organized King's 17 May sermon at the Cathedral of St. John the Divine (see "The Death of Evil upon the Seashore," pp. 256–262 in this volume).

To Septima Poinsette Clark

16 August 1956
[*Montgomery, Ala.*]

the school's twenty-fifth anniversary celebration a year later during the Labor Day weekend.

Mrs. S. P. Clark, Workshop Director
Highlander Folk School
Monteagle, Tennessee

Dear Mrs. Clark:

This is to acknowledge receipt of your very kind letter of July 30. Absence from the city for several days has delayed my reply.

Mrs. King and I were happy to learn of the invitation to the Highlander Folk School. Unfortunately, however, a series of previous committments make it impossible for us to accept this gracious invitation. It is with deepest regrets that we will be unable to attend.

We have long heard of the great and noble work being carried on by the Highlander Folk School. We look forward with great anticipation to the day that we will be able to accept such an invitation. I hope we will be able to come next summer.

Very sincerely yours,
M. L. King, Jr.,
President

MLK:j

TLc. MLKP-MBU: Box 14A.

To Homer Alexander Jack

20 August 1956
[*Montgomery, Ala.*]

In a 27 June letter, Jack mentioned to King an upcoming visit to Montgomery and offered to speak "on the life and meaning of Gandhi." King asked the Unitarian minister to fill Dexter's pulpit on 29 July, but Jack did not receive the invitation; he therefore cut his trip to the South short after visiting King, Sr., in Atlanta. On 1 August King again invited Jack to Montgomery, and on 12 August Jack delivered an address titled "From Gandhi to Montgomery: The Life and Teachings of Mahatma Gandhi." Gandhi saw passive resistance as a weapon against racism, Jack observed, and fought segregation successfully in South Africa for twenty years because he believed that "one determined individual, inspired by unquenchable faith, can stand up against the whole world and alter the course of history." Jack also compared Gandhi's protest methods with King's. "As with Gandhi, so with Dr. King—he confounds and baffles his opponents by the simple justice of his demands, by refusal to hate or retaliate." Jack's address was later excerpted in the Dexter Echo.[1]

---

1. "From Gandhi to Montgomery: The Life and Teachings of Mahatma Gandhi," *Dexter Echo,* 3 October 1956, pp. 1, 3.

Dr. Homer A. Jack, Minister   21 Aug
The Unitarian Church of Evanston   1956
1405 Chicago Avenue
Evanston, Illinois

Dear Dr. Jack:

May I express to you, on behalf of Dexter Avenue Baptist Church, our profound thanks for the signal contribution you made to our worship last Sunday
morning. I understand that your moving message was admirably attuned to the
occasion and, as you must have noted, made deep impact on the listeners. All
week long I have heard nothing but favorable comments concerning your message and your presence. I only regret that this engagement fell at a time when
most of our members were away on vacation. We will look forward to having you
again when our whole congregation will have the opportunity to hear you.

I would appreciate it very much if you could send a copy of your message. The
editor of our church paper has already requested a copy to be printed in the next
issue of the paper. Since I missed the message, it would mean so much if I could
at least read it. If this does not inconvenience you, we will look forward to your
sending it as soon as possible.

With all good wishes in your vital work, and with warm regards to you and Mrs.
Jack, in which Mrs. King joins me

Sincerely yours,
Martin L. King, Jr.,
Minister

MLK/j

P.S. Please send me Lillian Smith's address.

TLc. MLKP-MBU: Box 66.

To Marian and Nelson Fuson

21 August 1956
[*Montgomery, Ala.*]

*On 11 August Nelson Fuson, a Fisk physics professor who had been a conscientious
objector during World War II, and his wife, Marian, thanked King for his visits to
Fisk, noting that "several students we knew well needed just what you offered them in
understanding nonviolence now and in the struggle at hand." The Fusons also sent
King an etching of Gandhi.*

Mr. & Mrs. Fusons
1815 Morena Street
Nashville 8, Tennessee

Dear Mr. & Mrs. Fusons:

This is just a note to thank you for the etching of Mahatma Ghandi. This is the   351
first original picture that I have of Ghandi.

Due to my great admiration for Ghandi, this will remain one of the cherished gifts of my life. Please know that I will always remain grateful to you for your lasting contribution.

With warm personal regards, I remain

Sincerely yours,
Martin L. King, Jr.
President

MLK:j

TLc. MLKP-MBU: Box 17.

To Joffre Stewart

21 August 1956
[*Montgomery, Ala.*]

Stewart, who had written to King on 31 July, was a member of Peacemakers, a radical pacifist group founded in 1948. A delegation of Peacemakers had visited Montgomery to support the boycott.

Mr. Joffre Stewart
6114 S. May Street
Chicago 21, Illinois

Dear Mr. Stewart:

This is just a note to acknowledge receipt of your recent letter.

You make inquiry concerning the date that we decided to ask for complete desegregation on the bus. Unfortunately, I do not remember the exact date, but it came immediately after the Mayor announced the "get-tough policy." We had negotiated for several weeks to no avail. The City Commission insisted that what we were asking for could not be done on the basis of the present law; so we had no other alternative but to attack the structure of the law itself. It was at this time that we filed a suit in the Federal Court asking the Court to declare segregation unconstitutional in public transportation.[1]

Sincerely yours,
Martin L. King, Jr.,
President

MLK:j

TLc. MLKP-MBU: Box 65.

---

1. *Browder v. Gayle* was filed on 1 February 1956.

21 August 1956
Montgomery, Ala.

Billy Joe Nabors, an Alabama State College student, planned to enroll in the University
of Alabama. Nabors received guidance from Alabama Council on Human Relations
staff member Robert Hughes and FOR activist Glenn Smiley. On 15 August Smiley
asked King to alert his contacts in Tuscaloosa. Worried what Nabors's response might
be to a possible violent greeting, Smiley advised King to "spend some time" with
Nabors—"An hour or more might be the decisive factor in his remaining nonviolent in
the [face] of possible threats." After learning that the NAACP had decided not to
support his case, Nabors registered at Howard Law School instead.[1]

Rev. Glenn E. Smiley, Field Secretary
The Fellowship of Reconciliation
21 Audubon Avenue
New York 32, New York

Dear Glenn:

This is just a note to acknowledge receipt of your letter of August 15.

I was very happy to know of the approaching registration of Billy Joe Nabors in the University of Alabama. I was not aware of the fact that a Negro had been accepted in the University for the Fall Term. You can be assured that I will do everything possible to help in the present situation. I do not have any direct contact with the Leaders of the Negro Community in Tuscaloosa. However, I am sure that I can make such contact almost immediately.

The idea that you suggested concerning the possibility of Billy Joe Nabors coming to Montgomery to talk with me is a very good one. I will be more than happy to do this. If you could contact Mr. Nabors and see if he is interested in such an arrangement I would in turn contact him for such a meeting.

The idea of making the Sunday prior to Mr. Nabors registration in the University of Alabama a Day of Prayer is an excellent one. I will alert every church in the Community as well as the churches over the State to the need of making that Sunday a Day of Prayer for Billy Joe and the University of Alabama. Please feel free to contact me concerning any details that develop.

You have my prayers and best wishes for a great meeting in Chicago. Those of us who stand amid the bleak and desolate midnight of man's inhumanity to man are given new hope in the emerging day-break of Freedom and Justice through the noble work of such Organizations as F.O.R.

Sincerely yours,
[*signed*] Martin
Martin L. King, Jr.

MLK:hg

TLS. FORP-PSC-P.

---

1. See Robert Hughes to Glenn Smiley, 1 October 1956.

To Warren J. Bunn

24 August 1956
[*Montgomery, Ala.*]

*On 6 August Bunn had "strongly" urged the MIA to "continue the boycott until the
Supreme Court convenes in a body next year," even if a Supreme Court justice issued a
temporary ruling in favor of the boycotters.[1] If the court then ruled against the MIA
when it reconvened in October, Bunn and other members of the Brooklyn NAACP
feared that the boycott movement would suffer "complete demoralization and
disorganization." Bunn asked the MIA to "stand your ground, hold fast, and
wait . . . HELP IS ON THE WAY!" His labor and industry committee raised funds to
send a station wagon to Montgomery. In his answer King reports that the MIA had
decided to continue the boycott until the final ruling by the Supreme Court.*

Mr. Warren Bunn, Chairman of Labor & Industry Committee
Brooklyn Branch, NAACP
474 Summer Avenue
Brooklyn, New York

Dear Mr. Bunn:

This is just a note to acknowledge receipt of your very kind letter of August 6
making suggestions concerning our future strategy.

We are deeply grateful to you for these very helpful suggestions. We are very
happy to say that we decided some weeks ago to follow the very avenue that you
are recommending. The boycott will continue until a ruling comes down from
the Supreme Court.[2] This maybe a matter of several more months, but we intend
to stick it out to the finish.

We are very happy to know of your efforts in the direction of purchasing a
station wagon for Montgomery. Since we will have to go several months more, I
assure you that this will meet a real need.

Please know that we will always remain indebted to you and the fine people of
Brooklyn for your interest in our struggle for justice.

Sincerely yours,
M. L. King, Jr.,
President

MLK:j

TLc. MLKP-MBU: Box 63.

---

1. Warren J. Bunn (1914–1986) began his career as a factory worker in 1935. He worked for the E. R.
Squibb pharmaceutical company from 1939 until 1950, when he became an executive board member
of the AFL-CIO.

2. On 26 July the MIA executive board accepted the advice of its legal staff that "it would be wiser
to wait until the Supreme Court reconvenes this fall and render a decision on our case than to appeal
to one Supreme Court Justice for an immediate ruling on the same" (W. J. Powell, Minutes, MIA
Executive Board Meeting, 26 July 1956).

To Ernest Morgan

27 August 1956
[*Montgomery, Ala.*]

Mr. Ernest Morgan, President
Antioch Bookplate Company
Yellow Springs, Ohio

Dear Mr. Morgan:

This is just a note to acknowledge receipt of your letter of August 15 explaining the conditions confronting Koinonia Farm.

You can be assured that I will do everything possible to assist Koinonia Farm in the crisis that it is now confronting. I have always been deeply sympathetic with the noble work that is being done there. Just two nights ago, Howard Johnson, a resident of Koinonia, was our house guest. I was deeply moved as he unfolded to us the seriousness of the situation.

Thanks for your interest in Koinonia. I will be more than happy to comply with your request.

Cordially yours,
M. L. King, Jr.,
President

MLK:j
(Dictated by Rev. King, but signed in his absence.)

TLc. MLKP-MBU: Box 14.

From W. H. Jernagin

27 August 1956
Washington, D.C.

Jernagin continues his effort to convince King to become executive secretary of the National Fraternal Council of Churches, inviting him to discuss the matter at the upcoming meeting of the National Baptist Convention. King did not accept the position.

Reverend M. L. King, Jr.
309 S. Jackson Street
Montgomery, Alabama

My dear Reverend King:

Your letter of August 1 received while I was in Atlantic City, and contents duly noted. I regret very much that after thinking it through you feel that your leadership directly in the immediate community makes it necessary that you stay there. Of course, I had in mind for you to continue the leadership in that matter until it was through. As Executive Secretary of the National Fraternal Council of Churches you would be travelling over the country making contacts and could stop at Montgomery, Alabama any time you feel it is necessary, especially for the next year.

Do not think for a moment that I had in mind for you to discontinue your leadership in that movement, but that you would have a stronger force behind you in the final accomplishment of that task. Because the National Fraternal Council of Churches with 14 denominations and over 8 million members would be behind you in that task, as well as others which may occur.

We have a great fight on our hands in the South yet, and it takes a man like you with the spirit of God and non-violence to awaken the Negro community of America through the churches. Because two or three southern states already have made attempts to abolish the National Association for the Advancement of Colored People due to objection of its activities in their states; but, of course, there will always be a Negro church and a Negro preacher through whom you can work and keep informed of what they can do.[1] And by you and the N.A.A.C.P. working together, our cause will still have a defender.

Because of your fine work in Montgomery, you would not only attract the attention of the Negro church but you would also attract many white friends to help you put over the program of our race. And I do not know a better man in America who could do that as well as you. In fact this is your day and, also, this is your opportunity to become one of the leaders, not only of America, but of the world, in social adjustments.

I shall expect to see you in Denver. I will be stopping at the Park Lane Hotel. As soon as possible, we will arrange to have you speak with some of the Bishops of the various churches on this matter. Of course Bishop Green has written me that in case you did not accept, he had another man to recommend.[2] But I know that because of the fine spirit you exhibit in Montgomery that we do not have you equal at this time. Think over it, and I will see you in Denver.

Very truly yours,
[*signed*]
W. H. Jernagin

err

TLS. MKP-MBU: Box 63

---

1. Alabama, Louisiana, and Texas had obtained state court injunctions against NAACP activities.

2. Sherman Lawrence Greene (1886–?), an Atlanta resident and AME bishop for Georgia from 1951 to 1962, served as president of the National Fraternal Council of Churches. He was among the group of Atlanta leaders that King, Sr., assembled in February 1956 in an effort to persuade his son not to return to Montgomery.

To Dwight D. Eisenhower

27 August 1956
Montgomery, Ala.

*Two days after Montgomery minister and MIA executive board member Robert Graetz's
home was bombed, King and other Montgomery black leaders initiated correspondence
with the president, urging him to order an investigation of violence by white
supremacists acting with the complicity of local public officials. Presidential assistant
Maxwell M. Rabb acknowledged their letter on 25 October 1956; Department of Justice
officials responded on 7 September.[1]*

The President of the United States
Honorable Dwight D. Eisenhower
The White House
Washington, D.C.

Honorable Sir:

Continued threats, violence which has included bombings of homes on January 30, February 1, and August 24, 1956; the hangings in effigy of a Negro and a white man who "talked integration," and mass arrests authorized by city and state officials against Negroes, have tended to deprive Negroes of their civil rights and have left them without protection of the law here in Alabama.[2]

Public officials are members of White Citizens Councils whose purpose is to preserve segregation by economic reprisals against Negroes. These officials are doing nothing to prevent the violence. In fact, according to the local press, the Montgomery Journal (a copy of which is included), the city police of Montgomery led the procession to the down town public square when the effigies of the Negro and white man were hanged by a number of white men, some of whom were members of the White Citizens Councils. The effigies were allowed to remain there for over an hour before the mayor ordered them removed. Not one arrest was made in the case, yet there is a law against putting up signs of any kind in the down town area. (Newspaper pictures of the demonstrations and bombings are included).

As a result of the last bombing of a minister's home, the mayor attributed the incident to a publicity hoax on the part of Negroes to revive interest in the local Negro bus boycott against city transportation lines for abusive treatment.[3] (A fed-

---

1. See pp. 364–365 in this volume.

2. They refer to the bombings of the homes of King, E. D. Nixon, and Robert Graetz, respectively.

3. Gayle reportedly called the bombing "a publicity stunt," adding, "It seems strange that none of the occupants have been at home when other bombings have occurred" ("Graetz Denies Bomb Hoax," *Montgomery Advertiser*, 26 August 1956).

eral suit contesting the constitutionality of segregration laws on public intra-state transportation is at this time before the Supreme Court of the United States.) The "don't care" attitude of public officials toward such violence is manifesting itself throughout the city and state and encouraging hoodlums to continue. If something is not done to put a stop to it, further violence can be expected.

Hundreds of Negroes are being arrested daily on trumped-up charges and fined. The revival of the Ku Klux Klan is a constant threat and the robed members are allowed to demonstrate in the city without police interference whatsoever.

Thousands of Negroes in the city of Montgomery and the state of Alabama are deprived of their rights to vote, on the grounds that they "cannot successfully pass the test." As a result, unscrupulous men get into office on platforms of racial hate and provide no protection or justice for the minority race.

We, therefore, urge you to use the power of your office to see that the proper investigation is made in Montgomery and Alabama to the end that justice and law will prevail.

Respectfully yours,
[*signed*]
The Montgomery Improvement Association,
Reverend M. L. King, Jr., President
(50,000 members)
[*signed*]
Brotherhood of Sleeping Car Porters,
E. D. Nixon, President
[*signed*]
Inter-denominational Alliance,
Elder E. H. Mason, President
[*signed*]
Citizens Educational Committee,
Rufus Lewis, President

cc: U.S. Attorney General Herbert Brownell

THLS. WCFG-KAbE.

From Cecil A. Thomas

28 August 1956
Berkeley, Calif.

Thomas was one of Coretta Scott King's teachers in Marion, Alabama. As an administrator of the Stiles Hall University YMCA in Berkeley, he arranged King's appearance there on 15 May. Thomas reports on his efforts to build support for the bus

boycott and suggests that his wife, Fran, might assist King in writing a book.[1] *King*
responded to Thomas's letter on 2 October.[2]

28 Aug
1956

Dr. & Mrs. M. L. King
309 South Jackson St.
Montgomery, Alabama

Dear Martin and Coretta:

Our thoughts and prayers are very much with you these days as we read almost daily, of the things that are happening in Alabama. I have on my bulletin board the clipping of the A.P. release, yesterday, in the local paper which says "a Negro man was tossed into the air 'like a baby' and another was injured at a K.K.K. rally in Tuscaloosa."

We have followed with great interest the comments on the voting today on the "the freedom of choice plan."

The general reaction among our friends here is that it helped a great deal to have your speech in the August 3rd U.S. News and World Report and the article by Grover Hall attacking much of it.[3] We are glad that you encouraged Fran to type a copy of it, since some of the most interesting parts have been left out of the magazine article, as you probably noticed. So many people wanted to get your speech, so I got about 250 copies wholesale of the U.S. News and World Report and are letting people have them at the various meetings where we speak.

In two of the large White papers and two Negro newspapers, they used pictures of our group similar to the one I am enclosing from the Chronicle which has a very large circulation, especially on Sunday, when this article appeared. And as a result of these articles we have had more requests than we can even fill to come and show our colored slides and discuss what is happening in Montgomery. We have met with such groups as an open meeting in Rev. Bennett's church, a large noon meeting of the Fellowship of Reconciliation in San Francisco, a large

---

1. Cecil Thomas (1917–1969), born in Frankfort, Ohio, received his B.A. (1939) from Cedarville College in Ohio and his Ph.D. (1949) from Ohio State University. He and his wife, Fran Thomas, first became acquainted with Coretta Scott while teaching at Lincoln School in Marion, Alabama, between 1941 and 1943. Fran worked closely with Coretta and her older sister as their music instructor. They continued their relationship with Coretta Scott while she pursued music studies at Antioch College. Cecil Thomas was associate peace education secretary of the American Friends Service Committee from 1959 until 1966, when he became executive director of the National Committee on United States–China Relations.

2. See pp. 385–386 in this volume.

3. Thomas refers to the publication of King's prepared remarks to San Francisco's NAACP and a response to it by Grover C. Hall, editor of the *Montgomery Advertiser* (see King and Grover C. Hall, Jr., "Alabama's Bus Boycott: What It's All About," *U.S. News and World Report*, 3 August 1956, pp. 82–89).

NAACP membership meeting, four or five White churches and the Race Relations Committee of the Council of Churches through its Speakers Bureau are
encouraging all the churches in Berkeley have one member of the group come
to tell the story.[4] One church said they were sending $50 to you and when we read
in the paper of the arrest of some of the car pool drivers in Talahasee, we sent a
$20 offering from a meeting a couple of days ago to Rev. Steele.[5]

I hope that the short message from the 300 Quakers at our four day conference, showed some of the enthusiasm and real sense of support the group felt
after we discussed,—at great length with the entire group,—the spirit of the
approach which you are using. I am sure you will be hearing from some of these
Quakers from all up and down the west coast.

In fact, it was the kind of enthusiasm and interest evidenced there which
should make the {it} possible for us to bring Coretta to the west coast for some
concerts if she and Fran decide to try and work it out. Fran is still in Ohio and I
am not sure of what she is thinking about in regard to this but she will be back
this weekend.

I am also more certain than I was that if Martin and Fran decide that
they should experiment with Fran coming down to try to be of some help on the
book that we can get some real financial support to carry this idea along {from
Quakers.} The head of the American Friends Service Committee in southern California works closely with Mr. Hallock Hoffman, of the Fund for the Republic,
and he is interested in talking with him about financial support for the book and
for a documentary film, if you feel that now is the time to move ahead on either
one.[6]

Martin and Coretta, I want it very clearly understood that in no way am I urging
you to do any of these things if your spirit tells you that now is not the time. I
realize how busy you are and that you must make daily judgments as to what must
be done and what must be left undone. In no way have I made any commitments
but have tried to indicate that this is the situation with you. So if life is just to busy
or complicated to even think about these things now, please let me know so that
I will drop these matters. However, if this is the case we will stand by to help at
any time we can.

---

4. A group of white Bay Area activists accompanied the Thomas family and L. Roy Bennett, pastor
of San Francisco's First AME Zion Church and former MIA vice president, during a visit to Montgomery in late July. A photograph of their entourage appeared in the *San Francisco Chronicle* on 19 August 1956.

5. Thomas refers to Rev. C. K. Steele who headed a Tallahassee, Florida, bus boycott. On 26 May,
two Florida A&M female students refused to give up their seats and were arrested. On 28 May students
decided not to ride the buses and convinced local black residents to join the boycott. On 30 May
African-American church leaders organized the Inter-Civic Council (ICC) to continue the nonviolent
protest and elected Steele as president. See Steele to King, 23 October 1956, p. 404 in this volume.

6. In this letter to King Thomas enclosed a letter he had written to Hallock Hoffman on 27 August
in which he reported that King was "very interested" in writing a "short interpretative book about the
Montgomery movement, . . . but is handicapped because of time and limited resources for secretarial
help." Hoffman (1919—) served on the staff of the American Friends Service Committee from 1952 to
1954. He then joined the Fund for the Republic as a staff member and later became its secretary and
treasurer.

There is one important business matter which I would appreciate a reaction to in order that I can advise the executive secretary of the Council of Churches. He received a communication from a Harold Clements giving a Hope Street address asking for a list of churches in Berkeley and in California. He did not mention any connection with you or the M.I.A. or the Ministrial Association.[7] If this is a bona fide request in which you are interested, please let us know, so that we can cooperate with it, but I could not remember meeting Harold Clements while in Montgomery.

Almost every meeting where we talked about our Montgomery experience, we tell people of the meaningful experience we had in your home the morning, when you discussed the protest with us and lead us in prayer.

Probably you do not remember what you said but your prayer in which you asked for God's help as we worked on problems "gigantic in scope and chaotic in detail" made a lasting impression on us. Each one of us felt a little closer to God because of our close fellowship those few days with you, Martin and Coretta. I personally feel deeply in debt to you for challenging me to try to live more nearly in that spirit of reconciling love which Jesus exemplified. I shall always be grateful to you for this.

Sincerely yours,
[*signed*] Cecil
Cecil A. Thomas
Associate Secretary

CAT:jl

Enclosures

{P.S. Do you have the insurance worked out satisfactorily on the station wagons? Would appreciate pictures from you and Abernathys when they are available.}

TALS. MLKP-MBU: Box 67.

---

7. In his reply King reported that H. L. Clements was pastor of Mt. Zion AME Zion Church, L. Roy Bennett's former church, and an MIA executive board member (see King to Thomas, 2 October 1956, pp. 385–386 in this volume).

From Nannie H. Burroughs

28 August 1956
Washington, D.C.

Burroughs, a close friend of King's mother, Alberta Williams King, was the founder and president of the National Trade and Professional School for Women and Girls as well as president of the Woman's Auxiliary of the National Baptist Convention. A week before they would attend the group's annual convention in Denver, Burroughs asks

King if he knows of any teachers who had lost their jobs for being affiliated with the NAACP. She offers to employ such teachers at her school. King replied on 18 September.[1]

Rev. L. M. King, Jr.
309 South Jackson Street
Montgomery, Alabama

Dear Rev. King:

We are looking for two High School and Junior College teachers—one for English and History, and the other for Domestic Science and Sewing.

They must be Christian women of unimpeachable character. They must be personally clean and an example in sensible dress. There must be nothing slip-shod about them or their work.

It is reported that many teachers have not been reappointed because of their affiliation with the N.A.A.C.P. or other Civil Rights organizations

Do you know any such capable women who want to work in a Christian institution, in which they can help to develop fine womanhood for leadership.

Please let me know at once.

Sincerely yours,
[*signed*]
Nannie H. Burroughs, President

NHB/s

TLS. MLKP-MBU: Box 63A.

---

1. See pp. 370–371 in this volume.

From Kivie Kaplan

29 August 1956
Boston, Mass.

Longtime NAACP activist Kaplan was a leader of Reform Judaism and an executive of Boston's Colonial Tanning Company. He had established an acquaintance with King during the latter's years as a student in Boston and remained a close family friend.[1]

---

1. Kivie Kaplan (1904–1975), son of Lithuanian Jewish immigrants, joined the NAACP in 1932 and later succeeded Arthur Spingarn as president of the group, serving from 1966 until his death. He also served as vice chairman of the Union of American Hebrew Congregations.

Rev. Martin Luther King   30 Aug
530 So. Union St.   1956
Montgomery, Alabama

Dear Rev. King:

I haven't had a chance to write you, but I saw you and heard you at the Convention in San Francisco in June and I want to congratulate you on the most outstanding talk I have ever heard.

You certainly are a great help to the N.A.A.C.P. and I know that you did a wonderful job for our people in your city. Congratulations and keep up the good work!

I am very active in the N.A.A.C.P. and head up along with Dr. Mays the Life Membership drive and I am enclosing herewith one of our FIVE IMPORTANT BENEFITS pamphlet as well as our INVEST IN FREEDOM pamphlet, as well as other Life Membership pamphlets, and I hope that in your travels from time to time when you do run into important people, both White and Negro, who can afford to make an investment in freedom, that you will have our Life Membership drive in mind.

I realize your problems in Montgomery, but there are people who in addition to contributing to your fund, should be Life Members of our organization.

We prefer the cash, but we do accept payments over a period of either, two, three, five or even ten years at $50 a year.

Any help you can give us will certainly be appreciated.

I had hoped to invite you to stay at our home when you were coming up to the Ford Hall Forum in October, but Mrs. Kaplan and the writer are leaving for Europe on September 7th and will be out of the city when you come.

With best wishes, and kindest regards, I remain

Sincerely yours,
[*signed*]
Kivie Kaplan

kk:lf
encs

TAHLS. MLKP-MBU: Box 61.

From L. Harold DeWolf

30 August 1956
Boston, Mass.

DeWolf responds to his former student's 1 June letter, which has not been located.

Dr. Martin Luther King
The Montgomery Improvement Association
530-C South Union Street
Montgomery 8, Alabama

Dear Martin:

When I arrived at home I was delighted to find your personal letter of June 1st. You need have no misgivings about not having written earlier for I can well understand that your burden of work must be truly overwhelming in these days.

Your letter is a renewing inspiration to me as has been the marvelous leadership which you have given to our people in the south land during these last months. Indeed, the news concerning your leadership has gone throughout the world. I can testify that the self-discipline, courage, and faith of the people who are working with you in Montgomery have brought new courage and self-respect to many Christian people living under gross injustice in lands far across the sea.

Now that I am in the United States again I am wondering if there is anything that I could do which would be helpful to you. Please let me know. I shall be happy to share your reply ~~to~~ {with} others who I know would also be eager to assist you in this glorious struggle. Please call upon us.

May God continue to bless and sustain you and your family and associates and may He bring to you victory for <u>all</u> the people, for which you are making such great sacrifices.

With warmest personal regards, I am,

Cordially yours,
[*signed*] Harold DeWolf
L. Harold DeWolf

LHD:hh

TALS. MLKP-MBU: Box 15.

From Warren Olney III

7 September 1956
Washington, D.C.

Two Department of Justice officials, Assistant Attorney General Olney of the Criminal Division and Arthur B. Caldwell, chief of the division's Civil Rights Section, respond to the 27 August letter from Montgomery bus boycott leaders to President Eisenhower.[1]

---

1. Warren Olney III (1904–1978) was an Oakland, California, native who became a close associate of Earl Warren, serving with him in the Alameda County district attorney's office and, after Warren became California attorney general, as assistant attorney general. In 1953 Olney became assistant attorney general in charge of the U.S. Justice Department's criminal division. Olney helped draft the 1957 Civil Rights Act. Arthur Brann Caldwell (1906–1984) began working for the Department of Justice in 1935 and from 1951 to 1957 was chief of its Civil Rights Section. During the 1957 Little Rock desegregation crisis he was called upon to negotiate with Orval Faubus, governor of his home state of Arkansas.

Reverend M. L. King, Jr., President   8 Sept
The Montgomery Improvement Association   1956
530 South Union Street
Montgomery, Alabama

Dear Reverend King:

This acknowledges your letter of August 27, 1956 with respect to alleged threats
and violence directed against Negro citizens of Montgomery, including the
bombings of certain homes on January 30, February 1, and August 24 of this year.
Your letter also states that thousands of Negroes of the State of Alabama are being
deprived of the right to vote because of their race.

The information concerning the alleged violence, the activities of the White
Citizens Council and the local officers, does not appear to indicate violations of
federal criminal statutes. We are concerned however, with the statement concerning the alleged denial of the right to vote on the ground of race or color. If you
know of specific instances of this, and will furnish us with full information concerning the same, you may be assured that it will receive prompt and careful
consideration.

Sincerely,
WARREN OLNEY III
Assistant Attorney General
Criminal Division

By: [*signed*]
ARTHUR B. CALDWELL
Chief, Civil Rights Section

TLSr. MLKP-MBU: Box 66A.

From C. W. Kelly

8 September 1956
Denver, Colo.

*In an 18 July letter Kelly, pastor emeritus of Tuskegee's Greenwood Missionary Baptist
Church, had characterized King's leadership as a "missionary journey akin to Paul's
of old."* [1] *He added that "Paul never did it more effectively." Writing the day after
King delivered "Paul's Letter to American Christians" to an audience of ten thousand
at the seventy-sixth annual meeting of the National Baptist Convention in Denver,
Kelly*

---

1. Charles W. Kelly (1887–?), born in Columbia, Tennessee, received his B.A. from Fisk University
in 1913. After graduating from Oberlin Theological Seminary he became pastor of Tuskegee's Greenwood Missionary Baptist Church in 1920, serving there until his retirement in 1953. He was active in
the Tuskegee Civic Association and its several precursors. Kelly was close to Vernon Johns and other   365
Dexter pastors.

praises King's performance.[2] J. Pius Barbour also described the address in glowing terms: "Of course the center of attraction was THE KING. Never in the history of the Baptist Denomination has a young Baptist preacher captured the hearts and minds of the people as has young King. He just wrapped the convention up in a napkin and carried it away in his pocket."[3] Coretta Scott King sang at the gathering, and Alberta Williams King participated as organist for the Woman's Auxiliary. King responded to Kelly on 19 September, noting that "I always accept your compliments with profound gratitude and great humility."

My dear Friend, M. L:—

This brief word to say again how much I appreciated your message to the N.B.C. yesterday—It was indeed a masterpiece. You could hardly have improved on it. Your deliberateness, and calm dispassionate appeal to the very best in your huge audience, endeared you to their hearts with spiritual "hoops of steel." You will never be forgotten. The impression is everlasting. You spoke as a prophet and seer which you are—The imaginative "Letter from St. Paul" to American X[ns] was as vivid and real as any of the Pauline Epistles. You read the Epistle well, and be assured it will be "passed on to the churches," as the preachers will be talking about it always. Your emphasis on American X[ns] making little moral progress on their material progress, allowing their minds to outrun their hearts re— How right you were in your Epistle that they "were afraid to stand alone, and to be ostracised, capital's misuse of capitalism and their <u>love</u> of money, etc root of all evil re. How often have I stressed to my people their great error of "making a living instead of a life" I said just today, "If the white man was as smart in his heart as he is in his head, how much better off our world would be. The real body of X, the church, "has no disunity." The 256 denominations belie this fact. But we <u>must</u> have unity if not uniformity. And, so, on and on your Epistle rang true with truth, which gave it "power unto salvation" to your <u>believing</u> hearers. You may not have known it, but many, myself and others, along with Marshal Shepard wept like babies, and couldn't help ourselves, nor did we try.[4] My, boy, God used you because you can be used by Him—and like Joseph, God is with you, because <u>you</u> are with God.[5]

Keep on keeping on and may God bless and keep you Ever.

Sincerely
Yours + His
[*signed*] Chas W. Kelly

P.S. I was so happy, too, to hear your wife sing so feelingly.

ALS. MLKP-MBU: Box 66.

---

2. On 4 November King gave the sermon at Dexter, reprinted on pp. 414–420 in this volume. King later published a version of the sermon in *Strength to Love* (1963).

3. *National Baptist Voice*, September 1956.

4. Marshall Lorenzo Shepard, Sr. (1899–1967), was pastor of Mount Olivet Tabernacle Baptist Church in Philadelphia.

5. Matthew 1:23.

14 September 1956
[*Montgomery, Ala.*]

Having been warned by his doctor that exhaustion was threatening his health, King declines Terrill's invitation to give five lectures in November. Terrill, pastor of Zion Hill Baptist Church, was, like King, Sr., active in the Atlanta Missionary Baptist Association and the Atlanta District Sunday School and Baptist Training Union Congress, the sponsors of the annual Leadership Training School to which King was to give the evening chapel sermons.[1] Terrill had extended the invitation to King during the National Baptist Convention's annual meeting; he then confirmed it in a 17 September letter written before he received this letter from King. "To me," Terrill had written, "you are the kind of man who comes once in a lifetime and Atlanta will be out to hear you and give you the type of recognition that you so rightly deserve." King later agreed to participate in the 1957 training school, delivering the closing chapel sermon on 8 November.

Dr. L. M. Terrell
151 Chicomanga Place, S.W.
Atlanta, Georgia

Dear Dr. Terrell:

This is to confirm our conversation in Denver concerning the possibility of my coming to Atlanta to serve as guest speaker for your annual study course.

After returning to Montgomery and checking my schedule very scrutinizingly I find that circumstances make it necessary for me to decline your gracious invitation. The first reason is a very practical one. My physician has insisted that I slow up for my own health. Secondly, things will be of such a nature in Montgomery for the next two or three months that I cannot afford to be out of the city more than one or two days at a time. The third reason grows out of a rather large responsibility that I have undertaken. I am in the process of writing a book, and in order to complete it at the stipulated time it will be impossible for me to accept any more speaking engagements for the rest of the year. Please know that I regret this very deeply. It is even more regretable in the light of the fact that you have taken such a personal interest in me and the cause which I am representing. Moreover, it is regretable in the light of the fact that Atlanta is my home town. But with the present difficulties I am sure you will understand. If you will take

---

1. Terrill offered his sympathies to King in his 6 October reply: "We have not ceased praying for you for we understand the persecutions through which you are passing." Levi M. Terrill (1899–1971), born in Mobley, Mississippi, attended Morehouse with King, Sr. He earned a B.A. (1928) and a B.D. (1950) from Morehouse and an M.A. (1951) from Atlanta University. He taught at the Morehouse School of Religion from 1953 to 1971. He became president of the General Missionary Baptist Convention of Georgia in 1957 and then served as vice president of the National Baptist Convention for more than ten years. Terrill was among those King, Sr., convened to ask his son to leave Montgomery after the indictments in February 1956.

these factors under consideration and hold my invitation over until next year, I am sure the pressure of events will have let up by that time, and I will be very happy to serve you.

Very sincerely yours,
M. L. King, Jr.,
President

MLK:b

TLc. MLKP-MBU: Box 66.

To Warren Olney III

17 September 1956
[*Montgomery, Ala.*]

Olney replied to King's letter on 2 October. [1]

Honorable Warren Olney III
Assistant Attorney General
Criminal Division
United States Department of Justice
Washington, D.C.

Dear Mr. Olney:

This is to acknowledge receipt of your very kind letter of September 7. We are very happy to know of your concern with alleged denials of the right to vote on the ground of race or color in the State of Alabama. Enclosed you will find material to give concrete proof of the assertion that Negro citizens of Alabama face insuperable difficulties in attempting to gain the ballot. You will find enclosed a survey of voting practices in the State of Alabama made by the Southern Regional Council. [2] This is the most authentic study that has been made in this area in the last few months. Also enclosed is a list of all of the counties in the State of Alabama designating the number of white voters and the number of Negro voters.

---

1. See pp. 386–387 in this volume.

2. King enclosed a report entitled "Registration of Negro Voters in Alabama in 1954," written in 1956 by James E. Pierce, research secretary of the Alabama State Coordinating Association for Registration and Voting in Birmingham and member of the MIA executive committee. Pierce recounted some of the difficulties encountered by African Americans while attempting to register and surveyed voter registration numbers for Alabama counties. The report was commissioned by the Southern Regional Council, an Atlanta-based interracial organization that sought to improve southern race relations. It was the parent body of the Alabama Council on Human Relations and other state councils.

You will notice that in several counties there is not a single Negro voter. In most 18 Sept of these counties the Negroes outnumber the whites two or three to one. In one 1956 county, namely, Macon County, the officials of the state have absolutely refused to appoint a registration board simply because a number of Negroes sought to become registered voters.

We would appreciate your looking into this matter immediately. It is my conviction that foremost among the civil rights of citizens in a Democracy is the right to participate in the government through free exercise of the franchise. If the Federal Government does not step in to assure this right, it will probably never be given.

Sincerely yours,
M. L. King, Jr.,
President

MLK:b

enclosures
cc: Honorable Herbert Brownell, U.S. Attorney

TLc. MLKP-MBU: Box 66A.

Minutes of MIA
Executive Board Meeting, by W. J. Powell

18 September 1956
Montgomery, Ala.

These minutes, written by MIA recording secretary W. J. Powell, report on a special meeting called to discuss confidential information about an "anticipated or possible danger," perhaps a threat by the North Alabama White Citizens Council to disrupt the bus boycott. In the 21 September MIA newsletter editor Jo Ann Robinson reported that a leader of that group had announced plans to come to Montgomery on 16 September to "divulge plans on how 'they were going to break up the Negro bus boycott.'" She added that the engagement was "mysteriously cancelled."

Minutes of special meeting of the Executive Board of the Montgomery Improvement Association, Tuesday, September 18, 1956.

The meeting was called to order by the President at 11:00 A.M. Opening prayer was offered by the Rev. S. Sanders.

Those present were: Dr. M. L. King, Jr., H. H. Johnson, Rev. J. W. Bonner, A. Sanders, H. J. Palmer, R. B. McCain, G. Franklin Lewis, R. W. Hilson, R. J. Glasco, W. J. Powell, Robert Graetz, White, R. B. Binion, R. D. Abernathy, Mrs. A. W. West, Mrs. Erna Dungee, Mr. P. E. Conely, Mrs. Jimmie Lowe, Attorney Charles Langford, Mrs. Jo Ann Robinson, Mr. Rufus Lewis. Several ministers, not members of the board were voted the privilege of staying in the meeting.

Rev. Robert Graetz was presented to give information which was responsible for the calling of this committee.[1]

After Rev. Graetz had acquainted the body with confidential information which had ~~acquainted~~ come to him, the President stated that the course of action to be followed to meet the anticipated or possible danger was the question confronting the group.

After much discussion, it was moved and carried that this organization contact the U.S. Justice Department, the F.B.I., and influential local citizens in Washington, to acquaint them with the information which has come to us and seek their assistance and protection in this situation. It was further moved and carried that Governor James Folsom be contacted and informed of the situation before carrying out the decision of this body referred to immediately above.

The President appointed the following persons as members of the committee to contact the Governor: Rev. Robert Graetz, Mrs. Jo Ann Robinson, Attorney Charles Langford, Dr. M. L. King, Jr.

It was agreed that if a personal contact could be had in Washington with the Justice Department or F.B.I., the Rev. Robert Graetz and Dr. M. L. King, Jr. would constitute the committee.

Closing prayer was offered by Rev. G. Franklin Lewis.

The meeting then adjourned.

W. J. Powell, Secretary
M. L. King, Jr., President

TD. MLKP-MBU: Box 30.

---

1. Graetz may have presented information he received from Woodrow E. Draut, an agent in the Montgomery FBI office to whom Graetz reported on the bus boycott and received confidential information in return. Graetz considered the FBI as an ally whose activities deterred hostility and violence by local police and vigilantes. For more details on his participation in the bus boycott, see Graetz's autobiography, *Montgomery: A White Preacher's Memoir* (1991).

To Nannie H. Burroughs

18 September 1956
Montgomery, Ala.

Miss Nannie H. Burroughs, President
National Trade and Professional School for Women and Girls
Lincoln Heights
Washington 19, D.C.

Dear Miss Burroughs:

This is to acknowledge receipt of your very kind letter of August 28, making inquiry concerning two high school and junior college teachers. First I must apologize for being somewhat tardy in my reply. Absence from the city for several days accounts for the delay.

So far I have not been able to find qualified persons who are available for your two teaching positions. Up to this point we have not had too many teachers fired in the State of Alabama as the result of their affiliation in the NAACP and other civil rights organizations. Consequently, most of the teachers are still employed. However, I will be continually looking out for such persons, and if they are ever available I will be sure to contact you.

It was a real pleasure seeing you in Denver. Your remarks after my address were magnificent. You said in a few words more than most people could say in hours. It is always a real inspiration to listen to you. Let me thank you once more for the interest which you have taken in our struggle. I can assure you that your moral support and financial contributions have given me renewed courage and vigor to carry on.

With warm personal regards, I am

Sincerely yours,
[*signed*]
M. L. King, Jr.,
President

MLK:b

THLS. NHBP-DLC.

To William Cooper Cumming

18 September 1956
[*Montgomery, Ala.*]

King replies to one of the many letters he received after the prepared text of his 27 June speech to the NAACP appeared in U.S. News and World Report *on 3 August. In a 31 July letter Rev. Cumming had argued that the lengthy boycott had deepened "tensions and antagonisms" in Montgomery. While sympathetic with the boycott's aims, he suggested that tensions would ease if the MIA asked the bus company to run certain buses exclusively for African Americans.*

The Rev. William Cooper Cumming, Pastor
Westminster Presbyterian Church
Texarkana, Texas

Dear Rev. Cumming:

Thanks for your very kind letter of July 31, commenting on the article which appeared in The U.S. News and World Report. The idea of having the bus company to run a certain number of busses for Negroes only was once made as a suggestion but most of the people felt that that would be going backwards instead of forward. So the majority of people have the feeling that they would rather sacrifice by not riding the busses at all than accept any jim crow accommodations. At this point we are awaiting a decision from the United States Supreme Court which should be handed down within the next two or three months. We feel that this will clear up the whole matter.

Again let me thank you for your encouraging words. Such moral support and christian generosity are of inestimable value in the continuance of our humble efforts.

Sincerely yours,
M. L. King, Jr.,
President

MLK:mlb

TLc. MLKP-MBU: Box 67.

To Vernon Johns

18 September 1956
[*Montgomery, Ala.*]

On 27 September Johns, dean of the Maryland Baptist Center and King's predecessor at Dexter, accepted this invitation to return to his former church. On 9 December he delivered the anniversary sermon and the invocation at the closing meeting of the MIA's Institute on Nonviolence and Social Change.

Dr. Vernon Johns
Virginia State College
Petersburgh, Virginia

Dear Dr. Johns:

On the second Sunday in December 1956 Dexter Avenue Baptist Church will be observing her Seventy-ninth Anniversary. This is an annual event in which we seek to bring some of the outstanding preachers of the nation to deliver the sermon. We would like to extend the invitation to you to serve as guest preacher for this Seventy-ninth Anniversary Observance on Sunday, December 9 at the 11:00 O'clock Service. Both your presence and your message would be an inspiration to our church and the whole Montgomery Community. We hope very much that you will be able to accept the invitation. I would appreciate an early reply so that I can procede in setting up our church calendar.

Very Sincerely Yours,
M. L. King, Jr.

MLK/lmt

TLc. DABCC.

To Sally Canada

19 September 1956
[*Montgomery, Ala.*]

In an 8 September letter responding to King's U.S. News and World Report *article, Canada characterized King's writings as those of a "lunatic" and justified racial segregation on the grounds that "Negroes could never be equal to the whites—even the worst of them—that's God decision not the white man." Canada's letter was similar to many others King received.*

Mrs. Sally Canada
317 - 13th Street, Apt. 11
Huntington 1, W. Va.

Dear Mrs. Canada:

This is to acknowledge receipt of your recent letter in which you stated your views on segregation and the status of the Negro. I must confess that I am in total disagreement with your position. I feel that segregation is totally unchristian, and that it is against everything the Christian religion stands for. This, however, does not at all cause me to hate those who believe in segregation. I feel that we should seek to persuade the perpetrators of segregation through love, patience and understanding good will that it is wrong. God grant that the day will come when we all can live in this society as brothers and children of a common father on a non segregated basis. It is still true that in Christ there is neither Jew nor Gentile (Negro nor white) and that out of one blood God made all men to dwell upon the face of the earth.

Again, thank you for your interest and your willingness to correspond with me.

Cordially yours,
M. L. King, Jr.,
President

MLK: mlb

TLc. MLKP-MBU: Box 5.

To Manuel D. Talley

19 September 1956
[*Montgomery, Ala.*]

On 17 August Talley, action director of the Los Angeles—based National Consumers Mobilization,[1] informed King that in March his organization had considered a

---

1. Committed to nonviolence, the National Consumers Mobilization sought to protect consumers from discrimination in public places and in employment practices by investigating complaints, negotiating conflicts, pursuing litigation, and organizing consumer boycotts.

*sympathy boycott against Los Angeles Transit Lines, a subsidiary of National City
Lines, but now considered it unwise. Talley sought King's guidance on the question,
noting that the MIA's struggle was not with the bus company but against state and
local segregation ordinances.*

Mr. Manuel D. Talley, Action Director
National Consumers Mobilization
P.O. Box 6533
Los Angeles 55, California

Dear Mr. Talley:

Thanks for your very kind letter of August 17. First, let me apologize for being
somewhat tardy in my reply. Absence from the city plus the accumulation of a
flood of mail account for the delay.

After reading your letter I think you have analyzed the situation correctly. It is
true that the bus company has softened a great deal since the Supreme Court's
decision, and that the stumbling block which we confront at this time is really the
city officials of Montgomery. In the light of this, I would not advocate your boycotting the Los Angeles Transit Lines. We certainly appreciate your interest in
our struggle, and your willingness to help us at every point. Your moral support
has given us renewed vigor and courage to carry on. I am very happy to know of
your interest in the Tallahassee situation. I am sure that whatever you can do
there will be highly appreciated.

Sincerely yours,
M. L. King, Jr.,
President

MLK:mlb

TLc. MLKP-MBU: Box 63.

To Lafayette Dudley

19 September 1956
[*Montgomery, Ala.*]

*After reading King's April 1956 article "Our Struggle" for a research project, Dudley,
in a 3 September letter, praised King's "psychological, philosophical and sociological"
insights, adding that King's former roommate, Philip Lenud, had introduced them in
a Boston barbershop during the summer of 1955. Dudley noted that while attending
college he had "long pondered starting a crusade for my brothering [brethren?]" and
asked for King's advice: "Do you feel that I should get an early start before I finish
school?"[1] King encourages Dudley and suggests that he talk with two prominent*

1. Dudley attended Boston Junior College from September 1955 to May 1957.

clergymen at Boston University, Howard Thurman and Allan Knight Chalmers. On   20 Sept
15 December Dudley sent King a rambling letter in which he proposed forming a new   1956
organization to "motivate constructive social change."

Mr. Lafayette Dudley
33 Braddock Park
Boston, Massachusetts

Dear Lafayette:

Thanks for your very kind letter of September 3. I should say that I definitely remember meeting you in Boston through our mutual friend Philip Lenud. I am very happy to know of your progress and to know of your great interest in our struggle.

Since I have such an accumulation of mail before me as the result of being out of the city for several days, it will be impossible for me to go into any detailed discussions of the question which you raise. I do feel, however, that the time is always right to start a crusade for better human relations. If this is your interest I think it would be a fine idea to start now working in that direction. Many great movements have started in universities where students were dedicated to a great cause. As I remember the Wesley brothers started their reforms while students at Oxfor University in England which eventually led to the great Methodist Church.[2] I could point to so many other great movements that have been started by students with noble vision. I hope you will continue to consider this idea. Maybe at some future date I will have the opportunity to sit down and talk with you concerning the whole matter. In the meantime I would suggest that you talk with my good friends Dr. Howard Thurmond and Dr. Allen Knight Chalmers. Both of these men could give you excellent advice in this area.

With warm personal regards.

Sincerely yours,
M. L. King, Jr.,
President

MLK: mlb

TLc. MLKP-MBU: Box 16.

---

2. King refers to Charles Wesley (1707–1788) and John Wesley (1703–1791).

To Bayard Rustin

20 September 1956
[*Montgomery, Ala.*]

18 September of the Consultative Peace Council, a group composed of the major American peace organizations, which would take up the "Montgomery situation" as "the first and major item of the agenda." Rustin added that "first-hand information" from King would "do more than anything else to get these organizations working more vigorously in the interest of the Improvement Association." After receiving King's letter Rustin sent a copy to A. Philip Randolph with the notation, "Enclosed you will find a very interesting letter from Rev. King which I should like to share with you." [1]

Dear Bayard,

It was a real pleasure talking with you this morning. I must apologize for being somewhat tardy in my reply to your letter. Absence from the city plus the accumulation of a flood of mail account for the delay.

I will seek to answer your questions to the best of my ability. We may go about it by answering them one by one.

1. What is the immediate financial situation?

At present our finances are holding up fairly well. However, in the last three or four months our out-of-town contributions have dropped down tremendously. This is understandable in the light of the fact that the publicity on the Montgomery situation has lessened over the last few months. There is still need for all of the financial aid that we can get.

2. How much are you spending weekly?

We are spending at present approximately five thousand dollars ($5,000.00) weekly. Most of this money is used for the transportation system and the running of the office.

3. What does the financial picture look like for the future?

As I said above, we are still in need of financial aid. If we can continue to get a reasonable sum of money from outside sources I believe we will be able to raise enough in the local community to keep us going indefinitely. We seek at every point to cut down on expenses wherever we can, but the real problem is that as time goes on the wear and tear on the automobiles increases which leaves a tremendous repair bill.

4. What is the attitude of the people in the Negro community?

The people are just as enthusiastic now as they were in the beginning of the protest. They are determined never to return to jim crow buses. The mass meetings are still jammed and packed and above all the buses are still empty. Every now and then we will hear some complaint, but the vast majority of the people are dedicated to sacrificing and sticking out to the finish. I think also there is a growing commitment to the philosophy of non-violence on the part of the Negro community. Even those who were willing to get their guns in the beginning are gradually coming to see the futility of such an approach.

5. What are the major problems you are up against?

We are still confronting pressure from reaction forces. For instance there is still the attempt to block our transportation system. The policies have been cancelled

---

1. Rustin to Randolph, September 1956.

on more than half of our station wagons, and we have confronted insuperable difficulties trying to get them reinsured. You can see what it means to our transportation system to have about ten station wagons out of operation. We have had these station wagons out of operation for more than a week simply because they are not insured. This seems to be the major problem confronting us at this time.[2]

6. What is the effect of the White Citizens Council and Ku Klux Klan intimidation and action?

The actions of these two organizations in Alabama have given our people more determination to press on for the goal of integration. There is a general feeling that these organizations will destroy themselves through internal decay. There is good evidence for this view because these organizations are putting as much pressure on white people as they are on Negroes. (The white persons who don't agree with their point of view.)

7. What is the legal situation at present and what strategic plans have you for carrying on the struggle?

At present we are awaiting a decision of the Supreme Court. As you know the Federal District Court, in a decision back in May, declared segregation unconstitutional in public transportation. In order to delay the situation the city and state appealed the decision to the United States Supreme Court. The court will reconvene in October. Our lawyers feel that the Supreme Court will render its decision before Christmas or by January at the latest.[3] This case is a priority case since an injunction is involved, so it will be one of the first cases on the docket when the court reconvenes. We will continue to refuse to ride the buses until this decision has been rendered. While waiting for the decision we will use our mass meetings to put greater emphasis on non-violence as a way of life and as a technique and also seek to prepare the people to go back to integrated buses with a sense of dignity and discipline. We are also hoping to instill within the minds of the people the great implications of the bus protest. We are seeking to show that it is much larger than a bus situation, but that it is just one aspect of the total question of integration in the south.

The legal situation in which I am involved will probably continue this fall. It is probable that my case will come up in November in the state case appeal. The briefs have already been filed. They are so large that the cost to file the briefs was more than one thousand dollars ($1,000.00).

In order to carry on our legal battle we will continually need money. It seems

---

2. On 8 September 1956 several insurance companies announced the cancellation of policies covering seventeen of the twenty-four church station wagons used by MIA car pools. King later suggested that Citizens Councils had pressured the insurance companies to do so (see "We Are Still Walking," December 1956, p. 448 in this volume). On 27 November, with the assistance of an Atlanta insurance company, the MIA received a Lloyd's of London policy, retroactive to 18 September, for $11,000 per vehicle.

3. Following a hearing on 11 May, the federal district court in Montgomery ruled on 5 June against the city in *Browder v. Gayle*. The panel delayed enforcement until the city had exhausted its appeals. On 13 November the U.S. Supreme Court issued a per curiam opinion upholding the district court. Montgomery officials immediately petitioned the court to reconsider its ruling, indicating that they would continue to enforce segregation until all legal avenues had been exhausted. On 17 December the court rejected their petition.

to be the strategy of the White Citizens Council to keep us bogged down in litigation as much as possible. As one pro-segregationist said recently: "We are prepared for a century of litigation."

I hope this will in some way help you answer these pressing questions. I only regret that other pressing demands make it impossible for me to give more time to these questions. Feel free to contact me concerning any other questions. We are still deeply grateful to you for your encouraging words and your profound interest in our struggle. Whenever you feel the need to give some words of advice please feel free to do that.

With warm personal regards, I am

Very sincerely yours,
M. L. King, Jr.,
President

MLK:mlb

TLc. MLKP-MBU: Box 67.

To Wilbert J. Johnson

24 September 1956
[*Montgomery, Ala.*]

On 21 August Air Force sergeants Johnson, Johnnie Rainge, and Frank Garrett, stationed in Anchorage, Alaska, wrote to King after reading a magazine article discussing the use of Scripture by both integrationists and segregationists. They asked King to send biblical quotations used to justify integration and segregation for use in their Bible study. King identifies several passages that support integration and passes on an unidentified article listing those used by segregationists.

S/Sgt. Wilbert J. Johnson, AF 13 236 825
5039th Supply Squadron
Box 1002, APO 942
Seattle, Washington

Dear Sgt. Johnson:

Thanks for your letter of August 21, making inquiry concerning biblical scriptures being used to justify integration and/or segregation. Enclosed you will find an article which was sent to me recently with many biblical passages used to justify segregation. I am sending this with the assurance that you will send it back immediately for I must have it for my records.

As you can well see all of these quotations are blatant distortions of the true meaning of the scripture.

It seems to me that at least three New Testament passages reveal the fact that segregation is a tragic evil that is utterly unchristian. First Paul's declaration on

Mars Hill in which he states God has mad out of one blood all nations of men to live on the face of the earth.[1] Again Paul states there is neither Jew nor Greek, there is neither slave nor free, there is neither male nor female for you are all one in Christ Jesus.[2] Finally, it is expressed in the fact that Christ died for all mankind.

I hope these passages will help you in your studies together. Please give my regards to Mr. Garrett and Mr. Rainge.

Sincerely yours,
M. L. King, Jr.,
President

MLK:mlb

enclosures

TLc. MLKP-MBU: Box 60.

---

1. Acts 17:26.
2. Galatians 3:28.

From Harold Edward Pinkston

25 September 1956
Richmond, Va.

Pinkston, a divinity student at Virginia Union, had known King during the early 1950s while both assisted Rev. William H. Hester at Boston's Twelfth Baptist Church. He offers to transport King from the Richmond airport to Rev. Wyatt "Tee" Walker's home in Petersburg, Virginia, where King would stay before giving a speech to the Virginia state NAACP convention on 5 October. W. Lester Banks, the executive secretary of the state NAACP, thanked King on 8 November for his participation.

Hello "Mike,"

Greetings to you & Coretta and family. I sincerely hope everyone is fine and enjoying the best of blessings God can offer.

Mike, I was more than happy when my home-town brother and neighbor (N. Jersey) Tee Walker told me that you were coming this way. It'll really be good to see you again, and incline my ears to 'greater wisdom.'

I told "Tee" (Rev Walker) I'd be very happy to meet you at the airport next week (Fri I believe) and drive you over to Petersburg where he & family resides.

This King, I consider a unique previlege.

Talking with Mr. Lester Banks via phone, I requested the honor of meeting you upon arrival. He'll be writing you soon for your plane schedule, arrival, etc in order to inform me ~~of~~ immediately by phone.

Mars Hill in which he states God has mad out of one blood all nations of men to live on the face of the earth.[1] Again Paul states there is neither Jew nor Greek, there is neither slave nor free, there is neither male nor female for you are all one in Christ Jesus.[2] Finally, it is expressed in the fact that Christ died for all mankind.

I hope these passages will help you in your studies together. Please give my regards to Mr. Garrett and Mr. Rainge.

Sincerely yours,
M. L. King, Jr.,
President

MLK:mlb

enclosures

TLc. MLKP-MBU: Box 60.

I'd like to welcome you to our city again! If you have a few moments after your schedule is determined, I'd like to hear from you—you may count on my being there. I think you'll be coming in at <u>Byrd Airport</u> anyway.

Mike, oh yes, among other things I have yet a "lingering problem" I hope to be able to discuss with you en our route to Petersburg.

Hope to hear from you.

Fraternally,
[*signed*] "Pink" Boston '50–52

ALS. MLKP-MBU: Box 66A.

From Samuel S. Thomas

25 September 1956
Brunswick, N.C.

Thomas, a thirty-six-year-old North Carolina prison inmate convicted of perjury and illegal possession of whiskey, writes King of his hopes to become a minister after his release.[1] *King replied on 9 October.*[2]

Dr. M. L. King, Jr
Dexter Avenue Church
Montgomery, Ala

Dear Mr. King:

I followed the every movement of the MIA and thank God you emerged as a great leader and outstanding American. In February when you and 150 other citizens were arrested I was in Chicago and it electrified the people . . . Negroes in barrooms hotels night clubs cafes—paused and prayed for you . . . . . you won for God was on your side . . .

I have just finished reading the King Plan and I believe the eight points stressed will do us as a race a great deal of good . . . [3]

---

1. Samuel S. Thomas (1919–?), born in Thomasville, Georgia, graduated with a B.S. in social science from North Carolina A&T College in Greensboro and earned an M.S. from Columbia University in 1944. At the time of his conviction he owned a bail bond business in Greensboro. He was paroled from North Carolina's Central Prison on 2 April 1957 after serving nine months of a three-to-five-year sentence.

2. See pp. 397–398 in this volume.

3. The July 1956 edition of *Ebony* featured King's eight-point plan to "get rid of segregation in most areas of American life by 1963." His suggestions were: "Resist the evil of segregation in a passive, non-violent spirit"; "Use the weapon of love in our everyday relations"; "Mobilize for an all-out fight for first-class citizenship"; "Get out the vote"; "Continue legal and legislative fight"; "Awaken the church to its social responsibilities"; "Close the gap between the classes and the masses"; and "Be prepared." King expanded on the last point by advising African Americans to "skillfully and intellectually prepare ourselves to live in an integrated society" (quoted in Lerone Bennett, "The King Plan for Freedom," *Ebony,* July 1956, pp. 65–68).

When I left my home in St. Augustine to enter college I planned to finish college and then enter a seminary to prepare for the ministry. After gaining a M.A from Columbia I entered business . . I made a small fortune. At the age of 30 I had accumulated $100,000 cash and had three prosperous businesses—I forgot God—I quit the church, I worshipped my money—I mistreated my wife—(I began dating intimately 3 or 4 outside gals each week)—I became a pretty sorry individual.

26 Sept
1956

On October 12, 1955 I was arrested and charged with subordination of perjury . . I knew nothing about the charge . . I took the case to NC Supreme Court but they ruled against me . . . I had eight of best lawyers in this country but still had to come to prison. . . . I declare unto you, one week of prison life changed me. . . . It has shown me what a fool I was . . . My wife has stuck by me . . . For my adultrous acts I have asked her forgiveness—I have read the Bible through twice—I need some religious books.

The purpose of this letter is to ask you to recommend some good religious books and publishing houses from which I can purchase them—

Can you let me see your copy of "The Social Principles of Jesus" by Walter Rauschenbush.—This is a must book.[4] One question worries me—"Will the public accept a minister who is a former convict?

I plan to get out on parole on January 16, 1957—September 1957 if parole board allows me, I will enter school—

What seminary would you recommend?

Please take time out and answer my letter—please do not divulge contents of my letter to anyone for I want no sympathy from anyone.

I certainly hope that Mrs. King and your little girl are in the best of health.

[*signed*] Samuel S. Thomas
62172
Prison Number

AHLS. MLKP-MBU: Box 64.

---

4. Walter Rauschenbusch (1861–1918), a pioneering social gospel theologian and preacher, published *The Social Principles of Jesus* in 1916.

From Bayard Rustin

26 September 1956

Rustin encloses a memorandum he wrote entitled "A Message to American Christians" and proposes that King and Robert Graetz "sign something similar" for submission to Christian Century. *In the memorandum Rustin emphasized the moral and spiritual dimensions of the desegregation movement, while bemoaning the media's focus on legal and political issues. The Christian church had contributed to recent "fairly substantial" strides toward an integrated society, he argued, but it had "in its own life woefully fallen short of practicing what it has preached." He proposed six acts that would support the integration of the church and its community. A subsequent article by King, published in* Christian Century *on 6 February 1957 as "Nonviolence and Racial Justice," was not based on Rustin's draft.*

Dear Rev. King,

For some time I have been deeply disturbed with the manner in which Christian publications in this country have concentrated on the political aspects of racial change, and have tended to respond in their thinking for Christians as citizens rather than addressing themselves to the moral issues beneath the struggle.

It has occurred to me that perhaps you and Rev. Graetz might challenge a more profound approach. For what it is worth I enclose a memorandum for your study and consideration. If you and Rev. Graetz could jointly sign something similar to this and submit it to Dr. Harold Fey of the Christian Century (he is the editor, as you doubtless know), several things might occur:

The readers of Christian Century would undoubtedly begin a correspondence with the magazine; Montgomery protest and its Christian significance would be under debate and the real issue from the Christian viewpoint would be under discussion.

There, of course, may be reasons why this would not be a sound thing for you to do. I should, however, appreciate hearing from you.

Sincerely,
Bayard Rustin

TLc. BRP-DLC: Reel 3.

From Alma John

28 September 1956
New York, N.Y.

WWRL radio host John featured King's 12 August sermon at New York City's Mount Olivet Baptist Church on her show, a daily program for women called The Homemaker's Club. [1] *On 5 November King promised to send a tape recording of the sermon, adding that he was "very happy" to hear of the enthusiastic response it had elicited: "I am always glad to know that I can be of some little service."*

---

1. Alma Vessels John (1906–1986), born in Philadelphia, graduated from New York University and the Harlem Hospital School of Nursing, becoming a registered nurse in 1929. She worked at Harlem Hospital until 1939, when she was fired for trying to organize for better working conditions and higher wages. She later became the first African-American woman to become director of a school for practicing nurses in New York state and in 1946 became executive director of the National Association of Colored Graduate Nurses. Beginning in 1952 she hosted *The Homemaker's Club* on WWRL radio and later produced and hosted a half-hour television program, *Black Pride.* John interviewed guests such as Rosa Parks and Ella Fitzgerald and commented on health, education, and community issues.

The Reverand Martin Luther King   1 Oct
Pastor   1956
The Dexter Avenue Baptist Church
Montgomery Alabama

Dear Dr. King:

In my four years of broadcasting I have never had a more enthusiastic listener response than your sermon delivered at the Mt. Olivet Baptist church evoked!

It was a real pleasure to meet you and your sister personally and I do hope our paths will cross again before long.

Scores of people telephoned and many more wrote to ask whether you message was available on a record. Their requests have inspired me to visit churches in our several communities on Sunday mornings to record good sermons and I hope to make them available to interested listeners possibly mimeographed at first.

I plan to title them "Sermons to Live By." Several men have told me about the magnificent sermon you preached at Denver and I wonder if it would be possible for you to send me a tape recording of it.

One of my Jewish friends was so impressed with your message that he gave me a contribution to send you to assist in a small way your very important bus protest activity.

Should you wish to send him an acknowledgement his name is:
Mr. Sol Dason
Proprietor—Tru Walk Shoe Store
60–15 Roosevelt Ave.,
Woodside, 77
N.Y.
Please accept my very best wishes for continued success!

Sincerely,
[*signed*] Alma John
Director
The Homemaker's Club
Radio Station

WWRL

AHLS. MLKP-MBU: Box 60.

To Viva O. Sloan

1 October 1956
[*Montgomery, Ala.*]

*In a 17 September letter Viva Sloan, an MIA supporter from West Virginia, asked
King whether he considered Eisenhower or Stevenson "the safer or better leader as*   383

President . . . on the matter of desegregation." Believing that King knew "the feeling of the greater number of your people," Sloan promised to vote as he advised. King reports that he is "in a state of indecision." In other letters from the same period he indicated that "the Negro should be more of an independent voter . . . this would give him more bargaining power." He also explained that he was voting as a "private citizen" without taking a public stand, because the MIA received support from both Republicans and Democrats.[1]

Miss Viva O. Sloan
379 Baldwin Street
Morgantown, West Virginia

Dear Miss Sloan:

Thanks for your very kind letter of September 17, making inquiry concerning the way the Negro will vote in the coming election. I am of the impression that the Negro voter will go largely for the Democratic Party. I haven't fully decided which candidate I will vote for. In the past I have always voted the Democratic ticket. At this point I am still in a state of indecision. Stevenson seems to be more forthright on the race question than Eisenhower, but the Democratic Party is so inexplicably bound to the South that it does leave doubt in the minds of those interested in civil rights. Let us all hope that the candidate most concerned with the welfare for all people of America will win the election.

Sincerely yours,
M. L. King, Jr.,
President

MLK:mlb

P.S. There has been nothing published from this office taken from letters received from sympathizers in our cause.[2]

TLc. MLKP-MBU: Box 65.

---

1. King to E. F. Rodriguez, 19 September 1956; and King to Arnold Demille, October 1956.
2. Sloan had asked if the MIA had distributed a newspaper article she had written about the protest.

2 October 1956
[*Montgomery, Ala.*]

Responding to Thomas's letter of 28 August, King updates him about the situation in
Montgomery and expresses uncertainty about whether he can find time to write a
proposed book about the bus boycott.

Dr. Cecil A. Thomas, Associate Secretary
Stiles Hall
University Young Men's Christian Association
2400 Bancroft Way
Berkeley 4, California

Dear Cecil:

This letter is long over due. I have been intending to write you and Fran for
several weeks, but absence from the city and the accumulation of a flood of mail
prevented my reply. Please accept my deepest apologies. Coretta and I can never
adequately express our appreciation to you and Fran for the interest that you
have taken in us personally and the whole Montgomery struggle. I can assure you
that such moral support and christian generosity give us renewed courage and
vigor to carry on.

Things are going well around Montgomery. The community is still amazingly
united. We have had some recent difficulty with getting our station wagons insured. About three weeks ago the insurance company cancelled the policies on
all of our station wagons which made it impossible for us to leave them in operation. For a while it looked rather dark; it appeared that we would find no company to take the insurance. But finally a ray of light came in through the Lords
of London Insurance Company which willingly accepted the policy. Our station
wagons are now in operation once more. The Supreme Court reconvenes within
the next few days, and we are waiting now its verdict on the question of segregation in public transportation. We feel that the decision should come relatively
soon due to the fact our case is a priority case. (It is a priority case because an
injunction is involved.)

I am still deeply interested in writing the book that you and Fran have suggested. Nothing would satisfy me more but I am confronted with a great problem:
Instead of my work decreasing, in the last few weeks it has increased. My personal
correspondence is as high as ever, and the work of the Association is expanding
every day. Invitations for speaking engagements still come in in large numbers.
All of this causes me to wonder whether I would actually have the time to do such
a book. I would not like to accept the grant from the Fund for the Republic that
you have so graciously inquired about without knowing in advance that I could
complete the project. By the way, if the grant is given is there any stipulation
stating that the book must be published? In the light of these prevailing circum-

stances I would like for you to write me concerning your impressions. Frankly, I just don't see how I weill be able to do it in the next two or three months.

Give my best regards to Fran. Coretta and Yolanda are doing fine. Coretta appeared in a recital yesterday afternoon at our church and she sang to a full house.[1] The concert was brilliantly done and well accepted.

Sincerely yours,
M. L. King, Jr.,
President

MLK:mlb

P.S. You made inquiry concerning Rev. H. L. Clements. He is the pastor of the Mt. Zion A.M.E. Zion Church on Holt Street. He formerly pastored the church that Rev. Bennett pastors in San Francisco. He is a member of of the Executive Board of the Montgomery Improvement Association. So I am sure that his request is well founded.

TLc. MLKP-MBU: Box 67.

---

1. The concert at Dexter occurred on 30 September 1956 (see "Echo Echoes Recital," *Dexter Echo,* 3 October 1956, p. 4).

From Warren Olney III

2 October 1956
Washington, D.C.

Reverend M. L. King, Jr.
President, The Montgomery Improvement Association, Inc.
530-C South Union Street
Montgomery, Alabama

Dear Reverend King:

This acknowledges your letter of September 17, 1956, together with a document enclosed therein, entitled "Registration of Negro Voters in Alabama in 1954."

We are very glad to have the information set forth in the document, as well as that contained in your letter. However, any action which this Department may take must be based upon a specific complaint indicating that some particular person or persons have been deprived of rights protected by federal law. Since your letter refers to a general situation instead of specific individuals, we shall not be able to undertake the action you request. We shall, of course, be happy to consider any additional information which you may care to bring to our attention.

Sincerely,
WARREN OLNEY III
Assistant Attorney General
Criminal Division

By: [*signed*]
ARTHUR B. CALDWELL
Chief, Civil Rights Section

TLSr. MLKP-MBU: Box 23.

To Walter George Muelder

3 October 1956
Montgomery, Ala.

In a 16 September letter to King, Muelder noted that he had been following "with admiration and keen interest your leadership and experiences in the dramatic days of the past year." He invited King and his wife to "spend a week or so away from the daily tensions by coming to Boston and enjoying a quiet retreat." [1]

Dr. Walter G. Muelder, Dean
School of Theology
Boston University
745 Commonwealth Avenue
Boston 15, Massachusetts

Dear Dean Muelder:

Thanks for your very kind letter of September 16. Absence from the city has delayed my reply.

I cannot begin to express my deep appreciation to you and the whole School of Theology for the interest that you have taken in our struggle. Such moral support and christian generosity give me renewed courage and vigor to carry on.

---

1. Walter George Muelder (1907–), born in Boody, Illinois, received his B.S. (1927) from Knox College in Galesburg, Illinois, and his S.T.B. (1930) and Ph.D. (1933) from Boston University. Muelder was pastor of a Wisconsin church before moving to Kentucky to head the department of philosophy and Bible at Berea College. In 1940 he joined the faculty of the University of Southern California, returning to Boston University five years later to become a professor of social ethics and dean of the School of Theology, where he remained for years. Muelder edited and wrote many publications, including *Religion and Economic Responsibility* (1953).

Your gracious invitation, inviting me to come to Boston for a few days of rest, meditation, and fellowship, is one that appeals to me greatly. I can assure you that this would meet a real need in my life. Unfortunately, however, my schedule is so set up that such a retreat cannot be undertaken for the next two or three months. I did get an opportunity to get away for two or three weeks this summer, and it turned out to be very helpful for Mrs. King and me.

I am very sorry that my schedule made it impossible for me to accept the invitation to speak for the Zions Herald Banquet in December.[2] However, I will be in Boston the last of October to speak for the Ford Hall Forum.[3] I will look forward with great anticipation to seeing you and my many friends around Boston University. Please extend my best regards to the faculty members of the School of Theology.

With warm personal regards, I am
Sincerely yours,
[*signed*] Martin
Martin L. King, Jr.

MLK:mlb

TLS. WMP-MBU.

---

2. In his letter Muelder noted that the Wesleyan Association and the *Zion's Herald,* a publication of the Methodist Church, were inviting King to speak on 17 December.

3. On 28 October King delivered "A Realistic Look at Race Relations" at Jordan Hall for the Ford Hall Forum.

Robert L. Cannon
to Alfred Hassler and Glenn E. Smiley

3 October 1956
Nashville, Tenn.

Cannon reports to fellow field secretary Smiley and to Fellowship *editor Hassler on King's direction of the MIA's first nonviolent training session. After the session, which took place during a regular mass meeting on 1 October at Hutchinson Street Baptist Church, Cannon presented FOR's recently completed documentary film on the bus boycott,* Walk to Freedom.[1]

---

1. Robert L. Cannon worked out of Nashville as FOR's field secretary for the mid-South region during 1955 and 1956. In 1957 he moved to California to serve as a minister in the United Methodist church.

Mssrs. Hassler and Smiley   3 Oct
21 Audubon Ave.   1956
New York 32, N.Y.

Dear "Comrades":

Need I say it? The showing of our new movie to the mass meeting in Montgomery last Monday night was a howling success. I mean that literally as well as in its deeper sense. The meeting was, as usual, well-attended. The MIA leadership was in full force, including the new "hero" Pastor Graetz who came late and sat in the balcony. We were the only two white persons present.

A special significance was added to the premier showing. Either it was plain coincidence or something planned by King, but this meeting also marked the first in what is to be a series of mass training sessions in nonviolence. Now with the possibility looming that these people might wake up some morning to integrated busses, {Martin Luther} King and the MIA have decided to begin the process of ~~going~~ {training the people to go} back to integrated busses with as much creative goodwill and quiet determination as they carried out with the boycott. The showing of our film tied in beautifully with this new emphasis in the mass meetings. King, displaying the marvelous gift of leadership he has with the people, pointed out that the end of the boycott may be quite near. [*strikeout illegible*] Even tho our hopes must not be raised too high, he said, it is nevertheless important to consider how we ~~our~~ {are} to manage ourselves on integrated busses, because it is only to integrated busses that we plan to return (thundering applause here). Said King: "There will be some people who will not like this change and they will not hesitate to express themselves to you. There will possibly be some unpleasant experiences for us at the hands of people who will not immediately accept the idea of sitting with us on the bus. It is important that we begin to think seriously about how we are going to face up to these possibilities of abuse, slander, and embarrassment." Then the following took place:

King asked, "Now, I want just two persons to stand up and tell us how they plan to act on the busses. Suppose you sat down next to a white person on a bus. Suppose this person begin to make a fuss, calling you names, or even going so far as to shove you? What would you do?" The feelings over this were electric.

Two women stood up. King recognized one of them: "All right, Sister———" She began, "Well, if someone was to start calling me names, I guess I would be kinda upset, but mind you, I don't intend to move . . . I think I would just sit there and ignore her and let folks see how ignorant she was. But if she were to start pushin' me, maybe I would give her just a little shove."

At this point there were many murmurings of "No! No!" King then replied, "Thank you for your candid opinion. Now let me ask you this. If you were to shove this white person back, what would you achieve?" There were shouts of "Nothing!" in response to King, and the woman conceded the point. But King pursued it, addressing himself to the woman, "Now, do you agree with the opinion expressed here that nothing would be achieved by treating the white person in question the same way you are treated?" She agreed. "Then why," King asked, "Would you push that person back?" The woman replied, "Well, I guess I wouldn't."

389

The other woman was more forthright: She made this choice observation: "Now, I think most of us know the white folks pretty well. [*strikeout illegible*] We have to remember that they are not used to us, but we're used to them. It isn't going to do us any good to get mad and strike back, 'cause that's just what some of them <u>want</u> us to do. (Cries of 'That's right!') Now we've got this freedom. It is something they cain't take away from us. But we will <u>lose</u> it if we get mad and show them we are incapable of acting like good Christian ladies and gentlemen . . . " A wild applause followed this.

King then concluded, "This is good. Now you can see the seriousness of our task here. We are going to be doing some more of this in the meetings to come. Let's discuss and think this through together, for this is serious business. I want you to feel free to discuss and express your opinions about this, but I also want you to see what our Christian responsibility is to each other when we return to the busses of Montgomery."

The meeting was cut short in order to give more time to the film. King was most generous in his introduction. He pointed out how "the F.o.R. needs no introduction to us here. It is an organization of concerned Christians that has been with us from the very beginning." And so on. I was asked to say a few words of preface to the film. I pointed out how members and friends of the Fellowship have been thrilled and deeply moved by the courage and nonviolence of this movement for justice and human dignity. I mentioned how the F.o.R. for 40 years has sought to impress this same spirit upon the world. In commenting on the movie I tried to explain how because of its message—[*strikeout illegible*] "your message," I said—the lives of people who have come into contact with its making have been visibly moved. (Toward the beginning of my remarks I tried to ~~point out~~ bring the courage of Negro students at Clinton and Sturgis into the focus of the spirit of Montgomery.)

The thrill of seeing this movie with these history-making citizens of Montgomery will probably never be duplicated. I have often thought what it would be like to hear people cheer and applaud the virtues of nonviolence and Christian love the same way people go nuts over seeing "our boys" march to war or the impressive fluttering of Old Glory in the winds. That night my wondering was answered. The appearance of Rosa Parks on the screen brought the house down. King's remarks in his ~~church~~ church with the white reporter were followed by an ovation-like applause.[2] For me any shadow of a doubt that "Walking to Freedom" had "made its point" was quickly eliminated by King's whole-hearted reaction to the showing. He was obviously deeply moved and followed the showing with a brilliant, short summary of the power of nonviolence.

I got a thrilling indication of the priceless leadership this movement has ~~aft~~ when Ralph Abernathy got up and made this unforgettable remark:

---

2. The film depicts King telling the reporter, "We never intend to participate in violence. We depend solely on moral and spiritual forces."

"Children, I know how much this film has meant to you. But it is not something to be laughed at. When you see the feet of our people walking the streets with worn-out, scuffed, and turned in shoes you should feel <u>glad</u> inside and proud of those feet! You should have joy in your hearts for this movement and be able to say, 'Thank you, Jesus!'"

So went the premier showing of "Walking for Freedom." King is quite certain the MIA will buy a copy. I suggest you send down a copy immediately, because in any event they are willing to use the film under the second condition mentioned in Al's recent letter on the use of the film. Besides, Bob Graetz is eager to get his hands on it. We discussed this, and {he} plans to have it shown before white groups in Montgomery, Mobile, and Birmingham. And when Graetz says he will do it, it is as good as done. King agrees with my contention that there is ample need to show this film among the Negroes of Montgomery itself, because now a small percentage of the 46,000 or more Negroes attends the mass meetings. He has asked me to send him a note this week as a reminder to him to bring the matter of purchase before the MIA.

I felt lonely without you guys there, and I mean this. I was holding out a last-minute hope that at least one of you could make it. Anyway, I hope I have been able to convey to you a meaningful sense of the impact the film made on the mass meeting.

My thanks to you both for allowing me to represent you at such an event.

in fellowship,
[*signed*] Bob
Robert L. Cannon

THLS. FORP-PSC-P.

To Sylvester S. Robinson

3 October 1956
[*Montgomery, Ala.*]

Writing to an Atlanta attorney, King recounts how, en route to a speaking engagement at the Hampton Institute in Virginia, he "refused to eat under segregated conditions" at the Dobbs House restaurant at the Atlanta airport.[1] He told the manager who offered to seat King in a "dingy" segregated section that such practices in interstate transportation had been prohibited by a recent Supreme Court decision. Having missed his only opportunity for a meal that day, King notes that it was a "tragic inconvenience" and "an excellent case for a suit." On 15 October J. H. Carmichael,

---

1. Sylvester S. Robinson was a Howard Law School graduate with an office on Atlanta's Auburn Avenue. A member of Ebenezer Baptist Church and the Atlanta NAACP's executive committee, he handled the incorporation of the Southern Christian Leadership Conference (SCLC) in 1958.

*president of Capital Airlines, expressed regret about the incident, offering King
"genuine apologies for the delay and discomfort."*

*King's letter to Robinson was forwarded to C. Clayton Powell, chair of the Atlanta
NAACP's legal redress committee, who told King on 22 October that the group had
agreed to pursue the case and to obtain counsel to represent King. In his reply to Powell
on 30 October King reported that he was "very happy" to know that the NAACP was
taking up this "most significant case" and expressed his hope that it would reach the
courts "as soon as possible."* [2]

Atty. S. S. Robinson
175 Auburn Avenue
Atlanta, Georgia

Dear Atty. Robinson:

I am just getting to the point where I can set forth the information regarding the suit that I am interested in filing. I am not sure whether the suit will be toward the Dobbs House, which is the restaurant in the Atlanta Airport, or on Capitol Air Lines, which is the air lines that I used from Atlanta to Hampton, Virginia.

I left Montgomery, Alabama Thursday morning, September 27, via Eastern Air Lines en route to Hampton, Virginia. In Atlanta I changed from Eastern to Capitol Air Lines. Just as we were about to take off we discovered that we had generator trouble which necessitated our deplaning and going back in the waiting room. It was revealed that we would have to stay there three hours in order to give the mechanics time to install a new generator. Ordinarily, we would have eaten lunch on the plane, but since we were three hours late Capitol Air Lines issued a slip to all of the passengers on this plane giving them permission to purchase lunch in the Dobbs House. I was the only Negro passenger on the plane. Naturally I followed all of the other passengers into the Dobbs House. After getting in the Dobbs House I was taken to the back and offered a seat behind a dingy compartment which totally set me off from other passengers. I immediately refused, stating that I would rather go a week without eating before eating under such conditions. I immediately asked for the manager. I was introduced to the manager and we talked the matter over. His only answer was that it was a city ordinance and a state law that the races be segregated in restaurants, and under those conditions I could not be served in the main dining room. I talked with him about the fact that I was an interstate passenger. I also referred to the fact that segregation had been completely eliminated in diners on the train. None of this moved him enough to serve me. It ended up that I refused to eat under segregated conditions. It was not until 10:30 Thursday evening, after I

---

2. In 1959 King was again refused service at Dobbs House and indicated to an Atlanta attorney his willingness to give an affidavit regarding both incidents (King to Donald L. Hollowell, 31 August 1959, MLKP-MBU: Box 28). On 5 January 1960, before King had pursued his case, a federal district judge ruled against the restaurant and the city in *Coke v. City of Atlanta et al.,* a case involving a black Birmingham resident who was denied service at the restaurant. After this ruling King's father and several companions, returning to Atlanta from National Baptist Convention meetings in Arkansas, obtained service at Dobbs House, providing one of the first tests of the court decision (Donald L. Hollowell, interview with King Papers Project staff, 12 January 1995).

had spoken at Hampton Institute, that I was able to eat. After getting on the plane I discovered that there was no food there. I had left home very early without eating breakfast. By the flight being three hours late, I had to go directly from the airport to the platform to speak. It was that night after speaking that I had my first meal for the day. As you can see this was a tragic inconvenience. I think it is an excellent case for a suit.

Now I am sure that there is a question of witnesses. I talked with several of the waiters. All of them happened to have been colored. They gave me the impression that they would willingly serve as witnesses if a case came up. I don't have all of the names but you can contact the following two waiters and they will be very happy to refer you to the others who were present at the time: Mr. Claude Marshall, Dobbs House Number 2, The Atlanta Municipal Airport, Atlanta, Georgia. The head waiter who carried me to the back compartment to be served was Mr. Harry Wofford. He can be contacted at the same address. The white woman who served as hostess was very congenial. She stated outright that the whole thing had been embarrassing to her all along and that she hoped that it could be straightened out. It might be possible to get her to voluntarily serve as a witness. Her name is Mrs. Hilma Medlin. She would be ideal. She also can be contacted by calling or writing the Dobbs House. I am sure that these persons can be subpoenaed if they refuse to volunteer. I know the manager should be subpoenaed.

I believe these are the basic facts in the situation. If there are other points that need to be clarified please feel free to call me collect. I hope this suit can be filed immediately. I think your suggestion of having the NAACP take the case is a very fine one. Please let me hear from you concerning this whole matter.

Sincerely yours,
M. L. King, Jr.,
President

MLK:mlb

TLc. MLKP-MBU: Box 64A.

From Douglas E. Moore

3 October 1956
Durham, N.C.

An acquaintance from King's graduate school days at Boston University writes about his experiences as a proponent of Christian nonviolence and proposes "a regional group which utilizes the power of love and non-violence."[1] *On 7 December King's*

---

1. Douglas E. Moore (1928–), born in Hickory, North Carolina, earned his B.A. (1949) from North Carolina College and his S.T.B. (1953) and S.T.M. (1958) from Boston University. He served as pastor of several North Carolina churches from 1953 to 1960 and as executive secretary of the board of education of the North Carolina Conference of the Methodist Church (1956–1960). An NAACP activist, Moore led a 1957 desegregation sit-in in Durham, served on the executive board of SCLC, and in 1960 participated in the founding conference of the Student Nonviolent Coordinating Committee (SNCC).

secretary, Maude Ballou, wrote that his letter had been misplaced and would be
answered soon. That reply has not been found.

Dear King;

This is Doug Moore, graduate of Boston University's School of Theology of 1953. In that you get a heavy volume of mail, I thought that I would use this type of introduction in order that you might know who it is that is writing.

I believe the last time I saw you we were talking together with Jean Martain and ironically enough, as I recall, the discussion centered around whether or not there were many Negro women that we knew who were pacifist.

First let me commend you for the tremendous job that you have done in Montgomery. I feel that what you have done is in keeping with radical Christianity but also in keeping with personalism at its profoundest depth.

I would have written earlier but felt that it would be better to write after the great surge of popular feeling settled down.

The thing that you have acted out in mass in Montgomery, I have been putting into practice here in North Carolina and Virginia. I have consistently refused to move to the back of buses because I was a Christian and I have never used law as a threat against drivers, but relied completly upon the force of love and Christian witness.

My first encounter of this nature took place in Newport News, Virginia. This was on a local bus. After telling the person that I would not move, the driver got off the bus and stayed for twenty minutes then he got back on and drove off.

Once when I was coming from Richmond Va. the driver asked me to move but I refused as a Christian. He said to me, "Well, I will not be responsible for what happens to you," and to this I replied that I would die praying for him before I would move. Each time that he stopped he gave me a mean look but he only received a smile from me. We arrived in Greensboro with no difficulty. I would have died in that seat. Whenever a person threatens us with brutality and even death he is assuming that we value our lives more than eternal principles. I feel that my philosophical and theological belief in immortality comes to my aid in this situation as well as my Christian faith which does not conflict with the other two disciplines mentioned. When a man is afraid to die for what he believes to be true his concept of what is ultimately real is shallow.

I also reason from this point of view in that our government can call out young men to die for it; I feel that I as a Christian ought to be willing to die for Jesus Christ and truth. This I have expounded very forcefully in speaking at Bennett College, Lovingstone College, and will present the same challenge to the students at Clafin University in Orangeburgh this winter. I am to speak at Morgon College this Sunday when I then too shall present the challenge.

It is a strange thing that we will ask a man to bail out at forty thousand feet to perfect a military weapon but think it is neurotic if he is willing to die for justice.

Here in Durham I was asked to move to the rear and I refused as a Christian and the driver asked me for my ticket. Then he said "You are not an interstate passanger, go on to the back and give these White people your seat." I replied, "I know that I am not an interstate passenger; I am familiar with the Iren Morgan

Case of 1948 which said in essence that it was a burden on interstate commerce to segregate passengers; but as a Christian I refuse to move to the back. If I have to make a choice between Jesus or Ceasar and Ceasar in this instance being the state of North Carolina, then I will take Jesus." So the driver got off the bus which was an express and stayed thirty minutes trying to figure out with the company what to do. However, after this passing of time, he returned to the bus and drove off.

But one of the most memorable experiences that I have ever had occured in a little town in the center of North Carolina named Asheboro. This particular day I sat directly behind the driver and he of course asked me to move to the back. I again refused on the ground of being a Christian. Then he started to loud talk me, "I am not going to move this bus until you move." I have often thought that if he had said that to me ten years ago before I got to know the way of love I would have replied to him "I got news for you" but I said, "I am sorry you feel that way but as a Christian I can not move."

Then he went for the police and they came to see what was happening and I can recall the sherrif saying "Well, I an not going to arrest him." The driver had no other course to follow than to drive the bus. As we went down the road I sang some of my favorite spirituals and hymns and then I asked him if he were angry with me and he replied, "Don't say a word to me. You took advantage of me." To this I replied, "No my action was not directed at you but to the state of North Carolina who is responsible for the immoral segregation laws being on the books." As I got off the bus in Ramseur which is located in the country I told him that I loved him as a person.

When I arrived at where I was staying, I told my parishoners little grandson that I had sat on the front seat of the bus again but that was not enough, my job is not complete until I win the soul of the driver. At our regular morning worship we has a special prayer that this man might realize that my action was not directed at him but at the state of North Carolina.

About a month later I was on my way to Salisbury, N.C. and I had to make a bus change in Lexington, N.C. It had been raining all that week and was still raining that day. I saw a greyhound bus come into the yard and there was this driver. So I went out to wave at him. He stopped his bus and opened the door and said to me, "Preacher, which way are you going?" I told him which was in the opposite direction of the way he was going. Then he said this to me "Preacher, I have been having it pretty tough lately, will you pray for me? I told him I would at ten thirty that night when I remember others to our heavenly Father. He then replied, "Thanks very much preacher."

This is perhaps the most meaningful experience that I have ever had in the winning of a person on the other side of the fence.

I have maintained for years that one-hundred well disciplined persons could break the backbone of segregated travel in North Carolina in less than a year. Again whenever I speak at colleges or at special meetings this is the content of my message for I feel that so much of what students hear does not challenge them. To explore such topics I usually use these subjects "Who's in Your Gallery," "Facing the Rising Sun," or "Jesus or Ceasar."

My three years in North Carolina have been interesting. During that time I have picketed the New York Philhormonic orchestra because the Greensboro music company wanted to segregate me and I refused to go anywhere that I am denied full rights. Whenever I have an opportunity to speak on radio or on telvision I do the same thing that I do at the colleges. On one occasion they almost cut me off but the manager told me that that would been the worse thing they could have possibly done.

Well lets talk about something else and that is your coming to Durham October 15. You have a great opportunity to do us a great job. I have only been here since last June 10, prior to that I was in Leaksville, N.C., the Governors home town. While I was there we organized an N.A.A.C.P. chapter; a voters league and I helped the laundry workers organize and go out on strike. I was the most unpopular Methodist preacher in town, that is the White people thought so.

The people of Durham have a great class problem and in addition to this they are materialist. There is considerable exploitation of Negroes by Negroes. The buses in this city have been desegregated as far as policy goes but the Negroes still ride in the back from custom. Here the preachers could be of great help.

There are no Negro drivers and the line that the company makes its most money is in the Negro section. I would think that something could be worked out with the company. If you could give us the incentive we could create the right psychological moment.

I don't know what you schedule will be when you are here but if you had the time we might get together to discuss the possibility for a regional group which utilizes the power of love and non-violence. I was supposed to have attended the Atlanta meeting but at the time I was doing some teaching at Livingstone College, where Geogre B. Thomas is teaching. In addition to this I was also pastoring.

I feel that there is need of such a group because it cast the problem and it attacks in a new dimension. In talking with some of the top NAACP persons they felt that other forces must be used in this struggle.

A group of this nature would solidify our efforts and give a coherent philosophy behind what we are attempting to do. As you probably know there are not many Negroes or Whites who have a firm spiritual or intellectual grasp upon this whole idea of love and non-violence. This power has been in the Negro Church for generations.

Such a group would help to give us direction on national movements. For example it will help us to have a recognized spokesman rather than an opportunist like Adam C. Powell trying to interfere on something that he has neither the moral or intellectual power to do. Suggestion about days of prayers should have come from you and not him.

With your influence I think that we could do the job very well. I am anxious to hear how you feel about this for now is the time to make our move. Now I have been a member of the FOR many years, almost ten, and know many of its top men like John Swomley, A. J. Muste and Glen Smiley.[2] Whether or not we would

---

2. John M. Swomley, Jr. (1915–), born in Harrisburg, Pennsylvania, received his B.A. (1936) from Dickinson College, his M.A. (1939) and S.T.B. (1940) from Boston University, and his Ph.D. (1958) from the University of Colorado. From 1944 to 1952 he led the National Council Against Conscription. From 1953 to 1960 he served as national secretary of the Fellowship of Reconciliation.

want to patter a group along this line or be an affiliate of this group or establish an indegious all together could be worked out.

I feel that we can not let this get cold on us for the work that you have done in Montgomery is but the starting of a work that needs to be done throughout the South. To do this job that needs to be done there must be direction that is systematic, consistent and above all coherent and Christ like.

In that I am a new comer, although I finished college here and have a small mission church of 25 members, I doubt very seriously whether or not I will be able to see you at anytime personally. For those who love to laud it over celebrities and Durham most illustrative dignitaries will roll out the carpet for you, I have taken the liberty to speak to you about some of the things that are on my heart through the noisy keys of the typewriter.

Yours in Christ,
[*signed*]
Doug Moore

THLS. MLKP-MBU: Box 62.

To Samuel S. Thomas

9 October 1956
[*Montgomery, Ala.*]

Mr. Samuel S. Thomas, 62172
Camp 602
Brunswick, N. C.

Dear Mr. Thomas:

Thanks for your very kind letter of September 25. I read your letter with a great deal of interest and I am very happy to know that you have done a great deal of serious thinking while you have been in the process of serving a prison term. I was also happy to know of your interest in religion and your desire to become a minister. I would say that if you are definitely serious about this matter and you are willing to make the sacrifices necessary you have just as much right to enter the ministry as anybody else. Your experience in prison and the conversion which seems to have followed such an experience should give you a great deal of practical wisdom in guiding people who are grappling with the difficult decisions of life. I don't think there is anything wrong with a person who is serving a term in prison going into the ministry if that person is definitely reformed. You might be just a person to demonstrate to hundreds of thousands who are going wrong in our society the wisdom of going the right way. My only advice to you would be, be sure that you are serious and willing to confront all of the sacrifices of the ministry.

After checking through my books I find that I have loaned my copy of <u>The</u>

397

<u>Social Principles of Jesus</u> to a ministerial friend in Atlanta. I would be very happy to send it to you if I had it on hand at this time.

I was more than happy to receive your letter. Please know that you are in my prayers. I hope that God's richest blessings will be with you in all of your endeavors in the future.

Very sincerely yours,
M. L. King, Jr.,
Minister

MLK:mlb

TLc. MLKP-MBU: Box 64.

To Charles S. Johnson

11 October 1956
[*Montgomery, Ala.*]

King praises Johnson's article, "A Southern Negro's View of the South," which appeared in the New York Times Magazine *on 23 September. In the article Johnson asserted that most southern African Americans sought "full American citizenship" and believed that the region would experience "very little change except that brought about by a strong and higher authority." He also criticized the "provincial and isolationist" economy of the South and its failure to accept federal court decrees regarding integration. Accompanying the article was a photograph of King's March trial in Montgomery.*

Dr. Charles S. Johnson, President
Fisk University
Nashville, Tenn.

Dear Dr. Johnson:

This is just a note to say that I have just read your article which recently appeared in the New York Times. It is the best statement that I have read in this whole area. You evince a profound grasp of the whole subject. I am sure that the more this article is read it will bring about a greater understanding of the Negro's point of view as he struggles for first class citizenship. You combine in this article the fact finding mind of the social scientist with the moral insights of a religious prophet.

Sincerely yours,
M. L. King, Jr.,
Minister

MLK:mlb

TLc. MLKP-MBU: Box 17.

To Raleigh A. Bryant

15 October 1956
[*Montgomery, Ala.*]

Responding to a 25 September request by his friend Walter McCall, King recommends McCall to succeed the Reverend Ralph Mark Gilbert of First African Baptist Church in Savannah, Georgia. King sent a copy of this letter to McCall.[1] On 22 October Bryant told King that "a favorable response will be forthcoming," but McCall was not called to its pulpit.[2]

Mr. Raleigh Bryant, Clerk
The First African Baptist Church
23 Montgomery Street
Savannah, Georgia

Dear Mr. Bryant:

It came as a deep shock to me to learn of the sudden death of my very good friend Dr. Gilbert. In his passing both Savannah and the nation sustain a great loss.

I am sure that within the next few weeks you will begin thinking of calling a pastor to succeed the noble pastorate of Dr. Gilbert. I would like to suggest to the pulpit committee the name of The Rev. Walter R. McCall who is presently serving as Dean of Men at the Fort Valley State College, Fort Valley, Georgia. Rev. McCall is emminently qualified to fall in the footsteps of Dr. Gilbert. He has a rich academic background, having received the AB Degree from Morehouse College and the BD Degree from Crozier Theological Seminary. He is a very profound and dynamic preacher. After hearing him for several years I always go away deeply moved by his sermons. As a pastor, he would have few peers. He possesses a most radiant personality and the gift of dealing with people of all levels of life. Above all, he is a Christian gentleman. Everybody who knows Rev. McCall will agree that his character is above repute.

I can say all of these things without reservation because I know Rev. McCall very intimately. For more than ten years he has been one of my most intimate

---

1. King to Walter R. McCall, 15 October 1956. See also McCall to King, 29 October 1956, pp. 406–407 in this volume. Ralph Mark Gilbert (d. 1956), a graduate of the University of Michigan, became pastor of First African Baptist Church in 1939, where he remained until his death. A member of the NAACP, Gilbert organized a movement to hire the first African-American policeman in Georgia. On 13 June 1955, at Gilbert's request, King had arranged a meeting of Montgomery ministers during Gilbert's tour of the South for the New Standard Publishing Company.

2. Raleigh A. Bryant (1896–1984), born in Mariana, Florida, attended Florida A&M College. A World War I veteran, he joined the postal service in 1916 and worked there for forty-four years until his retirement. Gilbert also served as clerk of First African Baptist Church; after his retirement the church ordained him as a minister. Bryant moved to Atlanta in 1968, where he became an assistant pastor of Israel Baptist Church and aided services at Mount Vernon Baptist Church.

personal friends. We were classmates at Morehouse College and also at Crozier Theological Seminary. I can assure you that the First African Baptist Church would be richly benefitted in considering Rev. McCall as pastor. I hope you will find it possible to invite him to preach.

Your son Raleigh was a school mate of mine at Morehouse College. Please extend my best regards to him. You have my prayers and best wishes for God's guidance as you embark upon the seas of calling a pastor.

With every good wish, I am

Sincerely yours,
M. L. King, Jr.,
Minister

MLK:mlb
(Dictated by Rev. King but signed in his absence.)

TLc. MLKP-MBU: Box 16.

From Eleanor Roosevelt

17 October 1956
New York, N.Y.

Roosevelt expressed her interest in the Montgomery bus boycott in her "My Day" newspaper column of 14 May, which was based on her interview with Rosa Parks.[1] King's 5 November reply indicated that he was traveling when Roosevelt's telegram arrived.[2]

MARTIN LUTHER KING

309 SOUTH JACKSON MONTGOMERY ALA

HAVE BEEN MUCH INTERESTED IN WHAT YOU ARE DOING IN MONTGOMERY WOULD BE DELIGHTED IF YOU CAN COME TO SEE ME EITHER SUNDAY OCTOBER 21 AT 12 NOON OR TUESDAY OCTOBER 23 AT 4 PM MY APARTMENT 211 EAST 62 STREET NEW YORK CITY

ELEANOR ROOSEVELT

PWSr. MLKP-MBU: Box 64.

---

1. While serving as first lady from 1933 to 1945, Eleanor Roosevelt (1884–1962) endorsed the NAACP in 1934 and 1935 and campaigned vigorously for the Wagner Costigan Anti-Lynching Bill. In 1935 she began a syndicated column called "My Day," which reached millions of Americans every week. After leaving the White House, Roosevelt remained an active supporter of civil rights reform. President Harry S. Truman appointed her to the American delegation to the United Nations General Assembly in 1945. She served as chair of the U.N. Economic and Social Council's Commission on Human Rights the next year.

2. See pp. 420–421 in this volume.

NSB028   (02).

NS NA080 PD= NEW YORK NY 17 953AME=   1956 OCT 17 AM 9 15

MARTIN LUTHER KING=

   309 SOUTH JACKSON MONTGOMERY ALA=

HAVE BEEN MUCH INTERESTED IN WHAT YOU ARE DOING

IN MONTGOMERY WOULD BE DELIGHTED IF YOU CAN COME

TO SEE ME EITHER SUNDAY OCTOBER 21 AT 12 NOON OR

TUESDAY OCTOBER 23 AT 4 PM MY APARTMENT 211 EAST

62 STREET NEW YORK CITY=

       ELEANOR ROOSEVELT=

From T. J. Jemison

21 October 1956
Baton Rouge, La.

*Jemison, pastor of Mount Zion First Baptist Church in Baton Rouge and leader of
a brief bus boycott in 1953, invites King to deliver his church's annual Men's Day
address.[1] On 31 October King wrote agreeing to deliver the sermon on 18 November.*

Dr. M. L. King, Jr., Pastor
Dexter Avenue Baptist Church
308 South Jackson Street
Montgomery, Alabama

My dear Friend:

After our conversation via of the telephone earlier this evening, I thought I
would write and let you know just how important your coming to {us} would be.

First, our community like most other communities in United States want to
see and hear you. It will be more than a church engagement, it will be a community one.

Second, the people of Baton Rouge more than others could and would appreciate your coming because we too had a similar experience as to yours in Montgomery. Our refusal to ride lasted only eight days, therefore, we here know what
you and your supporters have been through for almost a year.

Third, it would mean much to our local church program and development.
We need the boost your coming would give. Please do all you can to help a friend
out if you can. I feel that if you can, you will.

Will take care of your round-trip flight ticket, all other expenses and will give
you a very nice honorarium.

Just as soon as you have made your decision, want you let me know, so that I
may go forward with the good news of your coming.

With kind greetings to Mrs. King, and a prayer for your continued health and
success, I am

Very sincerely yours,
[*signed*]
T. J. Jemison

TALS. MLKP-MBU: Box 61.

---

1. Theodore Judson Jemison (1919–) was general secretary of the National Baptist Convention and
son of a past president of the organization. During the spring of 1953 Jemison and others had successfully petitioned the Baton Rouge City Council to desegregate the buses, but the state attorney general
had ruled that the new city ordinance was in violation of state segregation laws. In June Jemison
helped found the United Defense League to organize a bus boycott to protest the ruling. The eight-
day boycott, featuring nightly mass meetings and a free car pool system, ended when the organizers
accepted a compromise seating arrangement that allowed most of the seats to be filled on a first-come,
first-served basis. On 8 December 1955, three days into the Montgomery boycott, King contacted Jemison for advice. He later expressed his appreciation for Jemison's "painstaking description" of the car
pools in Baton Rouge, calling his suggestions "invaluable" (*Stride Toward Freedom*, p. 75).

To L. Harold DeWolf

23 October 1956
[*Montgomery, Ala.*]

*King agrees to meet with his former dissertation advisor and interested Boston
University students for lunch on 30 October. King delivered "A Realistic Look at Race
Relations" to the Ford Hall Forum (which met in Boston University's Jordan Hall) on
28 October, but he canceled his subsequent engagements after receiving word of a
possible court injunction against the bus boycott.*[1]

Dr. L. Harold DeWolf
Boston University School of Theology
745 Commonwealth Avenue
Boston 15, Massachusetts

Dear Dr. DeWolf:

Thanks for your very kind letter of October 9. I would have answered this letter
long before now but absence from the city for several days has delayed my reply.

I will be more than happy to meet with a group of students for a discussion
session during my stay in Boston. It appears to me that the only possible time that
I could engage in such a session would be Tuesday noon at the lunch hour. All
other possibilities that you suggested conflict with engagements that I have already made. On Monday evening I have a commitment in Providence, Rhode
Island, and all day Monday and Tuesday morning I will be in the process of having
a general medical examination at Lahey Clinic. I will have to leave Boston about
six o'clock Tuesday afternoon for New York City. In the light of these prior commitments, the Tuesday noon hour seems to be the only possibility. If this can be
arranged you may feel free to go ahead with the plans.

I will be arriving in Boston Sunday afternoon around one or two o'clock. Since
I will have to be going back and forth to Lahey Clinic Monday and Tuesday I have
made arrangements to stop at the Statler Hotel. I will call you as soon as I arrive
at the hotel. I have just corresponded with Mrs. Levenberg, and she stated that
you have already talked with her concerning the hour that you will have me at
Jordan Hall.

I am looking forward with great anticipation to a rich fellowship with you and
your family and the whole Boston community.

Sincerely yours,
Martin L. King, Jr.

MLK:mlb

TLc. MLKP-MBU: Box 15.

---

1. Excerpts of King's speech, which Ballou sent on 25 October 1956 to Selma Levenberg of the
Forum, suggest that this address was similar to "The 'New Negro' of the South: Behind the Montgomery Story," published in the June 1956 issue of the *Socialist Call* (see pp. 280–286 in this volume).

From C. Kenzie Steele

23 October 1956
Tallahassee, Fla.

Steele, president of Tallahassee's Inter-Civic Council and leader of that city's five-month bus boycott, expresses regret that King was unable to speak in Tallahassee on 21 October as previously scheduled. King gave the Sunday sermon at Dexter that morning after a week-long speaking tour, but due to an unidentified "emergency" he was unable to attend the mass meeting in Tallahassee that evening. The day before, Steele and twenty other Inter-Civic Council activists had been fined for operating an unlicensed car pool. "We're going to keep walking," Steele announced; "the boycott of the buses will keep going on." [1]

Rev. M. L. King Jr.
520 Union Street
Montgomery, Alabama

Dear Mr. King:

We still have you on our agenda and are looking forward to your coming to Tallahassee in the near future.

There were over 1000 people to turn out Sunday to see and hear you. This shows how anxious the people here are to hear you speak.

We regret very much of the emergency you recognized on your arrival. We sincerely hope you have been successful in clearing them up by this time. We realize it is needless to mention, you have our solicitation and our support for every instant.

When you learn which day you will arrive here, wire us.

Sincerely yours,
[*signed*]
Rev. C. K. Steele, President of the Inter-Civic Council

CKS:jph

TLS. MLKP-MBU: Box 60.

---

1. "Outlaw Car Pool, Boycott Still On," *New York Amsterdam News,* 27 October 1956. Charles Kenzie Steele (1914–1980), born and raised in Gary, West Virginia, received his B.A. from Morehouse College in 1938. He served churches in Montgomery and Augusta, Georgia, before being called to Tallahassee's Bethel Baptist Church. He was head of the local NAACP when, in May 1956, he was elected president of the Inter-Civic Council, an organization formed to provide leadership for the city's bus boycott. In 1956 Steele and King participated in several nonviolence workshops, including panels at the National Baptist Convention's annual meeting, Tuskegee Institute, and the MIA's Institute on Nonviolence and Social Change. In early 1957 Steele was elected SCLC's first vice president at its founding meeting.

25 October 1956
Washington, D.C.

Presidential assistant and cabinet secretary Rabb acknowledges the 27 August letter
from King and other Montgomery black leaders to President Eisenhower.[1] Department
of Justice officials Warren Olney III and Arthur B. Caldwell had responded to the letter
on 7 September.

Reverend M. L. King, Jr.
530 S. Union Street
Montgomery Alabama

Dear Mr. King:

The President has asked me to thank you for your letter of recent date. We regret the delay in replying but your letter arrived while we were in San Francisco and due to the heavy volume of mail received, were unable to process your letter at an earlier date.

The situation in Montgomery has been followed with interest and the President appreciates having your views and analysis. I am advised that the Department of Justice is aware of the problem.

Sincerely,
[*signed*]
Maxwell M. Rabb

TLS. MLKP-MBU: Box 64.

---

1. Maxwell M. Rabb (1910–) was a Harvard-educated lawyer who served as Eisenhower's campaign manager in 1952. In 1958 he left the administration to join a New York law firm. He later served on the board of directors of the NAACP Legal Defense and Education Fund.

From B. J. Simms

26 October 1956
Montgomery, Ala.

Simms, a Baptist minister and Alabama State College professor, had served as director
of transportation for the MIA car pool for five months.[1] On 13 September the MIA

---

1. B. J. Simms (1904–), a native of Alabama, came to Montgomery in 1931 to attend Alabama State College. He served as the first principal of Alabama State Laboratory High School, a black high school in Montgomery. After receiving a scholarship (sponsored by Dexter Avenue Baptist Church) to pursue

executive board asked him to reimburse the organization for car pool funds that he had apparently misplaced, an action that may have prompted him to resign the post.[2] *Simms subsequently assumed a new leadership position as the MIA's promotional director.*

To the President and members of the Executive Committee of The Montgomery Improvement Association, Inc.

Dear Brethren:

For nearly seven months I have labored and given my all to the association and the people of Montgomery for the cause of freedom. I have done my best in spite of many hinderances and obstacles placed in my path. In spite of the above road blocks and difficulties in my path, I have labored without stint and given my all to the movement. I have now, after careful consideration, decided that I cannot, under the present conditions, continue in the position as Director of Transportation. I am therefore submitting my resignation to be effective at once or no later than Wednesday, October 31, 1956. In submitting my resignation I wish it known that I am not severing my association with the organization and that I will therefore continue to cooperate with all my heart towards the successful attainment of our goal of dignity and freedom for all.

In closing, I wish to thank all who supported me in my efforts to effect a workable transportation system for our people, for without your support and encouragement I could not have gone on under the existing conditions of which I have had to work.

Respectfully submitted
[*signed*]
(Rev.) B. J. Simms, Director
Transportation

TLS.MLKP-MBU: Box 30.

---

divinity studies at Oberlin College, Simms was ordained a Baptist minister in 1942 and received a master of theology from Oakland College. During World War II he helped establish a USO branch for African Americans. In 1946 Simms became chaplain of Alabama State and later a professor of history, while serving as an itinerant minister on weekends. Simms was appointed chair of the transportation committee to reform the car pool system and served on the MIA executive board. He was among those indicted for his role in the boycott.

2. W. J. Powell, Minutes, MIA Executive Board Meeting, 13 September 1956.

From Walter R. McCall

29 October 1956
Fort Valley, Ga.

McCall thanks King for recommending him to a Savannah church and indicates that two other churches are considering him as well. Several months later Atlanta's

Providence Baptist Church called him to its pulpit. McCall also praises fellow Baptist preacher and Morehouse graduate Charles Morton for his service during Fort Valley State College's Week of Prayer.[1]

30 Oct
1956

Dear Mike,

Thanks Ole Timer for the letter of recommendation. It was good and interesting. I hope it pays off. But if not, I do hope I can land at Providence in Atlanta or in the Ebenezer in Athens. Preferably Athens. I Think it has greater promise than either of the former. I have preached at all but First AB in Savannah.

All things are going smoothly, but work seems to hit me on all sides. We have just completed our Week of Prayer here, led by Chuck Morton. Believe me when I tell you: Morton has it. He needs to be heard by our people, and the American people at-large. Mike, Morton has it! He has established himself here in immeasurable fashion!

Norma is doing fine now since we have moved from the one room to a home of our own. Time will not permit me to say too much. Will write more later.

Remember not to become confident of **WHITE PEOPLE** collectively. They have no love in their hearts for Negroes. Stay out of public alone. Take no chances at any time.

Norma joins me in sending a hello to the family. With all good wishes for a good year ahead, I am

Sincerely,
[*signed*] Mac
A Pal

{WRM}

TALS. MLKP-MBU: Box 17.

---

1. Charles E. Morton (1926–) received his B.A. (1946) from Morehouse College, his B.D. (1949) from Union Theological Seminary, and his Ph.D. (1958) from Columbia University. He was a professor of religion and philosophy at Knoxville College in 1956, though he left shortly thereafter to become a professor at Dillard University. In 1963 he became minister of Metropolitan Baptist Church in Detroit.

To George Lawrence

30 October 1956
[*Montgomery, Ala.*]

Lawrence, executive chairman of In Friendship, had initiated a fund-raising campaign asking 1,200 churches to pledge $10 each week to the MIA "for the duration of the emergency in Montgomery." Lawrence had intended to meet with King and Bayard Rustin during King's 16 October stop at a New York airport, but illness forced him to ask by mail on 18 October for a list of MIA contributors. He also requested additional photographs of Coretta Scott King, who was scheduled to sing in an upcoming fund-raising concert on 5 December that also featured Duke Ellington and Harry Belafonte.

The Rev. George Lawrence
Friendship Baptist Church
144 West 131st Street
New York 27, New York

Dear George:

This is to acknowledge receipt of your letter of October 18. Absence from the city for a few days has delayed my reply.

We are very grateful to "In friendship" for the interest that it has taken in our struggle. I can assure you that we will long remember your coming to our aid at this time.

After checking with the secretary I find that we have the names of more than seven thousand persons and organizations that have contributed to our association in the past. It will entail a great deal of time to compile this list. The pressure of work in the office is of such a nature at this point that it will almost be impossible to get to it in the next few days. Please know that we regret this very deeply, and it is more regrettable in the light of the fact that the forwarding of such a list to you would greatly help our organization. But the volume of work before us at the present time makes it impossible to compile this list of some seven thousand persons and organizations. Be sure to let me know what else we can do to assist you in this project.

I have mentioned your request to Mrs. King concerning the additional glossy photographs. I am sure that she will be getting them to you in the next few days.

I hope things are going well with you. I too am sorry that I did not have the opportunity to see you in New York the other day.

With warm personal regards, I am

Sincerely yours,
M. L. King, Jr.,
President

MLK:b
(Dictated by Rev. King but signed in his absence.)

TLc. MLKP-MBU: Box 17.

To Earl Kennedy

30 October 1956
[*Montgomery, Ala.*]

On 18 October Kennedy, a 1941 Morehouse graduate and Detroit Republican activist, asked King about his position "relative to Negro people voting for Democratic candidates nationally." In Kennedy's view, Democratic control of the House and Senate would mean the "perpetuation of Senator Eastland's control, and the future possibility of a purged Supreme Court." King refuses to take a public stand in the November election, unlike his father, who a week earlier had declared from his pulpit that Eisenhower's position on civil rights was "firmer" than Stevenson's.[1]

1. "Rev. M. L. King, Sr., Announces His Support for Ike," *Birmingham World*, 20 October 1956.

Mr. Earl Kennedy, Chairman   31 Oct
First Congressional District   1956
Michigan Citizens for Eisenhower
400 North Capitol Avenue
Lansing, Michigan

Dear Mr. Kennedy:

Thanks for your very kind letter of October 18, making inquiry concerning my political position. Actually, I am not taking any public position in this election. In private opinion I find something to be desired from both parties. The Negro has been betrayed by both the Democratic and Republican Party. The Democrats have betrayed us by capitulating to the whims and caprices of the southern dixiecrats. The Republicans have betrayed us by capitulating to the blatent hypocrisy of conservative right wing northerners. This coalition of southern dixiecrats and right wing northern Republicans defeats every move toward liberal legislation in Congress. So we confront the problem of choosing the lesser of two evils. At this point I might say however, that I feel that the Negro must remain an independent voter, not becoming unduly tied to either party. He should seek to vote for the party which is more concerned with the welfare of all the people.

I was more than happy to hear from you, and of course I was very happy to know that you are an alumnus of Morehouse College. I hope it will be possible to meet you personally sometime in the near future.

Sincerely yours,
M. L. King, Jr.,
President

MLK:b
(Dictated by Rev. King but signed in his absence)

TLc. MLKP-MBU: Box 61.

Annual Report, Dexter Avenue Baptist Church

1 November 1955–31 October 1956
Montgomery, Ala.

In this introduction to his forty-page annual report King summarizes the church's accomplishments and thanks the congregation for supporting his leadership of the bus boycott. As leader of a movement with "international" dimensions, King notes that he has "often lagged behind in my pastoral duties" because demands on his time had "tripled." He therefore recommends that the church hire him an assistant. King's list of pastoral chores, which are not transcribed below, included 36 sermons preached at Dexter, 110 community and civic meetings attended, and 21 books and 96 periodicals read. King proposed a budget of $18,502 for the 1956–1957 fiscal year, considerably less than the $25,445 the church had spent the previous year. King presented this report at Dexter's annual meeting on 24 October, where it was received, according to one account, as "factual, informative, sincere, inspiring, and permeated with workable

409

and achievable recommendations, all of which were unanimously approved by the congregation."[1]

Introductory Expressions

We come again to the end of an old church year and the beginning of a new church year. As we stand at the point where the old and the new intersect, we are inevitably driven to think of past achievements and future challanges.

The 1955–56 church year has been a year of concrete spiritual advances in the life of Dexter. More than forty new members have joined the fellowship of Dexter this year. Fortunately, most of these new members are active participants in the life of the church, and have joined other members in inspiring worship services each Lord's Day.

Financially, we have done amazingly well. We have exceeded the high peak which was reached in the 1954–55 church year. Receipts from all sources have exceeded twenty-four thousand ($24,000.00). Of this amount we have given generously for benevolent purposes, missions, and education. Our building fund has now passed the twenty-five hundred dollar mark ($25,000.00).[2]

Toward the end of the church year we undertook a renovation program which exceeded six thousand dollars ($6,000.00). Through this renovation program several improvements were made in the parsonage and the church structure. The first unit of the church has taken a totally new face, with new rubber tile on the floor, new cellotex for the ceiling, new fluorescent lights, new venetian blinds, new tables, and new gas heaters.* In the vestibule of the church a new water fountain has been installed.† In the main sanctuary a new Grand Kimbell Piano has been added to beautify the worship services.

Many other wonderful things have taken place in the life of the church this year. Mention can only be made of a few. The church can now boast of the publication of a church paper. This church paper, known as the Dexter Echo, has served to meet a real need in the life of the church. Under the skilled and competent editorship of Mr. George Jones, the Dexter Echo serves to keep members and friends of Dexter abreast with all of the pertinent information concerning the church and its membership. Under the direction of the Scholarship Fund Committee, two scholarships of Seventy-five dollars each were given to two fine young

* These new gas heaters and their installation were made possible by a gift of $100.00 from the pastor's wife Mrs. Coretta S. King.
† This much needed water fountain was given as a gift to the church by Mr. John Brown and Mrs. Caressa Williams in memory of their father and mother, Mr. and Mrs. John Brown.

---

1. "Dexter in Annual Business Meeting," *Dexter Echo,* 31 October 1956, p. 1.
2. The financial report indicated that the building fund contained $2,495.11.

members of our church who are now freshmen in college.[3] Under the joint sponsorship of the Young Matrons Circle and the Ushers of the church Mrs. Coretta King was presented in a concert. This event proved to be one of the high points of the church year. It was both culturally and spiritually stimulating. The work of the Social and Political Action Committee continues to be superb. The entire membership has profited from the work of this committee. It has kept us informed on the major social and political issues of our time. The "special days" through the church year have again been tremendously successful. Through these special occasions we were fortunate enough to bring to Dexter some of the outstanding preachers and personalities of our nation. The various auxiliaries of the church are still active and working to further the total program of the church. All of these things represent the marvelous achievements of a church year that is now passing into history. New levels of spiritual development were reached in the 1955–56 church year that will remain in our thoughts so long as the chords of memory shall lengthen.

Certainly a personal word of thanks is in order at this point. As pastor, I would like to express my deepest appreciation to every member of Dexter for the cooperation given to my program and the personal courtesies extended to me and my family. Almost eleven months ago, through the force of circumstance, I was catapulted into the leadership position of a movement that has now risen to international propotions. Because of this new role, demands upon my time have tripled. The world-wide interest in the Montgomery Movement has made it necessary for me to do an extensive amount of traveling. Due to the multiplicity of duties that have come to me as a result of my involvement in the protest, I have often lagged behind in my pastoral duties. Yet, with a real sense of dedication to the cause, you have expressed a deep synpathetic understanding. You have carried on in my absence. You have given words of encouragement when I needed them most. Even when my life and the life of my family were in personal jeopardy, you were at my side. When we stood amid the bleak and desolate night of agony, you were always present with the bright morning of hope. For all of these things, I can not begin to thank you with words. I can only say that there are strong torrents of gratitude flowing from the depths of my heart which can never be captured by the thin vessels of words.

3. Teresa Anderson and Carolyn Motley received the scholarships.

As I bring this message to a close I must mention the job that lies ahead. As stated above, we reached new heights in the 1955–56 church year, but we must reach even greater heights in 1956–57. We have come a long, long way, but we have a long, long way to go. There are still gigantic spiritual mountains that we have not climbed. There are still uncharted continents of religious education that we have not explored. There are still unchurched persons in the community who are desperately in need of Christ. Let us rise up with bold determination to lift our church to new levels of spiritual achievement, and thereby bring the Kingdom of God nearer to our community. If we are to remain a great church we must never become a stagnant pool. Rather, we must be an ever flowing river.

M.L.K., Jr.

[*List of outstanding events, pastoral chores, sermons and lectures away from home, and new members omitted.*]

Recommendations

The following are recommendations submitted by the pastor for the 1956–57 church year:

1. In order to increase the membership of the church as well as extend the spiritual influence of the church throughout the community, a serious evangelistic champaign shall be continued, extending throughout the church year. This champaign shall be carried out by twenty-five evangelistic teams, each consisting of a captain and at least three other members. Each team shall be urged to bring in at least five new members within the church year. The team that brings in the highest number of members shall be duly recognized at the end of the church year. Each captain shall call his team together at least once a month to discuss findings and possibilities. [*List of team members is omitted.*]
2. In order to give the pastor some assistance in the multiplicity of duties that have accumulated as a result of his larger ministry to the community and the expanding program of the church, an assistant to the pastor shall be employed. The duties of this office shall be outlined by the pastor.
3. In order to meet the growing economic issues of our community and realize our great economic potential, a committee shall be appointed to pursue the idea of establishing a Credit Union in this church. This committee shall be requested to look into this matter immediately, and bring back concrete recommendations to the Official Board within the next month. The committee shall consist of the following persons: Mr. C. L. Dennard, Chairman; John Cannon, J. H. Gilchrist, C. Earl Anderson, P. M. Blair, F. W. Taylor, Sr., C. C. Beverly, Robert Nesbitt, Sr.

[*List of church members and officers is omitted, as is the detailed financial report.*]

TD. MLKP-MBU: Box 77.

31 October 1956
[*Montgomery, Ala.*]

King sends an unidentified sermon to help his younger brother prepare for his first sermon at Ebenezer Baptist Church in Atlanta, where he was to serve as assistant pastor under his father.[1]

Mr. A. D. King
501 Auburn Avenue
Atlanta, Georgia

Dear A. D.:

Enclosed is a copy of the sermon which I mentioned to you. I hope you will find it useful. I am looking forward with great anticipation to being with you on the evening of your initial sermon. I am sure everything will go extraordinarily well. Give my regards to the family. Coretta and I are doing fine.

Sincerely,
Martin

MLK:b

enclosure

TLc. MLKP-MBU: Box 61.

---

1. Alfred Daniel Williams King (1930–1969) attended Palmer Institute in North Carolina before receiving his B.A. (1959) at Morehouse College. His brother and father were among those who ordained him as a minister on 5 June 1957 at Ebenezer. He assisted his father at Ebenezer from December 1956 until early 1959, when he became pastor of Mount Vernon First Baptist Church in Newnan, Georgia. In 1963 A. D. King was pastor of Ensley's First Street Baptist Church and a leader of the Birmingham movement. On 11 May 1963 his parsonage was bombed along with the Gaston Hotel, where King, Jr., was staying. A. D. King later moved to Louisville, Kentucky, to become pastor of Zion Baptist Church. After his brother's death in 1968 A. D. returned to Atlanta to serve as co-pastor of Ebenezer with his father.

To Benjamin F. McLaurin

[*31 October 1956*]
[*Montgomery, Ala.*]

Threatened with the possibility of a city injunction charging the MIA with running an illegal jitney service, King sends McLaurin this telegram at 11 :30 P.M. canceling his speech at a rally the next day in Newark, sponsored by the New Jersey Committee for Civil Rights. The following day MIA attorneys filed a petition in U.S. District Court to

413

*enjoin the city from interfering with its car pool. At about 10:30 that night, the city
delivered its own petition asking Judge Eugene Carter to ban the MIA car pool because
it lacked a license.[1] On 2 November Judge Carter scheduled a hearing for 13 November.*

B F MCLAURIN
217 W 125TH ST.
ROOM 301

CITY OF MONTGOMERY IS PRESENTLY IN THE PROCESS OF SEEKING AN INJUNCTION AGAINST
THE MONTGOMERY IMPROVEMENT ASSOCIATION. THIS INJUNCTION IS EXPECTED TO BE ISSUED
TODAY. IN THE LIGHT OF THIS INJUNCTION IT WILL BE NECESSARY TO RE-ORGANIZE THE TOTAL
STRUCTURE OF OUR TRANSPORTATION SYSTEM. THIS ISSUE DEMANDS MY IMMEDIATE PERSONAL
ATTENTION. IT IS ABSOLUTELY NECESSARY FOR ME TO HAVE A SERIES OF MEETINGS AND AN
EXECUTIVE BOARD MEETING THIS AFTERNOON. IT IS THEREFORE NECESSARY FOR ME TO
CANCEL MY ENGAGEMENT IN NEWARK. I CAN ASSURE YOU THAT IT IS WITH DEEPEST REGRET
THAT THIS DECISION MUST BE MADE. I HAD LOOKED FORWARD WITH GREAT ANTICIPATION TO
A RICH EXPERIENCE IN NEWARK. HOWEVER, I AM SURE THAT YOU UNDERSTAND THE MANY
EMERGENCIES THAT ARISE IN THIS TYPE OF SITUATION I HOPE THAT MY ABSENCE WILL NOT
SERIOUSLY HAMPER YOUR PROGRAM. YOU HAVE MY PRAYERS AND BEST WISHES FOR A MOST
SUCCESSFUL MEETING.

REV M L KING JR

TWc. MLKP-MBU: Box 61.

---

1. Jo Ann Flirt, "Injunction Sought: City Requests Car Pool Halt," *Montgomery Advertiser*, 3 November 1956.

"Paul's Letter to American Christians,"
Sermon Delivered at Dexter Avenue Baptist Church

4 November 1956
Montgomery, Ala.

*In this Dexter sermon King reads a fictional letter from the apostle Paul to American
Christians of the mid–twentieth century. Loosely based on Paul's letter to the Romans,
King's sermon notes the gap between the nation's scientific progress and its ethical and
spiritual development. Deploring exploitative capitalism, spiritual arrogance, racial
segregation, and self-righteous egotism, he offers the remedy of Christian love. "Only
through achieving this love," King writes, "can you expect to matriculate into the
university of eternal life." King delivered the same sermon on 7 September at the
National Baptist Convention.[1]*

---

1. For details of the reception it found there, see C. W. Kelly to King, 8 September 1956, pp. 365–366 in this volume. King later published the sermon in revised form in *Strength to Love* (1963).

I would like to share with you an imaginary letter from the pen of the Apostle Paul. The postmark reveals that it comes from the city of Ephesus. After opening the letter I discovered that it was written in Greek rather than English. At the top of the first page was this request: "Please read to your congregation as soon as possible, and then pass on to the other churches."

For several weeks I have worked assiduously with the translation. At times it has been difficult, but now I think I have deciphered its true meaning. May I hasten to say that if in presenting this letter the contents sound strangely Kingian instead of Paulinian, attribute it to my lack of complete objectivity rather than Paul's lack of clarity.

It is miraculous, indeed, that the Apostle Paul should be writing a letter to you and to me nearly 1900 years after his last letter appeared in the New Testament. How this is possible is something of an enigma wrapped in mystery. The important thing, however, is that I can imagine the Apostle Paul writing a letter to American Christians in 1956 A.D. And here is the letter as it stands before me.

I, an apostle of Jesus Christ by the will of God, to you who are in America, Grace be unto you, and peace from God our Father, through our Lord and Savior, Jesus Christ.

For many years I have longed to be able to come to see you. I have heard so much of you and of what you are doing. I have heard of the fascinating and astounding advances that you have made in the scientific realm. I have heard of your dashing subways and flashing airplanes. Through your scientific genius you have been able to dwarf distance and place time in chains. You have been able to carve highways through the stratosphere. So in your world you have made it possible to eat breakfast in New York City and dinner in Paris, France. I have also heard of your skyscraping buildings with their prodigious towers steeping heavenward. I have heard of your great medical advances, which have resulted in the curing of many dread plagues and diseases, and thereby prolonged your lives and made for greater security and physical well-being. All of that is marvelous. You can do so many things in your day that I could not do in the Greco-Roman world of my day. In your age you can travel distances in one day that took me three months to travel. That is wonderful. You have made tremendous strides in the area of scientific and technological development.

But America, as I look at you from afar, I wonder whether your moral and spiritual progress has been commensurate with your scientific progress. It seems to me that your moral progress lags behind your scientific progress. Your poet Thoreau used to talk about "improved means to an unimproved end." How often this is true. You have allowed the material means by which you live to outdistance the spiritual ends for which you live. You have allowed your mentality to outrun your morality. You have allowed your civilization to outdistance your culture. Through your scientific genius you have made of the world a neighborhood, but through your moral and spiritual genius you have failed to make of it a brotherhood. So America, I would urge you to keep your moral advances abreast with your scientific advances.

I am impelled to write you concerning the responsibilities laid upon you to live as Christians in the midst of an unChristian world. That is what I had to do. That is what every Christian has to do. But I understand that there are many Christians in America who give their ultimate allegiance to man-made systems and customs. They are afraid to be different. Their great concern is to be accepted socially.

They live by some such principle as this: "everybody is doing it, so it must be alright." For so many of you Morality is merely group consensus. In your modern sociological lingo, the mores are accepted as the right ways. You have unconsciously come to believe that right is discovered by taking a sort of Gallop poll of the majority opinion. How many are giving their ultimate allegiance to this way.

But American Christians, I must say to you as I said to the Roman Christians years ago, "Be not conformed to this world, but be ye transformed by the renewing of your mind." [2] Or, as I said to the Phillipian Christians, "Ye are a colony of heaven." [3] This means that although you live in the colony of time, your ultimate allegiance is to the empire of eternity. You have a dual citizenry. You live both in time and eternity; both in heaven and earth. Therefore, your ultimate allegiance is not to the government, not to the state, not to nation, not to any man-made institution. The Christian owes his ultimate allegiance to God, and if any earthly institution conflicts with God's will it is your Christian duty to take a stand against it. You must never allow the transitory evanescent demands of man-made institutions to take precedence over the eternal demands of the Almighty God.

I understand that you have an economic system in America known as Capitalism. Through this economic system you have been able to do wonders. You have become the richest nation in the world, and you have built up the greatest system of production that history has ever known. All of this is marvelous. But Americans, there is the danger that you will misuse your Capitalism. I still contend that money can be the root of all evil.[4] It can cause one to live a life of gross materialism. I am afraid that many among you are more concerned about making a living than making a life. You are prone to judge the success of your profession by the index of your salary and the size of the wheel base on your automobile, rather than the quality of your service to humanity.

The misuse of Capitalism can also lead to tragic exploitation. This has so often happened in your nation. They tell me that one tenth of one percent of the population controls more than forty percent of the wealth. Oh America, how often have you taken necessities from the masses to give luxuries to the classes. If you are to be a truly Christian nation you must solve this problem. You cannot solve the problem by turning to communism, for communism is based on an ethical relativism and a metaphysical materialism that no Christian can accept. You can work within the framework of democracy to bring about a better distribution of wealth. You can use your powerful economic resources to wipe poverty from the face of the earth. God never intended for one group of people to live in superfluous inordinate wealth, while others live in abject deadening poverty. God intends for all of his children to have the basic necessities of life, and he has left in this universe "enough and to spare" for that purpose. So I call upon you to bridge the gulf between abject poverty and superfluous wealth.

I would that I could be with you in person, so that I could say to you face to

---

2. Romans 12:2.

3. Philippians 3:20: "For our citizenship is in heaven, from which we also eagerly wait for the Savior, the Lord Jesus Christ."

4. 1 Timothy 6:10.

face what I am forced to say to you in writing. Oh, how I long to share your
fellowship.

Let me rush on to say something about the church. Americans, I must remind
you, as I have said to so many others, that the church is the Body of Christ. So
when the church is true to its nature it knows neither division nor disunity. But I
am disturbed about what you are doing to the Body of Christ. They tell me that
in America you have within Protestantism more than two hundred and fifty six
denominations. The tragedy is not so much that you have such a multiplicity of
denominations, but that most of them are warring against each other with a claim
to absolute truth. This narrow sectarianism is destroying the unity of the Body of
Christ. You must come to see that God is neither a Baptist nor a Methodist; He is
neither a Presbyterian nor a Episcopalian. God is bigger than all of our denominations. If you are to be true witnesses for Christ, you must come to see that
America.

But I must not stop with a criticism of Protestantism. I am disturbed about
Roman Catholicism. This church stands before the world with its pomp and
power, insisting that it possesses the only truth. It incorporates an arrogance that
becomes a dangerous spiritual arrogance. It stands with its noble Pope who somehow rises to the miraculous heights of infallibility when he speaks *ex cathedra*. But
I am disturbed about a person or an institution that claims infallibility in this
world. I am disturbed about any church that refuses to cooperate with other
churches under the pretense that it is the only true church. I must emphasize the
fact that God is not a Roman Catholic, and that the boundless sweep of his revelation cannot be limited to the Vatican. Roman Catholicism must do a great deal
to mend its ways.

There is another thing that disturbs me to no end about the American church.
You have a white church and you have a Negro church. You have allowed segregation to creep into the doors of the church. How can such a division exist in the
true Body of Christ? You must face the tragic fact that when you stand at 11:00 on
Sunday morning to sing "All Hail the Power of Jesus Name" and "Dear Lord and
Father of all Mankind," you stand in the most segregated hour of Christian
America. They tell me that there is more integration in the entertaining world
and other secular agencies than there is in the Christian church. How appalling
that is.

I understand that there are Christians among you who try to justify segregation
on the basis of the Bible. They argue that the Negro is inferior by nature because
of Noah's curse upon the children of Ham. Oh my friends, this is blasphemy. This
is against everything that the Christian religion stands for. I must say to you as I
have said to so many Christians before, that in Christ "there is neither Jew nor
Gentile, there is neither bond nor free, there is neither male nor female, for we
are all one in Christ Jesus." [5] Moreover, I must reiterate the words that I uttered
on Mars Hill: "God that made the world and all things therein . . . hath made of
one blood all nations of men for to dwell on all the face of the earth." [6]

---

5. Galatians 3:28.
6. Acts 17:24, 26.

So Americans I must urge you to get rid of every aspect of segregation. The broad universalism standing at the center of the gospel makes both the theory and practice of segregation morally unjustifiable. Segregation is a blatant denial of the unity which we all have in Christ. It substitutes an "I-it" relationship for the "I-thou" relationship.[7] The segregator relegates the segregated to the status of a thing rather than elevate him to the status of a person. The underlying philosophy of Christianity is diametrically opposed to the underlying philosophy of segregation, and all the dialectics of the logicians cannot make them lie down together.

I praise your Supreme Court for rendering a great decision just two or three years ago. I am happy to know that so many persons of goodwill have accepted the decision as a great moral victory. But I understand that there are some brothers among you who have risen up in open defiance. I hear that their legislative halls ring loud with such words as "nullification" and "interposition." They have lost the true meaning of democracy and Christianity. So I would urge each of you to plead patiently with your brothers, and tell them that this isn't the way. With understanding goodwill, you are obligated to seek to change their attitudes. Let them know that in standing against integration, they are not only standing against the noble precepts of your democracy, but also against the eternal edicts of God himself. Yes America, there is still the need for an Amos to cry out to the nation: "Let judgement roll down as waters, and righteousness as a mighty stream." [8]

May I say just a word to those of you who are struggling against this evil. Always be sure that you struggle with Christian methods and Christian weapons. Never succumb to the temptation of becoming bitter. As you press on for justice, be sure to move with dignity and discipline, using only the weapon of love. Let no man pull you so low as to hate him. Always avoid violence. If you succumb to the temptation of using violence in your struggle, unborn generations will be the recipients of a long and desolate night of bitterness, and your chief legacy to the future will be an endless reign of meaningless chaos.

In your struggle for justice, let your oppressor know that you are not attempting to defeat or humiliate him, or even to pay him back for injustices that he has heaped upon you. Let him know that you are merely seeking justice for him as well as yourself. Let him know that the festering sore of segregation debilitates the white man as well as the Negro. With this attitude you will be able to keep your struggle on high Christian standards.

Many persons will realize the urgency of seeking to eradicate the evil of segregation. There will be many Negroes who will devote their lives to the cause of freedom. There will be many white persons of goodwill and strong moral sensitivity who will dare to take a stand for justice. Honesty impels me to admit that such a stand will require willingness to suffer and sacrifice. So don't despair if you are condemned and persecuted for righteousness' sake. Whenever you take a stand for truth and justice, you are liable to scorn. Often you will be called an

---

7. See Martin Buber, *I and Thou* (Edinburgh: T. and T. Clark, 1937).
8. Amos 5:24.

impractical idealist or a dangerous radical. Sometimes it might mean going to jail. If such is the case you must honorably grace the jail with your presence. It might even mean physical death. But if physical death is the price that some must pay to free their children from a permanent life of psychological death, then nothing could be more Christian.[9] Don't worry about persecution America; you are going to have that if you stand up for a great principle. I can say this with some authority, because my life was a continual round of persecutions. After my conversion I was rejected by the disciples at Jerusalem. Later I was tried for heresy at Jerusalem. I was jailed at Philippi, beaten at Thessalonica, mobbed at Ephesus, and depressed at Athens. And yet I am still going. I came away from each of these experiences more persuaded than ever before that "neither death nor life, nor angels, nor principalities, nor things present, nor things to come . . . shall separate us from the love of God, which is in Christ Jesus our Lord." [10] I still believe that standing up for the truth of God is the greatest thing in the world. This is the end of life. The end of life is not to be happy. The end of life is not to achieve pleasure and avoid pain. The end of life is to do the will of God, come what may.

I must bring my writing to a close now. Timothy is waiting to deliver this letter, and I must take leave for another church. But just before leaving, I must say to you, as I said to the church at Corinth, that I still believe that love is the most durable power in the world. Over the centuries men have sought to discover the highest good. This has been the chief quest of ethical philosophy. This was one of the big questions of Greek philosophy. The Epicurean and the Stoics sought to answer it; Plato and Aristotle sought to answer it. What is the *summon bonum* of life? I think I have an answer America. I think I have discovered the highest good. It is love. This principle stands at the center of the cosmos. As John says, "God is love." He who loves is a participant in the being of God. He who hates does not know God.[11]

So American Christians, you may master the intricacies of the English language. You may possess all of the eloquence of articulate speech. But even if you "speak with the tongues of man and angels, and have not love, you are become as sounding brass, or a tinkling cymbal."

You may have the gift of prophecy and understanding all mysteries.[12] You may be able to break into the storehouse of nature and bring out many insights that men never dreamed were there. You may ascend to the heights of academic achievement, so that you will have all knowledge. You may boast of your great institutions of learning and the boundless extent of your degrees. But all of this amounts to absolutely nothing devoid of love.

But even more Americans, you may give your goods to feed the poor. You may

---

9. In a speech to the National Committee for Rural Schools, King attributed this statement to Kenneth Clark, replacing "Christian" with "honorable" (see King, "Desegregation and the Future," 15 December 1956, p. 478 in this volume).

10. Romans 8:38–39.

11. 1 John 4:16.

12. 1 Corinthians 13:1–2.

give great gifts to charity. You may tower high in philanthropy. But if you have not love it means nothing. You may even give your body to be burned, and die the death of a martyr. Your spilt blood may be a symbol of honor for generations yet unborn, and thousands may praise you as history's supreme hero. But even so, if you have not love your blood was spilt in vain.[13] You must come to see that it is possible for a man to be self-centered in his self-denial and self-righteous in his self-sacrifice. He may be generous in order to feed his ego and pious in order to feed his pride. Man has the tragic capacity to relegate a heightening virtue to a tragic vice. Without love benevolence becomes egotism, and martyrdom becomes spiritual pride.

So the greatest of all virtues is love. It is here that we find the true meaning of the Christian faith. This is at bottom the meaning of the cross. The great event on Calvary signifies more than a meaningless drama that took place on the stage of history. It is a telescope through which we look out into the long vista of eternity and see the love of God breaking forth into time. It is an eternal reminder to a power drunk generation that love is most durable power in the world, and that it is at bottom the heartbeat of the moral cosmos. Only through achieving this love can you expect to matriculate into the university of eternal life.

I must say goodby now. I hope this letter will find you strong in the faith. It is probable that I will not get to see you in America, but I will meet you in God's eternity. And now unto him who is able to keep us from falling, and lift us from the fatigue of despair to the buoyancy of hope, from the midnight of desperation to the daybreak of joy, to him be power and authority, forever and ever. Amen.[14]

PD. MLKP-MBU: Box 119A.

------

13. 1 Corinthians 13:3.
14. Cf. Jude 24–25.

To Eleanor Roosevelt

5 November 1956
Montgomery, Ala.

King was unable to schedule a meeting with Roosevelt during 1956.

Mrs. Eleanor Roosevelt
211 East 62nd Street
New York, New York

Dear Mrs. Roosevelt:

On returning to Montgomery I discovered that you had sent a telegram to me requesting that I meet you in New York. I regret very deeply that my schedule was of such at the time that it was impossible for me to have the interview. I know nothing that I would have welcomed more. Let me express my personal appreciation to you for your interest in our struggle for justice. Please know that your moral support and Christian generosity are of inestimable value in the continuance of our struggle.

Very sincerely yours,
[*signed*]
M. L. King, Jr.,
President

MLK:b

Transcribed and signed in the absence of Rev. King.

TLSr. ERC-NHyF.

To Richard H. Dixon

8 November 1956
[*Montgomery, Ala.*]

Facing a 13 November circuit court hearing on the city's effort to shut down the car pool and a federal court hearing the following day on the MIA's request to enjoin the city's interference in MIA operations, King declines Dixon's invitation to speak in Pontiac, Michigan.[1] On 9 April 1956 Dixon had forwarded $700 to the MIA from the Oakland County Ministerial Fellowship, of which he was president.

The Rev. Richard H. Dixon, Jr.
Trinity Baptist Church
Wessen at Maple Street
Pontiac, Michigan

Dear Richard:

Thanks for your very kind letter of October 22. First, let me apologize for being so tardy in my reply. Absence from the city for several days accounts for the delay.

On returning to the city I discovered that we are once more confronted with court cases. In a desperate attempt to defeat our car pool the city has sought an injunction through the court. This means that for several days next week we will

---

1. Richard H. Dixon, Jr. (1923–), received his B.A. from Bishop College, his B.Th. from American Baptist Theological Seminary, and his B.D. from Colgate Seminary. He served as pastor of Trinity Baptist Church in Pontiac, Michigan, before being called to Macedonia Baptist Church in Mount Vernon, New York. He later headed the Westchester Urban League, the United Black Clergy of Westchester, and the Westchester Christian Leadership Conference. In 1964 Dixon accompanied King and his family to the Nobel Peace Prize ceremonies in Oslo, Norway.

be involved in court proceedings. In the light of this I have had to decline all invitations for speaking engagements for the next month or so. The injunction will mean that our whole transportation system will have to be reorganized. It is absolutely necessary that I be on hand to supervise this monumental responsibility. But for this, I would have been more than happy to come to Pontiac. Please know that I regret this very deeply.

I hope things are going well with you and your work in Pontiac. I was delighted to know that you plan to contribute five dollars a week to our cause from your church. This will go a long, long way in aiding us in our struggle. I will look forward to seeing you in the very near future.

With warm personal regards, I am

Sincerely yours,
M. L. King, Jr.,
President

MLK:b

Transcribed and signed in the absence of Rev. King.

TLc. MLKP-MBU: Box 66.

From Julius Waties Waring

9 November 1956
New York, N.Y.

King and Ralph Abernathy had invited Waring, a retired federal district judge, to attend the MIA's Institute on Nonviolence and Social Change in early December.[1] Waring had nullified South Carolina's white Democratic primary in 1947, and his 1951 dissent in a school desegregation case, Briggs v. Elliott, *helped set the stage for the Supreme Court's* Brown *decision in 1954.*

Messrs. M. L. King and Ralph D. Abernathy,
Montgomery Improvement Association,
530-C So. Union Street,
Montgomery, Alabama.

Gentlemen:

I wish to offer to you and the Montgomery Improvement Association my hearty congratulations on the great fight for freedom and the American Creed which

---

1. Julius Waties Waring (1880–1968), born in Charleston, South Carolina, received his B.A. (1900) from the College of Charleston. He served as assistant United States attorney in Charleston from 1914 to 1920 and as the city of Charleston's corporation counsel from 1933 to 1942. President Roosevelt appointed Waring to the federal bench in 1942, where he served until his retirement in 1952. He often endured harassment because of his pro–civil rights rulings.

you have made in Montgomery. You have shown the nation that decency and courage will eventually prevail. You have suffered vicious persecution and have undergone losses and privations. The immediate issue has not been won as yet but such faith and determination is bound to be triumphant and the persecutors must themselves by this time come to realize that they are fighting a cruel but losing effort. The entire nation salutes you and prays for your early relief and victory.

I thank you for your invitation to attend the anniversary meeting but regret that I cannot be there in person but I am there with you in spirit.

Sincerely,
[*signed*]
J. Waties Waring.

TLS. MLKP-MBU: Box 89.

From L. Harold DeWolf

9 November 1956
Boston, Mass.

Dear Martin,

It was a great pleasure to have you in our home. Our only regrets were that the time was so short and that the rest of your family could not be with you.

We are hoping that before long you can make some such arrangements as we talked of here, so that you and your family can come to Boston for a period of rest, spiritual renewal and writing. If this were planned some weeks ahead we think we could arrange for you to live in the Danielson guest house in Wellesley where you could have privacy together and a minimum of disturbance. At the same time you would be within easy commuting distance of the libraries and other facilities of the city.

Dean Muelder and I have talked together about this and we are confident that we could find means of relieving you of the financial burden of such an arrangement, if you can work out a scheme for the handling of your responsibilities in Montgomery for a time. Let us know when you see your way clear to plan dates and other details.

Your address in Boston was stirring and helpful to the causes which you so ably represent.

Our concerns and prayers will be with you through the difficult days ahead.

Fraternally yours,
[*signed*] Harold

TLS. MLKP-MBU: Box 15.

Address to MIA Mass
Meeting at Holt Street Baptist Church

[*14 November 1956*]
Montgomery, Ala.

On 13 November Judge Eugene Carter granted the city's request for a temporary injunction halting the car pool. In a dramatic turn of events, however, a brief recess during the all-day hearing turned into an informal celebration when a reporter informed King that the Supreme Court had affirmed Browder v. Gayle. *Later that evening, while forty carloads of Klan members rode through black neighborhoods, the MIA executive committee recommended that the boycott continue until the Supreme Court decision took effect. They also scheduled two concurrent mass meetings for the next day, one at Hutchinson Street Baptist Church, the other at Holt Street Baptist Church.*

On 14 November, after MIA attorneys argued unsuccessfully in federal district court for a temporary restraining order to prevent the city from interfering with the car pool, King addressed audiences in the packed churches—each mass meeting drew an estimated four thousand people—and asked the participants to vote on the leadership's recommendation. The motion carried unanimously at both meetings. A transcript of the second address appears below. Anticipating the imminent desegregation of city buses, King asks everyone to remain nonviolent during the first challenging days. Echoing Gandhi, he tells them that "I'm not asking you to be a coward. . . . You can be courageous and yet nonviolent." His address followed the Scripture reading by Rev. J. C. Parker, who read from 1 Corinthians 13.[1] Moses W. Jones, a Montgomery physician and the MIA's second vice president, introduced King as "the man that is loved by most people, hated by some people, and respected by all people."

Dr. Jones, members and friends of the Montgomery Improvement Association. I'm so happy to see you here this evening in such large numbers and such great enthusiasm. It reveals to all of us that after eleven months you are not tired [*Audience:*] (*No*) and that you are still determined to struggle and sacrifice for the great cause of justice. (*Yes*) I have said before that we have lived with this protest so long that we have learned the meaning of sacrifice and suffering. But somehow we feel that our suffering is redemptive. (*Yes*) We know that we have a moral obligation to press on for justice. Because of our love for democracy, we must press on. (*Yes*) We think of the fact that out of the two billion four hundred million people in the world, about a billion six hundred million of them live on two continents: Asia and Africa. About six hundred million in China, four hundred million in India and Pakistan, a hundred million in Indonesia, two hundred million in Africa, about eighty-six million in Japan. (*Yes*) And all of these people are looking over, across the seas, wondering what we have to say in America about

---

1. King later recalled the enthusiastic response Robert Graetz received when he read the same verses at the earlier mass meeting. See "We Are Still Walking," December 1956, p. 446 in this volume.

democracy. (*Yes*) And America is in a very vulnerable position. And because of
our love for democracy and our belief that democracy is the greatest form of
government that we have on earth, because of our determination not to allow
the world to turn to an evil communistic ideology, we must press on for justice.
(*Yes*) If it means going to jail we are willing to fill up the jail houses. [*loud applause*] We believe that.

Now I want to do two things now. I have a message, a statement rather, that I
would like to read to you, that I tried to put together and express a recommendation or two that we have from the executive board. After reading this statement I will have you to vote on the recommendations and if there are points that
you do not quite understand I would be very happy to try to clear them up for
you. And then after reading the statement and voting I have just another word or
two I want to say to you concerning our future attitudes and our strategy as we
move on.

For more than eleven months we, the Negro citizens of Montgomery, have
been engaged in a nonviolent protest against indignities and injustices experienced on city buses. We have felt all along that we have just cause and legal excuse
for such action. We simply decided to say en masse that we were tired of being
trampled over with the iron feet of oppression. (*Yes*) [*applause*]

All along we have sought to carry out the protest on high moral standards. Our
methods and techniques have been rooted in the deep soils of the Christian faith.
We have carefully avoided bitterness, and have sought to make love, even for our
opposers, a reality in our lives.

These eleven months have not at all been easy. Often we have had to stand
amid the surging murmur of life's restless sea; many days and nights have been
filled with jostling winds of adversity. Our feet have often been tired (*Yes*) and
our automobiles worn, but we have kept going with the faith that in our struggle
we have cosmic companionship, and that, at bottom, the universe is on the side
of justice.

Just yesterday we experienced a revelation of the eternal validity of this faith.
It was on this day that the Supreme Court of this nation affirmed that segregation
is unconstitutional in public transportation. This decision was simply a reaffirmation of the principle that separate facilities are inherently unequal, and that
the old *Plessy* Doctrine of separate but equal is no longer valid, either sociologically or legally. This decision came to all of us as a joyous daybreak to end the
long night of enforced segregation in public transportation.

Now what will be our mode of action in the light of this decision? After thinking
through this question very seriously—and I might say practically—the executive board of the Montgomery Improvement Association recommends that the
eleven-month-old protest against the city buses will be called off, and that the
Negro citizens of Montgomery, Alabama, will return to the buses on a non-
segregated basis. (*Yes*) [*applause*] Now this is important; let us hear the next part.
It is further recommended that this return to the buses will not take place until
the mandate from the United States Supreme Court is turned over to the federal
district court. It is true that this is purely a procedural matter, but it is a matter
that might be used by reactionary elements to plunge us into needless harassment and meaningless litigation. We have the assurance from authentic sources
that this mandate will come to Montgomery in a matter of just a few days. For

those three or four days we will continue to walk and share rides with friends.[2] [*applause*]

All of us have a basic responsibility to seek to implement this noble decision. Let all of us be calm and reasonable. (*Yes*) With understanding, goodwill, and Christian love (*That's right*) we can integrate the buses with no difficulties. (*Yes*) This is Montgomery's sublime opportunity. (*Yes*) We can now transform our jangling discords into meaningful symphonies of spiritual harmony.

This is the statement.[3] Now let us prepare to vote on what we have here, and this recommendation has two parts. Number one: that as a result of the Supreme Court's decision upholding the decision of the federal district court, that is, the decision outlawing segregation in public transportation, we will call off the protest and return to the buses on a non-segregated basis. That's the first part. The second part is that we will hold off returning to the buses for a few days, until the order or the mandate reaches Montgomery from the United States Supreme Court. Now [*applause*], now we stress the importance of this because there might be some difficulties developing by reactionary elements saying that you're not in your legal rights, we don't know whether this law is in effect or not. We don't mind getting arrested, it isn't that, it isn't that we are afraid to go back right today or tomorrow. It isn't that we are afraid of getting arrested, for we are used to going to jail now. [*applause*] But what we are saying, there is no need of us getting involved now into a long series of litigation and paying out a lot of money (*Yeah*), when we could just wait two or three days (*Yes*) and the mandate would be here from the Supreme Court. (*Yes*) So that is the burden of this recommendation, that we will wait so that nobody can say anything, they can't say that they didn't, they don't know a . . . [*recording interrupted*] All right, we have heard that unreadiness. All in favor of the motion as it stands before us, let it be known by standing on your feet. Just a minute; just a minute. Just a minute; I don't think you understood me. (*Quiet, quiet*) Just a minute. I'm not voting—we're not voting on the unreadiness. Is the mike on? (*No*) Oh, I'm sorry. I should have been talking louder. I didn't know it was off.

Now we are voting on the original motion, that we will turn, return to the buses of Montgomery, Alabama, on a non-segregated basis. That's number one. But that we will wait a few days until the mandate definitely gets to Montgomery before we return to the buses. Now we are ready to vote. All in favor of that motion let it be known by standing. Those opposed may do likewise. Be seated. Those opposed to the motion (*Quiet*), those opposed to the motion may do likewise. It seems that this is a unanimous, this is unanimously carried, so that you accept the motion. [*Brief discussion about public address system omitted.*]

Now my friends, I want to say just a few words to you in the way of advice and in the way of interpreting the spirit of our movement. And everything that I will say will be based naturally on this motion that has been carried, this decision that

---

2. A few days later the MIA learned that the city had petitioned the Supreme Court to reconsider its ruling, forcing the group to continue the bus boycott for several more weeks without its car pools. The Supreme Court order was not implemented until 21 December, at which point the MIA ended the bus boycott.

3. Cf. Statement on the Supreme Court Decision, 14 November 1956.

you have accepted. I should first make you intelligent on the legal status of our struggle. And I say that because we have had so many legal cases in the last few months that it's difficult to know which one we're talking about. So that I want to give you some interpretation of all of them that we are facing now. On yesterday we were in the circuit court of Alabama, dealing with the question of the legality of our transportation system. The city of Montgomery went to the court requesting an injunction restraining the Montgomery Improvement Association from operating a transportation system, along with the churches that operate station wagons. We were in court yesterday from about nine o'clock to six o'clock in the afternoon, the late afternoon. And at the end of that day, and that long day of arguing and witnessing, Judge Carter rendered his decision granting the injunction on the basis that the transportation system is illegal, that it is a private enterprise and without the proper licenses or without a franchise. So that a temporary injunction was issued, and this injunction was handed down. We immediately halted the car pool in order to comply. You can understand that—many persons would have been arrested, and not only that, we would have been cited for contempt of court and a lot of money would have been tied up and paid out. So that on the basis of this injunction, as law-abiding citizens, we abided by the injunction.

But not only that, another case came up today in the federal court. We were a little higher up today (*Yeah*): we had transcended the state and moved up to the federal court. Now the meaning of this was really to try to get a decision restraining the city from carrying on any court procedures to stop the car pool. That case was argued today from about ten o'clock to two-thirty or three o'clock. Judge Johnson rendered his decision this afternoon. I don't know the total text of the decision, but in substance the decision was that he did not grant the request of our attorneys. That is to say, he did not render a decision restraining the city from having any court procedures enjoining the Montgomery Improvement Association and these churches from operating.

So because of his decision the injunction is still on us, the temporary injunction, and that means that our car pool is still out of operation. The station wagons are not operating. We're not operating an organized car pool. Now this does not mean you do not have the right to aid friends, people living next to you, your friends, and we want to share rides among friends, not in any organized sense with dispatch stations and pickup stations, but we're going to continue to do that until we go back to the buses, until the mandate comes down. And I don't think any court will be—will attempt, I should say, I might even go on to say that I don't believe any court would be ambitious enough, to use Reverend Hubbard's words, to get an injunction against feet.[4] [*laughter and applause*] That's right.

So we're going to continue to walk and share rides for these next two or three or four days or so, and we're going to do it in the same spirit. Now, it might be necessary to call another mass meeting before our regular meeting Monday night, in order to give you direct instructions. Because if the mandate comes, say Friday, we might call you immediately. If not, we will go on with our regular mass

---

4. King refers to Hillman H. Hubbard, pastor of Bethel Baptist Church.

meeting Monday. But at any rate, we are still going and we're still in the spirit of this movement. [*applause*]

Now I want to say to you as we prepare to go back to the buses, we have before us some basic responsibilities and I want you to hear this. I want you to abide by it. Number one, I would be terribly disappointed if anybody goes back to the buses bragging about, we, the Negroes, have won a victory over the white people. [*applause*] If we do that we will bring about a lot of undue tension. (*Right*) And I want you to know anyway that the decision that was rendered by the Supreme Court yesterday was not a victory merely for fifty thousand Negroes in Montgomery. That's too small. (*Well*) It's not a victory merely for sixteen million Negroes over the United States. As I have said to you so many times, the tension in Montgomery is not so much a tension between Negro people and white people, but the tension is at bottom a tension between justice and injustice (*Yes*), a tension between the forces of light and the forces of darkness. And if that is a victory it will be a victory for justice and a victory for goodwill and a victory for the forces of light. So let us not limit this decision to a victory for Negroes. Let us go back to the buses in all humility and with gratitude to the Almighty God (*Yes*) for making this decision possible. (*Yes*) And I hope nobody will go out bragging (*All right*) and talking and taking some undue arrogance in going back to the buses. We can go back with humility. We can go back with meekness. (*Yeah*) And I don't feel, I don't believe meekness means that you are dried up in a very cowardly sense. But I believe it is something that gets in your soul so that you can stand and look at any man with a deep sense of humility, knowing that one day you shall inherit the earth.[5] (*Yes*) That's the meaning of meekness. That's what Jesus meant by it. So let us be meek and let us be humble and not go back with arrogance. Our struggle will be lost all over the South if the Negro becomes a victim of undue arrogance.

Then I want to stress to you the meaning of freedom, for as we struggle for freedom in America there is a danger that we will misinterpret freedom. We usually think of freedom from something, but freedom is also to something. (*That's right*) It is not only breaking aloose from some evil force, but it is reaching up for a higher force. Freedom from evil is slavery to goodness. And we must discover that freedom is more than a negative something. It is more than getting aloose from a negative, but it is becoming attached to a positive. I hope we will realize that. You know we talk a lot about our rights. And we ought to—we're supposed to, and we have certain unalienable rights. That's the glory of our Constitution: that all men are created equal and endowed by their Creator with certain unalienable rights, and that among these are life, liberty, and the pursuit of happiness. But not only must we become bogged down in rights, because if we stop there we might misuse our rights. We might use our rights to trample over other people's rights. (*That's right*) It's not only rights that we are seeking. We not only have the right to be free, we have a duty to be free. (*Yes*) And when you see freedom in sense of duty, it becomes greater than seeing it in terms of right, your right to be free. You have a duty to be free. And when you see that you have a duty to be free, you discover that you have a duty to respect those who don't even want you to have freedom. (*Yes*) That's the sense of duty. You come to see that

5. Cf. Matthew 5:5.

you must respect even that man who doesn't want you to sit next to him on the bus. (*Yes*) Somehow, freedom is this duty to respect *all* people, even though they don't love you, they don't respect you, but you respect them and you feel somehow that they can become better than they are. (*Yes*) That's the meaning of freedom. You have a duty to respect those—I don't mean you have to respect their opinions, I don't believe in respecting everybody's opinion. I don't respect anybody's opinion who thinks that I'm supposed to be kicked around and segregated. I don't respect their opinion. But I respect them as a personality, a sacred personality with the image of God within them. And although that image has been scarred, terribly scarred, although they, like the Protestant son—the prodigal son—have strayed away to some far country of sin and evil, I must still believe that there is something within them that can cause them one day to come to themselves (*That's right, Yes*) and rise up and walk back up the dusty road to the father's house. (*Yes*) And we stand there with outstretched arms. That's the meaning of the Christian faith. (*That's right, that's right*) That's the meaning of this thing. (*Yes*) Our Christian religion says somehow that a prejudiced mind can be changed. And I'd close up my books and stop preaching if I didn't believe that. (*Yes*) I want to tell you this evening that I believe that Senator Engelhardt's heart can be changed. (*Yes*) I believe that Senator Eastland's heart can be changed![6] (*Yes*) I believe that the Ku Klux Klan can be transformed into a clan for God's kingdom. (*Yes*) I believe that the White Citizens Council can be transformed into a Right Citizens Council! (*Yes*) I believe that. That's the essence of the Gospel.

I can see a Nicodemus running to Jesus saying, "What must I do to be saved?" and I can hear Jesus saying, "You must be born again." [7] (*Yes*) And the minute he says "You must," he means you *can* be born again. (*Yes*) We believe that. (*Praise God*) The fact that you must means you can. (*Yes*) We believe that, and we're going to live by that faith. (*Yes*) And we must go back to the buses with that faith. (*Yes*) I'll tell you, if we will go back to that faith, we will be able to stagger and astound the imagination of those who would oppress us. (*That's right*) They will look at you as a strange and peculiar people. (*Yes*) They will wonder what's wrong with you. (*Yes*) They will say that the methods of these people don't coincide with the usual methods. (*Yes*) They have some methods that broke aloose from the empire of eternity. (*Yes*) These methods have come down here to the colony of time, to keep them moving on. If we will do that, we will be able to astound the world. (*Yes*) And I believe that we will do it. (*Yes*) We will do it. We are going back to those buses, respecting even those who don't want us to go there and sit where we want to sit and where we have a right to sit. (*Yes*)

So remember that freedom is not only from something, but it is to something. We have a duty to be free. And when I say we have a duty to be free, I mean it just that way, that we have a duty because of God's command to all of us to keep the

---

6. Alabama state senator Sam Engelhardt, Jr., was chair of the Central Alabama Citizens Council. James Oliver Eastland (1904–1986), a native of Doddsville, Mississippi, served as a U.S. senator from 1943 to 1978. In 1955 Eastland helped organize a short-lived federation of Citizens Councils, addressing crowds throughout the South, including an estimated fifteen thousand in Montgomery on 9 February 1956. As chair of the Senate Judiciary Committee (1956–1978), he obstructed many attempts to enact federal civil rights legislation.

7. Cf. John 3:2–3.

whole of humanity level. You know in Greek culture, in Greek mythology, there was a goddess known as the Goddess of Nemesis. And the chief function of the Goddess of Nemesis was to keep everything and everybody on a common level. And when you got too high and above yourself, the Goddess of Nemesis was to pull you down. (*Yes*) And when you got too low and felt that you were too far down, the Goddess of Nemesis pulled you up. (*That's right*) And that's why we have a duty to be free because a lack of freedom gives the persons who are segregated a false sense of inferiority, and it gives those who are sitting up to the front of the bus, on the basis of the fact that they are white, a false sense of superiority. (*Yes*) And we have a right to level this thing off. [*applause*] We have a right to level, you see, we got to level it off. God doesn't want anybody to feel inferior. (*That's right, No*) Neither does he want anybody to feel superior. (*That's right*) We have a duty to ourselves for our self-respect and before the Almighty God to stand up for our freedom. (*Yes*) That is a duty that we have. (*That's right*) And I hope we will do it in that sense.

Now there's one other thing. We talked a lot about nonviolence, haven't we? (*Yes*) And I said it, I hope that we will live it now, because this is really the *practical* aspect of our movement. This is the *testing point* of our movement. (*That's right*) And if we go back to the buses and somehow become so weak that when somebody strikes us we gonna strike them back, or when somebody says an insulting word to us we gonna do the same thing, we will destroy the spirit of our movement— and I know it's hard, I know that. And I know you're looking at me like I'm somewhat crazy when I say that. [*laughter*] I know that. I know that. You see it's sort of the natural thing to do when you're hit. You feel that you're supposed to hit back. That's the way we're taught, we're brought up like that. And that is certainly a corollary of our Western materialism. We have been brought up on the basis that we live, that violence is the way to solve problems. And we unconsciously feel that we must do it this way and if we don't hit back we are not strong, we're weak. And that's the way we've been brought up. But I want to tell you this evening that the strong man is the man who will not hit back (*Yes*), who can stand up for his rights and yet not hit back. (*Yes*) Now I'm not asking you to be a coward. If cowardice was the alternative to violence, I'd say to you tonight, use violence. If that were the only alternative, I'd say, use violence. But I'm saying to you that cowardice is not the alternative. Cowardice is as evil as violence. (*Yes*) What I'm saying to you this evening is that you can be courageous and yet nonviolent. You can take a seat on the bus and sit there because it's your right to sit there and refuse to move, no matter who tells you to move, because it's your right, and yet not hit back if you are hit yourself. (*That's right*) Now that's what I call courage. (*Amen, Amen*) That's really courage. (*Yes*) And I tell you, if we hit back we will be shamed (*Let's hear it now*), we will be shamed before the world. (*That's right*) I'm serious about this. (*That's right*) I'm not telling you something that I don't live. (*That's right*) I'm not telling you something that I don't live. I'm aware of the fact that the Ku Klux Klan is riding in Montgomery.[8] I'm aware of the fact that a week never passes that somebody's not telling me to get out of town, or that I'm gonna

---

8. For King's description of the Klan's intimidation efforts, see "We Are Still Walking," December 1956, p. 447 in this volume.

be killed next place I move. But I don't have any guns in my pockets. I don't have any guards on my side. But I have the *God* of the Universe on my side. (*Yes*) [*ap-* *plause*] I'm serious about that. I can walk the streets of Montgomery without fear. (*Yes*) I don't worry about a thing. (*No*) They can bomb my house. They can kill my body. But they can never kill the spirit of freedom that is in my people. [*applause*]

I'm saying that because I believe it firmly and I'm not telling you something that I don't do myself. I'm telling you, I'm telling you to live by nonviolence. (*Yeah*) I say that that is the command before us. And there is still a voice crying through the vista of time, saying to every potential Peter, "Put up your sword!" [9] (*Yes*) History is replete with the bleached bones of nations (*Yeah*) that failed to follow the command of Jesus at that point. If we as Negroes succumb to the temptation of using violence in our struggle, unborn generations will be the recipients of a long and bitter night of—a long and desolate night of bitterness. And our only legacy to the future will be an endless reign of meaningless chaos. (*Yes*) I call upon you to choose nonviolence. (*Yeah*) Go back to the buses, and we're going in the next few days. And I'm not saying to you, go to the back of the bus. I want you to sit down on the bus. Sit down where a seat is convenient to sit down. Sit down because it's your right to sit down and you don't need to argue with anybody about sitting down, but just sit down on the bus.

Now I know that there's a danger here again, that we, you know, we've been going to the back so long. I mentioned a few minutes ago over at Hutchinson Street there was a psychologist in America by the name of John Watson and he became the father of behavioristic psychology.[10] And I remember at least this one thing about behaviorism or behavioristic psychology: Watson built up a great theory of conditioned response. And he even went over and got some, a theory from a Russian who had tested this stimuli-response theory with a dog, you know, and how that if you are conditioned to a certain thing for so long, you are going to respond that way.[11] You know you had just been working under this condition so long, you are just inevitably prone to respond that way. Now, there is the danger that we've been going to the back so long that we'll unconsciously get on the bus and just go to the back and perpetuate segregation. We've just been conditioned to do it so long that we'll just go straight to the back of the bus because we've been doing it, you see. Now I hope we can break the conditioning process now and just go on, on the bus and sit down, you see. Don't just go on to the back, that's what I'm trying to get over to you. Just take a seat. Now don't push over anybody. (*No*) You see, if there's a seat in the back, and there are no seats in the front, you naturally will take that seat. But now if there is a seat in the *front*, you see, you will take that one also, if it's convenient. (*Yes*) [*applause*] That's what I'm trying to say. We just gonna take seats.[12]

---

9. John 18:11.

10. King refers to John Broadus Watson (1878–1956). See King's description of the first mass meeting in "We Are Still Walking," December 1956, p. 446 in this volume; King, *Stride Toward Freedom*, pp. 161–162; and MIA Mass Meeting at Hutchinson Street Baptist Church, 14 November 1956.

11. King refers to the experiments of physiologist Ivan P. Pavlov (1849–1936), who won the Nobel Prize in 1904.

12. King and other MIA leaders led nonviolent training sessions to prepare for the return to the buses, later providing detailed instructions to returning riders. See Robert L. Cannon to Alfred Hass-

Now you know, in other southern cities this has worked, and we feel that it can work here. We feel that it can work here. I can name Durham, North Carolina, they—when the vague decision in the *Flemming's* case came down some months ago, they just discontinued segregation.[13] Little Rock, Arkansas; Charlotte, North Carolina; Dallas and Houston, Texas, and just several other cities that I can name. And I just feel, I don't believe for the world of me that all of the white people in Montgomery think that the world is coming to an end if the buses are integrated. I just don't believe that. [*laughter*] Now I know that the politicians will often make us—you know one frog in a pond can sound like a hundred (*Yes*)—and I know that they can make us feel that the world is coming to an end and the streets are going to be flowing with blood if we integrate the buses. But I don't believe that, and I know one thing, we aren't going to have it flowing with blood. We aren't going to do anything violent. We are going back in a real spirit of love and the Christian faith. And that's the thing that I think is the real challenge before us.

I say to you my friends, in conclusion, that we've been struggling for eleven months, but I want you to know that this struggle has not been in vain. It hasn't been in vain. If it has done any one thing in this community it has given us a new sense of dignity and destiny. (*That's right*) And I think that in itself it is a victory for freedom and a victory for the cause of justice. It has given us a new sense of dignity and destiny. And I want to urge you this evening to keep on keeping on. Keep on moving.

Doesn't mean that when the bus problem is solved all problems are solved. (*No*) There will be others. But we must keep on moving and keep on keeping on. There are some words that come down to us from Langston Hughes's "Mother to Son:"

> Well, son, I'll tell you:
> Life for me ain't been no crystal stair.
> It's had tacks in it,
> Splinters,
> Boards torn up,
> Places with no carpet on the floor—
> Bare.
> But all the time
> I'se been a-climbin' on,
> And reachin' landin's,
> And turnin' corners,
> And sometimes goin' in the dark
> Where there ain't been no light.
> So boy, don't you stop now.
> Don't you set down on the steps
> 'Cause you finds it's kinder hard.
> Don't you fall back, boy—
> For I'se still climbin',
> I'se still goin',
> And life for me ain't been no crystal stair.

---

ler and Glenn E. Smiley, 3 October 1956; and King, "Integrated Bus Suggestions," 19 December 1956; pp. 388–391 and 481–483 in this volume, respectively.

13. *Flemming v. South Carolina Electric and Gas Company* (1956).

Well, life for none of us has been a crystal stair, but we've got to keep going. We'll keep going through the sunshine and the rain. Some days will be dark and dreary, but we will keep going. Prodigious hilltops of opposition will rise before us, but we will keep going. Mountains of evil will stand in our path, but we will keep going. (*Yes*) Oh, we have been in Egypt long enough (*Well*), and now we've gotten orders from headquarters. The Red Sea has opened for us, we have crossed the banks, we are moving now, and as we look back we see the Egyptian system of segregation drowned upon the seashore. (*Yes*) We know that the Midianites are still ahead. We see the beckoning call of the evil forces of the Amorites. We see the Hittites all around us but, but we are going on because we've got to get to Canaan. (*Yes*) We can't afford to stop. (*Yes*) We've got to keep moving. So I want you this evening in a nonviolent sense, to go away [*remainder of sentence and an unknown number of additional sentences missing*] [14]

At. MLKJrP-GAMK.

---

14. King concluded his address at Hutchinson Street Baptist Church by saying: "Let us remember once more that Montgomery has been thrown into a peculiar position. It is a position in which we can well map out the strategy for the future of integration. It is unfortunate, that those people of good will—and there are hundreds of them in Montgomery—are afraid to speak out at this time. (*Yes*) And tonight as we go home, let us pray (*Yes*) that God will touch the hearts of some of these people (*We will, Amen*) and that through the constraining and compelling power of the holy spirit, they will have to speak (*Yes*)" (MIA Mass Meeting at Hutchinson Street Baptist Church, 14 November 1956).

From Benjamin Elijah Mays

14 November 1956
Atlanta, Ga.

This note was among the many congratulatory messages sent to King after the Supreme Court's 13 November ruling against bus segregation. King replied on 17 December to Mays's invitation to speak at Morehouse.

Dr. M. L. King, Jr.
309 South Jackson Street
Montgomery, Alabama

Dear Dr. King:

Just a note to congratulate you on the Supreme Court's Decision declaring segregation on the buses unconstitutional in Montgomery and Alabama. You have been a power of strength in this whole affair.

You recall you could not come to the college last year. Kindly let me kno if you can come in January, 1957. What about the 3rd or 4th? What about the 17th or 18th of January? If these dates are impossible, what about February 5, 6, 7, or 8th?

Kindly let me hear from you concerning same. With kindest regards and best wishes always, I am

Yours truly,
[*signed*]
Benjamin E. Mays
President
BEM:m

TLS. MLKP-MBU: Box 62.

From John M. Swomley

14 November 1956
New York, N.Y.

REV MARTIN LUTHER KING JR
MONTGOMERY IMPROVEMENT ASSN
~~309 SOUTH JACKSON ST~~ 530 S UNION ST
MONTGOMERY ALA

WE CAN IMAGINE THE REJOICING IN MONTGOMERY OVER THE SUPREME COURT DECISION OUTLAWING SEGRATION ON BUSSES YOUR NON VIOLENT STRUGGLE HAS MADE A MAJOR CONTRIBUTION TO THIS GREAT VICTORY FOR FREEDOM AND EQUALITY. OUR BEST WISHES AND PRAYERS FOR YOUR FUTURE WORK

JOHN M SWOMLEY
NATIONAL SECRETARY FELLOWSHIP OF RECONCILIATION

PHWSr. MLKP-MBU: Box 17.

To Ella J. Baker

14 November 1956
Montgomery, Ala.

Baker and A. J. Muste, who received a similar telegram, were involved in planning an In Friendship benefit concert for the MIA to be held 5 December in New York featuring, among others, Coretta Scott King.

MISS ELLA BAKER IN FRIENDSHIP
122 EAST 57 ST NYK

URGENT AND FLUID SITUATION HERE DEFINITELY REQUIRES CONSULTATIONS REMAINDER OF THIS WEEK. IF THIS CREATES PROBLEMS FOR YOU, PLEASE TELEGRAPH

MARTIN LUTHER KING RALPH D ABERNATHY

PWSr. MLKP-MBU: Box 14A.

From Ella J. Baker

14 November 1956
New York, N.Y.

REV MARTIN LUTHER KING JR
530 SOUTH UNION ST MONTGOMERY ALA

WE WILL MANAGE ON THIS END AND ONLY WISH WE WERE THERE TO SHARE THESE MOMENTS
OF TRIUMPH AND CHALLENGE WITH YOU

ELLA J BAKER

PHWSr. MLKP-MBU: Box 14A.

From Glenn E. Smiley

20 November 1956
New York, N.Y.

*FOR's field secretary asks for details regarding his participation in the MIA's Institute
on Nonviolence and Social Change, where Smiley served as forum moderator and
lecturer. He also informs King of FOR's plans to produce a comic book about the bus
boycott; the resulting publication, which appeared in late 1957,* was Martin Luther
King and the Montgomery Story.

Martin Luther King
309 S. Jackson
Montgomery, Ala.

Dear Martin:

I am anxiously looking forward to the December 4–7 dates and know that it
will be a significant event. Could I have more particulars about the sort of meetings contemplated, as far as my own participation is concerned? Are you going to
show the "Walk to Freedom" film again during this celebration? You have your
own copy, don't you?

I mentioned to your secretary over the telephone that I am available to come
down if at this time you wanted to push the matter of riding the buses, and
needed some white participation. Since I have not heard from you, I judge that
you are waiting on this particular matter. I would be in Michigan Nov. 26–29 and
after that time would be available to come down and help if you thought that you
needed me. Naturally, I would come at F.O.R. expense completely.

The Fund for the Republic is now actively interested in helping us to publish
the Story of Montgomery in comic book form, about which I had talked to you at
one time. As I said before, as soon as we have anything definite to submit to you,

we will do so for your approval and suggestions. We plan to publish a quarter of a million copies and they would sell for 10¢ each, but groups could buy them for considerably less than this and in this way could make a substantial profit for their own cause. I would assume that many Negro churches in the south, and all NAACP groups, protest movements, etc., would be anxious to promote such a deal because it will have two or three pages of explanation of the nonviolent techqnique and movement. We shall keep you informed about this.

Our best regards and prayers for the success of the movement.

Sincerely,
[*signed*] Glenn
Glenn E. Smiley

GES/hs

TLS. MLKP-MBU: Box 16.

From Ralph J. Bunche

21 November 1956
New York, N.Y.

King had apparently invited India's United Nations delegate Vengalil Krishnan Krishna Menon to participate in the MIA's Institute on Nonviolence and Social Change.[1] Menon did not attend.

Rev. M. L. King, Jr., 309 South Jackson Street Montgomery, Ala.

Dear Rev. King,

I have spoken twice to Krishna Menon about your invitation, urging him strongly to accept it. He has promised me to give it most serious consideration. I earnestly hope that he will come.

Sincerely yours,
[*signed*]
Ralph J. Bunche
Under Secretary

{P.S. What a <u>victory</u> you have had in the Supreme Court's full vindication of your fight for dignity! R–}

TALS. MLKP-MBU: Box 14.

---

1. Vengalil Krishnan Krishna Menon (1897–1974) led the India League from 1929 to 1947, thereafter becoming India's first high commissioner to the United Kingdom following the 1947 Indian Independence Act. He served as India's chief delegate to the United Nations between 1952 and 1960.

To Ruth Bunche and Aminda Wilkins

23 November 1956
Montgomery, Ala.

*King thanks Bunche and Wilkins for co-chairing the Montgomery Anniversary
Concert on 5 December. The benefit, sponsored by In Friendship and coordinated by
Stanley Levison and Bayard Rustin, was held at New York's Manhattan Center and
featured Coretta Scott King, Harry Belafonte, Duke Ellington, and Tallulah
Bankhead.[1]*

Mrs. Ralph J. Bunche and Mrs. Roy Wilkins
Co-Chairmen, Montgomery Anniversary Concert
"In Friendship"
122 East 57 Street
New York, 22, N.Y.

Dear Mrs. Bunche and Mrs. Wilkins:

I am very pleased to know that you are helping raise funds for Montgomery
through the Anniversary Concert on December 5th.

Your help comes at our most critical period. Our car pool has been destroyed
by legal action. Despite the Supreme Court's decision, the busses are still segregated, and influential people in places of great power have threatened violence
rather than comply with the court's decision. At present, therefore, Montgomery's 50,000 Negroes are forced to walk and must continue to do so until the
Supreme Court's mandate reaches the local courts. That may take a month, or
even longer.

Beyond this, we have 200 people who have driven in the car pool. They are
"marked men and women" and will have great difficulty finding work in Montgomery for a long time.

These factors mean that we are unfortunately in grave need of funds for carrying on the most critical phase of our struggle. I am sending out an urgent appeal but at present will not do so in New York. But hope that you will impress the
religious, labor and civic leaders that they can make a very real contribution now
by supporting the Anniversary Concert.

I can not tell you how much the people in our movement appreciate and, at

---

1. Coretta Scott King spoke at the event and sang a program of classical music and spirituals, including some of her husband's favorites such as "Honor, Honor" (see Speech at the Montgomery
Anniversary Concert, 5 December). Ruth Ethel Harris Bunche (1906–1988), wife of Ralph Bunche,
was a native of Montgomery and graduate of Miner Teachers College. She taught first grade in Washington, D.C., for many years before becoming more active in charitable organizations. Aminda "Minnie" Ann Badeau Wilkins was born in St. Louis and graduated from Chicago's Recreation Teaching
School in 1926. She then organized neighborhood programs for the National Urban League in Kansas
City, where she met and married Roy Wilkins. She later worked for New York City's departments of
social services and welfare.

this very moment, need your encouragement and support. With best regards to your husbands, I am

Very sincerely yours,
[*signed*] Martin L. King
Rev. Martin Luther King, Jr.
President

TLS. FORP-PSC-P.

To Albert S. Bigelow

24 November 1956
[*Montgomery, Ala.*]

> *On 6 November Bigelow, a Quaker pacifist and former Massachusetts housing official, wrote of his plan to vote for King in the presidential election. "Your struggle & suffering are long and growing harder," Bigelow added, "but please know that you have our love and admiration for your gallant, steadfast devotion to your high principles."* [1] *On 19 November King's secretary, Maude Ballou, thanked him for the letter.*

Mr. Albert S. Bigelow
Valley Road
Cos Cob, Connecticut

Dear Mr. Bigelow:

This is just a note to follow up the statement of my secretary in thanking you for your kind letter and your great contribution of three hundred dollars ($300.00). I can assure you that your moral support and encouraging remarks give us renewed vigor and courage to carry on. I was indeed flattered to know that you were writing my name in as President of the United States. I can assure you that your thinking of me in this sense gives me a deep feeling of humility and a new dedication to the cause of freedom.

Sincerely yours,
M. L. King, Jr.,
President

MLK:b

TLc. MLKP-MBU: Box 14.

---

1. Albert Smith Bigelow (1906?–1993) was born in Brookline, Massachusetts, and received degrees from Harvard and the MIT School of Architecture. He served as Massachusetts housing commissioner from 1947 to 1949. After becoming a Quaker in 1954 he participated in numerous protests concerning peace and social justice issues. In 1958 he tried to sail a thirty-foot ketch to a nuclear testing site in the Pacific; unsuccessful, he subsequently served a jail sentence for violating a court injunction. He accompanied John Lewis and other CORE members during the Freedom Rides in May 1961.

25 November 1956
New York, N.Y.

Four student activists request King's endorsement of an "Enroll for Freedom" campaign
designed to encourage students and youth to participate in the civil rights struggle and
to "accept the challenge and responsibility of building a really free America." King's
reply has not been located, but King may have agreed to serve as honorary chairman
of the "Enroll for Freedom" campaign.[1]

Dear Reverend King,

December 5th marks the first anniversary of the Montgomery Bus Boycott. On
that date IN FRIENDSHIP, an organization which has done much to aid the victims of racism, is sponsoring a concert at Manhattan Center in New York to commemorate this heroic struggle for dignity and for civil rights and to raise money
for the Montgomery Improvement Association.

Among the many groups working for this program are students and youth
who feel that it is our obligation to play a more effective role in the fight for
civil rights. Arising out of this project, therefore, a student committee has been
formed to launch an "ENROLL FOR FREEDOM" campaign on the college campus. We propose to present the names we collect to President Eisenhower on
Lincoln's birthday as an expression of support to this momentous struggle for
equality. Further details on the project are enclosed.

As an outstanding leader of your generation in the field of civil rights, we are
asking you to help our generation by endorsing this campaign. It is our hope that
the youth of this country will, through our efforts, become aware of their stake in
civil rights and will accept the challenge and responsibility of building a really
free America.

William Lusk, Columbia University
Marjorie Gettleman, CCNY
Naomi Friedman, Brooklyn College
Sheila [*Navarick*], Sarah Lawrence

TL. MLKP-MBU: Box 16.

---

1. A later FBI report stated that King was honorary chairman of the campaign, which the bureau
believed "was actually started by the Young Socialist League" (see J. Edgar Hoover to Herbert Brownell, 14 April 1958, in *Centers of the Southern Struggle: FBI Files on Montgomery, Albany, St. Augustine, Selma,*
and Memphis, ed. David J. Garrow [Frederick, Md.: University Publications of America], reel 2).

From Michael J. Quill and Matthew Guinan

27 November 1956
New York, N.Y.

*On 10 December Maude Ballou responded on King's behalf to this supportive letter
from the leaders of the Transport Workers Union.*

Dr. Martin King,
Montgomery, Alabama.

Dear Dr. King:

We are enclosing for your information a copy of a resolution on the recent
Supreme Court ruling which was adopted by the International Executive Board
of the Transport Workers Union of America. This board is the highest governing
body of our Union which represents 150,000 workers engaged in railroad, airline
and city passenger transportation throughout the United States.

Once again we want to take this opportunity to congratulate you for the mature
and courageous leadership you have given not only to the people of Alabama but
all Americans in the fight to wipe out the scourge of segregation from our national life.

We urge you not to hesitate to call upon the officers and membership of the
Transport Workers Union if we can be of any further help to your cause.

With best wishes,

Sincerely,
[*signed*]
Michael J. Quill,[1]
International President
[*signed*]
Matthew Guinan,[2]
Int'l. Secretary-Treasurer
encl.

mjq.rc.
oeiu-344-afl-cio

THLS. MLKP-MBU: Box 72.

---

1. Michael Joseph Quill (1905–1966) was born in Ireland, where he volunteered in the Irish Republican Army between 1919 and 1923; he moved to the United States in 1926. As a transit worker in New
York City he helped organize the Transport Workers Union of America (TWU) in 1934, becoming its
president a year later. From 1937 until his death he served as the union's international president. Quill
was also a member of the AFL-CIO's general executive board.

2. Matthew Guinan (1910–1995) emigrated to the United States from Ireland in 1929. He was a
trolley car operator in New York City when the TWU was organized. Joining the TWU staff in 1943,
Guinan later became its international executive vice president and secretary-treasurer. In 1966, after
Quill's death, he assumed the position of president.

From Roland E. Haynes

27 November 1956
Boston, Mass.

*Haynes, a fellow Baptist minister and Boston University alumnus, compliments King
on his speech at the Ford Hall Forum and encourages him to rest.[1] King replied on
17 December.*

The Reverend Martin Luther King
% The Dexter Avenue Baptist Church
Montgomery, Alabama

Dear "M. L.":

Congratulations to you and all who have continued to struggle and sacrifice
for the dignity of mankind and justice. I am sure that I voice the sentiment of all
of the fellows here and faculty members when I say to you God's richest Blessings
upon you and yours'.

For sometime I have wanted to write you and thank you for that most powerful
address (I call it a sermon) you gave to us at Ford Hall. It was brilliantly delivered.
And I believe M. L. that Dr. DeWolf came the closest in describing it in its essence—simply SUPERB. You need not worry about it being intellectually repre-
sentive of your learning and background. For indeed you caused the whole city
to take notes. Keep up the good work.

I sincerely hope, M. L. that you will take very seriously Dr. DeWolf's and Dean
Muelder's suggestion to take a rest at your earliest opportunity.[2] Now M. L. I personally realize that this is not as easy as it sounds. However, you study in through
as you generally do and let God help you to come to some decision.

This coming Christmas holidays, Minnie and I hope to be in Atlanta for a few
days. If you are going to be there, I would like very much to see you. Perhaps, we
could get together in an informal setting. I will see your Father and my dear
friend. It will be like old home folks getting together again. If you have time drop
me a line concerning your plans for the holidays.

I trust that Veretta's concert was a success.[3] And how is the baby? One wonders
how one can effectively play the role of Pastor, Husband, Father and Public
Leader when all every role demands so much from the individual. I am praying
that you will continue to give your all on the altar of God and live close to Him.

---

1. Roland Emerson Haynes (1928–) received his B.A. (1949) from Clark College in Atlanta and his
S.T.B. (1952), S.T.M. (1953), and Ph.D. (1961) from Boston University. He was a minister and professor
of psychology and religion at Clark College from 1957 to 1962. He then taught at several colleges in
South Carolina before joining the University of South Carolina faculty in 1972.

2. See Muelder to King, 16 September 1956; King to Muelder, 3 October 1956, pp. 387–388 in this
volume; and L. Harold DeWolf to King, 9 November 1956, p. 423 in this volume.

3. Haynes refers to Coretta Scott King's performance at the New York benefit concert on
5 December.

You have a rare talent and an ingenuis mind. I guess I sound like an old man talking to you in this fashion; but M. L., I am still very concerned in your health and the continued success of the movement not only from the standpoint of a fellow Negro but also as a believing Christian. Again, many thanks to you for your "superb" sermon; I remain,

Very Sincerely,
[*signed*]
Roland

THLS. MLKP-MBU: Box 15.

To Supporter

27 November 1956
Montgomery, Ala.

"Dollars For Freedom" Needed

Dear Friend:

During the week of December 3, 1956, the MIA will observe its first anniversary by conducting an Institute on <u>Non-Violence</u> and <u>Social Change</u>. Some of the outstanding thinkers and personalities of the nation have been invited to Montgomery to participate in this Institute. This is not to be construed as a victory celebration; rather it will be a week in which we will seek to rededicate the community and the nation to the principle of non-violence in the struggle for freedom and justice.

During the week of the Institute, the leaders of the Montgomery movement hope to raise enough funds to liquidate present financial obligations and meet the many financial responsibilities which lie ahead. We will need funds to give assistance to those individuals who sacrificed themselves in order to aid the movement. Many of them are "marked men" who will not be able to get work for some time. Ninety ministers and leaders of the protest movement still have cases pending in court and are subject to be tried any day on a charge of conspiracy against the city transportation lines. The president's case must still be appealed to the highest court in order to clear his name of false conspiracy charges. There is also the need for funds so that the MIA can continue to operate in the interest of the Negroes after the protest is ended, since the NAACP operation has been legally curtailed in Alabama. Since the ballot is one of the basic keys to the solution of the Negroes problem in the south, there is the urgent need to set up voting clinics throughout the community which will assist persons in registering and teach them voting procedures.

Because of these needs, a special request goes out to all people of goodwill for an anniversary contribution to be sent to the MIA during the week of December third. It is our hope that all churches, organizations, and individuals will make an "extra" liberal contribution for this most meeded cause.

If it is at all possible, we would be, indeed, honored to have you visit Montgomery during some period of this week and share in the rich fellowship that we are all anticipating. Again, we request your co-operation and speedy reply.

Cordially yours,
[*signed*]
Martin Luther King, Jr.,
President
[*signed*]
Ralph D. Abernathy,
Institute Chairman

TLS. NULR-DLC.

From Gil B. Lloyd

28 November 1956
Seattle, Wash.

The pastor of Mount Zion Baptist Church in Seattle urges King to run for president of the National Baptist Convention, citing the need for dynamic new leadership.[1] Lloyd's request reveals discontent with the leadership of J. H. Jackson among those Baptist ministers who wanted the group to promote civil rights. At the convention's September meetings a faction of delegates, including some of King, Sr.'s, closest friends, sought to limit Jackson's tenure as president, but the issue was tabled until the following year. On 7 January 1957 King, Jr., declined Lloyd's offer to organize support for a presidential campaign at the next convention meeting in Kansas City.

Dr. Martin Luther King, Jr.,
Pastor
Dexter Avenue Baptist Church
309 South Jackson Street
Montgomery Alabama

My Dear Dr. King:

This letter comes to ask your permission to form a committee to sponsor your name for the presidency of the National Baptist Convention, USA., Inc. As we stand at the threshold of momentous decision on Christian integration, while taking the long-range view of the future of our Negro Baptist ranks, we MUST

---

1. Gil Burton Lloyd (1916–), born in Nashville, Tennessee, earned his B.A. (1939) from Fisk University and his M.Ed. (1969) from Seattle University. Ordained in 1939, he served as an army chaplain and community worker in Chicago. He became pastor of Seattle's Mount Zion Baptist Church in 1954, staying there until 1957. From 1959 to 1986 he served as pastor of Cherry Hill Baptist Church in Seattle.

HAVE A NEW LEADERSHIP which embodies religious zeal with scholarship, group loyalty with clear thinking, and administration with integrity. Across the nation, your embodiment of these virtues is a fiat accompli. Under your leadership, our national body could develop a much-needed program of dynamic evangelism, education, missions, social action and finance. As I see it, without such a development at this particular insightful point of Negro-and-Baptist history in this country, our Baptist churches will miss their greatest opportunity since Reconstruction to enrich and broaden and stabilize their future.

With your permission I should like to organize a committee of approximately 25 to 50 across the country, to actively work for your nomination and election at Kansas City. There are no strings attached; you would have to approve our publicity and statements; and should a disruptive contest be foreseen, withdrawal would be a mutual agreement. This would be a voluntary movement on the committee's part. However, I should like your permission to launch the program during my Christmas mailing across the nation: because I have longed for a Baptist messiah like you since 1932!!

Respectfully, your Brother
[*signed*]
Gil Burton Lloyd

GBL/agw

TALS. MLKP-MBU: Box 61A.

To Lottie Mae Pugh

28 November 1956
[*Montgomery, Ala.*]

On 8 November Pugh, a student at the Booker T. Washington School in Suffolk, Virginia, had written to King about her wish "to work in an Orphan Home" after completing her high school education. She wanted "to know what qualities would you say one would have to possess in order to attain success in this field." She continued: "I admire the success you have won in your chosen field and that has prompted me to seek guidance from you."

Miss Lottie Mae Pugh
P.O. Box 854
Suffolk, Virginia

Dear Miss Pugh:

Thanks for your very kind letter of November 8. I was more than happy to hear from you. It is always encouraging to find young persons who are desirous of serving humanity. I am sure that there is a real need for persons to work in orphan homes. I would say that the basic qualities necessary for such a venture are conscientiousness, dedication to the cause of human need, soundness in thinking, a radiating personality, and genuine honesty. With these qualities I am sure that you will make a real success of your work in an orphan home.

You have my prayers and best wishes for a future filled with success.

Very sincerely yours,
M. L. King, Jr.,
President

MLK:mlb

THLc. MLKP-MBU: Box 64.

"We Are Still Walking"

December 1956
New York, N.Y.

Liberation, a new radical pacifist magazine, had published an article by King in its second issue.[1] Celebrating the boycott's first anniversary with a "Salute to Montgomery" by seven prominent political and religious leaders,[2] its December special issue included a firsthand account of "How It All Started" by MIA activist E. D. Nixon as well as King's report on the final stage of the protest. In this statement King contends that, despite its apparent legal and moral victory, the movement had entered its "most difficult" period. He asks everyone to return to the buses "not as a right but as a duty. If we go back as a right, there is a danger that we will be blind to the rights of others."

When the Supreme Court ruled on November 13th that segregated buses are illegal, it must have appeared to many people that our struggle in Montgomery was over. Actually, the most difficult stage of crisis had just begun.

For one thing the immediate response of some influential white people was to scoff at the court decision and to announce that it would never be put into effect. One pro-segregationist said: "We are prepared for a century of litigation." The leader of the Montgomery Citizens Council stated: "Any attempt to enforce this decision will inevitably lead to riot and bloodshed."[3] It is clear that all our tact and all our love are called for in order to meet the situation creatively.

Even more important, our own experience and growth during these eleven and a half months of united nonviolent protest has been such that we cannot be satisfied with a court "victory" over our white brothers. We must respond to the

---

1. See King, "Our Struggle," April 1956, p. 236–241 in this volume.
2. The "salutes" were written by Eleanor Roosevelt, Roy Wilkins, Ralph Bunche, A. Philip Randolph, Harry Emerson Fosdick, John Haynes Holmes, and Z. K. Matthews, a leader of the African National Congress in South Africa.
3. Luther Ingalls, quoted in "White Spokesmen Warn of Possible Violence," *Montgomery Advertiser,* 14 November 1956.

decision with an understanding of those who have opposed us and with an appreciation of the difficult adjustments that the court order poses for them. We must be able to face up honestly to our own shortcomings. We must act in such a way as to make possible a coming together of white people and colored people on the basis of a real harmony of interests and understanding. We seek an integration based on mutual respect. We have worked and suffered for non-segregated buses, but we want this to be a step towards equality, not a step away from it.

Perhaps if I tell you of our first mass meeting the night after the Supreme Court's decision, it will indicate what was going on in our minds.

After our opening hymm, the Scripture was read by Rev. Robert Graetz, a young Lutheran minister who has been a constant reminder to us in these trying months that white people as well as colored people are trying to expand their horizons and work out the day-to-day applications of Christianity. He read from Paul's famous letter to the Corinthians: " . . . though I have all faith, so that I could move mountains, and have not love, I am nothing. . . . Love suffereth long and is kind. . . . "

When he got to the words: "When I was a child, I spoke as a child, I understood as a child, I thought as a child, but when I became a man I put away childish things," the congregation burst into applause. Soon there was shouting, cheering, and waving of handkerchiefs. To me this was an exciting, spontaneous expression by the Negro congregation of what had happened to it these months. The people knew that they had come of age, that they had won new dignity. They would never again be the old subservient, fearful appeasers. But neither would they be resentful fighters for justice who could overlook the rights and feelings of their opponents. When Mr. Graetz concluded the reading with the words: "And now abideth faith, hope and love, but the greatest of these is love," there was another spontaneous outburst.[4] Only a people who had struggled with all the problems involved in trying to be loving in the midst of bitter conflict could have reacted in this way. I knew then that nonviolence, for all its difficulties, had won its way into our hearts.

Peculiar People

Later, when Rev. Abernathy spoke, he told how a white newspaper man had reproached him for this outburst on the part of the congregation. "Isn't it a little peculiar," he said, "for people to interrupt the Scripture that way?" "Yes it is," said Abernathy, "just as it is peculiar for people to walk in the snow and rain when there are empty buses available; just as it is peculiar for people to pray for those who persecute them; just as it is peculiar for the Southern Negro to stand up and look a white man in the face as an equal." Pandemonium broke loose.

In my talk, I tried to discuss the basic philosophy of our movement. It is

---

4. 1 Corinthians 13. King refers to the mass meetings held on 14 November 1956 at Hutchinson Street and Holt Street Baptist churches. See King's description of that evening in *Stride Toward Freedom*, pp. 161–162; and his address to the Holt Street mass meeting on pp. 424–433 in this volume.

summed up in the idea that we must go back on the buses not as a right but as a duty. If we go back as a right, there is a danger that we will be blind to the rights of others. We Negroes have been in a humiliating position because others have been chiefly concerned with insisting on their own rights. This is too narrow a basis for human brotherhood, and certainly will not overcome existing tensions and misunderstandings.

Secondly, if we insist on our "rights," we will return to the buses with the psychology of victors. We will think and say—by our manner if not our words—that we are the victors. This would be unworthy of us and a barrier to the growth we hope for in others.

In the past, we have sat in the back of the buses, and this has indicated a basic lack of self-respect. It shows that we thought of ourselves as less than men. On the other hand, the white people have sat in the front and have thought of themselves as superior. They have tried to play God. Both approaches are wrong. Our *duty* in going back on the buses is to destroy this superior-inferior relationship, from whichever side it is felt. Instead of accepting the division of mankind, it is our duty to act in the manner best designed to establish man's oneness. If we go back in this spirit, our mental attitude will be one that must in the long run bring about reconciliation.

There is a victory in this situation. But it is a victory for truth and justice, a victory for the unity of mankind.

These eleven months have not been at all easy. Our feet have often been tired. We have struggled against tremendous odds to maintain alternative transportation, but we have kept going with the faith that in our struggle we had cosmic companionship, and that, at bottom, the universe is on the side of justice. We must keep that perspective in the days that are immediately ahead.

Klan Stages Parade

The night the Supreme Court decision was handed down, the Ku Klux Klan tried to intimidate us. The radio announced that the Klan would demonstrate throughout the Negro community. There were threats of bombing and other violence. We decided that we would not react as we had done too often in the past. We would not go into our houses, close the doors, pull the shades, or turn off the lights. Instead we would greet them as any other parade.

When the Klan arrived—according to the newspapers "about forty carloads of robed and hooded members"—porch lights were on and doors open.[5] The Negro people had gathered courage. As the Klan drove by, people behaved much as if they were watching the advance contingent for the Ringling Brothers Circus or a Philadelphia Mummers Parade. Many walked about as usual; some simply watched; others relaxed on their stoops; a few waved as the cars passed by. This required a tremendous effort, but the Klan was so nonplussed that after a few short blocks it turned off into a side-street and disappeared into the night.

---

5. "Klan Stages Parade Here," *Montgomery Advertiser,* 14 November 1956.

Not all our problems are resolved that easily. A few hours after the Supreme Court decided in favor of non-segregated buses, the U.S. Circuit Court issued an injunction prohibiting us from continuing the car pool. This was a system whereby about 100 vehicles had picked up protesters at the Negro churches and had taken them to central locations. The court order deprived us of our chief method for transporting many Negroes to work or shopping centers from outlying districts.

Formal objections to the car pool included the charges that the cars were improperly insured and the drivers were "morally unsuitable." It is true that for a time some cars were without insurance—since the White Citizens Council brought pressure on the insurance companies to cancel the policies on cars being used in the pool. But this was remedied long before the court case, when Lloyds of London insured each car to the amount of $11,000. As evidence of the moral unfitness of the drivers, the city listed the numerous traffic tickets with which it had harassed us from the beginning. Despite this strange justice, we decided to comply with the court order.

Unlike the Supreme Court decision, which does not go into effect until the formal order is handed to the Montgomery officials, the injunction against the car pool was immediately operative. This means that at the present time—and for about a month—we have no car pool, and cannot, in good faith, ride the buses. As evidence of solidarity among Negroes, the leaders have decided either to put their cars in the garages, while the people must walk or to place their cars at the disposal of others. If people must walk, the leaders will walk with them.

Naturally, we were disappointed at the issuance of the injunction. There will be many sore feet in Montgomery—and many tasks unfilled because of lack of transportation. But as in the case of several previous persecutions it may work in the end to our benefit. Having destroyed the car pool, the defenders of segregation will be in no position to go to the courts and request delays in execution of the desegregation order. This was the method for getting around the Supreme Court order on integration of schools. It has succeeded to the extent that there is not a single integrated public school in the State of Alabama. But in the case of the buses it is hard to plead for "going slow yet a little longer" when Negroes must walk everywhere they go. To me this is further proof that human beings inevitably work against themselves when they work for selfish ends. Several weeks ago an editorial in the *Montgomery Advertiser* raised questions about the wisdom of the white segregationists pressing for the abolition of the car pool. The writer said he was not sure that this was the right thing to do. The answer is simple: you cannot do the right thing in the wrong context.

Growth on Both Sides

I do not mean to imply that all the white people are working for merely selfish ends. We have all inherited a situation that is extremely difficult. We are therefore gratified when we find members of the white population making a serious effort to change. There are many evidences of growth on the part of both white and Negro people in Montgomery.

A year ago the intolerable behavior of a prominent member of the white group was largely responsible for prolonging the protest. In fact, considerable tension arose from his initial intransigence. At the beginning we felt that this gentleman treated us rather rudely. But now he talks with us in a dignified and courteous manner and says that he understands us better. He told me that he respects persons who have deep convictions and are willing to stand up for them at the cost of personal suffering.

There are encouraging indications that hundreds of other white persons have come to feel similarly. They are under tremendous pressure to conform to the views of the more reactionary elements, or at least to remain discreetly aloof. But we are trying to encourage them to act firmly in line with their deeper convictions. That is why we are publicly asking all persons of good will to comply with the Supreme Court order.

One anonymous phone caller, whose voice I have come to recognize, has been calling me for months to insult and threaten me and then slam down the receiver. Recently he stayed on the 'phone for half an hour, giving me the opportunity to discuss the whole underlying problem with him. At the end of the call he said: "Reverend King, I have enjoyed talking with you, and I am beginning to think that you may be right." This willingness to change deeply ingrained attitudes buoys us up and challenges us to be open to growth, also.

Appeal to the Churches

We are appealing especially to church people to examine their lives in the light of the life and teachings of the great religious leaders. They teach that all men, whatever their race or color, are children of one Father and therefore brothers, one of another. He that loveth not his brother whom he hath seen can not love God whom he hath not seen.[6]

Churches, by disseminating these teachings, have had much to do with the increasing sensitiveness on the issue of race relations and the undoubted advances which have been made in recent years. However, the churches have fallen woefully short of practicing what they preach. They have contributed to the confusion, the hesitation, the bitterness and violence.

We are convinced that great gains can be made if religious men will seek to practice true love toward their brothers and sisters. This conviction underlies our own attempts to be fearlessly non-violent in the present situation. It is the basis on which we are appealing to our white brothers to see beyond the narrow concepts of the past.

Can Not Be Solved by Politics

Discussion has tended to concentrate on such aspects as Supreme Court decisions and the maintenance of law and order against mob rule. We do not wish to

---

6. King paraphrases 1 John 4:20.

minimize these issues. They have an important bearing on the peace of our land. But the racial problem, North and South, cannot be solved on a purely political level. It must be approached morally and spiritually. We must ask ourselves as individuals: What is the right thing to do, regardless of the personal sacrifices involved?

Within the Negro churches, one of the lessons we have learned is that the church is not living up to its full responsibilities if it merely preaches an other-worldly gospel devoid of practical social connotations. It must concern itself, as Jesus did, with the economic and social problems of this world, as well as with its other-worldly gospel. As our church has played a leading role in the present social struggle, it has won new respect within the Negro population.

Long Range Program

From this perspective, it is obvious that our interest in brotherhood extends far beyond the desegregation of the buses. We are striving for the removal of all barriers that divide and alienate mankind, whether racial, economic or psychological. Though we are deeply involved in the bus protest, we have also worked out a long-range constructive program. Recently we agreed on six continuing goals:

1. To establish the first bank in Montgomery to be owned and operated by Negroes. We have found that in the present situation many Negroes who are active in the protest have been unable to secure loans from the existing banks.

2. To organize a credit union. As a result of the protest, there is a strong desire among the Negroes to pool their money for great cooperative economic programs. We are anxious to demonstrate that cooperation rather than competition is the way to meet problems.

3. To expand the voting clinics, with which we have been trying not only to teach Negroes the techniques of registration and voting but also to provide impartial discussion of the underlying issues.

4. The establishment of training institutes in the methods and discipline of non-violent action. We have begun to see the tremendous possibilities of this method of tackling human problems.

5. Until the NAACP, which has been outlawed in Alabama, is able to function again in the State, we hope to be able to take on some aspects of the excellent work it has carried on.

6. To give aid to those who have sacrificed in our cause. Many of them are marked men and women who will be unable to get work in Montgomery for a long time. We cannot build a movement if we do not stand by those who are victims in the struggle. Spiritual solidarity is meaningless if it does not extend into economic brotherhood.

Unanticipated Results of Non-Violence

Everyone must realize that in the early days of the protest there were many who
questioned the effectiveness, and even the manliness, of non-violence. But as the

protest has continued there has been a growing commitment on the part of the entire Negro population. Those who were willing to get their guns in the beginning are coming to see the futility of such an approach.

The struggle has produced a definite character development among Negroes. The Negro is more willing now to tell the truth about his attitude to segregation. In the past, he often used deception as a technique for appeasing and soothing the white man. Now he is willing to stand up and speak more honestly.

Crime has noticeably diminished. One nurse, who owns a Negro hospital in Montgomery, said to me recently that since the protest started she has been able to go to church Sunday mornings, something she had not been able to do for years. This means that Saturday nights are not so vicious as they used to be.

There is an amazing lack of bitterness, a contagious spirit of warmth and friendliness. The children seem to display a new sense of belonging. The older children are aware of the conflict and the resulting tension, but they act as if they expect the future to include a better world to live in.

We did not anticipate these developments. But they have strengthened our faith in non-violence. Believing that a movement is finally judged by its effect on the human beings associated with it, we are not discouraged by the problems that lie ahead.

PD. *Liberation* 1 (December 1956): 6–9.

"Facing the Challenge of a New Age," Address Delivered at the First Annual Institute on Nonviolence and Social Change

3 December 1956
Montgomery, Ala.

The MIA's weeklong Institute on Nonviolence and Social Change, which became an annual event, featured seminars on nonviolent tactics, voter registration, and education.[1] Delivering the opening speech to an overflowing crowd at Holt Street Baptist Church, King declares that the success of the Montgomery movement has shattered many stereotypes. "We have gained a new sense of dignity and destiny," King asserts, as well as "a new and powerful weapon—nonviolent resistance." King sees the rise of the "new Negro" as heralding a "new world order" to replace the "old order" of colonialism, exploitation, and segregation. King's speech is similar to his August address to the Alpha Phi Alpha convention and his speech on 6 December to an NAACP gathering at Vermont Avenue Baptist Church in Washington, D.C.

---

1. Among the session leaders were T. M. Alexander, Glenn Smiley, T. J. Jemison, C. K. Steele, F. L. Shuttlesworth, B. D. Lambert, Carl Rowan, H. V. Richardson, Nannie Helen Burroughs, James B. Cobb, William Holmes Borders, Homer A. Jack, and John B. Culbertson. A mass religious service, with J. H. Jackson, president of the National Baptist Convention, as the main speaker, concluded the conference on Sunday, 9 December.

Significant variations are noted below between the notes taken by a person attending the Washington speech and the text that King prepared for his Holt Street remarks.[2]

I. INTRODUCTORY OBSERVATIONS

Presiding officer, members of the Montgomery Improvement Association, visiting friends, ladies and gentlemen.

One year ago we assembled in this church and voted unanimously to cease riding the buses of Montgomery until injustice had been eliminated in three definite areas of bus transportation. The deliberations of that brisk and cold night in December will long be stencilled on the mental sheets of succeeding generations. Little did we know on that night that we were starting a movement that would rise to international proportions; a movement whose lofty echos would ring in the ears of people of every nation; a movement that would stagger and astound the imagination of the oppressor, while leaving a glittering star of hope etched in the midnight skies of the oppressed. Little did we know that night that we were starting a movement that would gain the admiration of men of goodwill all over the world. But God still has a mysterious way to perform his wonders. It seems that God decided to use Montgomery as the proving ground for the struggle and triumph of freedom and justice in America. It is one of the ironies of our day that Montgomery, the Cradle of the Confederacy, is being transformed into Montgomery, the cradle of freedom and justice.

We have learned many things as a results of our struggle together. Our non-violent protest has demonstrated to the Negro, North and South, that many stereotypes he has held about himself and other Negroes are not valid. Montgomery has broken the spell and is ushering in concrete manifestations of the thinking and action of the new Negro.

Some of the basic things that we have learned are as follows: (1) We have discovered that we can stick together for a common cause; (2) Our leaders do not have to sell out; (3) Threats and violence do not necessarily intimidate those who are sufficiently aroused and non-violent; (4) Our church is becoming militant, stressing a social gospel as well as a gospel of personal salvation; (5) We have gained a new sense of dignity and destiny; (6) We have discovered a new and powerful weapon—non-violent resistance.

One of the amazing things about the protest that will long be remembered is the orderly way it has been conducted. On every hand you have evinced wise restraint and calm dignity. You have carefully avoided animosity, making sure that your methods were rooted in the deep soils of the Christian faith. Because of this, violence has almost been a non-existent factor in our struggle. For such "discipline, generations yet unborn will commend you.

If we are to be fair and honest we must also commend the white community at this point. If there had not been some discipline and moral sensitivity in the white

---

2. King, "Birth of a New Age," August 1956, pp. 339–346 in this volume; and Julian O. Grayson, notes on "Facing the Challenge of a New Age," 6 December 1956.

community, we would have had much more violence in Montgomery. All of this renews my faith in the vast possibilities of this community. I am aware of the fact that the vast majority of white persons of Montgomery and the state of Alabama sincerely believe that segregation is both morally and sociologically justifiable. But nobody has been able to convince me that the vast majority of white people in this community, or in the whole state of Alabama, are willing to use violence to maintain segregation. It is only the fringe element, the hoodlum element, which constitutes a numerical minority, that would resort to the use of violence.[3] I still have faith in man, and I still believe that there are great resources of goodwill in the southern white man that we must somehow tap. We must continue to believe that the most ardent segregationist can be transformed into the most constructive integrationist.

I cannot close these introductory expressions without giving a personal word of appreciation. I realize that words can never adequately express appreciation. Real appreciation must flow from the deep seas of the heart. But in my little way and with my stumbling words, I would like to express my deepest appreciation to each of you for following my leadership. The wonders that have come about in Montgomery this year were not due so much to my leadership, but to the greatness of your followship. The Executive Board has worked as a unit and has distinguished itself for peace and harmony. The Negro ministers of the city deserve the highest praise. They have worked indefatiguably and assiduously for the overall cause of freedom. They have been willing to forget denominations, and realize a deep unity of purpose. Above all, those of you who have walked and picked up rides here and there, must have a special place in freedom's hall of fame. There is nothing more majestic and sublime than the quiet testimony of a people willing to sacrifice and suffer for the cause of freedom. I am sure that God smiles upon each of you with an exuberant joy.

II. FACING THE CHALLENGE OF A NEW AGE

Those of us who live in the Twentieth Century are privileged to live in one of the most momentous periods of human history. It is an exciting age filled with hope. It is an age in which a new social order is being born. We stand today between two worlds—the dying old and the emerging new.

Now I am aware of the fact that there are those who would contend that we live in the most ghastly period of human history. They would argue that the rhythmic beat of the deep rumblings of discontent from Asia, the uprisings in Africa, the nationalistic longings of Egypt, the roaring cannons from Hungary, and the racial tensions of America are all indicative of the deep and tragic midnight which encompasses our civilization. They would argue that we are retrogressing instead

---

3. King apparently omitted these two sentences in his speech but later explained to a reporter that it was due to "a lack of time," adding that the passage "certainly still expresses my sentiments" ("King Labels 'Hoodlums' Bar to Racial Harmony," *Montgomery Advertiser*, 4 December 1956).

of progressing. But far from representing retrogression and tragic meaningless-
ness, the present tensions represent the necessary pains that accompany the birth
of anything new. Long ago the Greek philosopher Horaclitus[4] argued that justice emerges from the strife of opposites, and Hegel, in modern philosophy,
preached a doctrine of growth through struggle. It is both historically and biologically true that there can be no birth and growth without birth and growing
pains. Whenever there is the emergence of the new we confront the recalcitrance
of the old. So the tensions which we witness in the world today are indicative of
the fact that a new world order is being born and an old order is passing away.

We are all familiar with the old order that is passing away. We have lived with it
for many years. We have seen it in its international aspect, in the form of Colonialism and Imperialism. There are approximately two billion four hundred million (2,400,000,000) people in this world, and the vast majority of these people
are colored—about one billion six hundred million (1,600,000,000) of the
people of the world are colored. Fifty years ago, or even twenty-five years ago,
most of these one billion six hundred million people lived under the yoke of
some foreign power. We could turn our eyes to China and see there six hundred
million men and women under the pressing yoke of British, Dutch, and French
rule. We could turn our eyes to Indonesia and see a hundred million men and
women under the domination of the Dutch. We could turn to India and Pakistan
and notice four hundred ~~million~~ million brown men and women under the
pressing yoke of the British. We could turn our eyes to Africa and notice there
two hundred million black men and women under the pressing yoke of the British, the Dutch and the French. For years all of these people were dominated
politically, exploited economically, segregated and humiliated.

But there comes a time when people get tired. There comes a time when
people get tired of being trampled over by the iron feet of oppression. There
comes a time when people get tired of being plunged across the abyss of exploitation where they experience the bleakness of nagging despair. There comes
a time when people get tired of being pushed out of the glittering sunlight of
life's July and left standing in the piercing chill of an Alpine November. So in the
midst of their tiredness these people decided to rise up and protest against injustice. As a results of their protest more than one billion three hundred million
(1,300,000,000) of the colored peoples of the world are free today. They have their
own governments, their own economic system, and their own educational system.
They have broken loose from the Egypt of Colonialism and Imperialism, and they
are now moving through the wilderness of adjustment toward the promised land
of cultural integration. As they look back they see the old order of Colonialism
and Imperialism passing away and the new order of freedom and justice coming
into being.

We have also seen the old order in our own nation, in the form of segregation
and discrimination. We know something of the long history of this old order in
America. It had its beginning in the year 1619 when the first Negro slaves landed
on the shores of this nation. They were brought here from the soils of Africa. And

---

4. King refers to Heraclitus (ca. 500 B.C.).

unlike the Pilgrim Fathers who landed at Plymouth a year later, they were brought here against their wills. Throughout slavery the Negro was treated in a very inhuman fashion. He was a thing to be used not a person to be respected. He was merely a depersonalized cog in a vast plantation machine. The famous Dred Scott Decision of 1857 well illustrates the status of the Negro during slavery. In this decision the Supreme Court of the United States said, in substance, that the Negro is not a citizen of the United States; he is merely property subject to the dictates of his owner. Then came 1896. It was in this year that the Supreme Court of this nation, through the Plessy v. Ferguson Decision, established the doctrine of separate-but-equal as the law of the land. Through this decision segregation gained legal and moral sanction. The end results of the Plessy Doctrine was that it lead to a strict enforcement of the "separate," with hardly the slightest attempt to abide by the "equal." So the Plessy Doctrine ended up making for tragic inequalities and ungodly exploitation.

Living under these conditions, many Negroes came to the point of losing faith in themselves. They came to feel that perhaps they were less than human. The great tragedy of physical slavery was that it lead to the paralysis of mental slavery. So long as the Negro maintained this subservient attitude and accepted this "place" assigned to him, a sort of racial peace existed. But it was an uneasy peace in which the Negro was forced patiently to accept insult, injustice and exploitation. It was a negative peace. True peace is not merely the absence of some negative force—tension, confusion, or war; it is the presence of some positive force— justice, goodwill and brotherhood. And so the peace which presently existed between the races was a negative peace devoid of any positive and lasting quality.[5]

Then something happened to the Negro. Circumstances made it necessary for him to travel more. His rural plantation background was gradually being supplanted by migration to urban and industrial communities. His economic life was gradually rising to decisive proportions. His cultural life was gradually rising through the steady decline of crippling illiteracy. All of these factors conjoined to cause the Negro to take a new look at himself. Negro masses began to reevaluate themselves. The Negro came to feel that he was somebody. His religion revealed to him that God loves all of his children, and that every man, from a bass black to a treble white, is significant on God's keyboard. So he could now cry out with the eloquent poet:

> Fleecy locks and black complexion
> Cannot forfeit nature's claim
> Skin may differ, but affection
> Dwells in black and white the same
> And were I so tall as to reach the pole
> Or to grasp the ocean at a span,
> I must be measured by my soul,
> The mind is the standard of the man.[6]

---

5. These five sentences do not appear in Grayson's notes.

6. These lines are a composite of poems by William Cowper, "The Negro's Complaint" (1788), and Isaac Watts, "False Greatness" (1706). See note 5 to "The 'New Negro' of the South: Behind the Montgomery Story," June 1956, p. 283 in this volume.

With this new self respect and new sense of dignity on the part of the Negro, the South's negative peace was rapidly undermined. And so the tension which we are witnessing in race relations today can be explained, in part, by the revolutionary change in the Negro's evaluation of himself, and his determination to struggle and sacrifice until the walls of segregation have finally been crushed by the battering rams of surging justice.

Along with the emergence of a "new Negro," with a new sense of dignity and destiny, came that memorable decision of May 17, 1954. In this decision the Supreme Court of this nation unanimously affirmed that the old Plessy Doctrine must go. This decision came as a legal and sociological death blow to an evil that had occupied the throne of American life for several decades. It affirmed in no uncertain terms that separate facilities are inherently unequal and that to segregate a child because of his race is to deny him of equal protection of the law. With the coming of this great decision we could gradually see the old order of segregation and discrimination passing away, and the new order of freedom and justice coming into being. Let nobody fool you, all of the loud noises that you hear today from the legislative halls of the South in terms of "interposition" and "nullification," and of outlawing the NAACP, are merely the death groans from a dying system. The old order is passing away, and the new order is coming into being. We are witnessing in our day the birth of a new age, with a new structure of freedom and justice.

Now as we face the fact of this new emerging world, we must face the responsibilities that come along with it. A new age brings with it new challenges. Let us consider some of the challenges of this new age.

First we are challenged to rise above the narrow confines of our individualistic concerns to the broader concerns of all humanity. The new world is a world of geographical togetherness. This means that no individual or nation can live alone. We must all learn to live together, or we will be forced to die together. This new world of geographical togetherness has been brought about, to a great extent, by man's scientific and technological genius. Man through his scientific genius has been able to dwarf distance and place time in chains; he has been able to carve highways through the <u>stratosphere</u>. And so it is possible today to eat breakfast in New York City and dinner in Paris, France. Bob Hope has described this new jet age in which we live. It is an age in which we will be able to get a non-stop flight from Los Angeles, California to New York City, and if by chance we develop hiccups on taking off, we will "hic" in Los Angeles and "cup" in New York City. It is an age in which one will be able to leave Tokyo on Sunday morning and, because of time difference, arrive in Seattle, Washington on the preceding Saturday night. When your friends meet you at the airport in Seattle inquiring when you left Tokyo, You will have to say, "I left tomorrow." This, in a very humorous sense, says to us that our world is geographically one. Now we are faced with the challenge of making it spiritually one. Through our scientific genius we have made of the world a neighborhood; now through our moral and spiritual genius we must make of it a brotherhood. We are all involved in the single process. Whatever affects one directly affects all indirectly. We are all links in the great chain of humanity. This is what John Doane meant when he said years ago:

"No man is an island, entire of it selfe; every man
is a peece of the Continent, a part of the maine;

if a clod bee washed away by the Sea, Europe is the lesse,
as well as if a Promontorie were, as well as if a Mannor
of thy friends or of thine owne were; any mans death
diminishes me, because I am involved in Mankinde;
And therefore never send to know for whom the bell tolls;
it tolls for thee." [7]

A second challenge that the new age brings to each of us is that of achieving excellency in our various fields of endeavor. In the new age many doors will be opening to us that were not opened in the past, and the great challenge which we confront is to be prepared to enter these doors as they open. Ralph Waldo Emerson said in an essay back in 1871, "If a man can write a better book, or preach a better sermon, or make a better mouse trap than his neighbor, even if he builds his house in the woods the world will make a beaten path to his door." In the years to come this will be increasingly true.

In the new age we will be forced to compete with people of all races and nationalities. Therefore, we cannot aim merely to be good Negro teachers, good Negro doctors, good Negro ministers, good Negro skilled laborers. We must set out to do a good job, irrespective of race, and do it so well that nobody could do it better.

Whatever your life's work is, do it well. Even if it does not fall in the category of one of the so-called big professions, do it well. As one college president said, "A man should do his job so well that the living, the dead, and the unborn could do it no better." [8] If it falls your lot to be a street sweeper, sweep streets like Michelangelo painted pictures, like Shakespeare wrote poetry, like Beethoven composed music; sweep streets so well that all the host of Heaven and earth will have to pause and say, "Here lived a great street sweeper, who swept his job well." As Douglas Mallock says:

> If you can't be a pine on the top of the hill
> Be a scrub in the valley—but be
> The best little scrub by the side of the hill,
> Be a bush if you can't be a tree.
>
> If you can't be a highway just be a trail
> If you can't be the sun be a star;
> It isn't by size that you win or fail—
> Be the best of whatever you are [9]

A third challenge that stands before us is that of entering the new age with understanding goodwill. This simply means that the Christian virtues of love, mercy and forgiveness should stand at the center of our lives.[10] There is the danger that those of us who have lived so long under the yoke of oppression, those of us who have been exploited and trampled over, those of us who have had to stand amid the tragic midnight of injustice and indignities will enter the new age

---

7. John Donne, "Devotions upon Emergent Occasions" (1624).

8. King later identified his source as Morehouse president Benjamin Mays (see King, "Facing the Challenge of a New Age," 1 January 1957, Paul H. Brown Collection, in private hands).

9. Douglas Malloch, "Be the Best of Whatever You Are" (1926).

10. In his Washington speech King said he considered the third challenge "the most important."

with hate and bitterness. But if we retaliate with hate and bitterness, the new age will be nothing but a duplication of the old age. We must blot out the hate and injustice of the old age with the love and justice of the new. This is why I believe so firmly in non-violence. Violence never solves problems. It only creates new and more complicated ones. If we succumb to the temptation of using violence in our struggle for justice, unborn generations will be the recipients of a long and desolate night of bitterness, and our chief legacy to the future will be an endless reign of meaningless chaos.[11]

We have before us the glorious opportunity to inject a new dimension of love into the veins of our civilization. There is still a voice crying out in terms that echo across the generations, saying: "Love your enemies, bless them that curse you, pray for them that despitefully use you, that you may be the children of your Father which is in Heaven." [12] This love might well be the salvation of our civilization. This is why I am so impressed with our motto for the week, "Freedom and Justice through Love." Not through violence; not through hate; no not even through boycotts; but through love. It is true that as we struggle for freedom in America we will have to boycott at times. But we must remember as we boycott that a boycott is not an end within itself; it is merely a means to awaken a sense of shame within the oppressor and challenge his false sense of superiority. But the end is reconciliation; the end is redemption; the end is the creation of the beloved community. It is this type of spirit and this type of love that can transform opposers into friends. It is this type of understanding goodwill that will transform the deep gloom of the old age into the exuberant gladness of the new age. It is this love which will bring about miracles in the hearts of men.

Now I realize that in talking so much about love it is very easy to become sentimental. There is the danger that our talk about love will merely be empty words devoid of any practical and true meaning. But when I say love those who oppose you I am not speaking of love in a sentimental or affectionate sense. It would be nonsense to urge men to love their oppressors in an affectionate sense. When I refer to love at this point I mean understanding goodwill. The Greek language comes to our aid at this point. The Greek language has three words for love. First it speaks of love in terms of <u>Eros</u>. Plato used this word quite frequently in his dialogues. <u>Eros</u> is a type of esthetic love. Now it has come to mean a sort of romantic love. I guess Shakespeare was thinking in terms of <u>Eros</u> when he said "Love is not love which alters when it alteration finds, or bends with the remover to remove." It is an ever fixed mark that looks on tempest and is never shaken. It is a star to every wandering bark . . . [13] This is <u>Eros</u>. And then the Greek talks about <u>philia</u>. <u>Philia</u> is a sort of intimate affectionateness between personal

---

11. King altered these six sentences in his Washington address: "Love, justice, righteousness must be our companions as we enter the new age. We must continue in a spirit of passive resistance and non-violence. Violence would lead us into a night of bitterness. Ours must be a new demonstration of love. . . . We must seek to gain our freedom and equality through love; that is the essence of the victory for the 50,000 Negroes in Montgomery, Alabama. We are not out to defeat and humiliate the white man. We are trying to help him as well as ourselves establish justice in the world in a oneness under Christ Jesus."

12. Matthew 5:44–45.

13. William Shakespeare, "Sonnet CXVI" (1609).

friends. It is a sort of reciprocal love. On this level a person loves because he is loved, then the Greek language comes out with another word which is the highest level of love. It speaks of it in terms of <u>agape</u>. <u>Agape</u> means nothing sentimental or basically affectionate. It means understanding redeeming goodwill for all men.[14] It is an overflowing love which seeks nothing in return. It is the love of God working in the lives of men. When we rise to love on the <u>agape</u> level we love men not because we like them, not because their attitudes and ways appeal to us, but because God loves you. Here we rise to the position of loving the person who does the evil deed while hating the deed that the person does. With this type of love and understanding goodwill we will be able to stand amid the radiant glow of the new age with dignity and discipline. Yes, the new age is coming. It is coming mighty fast.[15]

Now the fact that this new age is emerging reveals something basic about the universe. It tells us something about the core and heartbeat of the cosmos. It reminds us that the universe is on the side of justice. It says to those who struggle for justice, "You do not struggle alone, but God struggles with you." This belief that God is on the side of truth and justice comes down to us from the long tradition of our Christian faith.[16] There is something at the very center of our faith which reminds us that Good Friday may occupy the throne for a day, but ultimately it must give way to the triumphant beat of the drums of Easter. Evil may so shape events that Caesar will occupy a palace and Christ a cross, but one day that same Christ will rise up and split history into AD and BC, so that even the life of Caesar must be dated by His name. There is something in this universe that justifies Carlyle in saying, "No lie can live forever." There is something in this universe which justifies William Cullen Bryant in saying, "Truth crushed to earth will rise again." There is something in this universe that justifies James Russell Lowell in saying:

> Truth forever on the scaffold
> Wrong forever on the throne
> Yet that scaffold sways the future
> And behind the dim unknown stands God
> Within the shadows keeping watch above his own.

---

14. Cf. Harry Emerson Fosdick, "On Being Fit to Live With," in *On Being Fit to Live With*, pp. 6–7: "Love in the New Testament is not a sentimental and affectionate emotion as we so commonly interpret it. There are three words in Greek for love, three words that we have to translate by our one word, love. *Eros*—'erotic' comes from it—that is one. . . . *Philia*—that is another Greek word. It meant intimate personal affectionateness and friendship. . . . But the great Christian word for love is something else: *agape*. . . . *Agape* means nothing sentimental or primarily emotional at all; it means understanding, redeeming, creative good will."

15. King elaborated on *agape* slightly differently in his Washington speech: "The other word for love of which I am speaking tonight is the word agape meaning the sacrificial, productive brotherly love as exemplified by Christ on the cross. I do not like Senator Eastland's attitude on the race question; I do not like the things he has said about us; I do not like the way he would treat us but I do love Senator Eastland with the love of God as a child of God. Agape should enter the new age with us with this true love of God in our hearts. Religion and spiritual love is the salvation of our new age. Toynbee in his massive work *A Study of History* thinks that it may be the Negro will inject love and understanding in our disintegrating society and save the world for a new age."

16. King added in Washington that "justice will be a reality here on earth."

And so here in Montgomery, after more than eleven long months, we can walk and never get weary, because we know there is a great camp meeting in the promised land of freedom and justice.[17]

I am about to close now. But before closing I must correct what might be a false impression. I am afraid that if I close at this point many will go away misinterpreting my whole message.[18] I have talked about the new age which is fastly coming into being. I have talked about the fact that God is working in history to bring about this new age. There is the danger, therefore, that after hearing all of this you will go away with the impression that we can go home, sit down, and do nothing, waiting for the coming of the inevitable. You will somehow feel that this new age will roll in on the wheels of inevitability, so there is nothing to do but wait on it. If you get that impression you are the victims of a dangerous optimism. If you go away with that interpretation you are the victims of an illusion wrapped in superficiality. We must speed up the coming of the inevitable.

Now it is true, if I may speak figuratively, that old man segregation is on his deathbed. But history has proven that social systems have a great last minute breathing power, and the guardians of a status-quo are always on hand with their oxygen tents to keep the old order alive. Segregation is still a fact in America. We still confront it in the South in its glaring and conspicuous forms. We still confront it in the North in its hidden and subtle forms. But if Democracy is to live, segregation must die. Segregation is a glaring evil. It is utterly unchristian. It relegates the segregated to the status of a thing rather than elevate him to the status of a person. Segregation is nothing but slavery covered up with certain nicities of complexity. Segregation is a blatant denial of the unity which we all have in Christ Jesus.

So we must continue the struggle against segregation in order to speed up the coming of the inevitable. We must continue to gain the ballot. This is one of the basic keys to the solution of our problem. Until we gain political power through possession of the ballot we will be convenient tools of unscrupulous politicians. We must face the appalling fact that we have been betrayed by both the Democratic and Republican parties. The Democrats have betrayed us by capitulating to the whims and caprices of the Southern Dixiecrats. The Republicans have betrayed us by capitulating to the blatant hypocracy of right-wing reactionary northerners. This coalition of Southern Democrats and Northern right-wing Republicans defeats every proposed bill on civil rights. Until we gain the ballot and place proper public officials in office this condition will continue to exist. In communities where we confront difficulties in gaining the ballot, we must use all legal and moral means to remove these difficulties.

We must continue to struggle through legalism and legislation. There are those who contend that integration can come only through education, for no other reason than that morals cannot be legislated. I choose, however, to be dialectical at this point. It isn't either education or legislation; it is both legislation and education. I quite agree that it is impossible to change a man's internal feelings merely through law. But this really isn't the intention of the law. The law does not seek to change ones internal feelings; it seeks rather to control the external

17. This line comes from the spiritual "A Great Meeting in the Promised Land."
18. Grayson's notes on King's Washington speech end at this point.

effects of those internal feelings. For instance, the law cannot make a man love me—religion and education must do that—but it can control his desire to lynch me. So in order to control the external effects of prejudiced internal feelings, we must continue to struggle through legislation.

Another thing that we must do in pressing on for integration is to invest our finances in the cause of freedom. Freedom has always been an expensive thing. History is a fit testimony to the fact that freedom is rarely gained without sacrifice and self-denial. So we must donate large sums of money to the cause of freedom. We can no longer complain that we don't have the money. Statistics reveal that the economic life of the Negro is rising to decisive proportions. The annual income of the American Negro is now more than sixteen billion dollars, almost equal to the national income of Canada. So we are gradually becoming economically independent. It would be a tragic indictment on both the self respect and practical wisdom of the Negro if history reveals that at the height of the Twentieth Century the Negro spent more for frivolities than for the cause of freedom. We must never let it be said that we spend more for the evanescent and ephemeral than for the eternal values of freedom and justice.

Another thing that we must do in speeding up the coming of the new age is to develop intelligent, courageous and dedicated leadership. This is one of the pressing needs of the hour. In this period of transition and growing social change, there is a dire need for leaders who are calm and yet positive; leaders who avoid the extremes of "hot-headedness" and "Uncle Tomism." The urgency of the hour calls for leaders of wise judgement and sound integrity—leaders not in love with money but in love with justice; leaders not in love with publicity, but in love with humanity; leaders who can subject their particular egos to the greatness of the cause. To paraphrase Holland's words:

> God give us leaders!
> A time like this demands strong minds, great hearts,
>   true faith and ready hands;
> Leaders whom the lust of office does not kill;
> Leaders whom the spoils of life cannot buy;
> Leaders who possess opinions and a will;
> Leaders who have honor; leaders who will not lie;
> Leaders who can stand before a demagogue and damn his
>   treacherous flatteries without winking!
> Tall leaders, sun crowned, who live above the fog
>   in public duty and private thinking.[19]

Finally, if we are to speed up the coming of the new age we must have the moral courage to stand up and protest against injustice wherever we find it. Wherever we find segregation we must have the fortitude to passively resist it. I realize that

---

19. Josiah Gilbert Holland, "Wanted" (1872). King substitutes "leaders" where Holland used "men" and omits the last five lines, but otherwise King recites the original accurately. On the verso of the page on which this poem appears King wrote, "The ~~issue~~ civil rights issue is not some evanescent ephemeral domestic issue which politicians can; it is an eternal moral issue which may well determine the destiny of our nation in the idealogical struggle with communism. The executive branch of the government is all to silent and apipithetic. The legislative branch is all too evasive and hypo-critical."

this will mean suffering and sacrifice. It might even mean going to jail. If such is the case we must be willing to fill up the jail houses of the South. It might even mean physical death. But if physical death is the price that some must pay to free their children from a permanent life of psychological death, then nothing could be more honorable.[20] Once more it might well turn out that the blood of the martyr will be the seed of the tabernacle of freedom.

Someone will ask, how will we face the acts of cruelty and violence that might come as results of our standing up for justice? What will be our defense? Certainly it must not be retaliatory violence. We must find our defense in the amazing power of unity and courage that we have demonstrated in Montgomery. Our defense is to meet every act of violence toward an individual Negro with the facts that there are thousands of others who will present themselves in his place as potential victims. Every time one school teacher is fired for standing up courageously for justice, it must be faced with the fact that there are four thousand more to be fired. If the oppressors bomb the home of one Negro for his courage, this must be met with the fact that they must be required to bomb the homes of fifty thousand more Negroes. This dynamic unity, this amazing self-respect, this willingness to suffer, and this refusal to hit back will soon cause the oppressor to become ashamed of his own methods. He will be forced to stand before the world and his God splattered with the blood and reeking with the stench of his Negro brother.

There is nothing in all the world greater than freedom. It is worth paying for; it is worth losing a job; it is worth going to jail for. I would rather be a free pauper than a rich slave. I would rather die in abject poverty with my convictions than live in inordinate riches with the lack of self respect. Once more every Negro must be able to cry out with his forefathers: "Before I'll be a slave, I'll be buried in my grave and go home to my Father and be saved." [21]

If we will join together in doing all of these things we will be able to speed up the coming of the new world—a new world in which men will live together as brothers; a world in which men will beat their swords into ploughshares and their spears into prunning-hooks;[22] a world in which men will no longer take necessities from the masses to give luxuries to the classes; a world in which all men will respect the dignity and worth of all human personality. Then we will be able to sing from the great tradition of our nation:

> "My country 'tis of thee, sweet land of liberty of thee I sing, Land where my fathers died, Land of the Pilgrims pride, From every mountain side, Let freedom ring."

This must become literally true. Freedom must ring from every mountain side. Yes, let it ring from the snow-capped Rockies of Colorado, from the prodigious hill tops of New Hampshire, from the mighty Alleghenies of Pennsylvania, from the curvaceous slopes of California. But not only that. Let Freedom ring from every mountain side—from every mole hill in Mississippi, from Stone Mountain

---

20. In a later speech King attributed this statement to Kenneth Clark (see "Desegregation and the Future," 15 December 1956, p. 478 in this volume).

21. King quotes a Negro spiritual, "Oh Freedom."

22. Isaiah 2:4.

of Georgia, from Lookout Mountain of Tennessee, yes, and from every hill and mountain of Alabama. From every mountain side let freedom ring.[23] When this day finally comes "The morning stars will sing together and the suns of God will shout for joy." [24]

TAD. MLKP-MBU: Box 3.

---

23. King may have adapted these seven sentences from Archibald J. Carey, Jr., who used a similar passage in his address to the 1952 Republican National Convention. Carey recited the song "My Country 'Tis of Thee" and then continued: "That's exactly what we mean—from every mountain side, let freedom ring. Not only from the Green Mountains and the White Mountains of Vermont and New Hampshire; not only from the Catskills of New York; but from the Ozarks in Arkansas, from the Stone Mountain in Georgia, from the Great Smokies of Tennessee and from the Blue Ridge Mountains of Virginia—Not only for the minorities of the United States, but for the persecuted of Europe, for the rejected of Asia, for the disfranchised of South Africa and for the disinherited of all the earth—may the Republican Party, under God, from every mountain side, LET FREEDOM RING!" (Carey, "Address to the Republican National Convention," 8 July 1952, AJC-ICHi).

24. Job 38:7.

To Charles Walker

5 December 1956
[*Montgomery, Ala.*]

In a 5 November letter FOR staff member Walker wrote that he spoke frequently "on the significance of Montgomery" and urged people to send funds to the MIA. He asked King if the MIA had other needs. He added that a Quaker delegation from Philadelphia had been "deeply moved" by their visit to Montgomery. They were helping, he continued, "to sensitize Quakers here to be more faithful to their own testimony on non-violence." [1]

Mr. Charles Walker
Regional Secretary
Fellowship of Reconciliation
2006 Walnut Street
Philadelphia 3, Pa.

Dear Mr. Walker:

This is just a note to acknowledge receipt of your very kind letter of November 5. First, I must apologize for being so tardy in my reply. Absence from the city and the accumulation of a flood of mail account for the delay.

---

1. Charles C. Walker (1920–), born in Gap, Pennsylvania, received his B.S. (1945) at Elizabethtown College (1941) and did graduate work at New York University. He was a staff member of the Fellowship of Reconciliation (1944–1956) and the American Friends Service Committee (1956–1970). He was

We are still gratified to know that you have continued in our struggle here in Montgomery. We are still facing problems, but they are gradually being solved. Our real problem now is to prepare the people to go back to integrated buses. As you know the Supreme Court's decision came down just a few weeks ago, and the city officials will attempt to circumvent the decision if at all possible. But we feel certain that the decision will go into effect as soon as the mandate comes down from Washington to the Federal District Court. Since our car pool is no longer in operation we will not need help from a friendly insurance agent. There are no particular needs confronting us at this time that are on my mind. Of course the general needs are still there, namely, prayer, moral support, and financial contributions. We will continue to need all of these things.

Again, let me express my appreciation to you for your moral support and Christian generosity. We will long remember your coming to our aid in this. I too wish it were possible for you to be in Montgomery during this week of the Institute on Non-Violence.

With every good wish, I am

Sincerely yours,
M. L. King, Jr.
Minister

MLK:mlb

(Dictated by Dr. King, but signed in his absence.)

TLc. MLKP-MBU: Box 16.

FOR's field secretary for the Middle Atlantic region when he wrote King. According to his wife's recollection, Walker spoke on Gandhi and nonviolence at Crozer Theological Seminary while King was a student there (Marian G. Walker to King Papers Project, 9 February 1994). Walker helped found *Liberation* magazine, the Gandhi Institute, World Peace Brigade, Committee for Nonviolent Action, and other organizations.

From Charles Walker

5 December 1956
Philadelphia, Penn.

MARTIN LUTHER KING

MONTGOMERY IMPROVEMENT ASSN

530 SOUTH UNION ST MONTGOMERY ALA

WE HONOR YOUR STRUGGLE ON THIS ANNIVERSARY. IN REMAINING FAITHFUL TO NONVIOLENCE IN THOUGHT AND ACTION THE PEOPLE OF MONTGOMERY HAVE MADE NEW HISTORY IN AMERICA AND A NEW CHAPTER IN THE HISTORY OF FREEDOM HAS BEEN WRITTEN

WALKER FELLOWSHIP OF RECONCILIATION

PWSr. MLKP-MBU: Box 17.

Congratulations

N8B032 PA113   1956 DEC 5   AM 9 41 (33).

P LLF110 CGN PD= PHILADELPHIA PENN 5 1010AME=

MARTIN LUTHER KING MONTGOMERY IMPROVEMENT ASSN=

   530 SOUTH UNION ST MONTGOMERY ALA=

WE HONOR YOUR STRUGGLE ON THIS ANNIVERSARY. IN

REMAINING FAITHFUL TO NON VIOLENCE IN THOUGHT AND

ACTION THE PEOPLE OF MONTGOMERY HAVE MADE NEW

HISTORY IN AMERICA AND A NEW CHAPTER IN THE HISTORY

OF FREEDOM HAS BEEN WRITTEN=

         CHARLES WALKER FELLOWSHIP OF RECONCILIATION=

         B Y   W E S T E R N   U N I O N

To Dorothy S. Bowles

5 December 1956
[*Montgomery, Ala.*]

In November Bowles asked to meet with King and Coretta Scott King while they were in New York for an 11 December United Negro College Fund–sponsored symposium entitled "The Negro Southerner Speaks." [1] *Bowles wrote that she and her husband, U.S. ambassador to India Chester Bowles, were going to India, and she knew "how interested many Indians will be to know more about the program of the Montgomery Improvement Association." King replies that his schedule probably does not allow time for a meeting.*

Mrs. Dorothy S. Bowles
Essex, Connecticut

Dear Mrs. Bowles:

This is to acknowledge receipt of your very kind letter of November 23.

I would be more than happy to have the personal interview with you while I am in New York City. However, due to pressing needs here in Montgomery, it seems that I will not arrive in New York until just a few hours before the Symposium and I will have to leave almost immediately afterwards. In the light of this I cannot make a definite commitment. If I find that it will be possible for me to be in New York longer than I now plan, I will be very happy to contact you for an appointment.

Thanks again for your interest in our struggle. Your encouraging words and great moral support are of inestimable value in the continuance of our struggle.

May I close by saying that I have long known of the great work of your husband. To my mind he is one of the greatest statesmen of our nation and of our age. His contribution to national and international relationships will remain in our thoughts so long as the cords of memory shall lengthen.

Very sincerely yours,
M. L. King, Jr.,
Minister

MLK:mlb

(Dictated by Dr. King but signed in his absence.)

TLc. MLKP-MBU: Box 15.

---

1. Dorothy Stebbins Bowles (1903–1989), born in Newton, Massachusetts, earned a B.A. from Vassar and an M.A. (1924) from Smith College. She became a social worker in Boston and later national secretary for the Junior League. Her husband, Chester Bowles (1901–1986), who served as ambassador to India from 1951 to 1953 and 1963 to 1969, wrote extensively on U.S. relations with developing nations.

10 December 1956
Montgomery, Ala.

*King testifies under oath to a Montgomery County Court clerk about an 11 July
confrontation with a Montgomery police officer at the railroad station. King, his wife,
and their friend Robert Williams attempted to walk through the white waiting room to
board a train for Nashville to attend a Race Relations Institute at Fisk University.
King probably prepared this deposition in response to a request from Mobile attorney
John L. LeFlore, who had informed NAACP staff and the U.S. Department of Justice
about the incident. King, Sr., reported being similarly harassed on three different
occasions at the Montgomery station, including once in September 1956 while traveling
with King, Jr., Coretta Scott King, and the Abernathys. On this occasion police officers,
who were apparently "stationed there to keep Negroes out of [the white] waiting room,"
threatened to arrest the group for "disturbing the peace."* [1]

Before me the undersigned authority personally came and appeared, and being by me first duly sworn, deposes and says:

My name is Martin Luther King, Jr. I am a minister and I am Pastor of The
Dexter Avenue Baptist Church located at 454 Dexter Avenue, Montgomery, Alabama. I reside at 309 South Jackson Street, Montgomery, Alabama.

On July 11, 1956, I was leaving Montgomery for Nashville, Tennessee as an interstate passenger. I decided to board the train by way of the general waiting room.
On entering the general waiting room a policeman stopped me at the door and
stated that I couldn't enter. I immediately told him that I was an interstate passenger, and on this basis had a right to enter the waiting room. He insisted that I go
to the colored waiting room. I continued to insist that I could not in all good
faith go to the colored waiting room since I was an interstate passenger. He held
me up for several moments arguing that the law of Alabama was totally against
the policy of Negro interstate passengers using the so-called white waiting room.
After five or ten minutes the time was drawing near for the train to leave. I told
him that I could not leave and go to the colored waiting room and that I would
just have to miss my train. At that time he said to me that he was going to take me
through the waiting room, but if I ever came back again he was going to "let me
have it." At one point he became so violent that he said that he wanted to "kill
up a few niggers anyway." Mr. Robert Williams, Professor of Music at The Alabama State College and my wife, Mrs. Coretta King, were with me at the time of
this incident.

Signed by:

TD. MLKP-MBU: Box 61.

---

1. King, Sr., to J. E. Tilford, 9 October 1956. Maude Ballou sent the deposition to LeFlore on 10
December 1956. See also LeFlore to King, 19 November 1956; King to LeFlore, 24 November 1956; and
Clarence Mitchell to Warren Olney III, 4 December 1956.

From L. Harold DeWolf

10 December 1956
Boston, Mass.

DeWolf asks if King is interested in a faculty appointment. On 4 January 1957 King replied: "I have had a great deal of satisfaction in the pastorate, and have almost come to the point of feeling that I can best render my service in this area, however, I can never quite get the idea out of my mind that I should do some teaching. In the light of this, I would certainly appreciate being recommended by you, and I would give such a recommendation the greatest consideration."

Dear Martin,

Would you be interested in considering a college faculty position? A seminary faculty position?

Requests for nominations come in, now and then, and it would be helpful to know the direction of your thinking.

We are all happy about the new Supreme Court decision and also the more vigorous enforcement of federal law in Tennessee.[1] We hope those weary feet in Montgomery can soon have some respite.

May God be with you always.

Ever—
[*signed*] Harold.

ALS. MLKP-MBU: Box 15.

---

1. DeWolf refers to the successful desegregation of the Clinton, Tennessee, high school on 10 December 1956 after several months of racial tension.

From Robert E. Hughes

10 December 1956
Birmingham, Ala.

As executive director of the Alabama Council on Human Relations, Hughes became acquainted with King, who agreed during 1955 to become first vice president of the council's Montgomery affiliate. Hughes occasionally preached at Dexter when King was obliged to be absent during the bus boycott, and he participated with King in a small biracial group of Montgomery ministers who met on Monday mornings to discuss religion and race. Hughes helped arrange the 8 December 1955 meeting between MIA leaders and the city commission. In mid-1956 Hughes moved the council's operations to Birmingham. In this letter he passes on news from Birmingham attorneys about the Supreme Court decision.

Dr. M. L. King   10 Dec
Pres., Montgomery Improvement Assn.   1956
S. Union St., Montgomery, Ala.

Dear Martin:

I have just talked to Attorney Orzelle Billingsley who has been in Washington, D.C. this past week. While there he talked to the clerk of the Supreme Court who stated that the Court would not announce its decision on a rehearing of the Montgomery case until next Mon. Dec. 17th. Naturally any mandate would not be sent down until after that date according to Billingsley. I mention this only in the event that someone in Mr. Shore's firm has not communicated this to you.

The Institute was very fine and certainly filled a gap among both groups in Montgomery as well as popularizing the idea over the South. All of you are to be heartily commended for this outstanding service.

Best wishes in these "last days" and call upon me if there is anything I can do.

Yours,
[*signed*] Bob
Rev. Robert E. Hughes
Exec. Director

TLS. MLKP-MBU: Box 13A.

From Joel Lawrence King

10 December 1956
Lansing, Mich.

King, a Lansing Baptist minister and the younger brother of King, Sr., praises his nephew's "marvelous" leadership in Montgomery and invites him to speak at the Lansing Civic Center Auditorium. King accepted the invitation and addressed a civil rights rally there on 17 February 1957, but his reply to his uncle has not been found. Ven King was Joel King's wife.

Dear M. L.

Just a few lines to let you hear from me, trust you, Coretta and the baby are well, which leaves us the same.

It was nice to me the Rev. Abernathy a few weeks ago, and to see you looking so well.

I was happy to see the very fine program that was carried out by your great organization last week. Seemingly that you had all of the "Tall Timbers" of the nation present. I am sure it was a great occassion for the city of Montgomery. Certainly you have done a marvelous job.

Things are moving along here in a very fine way. I have just filed my petition for councilman at large here in the city The outlook is good, people are giving   469 their support, both white and colored Greek and Jew. The election will be in February. (pray for the old Shepherd.) [1]

M. L. I am writing to you to extend an invitation to be our guest on either of these dates February, 17th or 24th. I feel its time for you to come to us. (Its almost a must) — people of all races are continually asking about your coming. I would like to make this one of the finest programs that they have had at this new huge Civic Center Auditorium. You can get some good (sugar) out of this deal if you would come at this time. Also I would like for you to bring Coretta to render several selections, along with the baby, since we haven't seen her, and you all spend some time with us.

Think about it and let me know, as it will take some time to work up my program and engage the Auditorium. Regards to wife and baby. Ven is fine.

Love,
[*signed*] Joel

AHLS. MLKP-MBU: Box 61.

---

1. Joel King was not elected as councilman.

To Medgar Wiley Evers

11 December 1956
[*Montgomery, Ala.*]

> *King responds to Evers's invitation to speak in Mississippi. Evers wrote King on 17 December to say that "our greatest inspiration was Sunday's mass meeting where thousands of liberty-loving Americans closed out the Institute. . . . Our only regret was that we were unable to attend all the previous sessions in which you had engaged."*

Mr. Medgar W. Evers, Field Secretary
National Association for the Advancement of Colored People
Mississippi State Office
Masonic Temple Building
1072 Lynch Street, Room 7
Jackson, Mississippi

Dear Mr. Evers:

This is to acknowledge receipt of your letter of November 13, inviting me to address the Jackson, Mississippi Branch of the NAACP. First, I must apologize for being so tardy in my reply. Absence from the city and the accumulation of a flood of mail account for the delay.

I have considered your request very seriously. It seems, however, that my schedule is too uncertain at this point to make any definite commitment. I am negotiating at this time on the possibility of being out of the country for about two months in the late Spring and early summer. I cannot accept any further engagements until this matter has been finally cleared up. I would suggest that you write me again around the first of February, and I can let you know then exactly whether or not I can come to Jackson. I wish it were possible to give you a definite answer at this time, but present conditions make it impossible.

It was a real pleasure having you in Montgomery yesterday. Your presence added much to the success of our meeting. You have my prayers and best wishes for continued success as you continue your struggle against the forces of evil and injustice in the state of Mississippi.

Yours very truly,
M. L. King, Jr.,
Minister

MLK:mlb

(Dictated by Dr. King but transcribed and signed in his absence.)

TLc. MLKP-MBU: Box 16.

"Desegregation and the Future," Address Delivered at the Annual Luncheon of the National Committee for Rural Schools

[*15 December 1956*]
[*New York, N.Y.*]

King delivers this address at New York City's Commodore Hotel to the annual luncheon of the National Committee for Rural Schools, an organization that sought to improve and equalize public education in the rural South. Labor leader Benjamin F. McLaurin, one of the organizers of the committee, and Jack Stetson, rector of the International Ladies Garment Workers Institute, presided over the event. Preceding King's address, Billy Flemming, a leader of the Clarendon County Improvement Association, reported on the desegregation movement in South Carolina and paid tribute to the courage of Judge J. Waties Waring, chair of the National Committee for Rural Schools. Social psychologist Kenneth Clark introduced King, observing of the Montgomery protest leaders that they had "the potential for truly great leadership; not just leadership of the American Negro, but . . . the potential for leadership of a spiritual, ethical and moral side of the American people who are sorely in need of such leadership."[1] Referring to his recent experience with segregated dining policies at the Atlanta airport, King claims that equality is not only quantitative but also qualitative, "not only a matter of mathematics and geometry" but "a matter of psychology."

---

1. For a complete transcript of this event, see Joseph F. Wilson, *Tearing Down the Color Bar* (New York: Columbia University Press, 1989), pp. 281–310.

Mr. Chairman, distinguished guests, ladies and gentlemen. I am delighted to have the opportunity of being here today and to be a part of this very rich fellowship. I'm very happy to share the platform with so many distinguished Americans, and I would like to say ditto to everything that has been said about these distinguished persons. I wish I had the time to make some statements about many of these persons because their names will long be remembered in America by those who are interested in freedom and human dignity.

Certainly, the name of Judge Waring and his wife will long be remembered, for his minority opinion has now become a majority opinion.[2] [*applause*] And I guess when he cast the dissenting vote in decision some years ago, there were those who said he was an impractical idealist. But history has proven that the impractical idealists of yesterday become the practical realists of today, and we are all indebted to him for what he has done in this nation.

And certainly, the very kind words that you have made about Rae Brandstein are greatly justifiable, but I have had the opportunity of knowing something of the work—of her work and the work of this great organization.[3] And I want to join you in expressing my personal appreciation to her and to all of her associates in this very fine and noble organization. Those of us who live in the southland have felt the influence, the inspiration, and the help that has come from this organization, and we are deeply grateful.

And I am indebted to my good friend Dr. Clark for this very generous introduction. I hope one day I will be able to live up to it.

Now the time is passing on and I want to have you think with me for a few moments from this subject: desegregation and the future. I think we're all concerned about the question of desegregation, and certainly we are all concerned about the future. And I want to speak about desegregation and the future.

On May seventeenth, 1954, the Supreme Court of this nation rendered in simple and unequivocal terms one of the most momentous decisions ever rendered in the history of this nation. To all men of goodwill, this decision came as a joyous daybreak to end the long night of human captivity. It came as a great beacon light of hope to millions of colored people throughout the world who had had a dim vision of the promised land of freedom and justice. It was a reaffirmation of the good old American doctrine of freedom and equality for all men. And this decision came as a legal and sociological deathblow to an evil that had occupied the throne of American life for several decades. Segregation has always been evil, and only the misguided reactionary clothed in the thin garments of irrational emotionalism will seek to defend it. Segregation is both rationally inexplicable and morally unjustifiable.

There are at least three basic reasons why segregation is evil. The first reason is that segregation inevitably makes for inequality. There was a time that we attempted to live with segregation. There were those who felt that we could live by a doctrine of separate but equal, and so back in 1896 the Supreme Court of this

---

2. Julius Waties Waring wrote the sole dissenting opinion in *Briggs v. Elliott,* a 1951 federal district court decision that the Supreme Court reversed in its *Brown v. Board of Education* decision of 1954.

3. Brandstein, executive secretary of the National Committee for Rural Schools, had arranged King's appearance (see King to Brandstein, 1 August 1956, pp. 332–333 in this volume).

nation, through the *Plessy v. Ferguson* decision, established the doctrine of separate but equal as the law of the land. But we all know what happened as a result
of that doctrine: there was always a strict enforcement of the separate without the
slightest intention to abide by the equal. And so as a result of the old *Plessy* doctrine, we ended up being plunged across the abyss of exploitation, where we experienced the bleakness of nagging injustice.

But even if it had been possible to provide the Negro with equal facilities in
terms of external construction and quantitative distribution, we would have still
confronted inequality. If it had been possible to give Negro children the same
number of schools proportionately and the same type of buildings as white children, the Negro children would have still confronted inequality in the sense that
they would not have had the opportunity of communicating with all children.
You see, equality is not only a matter of mathematics and geometry, but it's a
matter of psychology. It's not only a quantitative something, but it is a qualitative
something. And it is possible to have quantitative equality and qualitative inequality. The doctrine of separate but equal can never be.

I experienced this the other day. I was taking a flight to Virginia and took a
plane out of Montgomery and had to change in Atlanta, Georgia. And we got in
Atlanta and we were getting ready to take off and the train developed—the plane
developed a little motor trouble, and of course I was very happy that they discovered that trouble before we got in the air. [*laughter*] And so we had to get off and
go back into the waiting room, and it took about two or three hours to put in a
new transmission, I believe it was. We were to have lunch on the flight, and so
while we were waiting they gave all of us tickets to go in the Dobbs House in the
Atlanta airport and have lunch. I was the only Negro passenger on the plane, and
I followed everybody else going into the Dobbs House to get lunch.[4] When I got
there the—one of the waiters ushered me back, and I thought they were giving
me a very nice comfortable seat with everybody else. And I discovered they were
leading me to a compartment in the back. And this compartment was around
you, you were completely closed in, cut off from everybody else, so I immediately
said that I couldn't afford to eat there. I went on back and took a seat out in the
main dining room with everybody else and I waited there, and nobody served me.
I waited a long time, everybody else was being served. So finally I asked for the
manager, and he came out and started talking, and I told him the situation and
he talked in very sympathetic terms. And I never will forget what he said to me.
He said, "Now Reverend, this is the law; this is the state law and the city ordinance
and we have to do it. We can't serve you out here, but now, everything is the same.
Everything is equal back there; you will get the same food; you will be served out
of the same dishes and everything else; you will get the same service as everybody
out here." And I looked at him and started wondering if he really believed that.
And I started talking with him. I said, "Now, I don't see how I can get the same
service. Number one, I confront aesthetic inequality. I can't see all these beautiful
pictures that you have around the walls here. [*laughter*] We don't have them back
there." [*applause*]

---

4. For another account of this incident, see King to Robinson, 3 October 1956, pp. 391–393 in this
volume.

"But not only that, I just don't like sitting back there and it does something to me. It makes me almost angry. I know that I shouldn't get angry. I know that I shouldn't become bitter, but when you put me back there something happens to my soul, so that I confront inequality in the sense that I have a greater potential for the accumulation of bitterness because you put me back there. [*laughter*] And then not only that, I met a young man from Mobile who was my seat mate, a white fella from Mobile, Alabama, and we were discussing some very interesting things. And when we got in the dining room, if we followed what you're saying, we would have to be separated. And this means that I can't communicate with this young man. I am completely cut off from communication. So I confront inequality on three levels: I confront aesthetic inequality; I confront inequality in the sense of a greater potential for the accumulation of bitterness; and I confronted inequality in the sense that I can't communicate with the person who was my seat mate."

And I came to see what the Supreme Court meant when they came out saying that separate facilities are *inherently* unequal. There is no such thing as separate but equal. Separation, segregation, *inevitably* makes for inequality, and I think that is the first reason why segregation is evil, because it inevitably makes for inequality. [*applause*]

But not only that, segregation is evil because it scars the soul of both the segregated and the segregator. And I've said all along, as we struggle we must come to see that we are not merely trying to help the Negro. Segregation is as injurious to the white man as it is to the Negro. The festering sore of segregation debilitates the segregated as well as the segregator. It gives the segregated a false sense of inferiority, and it gives the segregator a false sense of superiority. It is equally damaging. And this is why we must forever take a stand against segregation, because it does something to the soul. And the Supreme Court came to see that also.

And thanks to the noble work of such persons as Dr. Kenneth Clark and other social psychologists who came to see, through long study, that segregation does something to the personality. That is why the Supreme Court said that segregation generates a sense and feeling of inferiority within children that distorts their personality. This is why the Negro parent must forever say to his child, "You are somebody, you belong, you count." Because the Negro child forever stands before a system that stares him in the face saying, "You are not equal to; you do not belong; you cannot be." Segregation distorts the personality of the segregated as well as the segregator.

Then there is a third reason why segregation is evil. That is because it ends up depersonalizing the segregated. That's the end results of segregation. The segregated becomes merely a thing to be used, not a person to be respected. He is merely a depersonalized cog in a vast economic machine. And this is why segregation is utterly evil and utterly un-Christian. It substitutes an "I/It" relationship for the "I/Thou" relationship.[5] It relegates the segregated to the status of a thing, rather than elevated to the status of a person, and so segregation will always be evil because it ends up depersonalizing the segregated.

---

5. King alludes to Martin Buber. See note 7 to "Paul's Letter to American Christians," 4 November 1956, p. 418 in this volume.

The Supreme Court decision of May seventeenth came in to correct a great evil. And thanks for this great decision, as a result of this decision, we can now gradually see old man segregation on his deathbed, if I may speak figuratively, and most of us are very happy to see the brother pass on because he has been a disturbing factor in the community for many years. [*laughter, applause*]

But this is not the only side of the story. We know all too well that there is another side. This decision has not gone without opposition. Many states have risen up in open defiance. We all know that the legislative halls of the South ring loud with such words as "interposition" and "nullification." And in so many sections of the South, a new modern form of the Ku Klux Klan has arisen in the form of white citizens councils. The methods of these councils range from threats and intimidation to actual economic reprisals against Negro men and women. Also these methods extend to white persons in the South who will dare take a stand for justice. These are the devotees of these councils so often stand up and preach sermons and give long talks about the nonviolence. They piously claim that they don't believe in violence, but we know all too well that their methods and public denouncements create the very atmosphere for violence. They must be held responsible for all of the terror, the mob rule, and brutal murders that have encompassed the South over the last several years. And I say to you this afternoon that it is an indictment on America and democracy that these ungodly and unethical and un-Christian and un-American councils have been able to exist all of these months without a modicum of criticism from the federal government. It is tragic. [*applause*] And so we must face the tragic fact that we are far from the promised land in the struggle for a desegregated society. Segregation is still a glaring fact in America. Yes, we still confront it in the South in its glaring and conspicuous forms. We still confront it in the North in its hidden and subtle forms. [*applause*]

Now it might be true, as I said, that old man segregation is on his deathbed, but as I said so often before, history has proven that social systems have a great last-minute breathing power and the guardians of the status quo are always on hand with their oxygen tents to keep the old order alive. [*laughter, applause*]

Segregation, segregation is still with us. We still confront it as a fact in this nation. So in the light of this great decision by the Supreme Court and the open opposition to it by reactionary and recalcitrant forces, the question which we now confront is this: How will we proceed to bring about a desegregated society in the future? What are we to do? What can we do to speed up the process of integration and make this whole move toward a desegregated society a final reality? What must we do to make it a reality in the future?

And I would like to take a few minutes to suggest two or three things that we must do, all of us, all people of goodwill. I think the first thing is this: we must continue to demand that the federal government will use all of its constitutional powers to enforce the law of the land. And I think this is one of the greatest areas that we must work in. It is tragic that the executive and legislative branches of our government have been so quiet in this whole movement. They have failed to follow the example so courageously set by the judicial branch. And now we must demand that the legislative and the executive branches of our government will take a definite stand and do something about enforcing these laws which are on the books. We all— [*applause*]

I know this afternoon our minds leap the mighty Atlantic and our minds and hearts go over to Hungary and we are concerned about what's happening there.

I'm sure that we are all grateful to our government for doing the right thing about Hungary and taking the proper attitude and being concerned about the Hungarians as they confront the desperate situation that they stand amid everyday.[6] But it is strange that the American government can be so much concerned about the Hungarians and have not the slightest concern about the Negroes in Mississippi and Alabama, in Georgia, in South Carolina. [*applause*]

Unless we in this nation wake up and decide to do something about the condition in America, we will never be able to defeat communism. We must do something about this problem. And I say that it is not just one party, but all of the political parties have a responsibility here. Actually, the Negro has been betrayed by both the Republican and the Democratic Party. [*applause*] The Democrats have betrayed him by capitulating to the whims and caprices of the southern Dixiecrats. The Republicans have betrayed him by capitulating to the blatant hypocrisy of reactionary right-wing northern Republicans. And this coalition of southern Dixiecrats and right-wing reactionary northern Republicans defeats every bill and every move towards liberal legislation in the area of civil rights. And if we are not careful, the same thing will happen in the next few days when Congress reconvenes. Nothing will be done about the filibuster and all of these other things that prevent any real move in the area of civil rights. We must be concerned enough all over this nation and demand that the federal government will become more aggressive, will rise up and take a stand and stop being so quiet and do something about the conditions which so many citizens of the South are confronting today.

There is a second thing which we must do in order to make segregation a dead factor and integration a reality in our society. And that is, we must continue to struggle through the courts, through legislation or legalism. Now I am aware of the fact that there are those who sincerely believe that this isn't the way. They would argue that you cannot legislate morals. Their contention is that integration must come into being through education. Well, I am sympathetic toward that view. I will agree that you can't legislate morals. I will agree that through the law you can't change one's internal feelings. But that isn't what we seek to do through the law. We are not seeking so much to change attitudes through the law, but to control behavior. We are not so much seeking to change one's internal feelings, but to control the external effects of those internal feelings. That's what we seek to do through the law. [*applause*]

I realize that the law cannot make an employer love me or have compassion for me, education and religion will have to do that, but it can at least keep him from refusing to hire me because of the color of my skin. And that is what we seek to do through the law. We seek to control the external effects of internal feelings that are prejudiced, and so we must continue to struggle through legalism. And at this point I must stress the need, the urgent need of our continuing to support the organization which has mastered the area of legal strategy, and that is the NAACP. [*applause*]

Let nobody fool you. They might outlaw the NAACP in Alabama. They might

6. King refers to the Hungarian revolution, which began on 23 October 1956. On 4 November 1956 the Soviet Union forcibly ended the rebellion.

outlaw the NAACP in Louisiana. They may outlaw it in Texas, and it looks like in Georgia they are getting ready to outlaw it. But it remains eternally true that this organization has done more to achieve the civil rights of Negroes than any other organization that we can point to [*applause*], and at this moment we cannot desert the NAACP. We must stand by it more than ever before. It might prove out that in future years this organization will prove to be America's greatest friend. By fighting its battles purely within the framework of legal democracy, it has saved the Negro from turning to foreign ideologies in order to solve his problems. We're all indebted to this great organization. [*applause*]

Now along with this, we've got to continue to go down in our pockets and give money for the cause of freedom. As you know, litigation is rising to heightening proportions every day, and it seems to be the strategy of the white citizens councils to delay integration as long as possible. I think they have about recognized now that segregation is dying, and they've conceded to that. They know as well as we know that segregation is on its deathbed, and what they are seeking to do now is to delay it as long as possible by keeping the Negro bogged down in litigation. As one attorney general said, I believe from Georgia, that "we are prepared for a century of litigation," and that's what they are attempting to do. And in order to block this stalling process, in order to block this delaying process, we must pile up great resources of money in order to block it. That means that we must continue to give generously and liberally for the cause of freedom. And I'm sure our hearts go out now to all of the organizations over the nation that have been concerned about these conditions. Negro people in the South will be confronted with many tragedies in these years of transition. They will confront economic reprisals and boycotts and threats and intimidation. And thanks to a great organization, like this organization, that has served to meet this real need, we need more of this. Because as this period of transition stands before us, many things will happen. We will need the aid and the cooperation of people of goodwill all over the nation. So I stress the need of continual financial support as we struggle for freedom and justice in America.

May I stress the need for courageous, intelligent, and dedicated leadership. I can never overlook this, for if we are to make a desegregated society a reality in the future, we will have to have dedicated, courageous, and intelligent leaders. In this period of transition and growing social change, we will need leaders who are positive and yet calm. Leaders who avoid the extremes of hotheadedness and Uncle Tomism. Leaders who somehow understand the issues. Leaders of sound integrity. Leaders not in love with publicity, but in love with justice. Leaders not in love with money, but in love with humanity. Leaders who can subject their particular egos to the greatness of the cause. God give us leaders. [*applause*] A time like this demands great souls with pure hearts and ready hands. Leaders whom the lust of office does not kill. Leaders whom the spoils of life cannot buy. Leaders who possess opinions and a will. Leaders who will not lie. Leaders who can stand before the demagogue and damn his treacherous flatteries without winking. Tall leaders, sun-crowned, who live above the fog in public duty and in private thinking.[7] This is one of the great needs of the hour, but as we move

---

7. In these four sentences King paraphrases the poem "Wanted" (1872) by Josiah Gilbert Holland.

on all over this nation we will need dedicated, courageous, and intelligent leaders.

And then I come to a final point. And I think this is probably more important than any of the others. If integration is to be a reality in the future, the Negro must decide himself to stand up courageously and protest against segregation wherever he finds it. Yes, we must depend on the law. We must depend on the courts. We must depend on financial support. But, in the final analysis, the Negro himself must assume the basic responsibility; for no other reason than laws cannot enforce themselves. The thing that we face now is to implement these laws. Segregation is already legally dead, but it is still factually alive. It confronted its legal death on May seventeenth, 1954. The problem which we confront now is to lift the noble precepts of our democracy from the dusty files of unimplemented court decisions, and the Negro himself must do something about this. And integration will not be some lavish dish that the white man will pass out on a silver platter while the Negro merely furnishes the appetite. He himself must be concerned. [*applause*]

So it means that we must rise up and protest courageously wherever we find segregation. Yes, we must do it nonviolently. We cannot afford to use violence in the struggle. If the Negro succumbs to the temptation of using violence in his struggle, unborn generations will be the recipients of a long and desolate night of bitterness and our chief legacy to the future will be an endless reign of meaningless chaos. There is still a voice crying out through the vista of time saying to every potential Peter, "Put up your sword." [8] History is replete with the bleached bones of nations and communities that failed to follow the command of Jesus at this point. No, violence is not the way. Hate is not the way. Bitterness is not the way. We must stand up with love in our hearts, with a lack of bitterness and yet a determination to protest courageously for justice and freedom in this land. [*applause*]

I realize that this will also mean suffering and sacrifice. It might even mean going to jail, but if such is the case we must be willing to fill up the jailhouses of the South. It might even mean physical death. But as Dr. Kenneth Clark said in a speech here last year, if physical death is the price that some must pay to free their children from a life of permanent psychological death, then nothing could be more honorable. We must somehow confront physical force with soul force and stand up courageously for justice and freedom. And this dynamic unity, this amazing self-respect, this willingness to suffer, and this refusal to hit back will cause the oppressors to become ashamed of their own methods and we will be able to transform enemies into friends. We will be able to emerge from the bleak and desolate midnight of injustice to the bright and glittering daybreak of freedom and goodwill. We can do this if we protest courageously, if we stand up with courage, if we stand up nonviolently. And this is the thing which will make integration a reality in our nation. This is the challenge that stands before all of us. If we will do this we will be able by the help of God to create a new world. A world in which men will be able to live together as brothers. A world in which men "will

---

8. John 18:11.

beat their swords into plowshares and their spears into pruning hooks." [9] A world
in which men will no longer take necessities from the masses to give luxuries to the classes. A world in which all men will respect the dignity and worth of all human personality. And that will be the day when all of us will be able to stand up and sing with new meaning: "My country 'tis of thee, / Sweet land of liberty, / Of thee I sing / Land where my fathers died, / Land of the pilgrim's pride, / From every mountain side, / Let freedom ring."

That must become literally true. Freedom must ring from *every* mountainside. And yes, let it ring from the snow-capped Rockies of Colorado. Let it ring from the prodigious hilltops of New Hampshire. Let it ring from the mighty Alleghenies of Pennsylvania. Let it ring from the curvaceous slopes of California. But not only that, from every mountainside, let freedom ring. Let it ring from every molehill in Mississippi, from every mountain and hill in Alabama, from Stone Mountain in Georgia, from Lookout Mountain in Tennessee, from every mountainside, let freedom ring. [10] And when that happens, the morning *stars* will sing together and the sons of God will shout for joy. [11] God bless you. [*applause*]

At. CSKC.

---

9. Isaiah 2:4.

10. King may have adapted these sentences from Archibald Carey, Jr.'s, address to the 1952 Republican National Convention (see note 23, "Facing the Challenge of a New Age," 3 December 1956, p. 463 in this volume).

11. Job 38:7.

To Roland E. Haynes

17 December 1956
[*Montgomery, Ala.*]

Mr. Roland Emerson Haynes
Boston University
School of Theology
745 Commonwealth Avenue
Boston 15, Mass.

Dear Roland:

Thanks for your very kind letter of November 27. It is a real pleasure hearing from you. I would have answered your letter before now, but absence from the city and an extremely busy schedule somewhat held me up.

I was more than delighted to have been in Boston and to have had the opportunity of seeing you. Also, it was a real pleasure seeing so many of my old professors. I have heard from Dr. DeWolf at least twice since that time. Things seem to be going very well with him.

I am still keeping in mind that much needed period of rest. Almost every time I plan to take such a rest something comes up to prevent it. Dr. DeWolf and Dean Muelder have made several offers for this rest period.

I hope everything goes well with you and your family. I plan to be in Atlanta toward the end of the Christmas Holidays. I hope it will be possible to see you and Minnie at that time.

Very sincerely yours,
M. L.

MLK:mlb

TLc. MLKP-MBU: Box 15.

To Benjamin Elijah Mays

17 December 1956
[*Montgomery, Ala.*]

King agrees to speak at Morehouse on 17 January 1957 (an engagement he later canceled). He criticizes his own performance in a New York City symposium sponsored by the United Negro College Fund.[1] On 21 December Mays replied with encouraging words: "I am very glad I had an opportunity to hear you on the panel in New York. I think you handled your part of the program exceptionally well."

Dr. Benjamin E. Mays, President
Morehouse College
Atlanta, Georgia

Dear Dr. Mays:

Thanks for your very kind letter of November 14, inviting me to speak at Morehouse College. First, I must apologize for being so tardy in my reply. Absence from the city and the accumulation of a flood of mail account for the delay. Please know that it was not due to sheer negligence but to the inevitable pressures of an involved situation.

After checking my schedule, I find that January 17, is the best date for me. If this date is satisfactory, I will proceed to place it on my calendar.

I will be in Atlanta on the first of January to deliver the Emancipation Address.[2] I hope it will be possible to see you at that time.

---

1 The symposium, entitled "The Negro Southerner Speaks," was held at Hunter College. Carl Rowan and two other newspaper reporters interviewed King, Atlanta University president Rufus Clement, and two other African-American southerners. Afterward Chester Bowles acclaimed King's leadership: "As Gandhi appealed to the basic decency, honesty, and democratic spirit of the British, so great new colored leaders will now appeal to the conscience and the decency of their white neighbors throughout the South" (see "Dr. King Speaks in New York City," *Dexter Echo,* 19 December 1956, p. 2).

2. King delivered "Facing the Challenge of a New Age" at Atlanta's Big Bethel AME Church.

It was a real pleasure seeing you in New York the other night. I only regret that I had to rush out so soon after the symposium to appear on a radio program.[3] I felt that the panel went over fairly well but I was somewhat disappointed with my own participation. I had the feeling all along that I did not get to answer the vital questions confronting the Southern Negro. In fact, I felt that the whole panel fell to grapple with the basic questions. All and all, however, the experience was very rich. I was very happy to meet so many white persons of financial means who are so intensely interested in our struggle for freedom and justice. I owe you a deep debt of gratitude for the contact.

With warm personal regards, I am

Sincerely yours,
M. L. King, Jr.,
Minister

MLK:mlb

TLc. MLKP-MBU: Box 62.

---

3. King and Rowan appeared on the NBC radio show "Tex and Jinx" from 10:35 P.M. to midnight (see Dorothy L. Barker to King, 7 December 1956).

"Integrated Bus Suggestions"

19 December 1956
[*Montgomery, Ala.*]

On 17 December the Supreme Court rejected city and state appeals of Browder v. Gayle *and ordered Montgomery's buses desegregated. Three days later, when the court order arrived by mail, the MIA held two mass meetings to formally call the bus boycott to an end and prepare for the next day when the protesters would return to the buses. After several weeks of well-attended nonviolent training sessions, King and Glenn Smiley prepared these guidelines for mass distribution.[1]*

This is a historic week because segregattion on buses now been declared un-constitutional. Within a few days the Supreme Court Mandate will reach Mont-gomery and you will be re-boarding <u>integrated</u> buses. This places upon us all a tremendous responsibility of maintaining, in face of what could be some un-pleasantness, a calm and loving dignity befitting good citizens and members of

---

1. King reprinted these suggestions in *Stride Toward Freedom*, pp. 164, 169.

our Race. If there is violence in word or deed it must not be our people who commit it.

For your help and convience the following suggestions are made. Will you read, study and memorize them so that our non-violent determination may not be endangered. First, some general suggestions:

1. Not all white people are opposed to integrated buses. Accept goodwill on the part of many.

2. The whole bus is now for the use of all people. Take a vacant seat.

3. Pray for guidance and commit yourself to complete non-violence in word and action as you enter the bus.

4. Demonstrate the calm dignity of our Montgomery people in your actions.

5. In all things observe ordinary rules of courtesy and good behavior.

6. Remember that this is not a victory for Negroes alone, but for all Montgomery and the South. Do not boast! Do not brag!

7. Be quiet but friendly; proud, but not arrogant; joyous, but not boistrous.

8. Be loving enough to absorb evil and understanding enough to turn an enemy into a friend.

NOW FOR SOME SPECIFIC SUGGESTIONS:

1. The bus driver is in charge of the bus and has been instructed to obey the law. Assume that he will cooperate in helping you occupy any vacant seat.

2. Do not deliberately sit by a white person, unless there is no other seat.

3. In sitting down by a person, white or colored, say "May I" or "Pardon me" as you sit. This is a common courtesy.

4. If cursed, do not curse back. If pushed, do not push back. If struck, do not strike back, but evidence love and goodwill at all times.

5. In case of an incident, talk as little as possible, and always in a quiet tone. Do not get up from your seat! Report all serious incidents to the bus driver.

6. For the first few days try to get on the bus with a friend in whose non-violence you have confidence. You can uphold one another by a glance or a prayer.

7. If another person is being molested, do not arise to go to his defense, but pray for the oppressor and use moral and spiritual force to carry on the struggle for justice.

8. According to your own ability and personality, do not be afraid to experiment with new and creative techniques for achieving reconciliation and social change.

9. If you feel you cannot take it, walk for another week or two. We have confidence in our people. GOD BLESS YOU ALL.

THE MONTGOMERY IMPROVEMENT ASSOCIATION
THE REV. M. L. KING, JR., PRESIDENT
THE REV. W. J. POWELL, SECRETARY

TD. MLKP-MBU: Box 2.

To W. A. Gayle

19 December 1956
[*Montgomery, Ala.*]

In a letter also sent to the other two commissioners, Clyde Sellers and Frank Parks, and to Police Chief G. J. Ruppenthal, King requests additional police patrols along bus routes to "prevent possible violence." Two days earlier the city commissioners had indicated that, although they had "no alternative but to recognize" the Supreme Court decision, they promised, "through every legal means at our disposal, to see that the separation of the races is continued on the public transportation here in Montgomery." In a thinly veiled attack on King they added that "it is hoped that those recent comers to Montgomery, who claim to be the leaders of the boycott-crusaders here, and who have day in and day out, in nearly every state in the Union for over a year, denounced the white race, will cease their hypocritical and unjustifiable attacks upon the people of Montgomery and their Board of Commissioners and will counsel the members of their race not to act unwisely."[1] *Ruppenthal rejected King's request for additional patrols, telling reporters that his department would provide "only regular protection."*[2]

The Honorable Mayor W. A. Gayle
City Hall
Montgomery, Alabama

Dear Mayor Gayle:

   We greatly appreciate all efforts which you have previously made to maintain the peace and to keep violence at a minimum, through your public statements

---

   1. Al McConagha, "City Bows to Court Decision, Pledges Fight for Segregation," *Montgomery Advertiser,* 18 December 1956; and Statement by Board of Commissioners, City of Montgomery, 17 December 1956. A week earlier, in an interview with Southern Regional Council representatives, King indicated that "the power structure of Montgomery is concerned about this situation. They seem more alert than they have in the past. They told the Negro leaders, 'Don't worry about the White Citizen's Councils, or the City Commission.' . . . The Negro community is ready with a quiet approach—a nonviolent one, to resume riding buses. The Mayor had said quietly that he would not permit violence" (Emory Via and Fred Routh, Memorandum to SRC staff, 17 December 1956).
   2. "'Regular Protection' Given 'Danger Zone,'" *Montgomery Advertiser,* 21 December 1956.

and otherwise. And we are hopefully looking forward to your continued efforts along these lines.

We understand that the Supreme Court's mandate concerning bus segregation has been mailed to the Federal District Court. As soon as the District Court issues the formal decree, we shall be returning to the busses.

Although we are hopeful that no violent incidents will occur, we must recognize that possibility. There is that element of violent-minded people, of both races, of which we must be mindful.

Past experience reveals that the only places where violence has occurred in connection with the busses has been at the end of lines and on very dark streets. And the hours after dark are potentially more dangerous than the daytime.

We, therefore, request that you use every precaution to prevent possible violence, and that you will insure that the above-mentioned danger zones will be patrolled with extra caution.

We reaffirm our basic conviction that violence is both impractical and immoral. We have been training our people to remain non-violent in word and deed, and not to return hate for hate. We believe that violence in our city will lead to a long and desolate night of bitterness, which will bring shame to generations yet unborn.

Thanking you for your cooperation, we remain

Yours truly,
The Executive Board of
The Montgomery Improvement
Association, by
(Rev.) Martin L. King, Jr.

MLK:mlb

THLc. MLKP-MBU: Box 22.

From William Holmes Borders

19 December 1956

Pastor for two decades of Atlanta's Wheat Street Baptist Church, Borders had known King since childhood. He spoke at the MIA's Institute on Nonviolence and Social Change two weeks earlier.[1]

---

1. William Holmes Borders (1905–1993), born in Macon, Georgia, earned his B.A. (1929) from Morehouse College, his B.D. (1932) from Garrett Theological Seminary, and his M.A. (1936) from Northwestern University. The following year he became pastor of Atlanta's Wheat Street Baptist Church, a few blocks from Ebenezer. Under his leadership, which lasted until his retirement in 1988, the church developed a complex of businesses, housing, and nonprofit organizations. Borders was a leader in many of Atlanta's civil rights campaigns, including its bus desegregation protest in 1957.

Rev. M. L. King, Jr.
Dexter Avenue Baptist Church
454 Dexter Avenue
Montgomery, Alabama

My dear Rev. King:

I received the annual report of your church. I read every line of the introductory experssions. I checked the outstanding events. I noted the number of outstanding speaking engagements. I scaned the financial record, the amount raised and spent. It is outstanding and wonderful.

It was kind of you to think of sending me a copy. May God continue to bless you that you may reach higher heights. Your future is unlimited. You have a Ph. D degree. You are beautifully married. You are humble. You are sweet. You have forty fruitful years before you. There is no position in any church, religious body, University and etc. which you could not fill. I have picked you for three outstanding positions in our race. I will be glad to risk my prophesy on that. May God bless you as you continue to grow.

Sincerely yours,
[*signed*]
William Holmes Borders

WHB:mw

TLS. MLKP-MBU: Box 14.

Statement on Ending the Bus Boycott

20 December 1956
[*Montgomery, Ala.*]

King reads a prepared statement to about 2,500 persons attending mass meetings at Holt Street and First Baptist Churches.[1] He urges "the Negro citizens of Montgomery to return to the busses tomorrow morning on a non-segregated basis." An audience question about segregated benches downtown prompted King to acknowledge that the Supreme Court ruling applied only on city buses.[2] A Birmingham News *account of the meetings reported that he admitted "it is true we got more out of this (boycott) than we went in for. We started out to get modified segregation (on buses) but we got total integration."[3] At six* A.M. *the following morning King joined E. D. Nixon, Ralph*

---

1. King later remembered that he had "carefully prepared [the statement] in the afternoon" before the meeting. It is reprinted in its entirety in *Stride Toward Freedom*, pp. 170–172. See also Excerpt, Statement on End of Bus Boycott, 20 December 1956.

2. Edward Pilley, "Acquiescence Keynote to Officials' 'Reaction,'" *Montgomery Advertiser*, 21 December 1956.

3. King, quoted in "Negro Woman Says She Was Slapped After Leaving Bus," *Birmingham News*, 21 December 1956.

Abernathy, and Glenn Smiley on one of the first integrated buses. During the initial day of desegregated bus seating there were only a few instances of verbal abuse and occasional violence. The Montgomery Advertiser *reported: "The calm but cautious acceptance of this significant change in Montgomery's way of life came without any major disturbances."*[4]

For more than twelve months now, we, the Negro citizens of Montgomery have been engaged in a non-violent protest against injustices and indignities experienced on city buses. We came to see that, in the long run, it is more honorable to walk in dignity than ride in humiliation. So in a quiet dignified manner, we decided to substitute tired feet for tired souls, and walk the streets of Montgomery until the sagging walls of injustice had been crushed by the battering rams of surging justice.

Often our movement has been referred to as a boycott movement. The word boycott, however, does not adequately describe the true spirit of our movement. The word boycott is suggestive of merely an economic squeeze devoid of any positive value. We have never allowed ourselves to get bogged in the negative; we have always sought to accentuate the positive. Our aim has never been to put the bus company out of business, but rather to put justice in business.

These twelve months have not at all been easy. Our feet have often been tired. We have struggle against tremendous odds to maintain alternative transportation. There have been moments when roaring waters of disappointment poured upon us in staggering torrents. We can remember days when unfavorable court decisions came upon us like tidal waves, leaving us treading in the deep and confused waters of despair. But amid all of this we have kept going with the faith that as we struggle, God struggles with us, and that the arc of the moral universe, although long, is bending toward justice.[5] We have lived under the agony and darkness of Good Friday with the conviction that one day the heightening glow of Easter would emerge on the horizon. We have seen truth crucified and goodness buried, but we have kept going with the conviction that truth crushed to earth will rise again.[6]

Now our faith seems to be vindicated. This morning the long awaited mandate from the United States Supreme Court concerning bus segregation came to Montgomery. This mandate expresses in terms that are crystal clear that segregation in public transportation is both legally and sociologically invalid. In the light of this mandate and the unanimous vote rendered by the Montgomery Improvement Association about a month ago, the year old protest against city busses

---

4. Bob Ingram, "Segregation Ends Quietly on Bus Line," *Montgomery Advertiser,* 22 December 1956.

5. This phrase, which became commonplace in King's oratory, may have come to his attention through John Haynes Holmes, "Salute to Montgomery," *Liberation* 1, no. 10 (December 1956): 5: "The great Theodore Parker, abolitionist preacher in the days before the Civil War, answered this doubt and fear when he challenged an impatient world, 'The arc of the moral universe is long, but it bends toward justice.'"

6. This line is from the poem *The Battlefield* (1839) by William Cullen Bryant.

is officially called off, and the Negro citizens of Montgomery are urged to return to the busses tomorrow morning on a non-segregated basis.

I cannot close without giving just a word of caution. Our experience and growth during this past year of united non-violent protest has been of such that we cannot be satisfied with a court "victory" over our white brothers. We must respond to the decision with an understanding of those who have oppressed us and with an appreciation of the new adjustments that the court order poses for them. We must be able to face up honestly to our own shortcomings. We must act in such a way as to make possible a coming together of white people and colored people on the basis of a real harmony of interests and understanding. We seek an integration based on mutual respect.

This is the time that we must evince calm dignity and wise restraint. Emotions must not run wild. Violence must not come from any of us, for if we become victimized with violent intents, we will have walked in vain, and our twelve months of glorious dignity will be transformed into an eve of gloomy catastrophy. As we go back to the busses let us be loving enough to turn an enemy into a friend. We must now move from protest to reconciliation. It is my firm conviction that God is working in Montgomery. Let all men of goodwill, both Negro and white, continue to work with Him. With this dedication we will be able to emerge from the bleak and desolate midnight of man's inhumanity to man to the bright and glittering daybreak of freedom and justice.

TD. MLKP-MBU: Box 2.

To Wyatt Tee Walker

20 December 1956
[*Montgomery, Ala.*]

On 12 December Walker invited King to preach at his church and suggested several dates. He added, "I could not close this letter without saying to you what a great inspiration and symbol you have been to me personally and many others so similarly dedicated."[1] King thanks Walker for the hospitality during his visit to Petersburg in early October and regretfully notes that he is already scheduled for the dates in question.

---

1. Wyatt Tee Walker (1929–), born in Brockton, Massachusetts, received his B.S. (1950) and B.D. (1953) from Virginia Union University and his D.Min. (1975) from Colgate-Rochester Divinity School. While minister of Virginia's Gillfield Baptist Church (1953–1960) Walker served as chairman of the local NAACP and director of the local CORE branch. He acted as SCLC's executive director from 1960 to 1964. After serving as pastor of New York City's Abyssinian Baptist Church for one year, Walker became pastor of Canaan Baptist Church of Christ in 1967. Walker also served as special assistant to New York governor Nelson Rockefeller.

The Rev. Wyatt Tee Walker, Minister
Gillfield Baptist Church
Perry Street
Petersburg, Virginia

Dear Tee:

Thanks for your very kind letter of December 12. It was a real pleasure hearing from you. Actually, I had been planning to write you for several weeks, but I could not find your address anywhere. Proctor promised to give it to me when I was in Richmond in November, but I forgot to remind him of it before leaving. So I am more than happy to have your letter before me, as well as your address.

First, I must express my deepest appreciation to you and your charming wife for making my stay in Petersburg such a comfortable. It was a real pleasure being in your palatial home and meeting your many friends. The fellowship was one that I will long remember.

After checking my schedule, I find that all of the possiblities that you mentioned fall within periods that I have made previous commitments. I am sure that this sounds strange to you, but my calendar reveals that I have accepted almost as many engagements as my schedule will allow for the whole of 1957. Please know that my non-acceptance at this point is not due to a lack of interest, but to the acceptance of already long standing engagements.

It might be possible, however, for me to take out one Sunday when I am in that vicinity and come to Petersburg. If such is at all possible, I will notify you in the very near future.

I hope things are going well with you. I was deeply impressed with your church and the great work that you are doing. You have my prayers and best wishes for continued success. ꜟ Give my regards to your lovely wife and also to your charming children. I will look forward to seeing you when I am at Union for the Week of Prayer.[2]

Very sincerely yours,
M. L. King, Jr.

MLK:mlb

TLc. MLKP-MBU: Box 17.

----

2. King was scheduled to speak at Virginia Union University in February 1957.

To Eugene Walton

20 December 1956
[*Montgomery, Ala.*]

Walton, a graduate student in public relations and communications at Boston
University, had been encouraged by Lafayette Dudley to share his fund-raising ideas

with King.[1] Concerned about "the plight of the NAACP in the South," Walton had written to King earlier in December that "there is a need for an independent fund raising organization to support it and the organizations that take over its function where it is banned." He proposed a structure for such an organization and suggested fund-raising techniques used by the Red Cross, which he had been researching.

Mr. Eugene Walton
Boston University
School of Public Relations
84 Exeter Street
Boston 16, Massachusetts

Dear Mr. Walton:

This is to acknowledge receipt of your kind letter of recent date. It was a real pleasure hearing from you, and knowing of your intense interest in the greater expansion of democracy for American Negroes.

Naturally I am quite interested in the fund raising aspect of the various movements which are fighting for the cause of freedom. This has always been a serious problem confronting most organizations of goodwill. I have always felt that this lack of gaining adequate funds is due to a lack of proper organization. So your letter came as a real encouragement to me. I would be interested to gain further insight into your proposals and also your experiences in this area. The NAACP is always in need of funds, and of course our organization here in Montgomery is in need of funds. Please feel free at any time to make suggestions.

I am very happy to know of Lafayette Duddley's growing interest in the cause of freedom. I am sure that you can be a real companion to him in such a noble venture. Please know that I am deeply interested in what you are doing and in all of your suggestions. Feel free to write me at any time.

Very sincerely yours,
M. L. King, Jr.,
President

MLK:mlb

TLc. MLKP-MBU: Box 15.

---

1. Eugene Walton (1930–) was born in Wichita Falls, Texas. He received two undergraduate degrees (1952, 1953) from the University of Washington and his M.S. (1957) from Boston University. After serving in several positions with the federal government, he became affirmative action coordinator for the Library of Congress. Walton had taught Dudley in Boston, where Dudley had met King in 1955. See King to Lafayette Dudley, 19 September 1956, pp. 374–375 in this volume; and Dudley to King, 15 December 1956.

To Daniel G. Hill

20 December 1956
[*Montgomery, Ala.*]

*On 10 December Hill, dean of Howard University's Rankin Chapel, had commended
King for his talks at the university on 6 December, when King delivered a morning
sermon, "Remember Who You Are?" followed by a dinner address, "The Three
Dimensions of a Complete Life." "It is difficult for us to estimate the tremendous
amount of inspiration and good which [accrued] to the students of Howard University
as a result of your visit," Hill commented.[1] On the evening of his Howard visit, King
also spoke at an NAACP mass meeting; over the course of the day, one newspaper
reported, more than four thousand people heard King's words.[2]*

Dean Daniel G. Hill
Howard University
Washington 1, D.C.

Dear Dean Hill:

Thanks for your very kind letter of December 10. Absence from the city has
delayed my reply.

Let me thank you again for your kind hospitality on my visit to the campus of
Howard University. I will long remember the rich fellowship we had together and
the total experience. My only regret is that an extremely busy schedule made it
necessary for me to rush in at the last moment and leave immediately after my
presentation.

After returning to Montgomery I became aware of the fact that our Institute
on Non-Violence and Social Change will be an annual event. It will take place
around the fifth of December of each year. In the light of this I find it necessary
to make some changes in the tentative commitment that I made with you in
Washington for the Annual Day of Prayer on Thursday, December 5, 1957. I am

---

1. Daniel G. Hill, Jr. (1896–1979), a native of Annapolis, Maryland, received an undergraduate
degree (1917) from the Lincoln University, a B.D. from the University of Denver, an M.A. (1932) from
the University of Oregon, an M.S.T. at Pacific School of Religion, and a Th.D. (1946) from Hill School
of Religion. Ordained in 1921, he served AME churches in Denver; Portland, Oregon; and Oakland,
California, before beginning teaching at Howard University in 1945. A year later he was appointed
dean of the chapel. He was dean of its school of religion from 1958 until retiring in 1964.

2. The NAACP address is "Facing the Challenge of a New Age" (see p. 451 in this volume). During
one of his three speeches that day King reportedly said: "There is a danger we will talk so much about
the Christian gospel we will forget that man is an animal and a product of nature. . . . I have heard
about the silver slippers and long white robes in heaven, but I am more concerned about shoes for
thousands of barefoot children and millions of people who go to bed hungry at night. I want to see
the golden streets up yonder, but I want to do something about the slums in Washington and Montgomery. I know about the new Jerusalem, but I want to know about the new Washington, the new
Montgomery and the new New York City" ("4,000 D.C. Citizens Hear Rev. M. L. King," *Baltimore Afro-
American*, 15 December 1956).

more than sorry that this conflict has arisen. I look forward with great anticipation to being able to come back to Howard University. If there is any other date
available in the Fall of 1957, I will be more than happy to consider it. Please feel
free to contact me concerning the possibility of such.

I have enjoyed very much reading "Well-Springs of Life." [3] You certainly did a
masterful job of editorship. You have my prayers and best wishes for continued
success in the noble work that you are doing.

With warm personal regards, I am

Sincerely yours,
M. L. King Jr.,
President

MLK:mlb

TLc. MLKP-MBU: Box 82.

---

3. Daniel G. Hill, ed., *Wellsprings of Life, and Other Addresses to College Youth* (Washington, D.C.: Howard University, 1956). Hill had given the book to King, suggesting that he could include King's 6 December 1956 sermon in a similar publication: Box 1.

From Bayard Rustin

23 December 1956

*Rustin sent King three short memos: a historical overview, "The Negroes' Struggle for
Freedom"; a memo on the importance and future of the Montgomery movement
(reprinted below); and a third that has not been located. In the following memo Rustin
refers to plans to form a regional "Congress of organizations" dedicated to nonviolent
mass action, an idea that he helped formulate with Ella Baker and Stanley Levison,
another New York activist.[1] As a first step toward initiating such an organization,
Rustin, writing on behalf of Levison, proposes a Southern Leadership Conference on
Transportation to bring together black leaders from around the South.[2] Rustin and
Levison also arrange to meet with Martin and Coretta during King's 29 December visit
to Baltimore to address the annual meeting of the Omega Psi Phi fraternity. Harris
and Clare Wofford also accompanied the group on its tour of Baltimore, which*

---

1. Stanley David Levison (1912–1979), born in New York City, studied at the University of Michigan,
Columbia University, and the New School for Social Research. He then earned his LL.B. (1938) and
LL.M. (1939) at St. John's University. Levison practiced law in New York City and managed a real estate
company and other investments. He was active in the American Jewish Congress and helped form In
Friendship with Ella Baker and Bayard Rustin.

2. This conference took place in Atlanta on 10–11 January 1957. At its next meeting a month later
in New Orleans the group elected King president and eventually changed its name to the Southern
Christian Leadership Conference (SCLC).

included a meeting with officers of the Christopher Reynolds Foundation to discuss a proposed visit by the Kings to Africa and India.[3]

Dear Martin:

Here are three separate but related papers which Stanley Levison and I felt you could use for the purpose we discussed by telephone.

We shall write you more fully soon on the Africa-India deal and shall send the kind of prospectus we feel would be excellent for the <u>Southern Leadership Conference on Transportation</u> that we feel should be called.

Sincerely,

P.S. I shall let you know more fully on the Conference either in Baltimore on Saturday or New York next Sunday.

Memo

A. Montgomery possessed three features which are not found in other movements or efforts:

1. It was organized; used existing institutions {as foundations} so that all social strata of the community were involved. It thus had the strength of unity which the school integration efforts have lacked, thereby leaving the fight to heroic but isolated individuals. Montgomery could plan tactics, seek advice and support, develop financial resources and encompass a whole community in a crusade dominating all other issues. The reason there were those who did not want to give up the boycott is due in part to the consciousness that this welding of a comprehensive, unified group had a quality not to be lost. The fellowship, the ideals, the joy of sacrifice for others and other varied features of the movement have given people something to belong to which had the inspiring power of the Minute Men, the Sons of Liberty, and other organized forms which were products of an earlier American era of fundamental change.

2. The actions of the people won the respect of their enemy. The achievement of unity, the intelligence in planning, the creation of a competent, complex system of transportation, the high level of moral and ethical motivation, all combined to give the closed mind of the white southerner an airing it has never before had. It is not only the Negroe's self-respect which was won—but the respect of white people, who though

---

3. The foundation eventually approved a $4,000 grant to help support the Kings' travels. They attended Ghana's independence ceremony in March 1957 and toured India during February and March 1959. See Stanley Levison, interview with James Mosby, 14 February 1970, Ralph J. Bunche Oral History Collection, Moorland-Spingarn Research Center, Howard University; Jack Clareman to A. Philip Randolph, 5 February 1957, APRC-DLC; and King to Christopher Reynolds Foundation, 7 March 1958, MLKP-MBU: Box 1.

they retain basic prejudice, have lost something in the course of this year
that begins their long struggle to genuine understanding. In short, Montgomery has contributed to the mental health and growth of the white man's
mind, and thus to the entire nation.

    3. Montgomery was unique in that it relied upon the active participa-
tion of people who had a <u>daily</u> task of action and dedication. The movement did not rely exclusively on a handful of leaders to carry through such
fundamental change.

B. The more advanced white people must be encouraged to develop more open
relations through various agencies so that a beginning toward Negro-White
relationships can be organized. Special recognition, in the form of honoring
speeches, or if possible, formal events, must be accorded such figures as Rev.
Turner of Clinton, Attorney Lee Grant, the superintendent of schools in Louisville.[4] It must be pointed out that their devotion to the principles of morality,
respect for law, the decent-minded human response to their fellow men, express the truest and finest traditions of our nation.

C. Similarly, the new southern Negro leaders must recognize that they built upon
the work of those men who for decades fought a more lonely fight . . . The
Randolphs, Wilkins, Bunches.

D. The movement must now widen to political areas. ~~Rpr~~ Representation in all
levels of political life from the exercise of the ballot to the holding of office
and participation in administrative agencies, is a next most vital step. (Here
consultation with men who led great national movements, such as Reuther,
Randolph, Potofsky, Quill, should be set up.[5] Note that all have a special social
outlook and all except Reuther represented minorities in trade union and
social life).

E. Regional groups of leaders should be brought together and encouraged to
develop forms of local organization leading to an alliance of groups capable
of creating a Congress of organizations. Such a Congress would create both
the alert leadership capable of reacting promptly and effectively to situations
and possessing ties to masses of people so that their action projects are backed
by broad participation of people who gain experience and knowledge in the
course of the struggles. We will be sending a prospectus on this ~~latter~~ later.
The final stage may be the [*strikeout illegible*] conference of leaders on transportation but its broader perspectives must be implicit in the deliberations.

F. The next stage must see the development of a strategy group of national
leaders who will be able to guide spontaneous manifestations into organized
channels. They will be able to analyze where concentration of effort will be
fruitful and while not discouraging any effort, be mobile enough to ~~through~~
throw reserves and support to areas where a breakthrough is achievable. The

---

    4. Rustin and Levison refer to Paul Turner, a Baptist minister who was severely beaten after escort-
ing black schoolchildren into a school in Clinton, Tennessee.

    5. Rustin and Levison refer to Walter P. Reuther (1907–1970), president of the United Automobile
Workers; A. Philip Randolph; Jacob Samuel Potofsky (1894–1979), president of the Amalgamated
Clothing Workers of America; and Michael Quill, international president of the Transport Workers
Union.

assessment of urban centers as areas of concentration should be studied against rural centers to determine possibilities of setting up practical goals so that the whole movement can balance successes with setbacks.

G. The fight of the Negro for integration and equality is a vital component in the fight of the common man, Negro and white, to realize higher living standards, higher education, and culture, and a deeper commitment to moral and ethical principles. It is contributing to the movement of America to achieve a nation capable of utilizing its vastly impressive industrial might for the benefit of all.

TLc. BRP-DLC: Reel 3.

"New Fields Await Negroes, King Tells Mass Meeting"

24 December 1956
Montgomery, Ala.

At 1:30 A.M. on 23 December King and his family were awakened by a shotgun blast shattering their front door, a harbinger of the violence that would plague Montgomery the following month. At Dexter's regular Sunday service that morning King "softly and without emotion" informed his congregation of the shooting, which injured no one and caused little damage. He told church members that he "would have liked to meet those who had done the shooting to tell them that surely they must know they could not solve problems that way. Without raising his voice, he added that even if he died his killers "would have 50,000 other Negroes here to 'get.'" He stated that "it may be that some of us have to die," but the struggle will continue. An observer reported that "there was no stir in the congregation, no sign that anyone was surprised."[1] At the mass meeting that evening, attended by several hundred, King outlines future integration efforts being considered by the MIA.

The head of the boycott supporting Montgomery Improvement Assn., last night outlined other fields which he said his group "is turning its efforts toward now that the city buses are integrated."[2]

Speaking at a mass meeting of Negroes, Rev. M. L. King, Jr., said the areas were:

1. "Recreation: We have none, but we must work toward being able to use all facilities with the same determination we worked on with the buses. Separate but equal always winds up with it being separate but far from equal. Oak Park, for example, would certainly be all right for us."

2. "Voting: The more Negroes we can get registered, the stronger we'll be. If a

---

1. George Barnett, "Shot Hits Home of Bus Bias Foe," *New York Times*, 24 December 1956.

2. See similar recommendations in the report of the MIA Future Planning Committee, 14 March 1957, MLKP-MBU: Box 2.

city commissioner or official doesn't please us, we can use our vote in a determining and decisive way."

3. "Internal areas. We must work within our race to raise economic, health and intellectual standings."

4. "Education. Here, we are going to lose many of our white friends that helped us during the bus boycott. Even still we must have integrated schools as the Supreme Court in 1954 ruled we can. That is when our race will gain full equality. We cannot rest in Montgomery until every public school is integrated."

The Negro minister urged that all Negroes return to riding the buses. "We must go back to the buses in big numbers. Then, perhaps, we might even be able to do something about the fares."

He said several people had complained because the fare was now 15 cents instead of the 10 cents when the Negroes first began their boycott. "Let me say, however, I would rather pay $2 to ride an integrated bus than pay one cent to ride a segregated one."

He cautioned bus riders to remain calm "in case there should be any violence. Get the facts, watch for people who look as if they might start trouble. If there are cars following the bus suspiciously, by all means, get the tag numbers.

"Without all of this, you don't have a case. Even if the police, perhaps, won't do anything there is always the FBI," he said.

PD. *Montgomery Advertiser*, 24 December 1956.

To Fred L. Shuttlesworth

[*26 December 1956*]
[*Montgomery, Ala.*]

Following the court-ordered desegregation of Montgomery buses, activists in Tallahassee, Birmingham, and other southern cities announced their intention to ride desegregated buses. On 26 December Tallahassee leader C. K. Steele, along with sixteen others, attempted to board city buses to test its segregation ordinance but called off the protest after confronting a shouting mob. The day after the Christmas night bombing of his parsonage, Fred Shuttlesworth and twenty-one others were arrested in Birmingham for violating that city's bus segregation law.[1] Following a two-hour mass meeting, Shuttlesworth decided to call off the protest, noting that "since the issue is properly one for the court we now believe that all purposes can be settled in the courts."[2] Later that

---

1. Fred Lee Shuttlesworth (1922–), born in Montgomery, earned his B.A. (1951) from Selma University and his B.S. (1953) from Alabama State College. In 1956, while pastor of Birmingham's Bethel Baptist Church, he founded and led the Alabama Christian Movement for Human Rights (ACMHR), which after the banning of the NAACP in Alabama engaged in direct-action protest against segregation. In early 1957 Shuttlesworth helped found the Southern Christian Leadership Conference (SCLC), in which the ACMHR became an important affiliate.

2. "Negroes at Tallahassee, Birmingham Halt Plans for Mass Demonstrations," *Montgomery Advertiser*, 28 December 1956.

*night at a second mass meeting Shuttlesworth read a telegram (a draft of which
appears below) from King asking the protesters to "keep riding" desegregated buses and
to "fill up the jails of Birmingham" if necessary. The four hundred participants then
voted unanimously to follow King's advice and continue the integration effort.
Although King's letterhead is from a hotel in Detroit, he notes in the text that he can't
get away from Montgomery, which suggests that the letter was written after he had
returned home from Detroit.*

Alabama Christian Movement for Human Rights,
Rev. F. L. Shuttlesworth,
President

    I had hoped to be with you in your meeting tonight, but important develop-
ments here in Montgomery made it impossible for me to get away. You are deeply
in my prayers and thoughts as you confront arrests, threats, bombings and all
types of humiliating experiences. Your wise restraint, calm dignity and unfliching
courage will be an inspiration to generations yet unborn. History records nothing
more majestic and sublime than the determined courage of a people willing to
suffer and sacrifice for the cause of freedom. The days ahead may be difficult,
but do not despair. Those of use who stand amid the bleak and desolate midnight
of man's inhumanity to man must gain consolation from the fact that there is
emerging a bright and glittering daybreak of freedom and justice. In closing I
must say to you, keep moving toward the goal of justice. Keep riding the buses on a
non-segregated basis. Keep living by the principle of non-violence. If necessary, fill
up the jails of Birmingham. ~~Remb~~ Remember. God lives! They that stand against
him stand in a tragic and an already declared minority. They that stand with him
stand in the glow of the world's bright tomorrows.

[*signed*]
M. L. King Jr.

ALS. MLKP-MBU: Box 71.

From Homer Alexander Jack

27 December 1956
Evanston, Ill.

*Reporting that five Quakers met with Indian prime minister Jawaharlal Nehru on
21 December, Jack endorses their hope that the Kings would visit India and recommends
as well a visit to the Gold Coast, which would become the independent nation of
Ghana in March 1957. The Kings traveled to Ghana for the event and two years later
toured India accompanied by James Bristol, one of the Quakers who had met with
Nehru.*

Alabama Christian Movement for Human Rights
Rev F L Shuttlesworth, President

I had hoped to be with you in your meeting
tonight, but important developments here in
Montgomery made it impossible for me to get
away. You are deeply in my prayers and thoughts
as you confront assaults, threats, bombings and
all types of humiliating experiences. Your wise
restraint, calm dignity and unflinching courage
will be an inspiration to generations yet unborn.
History records nothing more majestic and sublime
than the determined courage of a people willing
to suffer and sacrifice for the cause of freedom.
The days ahead may be difficult, but we
must stagnin. Those of us who stand out
the flat and steadfast midnight of man's

inhumanity to man must gain consolation
from the fact that there is emerging a bright
and glittering daybreak of freedom and justice.
So cling to what say to you, they never
stand the goal of justice. They obey the
laws on a non-segregated basis, they long
for the promise of non-violence of releasing
fill up the jails of Birmingham though
Remember. Oral time! They that stand
against who stand in a tragic and un
utterly declared minority. They that stand
with him stand in the glory of the
world's bright tomorrow.

M. L. King Jr.

Dr. and Mrs. Martin Luther King, Jr.
309 S. Jackson
Montgomery, Alabama

Dear Friends,

Just a word to tell you how thrilled I am at the relative ease in which the change-over was made in Montgomery. Your restraint has certainly paid off. It is good, too, to see other southern cities take up the fight.

You might be interested to know that the very morning last week when you were first riding the buses again, a Quaker group was in New York City having an interview with Prime Minister Nehru of India and telling him about your bus protest. I was not a member of the group, but I was in New York and understand that Nehru said he knew something about your movement.[1] The Quakers indicated that they hoped it would be possible for you to visit India soon. I think it would be a fine idea, but do not forget the possibility of the Gold Coast either!

Kindest regards.

Cordially,
[*signed*]
Homer A. Jack

HAJ:ej

TLS. MLKP-MBU: Box 66.

---

1. Dorothy M. Steere, one of the Quakers who talked with Nehru, had met with King during a visit to Montgomery in April. She later reported to King that Nehru "knew, of course, about the bus protest and had heard about your part in it, [but] unfortunately had not met you." When asked about a future visit by King to India, Nehru "responded with enthusiasm that he hoped this might be arranged" (Steere to King, 5 January 1957, MLKP-MBU: Box 65).

Each volume of *The Papers of Martin Luther King, Jr.* includes a Calendar of Documents that provides an extensive list of significant King-related material for the period. In addition to specifying those documents selected for publication, the calendar includes other research material relevant to the study of King's life and work. It is generated from an online database maintained at the King Project's Stanford University office.

Space limitations prevent listing all 3,500 documents from the online database; only the most important (approximately 1,300) have been selected by the editors for inclusion in the calendar. This inventory includes not only notable documents in the King collection at Boston University, but also those obtained from King's relatives and acquaintances and material gathered during an intensive search of over forty archives, such as that of the Amistad Research Center at Tulane University.

Owing to space constraints, full bibliographic citations are no longer provided in editorial annotations as they were in previous volumes: complete references for individual documents mentioned in headnotes, footnotes, and the Introduction will henceforth be found only in the calendar. The calendar includes significant King-authored material, selected correspondence and other ephemera regarding events in which King participated, and notes of meetings he attended. Relatively mundane documents such as routine office correspondence and most unsolicited letters of support are not listed in the calendar, though they remain available in the online database. The calendar also includes a sampling of the following types of documents: correspondence with friends, religious leaders, political leaders, and activists in civil rights organizations; historically significant MIA documents, such as legal and financial material; contemporary interviews; published articles with extensive King quotations; and other material documenting King's activities. The calendar also lists documents from earlier periods found too late for publication in prior volumes. Only those photographs or illustrations that appear in the volume are listed in the calendar.

Each calendar entry provides essential bibliographic information about the document. Italics and brackets indicate information determined by the editors based on evidence contained in the document; when the evidence is not conclusive, question marks are used as well. The entry adheres to the following format:

Date	Author (Affiliation). "Document Title." Date. Place of origin. (Physical description codes) Length. (Notes.) Archival location. King Papers Project identification number.
4/26/56	King, Martin Luther, Jr. (MIA). "Address at Mass Meeting at Day Street Baptist Church." [*4/26/56*]. [*Montgomery, Ala.*] (Vt) 11 min. (1 videocassette: analog.) CBSNA-CBSN. 560426–016.

Date. The date in the left margin is intended to aid the reader in looking up specific documents. Complete date information is provided in the entry. In those cases where the original document bears no date, the editors have assigned one and enclosed it in brackets. Those documents bearing range dates are arranged after precisely dated documents, unless logic dictates another order. The date of photographs is presented without brackets if the donor provided a date. The date of published or printed papers is the date of publication or public release rather than the date of composition.

Author. A standardized form of an individual's name (based on *Anglo-American Cataloging Rules*, 2d ed.) is provided in both the author and title fields. Forms of address are omitted unless necessary for identification, such as a woman who used only her husband's name. The calendar provides only one author for documents with multiple authors. For photographs, the photographer is considered the author. Since King's script is distinctive, his unsigned handwritten documents are identified as being of certain authorship. Institutional authorship is provided when appropriate.

Affiliation. Affiliation information is provided if the author wrote in his or her capacity as an official of an organization. No brackets or italics have been used in the affiliation field.

Title. In general, the title as it appears on the document is used, with minor emendations of punctuation, capitalization, and spelling for clarity. Phrases such as "Letter to," "Photo of," are used to create titles for otherwise untitled documents; in such titles, words are generally in lower-case letters and names are standardized. Published versions of earlier speeches contain the date of delivery in the title.

Place of Origin. This field identifies where the document was completed or, in the case of a published document, the place of publication. If the document does not contain the place of origin but the information can be obtained, it is provided in brackets; such information is offered only for documents written by King or those written on his behalf.

Physical Description Codes. This field describes the format of presentation, type of document, version of document, and character of the signature (see List of Abbreviations). Documents that consist of several formats are listed with the predominant one first.

Length. The number of pages or the duration of a recording is indicated.

Notes. In this optional field, miscellaneous information pertaining to the document is provided. This information includes enclosures to a letter; routing information (e.g., "Copy to King"), since King often received copies of correspondence addressed to others; and remarks concerning the legibility of the document or the authorship of marginalia. For tapes, information about the media used is also indicated in this field.

Archival Location. The location of the original document is identified using standard abbreviations based on the Library of Congress's codes for libraries and archives (see List of Abbreviations). When available, box numbers or other archival location identification are provided.

Identification Number. This nine-digit identification number, based on the date, uniquely identifies the document.

Documents that are published in the volume are set in boldface type. Entries for published documents contain bibliographic citations that adhere to the *Chi-*

5/21/54	Robinson, Jo Ann Gibson (Women's Political Council). "Letter to W. (William) A. Gayle." 5/21/54. Montgomery, Ala. (TLcS) 1 p. MCDA-AMC. 540521–000.
3/2/55	City of Montgomery Police Department. "Arrest report for Claudette Colvin." 3/2/55. (THFmS) 3 pp. (Amended 5/10/56.) DJG. 550302–001.
6/13/55	Gilbert, Ralph Mark (First African Baptist Church). "Letter to Martin Luther King, Jr." 6/13/55. Savannah, Ga. (TLS) 1 p. DABCC. 550613–000.
6/22/55	King, Martin Luther, Jr. (Dexter Avenue Baptist Church). "Letter to Ralph Mark Gilbert." 6/22/55. [*Montgomery, Ala.*] (TLc) 1 p. DABCC. 550622–001.
7/14/55	King, Martin Luther, Jr. (Dexter Avenue Baptist Church). "Letter to Mordecai Johnson." 7/14/55. [*Montgomery, Ala.*] (TLc) 2 pp. DABCC. 550714–001.
7/19/55	King, Martin Luther, Jr. (Dexter Avenue Baptist Church). "Letter to J. Pius Barbour." 7/19/55. [*Montgomery, Ala.*] (TLc) 2 pp. DABCC. 550719–000.
8/2/55	King, Martin Luther, Jr. "Letter to Major J. Jones." 8/2/55. [*Montgomery, Ala.*] (TLc) 1 p. DABCC. 550802–000.
8/8/55	Parks, Rosa. "Notes from Highlander Workshop." 8/8/55. Monteagle, Tenn. (AD) 13 pp. RPC-MiDW. 550808–001.
8/8/55	King, Martin Luther, Jr. (Dexter Avenue Baptist Church). "Letter to J. Pius Barbour." 8/8/55. [*Montgomery, Ala.*] (TLc) 1 p. DABCC. 550808–003.
8/10/55	King, Martin Luther, Jr. (Dexter Avenue Baptist Church). "Letter to Kelly Miller Smith." 8/10/55. [*Montgomery, Ala.*] (TLc) 1 p. DABCC. 550810–001.
8/15/55	King, Martin Luther, Jr. "Letter to Major J. Jones." 8/15/55. [*Montgomery, Ala.*] (TLc) 1 p. DABCC. 550815–000.
9/26/55	King, Martin Luther, Jr. (Dexter Avenue Baptist Church). "Letter to Gardner C. Taylor." 9/26/55. [*Montgomery, Ala.*] (TLc) 1 p. DABCC. 550926–000.
9/26/55	King, Martin Luther, Jr. (Dexter Avenue Baptist Church). "Letter to J. H. (Joseph Harrison) Jackson." 9/26/55. [*Montgomery, Ala.*] (TLc) 1 p. DABCC. 550926–001.
9/30/55	King, Martin Luther, Jr. (Dexter Avenue Baptist Church). "Letter to John Thomas Porter." 9/30/55. [*Montgomery, Ala.*] (TLc) 1 p. DABCC. 550930–000.
10/2/55	King, John W. "Letter to Martin Luther King, Jr." 10/2/55. Montgomery, Ala. (ALS) 1 p. DABCC. 551002–000.
10/3/55	Taylor, Gardner C. (Concord Baptist Church). "Letter to Martin Luther King, Jr." 10/3/55. Brooklyn, N.Y. (TLS) 1 p. DABCC. 551003–000.
10/5/55	King, Martin Luther, Jr. "Letter to John W. King." 10/5/55. [*Montgomery, Ala.*] (TLc) 1 p. DABCC. 551005–000.
10/20/55	Henderson, J. Raymond (Second Baptist Church and the Henderson Community Center). "Letter to Martin Luther King, Jr." 10/20/55. Los Angeles, Calif. (TLS) 1 p. DABCC. 551020–000.
10/24/55	Handy, W. T. (William Talbot), Jr. (Newman Methodist Church). "Letter to Martin Luther King, Jr." 10/24/55. Alexandria, La. (TLS) 1 p. DABCC. 551024–000.
10/24/55	Jones, Major J. (Fisk University). "Letter to Martin Luther King, Jr." 10/24/55. Nashville, Tenn. (TALS) 1 p. DABCC. 551024–001.
10/26/55	King, Martin Luther, Jr. "Letter to J. Raymond Henderson." 10/26/55. [*Montgomery, Ala.*] (TLc) 1 p. DABCC. 551026–001.
10/28/55	McCall, Walter R. (Fort Valley State College). "Letter to Martin Luther King, Jr." 10/28/55. Fort Valley, Ga. (ALS) 1 p. DABCC. 551028–000.
12/55	Dexter Avenue Baptist Church. "Social and Political Action Committee Digest." 12/55. Montgomery, Ala. (TD) 2 pp. MLKP-MBU: Box 77. 551200–009.
12/55	Alabama Council on Human Relations. "Montgomery Bus Boycott at a Glance." 12/55. Montgomery, Ala. (PD) 4 pp. ACHRP-GAU. 551200–011.
12/1/55	City of Montgomery Police Department. "Arrest report for Rosa Parks." 12/1/55. Montgomery, Ala. (THFmS) 3 pp. GEpFAR. 551201–000.
12/1/55	City of Montgomery Police Department. "Warrant for Rosa Parks." 12/1/55. Montgomery, Ala. (THFmS) 1 p. CMCR-AMC: File 4559. 551201–001.
12/2/55	[*Robinson, Jo Ann Gibson*] (Women's Political Council). "Leaflet, Another Negro woman has been arrested." [*12/2/55*]. (THD) 1 p. MCDA-AMC. 551202–001.
12/2/55	**[*Abernathy, Ralph, Martin Luther King, Jr., and Jo Ann Gibson Robinson*]. "Leaflet, Don't ride the bus." [*12/2/55*]. [*Montgomery, Ala.*](TD) 1 p. (551205–017 on verso.) MLKP-MBU: Box 6. 551202–000.**

12/4/55	Dexter Avenue Baptist Church. "Program, Sunday services." 12/4/55. Montgomery, Ala. (TD) 4 pp. DABCC. 551204–000.
12/5/55	**[Fields, U. (Uriah) J.] (Montgomery Improvement Association [MIA]). "Minutes, Founding meeting." 12/5/55. Montgomery, Ala. (TD) 2 pp. AAGR-A-Ar: SG 8423. 551205–002.**
12/5/55	**MIA. "Mass meeting at Holt Street Baptist Church." [12/5/55]. Montgomery, Ala. (At) 45 min. (1 sound cassette: analog.) MLKJrP-GAMK: Box 107. 551205–004.**
12/5/55	**"Photo of mass meeting at Holt Street Baptist Church." 12/5/55. Montgomery, Ala. From: Montgomery Advertiser, 6 December 1955. (PPh) 1 p. 551205–015.**
12/5/55	**Associated Press. "Photo of Rosa Parks, E. D. Nixon, Fred D. Gray." 12/5/55. Montgomery, Ala. (Ph) 1 p. APWW. 551205–020.**
12/5/55	City of Montgomery Police Department. "Arrest report for Fred Daniels." 12/5/55. Montgomery, Ala. (THFmS) 1 p. DJG. 551205–001.
12/5/55	Parks, Rosa, Defendant. "Judgment, City of Montgomery v. Rosa Parks." 12/5/55. Montgomery, Ala. (THFmS) 2 pp. CMCR-AMC: File 4559. 551205–006.
12/5/55	Parks, Rosa, Defendant. "Transcript, City of Montgomery v. Rosa Parks." 12/5/55. Montgomery, Ala. (THFmS) 3 pp. CMCR-AMC: File 4559. 551205–007.
12/5/55	King, Martin Luther, Jr. (MIA). "Notes, Agenda for mass meeting at Holt Street Baptist Church." [12/5/55]. [Montgomery, Ala.] (AD) 1 p. (551202–000 on recto.) MLKP-MBU: Box 6. 551205–017.
12/5/55	MIA. "Program, Mass meeting at Holt Street Baptist Church." Montgomery, Ala. 12/5/55. (TD) 1 p. AAGR-A-Ar: SG 8423. 551205–019.
12/6/55	Patton, W. C. (NAACP). "Memo to Roy Wilkins." 12/6/55. (THL) 1 p. NAACPP-DLC: Group III–A508. 551206–000.
12/7/55	Azbell, Joe. "At Holt Street Baptist Church: Deeply Stirred Throng of Colored Citizens Protests Bus Segregation." 12/7/55. Montgomery, Ala. From: Montgomery Advertiser, 7 December 1955. (PD) 1 p. 551207–000.
12/7/55	Durr, Virginia Foster. "Letter to Clark Foreman." 12/7/55. Montgomery, Ala. (TL) 2 pp. VFDP-MCR-S: Box 2. 551207–004.
12/7/55	Graetz, Robert (Trinity Lutheran Church). "Form letter to Christian Brothers." 12/7/55. Montgomery, Ala. (THLS) 1 p. RGP. 551207–006.
12/7/55	"Negro Minister Denies Effort to End Segregation On Buses." 12/7/55. Montgomery, Ala. From: Alabama Journal, 7 December 1955. (PD) 1 p. 551207–007.
12/7/55	Hallford. (U.S. Federal Bureau of Investigation). "Telegram to J. Edgar Hoover." 12/7/55. Mobile, Ala. (THWc) 1 p. MIAFBI-DJ. 551207–008.
12/8/55	**King, Martin Luther, Jr. (MIA). "Memo to the National City Lines, Inc." [12/8/55]. [Montgomery, Ala.] (TLc) 1 p. MLKP-MBU: Box 6. 551208–001.**
12/8/55	King, Martin Luther, Jr. (MIA). "Notes, Agenda for mass meeting at St. John AME Church." [12/8/55]. Montgomery, Ala. (AD) 1 p. MLKP-MBU: Box 6. 551208–003.
12/8/55	"Minutes, Meeting between contact committee of MIA and city and bus officials." 12/8/55. (TD) 1 p. AAGR-A-Ar: SG 8423. 551208–004.
12/8/55	MIA. "Resolution with proposals." [12/8/55]. (THD) 4 pp. (Marginal comments by King.) MLKP-MBU: Box 6. 551208–006.
12/9/55	Montgomery City Lines. "Notice to Bus Patrons." [12/9/55]. Montgomery, Ala. (PD) 1 p. JRC. 551209–001.
12/10/55	**King, Martin Luther, Jr. (MIA). "Statement of Negro Citizens on Bus Situation." [12/10/55]. [Montgomery, Ala.] (TD) 2 pp. RGP; copy of draft in MLKP-MBU: Box 30. 551210–001.**
12/12/55	**Whitaker, H. (Horace) Edward (New Hope Baptist Church). "Letter to Martin Luther King, Jr." 12/12/55. Niagara Falls, N.Y. (TAHLS) 1 p. (Marginal comments on verso by King.) DABCC. 551212–002.**
12/12/55	Morgan, Juliette. "Lesson From Gandhi." 12/12/55. Montgomery, Ala. From: Montgomery Advertiser, 12 December 1955. (PL) 2 pp. MLKP-MBU: Box 6. 551212–000.
12/12/55	MIA. "Program, Mass meeting at Bethel Baptist Church." 12/12/55. Montgomery, Ala. (TD) 1 p. AAGR-A-Ar: SG 8423. 551212–001.
12/13/55	[Parks, Rosa] (NAACP). "Minutes, Montgomery branch executive committee special meeting." 12/13/55. (AD) 2 pp. MNAACP-NN-Sc. 551213–003.
12/14/55	Garrison, James (Cab Company of the City of Montgomery). "Resolution on cab fares." [12/14/55?]. (TDS) 1 p. MLKP-MBU: Box 6. 551214–001.
12/15/55	King, Martin Luther, Jr. (MIA). "List of names to see mayor." [12/15/55]. [Montgomery, Ala.] (AD) 1 p. MLKP-MBU: Box 6. 551215–002.

12/15/55   Wynn, Daniel W. (Tuskegee Institute). "Letter to Martin Luther King, Jr." 12/15/55. Tuskegee, Ala. (TLS) 1 p. DABCC. 551215–003.

12/15/55   **MIA. "Program, Mass meeting at First Baptist Church." 12/15/55. Montgomery, Ala. (THD) 1 p. (Marginal comments by King.) MLKP-MBU: Box 6. 551215–000.**

12/15/55   **King, Martin Luther, Jr. "Letter to M. C. (Milton Cornelius) Ballenger." 12/15/55. [*Montgomery, Ala.*] (TLc) 1 p. DABCC. 551215–001.**

12/19/55   Patton, W. C. (NAACP). "Memo to Roy Wilkins and Gloster B. Current." 12/19/55. (TL) 2 pp. NAACPP-DLC. 551219–001.

12/19/55   MIA. "Program, Mass meeting at Hutchinson Street Baptist Church." 12/19/55. Montgomery, Ala. (TD) 1 p. MLKP-MBU: Box 6. 551219–002.

12/21/55   **King, Martin Luther, Jr. (Dexter Avenue Baptist Church). "Letter to Ralph W. Riley." 12/21/55. [*Montgomery, Ala.*] (TLc) 1 p. DABCC. 551221–000.**

12/21/55   **Carrington, Walter C. "Letter to Martin Luther King, Jr." 12/21/55. (ALS) 1 p. DABCC. 551221–004.**

12/21/55   King, Martin Luther, Jr. "Letter to Lucille B. Knapp." 12/21/55. [*Montgomery, Ala.*] (TLc) 1 p. DABCC. 551221–001.

12/21/55   Thomas, Jesse O. (Frontiers of America). "Letter to Martin Luther King, Jr." 12/21/55. Atlanta, Ga. (TLS) 1 p. DABCC. 551221–005.

12/21/55   Clark, Caesar (Good Street Baptist Church). "Letter to Martin Luther King, Jr." 12/21/55. Dallas, Tex. (TLSr) 1 p. DABCC. 551221–006.

12/22/55   Graetz, Robert. "Letter to Editor, *Time.*" 12/22/55. Montgomery, Ala. (THLc) 2 pp. (Copy to King.) MLKP-MBU: Box 107. 551222–000.

12/22/55   Riley, Ralph W. (American Baptist Theological Seminary). "Letter to Martin Luther King, Jr." 12/22/55. Nashville, Tenn. (TLS) 1 p. DABCC. 551222–010.

12/25/55   **Negro Ministers of Montgomery and Their Congregations. "To the Montgomery Public." 12/25/55. Montgomery, Ala. From: *Montgomery Advertiser–Alabama Journal*, 25 December 1955. (PD) 1 p. 551225–002.**

12/25/55   Dexter Avenue Baptist Church. "Program, Sunday services." 12/25/55. Montgomery, Ala. (TD) 4 pp. DABCC. 551225–003.

12/27/55   **King, Martin Luther, Jr. (MIA). "Letter to Archibald James Carey, Jr." 12/27/55. Montgomery, Ala. (TLSr) 1 p. (Contains enclosures 551227–002, -003.) AJC-ICHi: Box 29. 551227–001.**

12/27/55   **King, Martin Luther, Jr. (MIA). "Form letter to Supporter." 12/27/55. Montgomery, Ala. (TLSr) 1 p. (Enclosure in 551227–001.) AJC-ICHi: Box 29. 551227–002.**

12/27/55   "Legal Requirements Concerning the Segregation of Races on City Buses." [*12/27/55*]. (TD) 5 pp. (Enclosure in 551227–001.) AJC-ICHi: Box 30. 551227–003.

12/27/55   Wilkins, Roy (NAACP). "Letter to W. C. Patton." 12/27/55. (TLc) 1 p. NAACPP-DLC: Group III–A508. 551227–000.

12/28/55   King, Martin Luther, Jr. (Dexter Avenue Baptist Church). "Letter to H. (Horace) Edward Whitaker." 12/28/55. [*Montgomery, Ala.*] (TLc) 1 p. DABCC. 551228–001.

12/28/55   King, Martin Luther, Jr. (Dexter Avenue Baptist Church). "Letter to Caesar Clark." 12/28/55. [*Montgomery, Ala.*] (TLc) 1 p. DABCC. 551228–002.

12/29/55   King, Martin Luther, Jr. (MIA). "Advertisement, Day of Prayer." 12/29/55. Montgomery, Ala. (PD) 1 p. From: *Montgomery Advertiser*, 29 December 1956. 561229–001.

1956   **Dinnerstein, Harvey. "Drawing of African-American protesters marching." 1956. Montgomery, Ala. (AAwS) 1 p. HDBSD. 560000–113.**

1956   **Dinnerstein, Harvey. "Drawing of Rosa Parks." 1956. Montgomery, Ala. (AAwS) 1 p. HDBSD. 560000–115.**

1956   **Silverman, Burt. "Drawing of Martin Luther King, Jr." 1956. Montgomery, Ala. (AHAwS) 1 p. HDBSD. 560000–116.**

1956   **Silverman, Burt. "Drawing of protesters." 1956. Montgomery, Ala. (AAwS) 1 p. HDBSD. 560000–117.**

1956   Silverman, Burt. "Drawing of two protesters." 1956. Montgomery, Ala. (AAwS) 1 p. HDBSD. 560000–118.

1956   **Silverman, Burt. "Drawing of protester." 1956. Montgomery, Ala. (AAwS) 1 p. HDBSD. 560000–121.**

1956   **Silverman, Burt. "Drawing of Martin Luther King, Jr., and attorney at Montgomery bus boycott trial." 1956. Montgomery, Ala. (AHAwS) 1 p. HDBSD. 560000–122.**

1956   **Silverman, Burt. "Drawing of E. D. Nixon." 1956. Montgomery, Ala. (AAwS) 1 p. HDBSD. 560000–123.**

1956   **Silverman, Burt. "Drawing of Jo Ann Gibson Robinson." 1956. Montgomery, Ala. (AHAwS) 1 p. HDBSD. 560000–124.**

1956   **Dinnerstein, Harvey. "Drawing of protester." 1956. Montgomery, Ala. (AHAwS) 1 p. HDBSD. 560000–127.**

1956   King, Martin Luther, Jr. (MIA). "Membership list of committee on registration and voting." [*1956*]. [*Montgomery, Ala.*] (AD) 1 p. (560000–083 on verso.) MLKP-MBU: Box 6. 560000–060.

1956   King, Martin Luther, Jr. (MIA). "Membership list of committee on establishing bank and savings association." [*1956*]. [*Montgomery, Ala.*] (AD) 1 p. (560000–060 on recto.) MLKP-MBU: Box 6. 560000–083.

1956   King, Martin Luther, Jr. (MIA). "Membership list of committee on writing of the constitution." [*1956*]. [*Montgomery, Ala.*] (AD) 1 p. (Water damaged.) MLKP-MBU: Box 6. 560000–061.

1956   Pierce, James E. (Alabama State Coordinating Association for Registration and Voting). "Registration of Negro Voters in Alabama in 1954." [*1956*]. Birmingham, Ala. (TD) 18 pp. MLKP-MBU: Box 93. 560000–135.

1956   Merriam, Eve. "Montgomery, Alabama, Money, Mississippi, and other places." 1956. New York, N.Y. (PD) 37 pp. (Enclosure in 560330–011.) MLKP-MBU: Box 30. 560000–137.

1956   Shore, Herb (Fellowship of Reconciliation). "Walk to Freedom." 1956. Nyack, N.Y. (Vt) 15 min. (1 videocassette: analog.) Distributed by Fellowship of Reconciliation. 560000–138.

1/1/56   Dexter Avenue Baptist Church. "Program, Sunday services." [1/1/56]. Montgomery, Ala. (TD) 1 p. DABCC. 560101–001.

1/2/56   MIA. "Notes, Mass meeting at Holt Street Baptist Church." 1/2/56. Montgomery, Ala. (TD) 1 p. AAGR-A-Ar: SG 8423. 560102–000.

1/3/56   **Williams, Aubrey Willis (*Southern Farmer*). "Letter to Martin Luther King, Jr." 1/3/56. Montgomery, Ala. (ALS) 1 p. MLKP-MBU: Box 107. 560103–001.**

1/3/56   Mays, Benjamin Elijah (Morehouse College). "Letter to Martin Luther King, Jr." 1/3/56. Atlanta, Ga. (TALS) 1 p. MLKP-MBU: Box 119. 560103–000.

1/4/56   **Special agent in charge, Mobile (U.S. Federal Bureau of Investigation). "Memo to J. Edgar Hoover." 1/4/56. Mobile, Ala. (THL) 1 p. MIAFBI-DJ. 560104–001.**

1/5/56   MIA. "Program, Mass meeting at St. John AME Church." 1/5/56. Montgomery, Ala. (THD) 1 p. (Marginal comments by King.) MLKP-MBU: Box 6. 560105–000.

1/5/56   MIA. "Finance committee report for 12/5/55–1/2/56." 1/5/56. (TD) 2 pp. MLKP-MBU: Box 6. 560105–001.

1/8/56   Dexter Avenue Baptist Church. "Program, Sunday services." 1/8/56. Montgomery, Ala. (TD) 4 pp. MLKP-MBU: Box 76. 560108–000.

1/9/56   **Negro Ministers of Montgomery and Their Congregations. "Memo to the Commissioners of the City of Montgomery." [*1/9/56*]. [*Montgomery, Ala.*] (TD) 2 pp. MLKP-MBU: Box 6. 560109–004.**

1/9/56   MIA. "Notes, Mass meeting at Bethel Baptist Church." 1/9/56. Montgomery, Ala. (TD) 1 p. AAGR-A-Ar: SG 8423. 560109–003.

1/10/56   Drake, Fred (Tuscaloosa City Teacher's Association). "Letter to Martin Luther King, Jr." 1/10/56. Tuscaloosa, Ala. (TLS) 1 p. DABCC. 560110–007.

1/11/56   **Dickerson, Earl B. (Supreme Liberty Life Insurance Company). "Letter to Martin Luther King, Jr." 1/11/56. Chicago, Ill. (TLS) 1 p. MLKP-MBU: Box 107. 560111–000.**

1/12/56   Thomas, Norman. "Memo to Roy Wilkins." 1/12/56. (TLS) 2 pp. NAACPP-DLC. 560112–002.

1/15/56   Dexter Avenue Baptist Church. "Program, Sunday services." 1/15/56. Montgomery, Ala. (TD) 4 pp. MLKP-MBU: Box 76. 560115–000.

1/16/56   King, Martin Luther, Jr. "Letter to Fred Drake." 1/16/56. [*Montgomery, Ala.*] (TLc) 1 p. DABCC. 560116–000.

1/16/56   Durham, Barbee William (NAACP). "Letter to Martin Luther King, Jr." 1/16/56. Columbus, Ohio. (TLS) 1 p. MLKP-MBU: Box 106. 560116–001.

1/18/56   **Whitaker, H. (Horace) Edward (New Hope Baptist Church). "Letter to Martin Luther King, Jr." 1/18/56. Niagara Falls, N.Y. (THLS) 1 p. (Marginal comments on verso by King.) DABCC. 560118–005.**

504   1/18/56   Hughes, Robert E. "Interview by Anna Holden." 1/18/56. Montgomery, Ala. (TD) 9 pp. PV-ARC-LNT. 560118–004.

1/19/56 Johnson, Tom. "Rev. King Is Boycott Boss." 1/19/56. Montgomery, Ala. From: *Montgomery Advertiser*, 19 January 1956. (PD) 1 p. 560119–000.

1/19/56 Lee, Willie Mae. "Notes, MIA mass meeting at King Hill Baptist Church." 1/19/56. Montgomery, Ala. (TD) 1 p. PV-ARC-LNT. 560119–004.

1/20/56 Lewis, Rufus A. (MIA). "Interview by Donald T. Ferron." 1/20/56. Montgomery, Ala. (TD) 8 pp. PV-ARC-LNT. 560120–001.

1/20/56 Charles, Beatrice. "Interview by Willie Mae Lee." 1/20/56. Montgomery, Ala. (TAD) 5 pp. PV-ARC-LNT. 560120–002.

1/21/56 Ferron, Donald T. "Letter to Preston Valien." 1/21/56. Montgomery, Ala. (ALS) 2 pp. PV-ARC-LNT. 560121–002.

1/21/56 [MIA]. "Minutes of strategy committee meeting." [*1/21/56*]. (AHD) 4 pp. MLKP-MBU: Box 6. 560121–005.

1/22/56 King, Martin Luther, Jr. (MIA). "Press release, the bus protest is still on." [*1/22/56*]. [*Montgomery, Ala.*] (ALdS) 2 pp. MLKP-MBU: Box 6. 560122–001.

1/22/56 Dexter Avenue Baptist Church. "Program, Sunday services." 1/22/56. Montgomery, Ala. (TD) 4 pp. MLKP-MBU: Box 76. 560122–000.

1/23/56 King, Martin Luther, Jr. (MIA). "Agenda for board meeting." 1/23/56. [*Montgomery, Ala.*] (AD) 2 pp. MLKP-MBU: Box 6. 560123–002.

1/23/56 Ferron, Donald T. "Notes, MIA executive board meeting." 1/23/56. Montgomery, Ala. (TD) 4 pp. PV-ARC-LNT. 560123–005.

1/23/56 Durr, Virginia Foster. "Letter to Curtiss McDougall." 1/23/56. Montgomery, Ala. (TLS) 1 p. VFDP-MCR-S. 560123–003.

1/23/56 West, A. W. "Interview by Willie Mae Lee." 1/23/56. Montgomery, Ala. (TD) 3 pp. PV-ARC-LNT. 560123–006.

1/24/56 Wright, Allean. "Interview by Willie Mae Lee." 1/24/56. Montgomery, Ala. (TD) 2 pp. PV-ARC-LNT. 560124–001.

1/25/56 King, Martin Luther, Sr. "Letter to Hampton Z. Barker." 1/25/56. (TLc) 1 p. EBCR. 560125–000.

1/25/56 King, Martin Luther, Sr. "Letter to Sandy F. Ray." 1/25/56. (TLc) 1 p. EBCR. 560125–001.

1/25/56 Bynoe, John G. (Alpha Phi Alpha Fraternity). "Letter to Martin Luther King, Jr." 1/25/56. Boston, Mass. (TLS) 1 p. DABCC. 560125–005.

1/26/56 King, Martin Luther, Sr. "Letter to Martin Luther King, Jr." 1/26/56. (TLc) 1 p. EBCR. 560126–000.

1/26/56 King, Martin Luther, Jr., Defendant. "Complaint, *City of Montgomery v. Martin L. King*." 1/26/56. Montgomery, Ala. (TFmS) 2 pp. CMCR-AMC: File 4604. 560126–001.

1/27/56 Negro Ministers of Montgomery and Their Congregations. "To the Citizens of Montgomery." 1/27/56. Montgomery, Ala. From: *Montgomery Advertiser*, 27 January 1956. (PD) 1 p. 560127–005.

1/27/56 Glasco, R. J. (MIA). "Interview by Donald T. Ferron." 1/19/56, 1/27/56. Montgomery, Ala. (TD) 4 pp. PV-ARC-LNT. 560127–000.

1/27/56 Wilson, A. W. "Interview by Donald T. Ferron." 1/27/56. Montgomery, Ala. (TD) 2 pp. PV-ARC-LNT. 560127–001.

1/28/56 King, Martin Luther, Jr. (MIA). "Letter to Roy Wilkins." 1/28/56. Montgomery, Ala. (THLS) 1 p. RWP-DLC. 560128–000.

1/28/56 King, Martin Luther, Jr., Defendant. "Appeal Bond, *City of Montgomery v. Martin L. King*." 1/28/56. Montgomery, Ala. (THFmS) 2 pp. CMCR-AMC. 560128–002.

1/28/56 King, Martin Luther, Jr., Defendant. "Transcript, *City of Montgomery v. Martin L. King*." 1/28/56. Montgomery, Ala. (AFmS) 2 pp. CMCR-AMC: File 4604. 560128–003.

1/28/56 Fields, U. (Uriah) J. "Interview by Donald T. Ferron." 1/28/56. Montgomery, Ala. (TD) 2 pp. PV-ARC-LNT. 560128–005.

1/29/56 Graetz, Robert. "Interview by Donald T. Ferron." 1/29/56. Montgomery, Ala. (TD) 2 pp. PV-ARC-LNT. 560129–001.

1/29/56 Dexter Avenue Baptist Church. "Program, Sunday services." 1/29/56. Montgomery, Ala. (TD) 4 pp. DABCC. 560129–002.

1/30/56 Ferron, Donald T. "Notes, MIA executive board meeting." 1/30/56. (AD) 4 pp. PV-ARC-LNT. 560130–010.

1/30/56 King, Martin Luther, Jr. (Dexter Avenue Baptist Church). "Letter to H. (Horace) Edward Whitaker." 1/30/56. [*Montgomery, Ala.*] (TLc) 1 p. DABCC. 560130–000.

1/30/56 Lee, Willie Mae. "Notes, MIA mass meeting at First Baptist Church." 1/30/56. Montgomery, Ala. (TD) 3 pp. PV-ARC-LNT. 560130–011.

1/30/56	**United Press International. "Photo of Martin Luther King, Jr., R. L. Lampley, William. A. Gayle, and Clyde C. Sellers." 1/30/56. Montgomery, Ala. (Ph) 1 p. APWW. 560130–012.**
1/30/56	Durr, Virginia Foster. "Letter to Myles and Zilphia Horton." 1/30/56. Montgomery, Ala. (TLI) 1 p. HRECR-WHi: Box 11. 560130–001.
1/30/56	King, Martin Luther, Jr., Defendant. "Warrant, *City of Montgomery v. Martin L. King.*" 1/30/56. Montgomery, Ala. (THFmS) 2 pp. CMCR-AMC: File 4604. 560130–002.
1/30/56	Williams, Willard A. "Letter to Martin Luther King, Jr." 1/30/56. Newburg, Md. (ALS) 3 pp. MLKP-MBU: Box 67. 560130–003.
1/31/56	**Azbell, Joe. "Blast Rocks Residence of Bus Boycott Leader." 1/31/56. Montgomery, Ala. From: *Montgomery Advertiser*, 31 January 1956. (PD) 1 p. 560131–010.**
1/31/56	**Franklin, Pinkie S. "Letter to Martin Luther King, Jr." 1/31/56. Birmingham, Ala. (ALS) 1 p. MLKP-MBU: Box 17. 560131–002.**
1/31/56	**Barbour, J. Pius (Calvary Baptist Church). "Telegram to Martin Luther King, Jr." 1/31/56. Chester, Pa. (PWSr) 1 p. MLKP-MBU: Box 14. 560131–001.**
1/31/56	Lee, Willie Mae. "Bombing Episode." 1/31/56. Montgomery, Ala. (TD) 2 pp. PV-ARC-LNT. 560131–005.
1/31/56	Ferron, Donald T. "Notes, Joint MIA and NAACP meeting." 1/31/56. Montgomery, Ala. (TD) 1 p. PV-ARC-LNT. 560131–007.
2/56	King, Martin Luther, Jr. (MIA). "Agenda, Executive board meeting." [*1/56–2/56*]. [*Montgomery, Ala.*] (AD) 1 p. MLKP-MBU: Box 6. 560200–009.
2/56	King, Martin Luther, Jr. (MIA). "Financial recommendations." [*1/56–2/56*]. [*Montgomery, Ala.*] (AD) 1 p. MLKP-MBU: Box 6. 560200–010.
2/56	King, Martin Luther, Jr. (MIA). "Agenda, Executive board meeting." [*1/56–2/56*]. [*Montgomery, Ala.*] (TD) 1 p. MLKP-MBU: Box 6. 560200–011.
2/56	MIA. "Executive board list." [*2/56*]. (TD) 1 p. DJG. 560200–012.
2/1/56	**Jones, Major J. (Fisk University). "Letter to Martin Luther King, Jr." 2/1/56. Nashville, Tenn. (TALS) 1 p. MLKP-MBU: Box 119. 560201–000.**
2/1/56	**McCall, Walter R. (Fort Valley State College). "Letter to Martin Luther King, Jr." 2/1/56. Fort Valley, Ga. (TAHL) 1 p. DABCC. 560201–009.**
2/2/56	**Stanley, Frank L. (Alpha Phi Alpha Fraternity). "Letter to Martin Luther King, Jr." 2/2/56. Louisville, Ky. (THLS) 1 p. MLKP-MBU: Box 67. 560202–006.**
2/2/56	**Ferron, Donald T. "Notes, MIA executive board meeting." 2/2/56. Montgomery, Ala. (TD) 4 pp. PV-ARC-LNT. 560202–009.**
2/2/56	King, Martin Luther, Jr. "Letter to John G. Bynoe." 2/2/56. [*Montgomery, Ala.*] (TLc) 1 p. DABCC. 560202–000.
2/2/56	King, Martin Luther, Jr. "Letter to Owen D. Pelt." 2/2/56. [*Montgomery, Ala.*] (TLc) 1 p. DABCC. 560202–001.
2/2/56	Current, Gloster B. (NAACP). "Memo to Roy Wilkins." 2/2/56. (TL) 1 p. NAACPP-DLC: Group III–A273. 560202–002.
2/2/56	Griffin, Joseph L. (Macedonia Baptist Church). "Letter to Martin Luther King, Jr." 2/2/56. Denver, Colo. (TLS) 1 p. MLKP-MBU: Box 67. 560202–007.
2/2/56	Ferron, Donald T. "Notes, Joint MIA and NAACP meeting." 2/2/56. Montgomery, Ala. (AD) 2 pp. PV-ARC-LNT. 560202–011.
2/2/56	Durr, Clifford J. (Judkins). "Interview by Anna Holden." 2/2/56. Montgomery, Ala. (TD) 3 pp. PV-ARC-LNT. 560202–012.
2/2/56	Randolph, A. (Asa) Philip (Brotherhood of Sleeping Car Porters and Maids). "Telegram to James Elisha Folsom." 2/2/56. New York, N.Y. (PWSr) 2 pp. JEFAF-A-Ar. 560202–013.
2/3/56	Abernathy, Ralph. "Interview by Donald T. Ferron." 2/3/56. Montgomery, Ala. (TD) 3 pp. PV-ARC-LNT. 560203–001.
2/4/56	**King, Martin Luther, Jr. "Interview by Donald T. Ferron." 2/4/56. Montgomery, Ala. (TD) 3 pp. PV-ARC-LNT. 560204–003.**
2/4/56	**Grayson, Julian O. "Telegram to Martin Luther King, Jr." 2/4/56. Washington, D.C. (PWSr) 1 p. MLKP-MBU: Box 91. 560204–000.**
2/4/56	Burroughs, Nannie H. (National Baptist Convention, U.S.A., Inc., Woman's Auxiliary). "Letter to Alberta Williams King." 2/4/56. (TLc) 1 p. NHBP-DLC: Box 39. 560204–001.
2/5/56	**Britton, Milton. "Letter to Martin Luther King, Jr." [*2/5/56*]. Roxbury, Mass. (ALS) 2 pp. MLKP-MBU: Box 15. 560205–000.**
2/5/56	Parks, Rosa. "Interview by Willie Mae Lee." 2/5/56. Montgomery, Ala. (TD) 3 pp. PV-ARC-LNT. 560205–001.

2/5/56	Dexter Avenue Baptist Church. "Program, Sunday services." [*2/5/56*]. Montgomery, Ala. (TD) 4 pp. DABCC. 560205–002.
2/6/56	Palmer, H. J. "Interview by Donald T. Ferron." 2/6/56. Montgomery, Ala. (TD) 2 pp. PV-ARC-LNT. 560206–000.
2/6/56	MIA. "Notes, Mass meeting at Day Street Baptist Church." 2/6/56. (TD) 1 p. AAGR-A-Ar: SG 8423. 560206–001.
2/7/56	**King, Martin Luther, Jr. "Letter to Fred Drake." 2/7/56. [*Montgomery, Ala.*] (TLc) 1 p. DABCC. 560207–003.**
2/7/56	Robinson, Jo Ann Gibson. "Interview by Willie Mae Lee." 2/7/56. Montgomery, Ala. (TD) 4 pp. PV-ARC-LNT. 560207–005.
2/7/56	Folsom, James Elisha (Alabama Governor). "Letter to A. (Asa) Philip Randolph." 2/7/56. Montgomery, Ala. (TLc) 1 p. JEFAF-A-Ar. 560207–006.
2/7/56	Morgan, Juliette (Montgomery City Library). "Interview by Anna Holden." 2/7/56. Montgomery, Ala. (TD) 5 pp. PV-ARC-LNT. 560207–007.
2/8/56	Bratcher, A. L. (Mount Zion Baptist Church). "Letter to Martin Luther King, Jr." 2/8/56. Birmingham, Ala. (TLS) 1 p. MLKP-MBU: Box 91. 560208–000.
2/8/56	Ingalls, Luther. "Interview by Anna Holden." 2/8/56. Montgomery, Ala. (TD) 10 pp. PV-ARC-LNT. 560208–003.
2/9/56	Smith, Roland (National Baptist Training Union Board). "Letter to Martin Luther King, Jr." 2/9/56. Nashville, Tenn. (TLS) 4 pp. (Includes enclosures.) CSKC. 560209–000.
2/9/56	Meany, George (American Federation of Labor and Congress of Industrial Organizations [AFL-CIO]). "Telegram to Dwight D. (David) Eisenhower." 2/9/56. Miami Beach, Fla. (PWSr) 3 pp. WCFG-KAbE. 560209–004.
2/10/56	Citizens Council. "Preview of the Declaration of Segregation." 2/10/56. (TD) 1 p. MLKP-MBU: Box 17. 560210–002.
2/10/56	Gayle, W. (William) A. "Interview by Anna Holden." 2/10/56. Montgomery, Ala. (TD) 5 pp. PV-ARC-LNT. 560210–004.
2/10/56	Sellers, Clyde C. "Interview by Anna Holden." 2/10/56. Montgomery, Ala. (TD) 6 pp. PV-ARC-LNT. 560210–005.
2/11/56	**Proctor, Samuel D. (Dewitt) (Virginia Union University). "Letter to Martin Luther King, Jr." 2/11/56. Richmond, Va. (TLSr) 1 p. MLKP-MBU: Box 91. 560211–000.**
2/12/56	Dexter Avenue Baptist Church. "Program, Sunday services." 2/12/56. Montgomery, Ala. (TD) 4 pp. DABCC. 560212–000.
2/13/56	Men of Montgomery. "Outline of suggestions to end Montgomery bus boycott." 2/13/56. Montgomery, Ala. (TD) 3 pp. DJG. 560213–000.
2/13/56	Jett, Francis (United Packinghouse Workers). "Proceedings of the Montgomery, Ala., Bus Boycott Conference." 2/13/56. Chicago, Ill. (TD) 2 pp. UPW-WHi: Box 373. 560213–002.
2/13/56	MIA. "Notes, Mass meeting at First CME Church." 2/13/56. (TD) 1 p. AAGR-A-Ar: SG 8423. 560213–005.
2/14/56	Hunter, Roy. "Letter to Martin Luther King, Jr." 2/14/56. Baltimore, Md. (TALS) 2 pp. MLKP-MBU: Box 91. 560214–000.
2/15/56	Anonymous. "Letter to Martin Luther King, Jr." 2/15/56. Montgomery, Ala. (TL) 1 p. MLKP-MBU: Box 91. 560215–001.
2/15/56	Henderson, J. Raymond (Second Baptist Church and the Henderson Community Center). "Letter to Martin Luther King, Jr." 2/15/56. Los Angeles, Calif. (TLS) 1 p. MLKP-MBU: Box 91. 560215–005.
2/15/56	Tumbelston, Raimund L. (Crozer Theological Seminary). "Letter to Martin Luther King, Jr." 2/15/56. Chester, Pa. (TLS) 1 p. MLKP-MBU: Box 15. 560215–009.
2/16/56	**Wood, Marcus Garvey (Providence Baptist Church). "Letter to Martin Luther King, Jr." 2/16/56. Baltimore, Md. (TLS) 1 p. MLKP-MBU: Box 91. 560216–000.**
2/16/56	Gray, William H. (Herbert), Jr. (Bright Hope Baptist Church). "Letter to Martin Luther King, Jr." 2/16/56. Philadelphia, Pa. (TAHLS) 1 p. (Marginal comment by King.) MLKP-MBU: Box 16. 560216–001.
2/16/56	MIA. "Agendas of mass meetings." 12/6/55–2/16/56. (TDc) 5 pp. AAGR-A-Ar: SG 8423. 560216–002.
2/16/56	MIA. "Notes, Mass meeting at First Baptist Church." 2/16/56. (TD) 1 p. AAGR-A-Ar: SG 8423. 560216–014.

2/17/56	**Blanton, Sankey L. (Crozer Theological Seminary). "Letter to Martin Luther King, Jr." 2/17/56. Chester, Pa. (TLS) 1 p. MLKP-MBU: Box 91. 560217–000.**
2/17/56	Pugh, Thomas J. (Albany State College). "Letter to Martin Luther King, Jr., and Coretta Scott King." 2/17/56. Albany, Ga. (TLS) 1 p. MLKP-MBU: Box 91. 560217–001.
2/18/56	Bynoe, John G. (Alpha Phi Alpha Fraternity). "Letter to Martin Luther King, Jr." 2/18/56. Boston, Mass. (TLS) 1 p. MLKP-MBU: Box 91. 560218–000.
2/20/56	**Davis, George W. (Washington) (Crozer Theological Seminary). "Letter to Martin Luther King, Jr." 2/20/56. Chester, Pa. (ALS) 1 p. MLKP-MBU: Box 91. 560220–000.**
2/20/56	Abernathy, Ralph. "Memo to the Men of Montgomery." 2/20/56. Montgomery, Ala. (TLc) 1 p. DJG. 560220–002.
2/20/56	Horton, Myles. "Letter to Rosa Parks." 2/20/56. (THLc) 1 p. HRECR-WHi. 560220–005.
2/21/56	**King, Martin Luther, Jr., Defendant. "Indictment, *State of Alabama v. M. L. King, Jr., et al.*" 2/21/56. Montgomery, Ala. (THFmS) 3 pp. CMCR-AMC: File 7399. 560221–003.**
2/21/56	**Associated Press. "Photo of Ralph Abernathy, Fred D. Gray, Robert Graetz, and U. (Uriah) J. Fields." 2/21/56. Montgomery, Ala. (Ph) 1 p. APWW. 560221–019.**
2/21/56	Swomley, John M. "Letter to Wilson Riles." 2/21/56. (TLc) 2 pp. FORP-PSC-P. 560221–001.
2/21/56	King, Martin Luther, Jr., Defendant. "Capias, *State of Alabama v. M. L. King, Jr., et al.*" 2/21/56. Montgomery, Ala. (THFmS) 2 pp. (Executed 2/23/56.) CMCR-AMC: File 7399. 560221–017.
2/22/56	**Bunche, Ralph J. "Telegram to Martin Luther King, Jr." 2/22/56. Kew Gardens, N.Y. (PHWSr) 1 p. MLKP-MBU: Box 14. 560222–001.**
2/22/56	**Wilkins, Roy. "Telegram to Martin Luther King, Jr." 2/22/56. Jamaica, N.Y. (PHWSr) 1 p. MLKP-MBU: Box 67. 560222–013.**
2/22/56	**Associated Press. "Photo of Rosa Parks and D. H. Lackey." [*2/22/56*]. Montgomery, Ala. (Ph) 1 p. APWW. 560222–021.**
2/22/56	**"Photo of indicted boycott leaders at the state capitol." [*2/22/56*]. Montgomery, Ala. From: *Life*, 5 March 1956, pp. 42–43. (PPh) 1 p. 560222–037.**
2/22/56	Fisk University. "Program, Religious Emphasis Week." 2/18/56–2/22/56. Nashville, Tenn. (PD) 9 pp. MLKP-MBU: Box 89. 560222–000.
2/22/56	MIA. "Form letter to churches, clubs, and individuals." 2/22/56. Montgomery, Ala. (TLc) 1 p. MLKP-MBU: Box 105. 560222–003.
2/22/56	Peck, James, and Paula Peck. "Letter to Roy Wilkins." 2/22/56. New York, N.Y. (TLS) 1 p. NAACPP-DLC: Group III–A273. 560222–012.
2/22/56	Whitaker, H. (Horace) Edward. "Letter to Martin Luther King, Jr." 2/22/56. Niagara Falls, N.Y. (THLS) 1 p. MLKP-MBU: Box 67. 560222–015.
2/22/56	Corbett, J. Elliott (Community Methodist Church). "Letter to Martin Luther King, Jr." 2/22/56. McHenry, Ill. (AHLS) 2 pp. (Marginal comment by King.) MLKP-MBU: Box 15. 560222–032.
2/22/56	Powell, Adam Clayton. "Telegram to Dwight D. (David) Eisenhower." 2/22/56. Washington, D.C. (PHWSr) 2 pp. WCFO-KAbE: OF 142-A-6. 560222–033.
2/23/56	**Associated Press. "Photo of Ralph Abernathy, Martin Luther King, Jr., and D. H. Lackey." 2/23/56. Montgomery, Ala. (Ph) 1 p. APWW. 560223–025.**
2/23/56	**Associated Press. "Photo of Fred D. Gray, Orzelle Billingsley, Charles D. Langford, Arthur D. Shores, and Peter A. Hall." 2/23/56. Montgomery, Ala. (Ph) 1 p. APWW. 560223–026.**
2/23/56	**"Photo of Martin Luther King, Jr., at police station." [*2/23/56*]. Montgomery, Ala. From: *Life*, 5 March 1956, p. 41. (PPh) 1 p. 560223–028.**
2/23/56	Jackson, L. K. (St. Paul Baptist Church). "Letter to Martin Luther King, Jr." 2/23/56. Gary, Ind. (TLS) 1 p. MLKP-MBU: Box 91. 560223–000.
2/23/56	American Civil Liberties Union. "Press release, Montgomery indictment of Negroes unconstitutional." 2/23/56. New York, N.Y. (TD) 1 p. ACLUC-NjP. 560223–001.
2/23/56	Randolph, A. (Asa) Philip (Brotherhood of Sleeping Car Porters and Maids). "Telegram to E. D. Nixon." 2/23/56. Jacksonville, Fla. (PHWSr) 1 p. MLKP-MBU: Box 91. 560223–002.
2/23/56	NAACP. "Press release, NAACP support pledged to bus protest victims." 2/23/56. New York, N.Y. (TD) 2 pp. NAACPP-DLC: Group III–A273. 560223–003.

2/23/56 King, Martin Luther, Jr., Defendant. "Appearance Bond, *State of Alabama v. M. L. King, Jr., et al.*" 2/23/56. Montgomery, Ala. (HFmS) 2 pp. CMCR-AMC: File 7399. 560223–005.

2/23/56 Wilkins, Roy (NAACP). "Telegram to NAACP." 2/23/56. New York, N.Y. (PWSr) 1 p. NAACPP-DLC: Group III–A273. 560223–009.

2/23/56 Jackson, J. H. (Joseph Harrison) (National Baptist Convention, U.S.A., Inc.). "Telegram to Martin Luther King, Jr." 2/23/56. Miami, Fla. (PWSr) 1 p. MLKP-MBU: Box 63. 560223–010.

2/23/56 Burrus, Lloyd A. "Telegram to Martin Luther King, Jr." 2/23/56. Newburgh, N.Y. (PWSr) 1 p. MLKP-MBU: Box 14. 560223–016.

2/23/56 MIA. "Program, Mass meeting at First Baptist Church." [*2/23/56*]. Montgomery, Ala. (TD) 2 pp. HG-GAMK. 560223–017.

2/23/56 Jackson, J. H. (Joseph Harrison) (National Baptist Convention, U.S.A., Inc.). "Telegram to James Elisha Folsom." 2/23/56. Miami, Fla. (PWSr) 2 pp. JEFAF-A-Ar. 560223–021.

2/24/56 Phillips, Wayne. "Negroes Pledge to Keep Boycott." 2/24/56. New York, N.Y. From: *New York Times*, 24 February 1956. (PD) 2 pp. 560224–000.

2/24/56 Lawrence, Charles R. (Brooklyn College). "Letter to Martin Luther King, Jr." 2/24/56. Pomona, N.Y. (TLS) 2 pp. MLKP-MBU: Box 91. 560224–002.

2/24/56 Baker, Ella J. "Telegram to Martin Luther King, Jr." 2/24/56. New York, N.Y. (PHWSr) 2 pp. (Marginal comments by King.) MLKP-MBU: Box 14. 560224–006.

2/24/56 Carey, Archibald James, Jr. "Letter to Martin Luther King, Jr." 2/24/56. (TLc) 1 p. AJC-ICHi: Box 27. 560224–019.

2/24/56 Jones, William D. "Telegram to Martin Luther King, Jr." 2/24/56. Birmingham, Ala. (PWSr) 1 p. MLKP-MBU: Box 60A. 560224–007.

2/24/56 McKinney, Wade H. (Antioch Baptist Church). "Letter to Martin Luther King, Jr." 2/24/56. Cleveland, Ohio. (TLS) 2 pp. MLKP-MBU: Box 116. 560224–001.

2/24/56 Bertocci, Peter A. (Boston University). "Letter to Martin Luther King, Jr." 2/24/56. Boston, Mass. (ALS) 1 p. DABCC. 560224–028.

2/24/56 "Photo of Ralph Abernathy, Martin Luther King, Jr., and Bayard Rustin." 2/24/56. Montgomery, Ala. (Ph) 1 p. APWW. 560224–014.

2/24/56 King, Martin Luther, Jr., Defendant. "Agreement of Parties, *State of Alabama v. M. L. King, Jr., et al.*" 2/24/56. Montgomery, Ala. (THDS) 3 pp. (Filed 2/27/56.) CMCR-AMC: File 7399. 560224–008.

2/24/56 Swomley, John M. (Fellowship of Reconciliation). "Telegram to Martin Luther King, Jr." 2/24/56. New York, N.Y. (PHWSr) 1 p. MLKP-MBU: Box 65. 560224–009.

2/24/56 Nesbitt, J. E. "Telegram to Martin Luther King, Jr." 2/24/56. Los Angeles, Calif. (PWSr) 1 p. MLKP-MBU: Box 63. 560224–012.

2/24/56 Carter, Robert L. (Calvary Baptist Church). "Letter to Martin Luther King, Jr." 2/24/56. Haverhill, Mass. (TLS) 1 p. MLKP-MBU: Box 15. 560224–016.

2/24/56 Brown, Jesse H. "Letter to Martin Luther King, Jr." 2/24/56. Durham, N.C. (ALS) 1 p. MLKP-MBU: Box 14A. 560224–017.

2/25/56 Smith, Kelly Miller (First Baptist Church). "Letter to Martin Luther King, Jr." 2/25/56. Nashville, Tenn. (TLS) 1 p. MLKP-MBU: Box 119. 560225–001.

2/25/56 Arnold, Alphonzo A. (Phi Beta Sigma Fraternity). "Letter to Martin Luther King, Jr." 2/25/56. Roxbury, Mass. (TLS) 1 p. MLKP-MBU: Box 17. 560225–003.

2/25/56 Parks, Rosa. "Letter to Myles Horton." 2/25/56. Montgomery, Ala. (TLS) 1 p. HRECR-WHi: Box 22. 560225–007.

2/25/56 Blake, Eugene Carson (National Council of the Churches of the United States of America). "Telegram to S. S. (Solomon Snowden) Seay." 2/25/56. (THWc) 3 pp. NCCP-PPPrHi: Box 15. 560225–015.

2/25/56 Dixon, James Monroe. "Letter to Martin Luther King, Jr." 2/25/56. Sylacauga, Ala. (TLS) 1 p. MLKP-MBU: Box 16. 560225–016.

2/25/56 O'Bannon, Lester C. "Letter to Martin Luther King, Jr." 2/25/56. Boston, Mass. (ALS) 2 pp. MLKP-MBU: Box 63A. 560225–019.

2/25/56 Cargile, Loyce Furman. "Telegram to Martin Luther King, Jr." 2/25/56. Miami, Fla. (PWSr) 1 p. MLKP-MBU: Box 15. 560225–022.

2/26/56 Dexter Avenue Baptist Church. "Program, Sunday services." 2/26/56. Montgomery, Ala. (TD) 3 pp. DABCC. 560226–006.

2/27/56 Ferron, Donald T. "Notes, MIA mass meeting at Holt Street Baptist Church." 2/27/56. Montgomery, Ala. (AD) 4 pp. PV-ARC-LNT. 560227–020.

2/27/56 Lowe, Richard A. (National Negro Independent Civic and Political Association). "Letter to Martin Luther King, Jr." 2/27/56. New York, N.Y. (TALS) 1 p. MLKP-MBU: Box 91. 560227–000.

2/27/56 King, Martin Luther, Jr. "Letter to Lucille B. Knapp." 2/27/56. [*Montgomery, Ala.*] (TLc) 1 p. DABCC. 560227–003.

2/27/56 Jones, Edward A. (*Morehouse Alumnus*). "Letter to Martin Luther King, Jr." 2/27/56. Atlanta, Ga. (TLS) 1 p. MLKP-MBU: Box 62. 560227–006.

2/27/56 Clair, Alfred Petit (International Union of Mine, Mill, and Smelter Workers). "Telegram to Martin Luther King, Jr." 2/27/56. Perthamboy, N.J. (PWSr) 1 p. MLKP-MBU: Box 62. 560227–008.

2/27/56 Jones, J. Harold. "Notes, MIA mass meeting at Holt Street Baptist Church." 2/27/56. Montgomery, Ala. (AD) 3 pp. PV-ARC-LNT. 560227–019.

2/27/56 Morrow, E. (Everett) Frederick (U.S. White House). "Memo to Sherman Adams." 2/27/56. Washington, D.C. (TLI) 2 pp. WCFO-KAbE: OF 142-A. 560227–021.

2/28/56 King, Martin Luther, Jr. "Letter to William H. (Herbert) Gray, Jr." 2/28/56. [*Montgomery, Ala.*] (TLc) 1 p. DABCC. 560228–005.

2/28/56 [*Kelsey, George D.*] "Letter to Martin Luther King, Jr." [*2/28/56*]. (AHLd) 2 pp. GDKP. 560228–007.

2/28/56 Jones, Major J. (Fisk University). "Letter to Martin Luther King, Jr." 2/28/56. Nashville, Tenn. (TLS) 1 p. MLKP-MBU: Box 119. 560228–000.

2/28/56 McNeil, Jesse Jai (Tabernacle Baptist Church). "Recommendations approved by Baptist Ministers Conference of Detroit and Vicinity, regarding the Montgomery boycott." 2/28/56. Detroit, Mich. (THD) 1 p. (Enclosure in 560229–003.) MLKP-MBU: Box 91. 560228–001.

2/28/56 French, Edgar N. (MIA). "Minutes, Speakers Bureau meeting." 2/28/56. Montgomery, Ala. (TDS) 1 p. MLKP-MBU: Box 6. 560228–010.

2/28/56 Hebrew Union College, Jewish Institute of Religion. "Press release, Statement of solidarity with Montgomery bus boycott and with Negro fellow citizens." 2/28/56. Cincinnati, Ohio. (TAD) 2 pp. NAACPP-DLC: Group III–A273. 560228–011.

2/28/56 Smiley, Glenn E. (Fellowship of Reconciliation). "Letter to Muriel Lester." 2/28/56. (THLc) 1 p. FORP-PSC-P. 560228–013.

2/28/56 King, Martin Luther, Jr. (Dexter Avenue Baptist Church). "Interview by Glenn E. Smiley." [*2/28/56*]. [*Montgomery, Ala.*] (TTa) 4 pp. FORP-PSC-P. 560228–015.

2/28/56 Powell, Adam Clayton. "Telegram to Archibald James Carey, Jr." 2/28/56. New York, N.Y. (PHWSr) 2 pp. AJC-ICHi: Box 27. 560228–016.

2/28/56 Smiley, Glenn E. "Letter to Martin Luther King, Jr." 2/28/56. (ALS) 2 pp. MLKP-MBU: Box 57. 560228–018.

2/28/56 Jones, William (International Longshoremen and Warehousemen's Union). "Letter to Martin Luther King, Jr." 2/28/56. San Francisco, Calif. (PHWSr) 1 p. DABCC. 560228–019.

2/29/56 Neal, Alice. "Telegram to Martin Luther King, Jr." 2/29/56. Oakland, Calif. (PHWSr) 1 p. (Marginal comments by King.) MLKP-MBU: Box 91. 560229–001.

2/29/56 McNeil, Jesse Jai (Tabernacle Baptist Church). "Letter to Martin Luther King, Jr." 2/29/56. Detroit, Mich. (THLS) 1 p. (Marginal comments by King; contains enclosure 560228–001.) MLKP-MBU: Box 91. 560229–003.

2/29/56 Gray, William H. (Herbert), Jr. (Bright Hope Baptist Church). "Letter to Martin Luther King, Jr." 2/29/56. Philadelphia, Pa. (TLS) 1 p. MLKP-MBU: Box 91. 560229–000.

2/29/56 King, Martin Luther, Jr. "Letter to Wade H. McKinney." 2/29/56. [*Montgomery, Ala.*] (TLc) 1 p. DABCC. 560229–004.

2/29/56 Swomley, John M. "Letter to Glenn E. Smiley." 2/29/56. (TLc) 1 p. FORP-PSC-P. 560229–005.

2/29/56 Swomley, John M. "Letter to Glenn E. Smiley." 2/29/56. (THLc) 1 p. FORP-PSC-P. 560229–007.

2/29/56 King, Martin Luther, Jr., Defendant. "Agreement of Parties, *State of Alabama v. M. L. King, Jr.*" 2/29/56. Montgomery, Ala. (THDS) 4 pp. (Filed on 3/2/56.) CMCR-AMC: File 7399. 560229–009.

2/29/56 Smiley, Glenn E. (Fellowship of Reconciliation). "Letter to John M. Swomley and Alfred Hassler." 2/29/56. Montgomery, Ala. (THLc) 2 pp. FORP-PSC-P. 560229–012.

3/56 Barbour, J. Pius (*National Baptist Voice*). "Meditations on Rev. M. L. King, Jr., of Montgomery, Ala." 3/56. From: *National Baptist Voice*, March 1956. (PD) 2 pp. MLKP-MBU: Box 80. 560300–002.

3/56 Rustin, Bayard. "Letter to Coretta Scott King." [*3/56*]. New York, N.Y. (ALI) 1 p. MLKP-MBU: Box 91. 560300–010.

3/56 Morehouse College. "Alumnus Salutes Dr. M. L. King, Jr." 3/56. Atlanta, Ga. From: *Morehouse College Bulletin*, March 1956, p. 5. (PD) 1 p. MLKJrP-GAMK. 560300–012.

3/56 MIA. "List of executive board members." [*1/56–3/56*]. (TD) 2 pp. MLKP-MBU: Box 6. 560300–013.

3/56 King, Martin Luther, Jr. "Right of nonviolent protest." [*2/56–3/56*]. [*Montgomery, Ala.*] (At) 49 sec. (1 sound cassette: analog.) MMFR: Sync sound 48. 560300–018.

3/56 [*Du Bois, W. E. B. (William Edward Burghardt)*]. "Letter to Martin Luther King, Jr." [*3/56?*]. (TLc) 1 p. WEBD-MU. 560300–021.

3/1/56 Ferron, Donald T. "Notes, MIA mass meeting at Hutchinson Street Baptist Church." 3/1/56. Montgomery, Ala. (AD) 5 pp. PV-ARC-LNT. 560301–010.

3/1/56 King, Martin Luther, Jr., Defendant. "Demurrers, *State of Alabama v. M. L. King, Jr.*" 3/1/56. Montgomery, Ala. (THDS) 3 pp. CMCR-AMC: File 7399. 560301–005.

3/1/56 NAACP. "Press release, Powell prayer plan supported by NAACP." 3/1/56. New York, N.Y. (TD) 1 p. NAACPP-DLC: Group III–A273. 560301–006.

3/1/56 Goodman, Abram V. (Religious Council of the Five Towns and Rockaways). "Statement of support for Montgomery ministers." 3/1/56. Long Island, N.Y. (TD) 1 p. NAACPP-DLC: Group III–A273. 560301–007.

3/1/56 [*Smiley, Glenn E.*] "Letter to Helen Smiley." 3/1/56. Montgomery, Ala. (ALf) 2 pp. GESP. 560301–008.

3/1/56 Jones, J. Harold. "Notes, MIA mass meeting at Hutchinson Street Baptist Church." 3/1/56. Montgomery, Ala. (AD) 2 p. PV-ARC-LNT. 560301–011.

3/1/56 Swomley, John M. "Letter to Glenn E. Smiley." 3/1/56. (TLc) 1 p. BRP-DLC. 560301–014.

3/2/56 Powell, Adam Clayton (U.S. Congress. Senate). "Letter to Dwight D. (David) Eisenhower." 3/2/56. Washington, D.C. (THLS) 1 p. DDEP-KAbE. 560302–004.

3/2/56 Smiley, Glenn E. (Fellowship of Reconciliation). "Letter to John M. Swomley." 3/2/56. Montgomery, Ala. (ALS) 4 pp. BRP-DLC. 560302–005.

3/3/56 King, Martin Luther, Jr. (MIA). "Letter to Roy Wilkins." 3/3/56. [*Montgomery, Ala.*] (TLc) 2 pp. MLKP-MBU: Box 64. 560303–001.

3/3/56 King, Martin Luther, Jr. (MIA). "Letter to Archibald James Carey, Jr." 3/3/56. Montgomery, Ala. (TLS) 1 p. AJC-ICHi: Box 27. 560303–029.

3/3/56 King, Martin Luther, Sr. "Letter to James Timothy Boddie." 3/3/56. (TLc) 1 p. EBCR. 560303–003.

3/4/56 Schilling, S. Paul (Boston University). "Letter to Martin Luther King, Jr." 3/4/56. Boston, Mass. (TLS) 1 p. MLKP-MBU: Box 91. 560304–001.

3/4/56 Dawkins, Reuben S. "Letter to Martin Luther King, Jr." 3/4/56. Roxbury, Mass. (ALS) 2 pp. MLKP-MBU: Box 91. 560304–000.

3/4/56 Highlander Folk School. "Mrs. Rosa Parks Reports on Montgomery, Ala., Bus Protest." 3/4/56. Monteagle, Tenn. (TD) 5 pp. ACLUC-NjP. 560304–002.

3/4/56 [*MIA*]. "List of dispatch stations." [*2/27/56–3/4/56*]. Montgomery, Ala. (TD) 1 p. MLKP-MBU: Box 6. 560304–010.

3/5/56 Jackson, J. H. (Joseph Harrison) (National Baptist Convention, U.S.A., Inc.). "Letter to Martin Luther King, Jr." 3/5/56. Chicago, Ill. (THLS) 2 pp. MLKP-MBU: Box 91. 560305–002.

3/5/56 Carr, Leonard G. (National Baptist Convention, U.S.A., Inc.). "Letter to Martin Luther King, Jr." 3/5/56. Philadelphia, Pa. (THLS) 1 p. (Marginal comments by King.) MLKP-MBU: Box 91. 560305–003.

3/5/56 Guy, Eunice (Wiley College). "Letter to Martin Luther King, Jr." 3/5/56. Marshall, Tex. (ALS) 3 pp. MLKP-MBU: Box 91. 560305–008.

3/5/56 Pittard, Gwendolyn E. "Letter to Martin Luther King, Jr." 3/5/56. New York, N.Y. (AHLS) 2 pp. MLKP-MBU: Box 91. 560305–000.

3/5/56 Carey, Archibald James, Jr. "Letter to Martin Luther King, Jr." 3/5/56. Chicago, Ill. (TAHLS) 2 pp. (Marginal comments by King.) MLKP-MBU: Box 91. 560305–001.

3/5/56 King, Martin Luther, Jr. (Dexter Avenue Baptist Church). "Letter to Kelly Miller Smith." 3/5/56. [*Montgomery, Ala.*] (TLc) 1 p. DABCC. 560305–007.

3/5/56 [*Halstead, Fred*]. "Montgomery: Impressions and mass meeting notes." 3/4/56–3/5/56. Montgomery, Ala. (AD) 35 pp. FHP-WHi. 560305–027.

3/5/56 Taylor, Franklyn W. "MIA Audit Report for 12/7/55–2/27/56." 3/5/56. Montgomery, Ala. (TDS) 10 pp. RJGC. 560305–028.

3/6/56   **Miller, William Robert** (*Fellowship*). **"Letter to Martin Luther King, Jr." 3/6/56. (TLc) 1 p. WRMP-GAMK: Box 1. 560306–009.**

3/6/56   **Browning, Earline. "Letter to Martin Luther King, Jr." 3/6/56. Boise, Idaho. (AHLS) 2 pp. MLKP-MBU: Box 91. 560306–005.**

3/6/56   James, Julius (St. John Baptist Church). "Letter to Martin Luther King, Jr." 3/6/56. Gary, Ind. (TALS) 1 p. MLKP-MBU: Box 91. 560306–000.

3/6/56   Hoover, J. Edgar (U.S. Federal Bureau of Investigation). "Memo to Assistant Chief of Staff, Intelligence, Department of the Army." 3/6/56. (THL) 1 p. MIAFBI-DJ. 560306–012.

3/7/56   **Kilgore, Thomas G., Jr. (Friendship Baptist Church). "Letter to Martin Luther King, Jr." 3/7/56. New York, N.Y. (THLS) 1 p. MLKP-MBU: Box 91. 560307–001.**

3/7/56   **King, Martin Luther, Jr. (MIA). "Letter to J. H. (Joseph Harrison) Jackson." 3/7/56. [*Montgomery, Ala.*] (THLc) 1 p. MLKP-MBU: Box 91. 560307–003.**

3/7/56   Perry, Walter L. (British American Association of Coloured Brothers). "Letter to Martin Luther King, Jr." 3/7/56. Windsor, Ont., Canada. (THLS) 2 pp. (Marginal comment by King.) MLKP-MBU: Box 91. 560307–002.

3/7/56   Rustin, Bayard. "Notes of a conference: How outsiders can strengthen the Montgomery nonviolent protest." 3/7/56. Birmingham, Ala. (TAL) 2 pp. BRP-DLC. 560307–009.

3/7/56   Eubanks, John (NAACP). "Letter to Martin Luther King, Jr." 3/7/56. East St. Louis, Ill. (TLc) 1 p. NAACPP-DLC: Group III–A273. 560307–010.

3/7/56   Rabb, Maxwell M. "Letter to George Meany." 3/7/56. (TLc) 1 p. WCFG-KAbE. 560307–012.

3/7/56   Sheppard, Daphne A. (National Association of Business and Professional Women's Clubs). "Letter to Martin Luther King, Jr." 3/7/56. Brooklyn, N.Y. (TLS) 1 p. DABCC. 560307–013.

3/8/56   **Rustin, Bayard (*Liberation*). "Letter to Martin Luther King, Jr." 3/8/56. New York, N.Y. (TLS) 1 p. MLKP-MBU: Box 5. 560308–001.**

3/8/56   **King, Martin Luther, Jr. (MIA). "Letter to George D. Kelsey." 3/8/56. Montgomery, Ala. (TALS) 2 pp. (Includes enclosure.) GDKP. 560308–005.**

3/8/56   **Wilkins, Roy (NAACP). "Letter to Martin Luther King, Jr." 3/8/56. New York, N.Y. (TLS) 2 pp. MLKP-MBU: Box 67. 560308–006.**

3/8/56   Nunn, William G. (*Pittsburgh Courier*). "Letter to Martin Luther King, Jr." 3/8/56. Pittsburgh, Pa. (TLS) 1 p. MLKP-MBU: Box 91. 560308–000.

3/8/56   Swomley, John M. (Fellowship of Reconciliation). "Form letter to friend." 3/8/56. New York, N.Y. (TLS) 1 p. (Contains enclosure 560308–003.) MLKP-MBU: Box 91. 560308–002.

3/8/56   Fellowship of Reconciliation. "Press release, Statement by ministers urging action from Eisenhower." [*3/8/56*]. New York, N.Y. (THD) 2 pp. (Enclosure in 560308–002.) MLKP-MBU: Box 91. 560308–003.

3/8/56   MIA. Committee on Countywide Registration and Voting. "Memo to executive board." 3/8/56. Montgomery, Ala. (TD) 2 pp. MLKP-MBU: Box 84. 560308–010.

3/8/56   Wilkins, Roy (NAACP). "Telegram to Franklin H. Williams." 3/8/56. (PWSr) 1 p. NAACPP-DLC: Group III–A273. 560308–012.

3/8/56   James, Felix E. (Alabama State College). "Letter to Martin Luther King, Jr." 3/8/56. Montgomery, Ala. (THLS) 1 p. MLKP-MBU: Box 61. 560308–016.

3/9/56   King, Martin Luther, Jr. (MIA). "Letter to Claude Lee Saunders." 3/9/56. Montgomery, Ala. (TLS) 1 p. (560319–005 on recto.) MLKP-MBU: Box 2. 560309–002.

3/9/56   **Faulkner, William J. (Congregational Church of Park Manor). "Letter to Martin Luther King, Jr." 3/9/56. Chicago, Ill. (TAHLS) 1 p. MLKP-MBU: Box 15. 560309–003.**

3/9/56   Mason, Vivian C. (National Organization of Negro Women). "Telegram to Martin Luther King, Jr." 3/9/56. Washington, D.C. (THWc) 1 p. (Marginal comment by King.) MLKP-MBU: Box 91. 560309–000.

3/9/56   Jack, Homer Alexander. "To those interested in the nonviolent resistance aspects of the Montgomery, Alabama, protest against segregation on the city buses." 3/9/56. (TLc) 3 pp. BRP-DLC. 560309–008.

3/9/56   Diggs, Charles C., Jr. (U.S. Congress. Senate). "Letter to Dwight D. (David) Eisenhower." 3/9/56. Washington, D.C. (TLS) 2 pp. DDEP-KAbE. 560309–009.

3/10/56   **Smith, Lillian Eugenia. "Letter to Martin Luther King, Jr." 3/10/56. Neptune Beach, Fla. (TALS) 2 pp. MLKP-MBU: Box 65. 560310–002.**

3/10/56   Batten, Charles E. (Parish of the Epiphany). "Letter to Martin Luther King, Jr." 3/10/56. Winchester, Mass. (TLS) 1 p. MLKP-MBU: Box 64. 560310–005.

3/11/56   NAACP. "Press release, NAACP to continue support and legal assistance to bus protest movement." 3/11/56. Montgomery, Ala. (TD) 1 p. NAACPP-DLC: Group III–A273. 560311–002.

3/11/56   Dexter Avenue Baptist Church. "Program, Sunday services." 3/11/56. Montgomery, Ala. (TDf) 2 pp. DABCC. 560311–004.

3/12/56   Leishman, R. Murray (St. Andrew's University). "Letter to the Christian Ministers of Montgomery, Ala." 3/12/56. Fife, Scotland. (TLS) 2 pp. MLKP-MBU: Box 91. 560312–000.

3/12/56   King, Martin Luther, Jr. (MIA). "Letter to W. T. (William Talbot) Handy, Jr." 3/12/56. Montgomery, Ala. (TALS) 1 p. WTH. 560312–003.

3/12/56   Reed, Sam (State Penitentiary at Rockview). "Donation to MIA." 3/12/56. Bellefonte, Pa. (PHFmS) 2 pp. MLKP-MBU: Box 89. 560312–004.

3/12/56   Thomas, Norman. "Letter to Homer Alexander Jack." 3/12/56. (TLc) 1 p. NTC-NN. 560312–005.

3/12/56   Horton, Myles. "Letter to Rosa Parks." 3/12/56. (TLc) 1 p. HRECR-WHi. 560312–006.

3/12/56   Harlow, Bryce N. "Letter to Charles C. Diggs, Jr." 3/12/56. (THLc) 1 p. WCFO-KAbE. 560312–011.

3/13/56   Dockery, John (NAACP). "Telegram to Martin Luther King, Jr." 3/13/56. Stockton, Calif. (PWSr) 1 p. MLKP-MBU: Box 91. 560313–000.

3/13/56   King, Martin Luther, Jr. (Dexter Avenue Baptist Church). "Letter to J. Pius Barbour." 3/13/56. [*Montgomery, Ala.*] (TLc) 1 p. DABCC. 560313–004.

3/13/56   Wofford, Harris (Covington and Burling). "Letter to Martin Luther King, Jr." 3/13/56. Washington, D.C. (ALS) 1 p. MLKP-MBU: Box 91. 560313–005.

3/14/56   Chalmers, Allan Knight (Boston University). "Letter to Martin Luther King, Jr." 3/14/56. Boston, Mass. (TALS) 2 pp. MLKP-MBU: Box 91. 560314–000.

3/14/56   Thurman, Howard (Boston University Marsh Chapel). "Letter to Martin Luther King, Jr." 3/14/56. Boston, Mass. (TLS) 1 p. MLKP-MBU: Box 91. 560314–001.

3/14/56   MIA. Strategy Committee. "Recommendations to the executive committee." 3/14/56. (AD) 5 pp. MLKP-MBU: Box 2. 560314–004.

3/14/56   Redmon, J. F. (Mississippi Regional Council of Negro Leadership). "Letter to Martin Luther King, Jr." 3/14/56. Mound Bayou, Miss. (THLS) 1 p. MLKP-MBU: Box 64. 560314–005.

3/14/56   Walker, W. O. "Letter to Martin Luther King, Jr." 3/14/56. (TLc) 2 pp. NAACPP-DLC: Group III–A209. 560314–009.

3/15/56   King, Martin Luther, Jr. "Telegram to Dwight D. (David) Eisenhower." [*3/8/56–3/15/56*]. [*Montgomery, Ala.*] (TWd) 1 p. MLKP-MBU: Box 78. 560315–014.

3/15/56   King, Martin Luther, Jr. (MIA). "Press release, King urges exploratory White House conference." [*3/8/56–3/15/56*]. [*Montgomery, Ala.*] (TDd) 2 pp. MLKP-MBU: Box 78. 560315–015.

3/15/56   Mason, Vivian C. "Telegram to Martin Luther King, Jr." 3/15/56. Washington, D.C. (PWSr) 1 p. MLKP-MBU: Box 91. 560315–000.

3/15/56   Jack, Homer Alexander (Unitarian Church of Evanston). "Letter to Norman Thomas." 3/15/56. Evanston, Ill. (TLS) 1 p. NTC-NN. 560315–003.

3/15/56   Reddick, Lawrence Dunbar. "Bus Boycott in Montgomery: The Southern Negro Speaks Up." 3/15/56. Montgomery, Ala. From: *Dissent* 3 (Spring 1956): 1–11. (PHD) 12 pp. (Marginal comments by King.) MLKP-MBU: Box 76. 560315–005.

3/16/56   King, Martin Luther, Jr. (MIA). "Letter to Howard Thurman." 3/16/56. Montgomery, Ala. (TLS) 1 p. HTC-MBU: Box 43. 560316–008.

3/16/56   Jack, Homer Alexander (Unitarian Church of Evanston). "Letter to Martin Luther King, Jr., and Coretta Scott King." 3/16/56. Evanston, Ill. (TLS) 1 p. MLKP-MBU: Box 91. 560316–001.

3/16/56   Smiley, Glenn E. (Fellowship of Reconciliation). "Letter to Martin Luther King, Jr." 3/16/56. New York, N.Y. (TLS) 1 p. MLKP-MBU: Box 91. 560316–000.

3/16/56   King, Martin Luther, Jr. "Letter to Arthaniel Harris." 3/16/56. [*Montgomery, Ala.*] (TLc) 1 p. DABCC. 560316–003.

3/17/56   Harkins, Albert F. (First Universalist Society). "Letter to Martin Luther King, Jr." 3/17/56. Elgin, Ill. (TLS) 2 pp. MLKP-MBU: Box 17. 560317–000.

3/18/56   Rice, Thelma Austin (Dexter Avenue Baptist Church). "Letter to Martin Luther King, Jr." 3/18/56. Montgomery, Ala. (TALS) 2 pp. (Contains enclosure 560318–002.) MLKP-MBU: Box 119. 560318–001.

3/18/56 Dexter Avenue Baptist Church. "Comforting-sense of direction tidbits for our Pastor and club member." 3/18/56. Montgomery, Ala. (TADS) 15 pp. (Enclosure in 560318–001.) MLKP-MBU: Box 119. 560318–002.

3/18/56 Fellowship of Reconciliation. "Press release, Four hundred clergymen express support for Montgomery pastors." 3/18/56. New York, N.Y. (TD) 6 pp. ACLUC-NjP. 560318–000.

3/18/56 Dexter Avenue Baptist Church. "Program, Sunday services." 3/18/56. Montgomery, Ala. (TD) 4 pp. DABCC. 560318–007.

3/19/56 International Longshoremen and Warehousemen's Union. "Let Us Help Justice to Prevail." [3/19/56]. (TD) 1 p. (560319–006, 560309–002 on verso.) MLKP-MBU: Box 3. 560319–005.

3/19/56 King, Martin Luther, Jr. (MIA). "Letter to Claude Lee Saunders." 3/19/56. Montgomery, Ala. (TLSr) 1 p. (560319–005 on recto.) MLKP-MBU: Box 3. 560319–006.

3/19/56 Associated Press. "Photo of Rosa Parks and E. D. Nixon." 3/19/56. Montgomery, Ala. (Ph) 1 p. APWW. 560319–011.

3/19/56 Associated Press. "Photo of Martin Luther King, Jr., outside courthouse." 3/19/56. Montgomery, Ala. (Ph) 1 p. APWW. 560319–013.

3/19/56 King, Martin Luther, Jr. (MIA). "Letter to W. E. B. Du Bois." 3/19/56. Montgomery, Ala. (TLSr) 1 p. WEBD-MU. 560319–000.

3/19/56 MIA. "Program, Mass meeting at St. John AME Church." 3/19/56. Montgomery, Ala. (TD) 1 p. MLKP-MBU: Box 30. 560319–002.

3/19/56 King, Martin Luther, Jr., Defendant. "Order of Court Granting a Severance and Order Overruling Demurrer to Indictment, *State of Alabama v. M. L. King, Jr., et al.*" 3/19/56. (TD) 1 p. CMCR-AMC: File 7399. 560319–003.

3/20/56 Associated Press. "Photo of Martin Luther King, Jr., and supporters." 3/20/56. Montgomery, Ala. (Ph) 1 p. APWW. 560320–005.

3/21/56 Drake, St. Clair (Roosevelt University). "Letter to Martin Luther King, Jr." 3/21/56. Chicago, Ill. (TALS) 2 pp. (Includes enclosure.) MLKP- MBU: Box 91. 560321–000.

3/21/56 Nelson, William Stuart (Howard University). "Letter to Martin Luther King, Jr." 3/21/56. Washington, D.C. (TLS) 1 p. MLKP-MBU: Box 28. 560321–012.

3/21/56 Rustin, Bayard (War Resisters League). "Report on Montgomery, Alabama." 3/21/56. New York, N.Y. (PD) 4 pp. ACLUC-NjP. 560321–002.

3/21/56 King, Martin Luther, Jr., Defendant. "Motion to Exclude the State's Evidence, *State of Alabama v. M. L. King, Jr.*" 3/21/56. Montgomery, Ala. (THDS) 3 pp. CMCR-AMC: File 7399. 560321–006.

3/21/56 Ballou, Maude L. "Letter to Allan Knight Chalmers." 3/21/56. [*Montgomery, Ala.*] (TLc) 1 p. MLKP-MBU: Box 15. 560321–010.

3/21/56 Thomas, Julius A. (National Urban League). "Letter to Martin Luther King, Jr." 3/21/56. (TLc) 1 p. NULR-DLC. 560321–013.

3/22/56 King, Martin Luther, Jr., Defendant. "Transcript, *State of Alabama v. M. L. King, Jr.*" 3/19/56–3/22/56. Montgomery, Ala. (TD) 580 pp. AAGR-A-Ar: SG 8423. 560322–015.

3/22/56 King, Martin Luther, Jr., Defendant. "Judgment and Sentence of the Court, *State of Alabama v. M. L. King, Jr.*" 3/22/56. [*Montgomery, Ala.*] (THDd) 2 pp. CMCR-AMC: File 7399. 560322–003.

3/22/56 King, Martin Luther, Jr. "Reactions to conviction by the state of Alabama." [3/22/56]. [*Montgomery, Ala.*] (At) 3 min. (1 sound cassette: analog.) MMFR: Sync sound 103. 560322–030.

3/22/56 King, Martin Luther, Jr. (MIA). "Address to mass meeting at Holt Street Baptist Church." 3/22/56. Montgomery, Ala. (TTa) 1 p. MLKP-MBU: Box 80. 560322–001.

3/22/56 Stanley, Frank L. (Alpha Phi Alpha Fraternity). "Letter to Martin Luther King, Jr." 3/22/56. Louisville, Ky. (TLS) 2 pp. MLKP-MBU: Box 13A. 560322–002.

3/22/56 Associated Press. "Photo of Martin Luther King, Jr., and Coretta Scott King." 3/22/56. Montgomery, Ala. (Ph) 1 p. APWW. 560322–026.

3/22/56 Associated Press. "Photo of Martin Luther King, Jr., at mass meeting at Holt Street Baptist Church." 3/22/56. Montgomery, Ala. 1 p. APWW. 560322–027.

3/22/56 King, Martin Luther, Jr., Defendant. "Appeal Bond to Court of Appeals, *State of Alabama v. M. L. King, Jr.*" 3/22/56. Montgomery, Ala. (TFmS) 2 pp. CMCR-AMC: File 7399. 560322–004.

514 3/22/56 Holden, Anna. "Notes, Statements after decision, *State of Alabama v. M. L. King, Jr.*" 3/22/56. Montgomery, Ala. (TD) 1 p. PV-ARC-LNT. 560322–019.

3/22/56	Holden, Anna. "Notes, MIA mass meeting at Holt Street Baptist Church." 3/22/56. Montgomery, Ala. (TD) 7 pp. PV-ARC-LNT. 560322–020.
3/22/56	Holden, Anna. "Notes, *State of Alabama v. M. L. King, Jr.*" 3/19–3/22/56. Montgomery, Ala. (TD) 57 pp. PV-ARC-LNT. 560322–021.
3/22/56	King, Martin Luther, Jr. (MIA). "Letter to Charles C. Diggs, Jr." 3/22/56. Montgomery, Ala. (TLSr) 2 pp. (Includes enclosure.) CCDP-DHU: Box 43. 560322–023.
3/23/56	**King, Martin Luther, Jr. "Interview by Joe Azbell." [*3/23/56*]. [*Montgomery, Ala.*] (At) 2 min. (1 sound cassette: analog.) MMFR: Sync sound 48. 560323–015.**
3/23/56	**Cook, Samuel DuBois (Southern University). "Letter to Martin Luther King, Jr." 3/23/56. Baton Rouge, La. (TLS) 3 pp. MLKP-MBU: Box 91. 560323–000.**
3/23/56	**Gray, William H. (Herbert), Jr. (Bright Hope Baptist Church). "Letter to Martin Luther King, Jr." 3/23/56. Philadelphia, Pa. (THLS) 1 p. MLKP-MBU: Box 16. 560323–008.**
3/23/56	**Thomas, Norman. "Letter to Martin Luther King, Jr." 3/23/56. New York, N.Y. (TLS) 1 p. MLKP-MBU: Box 66. 560323–009.**
3/23/56	Alpha Phi Alpha Fraternity. "*Newsletter* 5, no. 4." 3/23/56. Chicago, Ill. (TD) 1 p. MLKP-MBU: Box 91. 560323–001.
3/23/56	Perry, Walter L. (British American Association of Coloured Brothers). "Letter to Martin Luther King, Jr." 3/23/56. Windsor, Ont., Canada. (THLS) 2 pp. MLKP-MBU: Box 91. 560323–003.
3/23/56	Sandberg, Edwin T. (Wartburg College). "Letter to Martin Luther King, Jr." 3/23/56. Waverly, Iowa. (TLS) 1 p. MLKP-MBU: Box 65. 560323–010.
3/25/56	[*Hilson, Ralph W.*] (MIA). "Montgomery Protest." 3/25/56. (THD) 5 pp. RWH. 560325–000.
3/26/56	Holden, Anna. "Notes, MIA mass meeting at Holt Street Baptist Church." 3/26/56. Montgomery, Ala. (TD) 7 pp. PV-ARC-LNT. 560326–007.
3/26/56	Collins, I. C. (Baptist Ministers Conference). "Letter to Martin Luther King, Jr." 3/26/56. Newark, N.J. (TLS) 2 pp. MLKP-MBU: Box 15. 560326–012.
3/26/56	Boddie, J. (James) Timothy (New Shiloh Baptist Church). "Letter to Martin Luther King, Jr." 3/26/56. Baltimore, Md. (TALS) 1 p. DABCC. 560326–014.
3/27/56	King, Martin Luther, Jr. (MIA). "Letter to J. F. Redmon." 3/27/56. [*Montgomery, Ala.*] (THLc) 1 p. MLKP-MBU: Box 64. 560327–005.
3/28/56	Banks, W. Lester (NAACP). "Letter to Martin Luther King, Jr." 3/28/56. Richmond, Va. (TAHLS) 1 p. MLKP-MBU: Box 62. 560328–004.
3/28/56	Kotelchuck, David (Students for Democratic Action). "Letter to Martin Luther King, Jr." 3/28/56. Washington, D.C. (TAHLS) 1 p. MLKP-MBU: Box 65. 560328–006.
3/28/56	Morgan, Gerald D. "Letter to Adam Clayton Powell." 3/28/56. (TLc) 3 pp. WCFO-KAbE. 560328–018.
3/29/56	**King, Martin Luther, Jr. "When Peace Becomes Obnoxious, Sermon delivered on 3/18/56 at Dexter Avenue Baptist Church." 3/29/56. Louisville, Ky. From: *Louisville Defender*, 29 March 1956. (PD) 1 p. 560329–000.**
3/29/56	MIA. "Program, MIA mass meeting at Hutchinson Street Baptist Church." 3/29/56. Montgomery, Ala. (TD) 1 p. HG-GAMK. 560329–002.
3/29/56	Black, Lucille (NAACP). "Letter to Martin Luther King, Jr." 3/29/56. New York, N.Y. (THLS) 1 p. MLKP-MBU: Box 62. 560329–003.
3/29/56	James, Arthur R. (United Baptist Convention of Delaware). "Letter to Martin Luther King, Jr." 3/29/56. Wilmington, Del. (THLS) 2 pp. MLKP-MBU: Box 15. 560329–005.
3/29/56	Harris, Arthaniel (Hunter's Chapel AME Zion Church). "Letter to Martin Luther King, Jr." 3/29/56. Tuscaloosa, Ala. (TLS) 1 p. DABCC. 560329–007.
3/30/56	Bunche, Ralph J. (NAACP Legal Defense and Education Fund). "Telegram to Martin Luther King, Jr." 3/30/56. New York, N.Y. (PWSr) 1 p. MLKP-MBU: Box 91. 560330–000.
3/30/56	Hatt, Ken (Methodist Youth Fellowship). "Letter to Martin Luther King, Jr." 3/30/56. Douglas, Ariz. (TALS) 1 p. MLKP-MBU: Box 60. 560330–006.
3/30/56	Cameron, Angus. (Cameron Associates, Inc.). "Letter to Martin Luther King, Jr." 3/30/56. New York, N.Y. (TLS) 1 p. (Contains enclosure 560330–012.) MLKP-MBU. 560330–011.
3/31/56	**"Quotable Quotes from Rev. King." 3/31/56. New York, N.Y. From: *New York Amsterdam News*, 31 March 1956. (PD) 1 p. 560331–013.**
4/56	**Weiner, Dan. "Photo of Martin Luther King, Jr., Coretta Scott King, and Yolanda Denise King on steps of Dexter Avenue Baptist Church." [*3/56–4/56*]. Montgomery, Ala. (Ph) 1 p. MAGPC. 560400–019.**

4/1/56 Wofford, Harris (Howard University School of Law). "Opinion Memorandum Assignment for the Howard University School of Law." 4/1/56. Washington, D.C. (TAD) 1 p. (Enclosure in 560425–008.) MLKP-MBU: Box 91. 560401–000.

4/1/56 Morris, Joseph C. "Montgomery on the March, a Symbol." 4/1/56. New York, N.Y. (PD) 4 pp. (Enclosure in 560427–007.) MLKP-MBU: Box 42. 560401–001.

4/2/56 Barbour, Worth Littlejohn. "Letter to Martin Luther King, Jr." 4/2/56. Minneapolis, Minn. (TAHLS) 1 p. MLKP-MBU: Box 14. 560402–001.

4/2/56 Gregg, Richard Bartlett. "Letter to Martin Luther King, Jr." 4/2/56. Jamaica, Vt. (ALS) 2 pp. MLKP-MBU: Box 17. 560402–004.

4/2/56 MIA. "Program, Mass meeting at Beulah Baptist Church." 4/2/56. Montgomery, Ala. (TD) 1 p. HJP-GAMK. 560402–000.

4/3/56 King, Martin Luther, Jr. "Letter to Frank L. Stanley." 4/3/56. [*Montgomery, Ala.*] (TLc) 1 p. DABCC. 560403–001.

4/3/56 King, Martin Luther, Jr. "Letter to Charles S. Morris II." 4/3/56. [*Montgomery, Ala.*] (TLc) 1 p. DABCC. 560403–003.

4/3/56 Smith, Lillian Eugenia. "Letter to Martin Luther King, Jr." 4/3/56. Neptune Beach, Fla. (TAHLS) 2 pp. MLKP-MBU: Box 65. 560403–005.

4/3/56 Thompson, Lafayette (First Baptist Church). "Letter to Martin Luther King, Jr." 4/3/56. Webster Groves, Mo. (THLS) 1 p. MLKP-MBU: Box 17. 560403–006.

4/3/56 Cober, Kenneth L. (American Baptist Convention). "Letter to Martin Luther King, Jr." 4/3/56. Philadelphia, Pa. (THLSr) 1 p. MLKP-MBU: Box 61. 560403–011.

4/3/56 King, Martin Luther, Jr. (MIA). "Letter to Loyce Furman Cargile." 4/3/56. [*Montgomery, Ala.*] (TLc) 1 p. MLKP-MBU: Box 15. 560403–015.

4/4/56 King, Martin Luther, Jr. (MIA). "Letter to Samuel D. (Dewitt) Proctor." 4/4/56. [*Montgomery, Ala.*] (TLc) 1 p. MLKP-MBU: Box 66. 560404–002.

4/7/56 Lowe, Richard A. (Lowe's Consolidated Enterprises). "Letter to Martin Luther King, Jr." 4/7/56. New York, N.Y. (ALS) 1 p. MLKP-MBU: Box 61. 560407–008.

4/9/56 King, Martin Luther, Jr. "Letter to J. Pius Barbour." 4/9/56. [*Montgomery, Ala.*] (TLc) 1 p. DABCC. 560409–001.

4/9/56 Gilmore, Edith. "Letter to Martin Luther King, Jr." 4/9/56. (THLS) 1 p. MLKP-MBU: Box 17. 560409–002.

4/9/56 McKinney, Samuel B. (Olney Street Baptist Church). "Letter to Martin Luther King, Jr." 4/9/56. Providence, R.I. (TLS) 1 p. MLKP-MBU: Box 63A. 560409–007.

4/9/56 Dixon, Richard H. (Trinity Baptist Church). "Letter to Martin Luther King, Jr." 4/9/56. Pontiac, Mich. (TLS) 1 p. MLKP-MBU: Box 66. 560409–008.

4/9/56 Wynn, Daniel W. (Tuskegee Institute). "Letter to Martin Luther King, Jr." 4/9/56. Tuskegee, Ala. (TLS) 1 p. DABCC. 560409–009.

4/10/56 Cober, Kenneth L. (American Baptist Convention). "Letter to Martin Luther King, Jr." 4/10/56. Philadelphia, Pa. (THLS) 2 pp. MLKP-MBU: Box 117. 560410–000.

4/10/56 King, Martin Luther, Jr. (Dexter Avenue Baptist Church). "Letter to Charles C. Diggs, Jr." 4/10/56. Montgomery, Ala. (THLc) 1 p. CCDP-DHU: Box 43. 560410–002.

4/10/56 Pan-Community Council. "Program, Annual forum." 4/10/56. Birmingham, Ala. (PHD) 12 pp. MLKP-MBU: Box 80. 560410–003.

4/10/56 Miller, William Robert (*Fellowship*). "Letter to Martin Luther King, Jr." 4/10/56. New York, N.Y. (TLS) 2 pp. MLKP-MBU: Box 16. 560410–005.

4/10/56 Whitaker, H. (Horace) Edward (New Hope Baptist Church). "Letter to Martin Luther King, Jr." 4/10/56. Niagara Falls, N.Y. (TLS) 2 pp. MLKP-MBU: Box 63. 560410–006.

4/10/56 Carey, Archibald James, Jr. "Letter to Martin Luther King, Jr." 4/10/56. Chicago, Ill. (TLS) 2 pp. MLKP-MBU: Box 15. 560410–009.

4/11/56 Proctor, Samuel D. (Dewitt) (Virginia Union University). "Letter to Martin Luther King, Jr." 4/11/56. Richmond, Va. (THLS) 1 p. MLKP-MBU: Box 66. 560411–003.

4/11/56 MIA. "Agenda, Executive board meeting." 4/11/56. (TD) 1 p. MLKP-MBU: Box 6. 560411–005.

4/12/56 Davis, James H. (United Transport Service Employees). "Letter to Martin Luther King, Jr." 4/12/56. Newark, N.J. (AHLS) 1 p. MLKP-MBU: Box 66A. 560412–004.

4/12/56 Wilkins, Roy (NAACP). "Letter to Martin Luther King, Jr." 4/12/56. New York, N.Y. (TLS) 1 p. MLKP-MBU: Box 62. 560412–003.

4/12/56   McMurray, Wayne D. (Asbury Park Press). "Letter to Martin Luther King, Jr."
           4/12/56. Asbury Park, N.J. (THLS) 1 p. (Marginal comment by King.) MLKP-
           MBU: Box 14. 560412–007.

**4/13/56 Smiley, Glenn E. (Fellowship of Reconciliation). "Letter to Martin Luther King,
           Jr." 4/13/56. New York, N.Y. (TAHLS) 2 pp. MLKP-MBU: Box 16. 560413–
           000.**

4/13/56   Muste, A. J. (Abraham Johannes) (Committee for Nonviolent Integration). "Let-
           ter to Benjamin Elijah Mays." 4/13/56. New York, N.Y. (TLS) 2 pp. (Contains
           enclosures 560413–002, –003.) BEMP-DHU. 560413–007.

4/13/56   Committee for Nonviolent Integration. "Nine Initial Projects." [4/13/56]. New
           York, N.Y. (TD) 3 pp. (Enclosure in 560413–007.) BEMP-DHU. 560413–002.

4/13/56   Committee for Nonviolent Integration. "Statement of purpose." [4/13/56].
           (TD) 2 pp. (Enclosure in 560413–007.) BEMP-DHU. 560413–003.

4/13/56   Glasco, R. J. (MIA). "Housing committee report." 4/13/56. Montgomery, Ala.
           (THDS) 2 pp. (Marginal comments by King.) MLKP-MBU: Box 6. 560413–006.

4/13/56   Ballou, Maude L. "Letter to Richard A. Lowe." 4/13/56. [Montgomery, Ala.] (TLc)
           1 p. MLKP-MBU: Box 61. 560413–008.

**4/14/56 Taylor, Jewelle. "Letter to Martin Luther King, Jr." 4/14/56. Washington, D.C.
           (TALS) 1 p. MLKP-MBU: Box 66. 560414–000.**

4/15/56   Durham, Barbee William (NAACP). "Press release, Martin Luther King, Jr.,
           speaks in Columbus." 4/15/56. Columbus, Ohio. (TD) 1 p. NAACPP-DLC:
           Group III–A273. 560415–001.

4/16/56   Horace, James L. (Baptist General State Convention of Illinois). "Letter to
           Martin Luther King, Jr." 4/16/56. (AHLS) 1 p. MLKP-MBU: Box 14. 560416–
           002.

4/16/56   Miller, William Robert (*Fellowship*). "Letter to Martin Luther King, Jr." 4/16/56.
           New York, N.Y. (TLS) 1 p. MLKP-MBU: Box 16. 560416–006.

4/16/56   MIA. "Program, Mass meeting at First Baptist Church." 4/16/56. Montgomery,
           Ala. (THD) 1 p. (Marginal comments by King.) MLKP-MBU: Box 30. 560416–
           007.

4/16/56   Peters, William. "Letter to Martin Luther King, Jr." 4/16/56. Pelham Manor, N.Y.
           (TLS) 1 p. MLKP-MBU: Box 64. 560416–008.

4/17/56   Barbour, Joseph P. "Letter to Martin Luther King, Jr." 4/17/56. Philadelphia, Pa.
           (ALS) 2 pp. MLKP-MBU: Box 91. 560417–000.

4/17/56   Austin, L. E. (*Carolina Times*). "Letter to Martin Luther King, Jr." 4/17/56. Dur-
           ham, N.C. (TLS) 1 p. MLKP-MBU: Box 15. 560417–006.

4/17/56   Abernathy, Ralph (MIA). "Letter to Archibald James Carey, Jr." 4/17/56. Mont-
           gomery, Ala. (TLS) 1 p. AJC-ICHi: Box 27. 560417–010.

4/17/56   King, Martin Luther, Jr. (MIA). "Letter to Donald G. Lothrop." 4/17/56. [Mont-
           gomery, Ala.] (TLc) 1 p. MLKP-MBU: Box 15. 560417–011.

4/18/56   King, Martin Luther, Jr. "Letter to Daniel W. Wynn." 4/18/56. [Montgomery,
           Ala.] (TLc) 1 p. DABCC. 560418–001.

4/18/56   Reynolds, Hobson R. (Improved Benevolent Protective Order of Elks of the
           World). "Letter to Martin Luther King, Jr." 4/18/56. Philadelphia, Pa. (THLS)
           2 pp. MLKP-MBU: Box 16. 560418–010.

**4/19/56 Randolph, A. (Asa) Philip. "Telegram to Martin Luther King, Jr." 4/19/56. New
           York, N.Y. (PHWSr) 1 p. (Marginal comment by King.) MLKP-MBU: Box 64A.
           560419–000.**

4/19/56   Diggs, Charles C., Jr. (U.S. Congress. House of Representatives). "Letter to Mar-
           tin Luther King, Jr." 4/19/56. Washington, D.C. (TLS) 1 p. MLKP-MBU:
           Box 16. 560419–003.

4/19/56   MIA. "Agenda, Meeting on constitution and trustees." [4/19/56]. Montgomery,
           Ala. (TD) 1 p. MLKP-MBU: Box 6. 560419–014.

**4/20/56 Diggs, Charles C., Jr. (U.S. Congress. House of Representatives). "Telegram to
           Martin Luther King, Jr." 4/20/56. Washington, D.C. (PWSr) 1 p. MLKP-MBU:
           Box 16. 560420–000.**

4/20/56   Offutt, Walter P., Jr. (Protestant Council). "Letter to Martin Luther King, Jr."
           4/20/56. New York, N.Y. (TLS) 1 p. MLKP-MBU: Box 64. 560420–008.

4/20/56   Newgent, William E. "Letter to Martin Luther King, Jr." 4/20/56. Washington,
           D.C. (TLS) 1 p. MLKP-MBU: Box 63. 560420–009.

4/21/56   Bross, John R. (Talladega College). "Letter to Martin Luther King, Jr." 4/21/56.
           Talladega, Ala. (THLS) 1 p. MLKP-MBU: Box 66. 560421–000.

4/21/56   Mays, Benjamin Elijah (Morehouse College). "Letter to Martin Luther King, Jr."
           4/21/56. Atlanta, Ga. (TLS) 1 p. MLKP-MBU: Box 62. 560421–001.

4/23/56 **Fisher, Dorothy Canfield. "Letter to Martin Luther King, Jr." 4/23/56. Arlington, Vt. (TAHLS) 2 pp. MLKP-MBU: Box 17. 560423–001.**

4/23/56 **Coleman, James P. (Mississippi Governor). "Telegram to Martin Luther King, Jr." [*4/23/56*]. Jackson, Miss. (PWSr) 1 p. MLKP-MBU: Box 15. 560423–008.**

4/23/56 Randolph, A. (Asa) Philip (Citywide Committee to Support Montgomery Bus Boycott). "Telegram to Martin Luther King, Jr." 4/23/56. New York, N.Y. (PWSr) 2 pp. MLKP-MBU: Box 64A. 560423–000.

4/23/56 MIA. "Program, Mass meeting at Dexter Avenue Baptist Church." 4/23/56. Montgomery, Ala. (THD) 2 pp. MLKP-MBU: Box 30. 560423–005.

4/23/56 Whitaker, H. (Horace) Edward (New Hope Baptist Church). "Letter to Martin Luther King, Jr." 4/23/56. Niagara Falls, N.Y. (TLS) 1 p. MLKP-MBU: Box 63. 560423–006.

4/24/56 **King, Martin Luther, Jr. (MIA). "Telegram to James P. Coleman." [*4/24/56*]. Montgomery, Ala. (THWc) 2 pp. MLKP-MBU: Box 15. 560424–020.**

4/24/56 **King, Martin Luther, Jr. (MIA). "Letter to Benjamin Elijah Mays." 4/24/56. [*Montgomery, Ala.*] (TLc) 1 p. MLKP-MBU: Box 62. 560424–013.**

4/24/56 **King, Martin Luther, Jr. (MIA). "Letter to Wayne D. McMurray." 4/24/56. [*Montgomery, Ala.*] (TLc) 1 p. MLKP-MBU: Box 14. 560424–015.**

4/24/56 **Associated Press. "Photo of Martin Luther King, Jr., at executive board meeting." 4/24/56. Montgomery, Ala. (Ph) 1 p. APWW. 560424–021.**

4/24/56 Guy, Eunice (Wiley College). "Letter to Martin Luther King, Jr." 4/24/56. Marshall, Tex. (TLS) 1 p. MLKP-MBU: Box 91. 560424–000.

4/24/56 King, Martin Luther, Jr. (MIA). "Letter to John R. Bross." 4/24/56. [*Montgomery, Ala.*] (THLc) 1 p. MLKP-MBU: Box 66. 560424–012.

4/24/56 King, Martin Luther, Jr. "Bus company's decision to end segregation on Montgomery City Lines." [*4/24/56*]. [*Montgomery, Ala.*] (At) 1 min. (1 sound cassette: analog.) MMFR: Sync sound 50. 560424–022.

4/25/56 **King, Martin Luther, Jr. (MIA). "Letter to William Peters." 4/25/56. [*Montgomery, Ala.*] (THLc) 2 pp. MLKP-MBU: Box 64. 560425–007.**

4/25/56 **Wofford, Harris. "Letter to Martin Luther King, Jr., Ralph Abernathy, and E. D. Nixon." 4/25/56. Alexandria, Va. (TAHLS) 1 p. (Contains enclosure 560401–000.) MLKP-MBU: Box 67. 560425–008.**

4/25/56 **Prattis, Percival Leroy (*Pittsburgh Courier*). "Letter to Martin Luther King, Jr." 4/25/56. Pittsburgh, Pa. (TLS) 1 p. MLKP-MBU: Box 64. 560425–009.**

4/25/56 King, Martin Luther, Jr. "Letter to Kenneth L. Cober." 4/25/56. [*Montgomery, Ala.*] (TLc) 1 p. DABCC. 560425–001.

4/25/56 King, Martin Luther, Jr. (MIA). "Letter to James H. Davis." 4/25/56. [*Montgomery, Ala.*] (THLc) 1 p. MLKP-MBU: Box 66. 560425–003.

4/25/56 Weston, Ross Allen (Unitarian Fellowship for Social Justice). "Letter to Martin Luther King, Jr." 4/25/56. (TLcS) 1 p. MLKP-MBU. 560425–004.

4/25/56 Griffin, Joseph L. (Macedonia Baptist Church). "Letter to Martin Luther King, Jr." 4/25/56. Denver, Colo. (THLS) 1 p. MLKP-MBU: Box 61. 560425–006.

4/25/56 McKinney, Samuel B. (Olney Street Baptist Church). "Letter to Martin Luther King, Jr." 4/25/56. Providence, R.I. (ALS) 1 p. MLKP-MBU: Box 63A. 560425–010.

4/26/56 **Brayboy, Jeanne Martin. "Letter to Martin Luther King, Jr." 4/26/56. Charlotte, N.C. (ALS) 3 pp. (Envelope included.) MLKP-MBU: Box 91. 560426–001.**

4/26/56 **King, Martin Luther, Jr. (MIA). "Letter to William E. Newgent." 4/26/56. [*Montgomery, Ala.*] (TLc) 1 p. MLKP-MBU: Box 63A. 560426–010.**

4/26/56 **Associated Press. "Photo of Martin Luther King, Jr., at MIA mass meeting at Day Street Baptist Church." 4/26/56. Montgomery, Ala. (Ph) 1 p. APWW. 560426–014.**

4/26/56 **King, Martin Luther, Jr. (MIA). "Address to mass meeting at Day Street Baptist Church." [*4/26/56*]. [*Montgomery, Ala.*] (Vt) 11 min. (1 videocassette: analog.) CBSNA-CBSN. 560426–016.**

4/26/56 Jones, E. Theodore (Virginia Union University). "Letter to Martin Luther King, Jr." 4/26/56. Richmond, Va. (TLS) 1 p. MLKP-MBU: Box 91. 560426–000.

4/26/56 Cooper, Floyd L. (NAACP). "Letter to Martin Luther King, Jr." 4/26/56. Portsmouth, Va. (THLS) 1 p. MLKP-MBU: Box 62. 560426–006.

4/26/56 MIA. "Agenda, Executive board meeting." 4/26/56. (TD) 1 p. MLKP-MBU: Box 30. 560426–007.

4/26/56 King, Martin Luther, Jr. (MIA). "Letter to Charles C. Diggs, Jr." 4/26/56. Montgomery, Ala. (TLS) 2 pp. (Includes enclosure.) CCDP-DHU: Box 43. 560426–008.

4/26/56 MIA. "Program, Mass meeting at Day Street Baptist Church." 4/26/56. Montgomery, Ala. (TD) 1 p. MLKP-MBU: Box 30. 560426–009.

4/27/56 Clark, Caesar (Good Street Baptist Church). "Letter to Martin Luther King, Jr." 4/27/56. Dallas, Tex. (TLS) 1 p. MLKP-MBU: Box 91. 560427–000.

4/27/56 King, Martin Luther, Jr. (MIA). "Letter to Norman Thomas." 4/27/56. [*Montgomery, Ala.*] (TLc) 1 p. MLKP-MBU: Box 66. 560427–005.

4/27/56 Deaderick, Janie (City Federation Colored Women's Club). "Telegram to Martin Luther King, Jr." 4/27/56. Nashville, Tenn. (PWSr) 1 p. MLKP-MBU: Box 62. 560427–006.

4/27/56 Morris, Joseph C. "Letter to Martin Luther King, Jr." 4/27/56. New York, N.Y. (TLS) 1 p. (Contains enclosure 560401–001.) MLKP-MBU: Box 62. 560427–007.

4/27/56 Maxwell, O. Clay (Mount Olive Baptist Church). "Letter to Martin Luther King, Jr." 4/27/56. New York, N.Y. (TLS) 2 pp. MLKP-MBU: Box 31A. 560427–010.

4/28/56 King, Martin Luther, Jr. "Letter to Samuel B. McKinney." 4/28/56. [*Montgomery, Ala.*] (TLc) 1 p. MLKP-MBU: Box 63A. 560428–005.

4/29/56 England, J. Martin. "Letter to Martin Luther King, Jr." 4/29/56. Somerville, N.J. (THLS) 1 p. MLKP-MBU: Box 16. 560429–001.

4/29/56 Foster, Hazel E. "Letter to Martin Luther King, Jr." 4/29/56. Cleveland, Ohio. (TLS) 1 p. (Enclosure in 560503–004.) MLKP-MBU: Box 31A. 560429–003.

4/29/56 Stephens, Fred E. (Ward African Methodist Episcopal Church). "Letter to Martin Luther King, Jr." 4/29/56. Los Angeles, Calif. (THLS) 1 p. MLKP-MBU: Box 67. 560429–002.

4/30/56 Mason, Vivian C. (National Council of Negro Women). "Letter to Martin Luther King, Jr." 4/30/56. Washington, D.C. (THLS) 1 p. MLKP-MBU: Box 63. 560430–012.

4/30/56 King, Martin Luther, Jr. "Letter to H. (Horace) Edward Whitaker." 4/30/56. [*Montgomery, Ala.*] (TLc) 1 p. MLKP-MBU: Box 63A. 560430–011.

4/30/56 King, Martin Luther, Jr. "Letter to Jesse Jai McNeil." 4/30/56. [*Montgomery, Ala.*] (TLc) 1 p. DABCC. 560430–001.

4/30/56 King, Martin Luther, Jr. (Dexter Avenue Baptist Church). "Letter to Albert F. Harkins." 4/30/56. [*Montgomery, Ala.*] (TLc) 1 p. DABCC. 560430–002.

4/30/56 King, Martin Luther, Jr. (Dexter Avenue Baptist Church). "Letter to A. L. Bratcher." 4/30/56. [*Montgomery, Ala.*] (TLc) 1 p. DABCC. 560430–003.

4/30/56 King, Martin Luther, Jr. (Dexter Avenue Baptist Church). "Letter to Caesar Clark." 4/30/56. [*Montgomery, Ala.*] (TLc) 1 p. DABCC. 560430–004.

4/30/56 Roosevelt, Eleanor. "Letter to Angus Cameron." 4/30/56. New York, N.Y. (TLS) 1 p. (Enclosure in 560521–000.) MLKP-MBU: Box 91. 560430–005.

4/30/56 MIA. "Program, Mass meeting at Holt Street Baptist Church." 4/30/56. Montgomery, Ala. (THD) 2 pp. HG-GAMK. 560430–006.

4/30/56 King, Martin Luther, Jr. (MIA). "Letter to Lucille Black." 4/30/56. Montgomery, Ala. (THLS) 1 p. NAACPP-DLC: Group III–A273. 560430–007.

4/30/56 King, Martin Luther, Jr. (MIA). "Letter to Joseph C. Morris." 4/30/56. [*Montgomery, Ala.*] (TLc) 1 p. MLKP-MBU: Box 62. 560430–009.

4/30/56 Rooks, Shelby (St. James Presbyterian Church). "Letter to Martin Luther King, Jr." 4/30/56. New York, N.Y. (TALS) 1 p. MLKP-MBU: Box 65. 560430–013.

4/56 King, Martin Luther, Jr. "Our Struggle." 4/56. New York, N.Y. From: *Liberation* 1 (April 1956): 3–6. (PD) 4 pp. 560400–001.

5/56 [*King, Martin Luther, Jr.*] "Letter to Jewelle Taylor." [*5/56*]. [*Montgomery, Ala.*] (TLc) 1 p. MLKP-MBU: Box 66. 560500–016.

5/56 Barbour, J. Pius (*National Baptist Voice*). "Religion in Montgomery, Alabama." 5/56. Philadelphia, Pa. From: *National Baptist Voice*, May 1956. (PD) 3 pp. DJG. 560500–002.

5/56 [*King, Martin Luther, Jr.*] "Draft, Walk for Freedom." [*3/56–5/56*]. [*Montgomery, Ala.*] (TDd) 3 pp. MLKP-MBU: Box 19. 560500–011.

5/56 King, Martin Luther, Jr. "Statement on the new Negro." [*4/56–5/56*]. [*Montgomery, Ala.*] (At) 4 min. (1 sound cassette: analog.) MMFR: Sync sound 1. 560500–014.

5/56 National Council of Negro Women. "Press release, Leaders conference held 26 May." 5/56. Washington, D.C. (TDf) 3 pp. NCNWR-DABW. 560500–017.

5/1/56 Nance, Earl E. (Greater Mt. Carmel Baptist Church). "Letter to Martin Luther King, Jr." 5/1/56. St. Louis, Mo. (TLS) 1 p. MLKP-MBU: Box 91. 560501–000.

5/1/56 King, Martin Luther, Jr. (MIA). "Letter to Roy Wilkins." 5/1/56. Montgomery, Ala. (TLSr) 1 p. NAACPP-DLC: Group III–A177. 560501–004.

5/1/56 King, Martin Luther, Jr. (MIA). "Letter to Richard Bartlett Gregg." 5/1/56. [*Montgomery, Ala.*] (TLc) 1 p. MLKP-MBU: Box 17. 560501–008.

5/1/56   **King, Martin Luther, Jr. (MIA). "Letter to Percival Leroy Prattis." 5/1/56. Montgomery, Ala. (TLSr) 1 p. PLPC-DHU. 560501–010.**

5/1/56   King, Martin Luther, Jr. (MIA). "Letter to Robert Cooley." 5/1/56. [*Montgomery, Ala.*] (TLc) 1 p. MLKP-MBU: Box 62. 560501–005.

5/1/56   McLaurin, Benjamin F. (Committee to Stage Madison Square Garden Civil Rights Rally). "Letter to Martin Luther King, Jr." 5/1/56. New York, N.Y. (TLS) 1 p. MLKP-MBU: Box 62. 560501–007.

5/1/56   King, Martin Luther, Jr. (MIA). "Letter to David Kotelchuck." 5/1/56. [*Montgomery, Ala.*] (TLc) 1 p. MLKP-MBU: Box 65. 560501–009.

5/2/56   **Bradford, Sadie (Sadie Beauty Shop). "Letter to Martin Luther King, Jr." 5/2/56. Gastonia, N.C. (ALS) 2 pp. MLKP-MBU: Box 16. 560502–004.**

5/2/56   King, Martin Luther, Jr. "The New Negro." [*5/2/56?*]. (At) 11 min. (1 sound cassette: analog.) MMFR: Sync sound 63. 560502–000.

5/2/56   Glass, Jesse. "Letter to Martin Luther King, Jr." 5/2/56. Chicago, Ill. (TALS) 1 p. MLKP-MBU: Box 17. 560502–001.

5/2/56   Morsell, John A. (NAACP). "Letter to Martin Luther King, Jr." 5/2/56. New York, N.Y. (TLS) 1 p. MLKP-MBU: Box 62. 560502–003.

5/2/56   Cayce, James B. (Ebenezer Baptist Church). "Letter to Martin Luther King, Jr." 5/2/56. Pittsburgh, Pa. (THLS) 1 p. MLKP-MBU: Box 16. 560502–005.

5/2/56   Rucker, James D. (National Baptist Sunday School and Baptist Training Union Congress). "Letter to Martin Luther King, Jr." 5/2/56. Rock Hill, S.C. (THLS) 1 p. MLKP-MBU: Box 14A. 560502–007.

5/3/56   King, Martin Luther, Jr. (MIA). "Letter to J. Evehard Carey." 5/3/56. Montgomery, Ala. (THL) 1 p. MLKJrP-GAMK. 560503–003.

5/3/56   Mays, Benjamin Elijah (Morehouse College). "Letter to Martin Luther King, Jr." 5/3/56. Atlanta, Ga. (TLS) 1 p. (Contains enclosure 560429–003.) MLKP-MBU: Box 31A. 560503–004.

5/3/56   Thomas, Lillie M. "Letter to H. (Horace) Edward Whitaker." 5/3/56. (TLc) 1 p. DABCC. 560503–006.

5/3/56   Stone, Candace. "Report on Community Prayer Service on Behalf of the Nonviolent Resistance Movement in Montgomery, Alabama." 5/3/56. Anderson, Ind. (TD) 12 pp. HG-GAMK. 560503–001.

5/4/56   Wilkins, Roy (NAACP). "Letter to Martin Luther King, Jr." 5/4/56. New York, N.Y. (THLS) 1 p. MLKP-MBU: Box 62. 560504–004.

5/4/56   King, Martin Luther, Jr. "Legitimacy of the struggle in Montgomery." [*5/4/56*]. [*Montgomery, Ala.*] (At) 2 min. (1 sound cassette: analog.) MMFR: Sync sound 48. 560504–011.

5/5/56   Morris, Joseph C. "Letter to Martin Luther King, Jr." 5/5/56. New York, N.Y. (TLS) 1 p. MLKP-MBU: Box 62. 560505–000.

5/6/56   **King, Martin Luther, Jr. (MIA). "Letter to Benjamin F. McLaurin." 5/6/56. [*Montgomery, Ala.*] (TLc) 1 p. MLKP-MBU: Box 62. 560506–001.**

5/7/56   **Randolph, A. (Asa) Philip (City-wide Committee to Stage Madison Square Garden Civil Rights Rally). "Letter to Martin Luther King, Jr." 5/7/56. New York, N.Y. (THLS) 2 pp. MLKP-MBU: Box 62. 560507–007.**

5/7/56   King, Martin Luther, Jr. (MIA). "Letter to Glenn E. Smiley." 5/7/56. [*Montgomery, Ala.*] (TLc) 1 p. MLKP-MBU: Box 17. 560507–000.

5/7/56   King, Martin Luther, Jr. (MIA). "Letter to Roy Wilkins." 5/7/56. Montgomery, Ala. (THLS) 1 p. NAACPP-DLC: Group III–A273. 560507–001.

5/7/56   Lawrence, George (Friendship Baptist Church). "Letter to Martin Luther King, Jr." 5/7/56. New York, N.Y. (THLS) 1 p. MLKP-MBU: Box 17. 560507–004.

5/7/56   King, Martin Luther, Jr. (MIA). "Letter to Anna C. Frank." 5/7/56. [*Montgomery, Ala.*] (TLc) 1 p. MLKP-MBU: Box 15. 560507–008.

5/7/56   Ballou, Maude L. "Letter to Vivian C. Mason." 5/7/56. [*Montgomery, Ala.*] (TLc) 1 p. MLKP-MBU: Box 63. 560507–012.

5/7/56   Wagner, Robert F. (New York City Mayor). "Proclamation for Day of Prayer and Thanksgiving." 5/7/56. New York, N.Y. (TD) 1 p. MLKP-MBU: Box 82. 560507–015.

5/7/56   King, Martin Luther, Jr. (MIA). "Letter to W. A. Gross." 5/7/56. [*Montgomery, Ala.*] (TLc) 1 p. MLKP-MBU: Box 17. 560507–016.

5/7/56   King, Martin Luther, Jr. "Letter to J. (James) Timothy Boddie." 5/7/56. [*Montgomery, Ala.*] (TLc) 1 p. DABCC. 560507–017.

5/7/56   King, Martin Luther, Jr. "Letter to the Young Men's Christian Association (YMCA)." 5/7/56. [*Montgomery, Ala.*] (TLc) 1 p. DABCC. 560507–018.

   5/8/56   **King, Martin Luther, Jr. (MIA). "Letter to William Robert Miller." 5/8/56. Montgomery, Ala. (THLS) 1 p. WRMP-GAMK: Box 1. 560508–006.**

5/8/56	King, Martin Luther, Jr. (MIA). "Letter to Jesse Hill, Jr." 5/8/56. [*Montgomery, Ala.*] (TLc) 1 p. MLKP-MBU: Box 14. 560508–014.
5/8/56	King, Martin Luther, Jr. (MIA). "Letter to Shelby Rooks." 5/8/56. [*Montgomery, Ala.*] (TLc) 1 p. MLKP-MBU: Box 65. 560508–016.
5/8/56	Diggs, Charles C., Sr. (Panorama of Progress). "Letter to Martin Luther King, Jr." 5/8/56. Detroit, Mich. (THLS) 2 pp. MLKP-MBU: Box 16. 560508–001.
5/8/56	King, Martin Luther, Jr. (MIA). "Letter to Jesse Glass." 5/8/56. [*Montgomery, Ala.*] (TLc) 1 p. MLKP-MBU: Box 17. 560508–002.
5/8/56	Wilkins, Roy (NAACP). "Letter to Martin Luther King, Jr." 5/8/56. New York, N.Y. (TLS) 1 p. MLKP-MBU: Box 62. 560508–004.
5/8/56	King, Martin Luther, Jr. (MIA). "Letter to L. E. Austin." 5/8/56. [*Montgomery, Ala.*] (TLc) 1 p. MLKP-MBU: Box 15. 560508–010.
5/8/56	King, Martin Luther, Jr. (MIA). "Letter to Walter P. Offutt, Jr." 5/8/56. [*Montgomery, Ala.*] (TLc) 1 p. MLKP-MBU: Box 64. 560508–013.
5/9/56	Dillard, Ernest C. (Committee to Aid the Montgomery, Alabama, Bus Protest). "Telegram to Martin Luther King, Jr." 5/9/56. Detroit, Mich. (PWSr) 2 pp. MLKP-MBU: Box 89. 560509–000.
5/9/56	King, Martin Luther, Jr. (MIA). "Letter to O. Clay Maxwell." 5/9/56. [*Montgomery, Ala.*] (TLc) 1 p. MLKP-MBU: Box 61. 560509–001.
5/9/56	Huger, James E. (Alpha Phi Alpha Fraternity). "Letter to Martin Luther King, Jr." 5/9/56. Chicago, Ill. (AHLS) 1 p. MLKP-MBU: Box 14. 560509–007.
5/9/56	Rustin, Bayard (War Resisters League). "Letter to Martin Luther King, Jr." 5/9/56. New York, N.Y. (THLS) 1 p. MLKP-MBU: Box 67. 560509–008.
5/10/56	King, Martin Luther, Jr. (MIA). "Letter to A. (Asa) Philip Randolph." 5/10/56. [*Montgomery, Ala.*] (TLc) 1 p. MLKP-MBU: Box 62. 560510–004.
5/10/56	King, Martin Luther, Jr. (MIA). "Letter to Harris Wofford." 5/10/56. [*Montgomery, Ala.*] (TLc) 1 p. MLKP-MBU: Box 67. 560510–007.
5/10/56	King, Martin Luther, Jr. (MIA). "Letter to Ross Allen Weston." 5/10/56. Montgomery, Ala. (TLS) 1 p. UUAR-MH-AH. 560510–000.
5/10/56	Dexter Avenue Baptist Church Finance Committee. "Financial Statement for November Through April." 5/10/56. Montgomery, Ala. (THD) 13 pp. (Marginal comments by King.) CKFC. 560510–001.
5/10/56	King, Martin Luther, Jr. "Telegram to Ross Allen Weston." [*5/10/56*]. Montgomery, Ala. (TWc) 1 p. MLKP-MBU: Box 66. 560510–011.
5/11/56	de la Brunelière, Henri Varin (Bishop of Martinique). "Letter to Martin Luther King, Jr." 5/11/56. Fort-de-France, Martinique. (TAHLS) 1 p. (Enclosure in 560522–009.) MLKP-MBU: Box 16. 560511–000.
5/11/56	Gilman, Howard B. (Universalist Church). "Letter to Martin Luther King, Jr." 5/11/56. East Syracuse, N.Y. (THLS) 1 p. MLKP-MBU: Box 66. 560511–002.
5/11/56	Henderson, J. Raymond (Second Baptist Church and the Henderson Community Center). "Letter to Martin Luther King, Jr." 5/11/56. Los Angeles, Calif. (TLS) 1 p. MLKP-MBU: Box 65. 560511–003.
5/11/56	Gayle, W. (William) A., Defendant. "Transcript of Record and Proceedings, *Aurelia S. Browder v. William A. Gayle.*" 5/11/56. Montgomery, Ala. (THDS) 71 pp. GEpFAR. 560511–005.
5/12/56	Smiley, Glenn E. "Minutes, Atlanta conference." 5/12/56. Atlanta, Ga. (TAD) 2 pp. FORP-PSC-P. 560512–000.
5/13/56	Poston, Ted. "The Boycott and the 'New Dawn.'" 5/13/56. New York, N.Y. From: *New York Post,* 13 May 1956. (PD) 1 p. 560513–000.
5/14/56	Muste, A. J. (Abraham Johannes). "The Magnolia Curtain?" 5/14/56. (TD) 2 pp. FORP-PSC-P. 560514–000.
5/14/56	George, B. T. "Letter to Martin Luther King, Jr." 5/14/56. Shreveport, La. (TLS) 1 p. MLKP-MBU: Box 17. 560514–001.
5/14/56	King, Martin Luther, Jr. (MIA). "Letter to George Lawrence." 5/14/56. [*Montgomery, Ala.*] (TLc) 1 p. MLKP-MBU: Box 17. 560514–003.
5/14/56	Berry, Carrie, and Velberta C. Chestnut (Alabama Association of Modern Beauticians). "Letter to Martin Luther King, Jr." 5/14/56. Selma, Ala. (THLS) 1 p. MLKP-MBU: Box 65. 560514–008.
5/14/56	Wilkins, Roy (NAACP). "Memo to files." 5/14/56. (TL) 1 p. NAACPP-DLC: Group III–A40. 560514–009.
5/14/56	Jones, Major J. (Fisk University). "Letter to Martin Luther King, Jr." 5/14/56. Nashville, Tenn. (TLS) 1 p. DABCC. 560514–010.
5/15/56	Banks, A. (Allen) A. (Second Baptist Church). "Letter to Martin Luther King, Jr." 5/15/56. Detroit, Mich. (TLS) 1 p. MLKP-MBU: Box 65. 560515–003.

5/16/56   King, Martin Luther, Jr. (MIA). "Letter to Roy Wilkins." 5/16/56. Montgomery, Ala. (THLSr) 1 p. NAACPP-DLC: Group III–A177. 560516–004.

5/16/56   King, Martin Luther, Jr. (MIA). "Letter to J. Raymond Henderson." 5/16/56. [*Montgomery, Ala.*] (TLc) 1 p. MLKP-MBU: Box 65. 560516–012.

5/16/56   Ballou, Maude L. (Dexter Avenue Baptist Church). "Letter to Joseph L. Griffin." 5/16/56. [*Montgomery, Ala.*] (TALc) 1 p. MLKP-MBU: Box 61. 560516–013.

5/16/56   King, Martin Luther, Jr. (MIA). "Letter to Velberta C. Chestnut." 5/16/56. [*Montgomery, Ala.*] (TLc) 1 p. MLKP-MBU: Box 65. 560516–017.

5/17/56   Johnson, Charles S. (Fisk University). "Letter to Martin Luther King, Jr." 5/17/56. Nashville, Tenn. (TLS) 1 p. MLKP-MBU: Box 17. 560517–006.

5/17/56   Greater New York Committee on a National Day of Prayer and Thanksgiving. "Announcement, Speech by Martin Luther King, Jr., at Service of Prayer and Thanksgiving at Cathedral of St. John the Divine." 5/17/56. New York, N.Y. (PD) 1 p. MLKP-MBU: Box 80. 560517–010.

5/17/56   King, Martin Luther, Jr. "The Death of Evil upon the Seashore, Sermon at the Service of Prayer and Thanksgiving at Cathedral of St. John the Divine." 5/17/56. New York, N.Y. (PD) 5 pp. MLKP-MBU: Box 10. 560517–001.

5/17/56   King, Martin Luther, Jr. "A Realistic Look at Race Relations, Speech at the Second Annual Dinner of the NAACP Legal Defense and Educational Fund." 5/17/56. New York, N.Y. (TAHDf) 7 pp. MLKJrP-GAMK: Box 107. 560517–000.

5/17/56   King, Martin Luther, Jr. "A Realistic Look at the Question of Progress in the Area of Race Relations, Speech at the Second Annual Dinner of the NAACP Legal Defense and Educational Fund." 5/17/56. New York, N.Y. (TD) 9 pp. MLKP-MBU: Box 5. 560517–003.

5/17/56   Cathedral of St. John the Divine. "Program, Service of Prayer and Thanksgiving." 5/17/56. New York, N.Y. (PHD) 4 pp. MLKP-MBU: Box 80. 560517–011.

5/17/56   Harlem Round Table Association. "Invitation, Presentation to Martin Luther King, Jr." 5/17/56. New York, N.Y. (PD) 1 p. MLKP-MBU: Box 21. 560517–016.

5/18/56   Miller, William Robert (*Fellowship*). "Letter to Martin Luther King, Jr." 5/18/56. New York, N.Y. (THLS) 1 p. MLKP-MBU: Box 61. 560518–006.

5/18/56   [*Lomax, Almena*]. "Mother's Day in Montgomery: Boycott Leader Serves His Congregation Toynbee, Langston Hughes, Emerson, and Jesus Christ and Is Received in Complete Consanguinity." 5/18/56. Los Angeles, Calif. From: *Los Angeles Tribune*, 18 May 1956. (PD) 1 p. 560518–009.

5/18/56   Reynolds, Hobson R. (Improved Benevolent Protective Order of Elks of the World). "Letter to Martin Luther King, Jr." 5/18/56. Philadelphia, Pa. (TLS) 1 p. MLKP-MBU: Box 16. 560518–002.

5/18/56   Lewis, Rufus A. (MIA). "Letter to MIA." 5/18/56. Montgomery, Ala. (TLS) 1 p. MLKP-MBU: Box 61. 560518–004.

5/20/56   Gregg, Richard Bartlett. "Letter to Martin Luther King, Jr." 5/20/56. Chester, N.Y. (TAHLS) 2 pp. MLKP-MBU: Box 17. 560520–002.

5/21/56   Cameron, Angus. "Letter to Martin Luther King, Jr." 5/21/56. New York, N.Y. (TLSr) 1 p. (Contains enclosures 560000–137, 560430–005.) MLKP-MBU: Box 91. 560521–000.

5/21/56   King, Martin Luther, Jr. (MIA). "Letter to Charles S. Johnson." 5/21/56. [*Montgomery, Ala.*] (TLc) 1 p. MLKP-MBU: Box 17. 560521–002.

5/22/56   King, Martin Luther, Jr. (MIA). "Letter to James E. Huger." 5/22/56. [*Montgomery, Ala.*] (TLc) 1 p. MLKP-MBU: Box 14. 560522–005.

5/22/56   Bunche, Ralph J. (NAACP Legal Defense and Educational Fund). "Letter to Martin Luther King, Jr." 5/22/56. New York, N.Y. (TLS) 1 p. MLKP-MBU: Box 63. 560522–000.

5/22/56   Mabrey, C. G. (Flo Enterprises). "Letter to Martin Luther King, Jr." 5/22/56. Greensboro, N.C. (TLSr) 1 p. MLKP-MBU: Box 62. 560522–003.

5/22/56   Martin, E. M. (Atlanta Life Insurance Company). "Letter to Martin Luther King, Jr." 5/22/56. Atlanta, Ga. (TLS) 1 p. (Contains enclosure 560522–011.) MLKP-MBU: Box 62. 560522–004.

5/22/56   Martin, E. M. (Atlanta Life Insurance Company). "Letter to Martin Luther King, Sr." 5/22/56. (TLc) 1 p. (Enclosure in 560522–004.) MLKP-MBU: Box 62. 560522–011.

5/22/56   Henderson, J. Raymond (Second Baptist Church and the Henderson Community Center). "Letter to Martin Luther King, Jr." 5/22/56. Los Angeles, Calif. (TLS) 1 p. MLKP-MBU: Box 65. 560522–006.

5/22/56   Laws, Clarence A. (NAACP). "Letter to Martin Luther King, Jr." 5/22/56. New Orleans, La. (TLS) 2 pp. (Contains enclosure 560511–000.) MLKP-MBU: Box 61. 560522–009.

5/22/56 Morris, T. (Dexter Avenue Baptist Church). "Scholarship committee report." 5/22/56. Montgomery, Ala. (TD) 1 p. MLKP-MBU: Box 77. 560522–010.

5/23/56 **King, Martin Luther, Jr. (MIA). "Letter to Hobson R. Reynolds." 5/23/56. [*Montgomery, Ala.*] (TLc) 1 p. MLKP-MBU: Box 16. 560523–003.**

5/23/56 King, Martin Luther, Jr. (MIA). "Letter to Charles C. Diggs, Sr." 5/23/56. [*Montgomery, Ala.*] (TLc) 1 p. MLKP-MBU: Box 16. 560523–000.

5/23/56 King, Martin Luther, Jr. (MIA). "Letter to Fred E. Stephens." 5/23/56. [*Montgomery, Ala.*] (TLc) 1 p. MLKP-MBU: Box 67. 560523–005.

5/24/56 **King, Martin Luther, Jr. (MIA). "Recommendations to executive board." 5/24/56. [*Montgomery, Ala.*] (TD) 2 pp. HG-GAMK. 560524–002.**

5/24/56 **King, Martin Luther, Jr. (MIA). "Letter to Lillian Eugenia Smith." 5/24/56. Montgomery, Ala. (TLS) 2 pp. LSP-GU: Box 65. 560524–005.**

5/24/56 **Horton, Myles (Highlander Folk School). "Letter to Martin Luther King, Jr." 5/24/56. Monteagle, Tenn. (THLS) 1 p. MLKP-MBU: Box 14A. 560524–011.**

5/24/56 Smiley, C. T. (Dexter Avenue Baptist Church). "Letter to Martin Luther King, Jr." 5/24/56. Montgomery, Ala. (TLc) 1 p. MLKP-MBU: Box 77. 560524–003.

5/24/56 King, Martin Luther, Jr. (MIA). "Letter to Howard B. Gilman." 5/24/56. [*Montgomery, Ala.*] (TLc) 1 p. MLKP-MBU: Box 66. 560524–009.

5/24/56 MIA. "List of executive board members." 5/24/56. Montgomery, Ala. (THD) 1 p. (Marginal comments by King.) MLKP-MBU: Box 6. 560524–012.

5/24/56 City-wide Committee to Stage Madison Square Garden Civil Rights Rally. "Announcement, Salute and Support the Heroes of the South." 5/24/56. New York, N.Y. (PD) 1 p. NAACPP-DLC: Group III–A177. 560524–014.

5/24/56 Thomas, Cecil A. (Young Men's Christian Association [YMCA]). "Letter to Martin Luther King, Jr., and Coretta Scott King." 5/24/56. Berkeley, Calif. (TALS) 2 pp. MLKP-MBU: Box 67. 560524–015.

5/25/56 King, Martin Luther, Jr. (MIA). "Letter to Dorothy Canfield Fisher." 5/25/56. [*Montgomery, Ala.*] (TLc) 1 p. MLKP-MBU: Box 17. 560525–000.

5/28/56 Fisk University. "Program, Eighty-second Annual Commencement." 5/26/56–5/28/56. Nashville, Tenn. (PHD) 18 pp. (Marginal comments by King.) MLKP-MBU: Box 80. 560528–000.

5/29/56 **King, Martin Luther, Sr. (Ebenezer Baptist Church). "Letter to Dexter Avenue Baptist Church." 5/29/56. Altanta, Ga. (TLS) 1 p. DABCC. 560529–005.**

5/29/56 Smith, Louis P. (Ford Hall Forum). "Letter to Martin Luther King, Jr." 5/29/56. Boston, Mass. (THLSr) 2 pp. MLKP-MBU: Box 17. 560529–001.

5/29/56 Thompson, Ernest (United Electrical, Radio and Machine Workers of America). "Letter to Martin Luther King, Jr." 5/29/56. New York, N.Y. (TLS) 1 p. MLKP-MBU: Box 66. 560529–002.

5/30/56 Nixon, E. D. (Edgar Daniel) (MIA). "Schedule of Out of State Deposits and Disbursements for 2/56–5/56." 5/30/56. Montgomery, Ala. (TD) 2 pp. RJGC. 560530–000.

5/31/56 **King, Martin Luther, Jr. (MIA). "Letter to E. (Edwin) T. Sandberg." 5/31/56. [*Montgomery, Ala.*] (TLc) 1 p. MLKP-MBU: Box 65A. 560531–009.**

5/31/56 **Associated Press. "Photo of a church-operated station wagon." 5/31/56. Montgomery, Ala. (Ph) 1 p. APWW. 560531–010.**

5/31/56 King, Martin Luther, Jr. (MIA). "Letter to Ken Hatt." 5/31/56. [*Montgomery, Ala.*] (TLc) 1 p. MLKP-MBU: Box 60. 560531–006.

5/31/56 MIA. "Agenda, Executive board meeting." 5/31/56. Montgomery, Ala. (THD) 1 p. (Marginal comments by King.) MLKP-MBU: Box 6. 560531–007.

5/56 **King, Martin Luther, Jr. "Walk for Freedom." 5/56. New York, N.Y. From: *Fellowship* 22 (May 1956): 5–7. (PD) 3 pp. 560500–000.**

6/56 **King, Martin Luther, Jr. "The 'New Negro' of the South: Behind the Montgomery Story." 6/56. New York, N.Y. From: *Socialist Call* 24 (June 1956): 16–19. (PD) 4 pp. MLKJrP-GAMK: Box 107. 560600–000.**

6/56 Silver, Theodore. "Rev. M. L. King: Alabama Moses." 6/56. Chicago, Ill. From: *American Negro* 1 (June 1956): 13–15. (PD) 3 pp. MLKP-MBU. 560600–001.

6/56 Miller, Robert H. (National Negro Funeral Directors Association). "Dr. Martin Luther King to Address Cleveland Meet." 6/56. Chicago, Ill. From: *National Funeral Director and Embalmer* 9 (June 1956): 4, 15. (PD) 2 pp. MLKP-MBU: Box 80. 560600–009.

6/56 Rustin, Bayard (War Resisters League). "Back from 'Bama." 5/56–6/56. New York, N.Y. From: *WRL News* 78 (May–June 1956): 2. (PD) 1 p. JNS-PSC-P. 560600–015.

6/1/56 **King, Martin Luther, Jr. (MIA). "Letter to Arthur R. James." 6/1/56. [*Montgomery, Ala.*] (TLc) 2 pp. MLKP-MBU: Box 15. 560601–006.**

6/1/56 **Peck, James (Committee for Nonviolent Integration). "Letter to Martin Luther King, Jr." 6/1/56. New York, N.Y. (TLS) 1 p. MLKP-MBU: Box 63A. 560601–010.**

6/1/56 **King, Martin Luther, Jr. (MIA). "Letter to J. Raymond Henderson." 6/1/56. [*Montgomery, Ala.*] (TLc) 1 p. MLKP-MBU: Box 65. 560601–014.**

6/1/56 King, Martin Luther, Jr. (MIA). "Letter to John A. Morsell." 6/1/56. [*Montgomery, Ala.*] (TLc) 1 p. MLKP-MBU: Box 62. 560601–002.

6/1/56 Alexandre, Clement (Doubleday & Co.). "Letter to Martin Luther King, Jr." 6/1/56. New York, N.Y. (THLS) 1 p. MLKP-MBU: Box 34. 560601–005.

6/1/56 Smiley, Glenn E. "Letter to Martin Luther King, Jr." 6/1/56. Tifton, Ga. (THL) 1 p. MLKP-MBU: Box 65. 560601–007.

6/1/56 Stephens, Fred E. (Ward African Methodist Episcopal Church). "Letter to Martin Luther King, Jr." 6/1/56. Los Angeles, Calif. (TLS) 1 p. MLKP-MBU: Box 67. 560601–011.

6/1/56 Savage, Augustus (*American Negro*). "Letter to Martin Luther King, Jr." 6/1/56. Chicago, Ill. (TLS) 1 p. MLKP-MBU: Box 14. 560601–012.

6/3/56 Moore, Juanita. "Letter to Martin Luther King, Jr." 6/3/56. Baltimore, Md. (ALS) 2 pp. MLKP-MBU: Box 62. 560603–000.

6/4/56 **King, Martin Luther, Jr. (MIA). "Letter to Ross Allen Weston." 6/4/56. Montgomery, Ala. (TLS) 1 p. UUAR-MH-AH. 560604–000.**

6/4/56 **King, Martin Luther, Jr. (MIA). "Letter to George Lawrence." 6/4/56. [*Montgomery, Ala.*] (TLc) 1 p. MLKP-MBU: Box 17. 560604–001.**

6/4/56 **King, Martin Luther, Jr. (MIA). "Letter to William J. Faulkner." 6/4/56. [*Montgomery, Ala.*] (TLc) 1 p. MLKP-MBU: Box 15. 560604–007.**

6/4/56 **King, Martin Luther, Jr. (MIA). "Letter to Myles Horton." 6/4/56. [*Montgomery, Ala.*] (TLc) 1 p. MLKP-MBU: Box 14A. 560604–010.**

6/4/56 **Hiller, Helen M. "Letter to Martin Luther King, Jr." 6/4/56. Mattapoisett, Mass. (ALS) 2 pp. MLKP-MBU: Box 60. 560604–017.**

6/4/56 King, Martin Luther, Jr. (MIA). "Letter to Milton Britton." 6/4/56. [*Montgomery, Ala.*] (TLc) 1 p. MLKP-MBU: Box 16. 560604–002.

6/4/56 MIA. "List of executive board members." 6/4/56. Montgomery, Ala. (THD) 1 p. MLKP-MBU: Box 30. 560604–006.

6/4/56 MIA. "List of committees." 6/4/56. Montgomery, Ala. (TD) 1 p. MLKP-MBU: Box 6. 560604–009.

6/4/56 MIA. "Program, Mass meeting at Holt Street Baptist Church." 6/4/56. Montgomery, Ala. (TD) 1 p. MLKP-MBU: Box 6. 560604–011.

6/4/56 Pugh, Thomas J. (Albany State College). "Letter to Martin Luther King, Jr." 6/4/56. Albany, Ga. (THLS) 1 p. MLKP-MBU: Box 64. 560604–013.

6/4/56 King, Martin Luther, Jr. (MIA). "Letter to Raimund L. Tumbleston." 6/4/56. [*Montgomery, Ala.*] (TLc) 1 p. MLKP-MBU: Box 15. 560604–015.

6/4/56 Lomax, Almena (*Los Angeles Tribune*). "Letter to Martin Luther King, Jr." 6/4/56. Los Angeles, Calif. (TALS) 1 p. MLKP-MBU: Box 61. 560604–018.

6/4/56 King, Martin Luther, Jr. (MIA). "Letter to James Monroe Dixon." 6/4/56. [*Montgomery, Ala.*] (TLc) 1 p. MLKP-MBU: Box 16. 560604–019.

6/4/56 King, Martin Luther, Jr (MIA). "Letter to Lester C. O'Bannon." 6/4/56. [*Montgomery, Ala.*] (TLc) 1 p. MLKP-MBU: Box 63A. 560604–020.

6/5/56 **King, Martin Luther, Jr. "Letter to Charles E. Batten." 6/5/56. [*Montgomery, Ala.*] (TLc) 1 p. MLKP-MBU: Box 64. 560605–009.**

6/5/56 King, Martin Luther, Jr. (MIA). "Letter to Charles S. Johnson." 6/5/56. [*Montgomery, Ala.*] (TLc) 1 p. MLKP-MBU: Box 17. 560605–000.

6/5/56 King, Martin Luther, Jr. (MIA). "Letter to Pinkie S. Franklin." 6/5/56. [*Montgomery, Ala.*] (TLc) 1 p. MLKP-MBU: Box 17. 560605–001.

6/5/56 Hill, Daniel G. (Howard University). "Letter to Martin Luther King, Jr." 6/5/56. Washington, D.C. (THLS) 1 p. MLKP-MBU: Box 82. 560605–003.

6/5/56 King, Martin Luther, Jr. (MIA). "Letter to J. Martin England." 6/5/56. Montgomery, Ala. (TLS) 1 p. JMEC. 560605–004.

6/5/56 King, Martin Luther, Jr. "Letter to J. Elliott Corbett." 6/5/56. [*Montgomery, Ala.*] (TLc) 1 p. MLKP-MBU: Box 15. 560605–007.

6/5/56 King, Martin Luther, Jr. "Letter to Cecil A. Thomas." 6/5/56. [*Montgomery, Ala.*] (THLc) 1 p. MLKP-MBU: Box 67. 560605–011.

6/5/56 King, Martin Luther, Jr. (MIA). "Letter to James B. Cayce." 6/5/56. [*Montgomery, Ala.*] (TLc) 1 p. MLKP-MBU: Box 16. 560605–014.

6/6/56 Ballou, Maude L. "Letter to W. Lester Banks." 6/6/56. [*Montgomery, Ala.*] (THLc) 1 p. MLKP-MBU: Box 63. 560606–006.

6/6/56	King, Martin Luther, Jr. (MIA). "Letter to William Robert Miller." 6/6/56. Montgomery, Ala. (TLSr) 1 p. WRMP-GAMK: Box 1. 560606–010.
6/6/56	King, Martin Luther, Jr. (MIA). "Letter to Joseph L. Griffin." 6/6/56. [*Montgomery, Ala.*] (TLc) 1 p. MLKP-MBU: Box 67. 560606–016.
6/7/56	MIA. "*Newsletter* 1, no. 1." 6/7/56. Montgomery, Ala. (TD) 3 pp. HG-GAMK. 560607–001.
6/7/56	Maxwell, O. Clay (Mount Olivet Baptist Church). "Letter to Martin Luther King, Jr." 6/7/56. New York, N.Y. (THLS) 1 p. MLKP-MBU: Box 61. 560607–003.
6/7/56	Hunter, Allan A. (Mt. Hollywood Congregational Church). "Letter to Martin Luther King, Jr." 6/7/56. Los Angeles, Calif. (THLS) 1 p. MLKP-MBU: Box 61. 560607–004.
6/7/56	Solow, Martin (*Nation*). "Letter to Martin Luther King, Jr." 6/7/56. New York, N.Y. (THLS) 1 p. MLKP-MBU: Box 62. 560607–005.
6/7/56	King, Martin Luther, Jr. (MIA). "Letter to Anna C. Frank." 6/7/56. [*Montgomery, Ala.*] (TLc) 1 p. MLKP-MBU: Box 63. 560607–006.
6/7/56	Sanders, Claude Lee (International Longshoremen and Warehousemen's Union). "Letter to Martin Luther King, Jr." 6/7/56. (THLS) 3 pp. MLKP-MBU: Box 65. 560607–012.
6/8/56	Moton, R. R. (Frontiers of America). "Letter to Martin Luther King, Jr." 6/8/56. Atlanta, Ga. (TLS) 1 p. MLKP-MBU: Box 60A. 560608–001.
6/8/56	King, Martin Luther, Jr. (MIA). "Letter to Juanita Moore." 6/8/56. [*Montgomery, Ala.*] (TLc) 1 p. MLKP-MBU: Box 62. 560608–003.
6/8/56	Handy, W. T. (William Talbot), Jr. (Newman Methodist Church). "Letter to Martin Luther King, Jr." 6/8/56. Alexandria, La. (THLS) 1 p. MLKP-MBU: Box 63. 560608–004.
6/8/56	Rooks, Shelby (St. James Presbyterian Church). "Letter to Martin Luther King, Jr." 6/8/56. New York, N.Y. (THLS) 1 p. MLKP-MBU: Box 65. 560608–006.
6/10/56	Second Baptist Church. "Program, Sunday services." 6/10/56. Los Angeles, Calif. (PTD) 4 pp. MLKP-MBU: Box 80. 560610–000.
6/10/56	Killens, John Oliver. "Letter to Martin Luther King, Jr." 6/10/56. Brooklyn, N.Y. (THLS) 1 p. MLKP-MBU: Box 61. 560610–003.
6/11/56	MIA. "Program, Mass meeting at Hutchinson Street Baptist Church." 6/11/56. Montgomery, Ala. (TD) 1 p. HG-GAMK. 560611–000.
6/11/56	Johnson, Charles S. (Fisk University). "Letter to Martin Luther King, Jr." 6/11/56. Nashville, Tenn. (TLS) 1 p. MLKP-MBU: Box 60A. 560611–002.
6/11/56	Smiley, Glenn E. (Fellowship of Reconciliation). "Letter to Martin Luther King, Jr." 6/11/56. New York, N.Y. (THLS) 1 p. MLKP-MBU: Box 16. 560611–003.
6/11/56	Catlos, Edward (Chicago Baptist Association). "Letter to Martin Luther King, Jr." 6/11/56. Chicago, Ill. (TLS) 1 p. MLKP-MBU: Box 15. 560611–009.
6/11/56	Mickleburg, Bruce (*Horizons*). "Telegram to Martin Luther King, Jr." 6/11/56. Toronto, Ont., Canada. (PWSr) 1 p. MLKP-MBU: Box 28. 560611–012.
6/11/56	King, Martin Luther, Jr. (Dexter Avenue Baptist Church). "Letter to Thelma H. Anderson." 6/11/56. [*Montgomery, Ala.*] (TLc) 1 p. DABCC. 560611–013.
6/11/56	King, Martin Luther, Jr. (Dexter Avenue Baptist Church). "Letter to Samuel D. (Dewitt) Proctor." 6/11/56. [*Montgomery, Ala.*] (TLc) 1 p. DABCC. 560611–014.
6/12/56	Williams, Dolores. "Letter to Martin Luther King, Jr." 6/12/56. Montgomery, Ala. (TLS) 1 p. DABCC. 560612–005.
6/13/56	**Weaver, Archie L. (Second Ward Improvement Association). "Letter to Martin Luther King, Jr." 6/13/56. Chicago, Ill. (THLS) 1 p. MLKP-MBU: Box 67. 560613–005.**
6/13/56	Schader, Annemarie. "Letter to Martin Luther King, Jr." 6/13/56. Zurich, Switzerland. (TAHLS) 2 pp. MLKP-MBU: Box 89. 560613–001.
6/13/56	King, Martin Luther, Jr. (MIA). "Letter to Martin Solow." 6/13/56. [*Montgomery, Ala.*] (TLc) 1 p. MLKP-MBU: Box 62. 560613–002.
6/13/56	Lee, J. (James) Oscar (National Council of the Churches of Christ in the United States of America). "Letter to Martin Luther King, Jr." 6/13/56. New York, N.Y. (TLS) 2 pp. MLKP-MBU: Box 63. 560613–003.
6/14/56	Hawley, Peter K. "Letter to Martin Luther King, Jr." 6/14/56. New York, N.Y. (ALS) 1 p. MLKP-MBU: Box 60. 560614–003.
6/15/56	**Lawrence, George (Friendship Baptist Church). "Letter to Martin Luther King, Jr." 6/15/56. New York, N.Y. (THLS) 2 pp. MLKP-MBU: Box 17. 560615–000.**
6/15/56	Parks, Rosa (MIA). "Letter to Ernest Thompson." 6/15/56. (TLc) 1 p. MLKP-MBU: Box 66. 560615–001.

6/15/56   Poston, Ted (*New York Post*). "The Negroes of Montgomery." 6/15/56. Montgomery, Ala. From: *New York Post*, 15 June 1956. (PD) 2 pp. 560615–003.

6/18/56   Fields, U. (Uriah) J. "Press Release, Reverend Fields's retraction." 6/18/56. Montgomery, Ala. (TD) 1 p. HJP-GAMK. 560618–000.

6/18/56   Smiley, Glenn E. (Fellowship of Reconciliation). "Letter to Martin Luther King, Jr." 6/18/56. New York, N.Y. (THLS) 1 p. MLKP-MBU: Box 16. 560618–003.

6/18/56   King, Martin Luther, Jr. (MIA). "Letter to Clement Alexandre." 6/18/56. [*Montgomery, Ala.*] (TLc) 1 p. MLKP-MBU: Box 34A. 560618–004.

6/18/56   Women's International League for Peace and Freedom. "Memo to Martin Luther King, Jr." 6/14/56–6/18/56. Washington, D.C. (TL) 1 p. (Enclosure in 560801–011.) MLKP-MBU: Box 67. 560618–006.

6/19/56   **King, Martin Luther, Jr. (MIA). "Letter to Jimmy and Ellen Hawley." 6/19/56. [*Montgomery, Ala.*] (TLc) 1 p. MLKP-MBU: Box 60. 560619–013.**

6/19/56   King, Martin Luther, Jr. (MIA). "Letter to James Gibbs." 6/19/56. [*Montgomery, Ala.*] (TLc) 1 p. MLKP-MBU: Box 17. 560619–003.

6/19/56   King, Martin Luther, Jr. (MIA). "Letter to Edward A. Jones." 6/19/56. [*Montgomery, Ala.*] (TLc) 1 p. MLKP-MBU: Box 62. 560619–007.

6/19/56   King, Martin Luther, Jr. (MIA). "Letter to Sadie Bradford." 6/19/56. [*Montgomery, Ala.*] (TLc) 1 p. MLKP-MBU: Box 16. 560619–010.

6/19/56   Gayle, W. (William) A., Defendant. "Judgment, *Aurelia S. Browder v. William A. Gayle.*" 6/19/56. Montgomery, Ala. (THDS) 3 pp. CMCR-AMC. 560619–014.

6/19/56   King, Martin Luther, Jr. (MIA). "Letter to Shelby Rooks." 6/19/56. [*Montgomery, Ala.*] (TLc) 1 p. MLKP-MBU: Box 65. 560619–015.

6/20/56   **King, Martin Luther, Jr. (MIA). "Letter to Annemarie Schader." 6/20/56. [*Montgomery, Ala.*] (TLc) 1 p. MLKP-MBU: Box 89. 560620–001.**

6/20/56   Smiley, Glenn E. (Fellowship of Reconciliation). "Letter to Martin Luther King, Jr." 6/20/56. New York, N.Y. (TALS) 1 p. (Contains p. 1 of 560620–011.) MLKP-MBU: Box 91. 560620–000.

6/20/56   [*Hassler, Alfred*]. "Notes, Series in *Montgomery Advertiser.*" [*6/20/56*]. (TD) 3 pp. FORP-PSC-P. 560620–011.

6/20/56   Gantt, Hermann. "Letter to Martin Luther King, Jr." 6/20/56. New York, N.Y. (AHLS) 2 pp. MLKP-MBU: Box 17. 560620–006.

6/20/56   Meyers, Irving (North Side Veterans Club). "Letter to Martin Luther King, Jr." 6/20/56. Chicago, Ill. (THLS) 1 p. MLKP-MBU: Box 63. 560620–008.

6/20/56   Ballou, Maude L. "Letter to Archie L. Weaver." 6/20/56. [*Montgomery, Ala.*] (TLc) 1 p. MLKP-MBU: Box 67. 560620–010.

6/21/56   Randolph, A. (Asa) Philip. "Letter to George D. Cannon." 6/21/56. (TLc) 1 p. APRC-DLC. 560621–001.

6/22/56   Handy, W. C. (Handy Brothers Music Company). "Letter to Lovie M. Rainbow." 6/22/56. New York, N.Y. (TLS) 1 p. (Enclosure in 560629–001.) MLKP-MBU: Box 64. 560622–000.

6/22/56   Inter-Civic Council of Tallahassee. "An Appeal to the People of Tallahassee for Moral Justice." 6/22/56. Tallahassee, Fla. From: *Capitol Post*, 26 June 1956. (PD) 1 p. FORP-PSC-P. 560622–001.

6/23/56   MIA. "*Newsletter* 1, no. 2." 6/23/56. Montgomery, Ala. (PD) 2 pp. HG-GAMK. 560623–002.

6/25/56   Taylor, Franklyn W. "MIA Audit Report for 3/1/56–5/31/56." 6/25/56. Montgomery, Ala. (TDS) 7 pp. RJGC. 560625–001.

6/25/56   Alexandre, Clement (Doubleday & Co.). "Letter to Martin Luther King, Jr." 6/25/56. New York, N.Y. (TLS) 1 p. MLKP-MBU: Box 34. 560625–003.

6/25/56   Greene, Homer. "Letter to Martin Luther King, Jr." 6/25/56. (THLS) 2 pp. MLKP-MBU: Box 17. 560625–004.

6/26/56   Diggs, Charles C., Jr. (Panorama of Progress). "Letter to Martin Luther King, Jr." 6/26/56. Detroit, Mich. (THLS) 1 p. DABCC. 560626–003.

6/27/56   **King, Martin Luther, Jr. (MIA). "The Montgomery Story, Address at the 47th Annual NAACP Convention." [*6/27/56*]. [*San Francisco, Calif.*] (At) 47 min. (1 sound cassette: analog.) MLKJrP-GAMK. 560627–003.**

6/27/56   King, Martin Luther, Jr. (MIA). "The Montgomery Story, Address at the 47th Annual NAACP Convention." 6/27/56. [*San Francisco, Calif.*] (AHD) 23 pp. NAACPP-DLC: Group III–B192. 560627–000.

6/27/56   Jack, Homer Alexander (Unitarian Church of Evanston). "Letter to Martin Luther King, Jr." 6/27/56. Evanston, Ill. (THLS) 1 p. MLKP-MBU: Box 66. 560627–002.

6/27/56 Peck, James (Congress of Racial Equality). "Letter to Martin Luther King, Jr." 6/27/56. New York, N.Y. (THLS) 1 p. (Marginal comments by King.) MLKP-MBU: Box 15. 560627–004.

6/28/56 Muste, A. J. (Abraham Johannes) (Fellowship of Reconciliation). "Form letter to supporters." 6/28/56. New York, N.Y. (TL) 2 pp. (Includes enclosure.) MLKP-MBU: Box 17. 560628–001.

6/29/56 Rainbow, Lovie M. "Letter to Martin Luther King, Jr." 6/29/56. Oberlin, Ohio. (ALS) 2 pp. (Contains enclosure 560622–000.) MLKP-MBU: Box 64. 560629–001.

6/29/56 Holleran, Mary P. (Hampton Institute). "Letter to Martin Luther King, Jr." 6/29/56. Hampton, Va. (TLS) 1 p. DABCC. 560629–003.

6/30/56 Simms, B. J. (MIA). "Memorandum to all day drivers." 6/30/56. (TL) 1 p. MLKP-MBU: Box 6. 560630–000.

7/56 **"Photo of Martin Luther King, Jr., Yolanda Denise King, and Coretta Scott King." [7/56]. Montgomery, Ala. (Ph) 1 p. MLKP-MBU: Box 43. 560700–004.**

7/56 Rustin, Bayard. "Letter to Martin Luther King, Jr." [6/56–7/56]. New York, N.Y. (TLS) 1 p. MLKP-MBU: Box 64A. 560700–008.

7/56 Bennett, Lerone (*Ebony*). "The King Plan for Freedom." 7/56. Chicago, Ill. From: *Ebony*, July 1956, pp. 65–68. (PD) 4 pp. 560700–011.

7/1/56 NAACP. "Program, 47th Annual Convention." 6/26/56–7/1/56. San Francisco, Calif. (PDf) 3 pp. NAACPP-DLC: Group III–A2. 560701–001.

7/2/56 King, Martin Luther, Jr. (MIA). "Letter to Louis P. Smith." 7/2/56. [*Montgomery, Ala.*] (TLc) 1 p. MLKP-MBU: Box 17. 560702–000.

7/3/56 **King, Martin Luther, Jr. (MIA). "Letter to W. T. (William Talbot) Handy, Jr." 7/3/56. Montgomery, Ala. (TLS) 1 p. WTH. 560703–000.**

7/3/56 Greene, Eleanor (*Redbook*). "Letter to Martin Luther King, Jr." 7/3/56. New York, N.Y. (TLS) 1 p. MLKP-MBU: Box 64. 560703–002.

7/3/56 King, Martin Luther, Jr. (MIA). "Letter to Daniel G. Hill." 7/3/56. [*Montgomery, Ala.*] (TLc) 1 p. MLKP-MBU: Box 82. 560703–003.

7/4/56 Diggs Enterprises, Inc. "Program, Panorama of Progress." 6/30/56–7/4/56. Detroit, Mich. (PD) 31 pp. MLKP-MBU: Box 80. 560704–000.

7/5/56 **King, Martin Luther, Jr. (MIA). "Letter to Glenn E. Smiley." 7/5/56. Montgomery, Ala. (TLS) 2 pp. FORP-PSC-P. 560705–001.**

7/5/56 **King, Martin Luther, Jr. (MIA). "Letter to Almena Lomax." 7/5/56. [*Montgomery, Ala.*] (THLc) 1 p. MLKP-MBU: Box 61. 560705–008.**

7/5/56 **King, Martin Luther, Jr. (MIA). "Letter to John Oliver Killens." 7/5/56. [*Montgomery, Ala.*] (TLc) 1 p. MLKP-MBU: Box 61. 560705–009.**

7/5/56 National Fraternal Council of Churches, U.S.A. "Program, 23d Annual Meeting." 7/3/56–7/5/56. Birmingham, Ala. (PHD) 5 pp. MLKP-MBU: Box 80. 560705–000.

7/5/56 King, Martin Luther, Jr. (MIA). "Letter to Charles S. Johnson." 7/5/56. [*Montgomery, Ala.*] (TLc) 1 p. MLKP-MBU: Box 17. 560705–003.

7/5/56 King, Martin Luther, Jr. (MIA). "Letter to Claude Lee Saunders." 7/5/56. [*Montgomery, Ala.*] (TLc) 1 p. MLKP-MBU: Box 65. 560705–010.

7/6/56 **King, Martin Luther, Jr. (MIA). "Letter to Helen M. Hiller." 7/6/56. [*Montgomery, Ala.*] (TLc) 1 p. MLKP-MBU: Box 60. 560706–000.**

7/6/56 King, Martin Luther, Jr. (MIA). "Letter to R. R. Morton." 7/6/56. [*Montgomery, Ala.*] (TLc) 1 p. MLKP-MBU: Box 17. 560706–001.

7/6/56 King, Martin Luther, Jr. "Letter to Mary P. Holleran." 7/6/56. [*Montgomery, Ala.*] (TLc) 1 p. DABCC. 560706–008.

7/8/56 New Hope Baptist Church. "Program, Morning worship." 7/8/56. Niagara Falls, N.Y. (PHD) 4 pp. MLKP-MBU: Box 80. 560708–000.

7/8/56 McColloch, Lois (Unitarian Fellowship for Social Justice). "Letter to Martin Luther King, Jr." 7/8/56. Pittsburgh, Pa. (TLS) 1 p. MLKP-MBU: Box 66. 560708–001.

7/8/56 Dexter Avenue Baptist Church. "Men's Day Program." 7/8/56. Montgomery, Ala. (TD) 4 pp. DABCC. 560708–004.

7/9/56 King, Martin Luther, Jr. (Dexter Avenue Baptist Church). "Letter to Homer Alexander Jack." 7/9/56. [*Montgomery, Ala.*] (TLc) 1 p. MLKP-MBU: Box 66A. 560709–000.

7/9/56 Smiley, Glenn E. (Fellowship of Reconciliation). "Letter to Martin Luther King, Jr." 7/9/56. New York, N.Y. (TLS) 1 p. MLKP-MBU: Box 82. 560709–002.

7/9/56 King, Martin Luther, Jr. (MIA). "Letter to Thomas J. Pugh." 7/9/56. [*Montgomery, Ala.*] (TLc) 1 p. MLKP-MBU: Box 64. 560709–004.

7/9/56   Rumford, Byron W. "Form letter to supporters." 7/9/56. (TALd) 1 p. (Copy to King.) MLKP-MBU: Box 67. 560709–006.

7/10/56   **King, Martin Luther, Jr. (MIA). "Letter to A. J. (Abraham Johannes) Muste." 7/10/56. [*Montgomery, Ala.*] (TLc) 1 p. MLKP-MBU: Box 17. 560710–005.**

7/10/56   **King, Martin Luther, Jr. (MIA). "Letter to Lovie M. Rainbow." 7/10/56. [*Montgomery, Ala.*] (TLc) 1 p. MLKP-MBU: Box 64. 560710–010.**

7/10/56   **King, Martin Luther, Jr. (MIA). "Letter to Homer Greene." 7/10/56. [*Montgomery, Ala*]. (TLc) 1 p. MLKP-MBU: Box 17. 560710–012.**

7/10/56   **King, Martin Luther, Jr. "Letter to J. Raymond Henderson." 7/10/56. [*Montgomery, Ala.*] (TLc) 1 p. MLKP-MBU: Box 65. 560710–013.**

7/10/56   King, Martin Luther, Jr. (MIA). "Letter to Bayard Rustin." 7/10/56. [*Montgomery, Ala.*] (TLc) 1 p. MLKP-MBU: Box 64A. 560710–002.

7/10/56   King, Martin Luther, Jr. "Letter to Hermann Gantt." 7/10/56. [*Montgomery, Ala.*] (TLc) 1 p. MLKP-MBU: Box 17. 560710–003.

7/10/56   King, Martin Luther, Jr. (MIA). "Letter to B. J. Fisher." 7/10/56. [*Montgomery, Ala.*] (TLc) 1 p. MLKP-MBU: Box 17. 560710–004.

7/10/56   King, Martin Luther, Jr. (MIA). "Letter to Henri Varin de la Brunelière." 7/10/56. [*Montgomery, Ala.*] (TLc) 1 p. MLKP-MBU: Box 16. 560710–007.

7/10/56   Hill, Daniel G. (Howard University). "Letter to Martin Luther King, Jr." 7/10/56. Washington, D.C. (TLS) 1 p. MLKP-MBU: Box 82. 560710–011.

7/11/56   King, Martin Luther, Jr. (MIA). "Letter to Lois McColloch." 7/11/56. [*Montgomery, Ala.*] (TLc) 1 p. MLKP-MBU: Box 66. 560711–002.

7/11/56   King, Martin Luther, Jr. (MIA). "Letter to Eleanor Greene." 7/11/56. [*Montgomery, Ala.*] (TLc) 2 pp. MLKP-MBU: Box 64. 560711–003.

7/11/56   Holleran, Mary P. (Hampton Institute). "Letter to Martin Luther King, Jr." 7/11/56. Hampton, Va. (TLS) 1 p. MLKP-MBU: Box 60. 560711–004.

7/11/56   King, Martin Luther, Jr. (MIA). "Letter to Hobson R. Reynolds." 7/11/56. [*Montgomery, Ala.*] (TLc) 1 p. MLKP-MBU: Box 16. 560711–005.

7/12/56   **Patterson, John (Alabama Attorney General). "Letter to Martin Luther King, Jr." 7/12/56. Montgomery, Ala. (TLSr) 1 p. (Signed by Edmond L. Rinehart.) MLKP-MBU: Box 62A. 560712–003.**

7/12/56   **"Photo of Martin Luther King, Jr., Institute of Race Relations." [*7/12/56*]. Nashville, Tenn. (Ph) 1 p. RR-ARC-LNT. 560712–007.**

7/13/56   Fullerton, Garry. "Little Chance Seen for Effective Boycott." 7/13/56. Nashville, Tenn. From: *Nashville Tennessean*, 7 July 1956. (PD) 1 p. CSJP-TNF: Box 39. 560713–003.

7/14/56   O'Bannon, Lester C. "Letter to Martin Luther King, Jr." 7/14/56. Boston, Mass. (AHLS) 3 pp. MLKP-MBU: Box 43. 560714–002.

7/14/56   American Missionary Association. "Program, 13th Annual Institute of Race Relations." 7/2/56–7/14/56. Nashville, Tenn. (PHD) 13 pp. (Marginal comments by King.) MLKP-MBU: Box 80. 560714–003.

7/16/56   Levison, Stanley D. "Letter to A. (Asa) Philip Randolph." 7/16/56. New York, N.Y. (TLS) 1 p. APRC-DLC. 560716–000.

7/16/56   Brandstein, Rae (National Committee for Rural Schools). "Letter to Martin Luther King, Jr." 7/16/56. New York, N.Y. (TALS) 1 p. MLKP-MBU: Box 63. 560716–004.

7/16/56   Weaver, Archie L. (Second Ward Improvement Association). "Letter to Martin Luther King, Jr." 7/16/56. Chicago, Ill. (THLS) 1 p. MLKP-MBU: Box 67. 560716–005.

7/16/56   McLaurin, Benjamin F. (Brotherhood of Sleeping Car Porters and Maids). "Letter to Martin Luther King, Jr." 7/16/56. New York, N.Y. (THLS) 1 p. (Marginal comment by King.) MLKP-MBU: Box 14. 560716–007.

7/17/56   King, Martin Luther, Jr. (MIA). "Letter to Mary P. Holleran." 7/17/56. [*Montgomery, Ala.*] (TLc) 1 p. MLKP-MBU: Box 60. 560717–005.

7/17/56   Ormsby, Robert J. (International Union, United Automobile, Aircraft, and Agricultural Implement Workers of America). "Letter to Martin Luther King, Jr." 7/17/56. Paterson, N.J. (THLS) 1 p. MLKP-MBU: Box 60. 560717–006.

7/18/56   Greene, Homer. "Letter to Martin Luther King, Jr." 7/18/56. Fort Benning, Ga. (TLS) 2 pp. (Envelope included.) MLKP-MBU: Box 17. 560718–003.

7/18/56   Lomax, Almena (*Los Angeles Tribune*). "Letter to Martin Luther King, Jr." 7/13/56, 7/18/56. Los Angeles, Calif. (TALS) 2 pp. MLKP-MBU: Box 61. 560718–004.

7/18/56   **King, Martin Luther, Jr. (Dexter Avenue Baptist Church). "From the Pastor's Desk." 7/18/56. Montgomery, Ala. From: *Dexter Echo*, 18 July 1956, pp. 1, 2. (TD) 2 pp. MLKP-MBU: Box 77. 560718–000.**

7/18/56	Kelly, C. (Charles) W. (Greenwood Missionary Baptist Church). "Letter to Martin Luther King, Jr." 7/18/56. Tuskegee, Ala. 6 pp. (ALS) MLKP-MBU: Box 66. 560718–006.
7/19/56	Picott, J. Rupert (Virginia Teachers Association). "Letter to Martin Luther King, Jr." 7/19/56. Richmond, Va. (TLS) 2 pp. MLKP-MBU: Box 66. 560719–003.
7/19/56	Wilkins, Roy (NAACP). "Letter to James Peck." 7/19/56. (TLc) 2 pp. NAACPP-DLC: Group III–A273. 560719–005.
7/20/56	Wilder, Craig S. (Wesley Methodist Church). "Letter to Martin Luther King, Jr." 7/20/56. Singapore. (TAHLS) 1 p. (Marginal comment by King.) MLKP-MBU: Box 89. 560720–000.
7/20/56	King, Martin Luther, Jr., Appellant. "Certificate of Appeal, *M. L. King, Jr., v. State of Alabama.*" 7/20/56. Montgomery, Ala. (TD) 1 p. CMCR-AMC: File 7399. 560720–005.
7/21/56	Jernagin, W. (William) H. (National Baptist Sunday School and Baptist Training Union Congress). "Letter to Martin Luther King, Jr." 7/21/56. Washington, D.C. (TLS) 2 pp. MLKP-MBU: Box 63. 560721–001.
7/23/56	**King, Martin Luther, Jr. "Non-Aggression Procedures to Interracial Harmony, Address at the American Baptist Assembly and American Home Mission Agencies Conference." [*7/23/56*]. Green Lake, Wis. (At) 29 min. ABAC-ABHSP. 560723–004.**
7/23/56	King, Martin Luther, Jr. (Dexter Avenue Baptist Church). "Letter to Members of Dexter Avenue Baptist Church." 7/23/56. Montgomery, Ala. (THLc) 1 p. DABCC. 560723–000.
7/25/56	Levy, James E. (NAACP). "Letter to Martin Luther King, Jr." 7/25/56. Cleveland, Ohio. (THLS) 1 p. MLKP-MBU: Box 63. 560725–000.
7/25/56	Fellowship of Reconciliation. "Announcement, Nonviolent workshops." 7/17/56–7/25/56. New York, N.Y. (TD) 1 p. BEMP-DHU. 560725–001.
7/26/56	Powell, W. (William) J. (MIA). "Minutes, Executive board meeting." 7/26/56. (TD) 2 pp. MLKP-MBU: Box 30. 560726–002.
7/26/56	MIA. "*Newsletter* 1, no. 3." 7/26/56. Montgomery, Ala. (TD) 3 pp. MLKP-MBU: Box 84. 560726–003.
7/26/56	Cook, Clair M. (National Religion and Labor Foundation). "Letter to Martin Luther King, Jr." 7/26/56. Columbus, Ohio. (TAHLS) 1 p. MLKP-MBU: Box 67. 560726–006.
7/26/56	Banyai, Ed (International Ladies' Garment Workers Union). "Letter to Martin Luther King, Jr." 7/26/56. Bethlehem, Pa. (TLS) 1 p. MLKP-MBU: Box 17. 560726–008.
7/27/56	Dove, Mabel. "Letter to Martin Luther King, Jr." 7/27/56. Accra, Gold Coast. (ALS) 3 pp. MLKP-MBU: Box 31. 560727–000.
7/28/56	Jack, Homer Alexander (Unitarian Church of Evanston). "Letter to Martin Luther King, Jr." 7/28/56. Evanston, Ill. (TLS) 1 p. MLKP-MBU: Box 66. 560728–000.
7/28/56	King, Martin Luther, Jr. "Letter to Major J. Jones." 7/28/56. [*Montgomery, Ala.*] (TLc) 1 p. DABCC. 560728–003.
7/30/56	**Clark, Septima Poinsette (Highlander Folk School). "Letter to Martin Luther King, Jr." 7/30/56. Monteagle, Tenn. (ALS) 1 p. MLKP-MBU: Box 14A. 560730–005.**
7/30/56	Murray, C. T. (Vermont Avenue Baptist Church). "Letter to Martin Luther King, Jr." 7/30/56. Washington, D.C. (TLS) 1 p. MLKP-MBU: Box 61. 560730–001.
7/30/56	Jones, Nathaniel R. (Youngstown Fair Employment Practice Committee). "Letter to Martin Luther King, Jr." 7/30/56. Youngstown, Ohio. (TLS) 1 p. MLKP-MBU: Box 16. 560730–003.
7/30/56	Mays, Benjamin Elijah (Morehouse College). "Letter to Martin Luther King, Jr." 7/30/56. Atlanta, Ga. (THLS) 1 p. MLKP-MBU: Box 62. 560730–006.
7/30/56	Talley, Manuel D. (National Consumers Mobilization). "Letter to Martin Luther King, Jr." 7/30/56. Los Angeles, Calif. (TLS) 1 p. MLKP-MBU: Box 63. 560730–007.
7/31/56	**Evers, Medgar Wiley (NAACP). "Letter to Martin Luther King, Jr." 7/31/56. Jackson, Miss. (TLS) 1 p. MLKP-MBU: Box 62. 560731–006.**
7/31/56	King, Martin Luther, Jr. (MIA). "Letter to Ed Banyai." 7/31/56. [*Montgomery, Ala.*] (TLc) 1 p. MLKP-MBU: Box 17. 560731–000.
7/31/56	King, Martin Luther, Jr. (MIA). "Letter to Ray Gibbons." 7/31/56. [*Montgomery, Ala.*] (TLc) 1 p. MLKP-MBU: Box 17. 560731–001.
7/31/56	King, Martin Luther, Jr. (Dexter Avenue Baptist Church). "Letter to O. Clay Maxwell." 7/31/56. [*Montgomery, Ala.*] (TLc) 1 p. MLKP-MBU: Box 61. 560731–002.

7/31/56   King, Martin Luther, Jr. (Dexter Avenue Baptist Church). "Letter to Edwin A. Brooks." 7/31/56. [*Montgomery, Ala.*] (TLc) 1 p. MLKP-MBU: Box 64. 560731–009.

7/31/56   King, Martin Luther, Jr. (Dexter Avenue Baptist Church). "Letter to Mrs. J. P. Drake." 7/31/56. [*Montgomery, Ala.*] (TLc) 1 p. MLKP-MBU: Box 13A. 560731–011.

7/31/56   Stewart, Joffre. "Letter to Martin Luther King, Jr." 7/31/56. Chicago, Ill. (ALS) 1 p. MLKP-MBU: Box 65. 560731–012.

7/31/56   King, Martin Luther, Jr. (MIA). "Letter to Robert J. Ormsby." 7/31/56. [*Montgomery, Ala.*] (TLc) 1 p. MLKP-MBU: Box 60. 560731–013.

7/31/56   King, Martin Luther, Jr. (MIA). "Letter to Dean Hutchinson." 7/31/56. [*Montgomery, Ala.*] (TLc) 1 p. (Enclosure in 560821–015.) MLKP-MBU: Box 15. 560731–014.

7/31/56   Cumming, William Cooper (Westminister Presbyterian Church). "Letter to Martin Luther King, Jr." 7/31/56. Texarkana, Tex. (TLS) 1 p. MLKP-MBU: Box 67. 560731–015.

8/56   Vaughan, David D. (Boston University). "Letter to Martin Luther King, Jr." [*8/56*]. Wolfeboro, N.H. (ALS) 2 pp. MLKP-MBU: Box 67. 560800–002.

8/56   Peters, William. "Our Weapon Is Love." 8/56. New York, N.Y. From: *Redbook*, August 1956, pp. 42–43, 71–73. (PD) 4 pp. 560800–006.

8/56   King, Martin Luther, Jr. "Letter to the 1956 Democratic National Convention Committee on Platform and Resolutions." [*8/56*]. (TLS) 2 pp. HRECR-WHi: Box 39. 560800–011.

8/1/56   **King, Martin Luther, Jr. (Dexter Avenue Baptist Church). "Letter to W. (William) H. Jernagin." 8/1/56. [*Montgomery, Ala.*] (TLc) 1 p. MLKP-MBU: Box 63A. 560801–008.**

8/1/56   **King, Martin Luther, Jr. (Dexter Avenue Baptist Church). "Letter to Rae Brandstein." 8/1/56. [*Montgomery, Ala.*] (TLc) 2 pp. MLKP-MBU: Box 63. 560801–009.**

8/1/56   **King, Martin Luther, Jr. (Dexter Avenue Baptist Church). "Letter to Clair M. Cook." 8/1/56. [*Montgomery, Ala.*] (TLc) 1 p. MLKP-MBU: Box 67. 560801–013.**

8/1/56   **Hope, E. S. (Edward Swain). "Letter to Martin Luther King, Jr." 8/1/56. (TLI) 1 p. MLKP-MBU: Box 60. 560801–015.**

8/1/56   King, Martin Luther, Jr. (Dexter Avenue Baptist Church). "Letter to Homer Alexander Jack." 8/1/56. [*Montgomery, Ala.*] (TLc) 1 p. MLKP-MBU: Box 66. 560801–005.

8/1/56   Stewart, Annalee (Women's International League for Peace and Freedom). "Letter to Martin Luther King, Jr." 8/1/56. Washington, D.C. (TLS) 1 p. (Contains enclosure 560618–006.) MLKP-MBU: Box 67. 560801–011.

8/1/56   King, Martin Luther, Jr. "Letter to H. (Horace) Edward Whitaker." 8/1/56. [*Montgomery, Ala.*] (TLc) 1 p. MLKP-MBU: Box 63. 560801–012.

8/1/56   Jemison, T. J. (Theodore Judson) (National Baptist Convention, U.S.A., Inc.). "Letter to Martin Luther King, Jr." 8/1/56. Baton Rouge, La. (THLS) 1 p. MLKP-MBU: Box 63. 560801–014.

8/1/56   King, Martin Luther, Jr. (MIA). "Letter to M. B. Powell." 8/1/56. [*Montgomery, Ala.*] (TLc) 1 p. MLKP-MBU: Box 64. 560801–017.

8/2/56   Ramsay, John G. (National Religion and Labor Foundation). "Letter to Martin Luther King, Jr." 8/2/56. Washington, D.C. (TLS) 1 p. MLKP-MBU: Box 66. 560802–001.

8/3/56   King, Martin Luther, Jr. "Alabama's Bus Boycott: What It's All About." 8/3/56. From: *U.S. News and World Report*, 3 August 1956, pp. 82, 87–89. (PD) 4 pp. (Printed version of 560627–003.) 560803–000.

8/3/56   Jack, Homer Alexander (Unitarian Church of Evanston). "Letter to Martin Luther King, Jr." 8/3/56. Evanston, Ill. (THLS) 1 p. MLKP-MBU: Box 66. 560803–002.

8/3/56   Barbour, J. Pius (Calvary Baptist Church). "Telegram to Martin Luther King, Jr." 8/3/56. Chester, Pa. (PHWSr) 1 p. MLKP-MBU: Box 15. 560803–005.

8/4/56   Wolfard, Mary. "Letter to MIA." 8/4/56. Berlin, Germany. (THLc) 1 p. MLKP-MBU: Box 67. 560804–002.

8/5/56   Koch, Mel (Young Men's Christian Association [YMCA]). "Letter to Martin Luther King, Jr., and Coretta Scott King." 8/5/56. Berkeley, Calif. (TLS) 1 p. MLKP-MBU: Box 67. 560805–002.

8/6/56	Bunn, Warren J. (NAACP). "Letter to Martin Luther King, Jr." 8/6/56. Brooklyn, N.Y. (THLS) 1 p. MLKP-MBU: Box 63. 560806–003.
8/7/56	Randolph, A. (Asa) Philip (Brotherhood of Sleeping Car Porters and Maids). "Letter to Martin Luther King, Jr." 8/7/56. New York, N.Y. (THLS) 1 p. MLKP-MBU: Box 64A. 560807–000.
8/7/56	Johnson, Carl R. "Letter to Martin Luther King, Jr." 8/7/56. Kansas City, Mo. (THLS) 1 p. MLKP-MBU: Box 62. 560807–002.
8/7/56	National Negro Funeral Directors Association. "Program, Annual Award Banquet." 8/7/56. Cleveland, Ohio. (PHD) 3 pp. MLKP-MBU: Box 81. 560807–003.
8/9/56	Kilgore, Thomas G. (Friendship Baptist Church). "Letter to Martin Luther King, Jr." 8/9/56. New York, N.Y. (TLSr) 1 p. MLKP-MBU: Box 61. 560809–002.
8/10/56	Brandstein, Rae (National Committee for Rural Schools). "Letter to Martin Luther King, Jr." 8/10/56. New York, N.Y. (TAHLS) 1 p. MLKP-MBU: Box 63. 560810–001.
8/11/56	**King, Martin Luther, Jr. "Testimony to Democratic National Convention, Committee on Platform and Resolutions." 8/11/56. Chicago, Ill. (TD) 10 pp. PDNC-MWalK: Box 104. 560811–005.**
8/11/56	King, Martin Luther, Jr. (MIA). "Statement before the Democratic National Convention Committee on Platform and Resolutions." 8/11/56. [*Chicago, Ill.*] (TD) 2 pp. MLKP-MBU: Box 3. 560811–001.
1956	**King, Martin Luther, Jr. "The Birth of a New Age, Address delivered on 8/11/56 at the 50th anniversary of Alpha Phi Alpha in Buffalo." 1956. Chicago, Ill. From: Charles H. Wesley, *Golden Anniversary Story of Alpha Phi Alpha Fraternity, Inc.* (Chicago: Alpha Phi Alpha, 1956), pp. 85–90. (PD) 4 pp. MLKP-MBU: Box 10. 560000–136.**
8/11/56	**"Photo of Martin Luther King, Jr., Frank Stanley, James Huger, and Raymond Pace Alexander." 8/11/56. Buffalo, N.Y. (Ph) 1 p. VSC. 560811–012.**
8/11/56	Alpha Phi Alpha Fraternity. "Program, 50th Anniversary Convention Banquet." 8/11/56. Buffalo, N.Y. (PD) 8 pp. MLKP-MBU: Box 80. 560811–002.
8/11/56	Fuson, Marian. "Letter to Martin Luther King, Jr." 8/11/56. Nashville, Tenn. (ALS) 3 pp. (Written on verso of a church pamphlet; includes envelope.) MLKP-MBU: Box 17. 560811–003.
8/14/56	Carr, Johnnie R. "The Montgomery Bus Protest." 8/14/56. (AHD) 11 pp. JRC. 560814–000.
8/15/56	**Morgan, Ernest (Antioch Bookplate Company). "Letter to Martin Luther King, Jr." 8/15/56. Yellow Springs, Ohio. (TALS) 1 p. MLKP-MBU: Box 14. 560815–005.**
8/15/56	Smiley, Glenn E. (Fellowship of Reconciliation). "Letter to Martin Luther King, Jr." 8/15/56. New York, N.Y. (TLS) 1 p. MLKP-MBU: Box 16. 560815–003.
8/15/56	Smiley, Glenn E. "Report from the South, II." 8/15/56. (TD) 4 pp. FORP-PSC-P. 560815–000.
8/15/56	King, Martin Luther, Jr. (MIA). "Letter to Annalee Stewart." 8/15/56. [*Montgomery, Ala.*] (TLc) 1 p. MLKP-MBU: Box 67. 560815–007.
8/16/56	**King, Martin Luther, Jr. (MIA). "Letter to O. Clay Maxwell, Sr." 8/16/56. [*Montgomery, Ala.*] (TLc) 1 p. MLKP-MBU: Box 61A. 560816–000.**
8/16/56	**King, Martin Luther, Jr. (MIA). "Letter to Septima Poinsette Clark." 8/16/56. [*Montgomery, Ala.*] (TLc) 1 p. MLKP-MBU: Box 14A. 560816–006.**
8/16/56	King, Martin Luther, Jr. (MIA). "Letter to Medgar Wiley Evers." 8/16/56. [*Montgomery, Ala.*] (TLc) 1 p. MLKP-MBU: Box 62. 560816–003.
8/16/56	King, Martin Luther, Jr. (Dexter Avenue Baptist Church). "Letter to Benjamin Elijah Mays." 8/16/56. [*Montgomery, Ala.*] (TLc) 1 p. MLKP-MBU: Box 62. 560816–008.
8/16/56	King, Martin Luther, Jr. (MIA). "Letter to Maurice McCrackin." 8/16/56. [*Montgomery, Ala.*] (TLc) 1 p. MLKP-MBU: Box 65. 560816–011.
8/17/56	Talley, Manuel D. (National Consumers Mobilization). "Letter to Martin Luther King, Jr." 8/17/56. Los Angeles, Calif. (TLS) 2 pp. MLKP-MBU: Box 63. 560817–000.
8/19/56	Schmoe, Ruth (Pacific Yearly Meeting and Improvement Association of the Religious Society of Friends). "Letter to MIA." 8/19/56. Seattle, Wash. (TLS) 1 p. MLKP-MBU: Box 65. 560819–001.
8/20/56	**King, Martin Luther, Jr. (Dexter Avenue Baptist Church). "Letter to Homer Alexander Jack." 8/20/56. [*Montgomery, Ala.*] (TLc) 1 p. MLKP-MBU: Box 66. 560820–000.**

8/20/56   King, Martin Luther, Jr. (MIA). "Letter to J. Rupert Picott." 8/20/56. [*Montgomery, Ala.*] (TLc) 1 p. MLKP-MBU: Box 66. 560820–001.

8/20/56   King, Martin Luther, Jr. (MIA). "Letter to Rae Brandstein." 8/20/56. [*Montgomery, Ala.*] (TLc) 1 p. MLKP-MBU: Box 63. 560820–002.

8/20/56   Wofford, Harris (Covington and Burling). "Letter to Martin Luther King, Jr." 8/20/56. Washington, D.C. (TLS) 1 p. MLKP-MBU: Box 67. 560820–003.

8/20/56   King, Martin Luther, Jr. (Dexter Avenue Baptist Church). "Letter to T. J. (Theodore Judson) Jemison." 8/20/56. [*Montgomery, Ala.*] (TLc) 1 p. MLKP-MBU: Box 63. 560820–004.

8/21/56   King, Martin Luther, Jr. (MIA). "Letter to Marian and Nelson Fuson." 8/21/56. [*Montgomery, Ala.*] (TLc) 1 p. MLKP-MBU: Box 17. 560821–003.

8/21/56   King, Martin Luther, Jr. (MIA). "Letter to Joffre Stewart." 8/21/56. [*Montgomery, Ala.*] (TLc) 1 p. MLKP-MBU: Box 65. 560821–012.

8/21/56   King, Martin Luther, Jr. (MIA). "Letter to Glenn E. Smiley." 8/21/56. Montgomery, Ala. (TLS) 1 p. FORP-PSC-P. 560821–001.

8/21/56   Mays, Benjamin Elijah (Morehouse College). "Letter to Martin Luther King, Jr." 8/21/56. Atlanta, Ga. (THLS) 1 p. MLKP-MBU: Box 62. 560821–008.

8/21/56   Johnson, Wilbert J. (U.S. Army). "Letter to Martin Luther King, Jr." 8/21/56. Seattle, Wash. (TLS) 1 p. MLKP-MBU: Box 60. 560821–009.

8/21/56   King, Martin Luther, Jr. (MIA). "Letter to James E. Huger." 8/21/56. [*Montgomery, Ala.*] (TLc) 1 p. MLKP-MBU: Box 14. 560821–010.

8/21/56   King, Martin Luther, Jr. (MIA). "Letter to Dean Hutchinson." 8/21/56. [*Montgomery, Ala.*] (TLc) 1 p. (Contains enclosure 560731–014.) MLKP-MBU: Box 15. 560821–015.

8/21/56   King, Martin Luther, Jr. (MIA). "Letter to Lillian Williams." 8/21/56. [*Montgomery, Ala.*] (TLc) 1 p. MLKP-MBU: Box 14A. 560821–016.

8/21/56   King, Martin Luther, Jr. (MIA). "Letter to Thomas G. Kilgore, Jr." 8/21/56. [*Montgomery, Ala.*] (TLc) 1 p. MLKP-MBU: Box 61. 560821–019.

8/22/56   King, Martin Luther, Jr. (Dexter Avenue Baptist Church). "Letter to David D. Vaughan." 8/22/56. [*Montgomery, Ala.*] (TLc) 1 p. MLKP-MBU: Box 67. 560822–003.

8/24/56   King, Martin Luther, Jr. (MIA). "Letter to Warren J. Bunn." 8/24/56. [*Montgomery, Ala.*] (TLc) 1 p. MLKP-MBU: Box 63. 560824–003.

8/24/56   King, Martin Luther, Jr. (MIA). "Letter to Craig S. Wilder." 8/24/56. [*Montgomery, Ala.*] (TLc) 1 p. MLKP-MBU: Box 89. 560824–000.

8/24/56   Hedgeman, Anna Arnold (New York City. Office of the Mayor). "Letter to Martin Luther King, Jr." 8/24/56. New York, N.Y. (TLS) 1 p. MLKP-MBU: Box 60. 560824–005.

8/27/56   King, Martin Luther, Jr. (MIA). "Letter to Ernest Morgan." 8/27/56. [*Montgomery, Ala.*] (TLc) 1 p. MLKP-MBU: Box 14. 560827–001.

8/27/56   Jernagin, W. (William) H. (National Baptist Sunday School and Baptist Training Union Congress). "Letter to Martin Luther King, Jr." 8/27/56. Washington, D.C. (TLS) 2 pp. MLKP-MBU: Box 63A. 560827–003.

8/27/56   King, Martin Luther, Jr. (MIA), E. D. (Edgar Daniel) Nixon, E. H. Mason, and Rufus Lewis. "Letter to Dwight D. (David) Eisenhower." 8/27/56. Montgomery, Ala. (THLS) 2 pp. WCFG-KAbE. 560827–004.

8/27/56   Cook, Clair M. (Religion and Labor Foundation). "Letter to Martin Luther King, Jr." 8/27/56. Columbus, Ohio. (TLS) 1 p. MLKP-MBU: Box 64A. 560827–000.

8/27/56   Thomas, Cecil A. (Young Men's Christian Association [YMCA]). "Letter to Hallock Hoffman." 8/27/56. Berkeley, Calif. (TALc) 3 pp. (Enclosure in 560828–003.) MLKP-MBU: Box 67. 560827–002.

8/28/56   Thomas, Cecil A. (Young Men's Christian Association [YMCA]). "Letter to Martin Luther King, Jr., and Coretta Scott King." 8/28/56. Berkeley, Calif. (TALS) 3 pp. (Contains enclosure 560827–002.) MLKP-MBU: Box 67. 560828–003.

8/28/56   Burroughs, Nannie H. (National Trade and Professional School for Women and Girls). "Letter to Martin Luther King, Jr." 8/28/56. Washington, D.C. (TLS) 1 p. MLKP-MBU: Box 63A. 560828–004.

8/28/56   McLaurin, Benjamin F. (Brotherhood of Sleeping Car Porters and Maids). "Letter to Martin Luther King, Jr." 8/28/56. New York, N.Y. (TLSr) 1 p. MLKP-MBU: Box 14A. 560828–005.

8/29/56   Kaplan, Kivie (NAACP). "Letter to Martin Luther King, Jr." 8/29/56. Boston, Mass. (TAHLS) 7 pp. (Includes enclosure.) MLKP-MBU: Box 61. 560829–000.

8/30/56	**DeWolf, L. Harold (Boston University). "Letter to Martin Luther King, Jr." 8/30/56. Boston, Mass. (TALS) 1 p. MLKP-MBU: Box 16. 560830–001.**
9/56	Barbour, J. Pius (*National Baptist Voice*). "Sermons and Addresses at the Convention." 9/56. Philadelphia, Pa. From: *National Baptist Voice*, September 1956. (PHD) 3 pp. MLKP-MBU: Box 80. 560900–001.
9/56	Dinnerstein, Harvey. "The Artist as Reporter: Drawings of the Montgomery Bus Boycott." 9/28/56–10/20/56. New York, N.Y. (PD) 8 pp. MLKP-MBU: Box 31. 560900–011.
9/56	King, Martin Luther, Jr. "To do list." [*9/56*]. [*Montgomery, Ala.*] (AD) 1 p. (560909–002 on recto.) MLKP-MBU: Box 14A. 560900–014.
9/1/56	Rodriguez, E. F. "Letter to Martin Luther King, Jr." 9/1/56. Chappaqua, N.Y. (TALS) 1 p. MLKP-MBU: Box 64A. 560901–000.
9/1/56	Thompson, Lafayette (First Baptist Church). "Letter to Martin Luther King, Jr." 9/1/56. Brentwood, Mo. (THLS) 1 p. MLKP-MBU: Box 17. 560901–002.
9/1/56	Stephens, Carlton M. (Stephens' Recording Service). "Letter to Martin Luther King, Jr." 9/1/56. Cleveland, Ohio. (TLS) 1 p. MLKP-MBU: Box 65. 560901–004.
9/2/56	Bly, Simon (Afro Arts Theatre Presents). "Letter to Martin Luther King, Jr." 9/2/56. New York, N.Y. (THLS) 1 p. MLKP-MBU: Box 13A. 560902–000.
9/3/56	Dudley, Lafayette. "Letter to Martin Luther King, Jr." 9/3/56. Boston, Mass. (TLS) 2 pp. MLKP-MBU: Box 16. 560903–000.
9/4/56	Graetz, Robert (Trinity Lutheran Church). "Letter to Herbert Brownell." 9/4/56. Montgomery, Ala. (TLc) 3 pp. HJP-GAMK. 560904–003.
1956	National Baptist Convention U.S.A., Inc., and Woman's Auxiliary. "Minutes for 9/7/56, 76th Annual National Baptist Convention." 1956. From: *Record of the 76th Annual National Baptist Convention*, 1956. (PD) 4 pp. SBHL-TNSB. 560000–134.
9/7/56	**Olney, Warren, III (U.S. Department of Justice). "Letter to Martin Luther King, Jr." 9/7/56. Washington, D.C. (TLSr) 1 p. (Signed by Arthur B. Caldwell.) MLKP-MBU: Box 66A. 560907–001.**
9/8/56	**Kelly, C. (Charles) W. (Greenwood Missionary Baptist Church). "Letter to Martin Luther King, Jr." 9/8/56. Denver, Colo. (ALS) 4 pp. MLKP-MBU: Box 66. 560908–002.**
9/8/56	Canada, Sally. "Letter to Martin Luther King, Jr." 9/8/56. Huntington, W.Va. (AHLS) 3 pp. MLKP-MBU: Box 5. 560908–000.
9/9/56	Macedonia Baptist Church. "Program, Sunday services." 9/9/56. Denver, Colo. (THD) 7 pp. MLKP-MBU: Box 80. 560909–001.
9/9/56	Williams, Lillian (City-wide Committee to Stage Madison Square Garden Civil Rights Rally). "Letter to Martin Luther King, Jr." 9/9/56. Jersey City, N.J. (THL) 1 p. (560900–014 on verso.) MLKP-MBU: Box 14A. 560909–002.
9/9/56	National Baptist Convention U.S.A., Inc. "Program, 76th Annual Session." 9/4/56–9/9/56. Denver, Colo. (PD) 9 pp. MLKP-MBU: Box 80. 560909–000.
9/10/56	Hefner, William K. "Letter to Martin Luther King, Jr." 9/10/56. Shelburne, Mass. (AHLI) 1 p. MLKP-MBU: Box 60. 560910–004.
9/10/56	Michaux, H. M. (Durham Business and Professional Chain). "Letter to Martin Luther King, Jr." 9/10/56. Durham, N.C. (TLS) 1 p. MLKP-MBU: Box 15. 560910–005.
9/11/56	Massey, Floyd (Pilgrim Baptist Church). "Letter to Martin Luther King, Jr." 9/11/56. St. Paul, Minn. (THLS) 2 pp. MLKP-MBU: Box 64. 560911–002.
9/12/56	King, Martin Luther, Jr. (MIA). "Letter to Simon Bly." 9/12/56. [*Montgomery, Ala.*] (TLc) 1 p. MLKP-MBU: Box 13A. 560912–000.
9/12/56	Banks, W. Lester (NAACP). "Letter to Martin Luther King, Jr." 9/12/56. Richmond, Va. (THLS) 2 pp. (Marginal comment by King.) MLKP-MBU: Box 63. 560912–002.
9/12/56	Austin, L. E. (*Carolina Times*). "Letter to Martin Luther King, Jr." 9/12/56. Durham, N.C. (TLS) 1 p. MLKP-MBU: Box 15. 560912–005.
9/12/56	Morong, Carrol O. (Quill Club). "Letter to Martin Luther King, Jr." 9/12/56. New York, N.Y. (TLS) 1 p. MLKP-MBU: Box 61. 560912–007.
9/12/56	Rustin, Bayard (War Resisters League). "Letter to Martin Luther King, Jr." 9/12/56. New York, N.Y. (TLS) 1 p. MLKP-MBU: Box 67. 560912–009.
9/12/56	Davidson, Eugene (NAACP). "Letter to Martin Luther King, Jr." 9/12/56. Washington, D.C. (TLS) 1 p. MLKP-MBU: Box 63. 560912–011.
9/13/56	King, Martin Luther, Jr. (MIA). "Letter to M. R. Austell." 9/13/56. [*Montgomery, Ala.*] (TLc) 1 p. MLKP-MBU: Box 17. 560913–002.

9/13/56 Smiley, Glenn E. (Fellowship of Reconciliation). "Letter to Martin Luther King, Jr., and Ralph Abernathy." 9/13/56. New York, N.Y. (THLS) 1 p. MLKP-MBU: Box 16. 560913–004.

9/13/56 Powell, W. (William) J. (MIA). "Minutes, Executive board meeting." 9/13/56. Montgomery, Ala. (TD) 2 pp. MLKP-MBU: Box 30. 560913–006.

9/13/56 Davis Galleries. "Letter to Roy Wilkins." 9/13/56. New York, N.Y. (THL) 3 pp. (Includes enclosures.) NAACPP-DLC: Group III–A273. 560913–008.

9/14/56 King, Martin Luther, Jr. (MIA). "Letter to L. (Levi) M. Terrill." 9/14/56. [*Montgomery, Ala.*] (TLc) 1 p. MLKP-MBU: Box 66. 560914–007.

9/14/56 King, Martin Luther, Jr. (MIA). "Letter to C. S. Reeder." 9/14/56. [*Montgomery, Ala.*] (TLc) 1 p. MLKP-MBU: Box 64. 560914–005.

9/14/56 Lee, J. (James) Oscar (National Council of the Churches of Christ in the United States of America). "Letter to Martin Luther King, Jr." 9/14/56. New York, N.Y. (TLS) 1 p. MLKP-MBU: Box 32A. 560914–006.

9/16/56 Muelder, Walter George (Boston University). "Letter to Martin Luther King, Jr." 9/16/56. Boston, Mass. (TLS) 1 p. MLKP-MBU: Box 15. 560916–000.

9/17/56 King, Martin Luther, Jr. (MIA). "Letter to Warren Olney III." 9/17/56. [*Montgomery, Ala.*] (TLc) 1 p. MLKP-MBU: Box 66A. 560917–003.

9/17/56 MIA. "Program, Mass meeting at First Baptist Church." 9/17/56. Montgomery, Ala. (THD) 1 p. MLKP-MBU: Box 30. 560917–005.

9/17/56 Sloan, Viva O. "Letter to Martin Luther King, Jr." 9/17/56. Morgantown, W.Va. (TAHLS) 1 p. MLKP-MBU: Box 65. 560917–006.

9/17/56 King, Martin Luther, Jr. (MIA). "Letter to Carrol O. Morong." 9/17/56. [*Montgomery, Ala.*] (TLc) 1 p. MLKP-MBU: Box 61. 560917–008.

9/17/56 King, Martin Luther, Jr. (MIA). "Letter to Eugene Davidson." 9/17/56. [*Montgomery, Ala.*] (TLc) 1 p. MLKP-MBU: Box 63. 560917–009.

9/17/56 Duckett, Alfred. "Telegram to Martin Luther King, Jr." 9/17/56. Chicago, Ill. (PHWSr) 1 p. MLKP-MBU: Box 16. 560917–011.

9/17/56 Terrill, L. (Levi) M. (Zion Hill Baptist Church). "Letter to Martin Luther King, Jr." 9/17/56. Atlanta, Ga. (TLS) 1 p. MLKP-MBU: Box 67. 560917–012.

9/18/56 Powell, W. (William) J. (MIA). "Minutes, Executive board meeting." 9/18/56. Montgomery, Ala. (TD) 1 p. MLKP-MBU: Box 30. 560918–002.

9/18/56 King, Martin Luther, Jr. (Dexter Avenue Baptist Church). "Letter to Nannie H. Burroughs." 9/18/56. Montgomery, Ala. (THLS) 1 p. NHBP-DLC. 560918–004.

9/18/56 King, Martin Luther, Jr. (MIA). "Letter to William Cooper Cumming." 9/18/56. [*Montgomery, Ala.*] (TLc) 1 p. MLKP-MBU: Box 67. 560918–006.

9/18/56 King, Martin Luther, Jr. "Letter to Vernon Johns." 9/18/56. [*Montgomery, Ala.*] (TLc) 1 p. DABCC. 560918–007.

9/18/56 Handy, W. T. (William Talbot), Jr. (Newman Methodist Church). "Letter to Martin Luther King, Jr., and Coretta Scott King." 9/18/56. Alexandria, La. (TLS) 1 p. MLKP-MBU: Box 91. 560918–000.

9/19/56 King, Martin Luther, Jr. (MIA). "Letter to Sally Canada." 9/19/56. [*Montgomery, Ala.*] (TLc) 1 p. MLKP-MBU: Box 5. 560919–000.

9/19/56 King, Martin Luther, Jr. (MIA). "Letter to Manuel D. Talley." 9/19/56. [*Montgomery, Ala.*] (TLc) 1 p. MLKP-MBU: Box 63. 560919–010.

9/19/56 King, Martin Luther, Jr. "Letter to Lafayette Dudley." 9/19/56. [*Montgomery, Ala.*] (TLc) 1 p. MLKP-MBU: Box 16. 560919–014.

9/19/56 King, Martin Luther, Jr. (MIA). "Letter to E. F. Rodriguez." 9/19/56. [*Montgomery, Ala.*] (TLc) 1 p. MLKP-MBU: Box 64A. 560919–002.

9/19/56 King, Martin Luther, Jr. (MIA). "Letter to C. (Charles) W. Kelly." 9/19/56. [*Montgomery, Ala.*] (TLc) 1 p. MLKP-MBU: Box 66. 560919–009.

9/20/56 King, Martin Luther, Jr. (MIA). "Letter to Bayard Rustin." 9/20/56. [*Montgomery, Ala.*] (TLc) 3 pp. MLKP-MBU: Box 67. 560920–000.

9/20/56 King, Martin Luther, Jr. (MIA). "Letter to Glenn E. Smiley." 9/20/56. [*Montgomery, Ala.*] (TLc) 1 p. MLKP-MBU: Box 16. 560920–007.

9/20/56 King, Martin Luther, Jr. (MIA). "Letter to L. E. Austin." 9/20/56. [*Montgomery, Ala.*] (TLc) 1 p. MLKP-MBU: Box 15. 560920–011.

9/21/56 MIA. "*Newsletter* 1, no. 4." 9/21/56. Montgomery, Ala. (TD) 3 pp. HJP-GAMK. 560921–001.

9/21/56 Ballou, Maude L. "Letter to W. Lester Banks." 9/21/56. [*Montgomery, Ala.*] (TLc) 1 p. MLKP-MBU: Box 63. 560921–004.

9/24/56 King, Martin Luther, Jr. (MIA). "Letter to Wilbert J. Johnson." 9/24/56. [*Montgomery, Ala.*] (TLc) 1 p. MLKP-MBU: Box 60. 560924–011.

9/24/56   Calhoun, J. H. (NAACP). "Letter to Martin Luther King, Jr." 9/24/56. Atlanta, Ga. (TLS) 1 p. MLKP-MBU: Box 62. 560924–004.

9/24/56   Feldman, Eugene. "Letter to Martin Luther King, Jr." 9/24/56. Winston Salem, N.C. (TLS) 2 pp. MLKP-MBU: Box 16. 560924–005.

9/24/56   King, Martin Luther, Jr. (MIA). "Letter to J. (James) Oscar Lee." 9/24/56. [*Montgomery, Ala.*] (TLc) 1 p. MLKP-MBU: Box 32A. 560924–014.

9/25/56   **Pinkston, Harold Edward (Virginia Union University). "Letter to Martin Luther King, Jr." 9/25/56. Richmond, Va. (ALS) 3 pp. MLKP-MBU: Box 66A. 560925–006.**

9/25/56   **Thomas, Samuel S. "Letter to Martin Luther King, Jr." 9/25/56. Brunswick, N.C. (AHLS) 2 pp. MLKP-MBU: Box 64. 560925–012.**

9/25/56   McCall, Walter R. (Fort Valley State College). "Letter to Martin Luther King, Jr." 9/25/56. Fort Valley, Ga. (TLS) 1 p. MLKP-MBU: Box 17. 560925–002.

9/25/56   Powell, W. (William) J. (MIA). "Minutes, Special committee meeting." 9/25/56. Montgomery, Ala. (TADS) 2 pp. MLKP-MBU: Box 30. 560925–008.

9/25/56   Olney, Warren, III (U.S. Department of Justice). "Letter to Robert Graetz." 9/25/56. Washington, D.C. (TLSr) 1 p. (Signed by Arthur B. Caldwell.) RGP. 560925–010.

9/26/56   **Rustin, Bayard. "Letter to Martin Luther King, Jr." 9/26/56. (TLc) 3 pp. (Includes enclosure.) BRP-DLC: Reel 3. 560926–005.**

9/26/56   MIA. "Agenda, Executive board meeting." 9/26/56. Montgomery, Ala. (THD) 1 p. (Marginal comments by King.) MLKP-MBU: Box 30. 560926–002.

9/27/56   **"Photo of Martin Luther King, Jr., at Hampton Institute." 9/27/56. Hampton, Va. (Ph) 1 p. MLK/BP-ViHaI. 560927–000.**

9/27/56   Smith, Kelly Miller (First Baptist Church). "Letter to Martin Luther King, Jr." 9/27/56. Nashville, Tenn. (TLS) 1 p. MLKP-MBU: Box 17. 560927–003.

9/27/56   Johns, Vernon (United Baptist Missionary Convention and Auxiliars of Maryland). "Letter to Martin Luther King, Jr." 9/27/56. Baltimore, Md. (TLS) 1 p. MLKP-MBU: Box 66. 560927–005.

9/27/56   Jumper, Iris (Hampton Institute). "Letter to Martin Luther King, Jr." 9/27/56. Hampton, Va. (ALS) 2 pp. MLKP-MBU: Box 60. 560927–006.

9/27/56   Rohrbough, Lynn (Cooperative Recreation Service). "Letter to Martin Luther King, Jr., and Coretta Scott King." 9/27/56. Delaware, Ohio. (TLS) 1 p. MLKP-MBU: Box 15. 560927–007.

9/27/56   King, Martin Luther, Jr. (MIA). "Letter to Carlton M. Stephens." 9/27/56. [*Montgomery, Ala.*] (TLc) 1 p. MLKP-MBU: Box 65. 560927–009.

9/27/56   King, Martin Luther, Jr. (MIA). "Letter to Almena Lomax." 9/27/56. [*Montgomery, Ala.*] (TLc) 1 p. MLKP-MBU: Box 61. 560927–010.

9/28/56   **John, Alma (WWRL radio station). "Letter to Martin Luther King, Jr." 9/28/56. New York, N.Y. (AHLS) 3 pp. (Includes enclosure.) MLKP-MBU: Box 60. 560928–001.**

9/28/56   Mathiason, David G. (Oberlin College). "Letter to Martin Luther King, Jr." 9/28/56. Oberlin, Ohio. (TLS) 2 pp. MLKP-MBU: Box 61. 560928–003.

9/28/56   Banks, W. Lester (NAACP). "Letter to Martin Luther King, Jr." 9/28/56. Petersburg, Va. (TLS) 1 p. MLKP-MBU: Box 63. 560928–004.

9/28/56   Schmitz, Helen C. (American Baptist Home Misson Boards). "Letter to Martin Luther King, Jr." 9/28/56. New York, N.Y. (THLS) 1 p. (Marginal comments by King.) MLKP-MBU: Box 14. 560928–006.

9/28/56   Powell, W. (William) J. (Old Ship AME Zion Church). "Letter to Martin Luther King, Jr." 9/28/56. Montgomery, Ala. (TLS) 1 p. DABCC. 560928–008.

9/29/56   DeWolf, L. Harold (Boston University). "Letter to Martin Luther King, Jr." 9/29/56. Boston, Mass. (TLS) 1 p. MLKP-MBU: Box 15. 560929–000.

9/30/56   Chamberlin, Roy B. (Talladega College). "Letter to Martin Luther King, Jr." 9/30/56. Talladega, Ala. (TLS) 1 p. MLKP-MBU: Box 66. 560930–000.

9/56   Rustin, Bayard. "Letter to A. (Asa) Philip Randolph." [*9/56*]. New York, N.Y. (ALS) 3 pp. (Contains 560920–000.) APRC-DLC. 560900–015.

10/56   King, Martin Luther, Jr. "Telegram to Arnold Demille." [*9/56–10/56*]. [*Montgomery, Ala.*] (TWc) 1 p. MLKP-MBU: Box 16. 561000–002.

10/56   MIA. "Program, Mass meeting at First Baptist Church." [*7/1/56–10/56*]. Montgomery, Ala. (TD) 2 pp. MLKP-MBU: Box 30. 561000–010.

10/56   MIA. "Program, Mass meeting at Beulah Baptist Church." [*5/56–10/56*]. Montgomery, Ala. (THD) 1 p. (Marginal comments by King.) MLKP-MBU: Box 30. 561000–011.

10/56   MIA. "Program, Mass meeting at Hutchinson Street Baptist Church." [*5/56–10/56*]. Montgomery, Ala. (TD) 1 p. HG-GAMK. 561000–012.

10/1/56   **King, Martin Luther, Jr. (MIA). "Letter to Viva O. Sloan." 10/1/56. [*Montgomery, Ala.*] (TLc) 1 p. MLKP-MBU: Box 65. 561001–004.**

10/1/56   Hughes, Robert E. (Alabama Council on Human Relations). "Letter to Glenn E. Smiley." 10/1/56. Homewood, Ala. (ALS) 2 pp. FORP-PSP-P. 561001–005.

10/1/56   MIA. "Program, Mass meeting at Hutchinson Street Baptist Church." 10/1/56. Montgomery, Ala. (TD) 1 p. RGP. 561001–003.

10/1/56   King, Martin Luther, Jr. "Letter to Cornell E. Talley." 10/1/56. [*Montgomery, Ala.*] (TLc) 1 p. MLKP-MBU: Box 67. 561001–006.

10/2/56   **King, Martin Luther, Jr. (MIA). "Letter to Cecil A. Thomas." 10/2/56. [*Montgomery, Ala.*] (TLc) 2 pp. MLKP-MBU: Box 67. 561002–008.**

10/2/56   **Olney, Warren, III (U.S. Department of Justice). "Letter to Martin Luther King, Jr." 10/2/56. Washington, D.C. (TLSr) 1 p. (Signed by Arthur B. Caldwell.) MLKP-MBU: Box 23. 561002–010.**

10/2/56   King, Martin Luther, Jr. (MIA). "Letter to Kelly Miller Smith." 10/2/56. [*Montgomery, Ala.*] (TLc) 1 p. MLKP-MBU: Box 17. 561002–003.

10/2/56   King, Martin Luther, Jr. (MIA). "Letter to L. Harold DeWolf." 10/2/56. [*Montgomery, Ala.*] (TLc) 1 p. MLKP-MBU: Box 15. 561002–006.

10/2/56   King, Martin Luther, Jr. (Dexter Avenue Baptist Church). "Letter to Lynn Rohrbough." 10/2/56. [*Montgomery, Ala.*] (TLc) 1 p. MLKP-MBU: Box 15. 561002–007.

10/3/56   **King, Martin Luther, Jr. (MIA). "Letter to Walter George Muelder." 10/3/56. Montgomery, Ala. (TLS) 1 p. WMP-MBU. 561003–000.**

10/3/56   **Cannon, Robert L. (Fellowship of Reconciliation). "Letter to Alfred Hassler and Glenn E. Smiley." 10/3/56. Nashville, Tenn. (THLS) 3 pp. FORP-PSC-P. 561003–001.**

10/3/56   **King, Martin Luther, Jr. (MIA). "Letter to Sylvester S. Robinson." 10/3/56. [*Montgomery, Ala.*] (TLc) 2 pp. MLKP-MBU: Box 64A. 561003–002.**

10/3/56   **Moore, Douglas E. "Letter to Martin Luther King, Jr." 10/3/56. Durham, N.C. (THLS) 4 pp. MLKP-MBU: Box 62. 561003–012.**

10/3/56   Dexter Avenue Baptist Church. "*Dexter Echo* 1, no. 7." 10/3/56. Montgomery, Ala. (TD) 4 pp. MLKP-MBU: Box 77. 561003–003.

10/3/56   Fowler, Elmer L. (Dorie Miller Memorial Foundation). "Letter to Martin Luther King, Jr." 10/3/56. Chicago, Ill. (TLS) 2 pp. MLKP-MBU: Box 61. 561003–004.

10/3/56   King, Martin Luther, Jr. (MIA). "Letter to Eugene Feldman." 10/3/56. [*Montgomery, Ala.*] (TLc) 1 p. MLKP-MBU: Box 16. 561003–005.

10/3/56   King, Martin Luther, Jr. (Dexter Avenue Baptist Church). "Letter to L. Harold DeWolf." 10/3/56. [*Montgomery, Ala.*] (TLc) 1 p. MLKP-MBU: Box 15. 561003–006.

10/3/56   King, Martin Luther, Jr. "Letter to Roy B. Chamberlin." 10/3/56. [*Montgomery, Ala.*] (TLc) 1 p. MLKP-MBU: Box 66. 561003–008.

10/3/56   King, Martin Luther, Jr. (MIA). "Letter to David G. Mathiasen." 10/3/56. [*Montgomery, Ala.*] (TLc) 1 p. MLKP-MBU: Box 61. 561003–011.

10/4/56   McCrackin, Maurice (St. Barnabas Church). "Letter to Martin Luther King, Jr." 10/4/56. Cincinnati, Ohio. (TLS) 1 p. MLKP-MBU: Box 65. 561004–001.

10/5/56   Cannon, Robert L. (Fellowship of Reconciliation). "Letter to Martin Luther King, Jr." 10/5/56. Nashville, Tenn. (TLS) 1 p. MLKP-MBU: Box 17. 561005–000.

10/5/56   Seymour, Whitney North (United Negro College Fund). "Letter to Martin Luther King, Jr." 10/5/56. New York, N.Y. (TLS) 1 p. MLKP-MBU: Box 66. 561005–003.

10/6/56   Terrill, L. (Levi) M. (Zion Hill Baptist Church). "Letter to Martin Luther King, Jr." 10/6/56. Atlanta, Ga. (TLS) 1 p. MLKP-MBU: Box 67. 561006–000.

10/8/56   King, Martin Luther, Jr. (Dexter Avenue Baptist Church). "Letter to Elmer L. Fowler." 10/8/56. [*Montgomery, Ala.*] (TLc) 1 p. MLKP-MBU: Box 61. 561008–002.

10/8/56   King, Martin Luther, Jr. (Dexter Avenue Baptist Church). "Letter to Alonzo G. Moron." 10/8/56. [*Montgomery, Ala.*] (TLc) 1 p. MLKP-MBU: Box 60. 561008–004.

10/8/56   King, Martin Luther, Jr. (Dexter Avenue Baptist Church). "Letter to Joseph L. Griffin." 10/8/56. [*Montgomery, Ala.*] (TLc) 1 p. MLKP-MBU: Box 61. 561008–006.

10/8/56   King, Martin Luther, Jr. (MIA). "Letter to W. Lester Banks." 10/8/56. [*Montgomery, Ala.*] (TLc) 1 p. MLKP-MBU: Box 63. 561008–007.

10/9/56	**King, Martin Luther, Jr. (Dexter Avenue Baptist Church). "Letter to Samuel S. Thomas." 10/9/56. [*Montgomery, Ala.*] (TLc) 1 p. MLKP-MBU: Box 64. 561009–006.**
10/9/56	DeWolf, L. Harold (Boston University). "Letter to Martin Luther King, Jr." 10/9/56. Boston, Mass. (TLS) 1 p. MLKP-MBU: Box 15. 561009–000.
10/9/56	King, Martin Luther, Sr. "Letter to J. E. Tilford." 10/9/56. (TLc) 2 pp. EBCR. 561009–003.
10/9/56	King, Martin Luther, Jr. (MIA). "Letter to Mary Wolfard." 10/9/56. [*Montgomery, Ala.*] (TLc) 1 p. MLKP-MBU: Box 67. 561009–009.
10/10/56	Glasco, R. J. (MIA). "Financial report, 9/13/56–10/8/56." 10/10/56. Montgomery, Ala. (TD) 1 p. RJGC. 561010–000.
10/10/56	Proctor, Samuel D. (Dewitt) (Virginia Union University). "Letter to Martin Luther King, Jr." 10/10/56. Richmond, Va. (TLS) 1 p. MLKP-MBU: Box 66. 561010–006.
10/10/56	King, Martin Luther, Jr. (Dexter Avenue Baptist Church). "Letter to Roy B. Chamberlin." 10/10/56. [*Montgomery, Ala.*] (TLc) 1 p. MLKP-MBU: Box 66. 561010–009.
10/10/56	MIA. "Agenda and minutes, Executive board meeting." 10/10/56. Montgomery, Ala. (THD) 2 pp. RGP. 561010–011.
10/10/56	Hall, Grover C. (*Montgomery Advertiser*). "Letter to Martin Luther King, Jr." 10/10/56. Montgomery, Ala. (TALS) 1 p. MLKP-MBU: Box 62. 561010–014.
10/10/56	King, Martin Luther, Jr. (Dexter Avenue Baptist Church). "Letter to Henry Parker." 10/10/56. [*Montgomery, Ala.*] (TLc) 1 p. MLKP-MBU: Box 64. 561010–015.
10/10/56	King, Martin Luther, Jr. (Dexter Avenue Baptist Church). "Letter to Ralph Henry." 10/10/56. [*Montgomery, Ala.*] (TLc) 1 p. MLKP-MBU: Box 60. 561010–016.
10/10/56	King, Martin Luther, Jr. (Dexter Avenue Baptist Church). "Letter to Malcolm G. Dade." 10/10/56. [*Montgomery, Ala.*] (TLc) 1 p. MLKP-MBU: Box 65. 561010–017.
10/11/56	**King, Martin Luther, Jr. (Dexter Avenue Baptist Church). "Letter to Charles S. Johnson." 10/11/56. [*Montgomery, Ala.*] (TLc) 1 p. MLKP-MBU: Box 17. 561011–001.**
10/11/56	Talley, Cornell E. (Pennsylvania Baptist State Convention). "Letter to Martin Luther King, Jr." 10/11/56. Pittsburgh, Pa. (TLS) 1 p. MLKP-MBU: Box 91. 561011–000.
10/12/56	Wilkes, Warren G. (Baptist Ministers Brotherhood). "Letter to Martin Luther King, Jr." 10/12/56. Camilla, Ga. (TLS) 1 p. MLKP-MBU: Box 14. 561012–000.
10/15/56	**King, Martin Luther, Jr. (Dexter Avenue Baptist Church). "Letter to Raleigh A. Bryant." 10/15/56. [*Montgomery, Ala.*] (TLc) 1 p. MLKP-MBU: Box 16. 561015–004.**
10/15/56	King, Martin Luther, Jr. "Letter to Walter R. McCall." 10/15/56. [*Montgomery, Ala.*] (TLc) 1 p. MLKP-MBU: Box 17. 561015–002.
10/15/56	Carey, Archibald James, Jr. "Letter to Martin Luther King, Jr., and Coretta Scott King." 10/15/56. Chicago, Ill. (TLS) 1 p. MLKP-MBU: Box 91. 561015–000.
10/15/56	Carmichael, J. H. (Capital Airlines). "Letter to Martin Luther King, Jr." 10/15/56. Washington, D.C. (TLS) 1 p. MLKP-MBU: Box 15. 561015–009.
10/15/56	Bonner, J. H. (MIA). "Recommendations of the ways and means committee." 10/15/56. (ADS) 1 p. MLKP-MBU: Box 6. 561015–011.
10/15/56	Ballou, Maude L. "Letter to Helen C. Schmitz." 10/15/56. [*Montgomery, Ala.*] (TLc) 1 p. MLKP-MBU: Box 14. 561015–014.
10/15/56	King, Martin Luther, Jr. (Dexter Avenue Baptist Church). "Letter to L. (Levi) M. Terrill." 10/15/56. [*Montgomery, Ala.*] (TLc) 1 p. MLKP-MBU: Box 67. 561015–015.
10/16/56	Lenud, Phillip M. "Telegram to Martin Luther King, Jr." 10/16/56. Worcester, Mass. (PWSr) 1 p. MLKP-MBU: Box 61. 561016–002.
10/17/56	**Roosevelt, Eleanor. "Telegram to Martin Luther King, Jr." 10/17/56. New York, N.Y. (PWSr) 1 p. MLKP-MBU: Box 64. 561017–001.**
10/17/56	King, Martin Luther, Jr. (MIA). "Telegram to Glenn E. Smiley." 10/17/56. (TWSr) 1 p. FORP-PSC-P. 561017–000.
10/17/56	Ballou, Maude L. (MIA). "Telegram to Eleanor Roosevelt." [*10/17/56*]. [*Montgomery, Ala.*] (PWc) 1 p. MLKP-MBU: Box 64. 561017–002.
10/18/56	Rustin, Bayard (*Liberation*). "Letter to Martin Luther King, Jr." 10/18/56. New York, N.Y. (TLS) 2 pp. MLKP-MBU: Box 64A. 561018–001.

10/18/56   Lawrence, George (Friendship Baptist Church). "Letter to Martin Luther King, Jr." 10/18/56. New York, N.Y. (TLS) 1 p. MLKP-MBU: Box 17. 561018–002.

10/18/56   Kennedy, Earl (Michigan Citizens for Eisenhower). "Letter to Martin Luther King, Jr." 10/18/56. Detroit, Mich. (TLS) 1 p. MLKP-MBU: Box 61. 561018–003.

10/18/56   Willingham, Edward B. (American Baptist Foreign Mission Society). "Letter to Martin Luther King, Jr." 10/18/56. New York, N.Y. (TLS) 1 p. MLKP-MBU: Box 18. 561018–004.

10/18/56   Schuyler, George S. (*Pittsburgh Courier*). "Letter to Martin Luther King, Jr." 10/18/56. New York, N.Y. (TLS) 1 p. MLKP-MBU: Box 61. 561018–005.

10/19/56   Vivian, C. Tindall (National Baptist Sunday School Publishing Board). "Letter to Martin Luther King, Jr." 10/19/56. Nashville, Tenn. (TLS) 1 p. MLKP-MBU: Box 67. 561019–001.

10/19/56   Olivet Baptist Church. "Announcement, Coretta Scott King in Recital." 10/19/56. Chicago, Ill. (PHD) 1 p. AJC-ICHi: Box 29. 561019–002.

10/19/56   Smiley, Glenn E. "Memo to Alfred Hassler." 10/19/56. (THLc) 2 pp. FORP-PSC-P. 561019–003.

10/20/56   Bell, Ada Pace. "Letter to Martin Luther King, Jr." Berkeley, Calif. (ALS) 3 pp. MLKP-MBU: Box 14. 561020–000.

10/21/56   **Jemison, T. J. (Theodore Judson) (Mount Zion First Baptist Church). "Letter to Martin Luther King, Jr." 10/21/56. Baton Rouge, La. (TALS) 1 p. MLKP-MBU: Box 61. 561021–000.**

10/22/56   King, Martin Luther, Jr. (MIA). "Letter to M. R. Austell." 10/22/56. [*Montgomery, Ala.*] (TLc) 1 p. MLKP-MBU: Box 17. 561022–001.

10/22/56   Bryant, Raleigh A. (First African Baptist Church). "Letter to Martin Luther King, Jr." 10/22/56. Savannah, Ga. (TLS) 1 p. MLKP-MBU: Box 16. 561022–003.

10/22/56   Powell, C. Clayton (NAACP). "Letter to Martin Luther King, Jr." 10/22/56. Atlanta, Ga. (TLc) 1 p. MLKP-MBU: Box 63. 561022–004.

10/22/56   King, Martin Luther, Jr. "Letter to Phillip M. Lenud." 10/22/56. [*Montgomery, Ala.*] (TLc) 1 p. MLKP-MBU: Box 61. 561022–006.

10/22/56   Dixon, Richard H. (Trinity Baptist Church). "Letter to Martin Luther King, Jr." 10/22/56. Pontiac, Mich. (TLSr) 1 p. MLKP-MBU: Box 66. 561022–008.

10/23/56   **King, Martin Luther, Jr. "Letter to L. Harold DeWolf." 10/23/56. [*Montgomery, Ala.*] (TLc) 1 p. MLKP-MBU: Box 15. 561023–001.**

10/23/56   **Steele, C. Kenzie (Inter-Civic Council). "Letter to Martin Luther King, Jr." 10/23/56. Tallahassee, Fla. (TLS) 1 p. MLKP-MBU: Box 60. 561023–004.**

10/23/56   Stright, Hayden L. (Minnesota Council of Churches). "Letter to Martin Luther King, Jr." 10/23/56. Minneapolis, Minn. (TLS) 1 p. MLKP-MBU: Box 62. 561023–003.

10/24/56   King, Martin Luther, Jr. (MIA). "Letter to Howard B. Gilman." 10/24/56. [*Montgomery, Ala.*] (TLc) 1 p. MLKP-MBU: Box 17. 561024–001.

10/24/56   King, Martin Luther, Jr. (Dexter Avenue Baptist Church). "Letter to Warren G. Wilkes." 10/24/56. [*Montgomery, Ala.*] (TLc) 1 p. MLKP-MBU: Box 14. 561024–002.

10/24/56   King, Martin Luther, Jr. "Letter to T. J. (Theodore Judson) Jemison." 10/24/56. [*Montgomery, Ala.*] (TLc) 1 p. MLKP-MBU: Box 61. 561024–003.

10/24/56   Kleinbaum, Max M. (Brandeis University). "Telegram to Martin Luther King, Jr." 10/24/56. Waltham, Mass. (PWSr) 1 p. MLKP-MBU: Box 15. 561024–005.

10/24/56   MIA. "Minutes, Executive board meeting." 10/24/56. Montgomery, Ala. (AD) 3 pp. MLKP-MBU: Box 6. 561024–008.

10/24/56   King, Martin Luther, Jr. (MIA). "Letter to Mr. and Mrs. H. M. Michaux." 10/24/56. [*Montgomery, Ala.*] (TLc) 1 p. MLKP-MBU: Box 62. 561024–011.

10/24/56   Corbett, Gordon L. (Presbyterian Church). "Letter to Martin Luther King, Jr." 10/24/56. Glens Falls, N.Y. (TLS) 1 p. MLKP-MBU: Box 15. 561024–012.

10/24/56   MIA. "Agenda, Executive board meeting." 10/24/56. Montgomery, Ala. (THD) 1 p. (Marginal comments by King.) MLKP-MBU: Box 30. 561024–013.

10/25/56   **Rabb, Maxwell M. (U.S. White House). "Letter to Martin Luther King, Jr." 10/25/56. Washington, D.C. (TLS) 1 p. MLKP-MBU: Box 64. 561025–000.**

10/25/56   Ballou, Maude L. (MIA). "Letter to Selma Levenberg." 10/25/56. [*Montgomery, Ala.*] (TLc) 1 p. (Contains enclosure 561025–003.) MLKP-MBU: Box 19. 561025–001.

10/25/56   [*King, Martin Luther, Jr.*] "Quotable excerpts." [*10/25/56*]. [*Montgomery, Ala.*] (TDf) 2 pp. (Enclosure in 561025–001.) MLKP-MBU: Box 19. 561025–003.

10/26/56   **Simms, B. J. (MIA). "Letter to Martin Luther King, Jr., and the executive committee." 10/26/56. Montgomery, Ala. (TLS) 1 p. MLKP-MBU: Box 30. 561026–001.**

10/27/56	Ministerial Association. "Memo to Ministers." [*10/26/56–10/27/56*]. Montgomery, Ala. (TL) 1 p. HJP-GAMK. 561027–000.
10/29/56	**McCall, Walter R. (Fort Valley State College). "Letter to Martin Luther King, Jr." 10/29/56. Fort Valley, Ga. (TALS) 1 p. MLKP-MBU: Box 17. 561029–001.**
10/29/56	King, Martin Luther, Jr. (Dexter Avenue Baptist Church). "Letter to Samuel D. (Dewitt) Proctor." 10/29/56. [*Montgomery, Ala.*] (TLc) 1 p. MLKP-MBU: Box 66. 561029–002.
10/29/56	King, Martin Luther, Jr. (Dexter Avenue Baptist Church). "Letter to Ivis Jumper." 10/29/56. [*Montgomery, Ala.*] (TLc) 1 p. MLKP-MBU: Box 60. 561029–003.
10/29/56	Mathiasen, David (Oberlin College). "Letter to Martin Luther King, Jr." 10/29/56. Oberlin, Ohio. (TLS) 1 p. MLKP-MBU: Box 61. 561029–008.
10/29/56	King, Martin Luther, Jr. (MIA). "Letter to Grover C. Hall." 10/29/56. [*Montgomery, Ala.*] (TLc) 1 p. MLKP-MBU: Box 62. 561029–009.
10/29/56	King, Martin Luther, Jr. (MIA). "Letter to Floyd Massey." 10/29/56. [*Montgomery, Ala.*] (TLc) 1 p. MLKP-MBU: Box 64. 561029–011.
10/30/56	**King, Martin Luther, Jr. (MIA). "Letter to George Lawrence." 10/30/56. [*Montgomery, Ala.*] (TLc) 1 p. MLKP-MBU: Box 17. 561030–000.**
10/30/56	**King, Martin Luther, Jr. (MIA). "Letter to Earl Kennedy." 10/30/56. [*Montgomery, Ala.*] (TLc) 1 p. MLKP-MBU: Box 61. 561030–002.**
10/30/56	Berger, Jean (Middlebury College). "Letter to Martin Luther King, Jr." 10/30/56. Middlebury, Vt. (TLS) 1 p. MLKP-MBU: Box 61. 561030–001.
10/30/56	King, Martin Luther, Jr. (MIA). "Letter to C. Clayton Powell." 10/30/56. [*Montgomery, Ala.*] (TLc) 1 p. MLKP-MBU: Box 63. 561030–003.
10/30/56	Wynn, Daniel W. (Tuskegee Institute). "Letter to Martin Luther King, Jr." 10/30/56. Tuskegee, Ala. (TLS) 1 p. MLKP-MBU: Box 67. 561030–004.
10/31/56	**King, Martin Luther, Jr. (Dexter Avenue Baptist Church). "Annual Report, Dexter Avenue Baptist Church." 11/1/55–10/31/56. Montgomery, Ala. (TD) 42 pp. MLKP-MBU: Box 77. 561031–000.**
10/31/56	**King, Martin Luther, Jr. "Letter to Alfred Daniel King." 10/31/56. [*Montgomery, Ala.*] (TLc) 1 p. MLKP-MBU: Box 61. 561031–005.**
10/31/56	**King, Martin Luther, Jr. (MIA). "Telegram to Benjamin F. McLaurin." [*10/31/56*]. [*Montgomery, Ala.*] (TWc) 2 pp. MLKP-MBU: Box 61. 561031–006.**
10/31/56	Dexter Avenue Baptist Church. "*Dexter Echo* 1, no. 9." 10/31/56. Montgomery, Ala. (TD) 4 pp. MLKP-MBU: Box 77. 561031–002.
10/31/56	King, Martin Luther, Jr. (MIA). "Letter to T. J. (Theodore Judson) Jemison." 10/31/56. [*Montgomery, Ala.*] (TLc) 1 p. MLKP-MBU: Box 66. 561031–003.
10/31/56	King, Martin Luther, Jr. (MIA). "Letter to George S. Schuyler." 10/31/56. [*Montgomery, Ala.*] (TLc) 1 p. MLKP-MBU: Box 61. 561031–008.
11/56	King, Martin Luther, Jr. "Job description for promotional director." [*11/56*]. [*Montgomery, Ala.*] (AD) 1 p. MLKP-MBU: Box 30. 561100–003.
11/56	King, Martin Luther, Jr. "Job description, public relations committee." [*11/56*]. [*Montgomery, Ala.*] (AD) 1 p. MLKP-MBU: Box 30. 561100–004.
11/56	King, Martin Luther, Jr., and Abernathy, Ralph (MIA). "Telegram to Lillian Eugenia Smith." [*11/56*]. Montgomery, Ala. (PWSr) 2 pp. LSP-GU. 561100–006.
11/56	King, Martin Luther, Jr. (MIA). "Non-Violent Procedures to Inter-racial Harmony." 11/56. Dryden, N.Y. From: *Empire State Universalist* (November 1956): 7–10. (PD) 4 pp. UUAR-MH-AH. 561100–007.
11/1/56	King, Martin Luther, Jr. (MIA). "Letter to William L. Bentley." 11/1/56. [*Montgomery, Ala.*] (TLc) 2 pp. MLKP-MBU: Box 14. 561101–001.
11/1/56	King, Martin Luther, Jr. (MIA). "Letter to Ada Pace Bell." 11/1/56. [*Montgomery, Ala.*] (TLc) 1 p. MLKP-MBU: Box 14. 561101–002.
11/1/56	King, Martin Luther, Jr. (MIA). "Letter to Edward B. Willingham." 11/1/56. [*Montgomery, Ala.*] (TLc) 1 p. MLKP-MBU: Box 18. 561101–007.
11/1/56	King, Martin Luther, Jr. (MIA). "Letter to William E. Stevenson." 11/1/56. [*Montgomery, Ala.*] (TLc) 1 p. MLKP-MBU: Box 61. 561101–010.
11/1/56	King, Martin Luther, Jr. (MIA). "Letter to C. Tindall Vivian." 11/1/56. [*Montgomery, Ala.*] (TLc) 1 p. MLKP-MBU: Box 67. 561101–011.
11/2/56	King, Martin Luther, Jr. (MIA). "Letter to Anna Arnold Hedgeman." 11/2/56. [*Montgomery, Ala.*] (TLc) 1 p. MLKP-MBU: Box 60. 561102–003.
11/4/56	**King, Martin Luther, Jr. (Dexter Avenue Baptist Church). "Paul's Letter to American Christians, Sermon at Dexter Avenue Baptist Church." 11/4/56. Montgomery, Ala. (PD) 7 pp. MLKP-MBU: Box 119A. 561104–000.**
11/5/56	**King, Martin Luther, Jr. (MIA). "Letter to Eleanor Roosevelt." 11/5/56. Montgomery, Ala. (TLSr) 1 p. ERC-NHyF. 561105–007.**

11/5/56   King, Martin Luther, Jr. (MIA). "Letter to Alma John." 11/5/56. [*Montgomery, Ala.*] (TLc) 1 p. MLKP-MBU: Box 60A. 561105–000.

11/5/56   Walker, Charles (Fellowship of Reconciliation). "Letter to Martin Luther King, Jr." 11/5/56. Philadelphia, Pa. (TLS) 2 pp. MLKP-MBU: Box 16. 561105–001.

11/5/56   MIA. "Program, Mass meeting at First Baptist Church." 11/5/56. Montgomery, Ala. (TD) 1 p. HG-GAMK. 561105–002.

11/5/56   King, Martin Luther, Jr. (MIA). "Letter to Jean Berger." 11/5/56. [*Montgomery, Ala.*] (TLc) 1 p. MLKP-MBU: Box 61. 561105–003.

11/5/56   King, Martin Luther, Jr. (MIA). "Letter to L. Harold DeWolf." 11/5/56. [*Montgomery, Ala.*] (TLc) 1 p. MLKP-MBU: Box 15. 561105–005.

11/5/56   King, Martin Luther, Jr. (MIA). "Letter to J. Rupert Picott." 11/5/56. [*Montgomery, Ala.*] (TLc) 1 p. MLKP-MBU: Box 66. 561105–006.

11/5/56   Durr, Virginia Foster. "Letter to Myles Horton." 11/5/56. Montgomery, Ala. (TL) 1 p. HRECR-WHi: Box 11. 561105–008.

11/5/56   King, Martin Luther, Jr. (MIA). "Letter to Samuel D. (Dewitt) Proctor." 11/5/56. [*Montgomery, Ala.*] (TLc) 1 p. MLKP-MBU: Box 64. 561105–015.

11/5/56   Stewart, Annalee (Women's International League for Peace and Freedom). "Letter to Martin Luther King, Jr." 11/5/56. Washington, D.C. (TLS) 1 p. MLKP-MBU: Box 67. 561105–016.

11/5/56   King, Martin Luther, Jr. (MIA). "Letter to Gordon L. Corbett." 11/5/56. [*Montgomery, Ala.*] (TLc) 1 p. MLKP-MBU: Box 15. 561105–017.

11/6/56   Bigelow, Albert S. "Letter to MIA." 11/6/56. Cos Cob, Conn. (ALS) 1 p. MLKP-MBU: Box 14. 561106–000.

11/7/56   Glasco, R. J. (MIA). "Financial report, 10/9/56–10/31/56." 11/7/56. Montgomery, Ala. (TD) 1 p. RJGC. 561107–000.

11/7/56   King, Martin Luther, Jr. (MIA). "Letter to Carnell E. Talley." 11/7/56. [*Montgomery, Ala.*] (TLc) 1 p. MLKP-MBU: Box 67. 561107–005.

11/8/56   **King, Martin Luther, Jr. (MIA). "Letter to Richard H. Dixon." 11/8/56. [*Montgomery, Ala.*] (TLc) 1 p. MLKP-MBU: Box 66. 561108–006.**

11/8/56   King, Martin Luther, Jr. (MIA). "Letter to Carl R. Johnson." 11/8/56. [*Montgomery, Ala.*] (TLc) 1 p. MLKP-MBU: Box 60A. 561108–000.

11/8/56   King, Martin Luther, Jr. (MIA). "Letter to J. H. Calhoun." 11/8/56. [*Montgomery, Ala.*] (TLc) 1 p. MLKP-MBU: Box 62. 561108–001.

11/8/56   Banks, W. Lester (NAACP). "Letter to Martin Luther King, Jr." 11/8/56. Richmond, Va. (THLS) 2 pp. MLKP-MBU: Box 63. 561108–002.

11/8/56   Pugh, Lottie Mae (Booker T. Washington School). "Letter to Martin Luther King, Jr." 11/8/56. Suffolk, Va. (TLS) 1 p. MLKP-MBU: Box 64. 561108–005.

11/8/56   MIA. "Transportation payroll, 11/1/56–11/8/56." [*11/8/56*]. Montgomery, Ala. (AD) 3 pp. MLKP-MBU: Box 6. 561108–007.

11/9/56   **Waring, Julius Waties. "Letter to Martin Luther King, Jr., and Ralph Abernathy." 11/9/56. New York, N.Y. (TLS) 1 p. MLKP-MBU: Box 89. 561109–000.**

11/9/56   **DeWolf, L. Harold (Boston University). "Letter to Martin Luther King, Jr." 11/9/56. Boston, Mass. (TLS) 1 p. MLKP-MBU: Box 15. 561109–002.**

11/13/56   Williams, M. C. (Inter-Civic Council). "Telegram to Martin Luther King, Jr." 11/13/56. Tallahassee, Fla. (PWSr) 1 p. MLKP-MBU: Box 60. 561113–007.

11/13/56   Evers, Medgar Wiley (NAACP). "Letter to Martin Luther King, Jr." 11/13/56. Jackson, Miss. (TLS) 1 p. MLKP-MBU: Box 16. 561113–008.

11/14/56   **King, Martin Luther, Jr. (MIA). "Address to mass meeting at Holt Street Baptist Church." [*11/14/56*]. Montgomery, Ala. (At) (1 sound cassette: analog.) MLKJrP-GAMK: Box 107. 561114–013.**

11/14/56   **Mays, Benjamin Elijah (Morehouse College). "Letter to Martin Luther King, Jr." 11/14/56. Atlanta, Ga. (TLS) 1 p. MLKP-MBU: Box 62. 561114–011.**

11/14/56   **Swomley, John M. (Fellowship of Reconciliation). "Telegram to Martin Luther King, Jr." 11/14/56. New York, N.Y. (PHWSr) 1 p. MLKP-MBU: Box 17. 561114–002.**

11/14/56   **King, Martin Luther, Jr., and Ralph Abernathy. "Telegram to Ella J. Baker." 11/14/56. Montgomery, Ala. (PWSr) 1 p. MLKP-MBU: Box 14A. 561114–008.**

11/14/56   **Baker, Ella J. "Telegram to Martin Luther King, Jr." 11/14/56. New York, N.Y. (PHWSr) 1 p. MLKP-MBU: Box 14. 561114–006.**

11/14/56   King, Martin Luther, Jr. (MIA). "Response to Supreme Court decision on transportation." [*11/14/56*]. [*Montgomery, Ala.*] (At) 2 min. (1 sound cassette: analog.) MMFR: Sync sound 63. 561114–001.

11/14/56   King, Martin Luther, Jr. (MIA). "Statement on recommending the end of bus boycott." 11/14/56. [*Montgomery, Ala.*] (TD) 1 p. MLKP-MBU: Box 2. 561114–003.

11/14/56	MIA. "Program, Mass meeting at Holt Street Baptist Church." 11/14/56. Montgomery, Ala. (TD) 1 p. MLKP-MBU: Box 30. 561114–009.
11/14/56	King, Martin Luther, Jr. "Telegram to A. J. (Abraham Johannes) Muste." 11/14/56. Montgomery, Ala. (PWSr) 1 p. MLKP-MBU: Box 14A. 561114–010.
11/14/56	Jemison, T. J. (Theodore Judson) (National Baptist Convention U.S.A. Inc.). "Letter to Martin Luther King, Jr." 11/14/56. Baton Rouge, La. (TLS) 1 p. MLKP-MBU: Box 63. 561114–012.
11/14/56	Dexter Avenue Baptist Church. "*Dexter Echo* 1, no. 10." 11/14/56. Montgomery, Ala. (TD) 4 pp. MLKP-MBU: Box 77. 561114–018.
11/14/56	MIA. "Excerpts, Mass meeting at Hutchinson Street Baptist Church." [*11/14/56*]. [*Montgomery, Ala.*] (At) 7 min. (1 sound cassette: analog.) MMFR: Sync sound 63, 125. 561114–024.
11/14/56	MIA. "Excerpts, Mass meeting at Hutchinson Street Baptist Church." [*11/14/56*]. Montgomery, Ala. (Vt) 4 min. (1 videocassette: analog.) NBCC-NNNBC. 561114–026.
11/15/56	Ballou, Maude L. "Letter to Julius Waties Waring." 11/15/56. [*Montgomery, Ala.*] (TLc) 1 p. MLKP-MBU: Box 89. 561115–001.
11/15/56	MIA. "Press release, Prominent Americans to participate in Montgomery Institute on Nonviolent Social Change." 11/15/56. Montgomery, Ala. (THD) 2 pp. BRP-DLC. 561115–011.
11/17/56	Floyd, Raymond B. (United Clubs of New Orleans). "Letter to Martin Luther King, Jr." 11/17/56. New Orleans, La. (TALS) 2 pp. MLKP-MBU: Box 66. 561117–001.
11/17/56	Cole, William J. "Letter to Martin Luther King, Jr." 11/17/56. Chicago, Ill. (ALS) 1 p. MLKP-MBU: Box 15. 561117–002.
11/18/56	Mount Zion First Baptist Church. "Program, Annual Men's Day." 11/18/56. Baton Rouge, La. (PHD) 4 pp. MLKP-MBU: Box 80. 561118–001.
11/18/56	Omega Psi Phi Fraternity. "Program, Omega Psi National Achievement Week Observance." 11/18/56. Montgomery, Ala. (PHD) 4 pp. MLKP-MBU: Box 80. 561118–002.
11/19/56	MIA. "Program, Mass meeting at Beulah Baptist Church." 11/19/56. Montgomery, Ala. (TD) 1 p. HG-GAMK. 561119–000.
11/19/56	Ballou, Maude L. "Letter to Albert S. Bigelow." 11/19/56. [*Montgomery, Ala*]. (TLc) 1 p. MLKP-MBU: Box 14. 561119–001.
11/19/56	Stebman, Betty J. (United Negro College Fund). "Letter to Martin Luther King, Jr." 11/19/56. New York, N.Y. (TLS) 1 p. MLKP-MBU: Box 61. 561119–003.
11/19/56	LeFlore, John L. "Telegram to Martin Luther King, Jr." 11/19/56. Mobile, Ala. (PWSr) 1 p. MLKP-MBU: Box 61. 561119–004.
11/20/56	**Smiley, Glenn E. (Fellowship of Reconciliation). "Letter to Martin Luther King, Jr." 11/20/56. New York, N.Y. (TLS) 2 pp. MLKP-MBU: Box 16. 561120–000.**
11/20/56	Young, Jessie. "Letter to Martin Luther King, Jr." 11/20/56. Richmond, Va. (TLS) 1 p. MLKP-MBU: Box 67. 561120–007.
11/21/56	**Bunche, Ralph J. (United Nations). "Letter to Martin Luther King, Jr." 11/21/56. New York, N.Y. (TALS) 1 p. MLKP-MBU: Box 14. 561121–000.**
11/21/56	MIA. "Minutes, Executive board meeting." 11/21/56. Montgomery, Ala. (TD) 1 p. MLKP-MBU: Box 30. 561121–003.
11/21/56	King, Martin Luther, Jr. (MIA). "Form letter to potential participants of the Institute on Nonviolence and Social Change." 11/21/56. Montgomery, Ala. (TLS) 1 p. BRP-DLC. 561121–004.
11/21/56	Hairston, Otis L. (Shaw University). "Letter to Martin Luther King, Jr." 11/21/56. Raleigh, N.C. (TLS) 1 p. MLKP-MBU: Box 65. 561121–005.
11/21/56	King, Martin Luther, Jr. (MIA). "Form letter to Reverend." [*11/21/56*]. [*Montgomery, Ala.*] (TLc) 2 pp. BRP-DLC. 561121–007.
11/23/56	**King, Martin Luther, Jr. (MIA). "Letter to Ruth Bunche and Aminda Wilkins." 11/23/56. Montgomery, Ala. (TLS) 1 p. FORP-PSC-P. 561123–000.**
11/23/56	Bowles, Dorothy S. "Letter to Martin Luther King, Jr." 11/23/56. Essex, Conn. (TALS) 1 p. MLKP-MBU: Box 15. 561123–002.
11/23/56	Corbett, Miriam R. (American Baptist Convention's Council on Christian Social Progress). "Letter to Martin Luther King, Jr." 11/23/56. New York, N.Y. (TLS) 2 pp. MLKP-MBU: Box 61. 561123–006.
11/24/56	**King, Martin Luther, Jr. (MIA). "Letter to Albert S. Bigelow." 11/24/56. [*Montgomery, Ala.*] (TLc) 1 p. MLKP-MBU: Box 14. 561124–000.**
11/24/56	King, Martin Luther, Jr. (MIA). "Letter to John L. LeFlore." 11/24/56. [*Montgomery, Ala.*] (TLc) 1 p. MLKP-MBU: Box 61. 561124–002.

11/25/56   **Lusk, William (Columbia University), Marjorie Gettleman (City College of New York), Naomi Friedman (Brooklyn College) and Sheila Navarick (Sarah Lawrence College). "Letter to Martin Luther King, Jr." 11/25/56. New York, N.Y. (TL) 1 p. MLKP-MBU: Box 16. 561125–000.**

11/26/56   King, Martin Luther, Jr., and Abernathy, Ralph (MIA). "Form letter to supporter." 11/26/56. Montgomery, Ala. (TLc) 1 p. MLKP-MBU: Box 91. 561126–000.

11/26/56   MIA. "*Newsletter* 1, no. 5." 11/26/56. Montgomery, Ala. (TD) 3 pp. DABCC. 561126–001.

11/26/56   King, Martin Luther, Jr. (Dexter Avenue Baptist Church). "Letter to Harold E. Fey." 11/26/56. [*Montgomery, Ala.*] (TLc) 1 p. MLKP-MBU: Box 15. 561126–009.

11/26/56   King, Martin Luther, Jr. (MIA). "Letter to Otis L. Hairston." 11/26/56. [*Montgomery, Ala.*] (TLc) 1 p. MLKP-MBU: Box 65. 561126–014.

11/27/56   **Quill, Michael J., and Matthew Guinan (Transport Workers Union of America). "Letter to Martin Luther King, Jr." 11/27/56. New York, N.Y. (THLS) 1 p. (Marginal comment by King.) MLKP-MBU: Box 72. 561127–001.**

11/27/56   **Haynes, Roland E. (Boston University). "Letter to Martin Luther King, Jr." 11/27/56. Boston, Mass. (THLS) 2 pp. MLKP-MBU: Box 15. 561127–003.**

11/27/56   **King, Martin Luther, Jr., and Ralph Abernathy (MIA). "To supporter." 11/27/56. Montgomery, Ala. (TLS) 1 p. NULR-DLC. 561127–006.**

11/27/56   Lloyd's of London. "Insurance Policy for Christian Churches of Montgomery, Ala." 11/27/56. London, England. (PHDS) 9 pp. TMA. 561127–000.

11/27/56   King, Martin Luther, Jr. (Dexter Avenue Baptist Church). "Letter to Miriam R. Corbett." 11/27/56. [*Montgomery, Ala.*] (TLc) 1 p. MLKP-MBU: Box 15. 561127–005.

11/28/56   **Lloyd, Gil B. (Mount Zion Baptist Church). "Letter to Martin Luther King, Jr." 11/28/56. Seattle, Wash. (TALS) 1 p. MLKP-MBU: Box 61A. 561128–000.**

11/28/56   **King, Martin Luther, Jr. (MIA). "Letter to Lottie Mae Pugh." 11/28/56. [*Montgomery, Ala.*] (THLc) 1 p. MLKP-MBU: Box 64. 561128–005.**

11/28/56   King, Martin Luther, Jr. "Letter to Daniel G. Hill." 11/28/56. [*Montgomery, Ala.*] (TLc) 1 p. MLKP-MBU: Box 82. 561128–007.

11/29/56   Powell, W. (William) J. (MIA). "Minutes, Executive board meeting." 11/29/56. (TD) 1 p. MLKP-MBU: Box 30. 561129–001.

11/30/56   Sims, William (United Steelworkers of America). "Letter to Martin Luther King, Jr." 11/30/56. Indiana Harbor, Ind. (TLS) 1 p. MLKP-MBU: Box 66. 561130–001.

12/56   **King, Martin Luther, Jr. "We Are Still Walking." 12/56. New York, N.Y. From: *Liberation* 1 (December 1956): 6–9. (PD) 4 pp. 561200–003.**

12/56   Dexter Avenue Baptist Church. "*Dexter Echo*, Special Anniversary Edition." [*12/56*]. Montgomery, Ala. (THD) 4 pp. (Marginal comments by King.) DABCC. 561200–005.

12/56   "Announcement, Negroes can now sit anywhere on buses." [*12/56*]. (PD) 1 p. FORP-PSC-P. 561200–014.

12/56   Ware, J. L. (James Lowell) (Emancipation Association of Birmingham and Vicinity). "Letter to Martin Luther King, Jr." [*12/56*]. Birmingham, Ala. (TLS) 1 p. MLKP-MBU: Box 16. 561200–018.

12/56   Walton, Eugene (Boston University). "Letter to Martin Luther King, Jr." [*12/56*]. Boston, Mass. (TLS) 1 p. MLKP-MBU: Box 15. 561200–020.

12/56   MIA. "List of executive board members." [*8/56–12/56*]. Montgomery, Ala. (TD) 2 pp. MLKP-MBU: Box 30. 561200–021.

12/56   MIA. "By-Laws." [*6/56–12/56*]. Montgomery, Ala. (PD) 3 pp. HJP-GAMK. 561200–022.

12/56   MIA. "Constitution and By-Laws." [*6/56–12/56*]. Montgomery, Ala. (THD) 3 pp. MLKP-MBU: Box 3. 561200–023.

12/3/56   **King, Martin Luther, Jr. (MIA). "Facing the Challenge of a New Age, Annual address at the first annual Institute on Nonviolence and Social Change." 12/3/56. Montgomery, Ala. (TAD) 22 pp. MLKP-MBU: Box 3. 561203–000.**

12/3/56   Henderson, J. Raymond (Second Baptist Church). "Letter to Louis J. Warner." 12/3/56. Los Angeles, Calif. (THLc) 1 p. (Copy to King.) MLKP-MBU: Box 65. 561203–003.

12/3/56   Fox, E. L. (Interdenominational Ministerial Alliance). "Telegram to Martin Luther King, Jr." 12/3/56. Gulfport, Miss. (PHWSr) 1 p. MLKP-MBU: Box 60. 561203–007.

12/4/56   Reddick, Lawrence Dunbar. "Montgomery Movement: An Historian's View; Speech at Institute for Nonviolence and Social Change." 12/4/56. Montgomery, Ala. (TD) 6 pp. HG-GAMK. 561204–000.

12/4/56   King, Martin Luther, Jr. (MIA). "Letter to Jessie Young." 12/4/56. [*Montgomery, Ala.*] (TLc) 1 p. MLKP-MBU: Box 67. 561204–009.

12/4/56   Mitchell, Clarence. "Letter to Warren Olney III." 12/4/56. Washington, D.C. (TLc) 3 pp. WCFG-KAbE. 561204–012.

12/5/56   King, Martin Luther, Jr. (Dexter Avenue Baptist Church). "Letter to Charles Walker." 12/5/56. [*Montgomery, Ala.*] (TLc) 1 p. MLKP-MBU: Box 16. 561205–000.

12/5/56   Walker, Charles (Fellowship of Reconciliation). "Telegram to Martin Luther King, Jr." 12/5/56. Philadelphia, Pa. (PWSr) 1 p. MLKP-MBU: Box 17. 561205–002.

12/5/56   King, Martin Luther, Jr. (Dexter Avenue Baptist Church). "Letter to Dorothy S. Bowles." 12/5/56. [*Montgomery, Ala.*] (TLc) 1 p. MLKP-MBU: Box 15. 561205–006.

12/5/56   Smith, Lillian Eugenia. "The Right Way Is Not a Moderate Way." 12/5/56. Montgomery, Ala. (THD) 9 pp. (Marginal comments by King.) MLKP-MBU: Box 6. 561205–001.

12/5/56   In Friendship. "Announcement, Coretta Scott King concert, Salute to Montgomery." 12/5/56. (PHD) 1 p. FORP-PSC-P. 561205–003.

12/5/56   Townsend, Francis E. "Letter to Martin Luther King, Jr." 12/5/56. Washington, D.C. (TLS) 1 p. MLKP-MBU: Box 65. 561205–011.

12/5/56   King, Coretta Scott. "Speech at the Montgomery Anniversary Concert." [*12/5/56*]. (THD) 2 pp. CB-CtY. 561205–012.

12/5/56   In Friendship. "Program, Montgomery Anniversary Concert." 12/5/56. New York, N.Y. (TD) 1 p. FSTC. 561205–016.

12/6/56   [*Grayson, Julian O.*] "Notes, Martin Luther King, Jr., Speech: Facing the Challenge of a New Age." 12/6/56. Washington, D.C. (AD) 14 pp. JOG. 561206–001.

12/6/56   Maxwell, O. Clay, Jr. (Baptist Ministers Conference, Greater New York and Vicinity). "Letter to Martin Luther King, Jr." 12/6/56. New York, N.Y. (THLS) 2 pp. MLKP-MBU: Box 14. 561206–002.

12/6/56   Jackson, L. K. (General Missionary Baptist State Convention, Inc.). "Letter to Martin Luther King, Jr." 12/6/56. Gary, Ind. (THLS) 1 p. MLKP-MBU: Box 17. 561206–004.

12/6/56   Blake, Eugene Carson (National Council of the Churches of Christ in the United States of America). "Letter to Martin Luther King, Jr." 12/6/56. (TLc) 1 p. (Included in "Communications Authorized by the General Board, December 4–5, 1956, and Replies Received.") NCCP-PPPrHi: Box 20. 561206–014.

12/7/56   Ballou, Maude L. "Letter to Medgar Wiley Evers." 12/7/56. [*Montgomery, Ala.*] (TLc) 1 p. MLKP-MBU: Box 16. 561207–003.

12/7/56   Mays, Benjamin Elijah (Morehouse College). "Letter to Martin Luther King, Jr." 12/7/56. Atlanta, Ga. (TLS) 1 p. MLKP-MBU: Box 62. 561207–004.

12/7/56   Mays, Benjamin Elijah. "Telegram to Martin Luther King, Jr." 12/7/56. Atlanta, Ga. (PWSr) 1 p. MLKP-MBU: Box 62. 561207–005.

12/7/56   Ballou, Maude L. (MIA). "Letter to Douglas Moore." 12/7/56. [*Montgomery, Ala.*] (TLc) 1 p. MLKP-MBU: Box 62. 561207–007.

12/7/56   Barker, Dorothy L. (United Negro College Fund). "Telegram to Martin Luther King, Jr." 12/7/56. New York, N.Y. (PWSr) 1 p. MLKP-MBU: Box 66. 561207–008.

12/9/56   MIA. "Program, Institute on Nonviolence and Social Change." 12/3/56–12/9/56. Montgomery, Ala. (PD) 8 pp. HJP-GAMK. 561209–000.

12/9/56   Howard University. "Program, Religious Emphasis Week." 12/2/56–12/9/56. Washington, D.C. (PHD) 4 pp. MLKP-MBU: Box 80. 561209–001.

12/9/56   King, Martin Luther, Jr. (MIA). "Letter to Betty J. Stebman." 12/9/56. Montgomery, Ala. (TLc) 1 p. MLKP-MBU: Box 61. 561209–005.

12/10/56   King, Martin Luther, Jr. "Sworn deposition on station incident on 7/11/56." 12/10/56. Montgomery, Ala. (TD) 2 pp. MLKP-MBU: Box 61. 561210–000.

12/10/56   DeWolf, L. Harold (Boston University). "Letter to Martin Luther King, Jr." 12/10/56. Boston, Mass. (ALS) 1 p. MLKP-MBU: Box 15. 561210–007.

12/10/56   Hughes, Robert E. (Alabama Council on Human Relations [ACHR]). "Letter to Martin Luther King, Jr." 12/10/56. Birmingham, Ala. (TLS) 1 p. MLKP-MBU: Box 13A. 561210–008.

12/10/56   King, Joel Lawrence. "Letter to Martin Luther King, Jr." 12/10/56. Lansing, Mich. (AHLS) 2 pp. (Marginal comment by King.) MLKP-MBU: Box 61. 561210–013.

12/10/56   Ballou, Maude L. "Letter to Michael J. Quill." 12/10/56. [*Montgomery, Ala.*] (TLc) 1 p. MLKP-MBU: Box 121. 561210–003.

12/10/56   Ballou, Maude L. (MIA). "Letter to John L. LeFlore." 12/10/56. [*Montgomery, Ala.*] (TLc) 1 p. MLKP-MBU: Box 61. 561210–014.

12/10/56   Bunn, Warren J. (NAACP). "Telegram to Martin Luther King, Jr." 12/10/56. Brooklyn, N.Y. (PWSr) 1 p. MLKP-MBU: Box 62. 561210–015.

12/10/56   Hill, Daniel G. (Howard University). "Letter to Martin Luther King, Jr." 12/10/56. Washington, D.C. (TLS) 1 p. MLKP-MBU: Box 82. 561210–016.

12/11/56   King, Martin Luther, Jr. (Dexter Avenue Baptist Church). "Letter to Medgar Wiley Evers." 12/11/56. [*Montgomery, Ala.*] (TLc) 1 p. MLKP-MBU: Box 16. 561211–004.

12/11/56   King, Martin Luther, Jr. (Dexter Avenue Baptist Church). "Letter to Raymond B. Floyd." 12/11/56. [*Montgomery, Ala.*] (TLc) 1 p. MLKP-MBU: Box 66. 561211–002.

12/11/56   King, Martin Luther, Jr. (Dexter Avenue Baptist Church). "Letter to J. D. Thompson." 12/11/56. [*Montgomery, Ala.*] (TLc) 1 p. MLKP-MBU: Box 63. 561211–005.

12/11/56   United Negro College Fund. "Negro Southerner Speaks: A Symposium." 12/11/56. New York, N.Y. (PD) 4 pp. UNCFR-GAU. 561211–006.

12/12/56   Walker, Wyatt Tee (Gillfield Baptist Church). "Letter to Martin Luther King, Jr." 12/12/56. Petersburg, Va. (TLSr) 1 p. MLKP-MBU: Box 17. 561212–000.

12/12/56   Atwood, Rufus B. (Kentucky State College). "Letter to Martin Luther King, Jr." 12/12/56. Frankfort, Ky. (TLS) 1 p. MLKP-MBU: Box 61. 561212–004.

12/14/56   Doubleday & Co. "Memorandum of Agreement Between Martin Luther King, Jr., and Doubleday & Co." 12/14/56. Garden City, N.Y. (PTD) 7 pp. (Enclosure in 561219–013.) MLKP-MBU: Box 78. 561214–003.

12/15/56   King, Martin Luther, Jr. "Desegregation and the Future, Address at the Annual Luncheon of the National Committee for Rural Schools." [*12/15/56*]. [*New York, N.Y.*] (At) 40 min. (2 sound cassettes: analog.) CSKC. 561215–004.

12/15/56   Bunn, Warren J. (NAACP). "Letter to MIA." 12/15/56. Brooklyn, N.Y. (TAHL) 1 p. MLKP-MBU: Box 62. 561215–000.

12/15/56   Dudley, Lafayette. "Letter to Martin Luther King, Jr." 12/15/56. Boston, Mass. (TAHLS) 2 pp. MLKP-MBU: Box 16. 561215–003.

12/17/56   King, Martin Luther, Jr. "Letter to Roland E. Haynes." 12/17/56. [*Montgomery, Ala.*] (TLc) 1 p. MLKP-MBU: Box 15. 561217–001.

12/17/56   King, Martin Luther, Jr. (Dexter Avenue Baptist Church). "Letter to Benjamin Elijah Mays." 12/17/56. [*Montgomery, Ala.*] (TLc) 1 p. MLKP-MBU: Box 62. 561217–005.

12/17/56   Via, Emory, and Fred Routh (Southern Regional Council). "Memo to central staff." 12/17/56. (THL) 3 pp. ASRC-GAU. 561217–002.

12/17/56   Montgomery Board of Commissioners. "Statement on Supreme Court decision on bus segregation in Montgomery." 12/17/56. (TD) 2 pp. DJG. 561217–003.

12/17/56   Evers, Medgar Wiley (NAACP). "Letter to Martin Luther King, Jr." 12/17/56. Jackson, Miss. (TLS) 1 p. MLKP-MBU: Box 16. 561217–004.

12/18/56   King, Martin Luther, Jr. (MIA). "Letter to William Sims." 12/18/56. [*Montgomery, Ala.*] (TLc) 1 p. MLKP-MBU: Box 66. 561218–005.

12/18/56   King, Martin Luther, Jr. (Dexter Avenue Baptist Church). "Letter to William J. Cole." 12/18/56. [*Montgomery, Ala.*] (TLc) 1 p. MLKP-MBU: Box 15. 561218–007.

12/18/56   King, Martin Luther, Jr. "MIA plans following Supreme Court decision on desegregation." [*12/18/56*]. [*Montgomery, Ala.*] (At) 2 min. (1 sound cassette: analog.) MMFR: Sync sound 63. 561218–009.

12/19/56   King, Martin Luther, Jr. (MIA). "Integrated Bus Suggestions." 12/19/56. [*Montgomery, Ala.*] (TD) 1 p. MLKP-MBU: Box 2. 561219–001.

12/19/56   King, Martin Luther, Jr. (MIA). "Letter to W. (William) A. Gayle." 12/19/56. [*Montgomery, Ala.*] (THLc) 2 pp. MLKP-MBU: Box 22. 561219–010.

12/19/56   Borders, William Holmes. "Letter to Martin Luther King, Jr." 12/19/56. (TLS) 1 p. MLKP-MBU: Box 14. 561219–014.

12/19/56   Glasco, R. J. (MIA). "Financial committee report, 11/1/56–12/15/56." 12/19/56. Montgomery, Ala. (THD) 2 pp. RJGC. 561219–002.

12/19/56   Dexter Avenue Baptist Church. *Dexter Echo* 1, no. 12." 12/19/56. Montgomery, Ala. (PD) 4 pp. DABCC. 561219–004.

12/19/56   King, Martin Luther, Jr. (MIA). "Letter to Clyde C. Sellers." 12/19/56. [*Montgomery, Ala.*] (THLc) 2 pp. MLKP-MBU: Box 22. 561219–008.

12/19/56   King, Martin Luther, Jr. (MIA). "Letter to G. J. Ruppenthal." 12/19/56. [*Montgomery, Ala.*] (TLc) 1 p. MLKP-MBU: Box 22. 561219–009.

12/19/56   King, Martin Luther, Jr. (MIA). "Letter to Frank Parks." 12/19/56. [*Montgomery, Ala.*] (THLc) 2 pp. MLKP-MBU: Box 22. 561219–011.

12/19/56	Bennetts, Chaucy (Doubleday & Co.). "Letter to Martin Luther King, Jr." 12/19/56. New York, N.Y. (TLS) 1 p. (Contains enclosure 561214–003.) MLKP-MBU: Box 78. 561219–013.
12/19/56	King, Martin Luther, Jr. (MIA). "Letter to Francis E. Townsend." 12/19/56. [*Montgomery, Ala.*] (TLc) 1 p. MLKP-MBU: Box 65. 561219–015.
12/19/56	MIA. "Program, Mass meeting at Mount Zion AME Zion Church." 7/1/56– 12/19/56. Montgomery, Ala. (TD) 1 p. HJP-GAMK. 561219–017.
12/20/56	**King, Martin Luther, Jr. (MIA). "Statement on ending the bus boycott." 12/20/56. [*Montgomery, Ala.*] (TD) 1 p. MLKP-MBU: Box 2. 561220–000.**
12/20/56	**King, Martin Luther, Jr. "Letter to Wyatt Tee Walker." 12/20/56. [*Montgomery, Ala.*] (TLc) 1 p. MLKP-MBU: Box 17. 561220–004.**
12/20/56	**King, Martin Luther, Jr. (MIA). "Letter to Eugene Walton." 12/20/56. [*Montgomery, Ala.*] (TLc) 1 p. MLKP-MBU: Box 15. 561220–015.**
12/20/56	**King, Martin Luther, Jr. (MIA). "Letter to Daniel G. Hill." 12/20/56. [*Montgomery, Ala.*] (TLc) 1 p. MLKP-MBU: Box 82. 561220–017.**
12/20/56	Klein, Edward E. (Stephen Wise Free Synagogue). "Letter to Martin Luther King, Jr." 12/20/56. (TLS) 1 p. MLKP-MBU: Box 65. 561220–006.
12/20/56	King, Martin Luther, Jr. (MIA). "Letter to Harold V. Jensen." 12/20/56. [*Montgomery, Ala.*] (TLc) 1 p. MLKP-MBU: Box 17. 561220–007.
12/20/56	Baker, Ella J. (In Friendship). "Letter to Martin Luther King, Jr." 12/20/56. New York, N.Y. (TL) 1 p. MLKP-MBU: Box 17. 561220–008.
12/20/56	King, Martin Luther, Jr. (MIA). "Excerpt, Statement on end of bus boycott." [*12/20/56*]. Montgomery, Ala. (Vt) 5 min. (1 videocassette: analog.) CBSNA-CBSN. 561220–032.
12/21/56	**Associated Press. "Photo of Martin Luther King, Jr., Glenn E. Smiley, and Ralph Abernathy." 12/21/56. Montgomery, Ala. (Ph) 1 p. APWW. 561221–007.**
12/21/56	Mays, Benjamin Elijah (Morehouse College). "Letter to Martin Luther King, Jr." 12/21/56. Atlanta, Ga. (TLS) 1 p. MLKP-MBU: Box 62. 561221–002.
12/21/56	Jackson, J. H. (Joseph Harrison) (National Baptist Convention, U.S.A., Inc.). "Letter to Martin Luther King, Jr." 12/21/56. Chicago, Ill. (TLS) 1 p. MLKP-MBU: Box 63. 561221–003.
12/22/56	**Associated Press. "Photo of African-American bus riders." 12/22/56. Montgomery, Ala. (Ph) 1 p. APWW. 561222–003.**
12/22/56	Wesley, Carter (Informer Group of Newspapers). "Letter to Martin Luther King, Jr." 12/22/56. Houston, Tex. (TLS) 2 pp. MLKP-MBU: Box 52. 561222–000.
12/23/56	**[*Rustin, Bayard*]. "Letter to Martin Luther King, Jr." 12/23/56. (TLc) 1 p. (Contains enclosures 561223–001, –003.) BRP-DLC: Reel 3. 561223–002.**
12/23/56	**[*Rustin, Bayard*]. "Memo on Montgomery movement." [*12/23/56*]. (TD) 2 pp. (Enclosure in 561223–002.) BRP-DLC: Reel 3. 561223–003.**
12/23/56	[*Rustin, Bayard*] "Negroes Struggle for Freedom." [*12/23/56*]. (TD) 3 pp. (Enclosure in 561223–002.) BRP-DLC: Reel 3. 561223–001.
12/24/56	**"New Fields Await Negroes, King Tells Mass Meeting." 12/24/56. Montgomery, Ala. From: *Montgomery Advertiser*, 24 December 1956. (PD) 1 p. 561224–005.**
12/24/56	King, Martin Luther, Jr. "Letter to Rufus B. Atwood." 12/24/56. [*Montgomery, Ala.*] (TLc) 1 p. MLKP-MBU: Box 61. 561224–003.
12/25/56	Schilling, S. Paul (Boston University). "Letter to Martin Luther King, Jr." 12/25/56. Newton, Mass. (ATDS) 3 pp. MLKP-MBU: Box 65. 561225–002.
12/26/56	**King, Martin Luther, Jr. "Letter to Fred L. Shuttlesworth." [*12/26/56*]. [*Montgomery, Ala.*] (ALS) 2 pp. MLKP-MBU: Box 71. 561226–010.**
12/26/56	King, Martin Luther, Jr. (MIA). "Letter to Warren J. Bunn." 12/26/56. [*Montgomery, Ala.*] (THLc) 1 p. MLKP-MBU: Box 63. 561226–001.
12/26/56	Boddie, J. (James) Timothy (United Baptist Missionary Convention and Auxiliaries of Maryland). "Letter to Martin Luther King, Jr." 12/26/56. Baltimore, Md. (TLS) 1 p. MLKP-MBU: Box 66. 561226–006.
12/26/56	King, Martin Luther, Jr. "Letter to Marion H. Bluitt." 12/26/56. [*Montgomery, Ala.*] (TLc) 1 p. MLKP-MBU: Box 65. 561226–009.
12/27/56	**Jack, Homer Alexander (Unitarian Church of Evanston). "Letter to Martin Luther King, Jr., and Coretta Scott King." 12/27/56. Evanston, Ill. (TLS) 1 p. MLKP-MBU: Box 66. 561227–003.**
12/27/56	Sloan, Viva A. "Letter to Martin Luther King, Jr." 12/27/56. Morgantown, W.Va. (TAHLS) 2 pp. MLKP-MBU: Box 65. 561227–005.
1/4/57	King, Martin Luther, Jr. "Letter to L. Harold DeWolf." 1/4/57. (Tlc) [*Montgomery, Ala.*] MLKP-MBU: Box 15. 570104–005.

Boldfaced page numbers in entries indicate that the material can be found in documents authored by Martin Luther King, Jr. Italicized page numbers in entries indicate the location of the main biographical entry for an individual, beginning with the volume number if other than the present volume.

Abernathy, Juanita, 12, **289**

Abernathy, Ralph, 39, 41, 46, *69n*, 80, 92, 103, 113, 120n, 133, 135, 144, **145–46,** 150, 153, 213, 214, 215, 226, **289,** 349–50, 369, 390–91, 422, 434, **446,** 467, 469, 501, 506, 508, 509, 517, 518, 534, 539, 540, 542, 545, illus.

aboard desegregated bus, 29, 53, 485–86

at boycott planning meetings, 3, 4, 18, 67

on bus boycott resolutions, 76–78, **192**

at Chicago Coliseum rally, 44, 295

as King, Jr.'s representative, 12, 15–16, **124n,** 144, **247**

at MIA founding meeting, 4, 36, 69, 70

Acts, 233n, 379n, **417**

Adair, Euretta, 13, 235

Adams, Sherman, 510

African Americans

as American citizens, 26, 74, **398**

as bus drivers, 92, **124–25,** 225, 226, **240**

deprived of voting rights, **358,** 365, **368–69,** 386–87

history of, **281–82, 300, 322–23, 341**

new sense of dignity of, **237–39, 242, 273, 282–83, 285, 292, 301, 305, 324, 341, 446, 447, 452, 455–56**

nonviolence commitment of, **376, 451**

political party choices of, **384, 409, 460, 476**

preparing for new world order, 265–66, **342–44,** 389, **457, 464**

responsibility for own advancement, 26, 204, **307, 345, 461, 478**

and spiritual revitalization, 266–67

supposed inferiority of, **236–37, 240,** 265, **282, 300–301, 323, 455**

use of economic boycott by, **224–25, 238**

Afro Arts Theatre, 50, 533

Agape, **306, 327, 459**

See also Love

Alabama Christian Movement for Human Rights (ACMHR), 27, 48, 54, 495n

Alabama Council on Human Relations (ACHR), 3, 36, 50, 78n, **123,** 126, 194, 353, 368n, 468, 501, 536, 543

Alabama Negro Baptist Center (Montgomery), 40, 85n, 120, 121

Alabama Public Service Commission, 45, 48–49, **82**

Alexander, Raymond Pace, **339,** 531, illus.

Alexander, T. M., 451n

Alexandre, Clement, 222n, 524, 526

Alford, Willie Frank, 69, 70, *70n,* 71, 109, 110

Alpha Phi Alpha fraternity, 118, 183, 505, 508, 514, 515, 521, illus.

Alpha Award of Honor from, **269–70,** 339

"The Birth of a New Age" address to, **339–46,** 531

financial support from, 26, 118–19, 201

American Baptist Assembly, 49, 321, 529, 541

American Civil Liberties Union, 206n, 508

American Federation of Labor and Congress of Industrial Organizations (AFL-CIO), 216–17n

American Friends Service Committee, 182n, 360, 463–64n

American Home Mission Agencies Conference (Green Lake, Wisconsin)

King, Jr.'s address to, 49, **321–28,** 529, 535

American Missionary Association, 528

American Socialist Party, 206, 280

Amos, 73, **286, 418**

Anderson, C. Earl, 412

Anderson, Marian, 270

Anderson, Teresa, 411n

Anderson, Thelma H., 525

Anti-boycott statute (1921), 14–15, 41–42, 133, **152, 305**

See also Economic boycott

Antioch Baptist Church (Cleveland), 141

Aristotle, 204, **300, 323**

Arnold, Alphonzo A., 509

Asbury Park Press, **223,** 517

Associated Press, 100, 102, 508, 514, 518, 523, 545, illus.

Atlanta Daily World, 215

Atlanta District Sunday School and Baptist Training Union Congress, 367

Atlanta Life Insurance Company, 250

Atlanta Missionary Baptist Association, 367

Atlanta Municipal Airport, 393. *See also* Dobbs House restaurant (Atlanta)

Atwood, Rufus B., 544, 545

Austell, M. R., 533, 538
Austin, L. E., 517, 521, 533, 534
Azbell, Joe, 35, 114–15, 502, 506
    King, Jr.'s interview with, **202–3**, 515

Baber, George W., 152–53
Bagley, James H., 4, **80,** *80n*
Baker, Ella J., 19, 138n, *139n,* 491
    King, Jr.'s correspondence with, 139, **434,** 435,
        509, 540, 545
Ballenger, Milton Cornelius, **87,** *87n,* 503
Ballou, Maude L., 13, 162, 226n, 294–95, 403n,
    440
    correspondence of, 235, 438, 467n, 514, 517,
        520, 522, 524, 526, 534, 537, 538, 541, 543
Baltimore Afro-American, 20, 32
Bankhead, Tallulah, 437
Banks, Allen A., Jr., *2:236n,* 27, 521
Banks, W. Lester, 379, 515, 524, 533, 534, 535,
    536, 540
Banyai, Ed, 529
Baptist Ministers Conference (Detroit), 149, 510
Baptist Ministers Conference (Montgomery),
    44, 76n, 92, 97–98, 107–8, 149–50, 156
Baptist Ministers Conference (New York), 543
Baptist Ministers Conference (Philadelphia), 145
Barbour, J. Pius, *1:125n,* 16–17, 28, 33, 44, 210,
    366, 510, 519, 533
    King, Jr.'s correspondence with, 116, **171–72,**
        501, 506, 513, 516, 530
Barbour, Joseph P., 517
Barbour, Worth Littlejohn, *210n,* 210–11, 516
Barker, Dorothy L., 543
Barker, Hampton Z., 105, 505
Barth, Karl, *1:230n,* 203
Baton Rouge bus boycott, 7, 402
Batten, Charles E., *1:126n,* 210n, **294,** 513, 524
Beirut, 334
Belafonte, Harry, 139, 408, 437
Bell, Ada Pace, 538, 539
Bell Street Baptist Church (Montgomery), 48,
    230
Bennett, L. Roy, 3–4, 68, *68n,* 69, 70, 84, 93,
    103, 108, 122, 133, 145, 359–60, **386**
Bennett, Lerone, 380n, 527
Bennetts, Chaucy, 545
Bentley, William L., 539
Berger, Jean, 539, 540
Berry, Carrie, 521
Bertocci, Peter A., *2:197n,* 142–43, 509
Bethel AME Church (Detroit), 45
Bethel Baptist Church (Montgomery), 36, 38,
    42, 85n 502, 504
Bethune, Mary McLeod, 235, *235n,* 270
Beulah Baptist Church (Montgomery), 37, 39,
    44, 48, 52, 516, 535, 541
Beverly, C. C., 412

Biblical interpretation, **282, 300, 323, 378–79,**
    417
Bigelow, Albert S., 32n, **438,** *438n,* 540, 541
Billingsley, Orzell, 184, *184n,* 194, 469, 508,
    illus.
Binion, R. B., 110, 120, 369
Birmingham bus boycott, 27, 31, 54, **495–96**
Birmingham Hungry Club, 44
Black, Hugo, 52
Black, Lucille, 515, 519
Blair, P. M., 412
Blake, Eubie, 317
Blake, Eugene Carson, 509, 543
Blanton, Sankey L., *1:391–92n,* 130–31, 508
Bluitt, Marion H., 545
Bly, Simon, 533
Boddie, Charles Emerson, 84, *84n,* 211
Boddie, James Timothy, *2:210n,* 84, 511, 515,
    520, 545
Bond, Horace Mann, 32
Bonner, J. W., 70, *70n,* 79, 369
Borders, William Holmes, 32, 451n, *484n,* 484–
    85, 544
Boston University, 118, 215, 228, 330, **388,** 394,
    403, 530, 535, 537
Bowles, Chester, 466, 480n
Bowles, Dorothy S., **466,** *466n,* 541, 543
Bradford, Sadie, 246, *246n,* 520, 526
Brandstein, Rae, *332n,* **332–33, 472,** 528, 530,
    531, 532
Bratcher, A. L., 507, 519
Brayboy, Jack S., 228
Brayboy, Jeanne Martin, *228n,* 228–29, 518
Bricklayers Union, 85n
Briddell, David W., 157, *157n*
Briggs v. Elliott, 422, 472n
Bright Hope Baptist Church (Philadelphia), 205
Bristol, James, 496
British-American Association of Colored Broth-
    ers (Windsor, Ontario), 50, 512, 515
Britton, Milton, 17n, *126n,* 126–27, 506, 524
Brooks, Edwin A., 530
Brooks, Estella, 90n
Brooks, Hilliard, 90
Brooks, J. T., 40
Brooks, Phillips, 260n
Bross, John R., 517, 518
Brotherhood of Sleeping Car Porters, 3, 69n,
    216–17n, 246n, 248, 332, 358, 506, 508, 528,
    531, 532
Browder, Aurelia S., 111n
Browder et al. v. Gayle, 40, 44, 46, 90n, 111, **352,**
    521, 526
    federal district court ruling on, 23–24, 47–48,
        303, 377
    NAACP's role in, 11, 25, 111–12, 121–22,
        165–66, **243–44**

Jeanatta Reese's withdrawal from, 43, 120–21, 145

Supreme Court ruling on, 29, 52, 377n, **425, 455,** 481, **486**

Brown, Jesse H., 509

Brown, John, 410n

Brownell, Herbert, 53, 156n, 369, 533

Browning, Earline, 160, 512

Brown v. Board of Education, 35, 43, 111n, 184n, 217, 283n, 422

implementation of, 28, 307n, 335, 336, **338**

second anniversary of, 46, 256, 258, 280

Supreme Court's ruling on, **261, 283, 456, 472**

See also School desegregation

Brunner, Emil, 203, 204

Bryant, Raleigh A., *399n,* **399–400,** 537, 538

Bryant, William Cullen, **259, 306, 328, 344, 459,** 486n

Buber, Martin, 203, 418n, 474n

Bunche, Ralph J., *134n,* 270, 445n

King, Jr.'s correspondence with, 134, 436, 508, 515, 522, 541

Bunche, Ruth, *437n,* **437–38,** 541

Bunn, Warren J., **354,** *354n,* 531, 532, 544, 545

Burks, Mary Fair, 3n

Burroughs, Nannie H., *2:282n,* 32, 361–62, **370–71,** 451n, 506, 532, 534

Burrus, Lloyd A., 509

Bus boycott. *See* Baton Rouge bus boycott; Birmingham bus boycott; Montgomery bus boycott; Tallahassee bus boycott

Bus drivers, 89–91, 92, **124–25,** 225, 226, **240**

Bus segregation

Alabama legislation on, 42, **82**

federal district court rulings on, 23–24, 35, 47–48, **303, 377**

municipal code on, 7, 72, **82**

Supreme Court rulings on, 23, 29, 45, 52, 217n, 219, **231,** 377n, **425**

as oppression, 5, **71–72,** 77, **80,** 135–36, 184, **277, 283, 301–2, 303, 425, 431**

See also Baton Rouge bus boycott; Birmingham bus boycott; Montgomery bus boycott; Montgomery City Lines; Segregation; Tallahassee bus boycott

Bynoe, John G., 505, 506, 508

Caldwell, Arthur B., 364, *364n,* 387, 405, 535, 536

Calhoun, J. H., 535, 540

Cameron, Angus, 515, 519, 522

Canada, Sally, **373,** 533, 534

Cannon, George D., 30n, 526

Cannon, John, **412**

Cannon, Robert L., 214n, 388–91, 431n, 536

Capitalism, 366, **416**

Capitol Airlines, **392**

Capitol Post, 526

Carey, Archibald James, Jr., *2:560–61n,* 99, 178, 463n, 479n, 510, 517

King, Jr.'s correspondence with, **93–95,** 139–40, **152–53,** 503, 509, 511, 516, 537

Carey, J. Evehard, 520

Cargile, Loyce Furman, 509, 516

Carlyle, Thomas, **259,** 260n, **306, 344, 459**

Carmichael, J. H., 391–92, 537

Carolina Times, 517, 533

Car pools, 36–37, 405–6, 523, illus.

canceled insurance policies on, **377, 385, 448**

cost of, **152, 153, 251, 304**

court's injunction against, 51, 52, **413–14, 421–22,** 424, **427, 448**

funding of, 166, **238, 354**

operation of, 77, **79,** 84, **187, 304,** 511

police harassment of, 9, 39, **125,** 144

Carr, Johnnie R., 13, 531

Carr, Leonard G., *2:261n,* 156, 511

Carrington, Walter C., 17n, 26n, *88n,* 88–89, 503

Carter, Eugene, 41, 42

and car pool injunction, 51, 52, 414, 424, **427**

and King, Jr.'s trial, 16, 43, 183–85, 198, **199–200**

Carter, Harold, 131

Carter, Robert L., 184, *184n,* 509

Cathedral of St. John the Divine (New York), 22, 257, **291**

"Death of Evil upon the Seashore" sermon at, 46, 256, **258–62,** 296, 522

Catholicism, **417**

Catlos, Edward, 525

Cayce, James B., 520, 524

CBS News, 230

Central Baptist Church (Delaware), 286

Chakravarty, Amiya, 169–70n

Chalmers, Allan Knight, *173n,* 173–74, 330, **375,** 513, 514

Chamberlin, Roy B., 535, 536, 537

Chambers, T. M., **289**

Charles, Beatrice, 505

Chauri Chaura, 268

Chestnut, Velberta C., 521, 522

Chicago Area Conference of Religious Liberals, 44

Christian Century, 381, 382

Christian church, 381–82, **417**

Christian mission, **416, 429**

Gandhian synthesis with, 17, 21, 89, **209n**

nonviolent protest as expression of, 5–6, 10–11, 28, **72, 73–74,** 89, 108, 137–38, 142–43, 144, **200, 208,** 394–95, **418, 425**

opposed to segregation, 27–28, **373,** 394–95, **418, 460, 474**

social and political responsibilities of, 2, 6, **449, 450,** 490n

Christopher Reynolds Foundation, 492
Church of the Master (New York), 274, **292**
Citizens Club (Montgomery), 85n
Citizens Coordinating Committee (Montgomery), 108
Citizens Councils, 41, 124, 429, 507
　city commissioners' membership on, 8, 38, 39, 107, 120
　tactics of, 174, **238, 322n, 357–58,** 365, 369, **377, 445, 448, 475**
Citizens Educational Committee (Montgomery), 358
Citizenship, 26, 74–75, 107, **336–38, 369, 398**
　See also Integration; Voting rights
City of Montgomery v. Martin L. King, 106, 505
Civil disobedience, 225, 226
Civil rights. *See* Citizenship
Civil Rights Act (1957), 364n
Civil Rights Congress (CRC), 156
Clair, Alfred Petit, 510
Clareman, Jack, 492n
Clark, Caesar, 503, 519
Clark, Kenneth Bancroft, 307n, **333,** *333n,* 419n, 462n, 471, **472, 474, 478**
Clark, Mamie Phipps, **333**
Clark, Septima Poinsette, 274n, 328–29, *329n,* **349–50,** 529, 531
Clement, Harold L., 361, **386**
Clement, Rufus E., 14, 480n
Cobb, James B., 451n
Cober, Kenneth L., 516, 518
Cohen, Morris R., 204
Coke v. City of Atlanta et al., 392n
Cole, David H., 178
Cole, Nat King, 317n
Cole, William J., 541, 544
Coleman, James P., 220, *220n,* **221,** 518
Collins, I. C., 515
Colonialism, 22, **260–61, 308–9, 324–25, 340–41, 454**
Colvin, Claudette, 3n, 5, 35, 90, 91, 111, **123,** 501
Committee for Nonviolent Integration (CNI), 18–19, 288, 517
Committee to Aid the Montgomery, Alabama, Bus Protest (Detroit), 252
Communism, 22–23, 144, 156, **318, 416**
Concord Baptist Church (Brooklyn), 43, 314
　King, Jr.'s address at, **209–10**
Conley, P. E., 369
Congress of Racial Equality (CORE), 18, 20, 163n, 170, 178n, 236, 288n, 487n, 527
Consultative Peace Council, 376
Cook, Clair M., **333–34,** *334n,* 529, 530, 532
Cook, Samuel DuBois, *203n,* 203–4, 515
Cooley, Robert, 520
Cooper, Floyd L., 518
Cooper, Homer, 256

Corbett, Gordon L., 538, 540
Corbett, J. Elliott, 508, 524
Corbett, Miriam R., 541, 542
Corinthians (1), 20n, 212, 424, 446n, **419,** 420n
Courts, Gus, 248
Cowper, William, 74n, 265n, 283n, 301n, 324n, 341n, 455n
Crenshaw, Jack, 78n, **80,** *80n,* **124**
The Crisis, 108–9n, 180n
Crockett, Roosevelt David, *2:240n,* 229
Crozer Theological Seminary, 16, 126, 130–31, **224,** 232, 294
Culbertson, John B., 451n
Cumming, William Cooper, **371–72,** 530, 534
Cunningham, Evelyn, 227
Current, Gloster B., 503, 506
Curry, M. K., 263–64

Dabbs, James McBride, 338n
Dade, Malcolm G., 537
Daniels, Fred, 70, 71, 74, **75,** 502
Davidson, Eugene, 533, 534
Davis, George Washington, *1:225n,* 131, 508
Davis, James H., 212–13, 516, 518
Davis, Jerome Dean, 256
Davis, Mildred J., 131
Dawkins, Reuben S., 511
Dawson, William L., 93, *95n*
Day Street Baptist Church (Montgomery), 37, 40, 45, **230–32,** 507, 518, 519, illus.
Deaderick, Janie, 519
Deats, Paul, Jr., *142n,* 142–43
De la Brunelière, Henri Varin, 254–55, 521, 528
Dellinger, David, 19n
Delta Sigma Theta, 54
Demille, Arnold, 535
Democracy, 107, 268, **416, 424–25**
　and segregation, **232, 252, 284, 308, 337–38, 345, 460**
　right to protest in, 6–7, **71, 72–73,** 136n, 198
Democratic National Convention (August 1956), **336–38**
Democratic Party, **384, 408–9, 460, 476**
Dennard, Cleveland L., 412
Desegregation. *See* Integration
DeWolf, L. Harold, *2:5–6n,* 33, 51, 154, 441, **479–80**
　King, Jr.'s correspondence with, 363–64, **403,** 423, 468, 533, 535, 536, 537, 538, 540, 543
Dexter Avenue Baptist Church (Montgomery), 1–2, **229–30,** 275–76, 501, 502, 514, 515, 518, 521, 523, 527, 529, illus.
　guest speakers at, 43, 44, 49, 50, 51, 86, **87–88,** 143, 171–72, **351, 372**
　mass meeting at, 3–4, 35, 67
　1955–56 annual report of, 2n, 14n, **409–12,** 539

1956–57 recommendations for, **412**

sermons at, **207–8, 414–20,** 439, 494

Seventy-eighth Anniversary program at, **87–88**

Sunday services of, 502, 503, 504, 505, 507, 509, 513, 514

supportive of King, Jr., 13–14, 179–80

Dexter Echo, **320–21,** 350, 386n, **410–11,** 536, 539, 541, 542, 544

Dickerson, Earl Burrus, 95, *98n,* 98–99, 504

Diggs, Charles C., Jr., 15, 175–76n, 183, *218n,* 512, 513

King, Jr.'s correspondence with, 218, 515, 516, 517, 518, 526

Diggs, Charles C., Sr., 521, 523

Diggs Enterprises, Inc., 49, 218n, 527

Dillard, Ernest C., 252, *252n,* 521

Dinnerstein, Harvey, 503, 504, 533, illus.

Dissent, 513

Dixon, James Monroe, 509, 524

Dixon, Richard H., *421n,* **421–22,** 516, 538, 540

Dobbs House restaurant (Atlanta), 391, **392–93, 473–74**

Dockery, John Isaac, *170n,* 170–71, 513

Donne, John, 342n, **456–57**

Dorie Miller Memorial Foundation (Chicago), 53, 222n, 524, 526, 536

Doubleday & Co., 544

Dove, Mabel, 529

Drake, Fred, *127n,* **127–28,** 504, 507

Drake, John Gibbs St. Clair, *181n,* 181–82, 514

Drake, Mrs. J. P., 530

Draut, Woodrow E., 370n

Dred Scott v. John F. A. Sandford, **282, 300, 322– 23, 341, 455**

Du Bois, William Edward Burghardt, 22, **180,** *180n,* 511, 514

Duckett, Alfred, 534

Dudley, Lafayette, **374–75, 488–89,** 533, 534, 544

Dungee, Erna A., 69, *69n,* 102, 369

Durham, Barbee William, 504, 517

Durr, Clifford Judkins, 3, 506

Durr, Virginia Foster, 3, 502, 505, 506, 540

Eastland, James Oliver, **429,** *429n*

Ebenezer Baptist Church (Atlanta), 1, 12, 38, 47, 275–76, 413, 523

Ebenezer Baptist Church (Pittsburgh), 47

Ebony, 49, 380n, 527

Economic boycott, 15, **125,** 136, 198, **224–25, 238**

indictments for, 14–15, 41–42, 133, **152, 279, 305,** 367n

See also Baton Rouge bus boycott; Birmingham bus boycott; Montgomery bus boycott; Tallahassee bus boycott

Egypt, **259, 260, 261, 340, 344, 433**

Eichelberger, James William, Jr., **95,** *95n*

Eisenhower, Dwight David, 41, 43, 270n, 507, 508, 511, 512

appeals for intervention to, 28–29, 50, 405

King, Jr.'s correspondence with, **175–77, 357– 58,** 513, 532

as presidential candidate, **384,** 409

Ellington, Duke, 139, 408, 437

Emerson, Ralph Waldo, 265–66, **343, 457**

Employment discrimination, 216–17n, 328–29, 361–62, **371**

Engelhardt, Sam, Jr., **429**

England, J. Martin, 232–33, *232–33n,* 347, 519, 524

Ephesians, 300n, 323n

Eros, **327, 458**

Eubanks, John, 512

Evers, Medgar Wiley, 329–30, *329–30n,* **470– 71,** 529, 531, 540, 543, 544

Evil, **258–61, 306, 328, 459, 472–74**

Exodus, 258

Farmer, James, 18–19

Farris, Christine King. *See* King, Christine

Faubus, Orval, 364n

Faulkner, William (author), 44, **209, 241**

Faulkner, William J. (minister), *167n,* 167–68, **292,** 512, 524

FBI. *See* United States Federal Bureau of Investigation

Federal government

civil rights role of, **336, 337, 338, 369**

Federal Home Loan Bank (Greensboro), **271**

Federation of Colored Women's Clubs (Montgomery), 235n, 519

Feldman, Eugene, 535, 536

Fellowship, 20, 21, 46, 158, 249, 311n, 511, 516

"Walk for Freedom" article in, **277–80,** 523

Fellowship of Reconciliation (FOR), 18, 158, 183, 316n, 463–64n, 512, 514, 526, 527, 529, 536, 539

bus boycott role of, 19, 136–37, 138

comic book of, 435–36

nonviolence conferences of, 30, 46, 49, 311, **312**

and school desegregation, **353**

Walk to Freedom film of, 51, 214, 388, 390–91, 504

Ferré, Nels, 203

Ferron, Donald T., 4n, 7n, 13n, 15n, 506, 507

King, Jr.'s interview with, **123–26,** 506

MIA executive board meeting notes of, 9n, 10n, 11n, 14n, 101–4, 109–12, 119–22, 505, 506

MIA mass meeting notes of, 16n, 144–45, 150, 151, 509, 511

Fey, Harold E., 382, 542

Index Fields, Uriah J., 4n, 15, *68n*, 71, 81, 93, **229–30, 319,** 505, 508, 526
  charges against MIA by, 24–25, 48, 289n, 294–95
  MIA founding meeting minutes of, 68–70, 502
Financial institutions, **271–72, 450**
First African Baptist Church (Savannah), 399, 538
First Baptist Church (Montgomery), 69n, **145**
  King, Jr.'s addresses at, **113–14,** 135–36, **485–87**
  MIA headquarters at, 85n, 120, 121
  MIA mass meetings at, 37, 40, 41, 42, 44, 50, 52, 53, 84–85; notes on, 505, 507; programs of, 503, 509, 517, 534, 535, 540
First CME Church, 507
Fisher, B. J., 528
Fisher, Dorothy Canfield, 219–20, 518, 523
Fisk Memorial Chapel (Nashville), 41
Fisk University (Nashville), 47, 49, 101–2, 255–56, 351, 508, 523, 525, illlus.
Flemming, Billy, 471
Flemming v. South Carolina Electric and Gas Company, 35, 45, 217n, **432**
Florida A & M, 47, 360
  See also Tallahassee bus boycott
Floyd, Raymond B., 541, 544
Folsom, James Elisha, 40, 43, 50, 120n, **125,** 370, 506, 507, 509
FOR. *See* Fellowship of Reconciliation
Ford Hall Forum, 51, 363, **388,** 403, 441, 523
Foreman, Clark, 502
Fosdick, Harry Emerson, *1:140n,* 259n, 260n, 262, 445n, 459n
Foster, Hazel Elora, 20n, 233–34, *234n,* 519
Fowler, Elmer L., 536
Fox, E. L., 542
Frank, Anna C., 15n, 520, 525
Franklin, B. W., 45
Franklin, Pinkie Smith, 32n, *115n,* 115–16, 506, 524
Frazer, G. Stanley, **124**
Freedom, 204, **462**
  as duty *vs.* right, **428–30, 447**
  history of struggle for, **281–82, 300, 322–23, 324–25, 341**
  See also Integration; Justice
French, Edgar Nathaniel, 69, *69n,* 70, 71, 74–76, **93,** 133, 510
Friedman, Naomi, 439, 542
Friendship House (Philadelphia), 16
Frontiers of America, 525
Fullerton, Garry, 528
Fund for the Republic, 360, **385,** 435
Fuson, Marian, **351–52,** 531, 532
Fuson, Nelson, **351–52,** 531, 532

Gandhi, Mohandas K., 16–17, 19–20, 181, 182–83, 171, 204, **210n,** 211, 212, 224, 233, 234, **254,** 268–69, **285, 307, 328, 351–52,** 480n

Gandhian ideas
  and bus boycott, 178, 182–83, **276, 285**
  and Christian ideals, 17, 21, 89, **209n**
  and civil disobedience, 225, 226
  on constructive work, 212, 268
  Juliette Morgan's letter on, 17, 36, 502
  See also King, political and social ideas of; Nonviolent resistance
Gantt, Hermann, 526, 528
Garrett, Frank, 378
Garrison, James, 502
Gayle, William A., *80n,* 107, 501, 506, 507, 521, 526, 544, illus.
  on bombing incident, 115, 193n, **357**
  and bus boycott negotiations, 3n, 8, 37, 39, **80,** 97, 103, **123–24, 188, 240**
  and bus desegregation, **483–84**
  "get tough" policy of, 9, **304–5, 352**
    See also *Browder et al. v. Gayle*
General Acts of Alabama (18 July 1947), **82**
George, B. T., 521
Gettleman, Marjorie, 439, 542
Ghana, 492n, 496
Gibbons, Ray, 529
Gibbs, James L., 526
Gibbs, James Lowell, Jr., 216
Gibbs, Jewelle Taylor. *See* Taylor, Jewelle
Gilbert, Ralph Mark, 399, *399n,* 501
Gilchrist, J. H., 412
Gilman, Howard B., 521, 523, 538
Gilmore, Edith, 222n, 516
Gilmore, Georgia, 184
Glasco, Roseby James, Sr., 7, 23n, 70, *70n,* 78, 85, 121, 150, **189,** 369, 505, 517, 537, 540, 544
Glass, Jesse, 520, 521
God
  Christian allegiance to, **416**
  as love, **327, 459**
  as process of integration, 264, 266, **430**
  and struggle for justice, **73–74,** 151, **200, 327–28, 459**
Goldstein, Israel, 47, 253
Good, **259–61, 306, 328**
Goodman, Abram V., 511
Goodman, Paul, 19n
Good Street Baptist Church (Dallas), 45
Graetz, Robert S., 184, **193,** *193n,* 369, 381, 382, 502, 503, 505, 508, 533, 535, illus.
  in contact with FBI, 370
  harassment of, 28, 29, 50, 193n, 357
  at MIA's nonviolent training session, 389, 391
  scripture reading by, 424n, **446**
Gray, Fred D., 68, *68n,* 80, 102, 173, 502, 508, illus.
  and *Browder v. Gayle,* 40, 41, 43, 109, 111, 112, 120, **123, 303**
  and MIA, 69, 70, 97–98, 104
  and Rosa Parks's appeal, 35, 36, 68

Gray, William Herbert, Jr., *1:210n,* **145–46,** 205, 507, 510, 515

Grayson, Julian O., 126, *126n,* 452n, 506, 543

Greater New York Committee for a National Day of Prayer and Thanksgiving, **256, 257, 291,** 522

Greene, Eleanor, 527, 528

Greene, Homer, 23, **317–18,** 526, 528

Greene, Sherman Lawrence, 356, *356n*

Greenwood Missionary Baptist Church (Tuskegee), 365, 529

Gregg, Richard Bartlett, 169–70n, *211n,* 212, 268–69, 516, 519, 522
   The Power of Nonviolence, 19, 211, **244–45,** 267

Griffin, Joseph L., 506, 518, 522, 525, 536

Gross, W. A., 520

Guinan, Matthew, 440, *440n,* 542

Guy, Eunice, *157n,* 157–58, 511, 518

Hairston, Otis L., 541, 542

Hall, Grover C., 359, 537, 539

Hall, Peter A., 42, 184, *184n,* 508, illus.

Halstead, Fred, 511

Hampton Institute (Virginia), 51, 391, **392,** 527, 528, 535, illus.

Handy, Ruth, **310**

Handy, William Christopher, **317,** *317n,* 526

Handy, William Talbot, Jr., *2:160–61n,* **310–11,** 501, 513, 525, 527, 534

Hardin, George C., 220n

Harkins, Albert F., 178, 513, 519

Harlem Round Table Association, 522

Harlem Writers Guild, 314n

Harlow, Bryce N., 176n, 513

Harper and Row, 222n

Harrington, Donald, 288n

Harris, Arthaniel, 513, 515

Hassler, Alfred, 14n, 20n, 214n, 311, *311n,* 388, 431–42n, 510, 526, 536, 538

Hastie, William, 256

Hatt, Ken, 515, 523

Hawley, Jimmy, **297–98,** 526

Hawley, Ellen, **297–98,** 526

Hawley, Peter K., 297, 525

Hayes, Joshua William, 92, *92n*

Haynes, Roland E., *2:161–62n,* 441n, 441–42, **479–80,** 542, 544

Hebrews, 267n

Hebrew Union College, Jewish Institute of Religion, 510

Hedgeman, Anna Arnold, 532, 539

Hefner, William K., 533

Hegel, Friedrich, **281, 454**

Henderson, J. Raymond, *2:555n,* 27, 105
   King, Jr.'s correspondence with, 25n, **289–90, 318–19,** 501, 507, 521, 522, 524, 528, 542

Henderson, Velva, **319**

Henry, Ralph, 537

Heraclitus, **454**

Herron, Shaun, 157n

Hester, William H., 379

Highlander Folk School (Tennessee), 3, 274, 275n, **292–93,** 329, 348, **349–50,** 501, 511, 529

Hill, Daniel G., *490n,* **490–91,** 524, 527, 528, 542, 544, 545

Hill, Jesse, Jr., **250,** *250n,* 521

Hiller, Helen M., 293, **315,** 524, 527

Hilson, Ralph W., 85, 369, 515

Hinduism, **259**

Hines, Ralph H., 85n

Hoffman, Hallock, 360, 532

Holden, Anna, 102n, 149n, 183n, 198n, 199n, 200n, 201n, 338n, 504, 506, 507, 514, 515

Holland, Josiah Gilbert, 346n, **461,** 477n

Holleran, Mary P., 527, 528

Hollowell, Donald L., 392n

Holmes, John Haynes, 445n, 486n

Holt Street Baptist Church (Montgomery), 17, 53, illus.
   first MIA mass meeting at, 4, 11n, 36, 67, 68, 71–79, **191, 195, 239, 302–3, 451;** notes on, 502
   King, Jr.'s speeches at, 5–7, **71–74, 199–200, 424–33, 451–63, 485–87,** 514, 540
   MIA mass meetings at, 42, 43, 46, 47, 52, 144–45; notes on, 509, 510, 515; programs of, 504, 519, 524, 541
   King, Jr.'s address to, **322–28**

Hoover, J. Edgar, 96, 502, 504, 512

Hope, Edward Swain, *334n,* 334–35, 530

Hope, John, 334, 335

Horace, James L., 517

Horton, Myles, *274n,* 329n, 506, 508, 509, 513, 540
   King, Jr.'s correspondence with, 274–75, **292–93,** 523, 524

Horton, Zilphia, 506

Hosea, 74

Houser, George, 169–70n

Howard, Theodore Roosevelt Mason, 248, *248n*

Howard University (Washington, D.C.), **490–91,** 516, 524, 528, 543

Hubbard, Hillman H., 40, 92, *92n,* 103, 104, 108, 120n, 122, **427**

Huger, James E., 119n, 201, *269n,* **269–70,** 521, 522, 531, 532, illus.

Hughes, Langston, **267,** 310n, **432**

Hughes, Robert E., 194, *194n,* 353, 468–69, 504, 536, 543

Hungary, **475–76**

Hunter, Allan A., 525

Hunter, Roy, 507

Hunter's Chapel AME Zion Church (Tuscaloosa), 46

Hurley, Ruby, 108–9n, 121, *121n,* 122

Hutchinson, Dean, 530, 532

Hutchinson Street Baptist Church (Montgomery)
mass meetings at, 37, 42, 44, 51, 52, 53, 150,
151, 388, 424, 433n, 446n, 541; notes on,
511, 541; programs of, 503, 515, 525, 536

Imperialism. *See* Colonialism
Improved Benevolent Protective Order of Elks
of the World, 50, **270–71**
India, 492n, 496, 498
Indian independence movement, 17, 21–22, 36,
211–12, 234, 268, **307, 328**
See also Gandhi, Mohandas K.; Gandhian ideas
In Friendship, 138n, 491n
founding of, 19, 42, 139
MIA fundraising by, **408–9, 434, 437–38,** 439
Ingalls, Luther, 37, **124,** 445n, 507
Institute on Nonviolence and Social Change, 30,
53, 372, 404n, 422, 435, 436, **442,** 451n, 469,
484, **490,** 541, 543
King, Jr.'s address to, 52, **451–63,** 542
Integration
based on mutual respect, **446, 487**
bus boycott and, 7–8, 11, 31–32, **277n, 303,
378–79, 481–83,** 491–93
Christian basis for, 27–28, **373, 418, 460, 474**
government's role in, 175, **284, 307, 345, 460–
61, 475, 476**
individual responsibility for, 26, 204, **307, 345,
461, 478**
monetary sacrifice for, **345, 461, 477**
moral dimensions of, 381–82
nonviolent implementation of, 389–90, **430,
431, 432, 481–83, 484, 487**
preparation needed for, 265–66, **342–44, 464**
progress in, **280–81, 341–342, 456, 460**
reactionary resistance to, **322, 336–37,** 347–
48, **376–77, 418, 445, 447, 475**
"State of the Race" Conference on, 216–17
as victory for justice, **232, 305–6, 326, 337,
344, 418, 428, 447**
white community's acceptance of, **448–49**
See also Freedom; Justice
Inter-Civic Council (Tallahassee), 47, 51, 53,
360n, 404, 526
Interdenominational Ministerial Alliance
(Montgomery), 4, 68n, 93, 97–98, 108, 358
Interdenominational Ministerial Union (Wil-
mington, Delaware), **287**
International Ladies' Garment Workers' Union,
529
International Longshoremen and Warehouse-
men's Union, 147, 510, 514, 525
Interstate Commerce Commission, 35, 38
Isaiah, 462n, 479n
Israel, **259–60**
I Was There by the Grace of God (Seay, Sr.), 111n

Jack, Homer Alexander, 20, 178, *178n,* 513
at Institute on Nonviolence and Social Change,
30, 451n
King, Jr.'s correspondence with, **350–51,** 496,
498, 513, 526, 527, 529, 530, 531, 545
on Montgomery movement, 169, 178–79,
206n, 512
on northern experts
Jackson, Emory, *2:328n,* **76**
Jackson, Joseph Harrison, *2:573n,* 33, 53, **162–
63,** 242, 443, 451n
King, Jr.'s correspondence with, 154–55, 501,
509, 511, 512, 545
MIA and, 27, **93–95,** 154–55
Jackson, L. K., 508, 543
Jackson, Maynard H., 250n
James, Arthur R., *286n,* **286–87,** 515, 523
James, Felix E., 512
James, Julius, *2:337n,* 512
James, William, **300, 323**
Jayaswal, Mishree Lal, **316**
Jefferson, Thomas, **286**
Jemison, Theodore Judson, 7, 27, 30, 36, *402n,*
451n
King, Jr.'s correspondence with, 402, 530, 532,
538, 539, 541
Jensen, Harold V., 545
Jernagin, William H., 33n, *331n,* **331–32,** 355–
56, 529, 530, 532
Jesus Christ, **6,** 72–73, 130, 172n, 199, **208, 224,**
234, **259, 325–26, 328, 344, 361, 395, 417,
428, 429, 431**
Jet, 88, 157
Jett, Francis, 140n, 507
Job, 295n, 310, 479n
John, Alma Vessels, *382n,* 382–83, 535, 540
John (New Testament), **419, 429n, 431n, 449n,
478n**
Johns, Vernon H., 53, 365n, **372,** 534, 535
Johnson, Arthur, 150
Johnson, Carl R., 531, 540
Johnson, Charles Spurgeon, 255–56, **398,** 522,
524, 525, 527, 537
Johnson, H. H., 84, 85, *85n,* 369
Johnson, Howard, **355**
Johnson, Mordecai, 16, 501
Johnson, Tom, 38, 104, 505
Johnson, Wilbert J., **378–79,** 532, 534
Jones, E. Theodore, 518
Jones, Edward A., 510, 526
Jones, George W., 320, **411**
Jones, J. Harold, 15n, 16n, 144n, 151n, 510, 511
Jones, Major J., *2:306n,* 116–17, 501, 506, 510,
521, 529
Jones, Mattie Parker, 116
Jones, Moses W., 424
Jones, Nathaniel R., 529

Jones, Walter B., 46, 47, 49, 53
Jones, William D. (student), 140–41, 509
Jones, William (labor union steward), 148, 510
Jordan, Clarence, 347
Journal of Religious Thought, 182n
Journey of Reconciliation (1947), 20, 163n, 288n
    See also Congress of Racial Equality
Judaism, **259**
Jude, 420n
Jumper, Iris, 535, 539
Justice
    and democracy, **424–25**
    and God, 151, **200, 327–28, 459, 486**
    and integration, **232, 305–6, 326, 337, 344,
        418, 428, 447**
    and love, 6, 21, **73–74,** 136, 154, **221, 279, 306**
    and nonviolent resistance, **73,** 146, **325, 327,
        486**
    and peace, **207–8, 221, 282, 323, 455**
    sacrifices for, 26, **78–79, 114, 200, 279, 307,
        418–19, 461–62, 478**
    as spiritual principle, 268–69

Kaplan, Kivie, *362n,* 362–63, 532
Kelly, Charles W., 12n, 28n, *365n,* 365–66,
    414n, 529, 533, 534
Kelsey, George D., *1:155n,* 146, **164–65,** 510,
    512
Kennedy, Earl, 29n, **408–9,** 538, 539
Kennedy, John Fitzgerald, 225n
Kilgore, Thomas G., Jr., *2:268n,* 26, 27, 151n,
    291, 296–97
    King, Jr.'s correspondence with, 160, 162, 512,
        531, 532
Killens, John Oliver, *314n,* **314–15,** 525, 527
Kinds, William K., 102, 103
King, Alberta Williams (King, Jr.'s mother), 11,
    15n, 50, 183, 201, 361, 366, 506
King, Alfred Daniel (King, Jr.'s brother), 11, 40,
    413, *413n,* 539
King, Christine (King, Jr.'s sister), 11, 40, *158n*
King, Coretta Scott (King, Jr.'s wife), 14, 130,
    172, 183, 199, 204, 211, 216, 242, **289, 327,
    311, 359n, 360,** 410n, 467, 508, 511, 513, 514,
    515, 523, 527, 535, 537, 543, 545, illus.
    bombing at home of, 11n, 40, 114–15
    on bus boycott, 13, 198
    concerts by, 50, 51, 52, 139, 366, **386,** 407–8,
        411, 434, 437, 441, 538, 543
King, Joel Lawrence (King, Jr.'s uncle), *2:224–
    25n,* 469–70, 543
King, John W., 501
King, Martin Luther, Jr.
    awards to, 46, 47, 49, 50, 52, 53, 54, 255–56,
        269–71, 290–91, 333, **334**
    bombing at home of, 10–11, 40, 115, **188,
        240, 278–79, 305**
    at boycott planning meeting, 3–4, 35, 67
    in civil rights network, 2–3, 25–27
    congratulatory notes on desegregation ruling
        to, 433–34, 436, 440
    Dexter congregation's support of, 13–14,
        179–80, **411**
    and Dobbs House incident, 51, 391, **392–93,
        473–74**
    FBI investigation of, 96, 502, 504, 512
    as head of MIA, 4–5, 8–9, 36, 68, 104
    illustrations of, 506, 508, 509, 514, 515, 518,
        527, 528, 531, 535, 545, illus.
    integrated bus suggestions of, 389–90, **481–83**
    leadership of, 10, 16, 32, 129–30, 138, 140,
        141, 142–43, 144, 146, 154, 156, 168, 181,
        182, 202, 215–16, 364
    and Madison Square Garden rally, **246–47,**
        248, **253**
    at MIA executive board meetings, 39, 45, 102–
        4, 109–12, 120–22, **271–73;** agendas on,
        505, 506; restructuring recommendations
        to, 30n, **271–73,** 523
    at MIA founding meeting, 4–5, 35–36, 69–
        70, **189–90**
    at MIA mass meetings, 5–7, 11, 29, 36, 37, 38,
        39, 40, 42–48, 50–54, **71–74,** 75, **76,** 77,
        78–79, 199–201, 267n, **424–33, 485–87,
        494–95,** 501–7, 514–19, 545
    on Montgomery's intimidation tactics, 28–29,
        114, 120, **239–40, 304–5**
    on NAACP, **243–44, 476–77**
    and National Baptist Convention presidency,
        33, 242–43, 443–44
    and National Fraternal Council of Churches,
        331, 355–56
    in negotiations with city, 7, 36, 37, 38, 41, **101,**
        102–3, **123–25, 186–87, 277n**
    oratorical skills of, 11–12, 28, 365–66
    on personal fears, **202–3**
    on *The Power of Nonviolence,* **244–45**
    and railroad station incident, 49, **467,** 543
    representative role of, 15–16, **124n,** 144, 184
    on security measures, 40, 120, 121
    shooting at home of, 53, **494**
    speeding citation of, 9, 39, 106, **200n, 240,
        304–5,** 505, 506
    spiritual crisis of, 9–10, 39
    statements of, 511, 514, 518, 519, 520, 540,
        544, 545
    subpoenaed in NAACP case, 319–20, **331**
    travel to Ghana and India by, 492n, 496, 498
    trial of, 14–16, 41–43, 49, 90n, 183–85, 132–
        33, 197, 198, **199–201, 279, 305,** 367n, 505,
        508, 509, 511, 514, 515, 529; testimony at,
        185–96
    on U.S. presidential candidates, **384, 408–9**
    on *Walk to Freedom* film, 390, 391

Index

King, Martin Luther, Jr., interviews of, 53, 54
  with Joe Azbell, **202–3,** 515
  with Donald T. Ferron, 7n, **123–25,** 506
  with Glenn E. Smiley, 42, **249,** 277, 278n, 510
King, Martin Luther, Jr., ministry of, 33, **229–30,**
  409–12
  and lay participation, 1–2, **320–21**
  and religious emotionalism, 11–12, 264
  in social gospel tradition, 1, 6, **114,** 490n
  See also Dexter Avenue Baptist Church
King, Martin Luther, Jr., political and social
  ideas of
  on acceptance of sacrifice, 26, **78–79, 114,**
    200, 279, 307, 345, 418–19, 461–62, 477
  on brotherhood of man, **261–62, 342, 450,**
    456–57, 462, 478–79
  on capitalism, 366, **416**
  on career preparation, **343, 457**
  Christian principles and, 2, 5–6, 10–11, 21,
    28, **72, 73–74**
  and communism, 22–23, 144, **318, 416**
  on federal government's civil rights role, **337,**
    338, 366, 369
  Gandhian ideas and, 16–17, 19–22, 350
  and good *vs.* evil, **200, 258–61, 306, 328, 459**
  and human dignity, **79, 94, 209–10, 236–37,**
    238, 242, 273, 285, 301, 324, 341–42, 446
  on individual responsibility for integration,
    26, **307, 345, 461, 478**
  on leadership, 31, **309, 315, 345–46, 461,**
    477–78
  on legislative controls, **284, 307, 345, 460–61,**
    475, 476
  on meaning of freedom, **428–30,** 447
  on peace and justice, 29, **207–8, 221, 282,**
    323, 455
  on political parties, 29, **384, 409, 460, 476**
  on preparing for new world order, 265–66,
    342–44, 453–54
  on race relations, **237, 280–81, 322, 324, 450,**
    456, 460
  on right to protest, 6–7, **72–73,** 135–36, 198
  on separate-but-equal doctrine, **283, 323n,**
    341, 425, 455, 472–73, 474
  on slavery, **282, 300, 323, 341**
  on states' rights, **337**
  on student movements, **375**
  in testimony to the Democratic National Con-
    vention, 28, 50, 335, **336–38,** 531
  and voting rights concerns, 2, 29, **337, 345,**
    369, 386–87, **442, 460**
  on world struggle against colonialism, **260–**
    61, 308–9, 324–25, 340–41, 454
  See also Democracy; Gandhian ideas; Integra-
    tion; Nonviolent resistance; Segregation;
    Violence
King, Martin Luther, Jr., press releases of, 555,
  513, 514, 518, 519, 520

"The Bus Protest Is Still On," 8n, **100–101,** 505
"Statement of Negroes on Bus Situation," **81–**
  83, 502
King, Martin Luther, Jr., published works of
  "From the Pastor's Desk," **321–22,** 528
  "Nonviolence and Racial Justice," 382
  "Our Struggle," 7n, 19n, 31n, 44, 163, **236–**
    41, 374, 445n, 519
  Strength to Love, 127n, 258n, 260n, 414n
  Stride Toward Freedom, 1, 2n, 4n, 5n, 7n, 8n,
    9–10, 11n, 12n, 13n, 14n, 15n, 16n, 17n,
    22, 24n, 25n, 39, 71, 124n, **125n,** 135n,
    173n, 222, 272n, 431n, 446n, 481n
  "Walk for Freedom," 21, 46, **249, 277–80,**
    519, 523
  "We Are Still Walking," 52, 377n, 424n, 430n,
    431n, **445–51,** 542
King, Martin Luther, Jr., religious ideas of
  on biblical interpretation, **282, 300, 323, 378–**
    79, 417
  on Christian allegiance to God, **416**
  Gandhian ideas and, 17, 21, **209n**
  on God as process of integration, 264, 266, **430**
  on good *vs.* evil, **200, 258–61, 306, 328, 459**
  on love as highest good, **419–20**
  and love and justice, 6, 17, 21, **73–74,** 136,
    200, 221, 279, 458
  on redemptive love, **278, 305–6, 327**
  on Roman Catholicism, **417**
  and scientific progress *vs.* spiritual develop-
    ment, **415–16**
  and struggle for justice, 151, **200, 327–28,**
    459, 486
King, Martin Luther, Jr., sermons of, 35, 37, 38,
  39, 40, 41, 42, 44, 45, 46, 47, 48, 50, 51, 52, 53,
  262
  "The Death of Evil upon the Seashore," 22,
    38, 46, 256, **258–62,** 296, 328n, 522
  "Loving Your Enemies," 17, 127
  "Paul's Letter to American Christians," 27–
    28, 50, 52, 365–66, **414–20,** 474n, 539
  "Rediscovering Lost Values," 17n, 50, 261n,
    348n, 382–84
  "Remember Who You Are," 52–53, 490
  "The Role of the Negro Mother in Preparing
    Youth for Integration," 46, **264–67**
  "The Three Dimensions of a Complete Life,"
    41, 53, 203n, 490
  "When Peace Becomes Obnoxious," 43, 44,
    207–8, 515
King, Martin Luther, Jr., speeches of, 41, 43, 44,
  45, 49, 50, 51, 52, 53, 54
  "The Birth of a New Age," 50, 261n, 269,
    281n, **339–46,** 452n, 531
  "The Declaration of Independence and the
    Negro," 44, 295n
  "Desegregation and the Future," 51, 53, 332n,
    346n, 419n, **471–79,** 544

"Facing the Challenge of a New Age," 8n, 23, 26, 30–31, 52, 53, 252, 261n, 281n, 306n, 342n, 343n, 346n, **451–63,** 480n, 490n, 530, 542, 543
  at MIA's first mass meeting, 5–7, **71–74, 76, 78–79,** 502
"The Montgomery Story," 48, 51, 252, 261n, 267n, 281n, **299–310,** 526, 530
"The 'New Negro' of the South: Behind the Montgomery Story,"48, 98n, 208n, 265n, **280–86,** 301n, 324n, 341n, 403n, 519, 523
"Non-Aggression Procedures to Interracial Harmony," 49, 51, 261n, 281n, 306n, **321–28,** 529, 539
"Quotable Quotes from Rev. King," **209–10,** 515
"A Realistic Look at Race Relations," 46, 51, 258, 388n, 403, 522
King, Martin Luther, Sr. (King, Jr.'s father), 1, 6, 28n, 38, 151n, 183, 201, 250n, 537
  bombing incident and, 11, 40
  on Dwight D. Eisenhower, 408
  King, Jr.'s correspondence with, 105, 505
  letter to Dexter Avenue Baptist Church from, 275–76, 523
  on Montgomery movement, 14–15, 46
  railroad station harassment of, 467
King, Yolanda Denise (King, Jr.'s daughter), 40, 83, 114, **311,** 320, 515, 527, illus.
King Hill Baptist Church (Montgomery), 39, 505
Klein, Edward E., 545
Kleinbaum, Max M., 538
Knapp, Lucille B., 503, 510
Koch, Mel, 530
Koinonia Farm (Americus, Georgia), 232–33n, 347–48, **355**
Kotelchuck, David, 515, 520
Krishna Menon, 436, *436n*
Ku Klux Klan, **73,** 322n, **358, 377,** 424, **429, 430, 447, 475**

Lackey, D. H., 508, illus.
Lambert, B. D., 150–51, **231,** 451n
Lampley, R L., 506, illus.
Langford, Charles D., 40, 42, 70, *70n,* 112, 122, 184, 369, 370, 508, illus.
Lawrence, Charles Radford, II, 18n, 19, *136n,* 136–38, 509
Lawrence, George, 258n, *291n*
  King, Jr.'s correspondence with, **291,** 296–97, **407–8,** 520, 521, 524, 525, 538, 539
Laws, Clarence A., 254, 522
Lee, George, 121n, 221n
Lee, James Oscar, 525, 534, 535
Lee, Willie Mae, 10n, 15n, 75, 102n, 113, 115, 505, 506, 507
LeFlore, John L., 467, 541, 543

Legislation and segregation, **284, 307, 345, 460–61, 475, 476**
Leishman, R. Murray, 513
Lenud, Philip M., 374, **375,** 537, 538
Lester, Muriel, 19n, 510
Levenberg, Selma, **403,** 538
Levison, Stanley David, 32, 54, 437, 491, *491n,* 492, 528
Levy, James E., 529
Lewis, G. Franklin, 369
Lewis, John, 438n
Lewis, Rufus A., 4, 7, 13n, 39, 68, *68n,* 84, 108, 113, 144, 358, 369, 505, 522, 532
Liberation, 19n, 44, 52, 163, 164, **236–41, 445–51,** 519, 542
Life, illus.
Lincoln, Abraham, **286**
Lloyd, Gil Burton, 33n, *443n,* 443–44, 542
Lloyd's of London, 50, 377n, **385, 448,** 542
Lomax, Almena, *263n,* **313,** 524, 527, 528, 535
  "Mother's Day in Montgomery," 263–67, 522
Lomax, Minnie, 313
Los Angeles Transit Lines, **374**
Los Angeles Tribune, 263, **313,** 522, 524
Lothrop, Donald G., 517
Louisville and Nashville Railroad, 38
Louisville Defender, 44, 201
  "When Peace Becomes Obnoxious," **207–8,** 515
Love, 204, 234, 266, **327, 419–20, 458–59**
  and justice, 6, 21, **73–74,** 136, 154, **221, 279, 306**
  in new world order, **344, 457–58**
  as redemptive, **278, 305–6**
  as regulating ideal, 15, 21, 146, 154, 198–99, **200, 230, 276, 305, 326**
  transformative power of, 17, 151, 233, **273**
Lowe, Jimmie, 235, 369
Lowe, Richard A., 162, 510, 516, 517
Lowell, James Russell, **260, 306, 328, 344,** 369, **459**
Lucy, Autherine, *128n,* **239,** 339
  at Madison Square Garden rally, 47, 248, 253
  and school desegregation, 40, 121n, 128, 207
Lusk, William, 439, 542
Lynne, Seybourn, 24n, 46

Mabrey, C. G., 522
McCain, R. B., 369
McCall, Paula, 407
McCall, Walter Raleigh, *1:327n,* 211, **399–400**
  King, Jr.'s correspondence with, 117–18, 406–7, 501, 506, 535, 537, 539
McColloch, Lois, 290n, 527, 528
McCormack, John W., 336
McCrackin, Maurice, 531, 536
McDonald, Susie, 111
McDougall, Curtiss, 505

Index

Macedonia Baptist Church (Denver), 50, 533
McKinney, Mary, 142n
McKinney, Samuel B., 142, *142n,* 516, 518, 519
McKinney, Virginia Ruth, 142, *142n*
McKinney, Wade H., *141n,* 141–42, 509, 510
McLaurin, Benjamin F., *246n,* 248, **253,** 332, 338n, 471
  King, Jr.'s correspondence with, **246–47, 413–14,** 520, 528, 532, 539
McMurray, Wayne D., **223,** 517, 518
McNeil, Jesse Jai, *2:239n,* 27, 45, 149–50, 218, 510, 519
Madison Square Garden rally (May 24), 47, 246, **247,** 248, **253,** 523
Malloch, Douglas, **457**
Mallory, Arenia C., 51
March on Washington Movement, 18, 246n
Maritain, Jacques, 203
Marshall, Thurgood, 52 111, *111n,* 134–35, 184n, 270, 339
  on school boycotts, 26n, 307n
Martain, Jean, 394
Martin, E. M., 250n, 522
Martin Luther King, Jr., Center for Nonviolence (Los Angeles), 137n
Martin Luther King, Jr., Center for Social Change, Inc., 203n, 250n
Martin Luther King, Jr., Film Project, 198
Marx, Karl, **144**
Mason, E. H., 85, 358, 532
Mason, Mrs. William Thomas, 256
Mason, Vivian C., *235n,* 235–36, 256, 512, 513, 519, 520
Massey, Floyd, 533, 539
Mathiason, David G., 535, 536, 539
Matthew (New Testament), 79, 115, **208,** 265n, 268n, 279, 293n, 305n, 325n, 428n, 528n
Matthews, Robert L., 79, 121–22
Matthews, Z. K., 445n
Maxwell, Lillie Bell, 349
Maxwell, O. Clay, 26, 258, *349n*
  King, Jr.'s correspondence with, 27n, **348–49,** 519, 521, 525, 529, 531, 543
Mays, Benjamin Elijah, *1:152n,* 14, 19n, 32, 128, 129, 169, 256, 288n, 343n, 363, 457n
  and Gandhian movement, 16, 233–34
  King, Jr.'s correspondence with, **222,** 433–34, **480–81,** 504, 517, 518, 520, 529, 531, 532, 540, 543, 544, 545
Meany, George, 41, 175–76n, 335, 507, 512
Media coverage
  of bus boycott, 4, 15, 35, 37, 40, 44, 49, 137, **224–25,** 230, **245,** 359
  international, 254–55, 334–35
  of King, Jr.'s trial, 183
  "Mother's Day in Montgomery," 263–67, **313,** 522

"Negroes Pledge to Keep Boycott," 135–36, 509
"Quotable Quotes from Rev. King," **209–10,** 515
  See also *Montgomery Advertiser*
Meharry Medical College (Nashville), 41
Men of Montgomery, 41, 145n, 187n, 507, 508
Menon, Vengalil Krishnan Krishna, 436, *436n*
Mercury Match Corporation (Zanesville, Ohio), 288
Merriam, Eve, 504
Messenger, 216–17n
Methodist Ministerial Alliance (Montgomery), 92, 97–98, 108
Meyers, Irving, 526
MIA. *See* Montgomery Improvement Association
Michaux, H. M., 533, 538
Mickleburg, Bruce, 525
Miller, Edith Lorraine, 262
Miller, Robert H., 523
Miller, William Robert, 20, *158n,* 280n
  King, Jr.'s correspondence with, 158–59, **249,** 262–63, 512, 516, 517, 520, 522, 525
Minneapolis Tribune, 102
Mississippi Regional Council of Negro Leadership, 220, 513
Mitchell, Clarence, 467n, 542, 543
Mitchell, Henry H., 28n
Montgomery: A White Preacher's Memoir (Graetz), 193n, 370n
Montgomery Advertiser, 4, 35, 40, **81–83,** 178, **202–3,** 214–15, **448,** 486n, 502, 503, 505
  "Blast Rocks Residence of Bus Boycott Leader," 11n, 114–15, 506
  "The Bus Protest Is Still On," **100–101**
  "Lesson from Gandhi" letter, 17, 36, 85n
  "New Fields Await Negroes, King Tells Mass Meeting," 494–95, 545
  "The Rev. King Is Boycott Boss," 38–39, 104
  suggested MIA column in, 311, **312**
  "To the Citizens of Montgomery," 39, 107–8, 505
  "To the Montgomery Public," 37, 89–93
  See also Media coverage
Montgomery Anniversary Concert (5 December 1956), 14n, 434, **437–38,** 439
Montgomery bus boycott, 508, 533
  in American tradition of protest, 6–7, **72–73**
  Chicago leaders' support of, **93–95,** 139–40, 153, 167
  and desegregation goal, 7–8, 11, **277n, 303**
  distanced from communism, 22–23, 144, 156, **318**
  economic reprisals for, **287, 437, 442, 450**
  FBI investigation of, 96
  and final Supreme Court ruling, 49, **354,** 371–**72, 377**

and FOR, 19, 51, 214, 388, 390–91, 504
fraternities' support of, 26, 118–19
historical significance of, 31–32, 491–93
Indian independence movement and, 17, 21–
22, 36, 178, 182–83, 211–12, **276, 285, 307,
328**
international interest in, 254–55, **298,** 334–
35, 521
King, Jr.'s proposed book on, 360, **385–86**
legal justification for, 184, **425**
as manifestation of "new Negro," **237–39,
283, 452**
MIA's resolutions on, 76–78, 191–92, 502
moral and ethical dimensions of, 5–6, **73–74,
305–6, 326, 428**
NAACP's position on, 11, 26n
National Deliverance Day observance of, 44,
147, 166n, 171, 212–13
noncoercive tactics of, 75, 78, 92, 184, **186,** 192
as non-economic protest, 15, **125,** 136n, 198,
486
number of participants in, **238, 302**
outsiders' role in, 18, 19, 20, 137–38, 163,
169–70, 178, 206, **239,** 520
planning for, 3–4, 35, 67–70, **190, 302**
and race, 15, 107, 136, 137, **176, 278, 428**
in Tallahassee, 27, 29, 47, 48, 51, 53–54, 360,
404
unified support for, **73, 74, 76, 239–40, 302**
white support for, 95, 97, 136n, 137, 138,
168–69, 170, 211, **304,** 435–36, **448–49**
women's role in, 12–13
WPC's leaflet on, 3, 35, 67, 80n, **189,** 190n,
501
See also Car pools; Montgomery Improvement
Association; Nonviolent resistance
Montgomery City Code. *See* Montgomery municipal code
Montgomery City Commission, 504, 544
and car pool injunction, 51, 52, **413–14, 421–
22,** 424, **427**
as Citizens Council members, 8, 38, 39, 107,
120
erroneous settlement reports by, 8, **101,** 102–3
intimidation by, 9, 28–29, **114,** 120, **239, 240,
304–5**
MIA's negotiations with, 36, 37, 38, 41, 97–98,
123–25, 186–87, 239, 277n, 468
in noncompliance with desegregation ruling,
45, 46, **231, 374,** 377n, 483, 544
and violence, 40, **357–58,** 365
Montgomery City Lines, Inc., 37–38, 90, 225,
226, 502
compliance with desegregation ruling, 23, 45,
46, 217n, 219, **374**
grievances against, **81–83,** 89–91
initial one-day boycott of, 4, 67, 190n

MIA's boycott resolution to, 76–78, 191–92,
502
MIA proposal to, 7, 36, **80–81,** 91–92, **93–94,
187**
reduced services on, 36, 44, 49
resumption of full services on, 29, 53, 485–86
seating policy of, **72,** 77, **80,** 82n, 90, **301–2**
See also Bus segregation; Montgomery bus
boycott
Montgomery Improvement Association (MIA),
7–8, 11, 12–13, 15, **189,** 502, 504, 540, 542
Alpha Phi Alpha fraternity's contributions to,
26, 118–19, 201–2
anniversary of, 14n, 30–31, 52, 434, **437–38,**
439
bus boycott resolutions of, 76–78, 191–92, 502
bus seating proposal of, 7, 36, **80–81,** 91–92,
103–4, **123, 124–25, 176, 187, 195, 303**
city's attempted intimidation of, 9, 28–29,
114, 120, **239–40, 304–5**
executive board meetings of, 24n, 39, 40, 411,
45, 47, 49, 50, 51, 101–4, 109–12, 119–22,
253, **271–73,** 354n, 523, 542, illus; agendas
of, 505, 516, 518, 535, 537, 538; and members list, 506, 511, 524; minutes of, 120–22,
369–70, 406n, 502, 505, 506, 529, 534, 538,
541
expanded civil rights concerns of, 29–32, **450,**
512
U. J. Fields's charges against, 24–25, 48, 289n,
294–95
financial needs of, **152, 153,** 191, 196, **280n,
287, 376,** 506
financial reports of, 23, 506, 540, 544
first mass meeting of, 5–7, 36, **71–74,** 75, **76,**
77, **78–79, 302–3, 452,** 502
founding meeting of, 4–5, 35–36, 68–70,
189–90; minutes of, 68–70
fundraising by, 23, 25–27, 288, **317, 407–8,
437–38,** 439, **442–43,** 489
indicted leaders of, 14–15, 41–42, **240, 305**
insurance policies of, **377, 385,** 448
integrated bus suggestions of, **481–83,** 544
lobbying of National City Lines by, **93–95,**
98–99
membership of, **185, 186, 192–93, 302**
NAACP's financial/legal support of, 25–26,
42, **109,** 134–35, **152,** 165–66, 173, **243–44,**
506
negotiating with city officials, 36, 37, 38, 41,
123–26, 186–87, 230, 468
newsletter, of, 24, 48, **272,** 525, 526, 529, 534,
542
nonviolent training session of, 389–90, 481
suggested newspaper column of, 311, **312**
transferred headquarters of, 85n, 120, 121,
287, 295

Index

Montgomery Improvement Association (MIA) (*continued*)
  See also Institute on Nonviolence and Social Change; King, Martin Luther, Jr., speeches of; Montgomery bus boycott
Montgomery movement. *See* Montgomery bus boycott
Montgomery municipal code, 7, **72, 82**
  See also Bus segregation; Montgomery City Lines, Inc.
Montgomery Police Department, 9, 39, 144, 501, 502
Montgomery's Prayer and Pilgrimage Day (24 February), 42, 140–41
Montgomery to Memphis (film), 198
Moore, Amzie, 139
Moore, Douglas E., *393n*, 393–97, 536, 543
Moore, Gladys, 16, 184
Moore, Juanita, 524, 525
Morehouse College (Atlanta), 16, 46, 142, 203, **222,** 234, 316, **400, 480,** 511, 529
Morgan, Ernest, *347n*, 347–48, **355,** 531, 532
Morgan, Gerald D., 515
Morgan, Juliette, 17, 36, 85n, 502, 507
Moron, Alonzo G., 536
Morong, Carrol O., 533, 534
Morris, Charles S., II, 516
Morris, Joseph C., 516, 519, 520
Morris, T., 523
Morrow, Everett Frederick, 510
Morsell, John A., 520, 524
Morton, Charles, 407, *407n*
Mosely, Benjamin F., 102
Motley, Carolyn, 411n
Moton, R. R., 525, 527
Mount Olivet Baptist Church (New York City), 50, 525
  King, Jr.'s sermon at, **348–49,** 382–84
Mount Zion AME Zion Church (Montgomery), 37, 51, 68, **190,** 545
Mount Zion First Baptist Church (Baton Rouge), 52, 541
Muelder, Walter George, *387n*, **387–88,** 423, 441, **480,** 534, 536
Murray, C. T., 529
Muste, Abraham Johannes, 18, 19n, 20, 30, 236n, 288n, **316,** *316n,* 396, 434, 517, 521, 527, 528, 541
Myrdal, Gunnar, 134n

NAACP. *See* National Association for the Advancement of Colored People
Nabors, Billy Joe, **353**
Nance, Earl E., *242n*, 242–43, 519
Nashville Tennessean, 528
National Association for the Advancement of Colored People (NAACP), 88n, 128n, 139n,
148n, 180n, 184, **243–44,** 248, 309n, 319–20n, 362, 363, 392, **442, 450, 476–77,** 502, 503, 504, 506, 509, 511, 512, 513, 516, 518, 520, 521, 531, 533, 535, 538, 540, 544
  banned activities of, 45, 47, 48, 49, 50, 356
  and *Browder v. Gayle,* 11, 25, 111–12, 121–22, 165–66
  on bus boycott, 11, 26n
  employment discrimination against members of, 328–29, 361–62, **371**
  financial / legal assistance from, 42, **109,** 134–35, **152,** 165–66, 173, 508
  47th Annual Convention of, 299, **319,** 329–30, 526, 527
  fundraising concerns of, 25–26, 166, **488–89**
  King, Jr.'s addresses to, 7, 44, 49, 51, 53, 258, **280–86, 299–310, 470–71,** 490n, 522
  King, Jr.'s connections with / support of, 3, 25–26, **244, 345, 476–77**
  Legal Defense and Education Fund of, 46, 173n, 280, 522
  and Rosa Parks case, 36
  press releases from, 511, 513
National Association of Business and Professional Women's Clubs (Brooklyn), 43, 209, 512
National Baptist Convention, U.S.A., Inc., 27, 33, 38, 154–5, 291n, 318, **332,** 349, 367, 392n, 402n, 530, 533
  King, Jr.'s sermon at, 50, 365–66, **414–20**
  presidency of, 242–43, 443–44
National Baptist Sunday School and Baptist Union Training Congress, 105n, 289, 331n, 349n, 529, 532
National Baptist Voice, 17n, 24n, 170–71, 258, 519, 533
National City Lines, Inc. (Chicago), 7n, 37, 374
  compliance with desegregation ruling, 230, **231, 232**
  MIA lobbying committee and, 41, **93–95,** 98–99
  MIA's negotiations with, 45, **80–81, 187,** 502
National Committee for Rural Schools, 246n, **332–33,** 419n, 528, 531
  "Desegregation and the Future" address to, **471–79,** 544
National Consumers Mobilization, 373–74, 529, 531
National Council of Negro Women (NCNW), 47, 179n, 235, 519
National Council of the Churches of Christ in the United States of America, 525, 534, 543
National Deliverance Day of Prayer (28 March), 44, 148, 166n, 171, 212–13
National Fraternal Council of Churches, U.S.A., 49, **331,** 355–56, 527
National Negro Funeral Directors Association, 50, 523, 531

National Religion and Labor Foundation, 333, **334,** 529, 530, 532

National Trade and Professional School for Women and Girls, 361–62, 532

National Urban League, 255n, 514

National Youth Administration, Division of Negro Affairs, 235n

Navarick, Sheila, 439, 542

Neal, Alice, 147–148, 510

Negro American Labor Council, 246n

Nehru, Jawaharlal, 496, 498

Nelson, William Stuart, 20, *182n,* 182–83, 288n, 514

Nesbitt, J. E., 509

Nesbitt, Robert, Sr., *2:256n,* 412

Newgent, William E., **229–30,** 517, 518

New Hope Baptist Church (Niagara Falls), 49, 83, 527

New York, 18–19

New York Amsterdam News, 515

New York Post, 33, 521, 525

New York Times, 15, 102n, 135, 137, 183, 198, 220n, 509, illus.

New York Times Magazine, 398

Niebuhr, Reinhold, 6n, 181, 203

Nixon, Edgar Daniel, 3, 15n, 18, 25, *69n,* 110–11, 163, 217n, 226, 358, 445, 502, 504, 508, 514, 518, 523, 532, illus.
  aboard desegregated bus, 29, 53, 485–86
  bomb threats against, 40, 119, **240, 305**
  indictment of, 14, 133
  and Madison Square Garden rally, 47, **247,** 248, 253
  at MIA founding meeting, 4, 35, 69, 70
  at MIA's first mass meeting, 79
  on seating compromise proposal

Nonviolent resistance
  African Americans' commitment to, **376, 451**
  J. Pius Barbour on, 171, 172
  as Christian action, 5–6, 10–11, 15, 28, **72, 73–74,** 89, 108, 137–38, 142–43, 144, **200, 208,** 394–95, **418, 425**
  Christian and Gandhian synthesis of, 16–17, 21, 89, **209n, 224**
  as legal action, **73,** 115, **337**
  MIA training session on, 389–90
  as nonretaliatory, **233, 238, 241, 305, 326n**
  and protest as fundamental right, 6–7, **71, 72–73**
  redemptive elements of, 233, **278, 305–6,** 395
  Bayard Rustin on, 17–19, 31–32, 163–64
  Glenn E. Smiley on, 19–20
  South's response to, 168–69, 170
  as spiritual movement, 208, 268–69, **278, 306, 325**
  and triumph of justice, **73,** 146, **325, 327, 486**
  unanticipated results of, **450–51**

See also Baton Rouge bus boycott; Birmingham bus boycott; Gandhian ideas; Institute on Nonviolence and Social Change; Montgomery bus boycott; Tallahassee bus boycott

Nunn, William G., 512

Oakland County Ministerial Fellowship, 421

O'Bannon, Lester C., 509, 524, 528

Offutt, Walter P., Jr., 517, 521

Olivet Baptist Church (Chicago), 154–55, **162–63,** 538

Olney, Warren, III, 29n, *364n,* 364–65, **368–69,** 386–87, 405, 467n, 533, 534, 535, 536, 542, 543

Omega Psi Phi fraternity, 52, 54, 491, 541

Ormsby, Robert J., 528, 530

Owen, C. C., 45, 47–48

Palmer, Hustis James, 120, *120n,* 122, 369, 507

Pan-Community Council (Birmingham), 44, 516

Panorama of Progress (Detroit), 49, 218n, 317n, 526

Parker, Henry, **124,** 537

Parker, Joseph C., Sr., *2:257n,* 89, 93, 424

Parker, Theodore, 486n

Parks, Franklin Warren, 37, 39, **80,** *80n,* 483, 544

Parks, Rosa, *2:572n,* 67, 70, 71, 122, 235, 274–75, **299, 317–18,** 390, 501, 502, 503, 508, 509, 511, 513, 514, 525, illus.
  arrest and conviction of, 4, 14, 35, 68, 81, 90, 112, **123,** 166, **239,** 501
  at Madison Square Garden rally, 47, **247,** 253
  NAACP and, 3, 36, 166, **243–44**
  personal qualities of, **72, 237**
  Eleanor Roosevelt and, 46, 275n, 400
  on segregated bus, 1, 74–75, **302**

Passive resistance. *See* Nonviolent resistance

Patterson, John, 44, 47, 49, 121n, *319n,* 319–20, 331n, 528

Patterson, William L., 156

Patton, W. C., 11n, 36, 122n, 502, 503

Paul (New Testament), **300, 323,** 366, **378–79,** 424, **446**
  and "Paul's Letter to American Christians" sermon, 28n, **414–20**

Pavlov, Ivan P., 431n

Peace, and justice, **207–8, 221, 282, 323, 455**

Peace Corps, 225n

Peacemakers (pacifist group), 352

Peck, James, 20, 26n, *288n,* 288–89, 508, 524, 527, 529

Peck, Paula, 26n, 508

Pelt, Owen D., 41, 151n, 506

Pennsylvania State Baptist Convention, 51

Perry, Walter L., 512, 515

Peters, William, 49, *224n,* **224–25,** 517, 518, 530

Philia, **327, 458–59**

Philip, Lee, 233
Philippians, **416**
Phillips, Wayne, 135, 509
Phylon, 180 n, 181 n
Pickett, Clarence Evan, 220, 293
Picott, J. Rupert, 529, 532, 540
Pierce, James E., 85, *85 n,* **272,** 368 n, 504
Pike, James A., 258, 296
Pinkston, Harold Edward, *2:298 n,* 379–80, 535
Pittard, Gwendolyn E., 511, 518
Pittsburgh Courier, 227–28, **245,** 512
Pius XII, 255
Platonism, **259, 327**
Plessy v. Ferguson, **283, 323 n, 341, 425, 455, 473**
Porter, John Thomas, *2:569 n,* 12 n, 501
Poston, Ted, 33, 521, 526
Potofsky, Jacob Samuel, 493
Powell, Adam Clayton, 47, 148, *148 n,* 175–76 n,
    220, 253, 396, 508, 510, 511, 515
Powell, C. Clayton, 392, 538, 539
Powell, M. B., 530
Powell, William J., 85, *85 n,* 354 n, 369–70, 406 n,
    529, 534, 535, 542
Prattis, Percival Leroy, *227 n,* 227–28, **245,** 256,
    518, 520
Press coverage. *See* Media coverage
Proctor, Samuel Dewitt, *2:158 n,* 49, 128–29,
    142, 488, 507, 516, 525, 537, 539, 540
Progressive National Baptist Convention, 291 n
Protestant Council (New York), 248, **291,** 349 n,
    517
Protestantism, **417**
Protest movement. *See* Nonviolent resistance
Psalm 34, 71
Psalm 46, 74
Pugh, Lottie Mae, **444–45,** 540, 542
Pugh, Thomas J., *2:568 n,* 508, 524, 527
Pullman Palace Car Company, 216–17 n

Quakers, 219–20, 360, 464, 498
Quill, Michael J., 440, *440 n,* 493, 542, 543

Rabb, Maxwell M., 357, 405, *405 n,* 512, 538
Race relations, 213–14, **450**
    attitudes on progress in, **280–81, 460**
    and boycott, 15, 107, 136, 137, **176, 278, 428**
    reasons for crisis in, **237, 322, 324, 456**
    See also Bus segregation; Integration;
        Segregation
Radcliffe College, 215–16
Rainbow, Lovie M., **317,** 526, 527, 528
Rainge, Johnnie, 378
Ramsay, John G., 530
Randolph, Asa Philip, 15 n, 18 n, 30, 138, 139,
    216–17 n, 246 n, 299, 335, 376, 445 n, 492 n,
    493, 506, 507, 508, 526, 535
    King, Jr. and, 25, 216–17, 247–48, **252–53,**
        517, 518, 520, 521, 531

and Madison Square Garden rally, 47, 247–
    48, **253**
Rauschenbusch, Walter, 381, **397–98**
Ray, Sandy F., *1:103 n,* 151 n, **209,** 505
Razaf, Andy, 317
Redbook, 49, **224–25,** 527, 529, 530
Reddick, Lawrence Dunbar, 272, *272 n,* 513, 542
Redmon, J. F., 221 n, 513, 515
Red Sea, **259–60, 261**
Reed, Sam, 513
Reeder, C. S., 534
Reese, Jeanatta, 40, 41, 43, 111, 120, 145
Republican National Convention (1952), 463 n,
    479 n
Republican Party, 29, **409, 460, 476**
Reuther, Walter P., 335, 493
Revelations, 115, 262 n, 267 n, 346 n
Reynolds, Hobson R., *270 n,* **270–71,** 517, 522,
    523, 528
Rice, Doc C., 102, 103
Rice, Thelma Austin, *179 n,* 179–80, 513
Richardson, H. V., 451 n
Riles, Wilson, 137 n, 214, 508
Riley, Ralph W., *2:300–301 n,* 36, **87–88,** 503
Rinehart, Edmond L., 528, 530
Rives, Richard, 24 n, 46
Robeson, Paul, 22
Robinson, Jo Ann Gibson, *80 n,* 235, 369, 504,
    507, illus.
    bus boycott leaflet of, 3, 35, 67, 501
    as MIA negotiator, 13, 50, 370
    as MIA newsletter editor, 24, 48, **272**
Robinson, Ruth Odessa, **310–11**
Robinson, Sylvester S., *391 n,* **391–93,** 473 n, 536
Rodriguez, E. F., 384 n, 533, 534
Rogers, Sidney, **317–18**
Rohrbough, Lynn, 535, 536
Roman Catholicism, **417**
Romans, **416, 419**
Rooks, Shelby, **251,** *251 n,* 519, 521, 525, 526
Roosevelt, Eleanor, 47, 253, *400 n,* 445 n, 519
    King, Jr.'s correspondence with, 400, 401,
        420–21, 537, 539
    and Rosa Parks, 46, 275, 400
Roosevelt, Franklin Delano, 75, 216–17 n, 270 n,
    422 n
Routh, Fred, 483 n, 544
Rowan, Carl Thomas, 8, 53, 100, *100–101 n,* 102,
    451 n, 480 n, 481 n
Rucker, James D., 520
Rumford, Byron W., 528
Ruppenthal, G. J., 37, 38, 483, 544
Rustin, Bayard, 14 n, 20, 22, 42, 51, 54, 137,
    137 n, *163 n,* 236, 288, 316, 381–82, 407, 437,
    509, 511, 512, 514, 523
    bus boycott role of, 18–19, 43, 137
    on future integration plans, 493–94
    as Gandhian proponent, 17–18, 169

King, Jr.'s correspondence with, 163–64, 222 n, **375–78, 381–82,** 491–94, 512, 521, 527, 528, 533, 534, 535, 537, 545

and Madison Square Garden rally, **247,** 248, **253**

on Montgomery movement's importance, 31–32, 491–93, 545

St. John AME Church (Montgomery), 36, 38, 43, 51, 53, 502, 504, 514

Sandberg, Edwin T., 21 n, *276 n,* **276–77,** 515, 523

Sanders, A., 369

San Francisco Chronicle, 359

Saunders, A., 151 n

Saunders, Claude Lee, 512, 514, 525, 527

Savage, Augustus, 524

Schader, Annemarie, **298–99,** 525, 526

Schilling, S. Paul, *2:334 n,* 153–54, 511, 545

Schmitz, Helen C., 535, 537

Schmoe, Ruth, 531

School desegregation
  in Tennessee, 468
  at University of Alabama, 40, 128, **207, 239, 353**
  use of boycotts in, 26 n, 307 n
  See also *Brown v. Board of Education*

Schuyler, George S., 538, 539

Scott, John B., 4, 68

Scott, Obadiah, 11, 40

Scottsboro Defense Committee, 173 n

Seay, Solomon Snowden, Sr., 111, *111 n,* 112, 113, 121, 122, 509

Second Baptist Church (Los Angeles), 48, 105 n, 289, **319,** 525

Segregation, **286,** 380 n, **392–93,** 417, 460, 467, **473–74**
  African Americans' attitude toward, 216, **451**
  Christianity's resistance to, 27–28, **373,** 394–95, **418**
  democracy's opposition to, **232, 252, 284, 308, 337–38, 345**
  inferiority elements of, **236–37,** 265
  legislation to eliminate, **284, 307, 345, 460–61, 475, 476**
  misuse of Bible to justify, **282, 300, 323, 378**
  as old world order, **341–42, 344–45, 454–55**
  See also Bus segregation

Sellers, Clyde Chapman, 37, 38, *80 n,* 115, 483, 506, 507, 544
  and bus boycott activities, 4, 45, **304**
  MIA negotiations with, **80, 101,** 102

Seymour, Whitney North, 536

Shepard, Marshall Lorenzo, Sr., 366

Sheppard, Daphne A., 512

Shiloh Baptist Church (Chicago), 41

Shore, Herb, 504

Shores, Arthur David, 42, 135, *135 n,* **152,** 184, 185–89, 194, 196, 339, 469, 508, illus.

Shurtleff College, 87

Shuttlesworth, Fred Lee, 27, 30, 31, 32, 54, 451 n, *495 n,* **495–96,** 545

Silver, Theodore, 523

Silverman, Burt, 503, 504, illus.

Simms, B. J., 405–6, *405–6 n,* 527, 538

Sims, William, 542, 544

Sixteenth Street Baptist Church (Birmingham), 116

Slavery, **282, 300, 322–23, 341**

Sloan, Viva O., **383–84,** 534, 536, 545

Smiley, C. T., 523

Smiley, Glenn E., 18 n, 19 n, 20 n, 30, 151 n, 211, 213–14, **245,** 388–90, 396, 451 n, 511, 521, 536, 538, 545
  aboard desegregated bus, 29, 53, 485–86
  bus boycott role, 137, 138
  King, Jr.'s correspondence with, **311–12, 353,** 432 n, 435–36, 481, 510, 513, 517, 520, 523, 524, 525, 526, 527, 531, 532, 534, 537, 541, 545, illus.
  King, Jr.'s interview with, 42, 249, 277, 278 n, 510
  on King, Jr.'s nonviolence stance, 14 n, 17–18

Smiley, Helen, 151 n, 511

Smith, A. Maceo, 256

Smith, Alberta, 90
  See also Smith, Mary Louise

Smith, Kelly Miller, *2:570 n,* 43, 143, 501, 509, 511, 535, 536

Smith, Lillian Eugenia, 20, *168 n,* **177,** 219, 543
  King, Jr.'s correspondence with, 168–70, **273–74,** 512, 516, 523, 539

Smith, Louis P., 523, 527

Smith, Mary Louise, 35, 90 n, 111 n

Smith, Roland, *2:320 n,* 507

Social and Political Action Committee, Dexter Avenue Baptist Church, 2, **411,** 501

Socialist Call, 258 n, 280, 403 n, 523

Socrates, 204

Solow, Martin, 525

Southern Christian Leadership Conference (SCLC), 32, 69 n, 274 n, 329 n, 393 n, 487 n, 491 n, 495 n

Southern Farmer, 504

Southern Leadership Conference on Transportation, 491, 492
  See also Southern Christian Leadership Conference

Southern Regional Council (Atlanta), **368,** 483 n, 544

Southern University, 203

Spelman College, 142

Spingarn, Arthur, 362 n

Stanley, Frank L., Sr., *118 n,* 183, 207, **339,** 531 n, illus.
  King, Jr.'s correspondence with, 26 n, 118–19, 201–2, 506, 514, 516

State of Alabama v. M. L. King, Jr., et al., 90 n, 183–85, 508, 509, 510, 511, 514, 515
  King, Jr.'s testimony in, **185–95**

State of Alabama v. NAACP, 49, 319–20
State of the Race Conference (Washington, D.C.), 25, 45, 216–17
States' rights doctrine, **337**
Stebman, Betty J., 541, 543
Steele, C. Kenzie, 30, 32, *404n,* 451n, 538
 and Tallahassee bus segregation, 27, 31, 47, 54, 360, 404, 495
Steere, Dorothy M., 220n, 498n
Stephens, Carlton M., 533, 535
Stephens, Fred E., 264n, 519, 523, 524
Stetson, Jack, 471
Stevenson, Adlai, 335, **384**
Stevenson, William E., 539
Stewart, Annalee, 530, 531, 540
Stewart, Joffre, **352,** 530, 532
Stiles Hall University YMCA (Berkeley), 359
Stockton City Lines, 170–71
Stone, Candace, 520
Strength to Love (King, Jr.), 127n, 258n, 260n, 414n
Stride Toward Freedom: The Montgomery Story (King, Jr.), 9–10, 22, 39, **125n, 222,** 272n
Stright, Hayden L., 538
Student movements, **375,** 439
Subversive Activities Control Board, 156
Supreme Liberty Life Insurance Company (Chicago), 504
Swingler, Lewis O., 119n, 201
Swomley, John M., 14n, 18n, 20n, 137n, 396, *396n,* 434, 508, 509, 510, 511, 512, 540

Tallahassee bus boycott, 27, 29, 47, 48, 51, 53–54, 360, 404; integration attempts, 31, 495
Tallahassee City Transit Lines, 47, 48
Talley, Cornell E., 536, 537, 540
Talley, Manuel D., **373–74,** 529, 531, 534
Taylor, Franklyn W., 23, 412, 511, 526
Taylor, Gardner C., *2:162–63n,* 26, 28n, 209, 501
Taylor, Jewelle, *215n,* 215–16, **242,** 517, 519
"Telescope" (television program), 54
Templin, Ralph, 169–70n
Tennessee State University, 41
Terrill, Levi M., *367n,* **367–68,** 534, 536, 537
Thetford, William F., 38, 184, illus.
Thomas, Cecil A., 199, 358–61, *359n,* **385–86,** 523, 524, 532, 536
Thomas, Fran, 199, *359n,* 360, **385**
Thomas, Jesse O., 503
Thomas, Julius A., 514
Thomas, Lillie M., 106, 520
Thomas, Norman Mattoon, 18n, 206, *206n,* 504, 513, 515, 519
Thomas, Samuel S., *380n,* 380–81, **397–98,** 535, 537
Thompson, Ernest, 523, 525

Thompson, J. D., 544
Thompson, John B., 275
Thompson, Lafayette, 516, 533
Thoreau, Henry David, 204, **415**
Thrasher, Thomas R., **194,** 213, 214
Thurman, Howard, *2:583n,* 20, 169, 170, 174–75, **177,** 178, **375,** 513
Tilford, J. E., 467n, 537
Till, Emmett, 121n, 221n, 329–30n
Tillich, Paul, *2:24n,* 6n, 203, 262
Time, 503
Timothy (1), 416n
Tobias, Channing, 32
Totten, Kenneth E., 37, 80, 85n, **124**
Townsend, Francis E., 543, 545
Townsend, Willard S., 256
Toynbee, Arnold Joseph, 181, 266
Transport Workers Union of America (TWU), 44, 542
Trenholm, H. Councill, 117
Troup, Cornelius V., 118
Troup, Katie, 118
Truman, Harry S., 216–17n, 400n
Tumbelston, Raimund L., 507, 524
Turner, Paul, 493
Tuskegee Institute, 49, 52, 311, **312,** 404n

Union Methodist Church (Boston), 43, 173–74
Unitarian Fellowship for Social Justice, 46, **290–91**
United Auto Workers, 54, 252n
United Baptist Convention of Delaware, 286
United Defense League, 402n
United Electrical, Radio, and Machine Workers of America, 523
United Negro College Fund, 53, **466, 480–81,** 536, 541, 543, 544
United Packinghouse Workers Union (Chicago), 41, 507
United Press International, 506
United Steel Workers of America, 542
United States Congress, 517
United States Department of Justice, 29, 50, 357, 364–65, 386–87
United States District Court
 and bus desegregation ruling, 23–24, 47–48, **303, 377**
 and car pool injunction, 51, 52, **413–14, 427**
United States Federal Bureau of Investigation (FBI), 41, 50, 96, 370, 439n, **495,** 502, 504, 512
United States Fourth Circuit Court of Appeals, 35
United States Supreme Court
 Alabama Public Service Commission's appeal to, 48–49
 on *Browder v. Gayle,* 29, 52, 377n, 424
 on *Brown v. Board of Education,* **261, 283, 472**
 bus desegregation rulings of, 23, 29, 45, 52,

217n, 219, **231**, 377n, **425;** mandate on, 53, **425–26, 437,** 469, **481**
Dred Scott decision of, **282, 300, 322–23, 341, 455**
on *Flemming v. South Carolina Electric and Gas Company,* 45, 217n
on *Plessy v. Ferguson,* **283, 323n, 341, 455, 472–73**
United Transport Service Employees, AFL-CIO Skycap Local 297, 212–13
Universalist Convention (Cortland, New York), 51, 321–22
Universalist Ministers Association of America, 178
University of Alabama, 40, 128, **207, 239, 353**
University of Chicago, 295n
University of Georgia, 347
U.S. News and World Report, 49, 359, 371, **373**

Valien, Preston, 102n, 505
Vaughan, David D., 530, 532
Via, Emory, 544
Violence
    aftermath of, **326, 458, 478**
    immorality of, **278, 284–85, 325**
    nonretaliatory response to, **462**
    Southerners' fear of, **241**
    in Western culture, **430**
    of white supremacists, **357–58,** 365, **437, 453**
Virginia Teachers Association, 52, 529
Virginia Union University, **488**
Vivian, C. Tindall, 538, 539
Voting rights, 268
    denied to African Americans, **337, 358, 368–69**
    Justice Department's position on, 365, 386–87
    as MIA concern, 29–30, 44, **271, 442, 450,** 504, 512
    and political power, **345, 460**

Wagner, Robert F., 520
Wagner Costigan Anti-Lynching Bill, 400n
Walden, A. T., 134–35
Walker, Charles, 236n, **463–64,** *463–64n,* 540, 543
Walker, Marian G., 463–64n
Walker, Martha, 184
Walker, W. O., 513
Walker, Wyatt Tee, 51, 379, *487n,* **487–88,** 544, 545
Walk to Freedom (film), 51, 214, 388, 390–91, 504
Waller, Luther H., 39
Walls, William Jacob, **94,** *95n*
Walton, Eugene, 23n, **488–89,** *489n,* 542, 545
Walton, Norman W., **272,** *272n*
"Wanted" (Holland), 346n, **461**
Ware, James Lowell, **76,** *76n,* 542
Waring, Julius Waties, *422n,* 422–23, 471, **472,** 540, 541

Warner, Lewis J., 542
Warren, Earl, 364n
War Resisters League, 288n, 523, 533
Watson, John Broadus, **431**
Watts, Isaac, 265n, 283n, 301n, 324n, 341n, 455n
Weaver, Archie L., 294–95, 525, 526, 528
Weiner, Dan, 515
Wesley, Carter, 545
Wesley, Charles, **375**
Wesley, John, **375**
Wesleyan Association, 388n
West, Irene (Mrs. A. W.), 13, 15, 235, 369, 505
Weston, LaVerne, 157, *157n*
Weston, Ross Allen, **290–91,** 518, 521, 524
Whalum, Wendell, 158, *158n*
Wheat Street Baptist Church (Atlanta), 484
Whitaker, H. Edward, *2:158n,* 520
    King, Jr.'s correspondence with, 10n, 83–84, 99–100, **113,** 502, 503, 504, 505, 508, 516, 518, 519, 530
White, Viola, 90
White, Walter, **309**
White Citizens Councils. *See* Citizens Councils
Wieman, Henry Nelson, 264n
Wilder, Craig S., 529, 532
Wilkes, Warren G., 537, 538
Wilkins, Aminda, *437n,* **437–38,** 541
Wilkins, Roy, 11n, 15, *108–9n,* 335, 445n, 502, 503, 504, 506, 508, 509, 512, 521, 529, 534
    on fund-raising, 25–26, 166
    King, Jr.'s correspondence with, 122n, 134, 165–67, 505, 508, 511, 516, 519, 520, 522
    at Madison Square Garden rally, 47, 253
    and NAACP financial contributions, 44, **108–9, 152,** 173
    pledge of legal support from, 134–35, 165–66, **243–44**
Williams, A. D. (King, Jr.'s grandfather), 167, 168
Williams, Aubrey Willis, 95, 97, 504
Williams, Caressa, 410n
Williams, Dolores, 525
Williams, Franklin H., 166n, 512
Williams, Lillian, 532, 533
Williams, M. C., 540
Williams, Mary Lucy, 114
Williams, Robert, 14, 49, 106, 467
Williams, Willard A., 506
Willingham, Edward B., 538, 539
Wilson, A. W., 4n, 505
Wilson, Leonard, **207**
Wingfield, Mary, 90
Wofford, Clare, 20, 225, 491–92
Wofford, Harris Llewellyn, Jr., 20, 54, *225n,* 491–92, 516
    King, Jr.'s correspondence with, 225–26, **254,** 513, 518, 521, 532
Wolfard, Mary, 530, 537

Index

Women's International League for Peace and Freedom, 526, 530, 540
Women's Political Council (WPC), 69n, 80n, 235n
  bus boycott leaflet of, 3, 35, 67, **189,** 190n, 501
Wood, Marcus Garvey, 129–30, *129–30n,* 507
The World Tomorrow, 206n
Worthy, William, 20, 43
WPC. *See* Women's Political Council
Wright, Allean, 505
Wynn, Daniel W., *2:561–62n,* 503, 516, 517, 539

Young, Andrew, 250n
Young, Jessie, 541, 543
Young, Ronald R., *103n,* 103–4
Young Men's Christian Association (YMCA), 36, 71, 520, 523, 530, 532

Zion Baptist Church (Denver), 50
Zion's Herald, 388n
Zoroastrianism, **259**

Designer:	Steve Renick
Compositor:	G&S Typesetters, Inc.
Text:	10/12 Baskerville
Display:	Baskerville
Printer and Binder:	Edwards Brothers, Inc.